SOCIAL POLICY

─── AND ───

SOCIAL JUSTICE

MEETING THE CHALLENGES
OF A DIVERSE SOCIETY

BY **MICHAEL REISCH**

 **cognella**® | ACADEMIC PUBLISHING

Bassim Hamadeh, CEO and Publisher
Kassie Graves, Director of Acquisitions
Jamie Giganti, Senior Managing Editor
Jess Estrella, Senior Graphic Designer
Claire Benson, Project Editor
Elizabeth Rowe, Licensing Coordinator
Rachel Singer, Associate Editor
Joyce Lue, Interior Designer

ISBN: 978-1-5165-0604-0 (pbk) / 978-1-5165-0605-7 (br)

 **cognella**® | ACADEMIC PUBLISHING

CONTENTS BRIEF

PREFACE   vii

PART I: THE CONTEXT OF SOCIAL POLICY   1

CHAPTER 1   U.S. SOCIAL POLICY IN THE NEW CENTURY   5

CHAPTER 2   U.S. SOCIAL POLICY AND SOCIAL WELFARE:
A HISTORICAL OVERVIEW   53

CHAPTER 3   THE POLITICAL ECONOMY OF U.S. SOCIAL POLICY   115

CHAPTER 4   SOCIAL POLICY AND THE RACIAL REGULATION OF PEOPLE OF COLOR   137

CHAPTER 5   WOMEN AND SOCIAL POLICY   163

PART II: POLICY PRACTICE   193

CHAPTER 6   POLICY ANALYSIS   197

CHAPTER 7   FEDERAL AND STATE BUDGET BASICS FOR SOCIAL WORKERS   227

CHAPTER 8   POLICY ADVOCACY AT THE FEDERAL LEVEL: A CASE STUDY
OF AMERICORPS—HOW THE LITTLE GUYS WON   249

CHAPTER 9   STATE AND LOCAL POLICY ADVOCACY   269

CHAPTER 10   THE JUDICIARY AND SOCIAL POLICY   293

PART III: KEY AREAS OF SOCIAL POLICY   **315**

CHAPTER 11   SOCIAL SECURITY: PAST, PRESENT, AND FUTURE   319

CHAPTER 12   POVERTY AND UNEMPLOYMENT: DOES A "WORK FIRST"
              REMEDY WORK?   355

CHAPTER 13   WELFARE, WELFARE REFORM, & NEOLIBERAL PATERNALISM   383

CHAPTER 14   HEALTH AND MENTAL HEALTH POLICY   409

CHAPTER 15   HUMAN SERVICES IN THE U.S.: SAFETY NET PROGRAMS
              FOR RACIAL AND ETHNIC MINORITIES AND IMMIGRANT
              FAMILIES   433

GLOSSARY   457

ABOUT THE AUTHORS   475

INDEX   481

MICHAEL REISCH, PH.D., M.S.W., IS THE DANIEL THURSZ DISTINGUISHED PROFESSOR OF SOCIAL JUSTICE AT THE UNIVERSITY OF MARYLAND SCHOOL OF SOCIAL WORK.

PREFACE

Rapid and unpredictable changes on a global scale and hyper-partisan politics in the United States have created a tumultuous environment in which cultural, political, and civil conflict have become the "new normal." Media coverage of such issues as poverty and inequality, employment and health care, housing and homelessness, public education, climate change, terrorism, and police-community relations emphasizes the divisions that exist—both in the U.S. and around the world—along racial, ethnic, class, gender, religious, geographical and generational lines. Today, Americans cannot seem to find common ground even on issues where consensus once long reigned, such as the preservation of the Social Security system. In this environment, it is not surprising that controversial issues—abortion, Affirmative Action, same sex marriage, police violence, and the rights of transgender persons—cannot be resolved. Social and political movements at all points of the ideological spectrum—from the Tea Party to Occupy Wall Street to Black Lives Matter—focus on our differences rather than our common needs and aspirations. Nowhere is this clearer than in the political rhetoric of the 2016 Presidential campaign.

Yet these divisions are hardly new. Throughout its history, the United States has been a contentious multiracial, multicultural, and multi-religious nation. This diversity has frequently been a source of strength, vibrancy, energy, and creativity, and it continues to be. Yet, the nation's heterogeneity has also both facilitated and impeded its progress toward social justice and produced barriers to the development of a social welfare system that addresses the evolving needs of individuals, families, and communities effectively and efficiently.

Despite recurrent nostalgia for a mythic past when these divisions did not exist, there is no turning back. The United States, already the most diverse nation on Earth, if not in human history, will become even more diverse in the decades ahead. By the 2040s, a mere quarter century away, there will be no "majority" racial or ethnic population in the U.S. This demographic dynamic has already transformed social and political relations in states such as California and in virtually every major American city. In 2016, it is the not-so-underlying cause of both "racial panic" and cultural and social change.

These demographic changes are not occurring in isolation. At the same time, gender roles and societal attitudes toward sexual orientation have evolved rapidly during the past decade alone. These changes have produced new family constellations with new and different needs, and inspired new social policy developments on such issues as same sex marriage, parental leave, and universal pre-k programs.

In addition, the dependent portion of the U.S. population is steadily increasing. The "baby-boomers" have already begun to retire. This demographic wave will increase the fiscal pressures on already strapped programs such as Social Security and Medicare and stimulate new attitudes toward the retirement needs of elder Americans, even as the problems facing children, youth, and working age families continue to grow. A major challenge for the U.S. in the years ahead is how to avoid inter-generational conflict in responding to these diverse needs.

Finally, the forces unleashed by economic globalization will grow even more powerful in the future. They have already produced unprecedented socio-economic inequality and revealed the inadequacies of our nation's institutions and physical and social infrastructures. Much of the anger that has been expressed during the current political campaign is a reflection of Americans' growing insecurity about what the future holds for themselves and their children and increasing cynicism about the ability of our existing structures to develop effective responses to persistent problems.

In isolation, each of these changes would have significant consequences for social policies and for social work practice. Their combined effects—unpredictable though they may be—will surely be even more dramatic. The overall goal of this book, therefore, is to enable students and practitioners to confront these emerging realities by enhancing their understanding of the context, substance, underlying assumptions, and goals of contemporary U.S. social policy. It was written based on the belief that the best preparation for an uncertain future is to face reality squarely, honestly, critically, and knowledgeably.

PURPOSE OF THIS BOOK

Throughout my career I have been fortunate to teach and conduct research about social policy and to engage in policy advocacy. In recent years I noticed that I was increasingly dissatisfied with the texts that were available, particularly for introductory policy courses. Most of them lacked a clear theoretical framework and covered excluded and marginalized populations superficially. Few texts present content in a manner that stimulates critical thinking, self-reflection, and analysis. Students' backgrounds and changes in k-12 and undergraduate education also create obstacles to learning and teaching. Many social work students today have taken few courses in history, politics, and economics. Most of them have been taught to think descriptively, rather than analytically and conceptually. They often enter social work programs with the belief that studying social policy is not relevant to their interests in becoming effective practitioners. As a consequence of digital technology and the spread of social media, they frequently resist reading text-based materials, no matter how much professors pare down reading requirements.

While no book can respond satisfactorily to all of these concerns, this book represents an attempt to provide today's students and tomorrow's practitioners with a comprehensive, in-depth overview of U.S. social policy and the policymaking process. It includes the critical contextual components of social policy (history, ideology, political economy, and culture), the major substantive areas of policy (e.g., Social Security, health and mental health care, welfare), and content designed to strengthen students' skills in policy analysis, critical thinking, and advocacy. The authors are scholars and activists in the field who possess up-to-date knowledge, broad experience, and commitment to the social justice goals of social policy.

The book intentionally has a "hybrid" design that attempts to combine the best features of a standard text and an anthology. It has a strong theoretical foundation and consistent themes which are applied by expert scholars in their particular areas of research and practice. It also includes case studies to illustrate the impact of social policies, particularly on excluded and marginalized populations; analyses of the relation-ship between social justice and social policy, and of the roles that ideology and politics play in shaping social policies; and exercises to encourage the development of critical thinking and reflection. Each of the book's three parts begins with a brief introduction highlighting the key themes in the chapters that follow and how they fit within the book's overall framework.

Several themes run through the entire book. They include:

- The relationship of social policy to economic, social, and cultural transformation
- The impact of economic and social changes on conceptions of need and helping, which are ultimately reflected in social policy development
- The role of social policies and social services in promoting or preventing social and political change
- The ways in which cultural, racial, ethnic, gender, and religious identity affect the development and implementation of social policies
- The impact of the ongoing conflict between universal and population-specific conceptions of social welfare

While many of these themes have been expressed for years in scholarly discourse and public debates, they are of increasing importance today as the U.S. struggles to address the implications of global and domestic developments for our social welfare system. Given the enormity of demographic, cultural, and social changes underway, it is particularly important to hear the "voices" of populations that have largely been ignored throughout our history: racial, ethnic, religious, and sexual minorities, and women.

CHANGES IN THE SECOND EDITION

Since the publication of the first edition of *Social Policy and Social Justice*, there have been dramatic changes in U.S. social policy and the environment that shapes it. These include the full implementation of the Affordable Care Act and the legal and political controversies that continue to surround it; the impact of the Black Lives Matter Movement on race relations and the nation's perception of its criminal justice system; major Supreme Court decisions regarding such critical issues as voting rights, reproductive rights, marriage equality, and the limits of executive authority; persistent gridlock and hyper-partisanship in Congress and state legislatures; ongoing conflicts over immigration and economic policy; and the tumultuous, unprecedented, and as of this writing unpredictable consequences of the 2016 election campaign.

The second, substantially revised edition of the book integrates an analysis of these changes into each chapter with both up-to-date information and insightful interpretations of their implications by experts in the field. Its highlights include:

- An analysis of the ongoing effects of the Great Recession, globalization, trade and tax policies, and increasing socio-economic inequality on the nation's political climate.
- The emergence of environmental justice and climate change as key social policy issues.
- An assessment of the Obama Administration's overall impact on social policy and the future of social welfare and social work in the U.S.
- Discussions of how political stalemate has affected the budgeting process in Congress and how political polarization has shaped policy advocacy at the state and federal levels.
- The implications of the Black Lives Matter Movement for the development of race-conscious social policies in such fields as criminal and juvenile justice, education, and social services, and for women's leadership roles in the policy arena.

- The effects of political conflicts over marriage equality, reproductive rights, contraceptive services, and transgender rights on social policies that affect women.
- The consequences of recent Supreme Court decisions on health policies affecting women and low-income persons, the limits of executive authority, voting rights, state vs. federal power, and environmental regulation.
- The changing nature of work and workforce participation in the U.S. and its implications for trade, employment, and workplace policies.
- The relationship of increased chronic and deep poverty to people's health and life expectancy, and the persistent problem of homelessness.
- The impact of the Affordable Care Act on health care access, cost, and quality.
- The future of Social Security and Medicare in the context of Congressional failure to respond to their looming financial crises.
- An examination of the effects of welfare reform 20 years after its implementation.
- The challenges involved in developing effective social services for racial and ethnic minorities and immigrants in the context of rapid demographic and cultural changes.

A major feature of the book is the development of a complementary webpage that houses primary source materials, media artifacts, cases, interactive exercises, and links to useful websites. The webpage will be updated regularly to remain current. Other ancillary materials, available to instructors, include PowerPoint slides, test questions, case materials, class exercises, and suggestions for how to use the book and the webpage. To enliven the manuscript and illustrate the material presented, the book uses figures, tables, charts, photographs, and other graphics.

The original development of this book and the revisions to this second edition would not have been possible without the contributions of colleagues whose chapters combine in-depth substantive knowledge and astute insights. I thank them for their wisdom, hard work, and timely responses to my persistent requests. I would also like to thank the reviewers of the first edition, whose suggestions helped guide the production of this updated version and improved the book's content, clarity, and focus. Any errors in the manuscript are entirely my responsibility.

In addition, I would like to thank my research assistants at the University of Maryland, Pamela Parnell, MSW, and Katie Januario, MSW, who assisted with the first edition, for their help, patience, and good humor. Finally, I would like to thank the staff at Cognella for their assistance with all aspects of the book's production. Above all, I would like to thank Kassie Graves, Cognella's Acquisitions Editor, for her encouragement, wisdom, and ongoing support.

PART I

THE CONTEXT OF SOCIAL POLICY

Michael Reisch, PhD

The chapters in Part I provide a conceptual foundation for the rest of the book and a broad overview of its cross-cutting themes.

Chapter 1 begins by posing the provocative question: Why care for strangers? It then discusses the meaning of social welfare and social policy, and why social policies are needed in complex, modern societies. Next, it outlines the stages of social policy development and addresses how the social problems addressed by social policies are socially constructed. It presents several contemporary perspectives on social welfare, the major approaches to social policy, and the relationship between social policy and social justice. It analyzes the role of the state (government) in social policy formation and implementation and how social class and race influence the focus and goals of social policies. The chapter then presents models of policy development and key policy concepts and briefly discusses the roles of economics and politics on social policy. It presents a concise framework for the analysis of contemporary social policies and defines several key evaluative concepts; these tools are applied to specific policy areas, particularly in Part III. The chapter's themes are reinforced throughout the book, particularly in the brief chapter introductions and the longer introductions to each of the three sections.

Chapter 2 presents a broad historical overview of U.S. social policy, from colonial times to the present, including the policy initiatives and policy challenges that have emerged during the Obama Administration. The chapter's content emphasizes the economic, social, demographic, political, and cultural forces that shaped the evolution of the U.S. social welfare system and the relationship of these forces to struggles for social justice. More than in any other nation, the development of social welfare and social work in the United States reflects an ongoing synthesis of ideas derived from many different sources. These diverse sources have created a pluralistic social welfare system that is unusually complicated and often full of contradictions. The chapter includes content on the influence of racial, ethnic, and religious minorities; ideas derived from other nations and cultures; the role of women; and the impact of radicals and reformers on the development of social policy. It emphasizes the dynamic relationship that exists between majority and minority populations, institutions, and communities in the development of U.S. social policies and the relationship of social policy formation to changes in the nation's political-economy, demographics, and cultural environment. Understanding the impact and implications of this complex history is particularly important today in order for students, practitioners, scholars, policymakers, and the general public to respond effectively to the dramatic changes already underway in the 21st century United States. Because understanding history is critical to comprehending the complexity of current issues and contemporary policy debates, content on the history of social welfare and social policy is also included in Chapters 4 and 5 in Part I, and in the chapters in Part III that cover the evolution of Social Security, employment, welfare, and health and mental health policies.

Chapter 3 by Joel Blau begins with a presentation of the key features of the contemporary U.S. political-economy. It then dissects several conservative myths about the relationship between the economy and social welfare and discusses the relationship between the U.S. economy and social policy development and the current status of this relationship. Blau explores the interaction of social policy and the political economy of the contemporary United States—a complex interaction that involves both costs and benefits. These costs include taxes and the maintenance of an unemployed, and partly unemployable, segment of the population. The benefits include political quiescence, increased aggregate demand, and during economic downturns, the positive effects of countercyclical programs such as unemployment insurance. Because the long-standing requirement that social welfare benefits must provide less income to recipients than the lowest paying job (the concept of "less eligibility") circumscribes all these functions, the chapter places a special emphasis on how the multiple permutations of these functions sometimes conflict and sometimes mesh together. It also discusses the impact of globalization on the political–economic environment of the United States and provides the latest data on the role of social welfare in the U.S. political economy. The chapter concludes by assessing the connection between social policy and social justice—both today and in the future.

Chapter 4 by Jerome H. Schiele examines how throughout U.S. history the nation's social policies have intentionally and unintentionally regulated the lives of people of color and immigrants and identifies some strategies to render these policies more just in their treatment of these populations. The chapter applies a racism-centered perspective of social policy analysis—based on critical race theory and related conceptual frameworks—that are particularly well-suited to the current climate in which the "Black Lives Matter" movement has focused increased attention on racial inequality. A racism-centered perspective underscores the role that white racial hegemony has played historically in social policy development and implementation in the U.S. It uses racism as an "organizing theme" to explain how social policy development and implementation have disadvantaged people of color by advancing the shared but varied political, economic, and cultural interests of non-Hispanic white Americans, and highlights the racial control function of U.S. social policies that persists into the 21st century.

Chapter 4 also discusses how this racial control function has changed over time from more overt expressions that included explicit legal and other political restrictions to more contemporary forms of what many commentators refer to as color-blind racism. Specific examples from various groups of color are employed to illuminate this racial control function and demonstrate the shared and divergent consequences for people of color. Finally, the chapter offers some recommendations on how to alleviate and eliminate racism's effects on social policy development and implementation by highlighting several roles that social policy practitioners can assume as community organizers, policy formulators, analysts, and cultural mediators. Additional recommendations focus on the need to transform the political- economy of

American society by examining the limitations of its core values for bringing about greater inclusion and meaningful participation for all people.

Using conceptual frameworks derived from critical and postmodern theory, including neo-feminism, Chapter 5 by Susan J. Roll focuses on the impact of social policy on women in the United States and traces the relationship between women and social policy over the course of U.S. history. In addition, the chapter analyzes how U.S. social policies reproduce the social construction of women's roles, women's problems, and women's status in the nation's families, political economy, and society. While it acknowledges how social policies have perpetuated gender-based inequalities and oppression, the chapter also discusses how, through their individual and collective agency, women have influenced the development and implementation of policy—for example, in the ways they negotiated systems of charity and welfare and in the development of a "maternalist" model of social policy.

This chapter begins by presenting a framework for understanding the overall context of policy development and how it affects women. This is followed by a brief overview of the historical evolution of the major social policies that have shaped the experiences of American women. Through the use of several vivid examples, the third section discusses the role of women in affecting social policy, through both formal and informal means. The final section outlines several significant policy issues affecting women today. These help illustrate the processes by which social workers, as advocates, can influence the development and implementation of contemporary and future social policies in such major areas as employment, family policy, domestic violence, and welfare. The discussion of these policy areas complements and provides a context for more detailed discussions of these issues in subsequent chapters.

1

U.S. SOCIAL POLICY IN THE NEW CENTURY

Michael Reisch, PhD

INTRODUCTION: MAKING DIFFICULT POLICY DECISIONS

Why should we care for strangers? Under what circumstances should we care for them and to what extent? These may sound like unusual questions with which to begin a book written for prospective social workers and those in related health and human service fields, the so-called "helping professions." But, if you think about it, the questions are at the heart of systems of social welfare and the policies they produce. The answers to these questions reflect a society's values, the prevailing interpretation of its past, present, and future, and the priorities it establishes in the allocation of its finite resources. To illustrate these points, let's look at the following scenarios:

- Scenario 1: As a result of a "natural disaster," such as a hurricane, tornado, flood, fire, or earthquake, an entire community is destroyed. Its residents are displaced, their homes are in ruins, and whatever industry and commerce supported the community will take years to recover, if ever. While volunteer organizations, such as the Red Cross and local churches, can provide temporary assistance (food, shelter, health care), their resources and personnel are limited, and they serve, at best, as a short-term "fix" that cannot solve the community's long-term rebuilding problems. Under these circumstances, what role should local, state, and federal government play in assisting the community and its residents? Who has the responsibility to ameliorate this immediate situation and solve the

Figure 1.1 People Wading to Safety after Hurricane Katrina in New Orleans

community's long-term problems? When is it appropriate to spend revenues from taxpayers who do not live anywhere near this community to help these people whom taxpayers will probably never meet? How much help should be provided? Should all residents be helped equally or should other factors be taken into consideration? For example, if two homeowners lost their houses in the disaster, and one home was worth ten times the value of the other, should both homeowners receive the same amount of assistance? Or, what if a homeowner knowingly built a home in a flood plan, too close to the ocean, or on an earthquake fault, should society be obligated to help them rebuild? What is the rationale for helping (or not helping) them?

- Scenario 2: What if a disaster was the consequence of "human error"—such as the BP oil spill in the Gulf of Mexico, or institutional neglect—such as lead poisoning the water supply of Flint, Michigan, or a corporate decision to maximize profit—such as the transfer of manufacturing sites and jobs overseas? Such disasters create serious and lasting economic, public health, or environmental problems for affected communities, problems which then produce increased social and psychological distress that further exacerbate the crisis.

What role should government play in such crises? Which level of government has the primary responsibility to intervene? In what ways would this intervention be most effective? For how long should this intervention continue? How should it be paid for? Should all affected residents be assisted

Figure 1.2 Destruction Caused by a Tornado in Oklahoma

Figure 1.3 Daughters kneel and beg for their father to be rescued from a collapsed building after the 2008 Sichuan Earthquake in Dujiangyan, China. He was later found dead.

Figure 1.4 Unemployed Coal Miners in West Virginia

Figure 1.5 Barron Street, Delray Neighborhood, Detroit, Michigan (2010)

to the same extent? If not, what criteria should be used to determine how much aid they should receive and for how long?

- Scenario 3: Finally, what if the "disaster" was at the individual level, such as a veteran returning home who develops post-traumatic stress disorder (PTSD), a victim of domestic violence or sexual assault, a person who is permanently disabled due to a car accident, a child born with a hereditary illness, an individual who has abused drugs or alcohol, or a formerly incarcerated person who is now homeless and is attempting to reintegrate into his community, reestablish his family, and obtain decent

Figure 1.6 The Problem of Homelessness Has Persisted Since the Late 1970s

employment? Where does the responsibility lie to help these strangers? What role, if any, does individual responsibility play in determining who should be helped?

In each example, ask yourself:

1. To what extent should government assist the people in need of assistance?
2. What is government (or society) obligated to provide? What is the extent of individual responsibility?
3. Should all persons who are similarly affected be treated equally? What factors matter?
4. Who should have the authority to answer these questions?
5. Which perspective on social welfare and social policy does your answer reflect?
6. How do you justify your responses to the three different examples?

Every society grapples with these questions regularly on a massive scale. At best, its answers are consistent; they reflect consistent values, established through democratic means, rather than mere personal whimsy. Ideally, they are institutionalized, through legislation, judicial regulations, and administrative regulations, rather than the product of individual bias or caprice. Collectively, the answers to these questions comprise a society's social welfare system. Unfortunately, throughout its history the United States has not always lived up to these ideals. The failure to do so in the past and today produces patterns of inequality, social exclusion, injustice, and even oppression that require the collective action of concerned individuals, groups, and communities. This book will analyze some of these patterns and the reasons they exist, and suggest ways to disrupt and correct them. This chapter will define some key concepts and terms that will help establish the relationship between social policy and social justice.

THE MEANING OF SOCIAL WELFARE

Although every society must address problems such as those presented in the above scenarios, there is no universal definition of social welfare either in terms of its scope or limitations. Each society creates its own definition based on its history, culture, and current context. All societies acknowledge in their own way, however, that the concept of social welfare implies some recognition of human need and human interdependence, what Trattner (1999) termed collective responsibility for collective need. Ironically, although they may have been established to help strangers, systems of social welfare also create mechanisms of social control that perpetuate an unequal or unjust status quo. They so this through various means of distributing or redistributing material resources, power, opportunities, rights, and status, and through the process of "social reproduction" of prevailing economic, social, and political relationships and cultural values (Gorz, 2010; Foucault, 1979).

On close examination, therefore, systems of social welfare reveal a great deal about the societies that create them. They reflect a society's priorities and goals; its view of the reciprocal relationship between individuals and the community; its assumptions about human nature (e.g., whether people are "naturally" altruistic or selfish); its definition of human needs; its interpretations of the past; and its ideas about the nature and desirability of change. To implement these ideas, systems of social welfare create assigned roles, such as policymakers, social workers, and clients. These roles reflect and perpetuate cultural concepts of need and helping. Through their policies, social welfare systems determine who deserves to be helped and in what manner, whether certain individuals and groups should be treated differently, and if the receipt of assistance constitutes a legal entitlement (a right) or a reason to be marginalized and stigmatized.

The evolution of the U.S. social welfare system during the past several centuries reflects ongoing conflicts over broad values and goals, and the specific policies designed to achieve them. New issues have emerged due to changes in the nation's political-economy, demographic composition, and cultural norms, and new conceptual frameworks and vocabulary have been developed to address them. In contrast to this pattern of constant change, there have also been persistent ideological and political conflicts that seem to resist permanent resolution. One of these conflicts involves the tension between individual and societal responsibility for people's problems and how to respond to the wide range of human needs. For nearly a century, a related conflict centers on whether the nation should rely on market forces, the government, or the nonprofit sector to respond to these needs. On a more abstract level, these conflicts reflect different ideas about equality, freedom, and social justice. [*See Chapter 2 in this volume for a discussion of the history of U.S. social welfare and social policy.*]

WHAT IS A SOCIAL POLICY?

Definitions of the terms *policy, social policy,* and social welfare overlap and may be initially confusing. Some are quite expansive; others are more narrowly focused. Popple and Leighninger (2008) provide an example of both definitions. While "policies may be laws, public or private regulations, formal procedures, or simply normatively sanctioned patterns of behavior" (p. 34), the term *social policy* reflects a philosophic position that is often "synonymous with increasing government involvement in social life and the pursuit of greater equality, equity, and social justice" (p. 27). In the broadest sense, policies are part of "a system of laws, programs, benefits and services which strengthen or assure provisions for meeting social needs recognized as basic for the welfare of the population and for the functioning of the social order" (Friedlander & Apte, 1974, p. 4). They constitute the sum of a society's actions which affect individual and social development. As such, they both reflect and shape social norms of behavior. Social policies can also be construed as statements of social goals or appeals to do something comprehensive about a social problem such as poverty, which then are translated through social programs, often by acts of government, to effect change around specific issues.

According to Tropman (1984) in its simplest form a policy is "an idea reduced to writing, approved by legitimate authority, which gives direction or guidance" (p. 2). From this perspective, a policy could range from an organization's handbook of personnel practice, to a piece of legislation, executive order, or judicial decision. In addition, organizations develop policies, procedures, and guidelines that influence how government policies are implemented—for example, through eligibility regulations for the receipt of a benefit.

Jansson (2016) identifies eight policy sectors that comprise the network of U.S. social programs and policies: children and families; health; gerontology; mental health; education and job development; corrections; the safety net; and the global sector (p. 2). **Social welfare policies** constitute a smaller subset of social policies that regulate benefits to persons defined by society as "needy." These policies include cash assistance, health care, and housing subsidies, and assistance in such areas as education, transportation, child welfare, and environmental justice. Ideally, their goals are to optimize individual and family well-being and to redistribute societal resources more equitably. In the real world, however, they also serve the functions of social control and **social reproduction**—that is, they use societal institutions to replicate and perpetuate dominant cultural values and norms (Gorz, 2010; Jimenez, et al, 2015).

As Richard K. Caputo discusses in Chapter 6 of this volume, social policy can also be conceptualized in four other ways: as (a) an expression of a **philosophical concept or value position** about a society's purposes; (b) as a **product**, such as a law, regulation, or program guideline; (c) as a **process** of identifying issues, providing alternative explanations for problem causation, and various methods to solve problems; and (d) as a **framework for political or social action** around broader goals.

WHY DO WE NEED SOCIAL POLICIES?

What if we tried to resolve the questions raised by the three scenarios at the beginning of this chapter? What might be the results? What is the likelihood that different decisions would be made in each situation? When you consider these questions, it is clear that one reason for creating social policies is to enhance the consistency with which we respond to these circumstances. In an increasingly diverse nation of nearly 320 million people, without the guidelines and standards social policies provide our decisions would be random and probably ineffective, at best, highly discriminatory and unjust at worst.

Addressing the need for consistency is necessary, but insufficient in developing a clearer understanding of the purpose of social policies. Interpreting their overall purpose requires us to recognize that our environment is constantly changing and that these changes produce unprecedented problems and often exacerbate and complicate problems that have existed for some time. In other words, rapid and inevitable change produces costs—both material and social. The overarching question guiding social policy, therefore, is: Who should bear the costs of these changes (Kapp, 1972)? This is obviously a broad question, but it helps provide a foundation to understand the wider context of social policy development and implementation. Looking at social policies through a broader lens, particularly in an environment in which different policy areas are viewed in isolation from each other (the so-called "silo effect"), helps us recognize how social policies in one area, such as housing, affect and are affected by policies in other areas, such as employment and education.

Social policy development also involves deciding whether these costs should be absorbed by the private sector (the "market"), the non-profit sector, or the public sector (the "state"). If we decide that the state (government) should bear primary responsibility for covering these costs, what level of government should shoulder the greatest burden? If the private sector is to play a significant role in this regard, should the for-profit sector (e.g., corporations) or the nonprofit sector (e.g., social service agencies) play the major role?

Finally, as the three introductory scenarios illustrate, which costs should be absorbed at all? For example, to what extent should society absorb the costs of unemployment and retraining that result from the consequences of global economic changes, as discussed in Scenario 2? Or, as posed by Scenario 3, to what extent should society absorb the costs of individuals' personal misfortunes (bad luck) or bad choices?

Finally, by examining social policies through this broader lens we can understand more clearly:

1. How problem-solving strategies are developed and implemented at the local, state, national, and international levels
2. How the results of policies are measured, using what criteria, and by whom
3. How policies distribute resources, power, opportunities, rights, and status
4. How policies and the policy development process reflect conflicting interpretations of a society's past, different explanation of its current problems, and competing visions of its future.

FROM PRIVATE TROUBLES TO PUBLIC ISSUES: THE STAGES OF POLICY DEVELOPMENT

How do the problems described in the scenarios above become issues worthy of being addressed through social policy? There are several ways this could occur. It could occur as the "natural by-product" of widespread changes that affect large numbers of persons. Examples include mass unemployment during a recession or the impact of environmental pollution. Another is through growing awareness of the effects of demographic changes, such as increasing numbers of children, elderly persons, or immigrants; changing family patterns; or greater racial and ethnic diversity. A third is a consequence of unforeseen catastrophes such as natural disasters or epidemics. A fourth is a result of increasing discontent with the status quo due to changes in standards and expectations. Finally, issues emerge—usually gradually—because of the development of new societal priorities in response to the environmental changes described above, the influence of social movements and the conflicts they produce, or external threats.

This transition, from a private problem to a public issue worthy of societal intervention through social policy, occurs through various developmental stages. They can be summarized as follows:

1. *Recognition.* A private trouble (or problem), such as domestic violence or substance abuse, is converted into a public issue in numerous ways. It could occur as the consequence of socioeconomic changes

such as industrialization, the transition from a goods-producing to a service-oriented economy, or the advent of economic globalization. Demographic developments, such as changes in family size, gender roles, the aging of the population, or the racial and ethnic composition of the community, can also transform people's problems into issues of broader concern. Other sources of this transformation are unprecedented epidemics, environmental disasters, or external threats such as war and terrorism (Titmuss, 1958). Finally, increased dissatisfaction with the status quo resulting from new cultural norms and expectations, political conflicts, new scientific discoveries, or the introduction of new technologies can change our perceptions of private problems.

2. *Legitimation.* As a stage of policy development, **legitimation** refers to the process by which an issue becomes worthy of being placed on the public agenda—that is, it is an issue that society should address and attempt to resolve through its existing institutions. A private trouble can become a legitimate issue for a variety of reasons. New or different information could become available, for example, about the causes of mental illness as a result of research; or information that has existed for some time, such as the extent of police violence against African Americans, could be communicated more widely or more effectively through new channels such as social media. Old information could be interpreted in new ways because of the introduction of new cultural norms, new ideological perspectives, a new vocabulary, or the presence of new evaluators of the situation. Attitudes about same sex marriage are a good illustration of this type of transformation. New standards of behavior could emerge that affect societal expectations and social policies, such as Title IX regulations regarding acceptable conduct in the workplace. Finally, decision makers could acquire new values or prioritize social needs differently as a result of political or social pressure from advocacy groups or social movements. The passage of legislation extending rights to persons with disabilities is an excellent example of this process.

3. *Mobilization.* Once a private trouble is legitimized as a public issue, key actors inside and outside the political system must decide to do something about the problem because it will not disappear by itself and the situation is of sufficient urgency to demand prompt attention. Often such situations are characterized as a "crisis" (the HIV/AIDS crisis, for example) in order to justify increased public and political attention to the issue. At this juncture of the policy development process, the role of policy advocates is particularly critical. They must ensure that the public does not lose interest in the issue or become distracted by other matters or tangential concerns.

4. *Formulation.* At this stage, policy makers create an official, legally sanctioned plan to do something about the issue—such as a citywide plan to address homelessness. Various policy options are proposed—usually in the legislative arena—where conflicting interests, from inside and outside the policymaking apparatus, interact. In this stage, agenda setting is critical—it establishes policy goals, determines what alternatives are considered, assesses the cost of the policy, and defines the possible outcomes of the policymaking process.

5. *Implementation.* Once a policy is adopted at whatever level of government, it needs to be put into effect by the executive branch. Administrative departments draft regulations that stipulate the details of policy implementation. For example, if Congress appropriated funds for universal pre-k programs, the Department of Education and the Department of Health and Human Services would draft regulations regarding such details as eligibility requirements, mandated or optional components of these programs, health standards, and criteria for program staff. Once these regulations go into effect after a period for public commentary, the policies they shape are then translated into specific programs, a process that requires funding (through government budgets) and planning at the state and local levels, often with the assistance of private sector organizations. After these programs are implemented,

both the executive branch and external advocacy groups monitor the implementation process to ensure that policies are delivered in a manner consistent with administrative regulations and the legislature's intent. Lastly, the judicial system is often the final arbiter of whether policies are being implemented in a manner consistent with the law. The number of court cases involving the 2010 Affordable Care Act (ACA) is a good example of the latter. [*See Chapter 10 for further discussion of the role of the judiciary in social policy development.*]

6. *Evaluation.* Ideally, all policies and programs are periodically evaluated to determine to what extent they achieved their goals and objectives, and, if possible, what components of a policy or program were most critical to its success or failure. During the evaluation process, a set of similar-sounding concepts—effectiveness, efficiency, and effect—are used to measure a policy's impact. Understanding the differences between these similar-sounding terms is important to grasp the entirety of a policy or program's consequences.

Effectiveness refers to the extent to which a program's service or a policy's benefit achieves its original goals or terminal values. That is, did the policy actually address its target issue? Did the policy produce what it was intended to produce—e.g., a reduction in the number of persons who lacked health insurance or an increase in the number of families who obtained affordable, quality child care?

In comparison, assessing the **efficiency** of a policy involves identifying and measuring all short-term and long-term costs and benefits of the service or benefit it provides. This aspect of evaluation poses such questions as: How much did each child care "slot" cost? Which approach to increasing high school completion rates was most cost-effective? A focus on efficiency is often associated with the use of cost-benefit analyses and a utilitarian approach to social policy—that is, an approach that evaluates a policy in terms of its consequences (such as the maximization of the well-being of the most possible persons) rather than its underlying values (such as the right of all persons to a particular standard of living). Difficulties with this approach include distinguishing between short-term and long-term costs and benefits, weighing different types of costs and benefits (e.g., those that can be quantified and those of a more qualitative nature), and factoring in unforeseen or indirect consequences including the impact of policies on third parties—people who are not directly affected by the policy such as residents of neighborhoods in which halfway houses for homeless persons are developed.

Finally, measuring the **effect** of a social policy requires analyzing the extent to which a service or benefit achieved the goals associated with instrumental values—that is, its overall impact on society and not merely its consequences for the target population. There are numerous examples of policies whose effect and effectiveness varied considerably. China's one-child policy is a pointed example. Although it was highly *effective* in slowing the nation's population growth, in terms of its societal effect, the policy also produced several undesirable consequences, including a marked increase in voluntary abortion or the infanticide of female children, a gender imbalance among marriageable adults, a future labor shortage, and a lack of children available to assume filial caretaking responsibilities for elderly relatives.

7. *Feedback.* The implementation of a policy alters the original conditions in which the issue emerged and may transform the lives of persons it affects. At the same time, the context in which policies are implemented is constantly changing as well. A "feedback loop" is essential, therefore, to assess whether the original policy requires revision or may no longer be needed. This assessment has both objective components (i.e., those that can be determined through scientific observation) and subjective components (i.e.,

those that are influenced by political or ideological perspectives). A recent example concerned whether some of the core provisions of the 1965 Voting Rights Act that monitored states' election processes were still necessary. A sharply divided Supreme Court agreed with the states (primarily in the Southern U.S.) who argued that changes during the past half century rendered these legislative provisions unnecessary. In light of the numerous laws these states have subsequently passed, such as voter ID laws that restrict access to the ballot, those who argue that the original provisions of the Voting Rights Act should be retained could claim that the "feedback loop" in this particular instance was flawed.

Finally, to conclude this section, when assessing how a private trouble is transformed into a public issue (Mills, 1959), it is important to ask the following questions: How is the problem being defined at various stages of this process and for whom is it considered a problem? Who has the power to define the condition as a problem? What social, economic, political, cultural, and technological forces created this newfound awareness? What are the underlying assumptions about the nature of the issue? Who are the potential winners and losers if society attempts to address the issue through social policy? In what ways can the issue be defined differently? What are the implications of defining the issue in these different ways? Much like the assessment of a client or community's problem, how a public issue is framed influences from the outset how policy responses to the issue evolve. It is important, therefore, to recognize the role that the social construction of social problems plays in policy formulation.

EXERCISE: APPLYING THESE STAGES TO REAL WORLD PROBLEMS

Think about the following questions:

1. How would you apply the distinction between private troubles and public issues to the three scenarios described above?
2. Which of them are solely private matters?
3. Which of them constitute a public issue or falls somewhere in between?
4. How would you make the distinction?
5. What steps would be required to transform each problem into a public issue?

THE SOCIAL CONSTRUCTION OF SOCIAL PROBLEMS

Think about the issues that society considers important today such as those mentioned at the beginning of this chapter. Although we would like to believe otherwise, *none* of these issues are inevitably significant enough to require societal attention. Nor is the current interpretation of any of these issues the only way they could be explained and understood. Our views and responses to particular situations are shaped by our interpretation of history, and by their presentation in the media. They are also influenced by existing laws, customs, traditions, and values, including culturally-based biases. Concepts such as poverty, mental illness, crime, substance abuse, homelessness, and sexual deviance are not fixed. They are socially constructed for specific, if often unacknowledged purposes. Our current interpretation of these issues evolved as a result of a variety of environmental factors and shifting societal priorities. Conversely, many conditions are no longer viewed as problems or are now interpreted in significantly different ways—for example, homosexuality, divorce, single parenting, and women's participation in politics and the workforce.

The **social construction** of issues is, in effect, a subtle means of exercising control over societal institutions and the persons affected by their policy decisions. This occurs in several ways. It presents (and popularizes) false or misleading narratives about marginalized and socially excluded individuals and groups. It explains social problems in a manner that does not challenge existing structural arrangements or their underlying values. It interprets the goals and outcomes of policies on such issues as welfare, Social Security, same-sex marriage, and domestic violence in a manner that validates dominant cultural goals. As a consequence of social construction, social policies in virtually every society largely reflect the views and interests of the dominant groups.

EXERCISE: THE SOCIAL CONSTRUCTION OF SOCIAL PROBLEMS

1. Select one of the following issues:

   • Poverty
   • Unemployment
   • Substance Abuse
   • Homelessness
   • Crime
   • Mental Illness

2. Discuss how the social construction of this issue

   • Reflects dominant cultural concepts of need and "helping"
   • Stigmatizes some needs but not others
   • Maintains social roles and norms regarding race, class, gender, sexual orientation, ability status
   • Reinforces existing power dynamics in society
   • Combines social care and social control
   • Creates false narratives about excluded and marginalized groups
   • Interprets problems and their potential solutions in ways that maintain the status quo
   • Is a means of social control

PERSPECTIVES ON SOCIAL WELFARE AND SOCIAL POLICY

Because of their varied histories, even nations at similar stages of economic development have different perspectives on the purposes of social welfare and the desirable scope of social policy. These perspectives reflect their diverse ideologies and goals, and wide-ranging views on the relationship between government and the market and between individuals and the society as a whole. In short, they answer the question: who should bear the costs of change in significantly distinctive ways.

For example, throughout most of its history, dating back to the colonial era, U.S. social policy embodied a **residual view of social welfare**, based on values derived from conservative ideas about the state, a harsh view of human nature, and a desire to maintain the existing social structure. Its key features included minimal government intervention in the market economy, the preservation of individual freedom, the exaltation of self-reliance, and protection of the sanctity of private property (Jansson, 2014).

During the 20th century, the social welfare systems of many Western European nations, such as Great Britain, as well as Canada, Australia, and New Zealand evolved to reflect a liberal or **institutional view of social welfare**. Proponents of this perspective argued that the purpose of social policy is to ameliorate social and economic problems such as unemployment—what Titmuss (1958) referred to as the "diswelfares" of the market economy—promote greater equality of opportunity, and gradually expand the concept of citizenship beyond political rights to include social rights (Marshall, 1950). To some extent, U.S. social policies between 1933 and 1980 also reflected this perspective (Katz, 2001).

A third social democratic or **developmental view of social welfare** emerged in the Scandinavian nations during the 20th century and, for a time, in post-World War II Great Britain. Policies in such systems would not only seek to correct the "diswelfares" of the market economy, they would also attempt to eliminate poverty and enhance human well-being. In nations such as Sweden that have created a "social welfare state," social policies are not merely directed at specific populations in need; they are the basis of "cradle-to-grave" protections that support the normal process of human development at all stages of the life cycle (Chatterjee, 1996; Esping-Andersen, 2002; Fitzpatrick, 2001). The U.S. has adopted only a few policies of this nature: Medicare and Social Security for the elderly and, more recently, universal pre-k for young children.

During the past four decades, a **neoliberal** perspective on social welfare has emerged concurrently with the advent of economic globalization. Although neoliberals, like conservative supporters of residual systems, believe that government should play a smaller role in society and prefer market-oriented solutions to social problems, they recognize that specific social policies can advance the public good in a limited way. For example, they are likely to support increased funding for human capital development—such as education and job training—to make the United States more competitive in the global economy (Abramovitz, 2012; Stoesz, 2016).

CONTEMPORARY APPROACHES TO SOCIAL POLICY

These diverse perspectives on social welfare systems, in general, are often translated into differences in the scope (coverage) of social policies. Nations with institutional and developmental systems of social welfare rely upon **universal social policies**. These provide societal benefits to everyone regardless of income and other personal circumstances and, in most cases, without specific obligations being imposed on recipients, such as mandatory employment. By contrast, nations whose social welfare systems combine elements of residual and institutional perspectives favor **selective social policies**. Their benefits are determined by income (through a **means test**) or through membership in a specific age cohort, group with a common problem, or residency in a particular geographic area (a needs test). In the United States, Social Security, Medicare, and public education are examples of policies that reflect universality, while TANF (Temporary Assistance for Needy Families), Medicaid, and SNAP (formerly food stamps) are policies that reflect a selective approach. The differences between these approaches to social policy mirror debates over whether systems of social welfare should provide minimal or optimal assistance, take a reactive (or residual) approach versus a proactive (institutional or developmental) approach, and provide short-term (temporary) or long-term (permanent) benefits. They also determine whether benefits should be conditioned on other behaviors, such as work, and whether they should be provided in institutions or in people's homes.

Finally, a wide range of administrative issues shape how social policies are delivered. Should their implementation be centralized (like Social Security) or decentralized (like TANF)? Should their programs and services be integrated or segmented? Should these programs be delivered by the public or private sector? Should beneficiaries be involved in program design, implementation, and evaluation? Finally, how should social policies and programs be funded and at what level of government?

In the United States today, competing visions of social welfare and social policy produce more divisions than at any other time during the past century. In part, this is because U.S. social policy attempts to address two overarching goals that on the surface appear to contradict each other. On one hand, social policy serves as an instrument to support and sustain existing structures, institutions, and values (the so-called status quo) and to adapt these structures to dynamic internal and external environmental changes. At the same time, however, policies that are adopted (or fail to be adopted) alter that environment through the incentives or disincentives they create and the intended or unintended consequences they produce.

The contradictory roles played by social policy have several important implications. First, as Joel Blau points out in Chapter 3 of this volume, analysis of contemporary social policy must examine the interrelationship of economics, politics, and ideology. Although often obscured by the myth that the United States is a non-ideological society, this relationship exists in the ways our society addresses every issue it confronts. Second, issues of resource distribution and power are omnipresent at all levels of the policymaking and implementation processes, from the federal government to the day-to-day interactions of social workers and their clients. Third, in assessing current social policies and designing strategies to change them, analysts and advocates must recognize the contradiction involved in using the system to change itself and that policy change can be both qualitative (e.g., a shift in societal goals) and quantitative (i.e., an increase or decrease in the number of persons affected by a policy or the size of benefits they receive).

Fourth, the history of social policy, particularly in the United States, demonstrates the ongoing impact of various invidious "isms," such as racism, sexism, and homophobia, which lead to the exclusion, stigmatization and marginalization of many populations in need. Understanding both the historical and contemporary impact of these isms on policymaking is, therefore, vital. [*See Chapters 2, 4, 5, 12, 13, and 15 in this volume for specific examples.*]

Fifth, it is equally important to understand how various social problems are interconnected. For example, malnutrition in children due to poverty has been linked to the onset of chronic health and mental health problems and poor educational and employment outcomes; individuals' future employment status and income are consequences of their education and receipt of welfare benefits; drug abuse is associated with crime and family breakdown; and immigration and migration patterns are major consequences of economic globalization.

Finally, it is important to distinguish policies that designate particular ends and those that stipulate specific methods to achieve those ends. For the broader social welfare field, the fundamental question is not if change is to occur but how and under whose control?

To summarize, a nation's approach to social policy is informed by its views of

- the nature of society itself, whether it is individualistic or cooperative/collectivist at its core
- the socioeconomic system that determines how goods will be produced, distributed, and consumed;

- the legitimacy and effectiveness of the state (government) and its decision-making processes;
- individual and social morality, particularly as they affect human nature and human needs;
- the degree of mutual responsibility between individuals and society;
- the definition of community and its obligations;
- its value priorities and social goals;
- its history; and
- the nature, desirability, and preferred means and pace of change.

SOCIAL POLICY AND SOCIAL JUSTICE

As the above discussion indicates, values are at the foundation of social policy development. They shape the process of policy development every bit as much as the best evidence derived from research. One of the central value conflicts in the United States is the relationship between social policies and social justice. Since the early 20th century when proponents of social justice in the U.S. became more vocal expressing their concerns, activists and scholars have attempted to use social policies as instruments to achieve a more socially just society. These efforts have often been stymied, however, not only by powerful resistance, but also by the presence of considerable differences in how social justice is defined (Reisch, 2002). These ideological differences about the meaning of social justice inform the various perspectives on social welfare described above. They can be briefly characterized in the following ways:

- **Conservative views** of justice focus on the preservation of individual liberty, property rights, and economic and social order (Stoesz, 2014).
- **Liberal views** of justice emphasize the more equal distribution of societal benefits and burdens and the expansion of civil rights and civil liberties (Reisch, 2014).
- **Social Democratic conceptions** of justice promote the goals of social and economic equality and greater civic participation (Rawls, 1999).
- **Postmodern ideas** about social justice stress the inclusion of marginalized groups in socially just decision-making processes (Leonard, 1997).

During different periods, one or more of these perspectives has been dominant in the U.S. The promotion of social justice through social policies, therefore, has reflected several distinct interpretations of social justice. These include

- Fair play: a more equal distribution of rights and opportunities by removing discriminatory barriers (Ryan, 1981);
- Fair shares: more equal outcomes through redistributive taxation and spending policies (Rawls, 2001);
- A meritocracy: equal distribution of resources based on personal merit or productivity;
- A human needs or capabilities approach: unequal distribution based on unique individual needs or requirements, such as disability (Dover, 2016; Nussbaum, 2011);
- The preservation of privilege: unequal distribution based on status, political position, or religious beliefs;
- Compensation: unequal distribution based on compensatory principles to remedy past injustices, such as Affirmative Action (Kennedy, 2013; Sabbagh, 2011).

Given this complicated array of definitions of social justice, a recurrent issue for policymakers in the U.S. is: How can we apply a concept of social justice based on individual rights to solve problems that are created by group membership (e.g., race, gender, social class)? Today, the diverse values all claiming to reflect a social justice approach to social policy development and implementation include: the equal worth of all human beings; the equal right of people to be able to meet their basic needs; the importance of distributing opportunities and life chances as widely as possible; the reduction or elimination of unjustified inequalities; and the expansion of people's capabilities (Reisch & Garvin, 2016; Reisch, 2014; National Association of Social Workers, 1999; Nussbaum, 2011; Sen, 2009).

For more than a century in the United States, efforts to achieve these value-driven ends through social policy have taken various forms and produced mixed results. On the positive side, they have created a limited social safety net, expanded economic opportunities by removing a number of discriminatory barriers to employment and education, and enhanced access to health and mental health care. Some policies, such as Social Security, Medicare, and Medicaid, have modestly redistributed resources to the least advantaged members of society. Attempts to promote better balance between employment, family, education, and leisure and to promote greater security across the life cycle have been less successful. Social policies have only recently begun to address such needs as paid family leave, affordable child care, work/life balance, and support for caregivers of the elderly, infirm, and disabled.

As a result of advocacy efforts, in recent decades the goals of social policy have also been linked to the creation of a more egalitarian, multicultural, and democratic society (Marable, 2009). This type of society would pay greater attention to equitable decision making in determining the allocation of resources, the promotion of self-determination at the individual and community level, and the construction of an economic system centered on human needs and human rights rather than mere economic gain. It would represent an attempt to infuse policymaking with a common sense of ethics and values that challenge long-standing structures of oppression, power, and privilege within the dominant social and cultural order (Wilson, 2009).

In examining the substance of social policies and the means by which they are developed and implemented, it is important, therefore, to assess whether a policy is intended to have a **redistributive effect** as part of its overall strategy to promote social justice. Assessing the redistributive components of a social policy requires answering the following questions:

- Is this redistributive effect intentional?
- What resources does the policy attempt to redistribute?
- What are the consequences of this policy for third parties—intended and potential?
- Who benefits from the policy or is harmed by it directly or indirectly? How? To what extent?
- What type of cost is involved in implementing or failing to implement the policy (social, fiscal, other)? How much is the cost? Who pays the cost?
- To what extent does the policy involve a shift in power or an alteration of status, social roles, and cultural norms and values?

In the United States, two major concepts have often constrained the nation's ability to apply principles of social justice to the social policy arena: our concept of property and our concept of the state (or government). In combination, these two concepts produce an ideological superstructure that explains, defends, promotes, and reproduces existing systems, values, and institutions (Althusser & Balbar, 2009).

They determine who should bear the social and economic costs of change, how these costs should be calculated, and who makes these critical decisions.

Our concept of property determines the means by which our society produces, distributes, and consumes resources. This influences the nature of ownership of goods; ideas about what constitutes work and what types of work should be rewarded, and at what level; how we should distribute material resources; the kinds of social relationships that are preferred or required; and the focus of our cultural institutions. For example, our ideas about the sanctity of property influence our views about taxation, which in turn determine the revenues we have available to address issues that affect individuals, families, and communities. In addition, our notion that property ownership resides primarily in individuals or in entities like corporations that have the legal status of individuals informs our prevailing view that individual responsibility should be a cornerstone of our social policies.

The connection of our concept of property to our ideas about social policy and social justice has been taken for granted for so long that its existence is rarely acknowledged or disputed. The same cannot be said for our concept of the state. Since Independence, this concept has been a topic of ongoing, often violent conflict in our society. This conflict continues today as our political rhetoric frequently demonstrates.

THE STATE AND SOCIAL POLICY

Our concept of the state is linked to social policy development in two ways. First, it establishes the degree of responsibility government assumes for social welfare and human well-being through the regulation of the market economy, and the support government provides to the ancillary economic, social, and cultural institutions and relationships that preserve the prevailing distribution of societal goods. Second, it determines how the state will mediate the many conflicting interests and competing needs of individuals and groups in our increasingly diverse and complex society. The concept of the state also influences how power is distributed, the nature of formal authority in government and other major institutions, and our definition of individual and social responsibility.

Throughout history, a variety of different perspectives have been put forward about the role of the state. In the early modern period (roughly the 16th and 17th centuries), European proponents of absolute monarchies or divine right theory (like Thomas Hobbes) proclaimed that God was the sole source of political authority, and that His will could only be interpreted by humans, like kings, who possessed the authority to do so. This view prevails today in nations such as Iran and Saudi Arabia and has adherents among some fundamentalist Christians in the United States.

Advocates of natural law theory from ancient times through the Middle Ages, such as Plato, Aristotle, and Thomas Aquinas, regarded the state as a "natural phenomenon" whose existence must be presumed and whose authority could not be questioned. In a similar vein, 19th century adherents of force theory, such as the German philosophers Hegel and Nietzsche, regarded the state as the most powerful and total form of human organization, an institution distinctly above the people (Murphy, 2006). In its most extreme form, the application of force theory produced the totalitarian states of the 20th century.

By contrast, proponents of social contract theory, including John Locke, Jean-Jacques Rousseau, Thomas Jefferson, and 20th century philosophers such as John Rawls, posit that the state is the creation of all the individuals and groups within it and that those invested with state authority govern solely by the consent of the governed. These ideas are expressed clearly in the language of the U.S. Declaration of Independence and the Gettysburg Address. This concept of the state, which remains popular among 21st century liberals, regards it as an instrument that mediates class and racial/ethnic conflicts by applying the principle of "popular sovereignty." It is the primary principle underlying contemporary pluralist theories of policymaking (Lassman, 2011; Rawls, 1999).

Finally, in Marxist theory, the state is regarded as the "executive committee" of the ruling class. The implication of this theory is that the interests of the state are viewed as identical to those of ruling elites (Miliband, 1969). Ironically, members of both the Occupy and Tea Party movements, who represent different points on the political spectrum, may subscribe to this view even if they do not consciously embrace Marxism.

These different conceptions of the state produce four views of the relationship between the state and social policy and different perspectives on the state's connection to social welfare as a whole. One conception of this relationship, a contemporary corollary of social contract theory, regards the state as a neutral or benevolent force that balances competing interests, smooths over the inequalities of the socioeconomic system, and provides minimal regulation in a society dominated by the free market. This reflects a residual view of social welfare in which the state is a vehicle of last resort, after other societal institutions such as the family and the market have failed.

A second conception of the relationship between the state and social policy regards government as a positive, occasionally paternalistic force in society and a critical source of intervention in economic and social development. The state's role within this perspective, however, is limited to correcting the excesses of modernity. This leads to an institutional view of social welfare that formed the basis of social policy provision in the United States from the 1930s to the 1980s and is still somewhat influential today. (*See above discussion about concepts of social welfare.*) Its key features include:

- an increased role for government in the promotion of greater equality of opportunity and in responding to new and more complex human needs;
- a paternalistic focus on needs, not rights, through the adoption of policies that are, for the most part, selective rather than universal;
- an embrace of the concept of the "common good" as something greater than the aggregate good of individuals, coupled with the belief that the promotion of the common good is compatible with the preservation of individual freedom—in brief, the assumption that the state can "do good" without sacrificing anyone's interests (Gaylin, Glasser, Marcus, & Rothman, 1978);
- the state's efforts to reconcile class conflict and restore community—This was the view of government that shaped the ideas of leaders of the Progressive Movement, such as John Dewey, Louis Brandeis, and Jane Addams (Elshtain, 2002; Knight, 2005; Puckett, Harkavy, & Benson, 2007). [*See Chapter 2 in this volume.*];
- a belief that an expanding economy can achieve most desired social goals, including the reduction of poverty and inequality, without fundamentally restructuring the socioeconomic system—This belief was an underlying assumption of the policies developed during the New Deal and the War on Poverty and, to some extent, has shaped the policies of both Democratic and Republican administrations from the late 1970s to the present (Alperovitz, 2011) [*See Chapter 2 in this volume.*]; and
- a belief that no adversarial relationship exists between the state and recipients of services or benefits, because the state is exercising the collective will of the people in the interest of the common good (Mansbridge, 1980).

A third conception of the state, most popular in Scandinavian nations, sees it as a vehicle for economic and social transformation, the redistribution of resources, and the facilitation of human development at all stages of the life cycle. This conception underlies the policies of welfare states, based on a developmental view of social welfare, as discussed above. It relies on higher rates of taxation to support policies that provide a more extensive sense of social and economic security for its citizens (Russell, 2015).

Finally, since the 1980s there has been a resurgence of anti-statist, neoconservative views in the United States that have attacked many of the premises on which modern social policies are based. According to this perspective, most forms of social welfare provision restrict individual liberty and are destructive of human potential. They are unnecessary in a free market society and are, ultimately, antithetical to its purposes (Friedman, 1962). Neoconservatives also assert that in an increasingly competitive global economic system the United States can no longer afford the "inefficiencies" of the welfare state and that the provision of private social services through the market would be less costly, more effective, and more consistent with American cultural values of self-reliance and individual freedom. Opponents of the Affordable Care Act within both the Tea Party movement and Congress often rely on such arguments (Stoesz, 2014). [*See Chapter 14 in this volume.*]

In addition, unlike liberal proponents of institutional social welfare systems, and even their neoliberal counterparts, critics of government-funded policies argue that the preservation of freedom and the promotion of social equality are antithetical goals, and that state-sponsored efforts to create a more egalitarian society (e.g., through redistributive tax policies, welfare benefits, Affirmative Action) have deleterious economic, social, and moral effects. They reject the concepts of legal entitlements and human rights at the heart of the welfare state and do not regard disparities of income and wealth as excessive or socially harmful (Nozick, 1974). In fact, they are more concerned about the impact of a coercive state apparatus than about the impact of socioeconomic inequality. The recent budget blueprint approved by the Republican majority in the House of Representatives reflects this orientation clearly (Kogan & Shapiro, 2016).

SOCIAL CLASS AND SOCIAL POLICY

U.S. social policy has also been shaped by two persistent beliefs about the nature of American society. One is that the United States lacks the social class divisions of other industrialized nations, such as those in Europe; the other is that whatever boundaries exist between classes are very fluid. The former belief feeds the myth that the United States is a "middle-class nation." The latter is reflected in the frequent individually-focused "rags-to-riches" stories that saturate the media regularly.

As several chapters in this volume indicate, however, the distribution of resources, power, and life outcomes in U.S. society is very much related to factors of income and wealth. During the past three decades, the United States has become increasingly stratified. It is now more economically unequal than at any other time since the Great Depression (Drennan, 2015). The myth that most Americans are middle class obscures the existence of class differences and how recent changes in the nation's economy and policy decisions during the past several decades have affected the distribution of resources, life chances, and even life expectancy in the United States (Frankfurt, 2015; Stiglitz, 2013). For most Americans, therefore, even students of social policy, the term *social class* is ambiguous and often confusing.

To clarify this ambiguity, there are three ways to analyze the nation's class structure, each of which has different implications for how we can assess the relationship between social class and social policy. Each method of analysis, however, both reveals and masks different aspects of the nation's class structure.

One way to analyze class structure is by **income distribution**, which involves dividing all U.S. households into quintiles (fifths of the population). [*See Chapter 3 in this volume for further discussion of this issue.*] Many reports on income inequality by government agencies and nongovernmental research and advocacy organizations use this measure (Stone, Trisi, Sherman, & Debot, 2015). The problem with this method is that it raises as many questions as it answers. It is not clear, for example, how income should be defined. Should we count income from wages, from investments, and from government programs in the same way? Should nonmonetary income (e.g., food stamps, health benefits, educational vouchers) be included? Should individuals with the same income but very different types of jobs—for example, social workers and sanitation workers—be considered members of the same social class? A final problem with this approach is that measuring income alone does not reveal the effects of vast, often inter-generational racial differentials in the distribution of wealth, which have intensified since the Great Recession (Kochar & Fry, 2014; Shapiro, Meschede, & Osoro, 2013).

A second definition of social class, based on Marxist theory, emphasizes what Marx termed individuals' relationship to the "means of production"—land, capital, and labor. According to classical Marxism, industrial societies are divided into four primary classes: the haute bourgeoisie, who own the means of production (factories, banks, etc.); the petite bourgeoisie, which consists of small business owners, shopkeepers, and civil servants; the proletariat, people who work for wages (largely in factories); and the *lumpen proletariat*, beggars, criminals, and social deviants, who are sometimes referred to in contemporary society as the "underclass" (Marx, 1852). In response to dramatic changes during the 20th century in the nation's occupational structure, neo-Marxists have created an additional category, the "professional managerial class," which is situated between the two former divisions of the bourgeoisie (Ehrenreich & Ehrenreich, 1978). Yet, are all salaried workers in the same class? For example, should a social worker, public school teacher, or nurse who has a graduate degree be considered in the same class as a factory worker with a high school education (even if they earn the same wage)? Are they members of the same class as high salaried Wall Street executives or professional athletes?

Responding to this criticism, a third method of analyzing class structure has appeared in recent decades based on **sectoral divisions in the labor market**. According to this perspective, the labor market is divided into three sectors. The **primary sector** consists of big business and finance, which are largely capital intensive. It is characterized by relatively high wages and, in some manufacturing industries, stronger unions (such as the United Auto Workers). The **secondary sector** is highly competitive, consisting of small and midsized businesses with few or no unions. This sector is labor intensive. The **tertiary sector** includes government and nonprofit organizations. It is also labor intensive and, among some government employees, increasingly unionized, although it requires large external infusions of capital, primarily through taxes and philanthropy. The professional/technical labor market described above cuts across all three sectors and has also been growing in recent years. More creative opportunities exist for these workers in the primary sector than in the secondary sector. These changes underlie the emphasis of some policymakers on job retraining and the importance of higher education. Nevertheless, according to this analytical framework, workers and their families in each sector require different types of support through social policies and programs.

RACE AND SOCIAL POLICY

Similar to the relationship between social class and social policy, two conflicting perspectives shape discussions of the role race plays in the construction of U.S. social policy. One perspective asserts that the economic changes of the past half century, combined with the expansion of social welfare programs and

Figure 1.7a Poverty Rates by Race and Hispanic Origin: 1959 to 2010

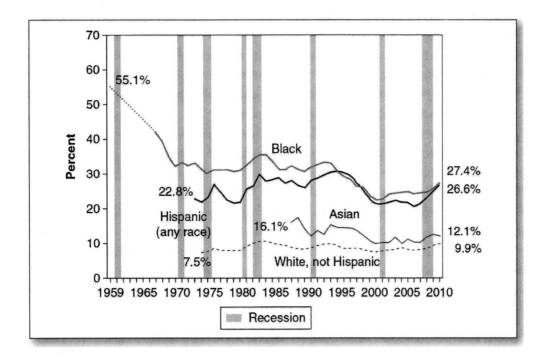

Source: U.S. Census Bureau.

Figure 1.7b Poverty Rates by Race and Hispanic Origin: 2000–2013

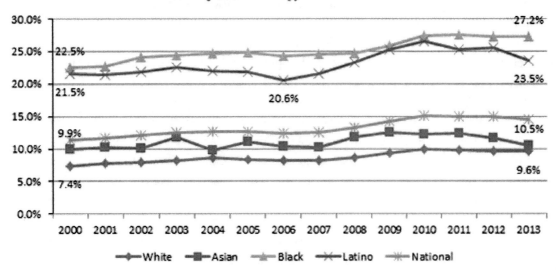

Source: U.S. Census Bureau.

the passage of antidiscrimination legislation, have raised the socioeconomic status of African Americans and other persons of color. Proponents of this view assert that these changes have substantially lowered the poverty and unemployment rates among these formerly marginalized groups, created a viable middle class among persons of color, and eliminated the need for compensatory programs such as Affirmative Action or antidiscrimination policies such as the 1965 Voting Rights Act because the United States is now a "post-racial" society (Kaplan, 2011). In its most extreme form, individuals who believe this myth oppose government-funded social programs on the grounds that they help only "others" who no longer need such assistance and ignore the needs of many hard-working Americans.

A second perspective is based on the premise that in the development of social policies and programs, African Americans and Latinos, in particular, are often equated with welfare recipients, criminals, substance abusers, and individuals who prefer government handouts to work or are qualified only for low-paying, low-responsibility jobs. According to this view, the failure of minorities of color to share fully in the nation's economic prosperity and to take advantage of existing opportunities results from their cultural, psychological, or moral shortcomings (Harding, 2016; Katiuzhinsky & Okech, 2014; Young, 2011; Marable, 2009; Wilson, 2009). Proponents of this myth prefer social policies and programs that correct individual behavior, such as job-readiness programs, parenting classes, and nutrition education.

The facts about race and social policy paint a very different picture from both of these interpretations. Although African Americans and Latinos have experienced some upward mobility in terms of occupational status since the 1960s, the class structure of the African American and Latino communities does not mirror that of the broader society. Official statistics reveal that African Americans and Latinos are still 2 1/2 to 3 times more likely to be poor than are whites and that substantial numbers live in deep poverty, less than 50% of the federal poverty line (U.S. Census Bureau, 2011, 2015; see Figures 1.7a and 1.7b). In addition, the distribution of wealth and health outcomes is even more skewed along racial lines (Shapiro, Meschede, & Osoro, 2013; Kochar & Fry, 2014; see Figure 1.8c). Recent economic developments, particularly globalization and the recession, and conscious policy choices have also had a disproportionately negative impact on persons of color. In combination, they have produced a marked decrease in the number of entry-level industrial jobs, cutbacks in public-sector employment (a major path to middle-class status for persons of color in the United States), reductions in expenditures on education and social services, and increased rates of incarceration and housing foreclosures (Alexander, 2010; Marable, 2009; Wilson, 2009). To a considerable extent, the response of the African American community to recent incidents of police violence has been fueled by its anger over these inter-connected developments. Figures 1.7a and 1.7b illustrate the persistent disparities in the poverty rates between whites and persons of color in the U.S.

As Jerome H. Schiele points out in Chapter 4 of this volume, the subordinate status of persons of color in the United States is not a historical aberration or the result of institutional deficiencies alone. It is an intrinsic part of the operations of the nation's socioeconomic system. Racial inequality and institutional racism, therefore, are not separate from the issue of class but, rather, closely related to it in the following ways.

First, policies and practices produced by institutional racism reduce the wages and employment prospects of *all* workers. (See Figures 1.8a, b, and c) They lower the floor on income while providing a "wedge issue" that divides workers with common interests along racial lines, thereby reducing the possibility of multiracial social justice coalitions. Second, they reduce the supply of essential public services, such as health care, education, and housing, to low- and middle-income individuals of all races because the "needy" are stereotyped as belonging primarily to certain less capable races or ethnic groups, a phenomenon intensified by increasing geographic segregation (Wright, Ellis, Holloway, &

Figure 1.8a US Unemployment Rate by Race, 2005–2015.

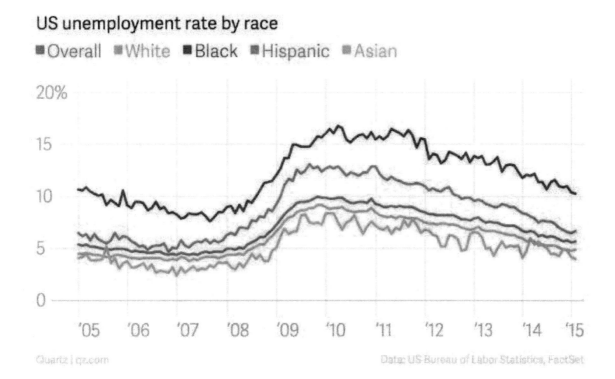

US unemployment rate by race

■Overall ■White ■Black ■Hispanic ■Asian

Quartz | qz.com   Data: US Bureau of Labor Statistics, FactSet

Figure 1.8b Trends in workers earning poverty-level wages, by race and ethnicity, 1973–2013.

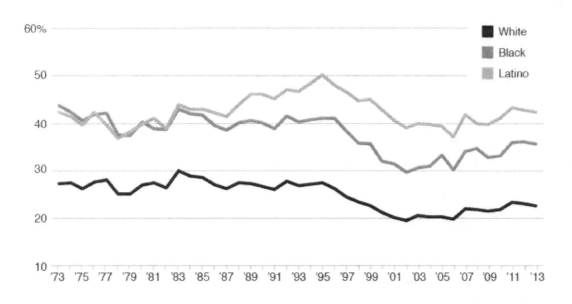

Source: U.S. Census Bureau.

Figure 1.8c Distribution of wealth by race and ethnicity.

Median Net Worth, by Race/Ethnicity, 2011

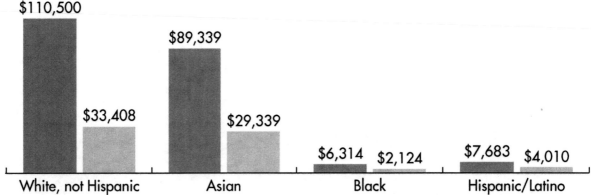

Note: Households headed by Other Races had a net worth of $19,023 (or $7,113 excluding home equity).

Source: U.S. Census Bureau, Survey of Income and Program Participation, 2008 Panel, Wave 10.

Wong, 2014; Baynton, 2001; Massey & Denton, 1993). Finally, the presence of racial conflict reduces political pressure on government to provide other public services that would have a progressive distributional effect and promote social justice.

MODELS OF POLICY DEVELOPMENT

There are several ways of analyzing the process of policy development—that is, the means by which a private trouble, through the phases described above and filtered through the lens of social construction, becomes a public issue. The most commonly used models are listed below.

> *Systems Model:* This approach focuses on the interaction of three components, what systems theorists refer to as inputs, throughputs, and outputs. Policy inputs include available resources, demographics, the distribution of power, and dominant value perspectives. They also include the impact of political parties, interest groups, policymakers, and the public's perception of the seriousness of the problem. Throughputs consist of the political "rules of the game," governmental and nongovernmental authority structures, and the interpretation of the issue by the media and key policymakers. Policy outputs include laws, regulations, budgets, judicial decisions, and the programs and services policies create.

Elite Model: The elite model is based on the assumption that a few individuals and groups dominate the policy-making process by shaping the agenda (Bottomore, 1991) and thereby limiting the possible outcomes of policy debate. One version of this model refers to the "Iron Triangle" of policy-making, which consists of major Congressional committees responsible for legislation in a particular area, the departments of the executive branch of government responsible for developing regulations and implementing legislative policies, and powerful inter-

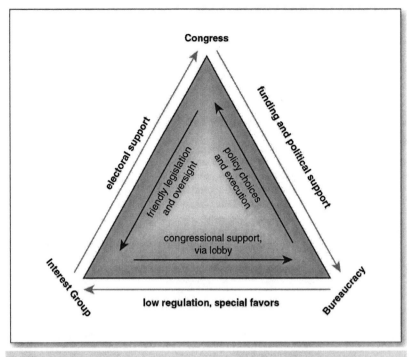

Figure 1.9 The Iron Triangle of Policymaking.

est groups that influence policy development and implementation through lobbying and political contributions (see Figure 1.9). The development of foreign and military policy is a prime example of how the elite model works. In the domestic sphere, education policy provides a useful illustration; here, the "iron triangle" consists of elected officials, the Department of Education, education experts in universities or think tanks, and teachers' unions.

Rational Choice Model: This model is popular today, particularly among market-oriented policy analysts who have adopted a neoliberal approach to social welfare and social policy development. Proponents of this approach regard policymaking as an objective process in which the costs and benefits of policy options can be quantified, measured, and used to inform policy decisions. They also assume that *all costs* can be calculated in this manner and that comparisons between different types of costs and benefits can be useful to policymakers in determining which policy options are most efficient and effective (Eriksson, 2011).

Interest Group Model: For many years, this model, which is based upon pluralist theory, has been a popular explanation of the policymaking process in the United States. It assumes that policy outcomes are the products of compromise between competing interest groups and that these groups have relatively equal access to decision-making circles. In addition, pluralist theorists assume that all parties will primarily work within the "system" and strive to reach common ground through negotiation. Although all sides in this competition for resources and influence engage in advocacy and popular education in their attempts to sway public opinion,

A Systems Model of Policy Change

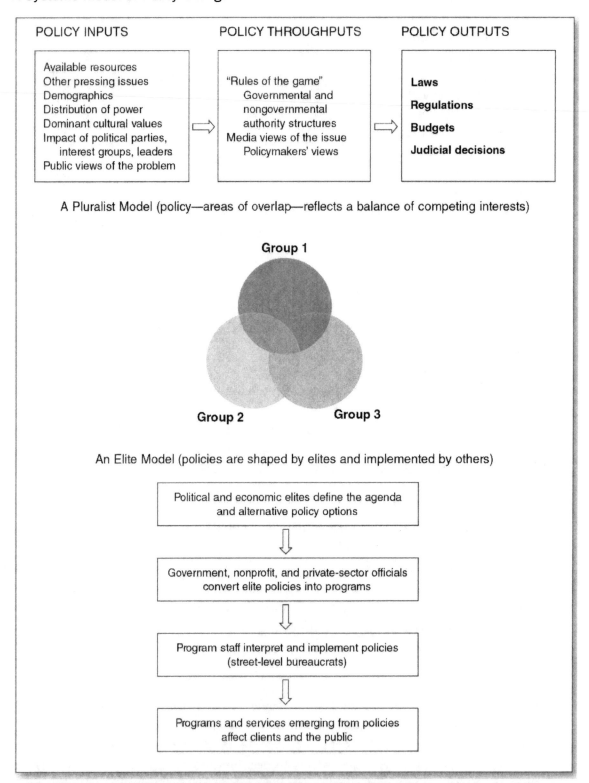

POLICY INPUTS	POLICY THROUGHPUTS	POLICY OUTPUTS

Available resources
Other pressing issues
Demographics
Distribution of power
Dominant cultural values
Impact of political parties,
    interest groups, leaders
Public views of the problem

"Rules of the game"
    Governmental and
    nongovernmental
    authority structures
Media views of the issue
Policymakers' views

Laws

Regulations

Budgets

Judicial decisions

A Pluralist Model (policy—areas of overlap—reflects a balance of competing interests)

Group 1

Group 2   **Group 3**

An Elite Model (policies are shaped by elites and implemented by others)

Political and economic elites define the agenda
and alternative policy options

Government, nonprofit, and private-sector officials
convert elite policies into programs

Program staff interpret and implement policies
(street-level bureaucrats)

Programs and services emerging from policies
affect clients and the public

Figure 1.10 Models of the Policy Development Process.

they remain committed to achieving some resolution of the issue (Lassman, 2011). The development of the Patient Protection and Affordable Care Act (ACA) of 2010 provides a clear recent illustration of the strengths and limitations of pluralism. [*See Chapter 14 in this volume for further discussion of the process by which the ACA was created.*]

Incremental Model: This explanation of policymaking, referred to by Charles Lindblom (1980) as "The Science of Muddling Through," complements the pluralist model. It views the evolution of social policy as a gradual process in which small steps are taken that, over time, produce major policy changes. The gradual expansion of Social Security from 1935 to the present is often cited as a good example of incremental policy development.

Conflict Model: Unlike the interest group or pluralist model, this model assumes that policies emerge from conflicts between forces that are unwilling or unable to reach consensus or to compromise. Through a variety of "contests," including elections, legislative battles, and judicial decisions, one side wins and determines the policy results. Conflict approaches assume that competing interests will use a variety of forms of advocacy, both inside and outside the "system," join forces with and mobilize social movement supporters to advance their cause and, if necessary, engage in protest tactics to arouse public opinion and change the view of policymakers in their favor (Acemoglu, Egorov, & Sonin, 2011). Examples of the use of conflict approaches include the labor struggles of the 1930s, the civil rights and feminist movements of the 1960s, the work of AIDS activists in the 1980s, and the Tea Party, Occupy Wall Street, and Black Lives Matter movements in recent years.

KEY POLICY CONCEPTS

Understanding social policy and the policymaking process requires some familiarity with frequently used policy concepts, so that the process does not remain solely the province of policy "wonks" or powerful institutional leaders. Some of these concepts refer to the nature of policy itself; others help explain key components of the policymaking process and the role of key players.

THE SOCIAL DIVISION OF WELFARE

When they think of social policy or social welfare most people imagine a system of benefits that primarily assist low-income persons. Policies such as welfare (TANF), Medicaid, food stamps (now called the Supplemental Nutritional Assistance Program, or SNAP), energy assistance, and subsidized housing often come to mind. This limited perspective on the nature of social policy often leads to the stigmatization of individuals and families who receive these benefits and reflects a misunderstanding about the extensive role that social policy plays in contemporary society.

In a classic article, the great British social policy theorist Richard Titmuss (1976) provided an alternative perspective called the **social division of welfare**. Titmuss argued that the purpose of a nation's social policy system is to promote redistribution—that is, efforts to redirect resources (both income and in-kind) to specific groups, which thereby affect their standard of living and quality of life. According to Titmuss, the issue of redistribution is addressed by social policy in three different ways. The most obvious type—social welfare—consists in the United States of direct payment to individuals (via cash assistance or in-kind benefits) through the Social Security retirement program, Unemployment Insurance, welfare, or veterans' benefits. In Great Britain, these benefits are often called "social services." Titmuss referred to them as forms of **social welfare**. In the United States, they are sometimes referred to generically as "welfare" and, at other times, as "entitlement programs." Note how both American labels contain subtle pejorative assumptions about the recipients of these benefits.

A second type of welfare, **fiscal welfare**, provides aid to people of *all* social classes through tax expenditures—that is, ways the government allows people to keep more of their income, provided they engage in certain behavior. Examples of fiscal welfare that assist individuals and families include exemptions for people who have dependent children, the home mortgage and property tax deductions for homeowners, the child care tax credit for families that have children in child care, and the Earned Income Tax Credit (EITC). [*See Chapter 7 and Chapter 12 this volume for further discussion of the EITC.*] Corporations, which are treated as "individuals" by the U.S. legal system, also receive a number of types of fiscal welfare, such as the oil depletion allowance, funds to promote overseas exports, and various subsidies to different industries. With the exception of the EITC, most fiscal welfare in the United States benefits the middle and upper classes.

The third form of welfare is **occupational welfare**, which consists of benefits people receive through their employment. Often called "fringe benefits," these benefits include health or life insurance, pensions, housing and transportation allowances, and child care. As Mimi Abramovitz (2001) has frequently pointed out, taking this broader view of the nation's social welfare system reveals that "everyone is on welfare." The irony, of course, is that only certain individuals are looked down on for receiving "welfare" benefits, while most of the population considers the benefits they receive as "natural," if they think of them at all. As some of the rhetoric expressed during the 2016 election campaign reflects, this misunderstanding fuels a great deal of the insecurity, anger, and mistrust underlying today's political conflicts.

TAXES AND SOCIAL POLICY

Either directly or indirectly, all three of these forms of "welfare" require a source of revenue and affect the distribution of tax burdens (or fiscal costs) in a society. In determining whether a given policy promotes social justice, it is important, therefore, to assess both the goals and substance of these policies and how they are funded. As discussed in Chapter 7, most policies in the United States are funded through taxes of some sort, which are collected at every level of government. One way to analyze if the impact of tax policy is just is to examine whether a given method of taxation is "progressive" or "regressive."

A progressive tax places a heavier burden on individuals or households with higher incomes. The federal income tax is the prime example of a moderately progressive tax. Higher earners pay a higher rate of taxes on their taxable "earned income" incomes (i.e., from wages), which is currently 39.6%. It is important to note that in 1980, the highest "marginal" tax rate was 70% and, in the prosperous 1950s it was 90%. This dramatic change is the result of tax cuts that have primarily benefited affluent Americans.

There are other features of tax policy, however, that make even the income tax considerably less progressive. Numerous tax expenditures (see "fiscal welfare" above), such as the home mortgage deduction and child care tax credit, provide a benefit primarily to middle- and upper-income households. In addition, certain types of income—so-called "unearned income," such as dividends, interest, and capital gains on the sale of stocks or real estate—are taxed at a different rate (currently 15–20%). These policies can create unjust outcomes as the following example illustrates.

Take two individuals, Mary and Mark, who each have a taxable income of $100,000/year (i.e., this is their income subject to federal and state taxes after all deductions are taken into account). Mary has a well-paying job as an executive of a major nonprofit social service organization. Her taxable income places her in the top tax bracket, so she pays about $35,000/year in federal income taxes alone. Mark is not employed and derives his income from a combination of real estate investments, stocks, and bonds he inherited from his parents. His taxable income is also $100,000/year, but unlike Mary, he pays only $15–20,000/year in federal taxes. (This example assumes that all other aspects of Mary's and Mark's tax returns are identical.) How would you rationalize this difference? What does it reveal about the justice of our tax system?

In contrast to progressive taxes, the impact of a **regressive tax** falls more heavily on lower-income households. Two common examples of regressive taxes are the "payroll tax" (which funds Social Security and Medicare) and the sales tax. All wage earners in the United States must pay the payroll tax, which is currently 7.65–8.55% (twice that for the self-employed). On the surface, this would appear to be equitable as it applies to everyone who is employed. However, this tax is regressive for two reasons. First, individuals whose income is derived entirely from capital gains do not pay this tax; only wage earners do. In addition, even those individuals whose income is primarily from wages pay the bulk of this tax on only the first $118,500 (in 2016) they earn. (They pay the Medicare portion of the payroll tax, 1.45%, on all earned income [salary] up to $200,000; this increases to 2.35% on earned income above $200,000.)

The same reasoning applies to sales taxes. All individuals, regardless of the size or source of their income, pay the same-percentage tax on those items their state (or county) taxes (e.g., clothing). Again, this would seem to be fair. Yet, analysts have demonstrated that while wealthier individuals may pay more sales tax each year in absolute dollars, lower-income persons pay a higher proportion of their income in sales taxes (Citizens for Tax Justice, 2012).

Two glaring examples of how the tax system can produce inequities came to light during the 2012 Presidential campaign. When Mitt Romney, the Republican candidate, released his tax returns, the public responded negatively to the revelation that he paid a much lower proportion of his (substantial) income than the average taxpayer. In another incident, billionaire investor, Warren Buffett, reported that he paid a lower overall tax rate than his secretary did. Unlike Romney, however, who justified his low tax rate in part by the large amount he contributed to charity, Buffett publicly decried the unfairness of a system in which his secretary paid a higher proportion of her income.

The manner in which the government collects taxes has become particularly significant for social policy development in recent decades for several reasons. First, federal and state tax cuts since the 1980s have resulted in middle- and lower-income households bearing a larger share of the nation's overall tax burden— that is, paying more to help fund government programs, from military expenditures to social services. As the chart in Figure 1.11 indicates, most of the benefits of recent tax cuts have gone to upper-income households.

Second, during the past several decades, as states have been given more and more responsibility for funding social policies—a process referred to as **policy devolution**—a higher percentage of social policies are now funded by state and local government. These levels of government rely more heavily on regressive taxes for their revenue (primarily the sales tax) than does the federal government (which relies primarily on the income tax). [*See Chapter 7 in this volume for further discussion of the relationship between tax policy and government spending.*]

Third, anti-tax movements during the past four decades (from the movement that produced California's landmark Proposition 13 in 1978 to today's Tea Party) and opposition to tax increases by the Republican Party and some segments of the Democratic Party, have made it increasingly difficult for governments to fund essential services, particularly in tough economic times, such as the Great Recession, when regular tax revenues have decreased (Skocpol & Williamson, 2012; Stocker, 1991). During and after the Great

Figure 1.11 U.S. Income Inequality, 1967–2011.

Historical US Income Inequality

Source: US Census Bureau, Income Limits for Each Fifth and Top 5 Percent of Households

(Current Dollars)

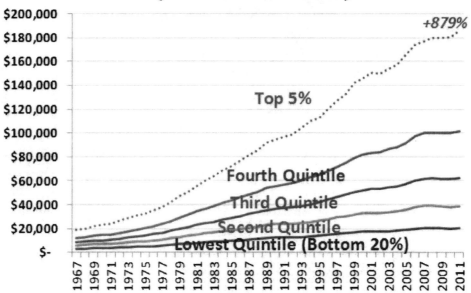

Recession, hundreds of thousands of public-sector employees—teachers, firefighters, police officers, and social workers—were laid off and many cities and counties eliminated long-standing programs, closed libraries and parks, and reduced service hours (Johnson, Oliff, & Williams, 2011). For the most part, these cuts have not been restored even as the economy has recovered somewhat. A fundamental social policy question for the future, therefore, is: How will the nation pay for the services required to maintain its competitiveness in a global economy and meet the basic needs of its growing and increasingly diverse population?

DEFICITS AND THE DEBT

There has been considerable controversy lately over the size of the federal deficit and the national debt and their impact on the overall health of the U.S. economy. [*See Chapters 3 and 7 in this volume for a more detailed discussion of these concepts.*] Since 2011, opposition to increasing the nation's debt ceiling, which used to be a mere formality, has become an instrument of policymaking, as conservative legislators demand spending cuts in return for their approval. (Ironically, at the end of the Clinton Administration, the federal government had a large surplus, and during the 2000 Presidential election policy debates centered on how that surplus should be used—to pay off the national debt within a generation or to secure the funding of Social Security and Medicare for the "baby boomers.") Without going into the details of how this surplus became a deficit, it is important to understand the distinction between the federal deficit and the national debt, and their implications for social policy.

The **deficit** refers to the *annual* difference between the revenues the federal government receives (primarily through taxes) and its total outlays or expenditures. Since the government cannot spend funds it does not have, in fiscal years when expenditures exceed revenues (most years since the 1930s), the government has to borrow money to make up the difference. Sometimes, government expenses are a form of investment in the future; the construction of bridges, roads, universities, and hospitals is a good example, as is the funding of long-term projects such as the space program and development of the Internet. (This is comparable to families borrowing money to buy a home or pay for college tuition.) The government makes up the difference between revenues and expenditures by selling Treasury bills and bonds to banks, foreign governments, and individual investors, who are essentially lending the government money. In order to induce them to do so, the government pays them interest. (To make this even simpler, think of your household budget. In those months when your expenses exceed your income, you may have to borrow money—often by charging purchases to a credit card. In return for lending you these funds, the credit card company charges you interest.) The total amount that the government owes to all its creditors, principal plus interest, accumulated over the years constitutes the national **debt**. Each year that the federal government runs a deficit, it must borrow more money and the national debt increases.

Unlike the federal government, state and local governments are generally prohibited by their constitutions or charters from running a fiscal deficit or from borrowing funds to pay for general operating expenses. They can borrow money (largely through the sale of bonds) only for capital projects such as road construction or the development of a new college campus. This is why increased fiscal pressures on state and local governments—the combined product of policy devolution, federal cutbacks, and economic slowdowns or recessions—have become so severe and pose a serious threat to the maintenance of adequate levels of spending for social policies and programs. [*See Chapter 7 this volume for further discussion of the federal budget process.*]

Figures 1.12a, 1.12b, and 1.12c illustrate how the government spends its revenues. In reviewing these charts, it is important to note the different perspectives they provide. For example, if you looked solely at Figure 1.12a, you would get the impression that Social Security, Medicare, and other so-called "entitlement programs" comprise the bulk of the Federal budget. This impression is often used to buttress arguments in favor of reining in spending on entitlements because of their impact on the federal budget deficit and the national debt. As discussed in Chapters 7 and 11, however, this would be a false impression. These mandatory expenditures (Figure 1.12b) are largely funded from targeted taxes, such as the payroll tax, not from general revenues. When this mandatory spending is subtracted from the total federal budget and only discretionary spending is analyzed (Figure 1.12c), a very different impression is revealed: Military expenditures (including veterans' benefits, some portion of expenditures on energy, e.g., for weapons research, and part of the interest for past military expenditures) now comprise nearly 2/3 of the budget. This demonstrates that the budget can be used both as a tool of policy development and for policy advocacy.

ECONOMICS AND SOCIAL POLICY

Economists differ on the impact of deficits and debt on the health of the nation. Some argue that excessive government borrowing reduces the amount of capital available to the private sector and raises interest rates on business and consumer loans. Others assert that, particularly during recessions or periods of economic slowdown, government spending is necessary to stimulate the economy by providing a floor

Figure 1.12a Total U.S. Federal Spending, Fiscal Year 2016.

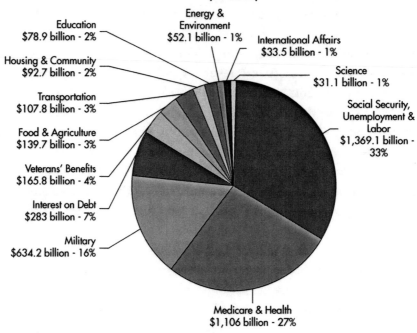

**President's Proposed $4.1 Trillion Total Spending Budget
(FY 2016)**

Education
$78.9 billion - 2%

Energy &
Environment
$52.1 billion - 1%

International Affairs
$33.5 billion - 1%

Housing & Community
$92.7 billion - 2%

Science
$31.1 billion - 1%

Transportation
$107.8 billion - 3%

Social Security,
Unemployment &
Labor
$1,369.1 billion -
33%

Food & Agriculture
$139.7 billion - 3%

Veterans' Benefits
$165.8 billion - 4%

Interest on Debt
$283 billion - 7%

Military
$634.2 billion - 16%

Medicare & Health
$1,106 billion - 27%

Source: OMB. National Priorities Project.

Figure 1.12b Mandatory U.S. Federal Spending, Fiscal Year 2016.

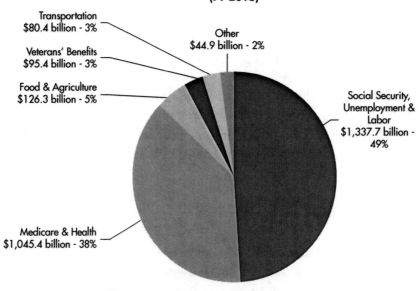

**President's Proposed $2.63 Trillion Mandatory Spending Budget
(FY 2016)**

Transportation
$80.4 billion - 3%

Other
$44.9 billion - 2%

Veterans' Benefits
$95.4 billion - 3%

Food & Agriculture
$126.3 billion - 5%

Social Security,
Unemployment &
Labor
$1,337.7 billion -
49%

Medicare & Health
$1,045.4 billion - 38%

Source: OMB. National Priorities Project.

Figure 1.12c Total U.S. Discretionary Spending, Fiscal 2016.

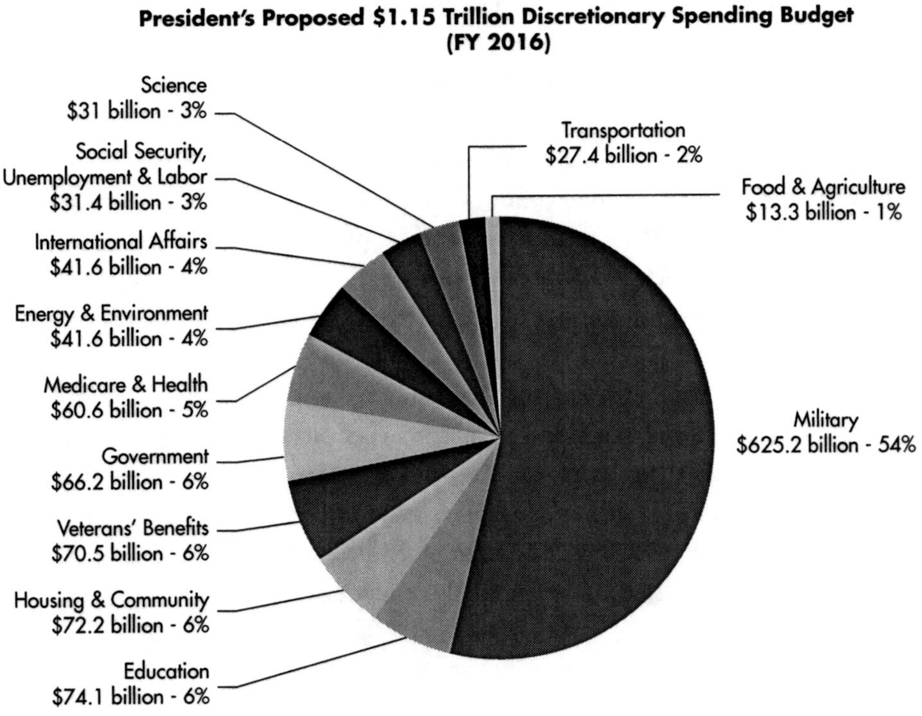

President's Proposed $1.15 Trillion Discretionary Spending Budget (FY 2016)

Science
$31 billion - 3%

Social Security,
Unemployment & Labor
$31.4 billion - 3%

International Affairs
$41.6 billion - 4%

Energy & Environment
$41.6 billion - 4%

Medicare & Health
$60.6 billion - 5%

Government
$66.2 billion - 6%

Veterans' Benefits
$70.5 billion - 6%

Housing & Community
$72.2 billion - 6%

Education
$74.1 billion - 6%

Transportation
$27.4 billion - 2%

Food & Agriculture
$13.3 billion - 1%

Military
$625.2 billion - 54%

Source: OMB. National Priorities Project.

on consumption and creating jobs. In addition, many analysts believe that only government possesses sufficient resources to make the investments in human capital development and physical infrastructure required by a global market system (Krugman, 2012; Reich, 2010).

Since the 1930s, the relationship of government to the economy in both Republican and Democratic Administrations has been guided primarily by one form of Keynesian economic theory or another. Based on the ideas of the British economist John Maynard Keynes (1936), Keynesians posit that modern, so-called "mixed economies" (i.e., those in which some items, such as consumer goods, are purchased in the marketplace, and others, such as education and social services, are at least partly funded by government) require some level of government intervention to regulate the business cycle and avoid the dramatic ups and downs that occurred throughout the 19th and early 20th centuries.

According to Keynesians, governments can accomplish this goal through three means:

1. *Monetary policy*—The Federal Reserve (in the U.S.) and central banks (in most other industrial nations), attempt to control the money supply to stimulate or "cool down" the economy when it is "overheated" (growing too fast). Since the 2007 recession, the Federal Reserve has kept interest rates at record low levels to make it easier for banks and businesses to obtain capital and for some consumers to acquire home mortgages in order to revive the flagging economy.

2. *Tax policy*—Tax cuts are designed to stimulate the economy in the midst of a recession while tax increases during a period of rapid economic growth attempt to slow it down and reduce the likelihood of inflation. During the past decade, the U.S. government has used tax policy to promote economic growth

in at least two ways: It has extended the Bush Administration's tax cuts and approved a temporary reduction in the payroll tax.

3.   *Government spending*—Government revenues are used to "prime the pump" of the economy and to maintain a floor on consumer spending, which accounts for about 70% of the nation's gross domestic product (GDP). The American Recovery and Reinvestment Act of 2009, which included a combination of tax rebates and government spending, is the most recent example of a government "stimulus package."

There are three schools of thought among Keynesians, each of which emphasizes a different perspective on government's role in regulating the economy. Conservative Keynesians focus on providing tax breaks for corporations to spur industrial production and economic growth, creating what is sometimes referred to as a "trickle-down" effect. Advocates of so-called "supply-side economics," although they emphasize the importance of shrinking the size of government, actually promote a form of conservative Keynesianism.

Liberal Keynesians, such as those who inspired the New Deal and the War on Poverty (see Chapter 2 in this volume), favor increased social expenditures and tax cuts or credits to individuals and families as a means to stimulate demand. These are primarily "top-down" efforts to redistribute income and wealth. Finally, Radical Keynesians support policies such as guaranteed full employment; controls on prices, rents, and interest rates; a major overhaul of the tax code; demilitarization of the nation's economy; and a general reordering of national priorities (Arestis & Sawyer, 2010; Ventelou, 2005).

POLITICS AND SOCIAL POLICY

As discussed throughout this volume, the development of social policies involves the resolution of fundamental issues about the current status and future direction of a society. In a democratic nation, this resolution occurs in the political arena at various levels and increasingly in the media. But what is this "political arena"? Many Americans have a narrow view of politics; they believe that it involves only electoral contests in which there are clear winners and losers. Yet, because politics is essentially about the acquisition and use of power, it is an inescapable feature of all aspects of our lives. Compare the following interpretation of "politics" with those with which you are familiar:

> A statement is political when either the content of the issue is viewed differently by people from different social groups ... or the decision has consequences for different social groups or both.... As long as society is differentiated along ethnic, sex, or social class lines, politics pervades all of social life. You are involved in politics and so is your mother (Goldberg & Elliott, 1980, p. 478).

According to this perspective, politics cannot be separated from practice or from the policies that shape the parameters of practice (Reisch & Jani, 2012). Instead, politics defines the issues with which policymakers will engage, determines the alternative solutions available, and establishes the criteria by which the success or failure of policies will be evaluated. Virtually every policy debate—whether at the local, state, national, or international level, or in the public, non-profit, or private for-profit sector—is, therefore, framed by political discourse. Because politics is at the core of all decisions about our priorities, conflicts recur over the respective roles of the legislative, executive, and judicial branches of government, about the appropriate balance of power between the federal government and the states, and regarding the most desirable relationship between government and the market. *How* these conflicts are resolved is just as important as *what* they resolve. In general, their resolution is the product of a combination of individual and group self-interest and the influence of wide-ranging ideological perspectives.

More specifically, politics determines how inclusive a policy will be—that is, whether it will be universal or selective in application. It reflects public opinion about government's potential to solve people's social and economic problems and the biases of policymakers toward certain issues, groups, or strategies. Politics determines whether the goals of a policy are considered feasible and whether we provide adequate resources to achieve them. Above all, politics influences who has the power to define a condition as a problem worthy of attention.

The politics of problem definition is reflected, therefore, in a variety of ways: in the history of how the problem was addressed, in the underlying assumptions about the causes of the problem, in defining the "population-at-risk" (see below), and in assessing which interventions are most likely to produce desired results, how they should be funded, and how they should be implemented.

POLITICAL FEASIBILITY

While many social policies may be desirable from a value-based perspective, or widely recognized as necessary, obstacles to their enactment may still exist. One barrier is the lack of adequate resources. Even in the best economic times, resources are finite and problems are seemingly without limit. Another obstacle is cultural intransigence—that is, resistance to a policy initiative because it challenges and overturns long-standing cultural norms. Recent examples include opposition to same-sex marriage or the rights of transgendered persons. In other eras, proponents of women's suffrage, supporters of civil rights for racial minorities, and advocates for organized labor encountered similar resistance.

Because political resistance to policy change is the norm, rather than the exception, policy advocates must consider the political feasibility of their goals when they consider which change strategies would be most effective. Political feasibility refers to the level of acceptability of a particular proposal within the *present* political context. Political partisanship, public opinion, entrenched ideological positions, groups' self-interest, and the existence of other policy priorities all determine the feasibility of a policy proposal. Political feasibility also influences how proponents frame a policy initiative to make its acceptance by policymakers and the general public more likely. For example, in promoting the Affordable Care Act, the Obama Administration emphasized how it would reduce the costs of health care far more than it focused on the humane or egalitarian aspects of the legislation. More recently, a rare bipartisan consensus is emerging in Congress and in a number of state legislatures about the need for criminal justice reform. This consensus did not develop because conservatives and liberals underwent an ideological conversion. Rather, what is gradually bringing disparate political forces together is mutual recognition of the staggering costs of imprisoning so many non-violent offenders in U.S. society.

The feasibility or acceptability of a policy proposal, therefore, can increase (or decline) as a result of changes in the environment. Advocates can shape public opinion through popular education campaigns or the use of media. They can also help mobilize groups that have a stake in policy change to pressure policymakers to take action. Their power is enhanced through the development of new organizations, such as coalitions, and the possibility of new rewards, including indirect benefits to the public. As the public views a particular issue with greater understanding and sympathy, the issue becomes more legitimate in its eyes. Recent changes in popular attitudes about marriage equality, climate change, and police-community relations in African American communities are good illustrations of this process.

Over the past 3–4 decades, as a result of global economic forces and the ideological rationales that have accompanied them, a major trend within the United States has been to shift the responsibility for social policy implementation from both federal and local governments to the private sector. This phenomenon, referred to as **privatization,** involves "shifting into non-governmental hands some or all roles in producing a good or service that was once publicly produced or might be publicly produced" (Bendick, 1997, p. 98). There are two broad categories of privatization. One version of privatization is sometimes referred to as "load shedding;" it involves the transfer of government services or costs to the private sector. The other—also the product of conscious policy decisions—reflects the goal of empowering so-called "mediating institutions" at the community level both to bridge the gap between the market and the state and to serve as a buffer that protects localities from their divisions (Berger & Neuhaus, 1977).

Although often used interchangeably, the transfer of responsibility from government to the private, nonprofit sector is a very different form of privatization from the transfer of the public sector's role to for-profit entities. The former reflects what Dennis Young (1999) termed the longstanding "complementary" and "supplementary" relationships between the nonprofit sector and government that uniquely exist in the U.S. In Young's formulation, the "complementary" relationship involves cooperation between nonprofits and the government to provide essential supports. Examples include government contracting for health and behavioral health care to nonprofit hospitals and community agencies. The "supplementary" relationships refers to the role nonprofits have traditionally played in filling gaps in services that neither government nor the market can provide or chooses to provide. Often, these services are for hard-to-reach or highly stigmatized populations, such as persons experiencing homelessness or persons with HIV/AIDS. The collaboration between government and the nonprofit sector, therefore, can be used for multiple purposes: to cut program costs (i.e., make services more cost efficient), promote increased service innovation, and provide services that are more responsive to community needs.

The increased use of for-profit entities to deliver essential programs and services, however, is a more recent development. It reflects the growing preference among U.S. policymakers for market-oriented solutions to social problems. Examples range from corporate implementation of welfare-to-work programs after welfare reform, managed care behavioral health programs, charter schools, and the construction of private prisons. Proponents of this approach argue that the for-profit sector can deliver services more efficiently, that competition keeps costs down, and that privatization protects people's freedom by preventing the expansion of the size and scope of government. Critics of this approach, however, assert that short-term cost savings have largely occurred by lowering employees' wages, reducing services, diminishing service quality, limiting access, and shifting the focus of programs to more affluent, fee-paying clients. They also maintain that privatization perpetuates the exclusion and marginalization of low-power, low-resource individuals and communities.

There are two aspects of this form of privatization that critics find particularly troubling. One is that it is part of a broader effort to shift control of formerly public assets (parks, airwaves) to the private, for-profit sector. This diminishes the common space collectively owned by all members of society and alters the meaning of community and a democratic society. A second consequence is that by applying market-oriented concepts and models to both public- and nonprofit-sector activities, agencies that used to be part of government (e.g., AMTRAK and the postal service) are now treated like corporations. Since the 1980s, this phenomenon of "marketization" has had a major impact on nonprofit social service agencies as well.

Researchers have found this trend has altered the mission and basic character of these organizations and produced greater competition for increasingly scarce resources at a time when more inter-organizational collaboration is needed (Alexander, 1999; Gronbjerg & Salamon, 2002).

EXERCISE: THE PRIVATIZATION OF SOCIAL POLICY & SOCIAL SERVICES

The privatization of social welfare programs raises a number of fundamental questions. Ask yourself:

1. When is it appropriate for a particular service to be privatized?
2. If the responsibility for policy implementation is transferred to the for-profit sector, what is an acceptable rate of profit?
3. How can the goal of profit (or revenue) enhancement be balanced with service quality?
4. To what extent should government regulate services delivered by the private sector or determine what constitutes an acceptable rate of profit?
5. Should such services be standardized—that is, treated like a commodity?
6. Which services should be coercive, and which should be voluntary?
7. Which approach to privatization best promotes social justice goals? How will services to the most difficult clients be assured?

Since the mid-1990s the emergence of two issues has further complicated the picture. One was the insertion of the "Charitable Choice" initiative into the 1996 welfare reform legislation; it required states to spend 10% of their TANF block grants through "faith-based" social service agencies. Although sectarian (religiously-based) organizations, such as Catholic Charities, Lutheran Social Services, and Associated Jewish Charities, have played a major role in social service delivery for decades and congregations of all religious faiths have provided valuable aid to needy populations throughout U.S. history (Cnaan & Boddie, 2002), recent policy initiatives have funded some religious organizations of a different nature. These faith-based organizations often have staff with fewer professional credentials and limited accountability for their actions, which have included using funds from government grants and contracts to engage in religious activities. Some critics have charged that the promotion of faith-based services threatens to breach the "church–state" wall and endanger the civil rights of religious minorities and LGBTQ (lesbian, gay, bisexual, transgender, and queer) persons, while delivering services of questionable effectiveness (Belcher, Fandetti, & Cole, 2004; Daly, 2006).

More recently—as discussed in Chapter 10 of this volume—sectarian organizations and family-owned companies have engaged in judicial challenges to the provision of the Affordable Care Act that requires employers to include coverage of contraceptives in the health insurance plans their employees receive. They have even refused to submit a form requesting a waiver of this requirement as part of a compromise proposed by the Obama Administration. The current standoff on this issue raises questions about the meaning of "religious freedom" and the extent to which the exercise of this freedom can be used to limit the rights of others.

A FRAMEWORK FOR POLICY ANALYSIS

To asseess the various dimensions of a social policy, Gilbert and Terrell (2013) developed a useful framework for policy analysis, a topic that will be discussed in greater detail in Chapter 6 of this volume. Their framework is constructed around four central questions:

1. *What kind of benefits does the policy offer?* Answering this question involves determining the nature, size, and frequency of the benefits it provides. Examples of policy benefits include cash assistance, in-kind benefits (e.g., food), services such as counseling or job training, vouchers (e.g., for housing or education), enhanced power, increased opportunity, and the promise of future assets (such as through Individual Development Accounts or IDAs).

2. *What are the criteria for receiving these benefits?* In other words, who is entitled to receive the benefits offered? This question refers to the eligibility criteria that have been established by the policy and the type of risks it covers. Criteria may include marital or employment status (past and present), geographic residence, family size, health, age, educational level, gender, military service, race/ethnicity, religion, IQ, or income.

3. *How are the policy's benefits delivered?* This involves examining the structure and character of the institutions developed to administer the policy. Subsidiary questions include: What level of government should deliver the benefits? What is the best mix of public, nonprofit, and private for-profit sector participation? Should policy implementation be centralized or decentralized? Should it be standardized or tailored to specific situations? Should a policy's benefits be delivered separately or integrated into other policy systems? Should the policy be delivered through a distinct, "categorical" program or folded into a "block grant"?

4. *How are the benefits financed?* For example, are they financed through taxes (and of what type?), fees, or charitable contributions? Who will bear the fiscal cost of the policy?

A fifth question might be: How is the policy evaluated and by whom? In other words, who determines if the policy is working as intended?

As you analyze the policies presented in this book, keep in mind (a) the range of alternatives within each dimension of the above questions; (b) the values underlying these alternatives; and (c) the assumptions or theories implicit in these alternatives (Gilbert & Terrell, 2013). Ask yourself: Is the policy fair (or just)? Does it fit within contemporary cultural norms? Have the policy's underlying assumptions been empirically tested? Are they feasible in the real world? Who benefits from the policy—directly or indirectly—from its current construction? What are the potential consequences for third parties, intended or unintended? Finally, is the policy as designed capable of achieving its intended goals (i.e., is it effective?) and is it reasonably efficient in terms of financial and social costs?

ADDITIONAL EVALUATIVE CONCEPTS

The following are some additional evaluative concepts that policymakers and advocates use to analyze social policy. [*Further details about the process of policy analysis can be found in Chapter 6 in this volume*]. As you read the chapters in Part III of this volume, which address specific areas of social policy, it would be useful to apply these concepts to both contemporary policies and proposals for policy change.

Since most social policies target a specific issue or problem, it is important to understand the **population-at-risk** the policy is attempting to address. **Population-at-risk** refers to the number and character of persons who are vulnerable to a particular social, economic, or environmental hazard. This could be determined by looking at such factors as gender, geography, age, ability status, occupation, sexual orientation, race/ethnicity, immigration status, and employment status. In determining the population-at-risk, it is important to ask two questions: (a) In what ways are we measuring risk? (b) What are the conditions that create this risk?

A related concept is **inclusiveness of coverage**. This measures the extent to which a defined population-at-risk is protected against a specific hazard—for example, how many persons who are currently jobless are receiving unemployment benefits? This concept is linked to the determination of eligibility for a specific benefit. Generally, the number of persons protected by a policy (in theory) is greater than the number actually receiving benefits. For example, in the United States, less than two-thirds of the individuals eligible to receive SNAP (food stamps) obtain this benefit.

Another way to examine the connection between a policy's goals and its impact is to assess the policy's **horizontal adequacy**. This measures the accessibility of a service or benefit to all persons who are eligible to receive it. It addresses the question: Does the policy reach the target population? In some instances, the horizontal adequacy of a policy changes over time. For example, when the Social Security Act was passed in 1935, it covered about 60% of the U.S. workforce. Today, it covers about 95%. [*See Chapter 11 in this volume for further details.*]

The receipt of an assigned benefit, however, does not mean that a service or benefit is sufficient to meet the needs of recipients. To determine the **vertical adequacy** of a policy, ask whether each recipient is covered satisfactorily. Again, using Social Security policy as an illustration, while the policy's horizontal adequacy is now very high, it is not yet vertically adequate. This is because the average retirement benefit (about $1,200/month) does not lift an individual above the federal poverty line.

The concepts of horizontal and vertical adequacy, however, do not assess the extent to which a particular policy promotes social justice. To do this, we need to apply the concept of **equity,** or fairness. Just as there are different definitions of social justice, so, too, there are different ways of examining the equity of a social policy.

One approach, **individual equity**, essentially states that "you get what you pay for." For example, the concept of individual equity is used to rationalize why higher wage earners receive higher Social Security retirement or unemployment insurance benefits, and why individuals who can afford "Cadillac" health insurance plans get superior coverage. By contrast, the concept of **social equity** is based on the premise that individuals should receive the benefits they need regardless of their past, current, or potential future contribution to society. This principle more closely aligns with the use of redistributive policies to achieve the goal of social justice.

Two related concepts are **horizontal** and **vertical equity**. According to the principle of **horizontal equity,** all persons **in the same circumstances** should be treated equally regardless of other factors (e.g., income or past contributions). This concept complements universal approaches to social policy.

The concept of **vertical equity** is used to justify the differential treatment of persons in different circumstances—for example, the allocation of greater resources to a person who has a more serious health condition or to a student who has special needs. According to Rawls (1999), vertical equity supports the idea of using policy as a redistributive tool in that it posits that inequalities in the distribution of societal resources are justified solely if they serve the needs of the least advantaged.

It is also important to distinguish between equity in benefits and equity in financing. A state's policy might distribute resources equitably—for example, through its funding for public schools. Yet, the state may collect the revenues to pay for these programs through inequitable means—for example, through greater reliance on regressive taxes, such as a sales tax.

Finally, although they sound alike, the concepts of equity and equality are not identical. Equality implies equal treatment *regardless* of circumstances. Equity, particularly social equity, implies differential treatment *according to* circumstances. In application, a policy based on equality without social equity would produce unfairness and inequality—if, for example, all children received the same allotment for their education, regardless of family income or their specific educational needs. Social equity, however, does not necessarily correlate with adequacy, particularly in times of fiscal austerity such as the present. In other words, people with greater needs might be given a larger share of available resources, but the resources available may still be insufficient to address these needs.

EXERCISE: APPLYING EVALUATIVE CONCEPTS

Select a program or service within your place of employment or internship and identify the policy on which it is based. Answer the following questions based on the evaluative framework and concepts discussed above:

1. What kind of benefits does the policy provide?
2. What are the eligibility criteria for receiving these benefits?
3. How are the benefits delivered?
4. How are the benefits financed?
5. What is the targeted population-at-risk?
6. How inclusive is the coverage of these benefits?
7. To what extent are the benefits provided horizontally adequate? To what extent are they vertically adequate?
8. To what extent are the benefits based on the concept of individual equity? To what extent are they based on the concept of social equity?

CONCLUSION: THE FUTURE OF SOCIALLY JUST SOCIAL POLICY

The Preamble to the U.S. Constitution commits the nation to the establishment of social justice. Given this commitment, why does the gap between this rhetoric and reality continue to grow? Although the remaining chapters of this book will address this question in more detail, several possible explanations are presented briefly here.

One is that the façade of national unity and a periodic focus on external enemies (as in the Cold War or the "global war on terror") often obscures, perhaps deliberately, the persistence of entrenched social inequalities. Another is that images of prosperity, promoted by Madison Avenue and the media, hide long-standing social divisions and isolate disadvantaged groups. Finally, to thwart efforts to address the structural causes of persistent inequality and injustice, proponents of social justice, including some social workers, have been frequently labeled subversive and marginalized both politically and culturally.

Developing socially just social policies in the future will require policymakers and policy advocates to take three critical steps. First, they must question and, where necessary, challenge the assumptions underlying contemporary views of social issues and the policies that address them. This includes recognizing that the social and cultural divisions in U.S. society are far more complex than generally conceived and that policy solutions to the problems these divisions create will be much more complicated than previously assumed (Reisch, 2008). We must also recognize that the expansion of social welfare benefits cannot by itself create a more egalitarian and socially just society. We must also strive to change our cultural norms and values through education and dialogue. In addition, we must acknowledge, however painfully, that dramatic developments such as globalization and climate change, our political system, as currently constructed, cannot correct contemporary problems that are occurring on an unprecedented scale (Reisch, 2013). This may require major revisions in the basic governing institutions of our society.

A second step involves moving beyond outdated assumptions about the goals of social policy and the policy development process. One of these assumptions is that divisions in U.S. society occur along a clear "majority–minority" axis. In fact, the definition of what constitutes a "minority group" has undergone rapid changes due to recent demographic and cultural developments. This requires us to adjust our social justice goals and policy framework, to reassess the relationship that currently exists between government and the market economy, and to stop dealing with major issues within current policymaking "silos."

A third step involves creating a revised vision of a socially just society that fits 21st century realities. This vision would emphasize both socially just means and ends. It would address both people's material needs and the non-material, often intangible assets they requires to achieve what Martha Nussbaum and Amartya Sen refer to as their capabilities (Sen, 2009; Nussbaum, 2011). Finally, it would reconcile an approach based on the concept of universal human rights with respect for cultural diversity (Wronka, 2014).

Discussion Questions

1. Identify a policy developed at the local, state, or federal level that affects the clients or constituents of the agency where you work or are placed as a student. What are the underlying assumptions of this policy about the causes of the problem(s) it is designed to address? In what ways do the policy's provisions reflect these assumptions?

2. In small groups, develop a budget for a family of four in your metropolitan area that you believe would enable them to lead a "minimally decent life." Compare your results with those of other groups. What assumptions did you make in constructing your budget? How did your results compare with the current federal poverty line? What does this exercise reveal about the adequacy of our social welfare system?

3. Select an issue about which you are concerned or which affects you and your family directly. If this issue is currently being addressed by social policy, how did the issue come to the attention of policymakers and the general public? If the issue is not being addressed, or is being addressed inadequately, how might advocates increase the public's awareness of the issue?

4. What is your definition of "social justice"? Select an issue you care about and discuss how you would apply your definition of social justice to the development of a social policy that addresses this issue.

5. Apply Gilbert and Terrell's analytical framework to the policy you identified in #1 above. Pay particular attention to the underlying assumptions of the policy and the alternatives that might be created to address the issue it is designed to address. Look at the alternatives proposed by policy research and advocacy organizations that have different ideological perspectives and identify their underlying assumptions.

Suggested Websites

GOVERNMENT RESOURCES

The Library of Congress (Thomas)—for legislative information: thomas.loc.gov

National Association of Counties: www.naco.org

National Conference of State Legislatures: www.ncsl.org

National Governors Association: www.nga.org

National League of Cities: www.nlc.org

Poverty Statistics at the Census Bureau: www.census.gov/hhes/www/poverty.html

U.S. Census Bureau: www.census.gov

U.S. Supreme Court Decisions: www.fedworld.gov/supcourt/index.htm

LIBERAL POLICY RESEARCH AND ADVOCACY GROUPS

Brookings Institution: www.brook.edu

Center on Budget and Policy Priorities: www.cbpp.org

Center for Law and Social Policy: www.clasp.org/

Economic Policy Institute: www.epinet.org

Families USA: www.familiesusa.org/

Urban Institute: www.urban.org

American Enterprise Institute: www.aei.org

Cato Institute: www.cato.org

The Heritage Foundation: www.heritage.org

Hudson Institute: www.hudson.org

MAJOR NEWSPAPERS

The Economist: www.economist.com

The New York Times: www.nytimes.com

The Washington Post: www.washingtonpost.com

Suggestions for Further Reading

Blau, J., with Abramovitz, M. (2014). *The dynamics of social welfare policy,* (4th ed.) New York: Oxford University Press.

Jansson, B. (2016). *Social welfare policy and advocacy: Advancing social justice through 8 policy sectors.* Thousand Oaks, CA: Sage Publications.

Jimenez, et al; Midgley & Livermore, Titmuss (1976) J., Pasztor, E.M., & Chambers, R.M., with Fujii, C.M. (2015). *Social policy and social change: Toward the creation of social and economic justice,* (2nd ed.) Thousand Oaks, CA: Sage Publications.

Katz, M. B. (2001). *The price of citizenship: Redefining the American welfare state.* New York: Henry Holt.

Klein, N. (2014). *This changes everything: Capitalism vs. the climate.* New York: Simon & Schuster.

Midgley, J., & Livermore, M. (Eds.). (2008). *The handbook of social policy,* (2nd ed.) Thousand Oaks, CA: Sage.

Nussbaum, M. C. (2011). *Creating capabilities: The human development approach.* Cambridge, MA: Harvard University Press.

Reich, R. B. (2010). *Aftershock: The next economy and America's future.* New York: Alfred A. Knopf.

Reichart, E. (2011). *Social work and human rights: A foundation for policy and practice,* (2nd ed.) New York: Columbia University Press.

Reisch, M. (ed.) (2014). *The Routledge international handbook of social justice.* London: Routledge.

Sen, A. (2009). *The idea of justice.* Cambridge, MA: Belknap Press of Harvard University Press.

Stiglitz, J. (2013). *The price of inequality.* New York: W.W. Norton.

Titmuss, R. M. (1958). *Essays on the welfare state.* London: Allen & Unwin.

Titmuss, R. M. (1976). *Commitment to welfare,* (2nd ed.) London: Allen & Unwin.

Abramovitz, M. (2001). Everyone is still on welfare: The role of redistribution in social policy. *Social Work, 44*(3), 297–308.

Abramovitz, M. (2012). Theorizing the neoliberal welfare state for social work. In M. Gray, J. Midgley, & S. Webb (Eds.), *The Sage handbook of social work*. Thousand Oaks, CA: Sage Publications.

Acemoglu, D., Egorov, G., & Sonin, K. (2011). *A political theory of populism.* Cambridge, MA: National Bureau of Economic Research.

Alexander, J. (1999). The impact of devolution on nonprofits: A multiphase study of social service organizations. *Nonprofit Management and Leadership, 10(1),* 57–70.

Alperovitz, G. (2011). *America beyond capitalism: Reclaiming our wealth, our liberty, and our democracy.* Boston, MA: Democracy Collaborative Press.

Althusser, L., & Balbar, E. (2009). *Reading capital.* London: Verso.

Arestis, P., & Sawyer, M. (Eds.). (2010). *21st century Keynesian economics.* New York: Palgrave Macmillan.

Baynton, D. C. (2001). Disability and the justification of inequality in American history. In P. K. Longmore & L. Umansky (Eds.), *The new disability history: American perspectives* (pp. 33–57). New York: New York University Press.

Belcher, J. R., Fandetti, D., & Cole, D. (2004). Is Christian religious conservatism compatible with the liberal social welfare state? *Social Work, 47*(3), 269–276.

Bendick, M. (1997). Privatizing the delivery of social welfare services. In S. Kamerman & A. Kahn (Eds.), *Privatization and the welfare state (pp. 97–120)*. Princeton, NJ: Princeton University Press.

Berger, P. L., & Neuhaus, R. J. (1977). *To empower people: The role of mediating structures in public policy.* Washington, DC: American Enterprise Institute.

Bottomore, T. (Ed.). (1991). *A dictionary of Marxist thought* (2nd ed.). Cambridge, MA: Blackwell Reference.

Center on Budget and Policy Priorities. (2011, November 28). *A guide to statistics in historical trends in income inequality.* Washington, DC: Author.

Chatterjee, P. (1996). *Approaches to the welfare state.* Washington, DC: NASW Press.

Citizens for Tax Justice. (2012, April 12). *Buffett rule bill before the Senate is a small step towards tax fairness.* Washington, DC: Author.

Cnaan, R., & Boddie, S. C. (2002). *The invisible caring hand: American congregations and the provision of welfare.* New York: New York University Press.

Daly, L. (2006). *God and the welfare state.* Cambridge: MIT Press.

Dover, M. A. (2016). Human needs: Overview. In C. Franklin (Ed.), *The encyclopedia of social work* (Electronic ed.). New York: Oxford University Press and National Association of Social Workers. Retrieved from doi: 10.1093/acrefore/9780199975839.013.554

Drennan, M.P. (2015). *Income inequality: Why it matters and why most economists didn't notice.* New Haven, CT: Yale University Press.

Ehrenreich, B., & Ehrenreich, J. (1978). The professional-managerial class. In P. Walker (Ed.), *Between labour and capital (pp. 1–45)*. Montreal: Black Rose Books.

Elshtain, J.B. (2002). *Jane Addams and the dream of American democracy: A life.* New York: Basic Books.

Eriksson, L. (2011). *Rational choice theory: Potential and limits.* New York: Palgrave Macmillan.

Esping-Andersen, G. (with Gallie, D., Hemerijck, A., & Myles, J.). (2002). *Why we need a new welfare state.* New York: Oxford University Press.

Fitzpatrick, T. (2001). *Welfare theory: An introduction.* New York: Palgrave.

Foucault, M. (1979). *Discipline and punish*, trans. A. Sheridan. New York: Vintage.

Frankfurt, H. (2015). *On inequality.* Princeton, NJ: Princeton University Press.

Friedlander, W. A., & Apte, R. Z. (1974). *Introduction to social welfare*, (4th ed.) Englewood Cliffs, NJ: Prentice Hall.

Friedman, M. (with Friedman, R. D.). (1962). *Capitalism and freedom.* Chicago: University of Chicago Press.

Gaylin, W., Glasser, I., Marcus, S., & Rothman, D. (1978). *Doing good: The limits of benevolence.* New York: Pantheon Books.

Gilbert, N., & Terrell, P. (2013). *Dimensions of social welfare policy*, (8th ed.) Boston: Pearson Higher Education.

Goldberg, G., & Elliott, J. (1980). Below the belt: Situational ethics for unethical situations. *Journal of Sociology and Social Welfare, 7*(4), 478–486.

Gorz, A. (2010). *Ecologica* (C. Turner, Trans.). Boston: Beacon Press.

Greenstein, R. (2012, March 21). *Statement of Robert Greenstein on Chairman Ryan's budget plan.* Washington, DC: Center on Budget and Policy Priorities.

Gronbjerg, K., & Salamon, L. M. (2002). Devolution, marketization and the changing shape of government-nonprofit relations. In L. M. Salamon (Ed.), *The state of nonprofit America (pp. 447–470).* Washington, DC: Brookings Institution.

Harding, D.J. (2016). Culture, poverty, and racial inequality: A new agenda? *Contemporary Sociology: A Journal of Reviews, 45*(3), 273–276.

House Budget Committee. (2012, March 20). *The path to prosperity: A blueprint for American renewal.* Washington, DC: U.S. House of Representatives.

Jansson, B. (2016). *Social welfare policy and advocacy: Advancing social justice through 8 policy sectors.* Thousand Oaks, CA: Sage Publications.

Jimenez, J., Pasztor, E.M., & Chambers, R.M., with Fujii, C.M. (2015). *Social policy and social change: Toward the creation of social and economic justice* (2nd ed.). Thousand Oaks, CA: Sage Publications.

Johnson, N., Oliff, P., & Williams, E. (2011, February 9). *An update on state budgets.* Washington, DC: Center on Budget and Policy Priorities.

Kaplan, H. R. (2011). *The myth of post-racial America: Searching for equality in the age of materialism.* Lanham, MD: Rowman & Littlefield Education.

Kapp, J. W. (1972). *The social costs of private enterprise.* New York: Schocken.

Katiuzhinsky, A., & Okech, D. (2014). Human rights, cultural practices, and state policies: Implications for global social work practice and policy. *International Journal of Social Welfare, 23*(1), 80–88.

Katz, M. B. (2001). *The price of citizenship: Redefining the American welfare state.* New York: Henry Holt.

Kennedy, R. (2013). *For discrimination: Race, Affirmative Action, and the law.* New York: Pantheon Books.

Keynes, J. M. (1936). *The general theory of employment, interest, and money.* London: MacMillan.

Knight, L.W. (2005). *Citizen: Jane Addams and the struggle for democracy.* Chicago: University of Chicago Press.

Kochar, R., & Fry, R. (2014). Wealth inequality has widened along racial, ethnic lines since end of Great Recession, *Pew Research Center, 12.*

Kogan, R., & Shapiro, I. (2016, March 28). *House GOP budget gets 62 percent of budget cuts from low- and moderate-income programs.* Washington, DC: Center on Budget and Policy Priorities.

Krugman, P. R. (2012). *End this depression now!* New York: W. W. Norton.

Lassman, P. (2011). *Pluralism*. Cambridge, UK: Polity.

Leonard, P. (1997). *Postmodern welfare: Reconstructing an emancipatory project*. Thousand Oaks, CA: Pine Forge Press.

Lindblom, C. E. (1980). *The policy-making process* (2nd ed.). Englewood Cliffs, NJ: Prentice Hall.

Lui, M., Robles, B., Leondar-Wright, B., Brewer, R., & Adamson, R. (with United for a Fair Economy). (2006). *The color of wealth: The story behind the U.S. racial wealth divide*. New York: New Press.

Maguire, D. C. (1980). *A new American justice: Ending the white male monopolies*. Garden City, NY: Doubleday.

Mansbridge, J. J. (1980). *Beyond adversary democracy*. New York: Basic Books.

Marable, M. (2009). *Beyond black and white: Transforming African-American politics* (2nd ed.). New York: Verso.

Marshall, T. H. (1950). *Citizenship and social class, and other essays*. Cambridge, UK: Cambridge University Press.

Marx, K. (1852). *The eighteenth Brumaire of Louis Napoleon*. Retrieved October 16, 2012, from http://www.marxists.org/archive/marx/works/1852/18th-brumaire/ch01.htm

Massey, D. S., & Denton, N. A. (1993). *American apartheid: Segregation and the making of the underclass*. Cambridge, MA: Harvard University Press.

Miliband, R. (1969). *The state in capitalist society*. New York: Basic Books.

Mills, C. W. (1959). *The sociological imagination*. New York: Oxford University Press.

Morone, J. A., & Jacobs, L. R. (Eds.). (2005). *Healthy, wealthy, and fair: Health care and the good society*. New York: Oxford University Press.

Murphy, M. C. (2006). *Natural law in jurisprudence and politics*. New York: Cambridge University Press.

National Association of Social Workers. (1999). *Code of ethics* (Rev. ed.). Washington, DC: Author.

Nozick, R. (1974). *Anarchy, state, and utopia*. New York: Basic Books.

Nussbaum, M. C. (2011). *Creating capabilities: The human development approach*. Cambridge, MA: Harvard University Press.

Popple, P. R., & Leighninger, L. (2008). *The policy-based profession: An introduction to social welfare policy analysis for social workers,* (4th ed.) Boston: Allyn & Bacon.

Puckett, J. L., Harkavy, I. & Benson, L. (2007). *Dewey's dream: Universities and democracies in an age of education reform*. Philadelphia: Temple University Press.

Rawls, J. (1999). *A theory of justice* (Rev. ed.). Cambridge, MA: Harvard University Press.

Rawls, J. (2001). *Justice as fairness: A restatement*. Cambridge, MA: The Belknap Press of Harvard University Press.

Reich, R. B. (2010). *Aftershock: The next economy and America's future*. New York: Alfred A. Knopf.

Reisch, M. (2002). Defining social justice in a socially unjust world. *Families in Society: The Journal of Contemporary Human Services, 83*(4), 343–354.

Reisch, M. (2008). From melting pot to multiculturalism: The impact of racial and ethnic diversity on social work and social justice in the U.S. *British Journal of Social Work, 38*(4), 788–804.

Reisch, M. (2014). Social justice and liberalism. In M. Reisch (ed.), *The Routledge international handbook of social justice* (pp. 132–146). London: Routledge.

Reisch, M. (2013). Not by the numbers alone: The effects of economic and demographic changes on social policy. In I. Colby, K. M. Sowers, & C. N. Dulmus (Eds.), *Social welfare policy: A foundation of social work*. Hoboken, NJ: Wiley.

Reisch, M. & Jani, J.S. (2012). The new politics of social work practice: Understanding context to promote change. *British Journal of Social Work*, 42(6), 1132–1150.

Russell, J.W. (2015). *Double standard: Social policy in Europe and the United States* (3rd ed.). New York: Rowman & Littlefield.

Ryan, W. (1981). *Equality.* New York: Pantheon.

Sabbagh, L. (2011). The paradox of decategorization: Deinstitutionalizing race through race-based Affirmative Action in the United States. *Ethnic and Racial Studies, 34*(10), 1665–1681.

Sen, A. (2009). *The idea of justice.* Cambridge, MA: Harvard University Press.

Shapiro, T., Meschede, T., & Osoro, S. (2013, February). The roots of the widening racial wealth gap: Explaining the black-white economic divide. *Institute on Assets and Social Policy.*

Skocpol, T., & Williamson, V. (2012). *The Tea Party and the remaking of Republican conservatism.* New York: Oxford University Press.

Stocker, F. D. (Ed.). (1991). *Proposition 13: A ten-year retrospective.* Cambridge, MA: Lincoln Institute of Land Policy.

Stoesz, D. (2014). Conservatism and social justice. In M. Reisch (ed.), *The Routledge international handbook of social justice* (pp. 147–159). London: Routledge.

Stoesz, D. (2015). *The dynamic welfare state.* New York: Oxford University Press.

Stone, C., Trisi, D., Sherman, A., & Debot, B. (2015, October 26). *A guide to statistics on historical trends in income inequality.* Washington, DC: Center on Budget and Policy Priorities.

Titmuss, R. M. (1958). *Essays on the welfare state.* London: Allen & Unwin.

Titmuss, R. M. (1976). *Commitment to welfare* (2nd ed.). London: Allen & Unwin.

Trattner, W. I. (1999). *From poor law to welfare state,* (6th ed.) New York: Free Press.

Tropman, J. E. (1984). *Policy management in the human services.* New York: Columbia University Press.

U.S. Census Bureau. (2010). Table H-2: Share of aggregate income received by each fifth and top 5 percent of households. Retrieved March 29, 2012, from http://www.census.gov/hhes/www/income/data/historical/household/index.html

U.S. Census Bureau. (2011). *Poverty in the United States.* Washington, DC: U.S. Government Printing Office.

Ventelou, B. (2005). *The millennial Keynes: An introduction to the origin, development, and later currents of Keynesian thought* (G. P. Nowell, Ed. & Trans.). Armonk, NY: M. E. Sharpe.

Wilensky, H. L., & Lebeaux, C. N. (1965). *Industrial society and social welfare: The impact of industrialization on the supply and organization of social welfare services in the United States.* New York: Free Press.

Wilson, W. J. (2009). *More than race: Being black and poor in the inner city.* New York: W. W. Norton.

Wright, R., Ellis, M., Holloway, S.R., & Wong, S. (2014). Patterns of diversity and segregation in the United States, 1990–2010. *The Professional Geographer, 66*(2), 173–182.

Wronka, J. (2014). Human rights as pillars of social justice. In M. Reisch (ed.), *The Routledge international handbook of social justice* (pp. 216–226). London: Routledge.

Young, D. (1999). Complementary, supplementary, or adversarial? A theoretical and historical examination of nonprofit-government relations in the United States. In E. Boris & E. Steuerle (Eds.), *Nonprofits and government: Collaboration and conflict* (pp. 31–67). Washington, DC: Urban Institute Press.

2

U.S. SOCIAL POLICY AND SOCIAL WELFARE
A Historical Overview

Michael Reisch, PhD

The social policies of a nation reveal a great deal about its preferred values and goals, the nature of its social relationships, and how it chooses to distribute power, resources, status, rights, and opportunities. These policies require the construction of specific roles—the needy, the helpers, and the benefactors—and reinforce these constructions through laws, customs, institutions, and traditions. While a range of environmental factors influence how social policies are developed and implemented, policies do not develop randomly or accidentally. They are designed to serve a purpose, often multiple purposes, although these purposes are rarely made explicit or even acknowledged. The U.S. system of social welfare and the social policies within it are no different in this regard.

Social policies in Western industrialized societies such as the United States have been shaped by four general trends. First, they evolved from informal systems of helping, guided by personal and familial relationships, long-standing customs, and oral traditions, to more formal structures with written policies and rule-governed programs. Second, over time their focus shifted from addressing small-scale, local issues to those of national and, ultimately, global significance. Third, their underlying assumptions have evolved from widely shared spiritual beliefs to an often conflict-ridden mixture of religious and secular values and scientific principles. Finally, as a result of this transformation, social policies have reflected increasingly complex definitions of need and more sophisticated ideas about helping.

U.S. social policies did not emerge from a single cultural or historical source. In fact, the ideas that shaped them reflect a dynamic synthesis of many different cultural norms. For example, while many commonly used social welfare terms (such as *charity* and *philanthropy*) have Greek or Roman origins, the first articulation of a concept of justice appeared in the Babylonian Code of Hammurabi. Buddhist teachings rejected social stratification before this idea was expressed in the Bible. Both the Old and New Testament proclaim the duty of giving and the right of *all* needy persons to receive help. In a similar manner, the Qur'an stresses the relationship between justice and mercy and the importance of hospitality, particularly to strangers. Finally, centuries-old mutual aid practices of African and Asian civilizations and the Native American concept of a "community of goods" influenced the U.S. social welfare system in ways that resonate to the present (Chew, 2000; Thakur, 1996).

Although all social welfare systems recognize, in some way, human interdependence, they also serve seemingly contradictory impulses. At times, they seek to correct problems created by rapid social and economic change or unanticipated disasters. Inspired by different definitions of social justice, they often include conscious efforts to redistribute resources, power, and status. Yet, as the chapters in this volume demonstrate, social policies also involve a variety of means by which elites exercise social control over individual and group behaviors, reinforce dominant cultural norms, and reproduce prevailing economic, social, and political relationships.

Social policy in the United States evolved somewhat differently from the pattern in other Western industrialized nations (Jansson, 2012; Katz, 2001). Until recently, it emphasized pragmatic rather than ideological solutions to social problems, relied more on state and local governments and the private sector than on the national government, and had modest, often incremental goals (Gilbert, 2002). These qualities produced a patchwork of largely means-tested programs instead of the systems of universal social welfare that exist in most Western European nations (Patterson, 2001; Lorenz, 2006; Russell, 2015). There are several explanations for this so-called **"American exceptionalism"**: the preference for market-oriented solutions to social problems; the cultural value of individualism; the absence of working class, social democratic parties to advocate for policy alternatives; and the use of policies to maintain class, racial, and gender hierarchies (Reisch, 2005).

Figure 2.1 Ancient Forms of Charity.

THE ROOTS OF U.S. SOCIAL WELFARE

For more than a millennium prior to the European colonization of the Americas, the Christian Church played a leading role in the establishment of Western social welfare. In the absence of powerful secular governments, it distributed charity in rural monasteries and urban parishes and created hospitals, the antecedents of modern social service agencies. Often formalized through canon (church) law or papal edicts, Christian charity carried on the Judaic and Islamic traditions of alms-giving (Thompson, 2014; Telushkin, 1994; Badawi, 1995) based on two important principles: Poverty was not a crime, and justice and mercy required society, particularly the affluent, to take responsibility for the care of the needy (Axinn & Stern, 1988). As early as the 14th century, formal social welfare systems emerged throughout Western Europe. Some were created by organized religion, others by local or central governments. Over the next several centuries, these systems expanded as European societies dealt with the consequences of frequent religious and dynastic wars and struggled through the tumultuous transition from feudalism to capitalism.

As a consequence of this transition, two sets of political–economic ideas emerged that had a particularly significant impact on social policies. One was the development of new conceptions of property, property rights, and social relations that a market economy (capitalism) required (Macpherson, 1985). The other reflected new views about the nature and purpose of the state (government). In combination, these perspectives defined the extent to which governments could (and should) regulate the market, respond to the human needs rapid socioeconomic changes produced, or redistribute resources and power more equitably. At the same time, dominant cultural values, both religious and secular, about the balance between individual and social responsibility, the importance of work, and the causes of poverty influenced the direction of social policies (Stern & Axinn, 2012).

A major example of this phenomenon occurred in Great Britain between 1349 and 1664. During this period, motivated both by humanitarian reasons and a desire to establish social order in a chaotic and rapidly changing environment, the British Parliament enacted legislation later known as the **Elizabethan Poor Laws.** Although these laws created a formal system of relief (welfare) for the poor, they also sought to control or reduce wages in order to support commercial development and to reassert traditional political authority in the face of frequent popular protests (Piven & Cloward, 1995). Their key features—most of which still exist in some form in the United States during the 21st century—can be summarized as follows:

- A distinction among categories of needy persons based on the causes of their need
- A distinction between the **"worthy" and "unworthy" poor**, largely based on a person's ability to work
- The establishment of a societal obligation to help the needy
- The incorporation of principles of family responsibility into legislation
- The establishment of local responsibility for the administration of social welfare
- The institution of coercive work and residency requirements to receive benefits
- The stigmatization of "pauperism" which was distinguished from poverty

The Poor Laws are significant for understanding the evolution of U.S. social policy because the North American colonies established by Great Britain in the 17th century adopted them as models for their own social welfare systems, often word-for-word. (Colonies that were established by France, Spain, Sweden, and the Netherlands similarly introduced versions of their social welfare systems, although with the exception of French-settled Louisiana these systems did not have a lasting impacton the U.S.) Consequently, long before the American Revolution, formal systems of poor relief—the antecedents to modern public assistance, child welfare, and even mental health services—were established in North America. Until the end of the 18th century, they provided aid through several different means: **outdoor relief** (i.e., assistance to people in their homes, for the so-called "worthy poor"), apprenticeship (for children), indenture (for both children and adults), and farming out (adults) through either auctioning off or contracting labor. The connection between the receipt of welfare and work-related obligations was, therefore, present from the beginning of the nation.

As they do today, American social policies served a dual role of compassion for the needy and protection of society from the social unrest that a lack of response to the needy might arouse (Pumphrey, 1959). Relief provisions in the American colonies continued the practices of the English Poor Laws: they categorized and stigmatized the needy, collected taxes to pay for aid, and maintained local responsibility and control of social welfare. As early as 1624, colonies began to provide aid to military veterans, establishing a precedent that has continued throughout U.S. history.

Just prior to the Revolutionary War (1776–1783), another form of assistance called **indoor relief** became increasingly popular. This type of aid included institutions such as the Pennsylvania Hospital in Philadelphia, the first American mental health facility, established in 1756 by Dr. Benjamin Rush, one of the future signers of the Declaration of Independence. Under the guise of providing medical care, education, or moral instruction, indoor relief also took the form of almshouses, workhouses, prisons, orphanages, and reformatories, all designed to protect the populace from certain classes of persons who annoyed or threatened them. Given prevailing views during this period about race, class, and gender, it is not surprising that a disproportionate number of persons in these institutions were women, recent immigrants from Europe, newly freed African Americans, and, of course, the poor (Rothman, 2002b).

Social policies in the newly independent United States of America, therefore, reflected the following characteristics:

- The importance of local control, at the town, village, or parish level
- The provision of limited assistance and the importance of maintaining the distinction between the "worthy" and "unworthy" poor
- Strict residency requirements and coercive work requirements for the receipt of aid
- The establishment of early public welfare systems in cities such as Boston
- A key role for churches, mutual aid societies, and so-called "voluntary" social service agencies.

This relatively simple system of social welfare would soon be tested by major environmental changes.

MAJOR TRENDS BETWEEN INDEPENDENCE AND THE CIVIL WAR, 1776–1861

During the first half of the 19th century, the population and geographic size of the U.S. expanded considerably. More than 6 million immigrants, largely fleeing political repression in Germany and Ireland, changed the demographics and cultural character of cities along the Atlantic coast (Gutman, 1976). The displacement of indigenous populations east of the Mississippi, the Louisiana Purchase, and the seizure of former Mexican territory after the U.S.-Mexican War opened up vast new lands for white settlement. The political dominance of what Abraham Lincoln called the "slave power" ensured that slavery continued to exist in Southern states and some Western territories (Foner, 2010). Technological advances, such as the introduction of mass production, the construction of an extensive physical infrastructure (railroads, canals, and stage routes), the creation of agricultural and commercial wealth by the use of slave labor, and the growth of a national banking system all spurred rapid, if uneven, economic development.

As the U.S. economy industrialized, the scale of urban social problems such as poverty, unemployment, homelessness, crime, and alcoholism increased dramatically and their character changed as well (Mandler, 1990). The nation's response to these problems was largely inadequate and soon came under attack from several quarters. As early as the late 18th century, influential leaders, such as Benjamin Franklin (1766), criticized existing systems of poor relief, whose costs doubled between 1760 and 1818, on both economic and moral grounds. Some critics asserted that the poor laws rationalized growing poverty and inequality, were ineffective and inequitable, impeded the development of a market economy, and created unsustainable costs. Others, like Franklin, claimed that relief encouraged socially irresponsible behavior and promoted dependency. Displaying increased distrust of impoverished immigrants, they equated their persistent poverty with moral deficiency. Some observers, such as the British mathematician and philosopher Jeremy Bentham, went further; he distinguished between poverty, which he regarded as the natural state of the laboring classes (Poynter, 1969), and pauperism—a distinction similar to the one made today between the working poor and the welfare poor, or the so-called "underclass," which is increasingly used as a rationale for disciplinary welfare policies and mass incarceration (Jones, 1992; Soss, Fording, & Schram, 2011; Alexander, 2010).

Inspired by these critics, legislatures in Northeast and Mid-Atlantic states approved major reforms of the Poor Laws between 1818 and the early 1830s. The *Report of the Committee on Pauper Laws* drafted by the Massachusetts State Legislature (Quincy, 1822) embodied many of the features of these reforms. Its five major underlying principles were:

1. Of all modes of providing for the poor, the most wasteful, the most expensive, and most injurious to their morals is that of supply in their own families.
2. The most economical mode is that of almshouses, having the character of workhouses; thus the poor are made to provide for their own support.
3. Of all modes of employing the labor of the pauper, agriculture affords the best, the most healthy, and the most profitable.
4. The success of [relief] establishments depends upon their being placed under the supervision of a Board of Overseers, constituted of the most substantial and intelligent inhabitants of the vicinity.
5. Of all the cause of pauperism, intemperance in the use of spirituous liquors is the most powerful and universal (pp. 25–28).

In addition to Massachusetts, legislatures in other states, such as New York and Maryland, recommended the termination of outdoor relief for all able-bodied persons; the transfer of administrative responsibility for relief from towns to counties; the creation of county superintendents of the poor; and the construction of almshouses and workhouses (forms of "indoor relief"). These institutions protected the public from the so-called "dangerous classes" while reinforcing the impression that society was helping individuals in need, ironically by removing them from the environment that created their problems in the first place.

Consequently, rather than attempting to change that environment, the expansion of indoor relief largely strengthened the perception that those being helped were somehow "deviant" because their behavior and values did not conform to prevailing cultural norms. By the mid- and late 19th century, reformers added scientific and pseudoscientific rationales to provide further support for these morally based ideas about the poor (Rothman, 2002a). Thus, the popularity of indoor relief during the 19th century established a moral justification for social policies designed to treat the indigent, insane, incarcerated, and intemperate that persists in the 21st century U.S.

By the 1830s and 1840s, however, some social critics began to argue that indoor relief was inadequate to meet the challenges of poverty and unemployment created by the cyclical economic depressions (then called "panics") that regularly afflicted the U.S. economy. At the time, observers estimated that up to one-third of the urban population of the United States lived in poverty and that unemployment during the frequent panics reached close to 50% (Stern & Axinn, 2012). Nor was indoor relief capable of responding effectively to frequent epidemics of infectious diseases, such as cholera, typhoid, or tuberculosis. As a result, even as they continued to construct large-scale social welfare institutions, state governments began to assume responsibility for the distribution of outdoor relief that had formerly been left to towns and counties.

Advocates for the poor, such as the Reverend Matthew Carey, rejected moral explanations for poverty and unemployment, and were among the first reformers to attribute chronic poverty and the numerous social problems it produced to low wages, unhealthy and unsafe working conditions, chronic unemployment, and overcrowded housing. In a pamphlet circulated to the leading citizens of Philadelphia, Carey (1833) wrote:

The erroneous opinions to which I have alluded are

1. That every man, woman, and grown child, able and willing to work may find employment;
2. That the poor, by industry, prudence, and economy, may at all times support themselves comfortably, without depending on eleemosynary aid;
3. That their sufferings and distresses chiefly, if not wholly, arise from their idleness, their dissipation, and their extravagance;
4. That taxes for the support of the poor, and aid afforded them by charitable individuals, or benevolent societies, are pernicious as, by encouraging the poor to depend on them, they foster their idleness and improvidence, and thus produce, or at least increase, the poverty and distress they are intended to relieve (pp. 3–5).

As social conditions worsened, especially in large coastal cities such as Baltimore, New York, and Philadelphia, private benevolent societies established by elites, self-help organizations, and mutual aid societies, particularly among new European immigrants from Germany and Ireland, and African Americans, sought to fill the gap created by tentative, insufficient, and ineffective government responses (Skocpol, Liazos, & Ganz, 2006). These voluntary organizations, which had first appeared in the late 18th century, were the ancestors of today's nonprofit social service agencies. A leading example is the Association for the Improvement of the Condition of the Poor (AICP), which was established in New York City in 1842 in response to the disastrous Panic of 1837. The AICP later merged with the New York Charity Organization Society (see below) to form the Community Service Society, the oldest continuously operated nonprofit social service organization in the United States. In 1853, the AICP issued an influential report on New York City's tenement housing that produced some modest reforms. Among its findings were the following:

In the lower wards there are thousands of poor persons, but comparatively few buildings suitable for their accommodation. And now, in their dilapidated state, many of these houses are

Figure 2.2 Children's Aid Society.

tenanted by miserably poor Irish and German emigrants … Large rooms have been divided by rough partitions into dwellings for two or three families—each perhaps taking boarders, where they wash, cook, eat, sleep, and die—and many of them prematurely because of the fearful circumstances in which they live. (AICP, 1853)

In the same year this report was published, Charles Loring Brace founded the **Children's Aid Society (CAS)** in New York City, now the oldest continuously operating nonprofit child welfare agency in the United States. In his memoirs (1872) Brace described the population the CAS served in a manner that reflects both his original motives and the values of the era's elites:

These boys and girls, it should be remembered, will soon form the great lower class of our city. They will influence elections; they may shape the policy of the city; they will assuredly, if

Figure 2.3 The "Child-Mother." frontispiece illustration from G.C. Needham, Street Arabs and Gutter Snipes (Boston, 1884) - Originally appeared in the memoir of Charles Loring Brace's The Dangerous Classes of New York. Brace was the founder of the Children's Aid Society.

unreclaimed, poison society all around them. They will help to form the great multitude of robbers, thieves, vagrants, and prostitutes who are now such a burden upon the law-respecting community.... In view of these evils ... we propose to give to these children work and to bring them under religious influence ... [so] the great temptations to this class arising from want of work may be removed (pp. 90–93)

Two decades earlier, the French aristocrat Alexis de Tocqueville (1835) perceptively noted following an extended visit to the United States, that the emergence of these "voluntary" (private, nonprofit) associations in the United States constituted a unique feature of American life, which continues to characterize "**American exceptionalism.**" Scholars have noted several reasons for the emergence of the voluntary sector in the United States during this period and for its ongoing importance in U.S. society, as illustrated in Table 2.1.

Other reform movements, whose leaders advocated with limited success for expanded government involvement, emerged in the U.S. immediately prior to the Civil War—particularly in the fields of mental health and welfare. For example, the 20-year campaign of a former teacher, Dorothea Dix, who is often considered the nation's first social worker, resulted in numerous state reforms in the treatment of persons with mental illness (Brown, 1998). Despite her tireless efforts, President Franklin Pierce (1854) vetoed a bill passed by Congress that would provide land for the construction of mental institutions. Pierce justified his veto on the grounds that he "cannot find any authority in the Constitution for

Table 2.1 Why the United States Developed a Nonprofit Sector (Hall, 1992).

Source	Societal Response
1. Ideas underlying the American Revolution	Resistance to encroachment of the central government on local matters
2. Lack of adequate government aid	Development of local services
3. Desire to maintain church/state separation	Establish "faith-based" services free of government interference
4. Spirit of independence and individualism	Development of self-help and **mutual aid organizations**
5. Leadership of secular and religious reformers	Emergence of advocacy organizations (women's suffrage, antislavery, temperance)

Figure 2.4 Dorothea Dix.

Figure 2.5 President Franklin Pierce.

making the Federal Government the great almoner of public charity throughout the U.S." (p. 1062). Pierce's veto established a precedent of federal non-involvement in social policy that, with few exceptions, lasted until the **New Deal** of the 1930s (Patterson, 2001; Stern & Axinn, 2012). As a result, it was not until a half century after the Civil War that the problems of low-income populations were seriously addressed, largely by state governments and the nonprofit sector. The lingering trauma of the Civil War, however, in which over 700,000 soldiers and sailors died, ultimately transformed the nation's ideas about social welfare (Faust, 2009).

THE CIVIL WAR AND SOCIAL WELFARE, 1861–1865 AND BEYOND

The unprecedented human tragedy of the Civil War inspired a variety of advances in U.S. social policy. Not surprisingly, the first social welfare initiatives during the war emerged from the private (voluntary) sector in response to the terrible conditions experienced by Union soldiers in their encampments, where more died from disease than from battlefield wounds. Private organizations, such as the U.S. Sanitary Commission and the American Red Cross, provided essential health and social services to the troops and helped them stay connected to their families. Many future leaders of the voluntary social service sector who later founded the social work profession, such as Josephine Shaw Lowell, the sister-in-law of Robert Gould Shaw, the officer immortalized in the film "Glory," began their careers in these organizations.

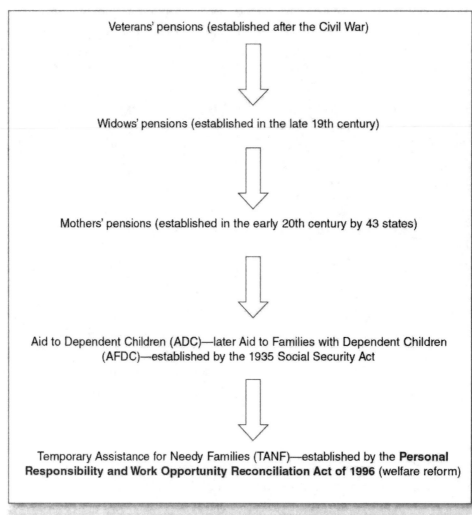

Figure 2.6 The Evolution of Modern Public Assistance in the United States.

One month after the conclusion of the war, the U.S. Bureau of Refugees, Freedmen, and Abandoned Lands (commonly referred to as the **Freedmen's Bureau**) was established in the War Department under the direction of General Oliver Howard. During its brief existence (1865–1871), the Freedmen's Bureau provided a wide range of social welfare, economic, and educational assistance to newly emancipated slaves in the South (Cimbala & Miller, 1999). Although the Bureau achieved some measurable successes, the combination of white Southerners' resistance in and out of Congress and the ambivalence of many Northerners about racial equality led to its demise. Five years later, the federal government retreated altogether from the broader project of Reconstruction that the Freedmen's Bureau symbolized, setting the stage for the reemergence of white supremacy and the legal marginalization of the African American population throughout the South, a condition that lasted well into the 20th century and which is reflected today in the recent passage of numerous "voter ID" laws. Thus, while civil rights legislation and Supreme Court decisions during the 1950s and 1960s abolished the "Jim Crow" laws established in the late 19th century, in many ways the United States is still dealing with the economic, political, and social consequences of the failure of Reconstruction (Foner, 1988; Also see Chapter 4 in this volume).

Another lasting consequence of the Civil War was the passage of veterans' pensions for men who had fought in the Union army; a few decades later, these were expanded to provide aid to their widows and orphans (Skocpol, 1992). Later, this policy was further modified to assist the widows and orphans of workers who had been killed in industrial accidents. Ultimately, "widows' pensions" became state-administered "mothers' pensions." Finally, through the 1935 Social Security Act, the Federal government established the Aid to Dependent Children (ADC) program that evolved into Aid to Families with Dependent Children (AFDC) and, more recently, Temporary Assistance to Needy Families (TANF). The evolution of veterans' pensions to modern forms of public assistance is illustrated in Figure 2.5.

INDUSTRIALIZATION AND SOCIAL WELFARE, 1865–1917

During the half century between the end of the Civil War in 1865 and U.S. entry into World War I in 1917, the United States was transformed from an agricultural, semirural, and largely insular society to a multicultural urban nation with international alliances that was the major industrial power in the world. These extraordinarily rapid changes were accompanied by the greatest wave of immigration any nation had every experienced—more than 23 million persons entered the United States during this period—as well as massive internal migration, particularly of African Americans, from rural areas in the South to Northern industrial centers. Inevitably, this dramatic transformation produced new, more severe, and in some cases unprecedented problems for which existing social policies were inadequate. The struggle to understand and address these problems inspired the emergence of a modern social welfare system and the creation of the profession of social work.

In addition to massive socioeconomic and demographic changes, there are other striking similarities between this period and our contemporary era. Repeated conflicts over the respective roles of the federal government and the states created barriers to the development of effective policy solutions to problems such as poverty, unemployment, and homelessness and produced striking variations in how state governments responded to these social problems. Proponents of religious and scientific explanations for poverty competed for influence in elite circles and among the general public. Debates persisted over the proper relationship between government and the market economy and between government and the nonprofit sector (Patterson, 2001).

One of the striking features of this period is how frequently contradictions appeared between the nation's expressed ideals and the reality of its social policies and programs. While the nation often celebrated its democratic heritage, it continued to deny political and civil rights to African Americans, Latinos, Native Americans, Asian and European immigrants, and women. As this excerpt from an earlier speech by Frederick Douglass reflects, the much-heralded American principle of equality under law contrasted starkly with the nation's glaring and growing social inequalities.

> What, to the American slave, is your 4th of July? I answer: a day that reveals to him, more than all other days in the year, the gross injustice and cruelty to which he is the constant victim. To him, your celebration is a sham; your boasted liberty, an unholy license; your national greatness, swelling vanity; your sounds of rejoicing are empty and heartless; your denunciations of tyrants, brass fronted impudence; your shouts of liberty and equality, hollow mockery; your prayers and hymns, your sermons and thanksgivings, with all your religious parades, and solemnity, are, to him, mere bombast, fraud, deception, impiety, and hypocrisy—a thin veil to cover up crimes

Figure 2.7 Frederick Douglass.

which would disgrace a nation of savages. There is not a nation on the earth guilty of practices, more shocking and bloody, than are the people of these United States, at this very hour (Douglass, July 4, 1852).

Similar contradictions appeared in the field of social welfare, particularly in the nation's cities—for example, between religious benevolence and the forced conversion practices of Protestant charities, and between the democratic sentiments of the earliest social workers and the racial and ethnic prejudices that were reflected in their assumptions about the populations they served (Park & Kemp, 2006; Reisch, 2008a; Boyer, 1978).

While it is important to understand this complex historical context, it is equally important not to interpret 19th or early 20th century concepts through a 21st century lens. Words such as *freedom*, *race*, *democracy*, and *community* had different meanings to people of this era. Like today, concepts such as social justice and social welfare were defined differently by different groups, as were ideologies such as feminism and socialism. Analyzing these concepts from a critical perspective is useful in assessing both the history of U.S. social welfare and social work and contemporary policy and practice issues.

One way to understand the evolution of social policies and social welfare during this period is by examining the relationship between the following concepts: context and change, continuity and conflict, and community and coercion.

THE CONTEXT OF CHANGE

During this critical half century, even as the U.S. struggled with the enduring trauma of the Civil War (Faust, 2009; Foner, 2010), it developed a *national economy* for the first time. In combination with the technological innovations that transformed transportation (a national railroad system, automobiles, and airplanes), communications (the invention of the telegraph and telephone), manufacturing processes (the assembly line), and the nature of urban life (electric lighting, mass transit systems), this had a profound impact on how people lived, the nature of their needs, and the forms of helping required to assist them (Kasson, 1980).

This transformation, however, went far beyond the economic and technological spheres. The physical and cultural environments of cities changed dramatically as a result of rapid population growth and increased racial, ethnic, and religious diversity. By the first decade of the 20th century, the majority of the population of cities such as New York and Chicago consisted of immigrants or the children of immigrants. Family life changed because of the transformation of work and gender roles and the separation of the public and private spheres of life that industrialization produced. New social problems, such as chronic unemployment, became more widespread. In addition, ideas from other cultures—European, Asian, and Latin American—began to influence the U.S. social welfare system (Carson, 1990; Takaki, 1994).

Although rapid change is the most striking feature of this period, the continuity of certain cultural and political divisions and the persistence of a variety of social conflicts also shaped social policy development. These conflicts emerged along several lines: urban industry versus rural agriculture; natives versus immigrants; capital versus labor; modern versus premodern views of society; and scientific versus religious interpretations of social problems (Hofstadter, 1992; Patterson, 2001). Many of these conflicts turned violent: Armed guards shot striking workers; white supremacist groups such as the Ku Klux Klan terrorized and lynched African Americans; and police attacked women demonstrating for voting rights (Wiebe, 1967). Particularly after the end of Reconstruction in 1876, there was sustained resistance to large-scale federal intervention in the social policy arena under the rubric of preserving so-called "states' rights." As in the 20th and 21st centuries, this justified the maintenance of systems of racial stratification and the failure of state and local governments to respond adequately and equitably to human needs. Consequently, just four decades after the passage of the Civil War Amendments barring slavery and making African Americans citizens, the United States was a more racially conscious and racially stratified society than at any other point in its history (Foner, 2002).

Faced with a range of unprecedented issues that were euphemistically termed the "Social Question," political leaders, social observers, and intellectuals formulated various explanations and rationalizations. For example, proponents of **Social Darwinism**—the attempt to apply the evolutionary theories of Charles Darwin to society—used pseudoscientific explanations to justify increasing socioeconomic inequality and to oppose social policies that would address issues such as poverty. One of its leading spokespersons, the distinguished sociologist William Graham Sumner (1883), expressed their perspective this way:

Figure 2.8 William Graham Sumner.

> Competition draws out the highest achievements in man.... It draws out the social scale upwards and downwards to great extremes and produces aristocratic social organizations in spite of all dogmas of equality.... [Consequently,] in an over-populated country the extremes of wealth and luxury are presented side by side with the extremes of poverty and distress.... The achievements of power are highest, the rewards of prudence, energy, enterprise, foresight, sagacity, and all other industrial virtues the greatest. On the other hand, the penalties of folly, weakness, error, and vice are most terrible. Pauperism, prostitution, and crime are the attendants of a state of society in which art, science, and literature reach their highest development.
>
> ... If we should try by any measures of arbitrary interference and assistance to relieve the victims

of social pressure from the calamity of their position we should only offer premiums to folly and vice and extend them further (pp. 7, 145).

The increasing fragmentation of American society along class, ethnic, racial, and religious lines also inspired a wave of nostalgia for a simpler, less conflict-ridden era. This was especially reflected in the desire of segments of the elite to re-create the mythic "organic community" of the past. It also influenced the development of the three major forms of nongovernmental social welfare that emerged during this period—the **Charity Organization Societies (COS)**, the **Settlement House Movement**, and the mutual aid and self-help organizations created by ethnic and immigrant groups. In different ways, they all focused on the goal of restoring or reconstructing a nostalgic vision of an "organic" American community (Bender, 1978).

Tensions emerged, however, between proponents of "old-style" charity, based on elite control, and promoters of "**scientific charity**" in the COS, who sought to apply modern principles of management and industry to the distribution of relief. In addition, differences arose between policymakers who favored indoor relief and those who argued that institutionally based assistance could not meet the burgeoning needs of the nation's poor (Katz, 1986; Patterson, 2001). Although they came from similar social backgrounds, conflicts also emerged between the leaders of the COS and the Settlement House Movement over the goals and desired extent of social reform, their underlying assumptions about the causes of social problems, the methods used to assist needy populations, the role of clients and constituents in social change efforts and in designing social services, and the role of the social work profession in American society (Wenocur & Reisch, 1989; Reisch & Andrews, 2002).

CHARITY AND COERCION

Within this desire to restore community there were strong, if hidden, elements of social control and cultural coercion. The former took its most visible form in the growth of urban police forces and the use of the National Guard and U.S. army to suppress strikes, riots, and other forms of popular protest (Boyer, 1978; Wiebe, 1967). On a cultural level, efforts increased to promote prohibition and to enforce stricter laws regulating "obscenity" and even the sale of contraceptives (Okrent, 2010; PBS Online, 2001). On a more subtle level, both public and private welfare agencies employed coercive methods to enforce compliance with dominant cultural norms or restrictive laws (Margolin, 1997). Impoverished families feared the specter of the poorhouse and resented the moralistic charity of the **friendly visitors** sent by the COS (Katz, 1996; Wagner, 2005). (See below)

THE PROGRESSIVE ERA (~1890–1917)

The dramatic changes summarized above inspired a broad-based reform movement at the turn of the 20th century—a period often called the **Progressive Era** because of the future-oriented perspective of the movement's leaders. Their efforts focused on responding to increased social need while recognizing for the first time the structural bases of the problems afflicting U.S. society. In fact, Jane Addams—one of the principal founders of the American Settlement House Movement—framed the central issue of the period: "In what attitude stand ye toward the present industrial system?" (Addams, 1895, p. 193).

There were three main developments during this period that shaped the course of U.S. social welfare: the growing dominance of the COS in the new social work profession; the influence of the Settlement House Movement on social reform; and the earliest efforts to pass state-sponsored social policies.

THE CHARITY ORGANIZATION SOCIETIES (COS)

The first COS in the United States was established by Reverend S. Humphreys Gurteen in Buffalo, New York, in 1877. By the early 20th century, there were hundreds of similar organizations in midsized and large cities east of the Mississippi. Their primary purpose was to rationalize the delivery of relief by applying new principles of organization derived from industry to the creation of "scientific charity." Although initially the COS were strongly influenced by moralistic conceptions of poverty and the poor, in less than two decades their leaders—such as Mary Richmond, who directed COS in Baltimore, Philadelphia, and New York—embraced the use of social science research and applied ideas drawn from multiple disciplines—including medicine, law, economics, and political science—to the development of what became known as social casework. This marked an early example of the use of what is now termed "evidence-based" or "evidence-informed" practice. By the First World War, through their connections to influential elites and the successful promotion of their ideas in major institutions, such as universities, and widely read publications, the COS transformed the distribution of relief and acquired a dominant role in the fledgling social work profession (Wenocur & Reisch, 1989).

The initial attitudes of leading COS spokespersons about social welfare "however" are reflected in the following statements:

> The less that is given, the better for everyone, the giver and the receiver, and, therefore, the conditions [for receipt of aid] must be hard, although never degrading. (Lowell, 1890, pp. 82–83)

> The four great causes of pauperism and of degraded city life have long seemed to me to be these: (1) Foul homes; (2) Intoxicating drink; (3) Neglect of child life; (4) Indiscriminate almsgiving. (Paine, 1893, pp. 25–26)

> No matter what efforts may be made by philanthropists and social economists for the removal of poverty, we must make up our minds that poverty in one shape or another will always exist among us.... It is in accordance with the economy of Divine Providence that men should exist in unequal conditions in society, in order to ensure the exercise of benevolent virtues. (Gibbons, 1891, pp. 387–388)

THE SETTLEMENT HOUSE MOVEMENT

By contrast, the Settlement House Movement had its origins in a variety of radical sources, including the writings of British thinkers such as William Morris, John Rustin, and Octavia Hill; the Social Gospel Movement among American Protestants; the philosophy of pragmatism developed by William James and John Dewey; 19th century feminism; and socialist ideas derived from European immigrants. The first **settlement house** in the United States, the Neighborhood Guild, was established in New York City in 1886; the most famous, Hull House, was founded in Chicago 3 years later by Jane Addams and Ellen Gates Starr, who at the time were only 29 and 30 years old, respectively.

Settlements were unique in their attempt to implement a more democratic conceptualization of community by bridging the class and ethnic boundaries that threatened to fragment U.S. society. Jane Addams

Figure 2.9 Jane Addams.

Figure 2.10 Ellen Gates Starr, Circa 1915.

Figure 2.11 Lillian Wald.

Figure 2.12 Hull House.

Figure 2.13 Florence Kelley.

Figure 2.14 Julia Lathrop.

Figure 2.15 Grace Abbott.

Figure 2.16 Edith Abbott.

Figure 2.17 W. E. B. Du Bois.

expressed this belief in democratic ideals succinctly: "The things that make men [sic] alike are far finer and better than the things that keep them apart" (Addams, 1910, p. 111). Inspired by such sentiments, settlement workers tried to increase social interaction between diverse classes and ethnic groups and stressed the importance of civic engagement. Resembling secular urban missionaries, they lived in the communities in which they worked, such as the lower East Side of New York City and the South Side of Chicago. Within two decades, hundreds of settlements had been established throughout the United States, including those organized by African Americans and Latinos, who were generally excluded from the settlements founded by and for white Americans (Iglehart & Becerra, 2011; Lasch-Quinn, 1993).

All settlements engaged in three types of activities. They provided concrete services such as health care and child care to neighborhood residents. They created a wide range of cultural and educational programs and, in doing so, laid the foundation for what later became social group work. Of most lasting significance,

Figure 2.18 First Lady Eleanor Roosevelt and Mrs. Henry Morgenthau, wife of the Secretary of the Treasury, visiting a self-help exchange in Washington, DC in Feburary 1939.

Figure 2.19 Sewing room in a Washington, DC self-help exchange.

they engaged in research-informed policy advocacy to promote a variety of social reforms. Their efforts produced such essential features of urban life as street lighting, public sanitation programs, expiration dating of milk, and construction of playgrounds and kindergartens. They were also instrumental in passing legislation that created juvenile courts, housing codes, public health measures, and the regulation of working conditions in factories and mines (Chambers, 1967; Davis, 1984).

In 1909, leaders of the settlement movement, such as Addams, Lillian Wald of the Henry Street Settlement in New York, Florence Kelley, Julia Lathrop, and Edith and Grace Abbott, persuaded President Theodore Roosevelt to host the first White House Conference on Children (Costin, 1983; Wald, 1909). This landmark event ultimately produced such important consequences as the creation of the Children's Bureau, and, ultimately, the 1921 Sheppard-Towner Act (which established the first federally funded maternal and child health clinics in the United States), and the 1935 Social Security Act. Settlement leaders also took controversial and frequently unpopular stands on such issues as women's suffrage, the lynching of African Americans in the South, civil rights (Jane Addams cofounded the National Association for the Advancement of Colored People with W. E. B. Du Bois), and opposition to U.S. entry into World War I (Reisch & Andrews, 2002).

Despite the different methods they employed, the COS and the settlements had much in common. Most of their early staff came from upper-middle-class and upper-class white Anglo-Saxon Protestant social backgrounds. Jane Addams' father was a colleague of Lincoln; Florence Kelley's father a member of Congress. (Mary Richmond was one of the few social work leaders of her generation who grew up in poverty.) In both organizations, women played major roles—a phenomenon with little precedent at the time. Both the COS and the settlements focused primarily on urban issues and made critical use of elite connections for political support and funding. Both were motivated by a desire to strengthen American communities, either by restoring order and applying scientific rationality to chaotic environments or by re-creating more "organic communities." Sadly, despite their appeal to democratic values, they largely excluded racial minorities and, in their early decades, allowed few members of ethnic immigrant groups or minority religions to assume leadership roles (Iglehart & Becerra, 2011; Wenocur & Reisch, 1989).

U.S. SOCIAL WELFARE BEFORE THE GREAT DEPRESSION

As a result of the influence of the settlement movement and its allies, during the first two decades of the 20th century the federal government and the states began to pass reform legislation, despite the generally conservative political and cultural climate, which made modest improvements in the conditions of low-income persons. These reforms established the foundation for more extensive government intervention during the New Deal of the 1930s. For example, the **Children's Bureau**, established in 1912 under the direction of former settlement house workers Julia Lathrop and Grace Abbott, represented the first tangible federal recognition of children's rights. Through its research and advocacy, the Bureau led a successful effort to pass the Sheppard-Towner Act in 1921, which lowered the maternal and infant mortality rate in the United States, which was higher at the time than in any other industrialized nation. The Children's Bureau also loosened the grip of the medical profession on health care policy and created the basis for future cooperation between the federal government and the states in the fields of child welfare, income maintenance, and public health (Sorensen, 2008).

At the same time, the establishment of widows' or **mothers' pensions** broke new ground in the development of government-funded programs of public assistance. By 1919, 39 states had established such programs. By 1935, when the Social Security Act was passed, all but Georgia and South Carolina had some program of this nature. Perhaps more than any social policy innovation in the early 20th century, mothers' pensions changed the nature of the relationship between government and the nonprofit sector by shifting the responsibility for the provision of cash assistance from private charities to the state. These programs also reflected the beginning of government recognition of family welfare needs, particularly the need for

Figure 2.20 Selected Global Events, 1922 to 1941.

1922: Mussolini seizes power in Italy and establishes a Fascist government.

January 1933: Hitler becomes Chancellor of Germany (through legal means) and quickly establishes the Nazi dictatorship.

1936: Spanish Civil War begins when General Francisco Franco initiates a rebellion against the democratically elected republican government. German military buildup begins.

1937: Sino-Japanese War begins. Japan occupies Manchuria.

1938: Germany annexes Austria and part of Czechoslovakia.

March 1939: Germany seizes the remainder of Czechoslovakia; the Spanish Republic falls to Franco's forces.

August 1939: Germany and the Soviet Union sign a non-aggression pact.

September 1, 1939: Germany invades Poland, and World War II begins.

December 7–11, 1941: Japan and Germany declare war on United States. United States enters World War II.

long-term support of fatherless children. Although they reflected institutional racism and sexism in their premises and implementation, mothers' pensions removed some of the stigma surrounding the receipt of public aid and broke down the 19th century preference for indoor relief over outdoor relief. Finally, by promoting the concept of social insurance, they created the policy basis for Title IV of the Social Security Act, which established the nation's Aid to Dependent Children (ADC) program and the foundation of a publically funded child welfare system (Katz, 2001).

Prior to the 1930s, efforts at the state level to establish unemployment insurance, workers' compensation programs, old-age assistance, and health and mental health policies were less successful. For several decades, the courts repeatedly declared state policies in these areas unconstitutional. In 1908, however, the first federal unemployment insurance law was passed; by 1920, similar laws were enacted in 43 states. Most of these laws, however, merely provided incentives for employers to retain their workers. Only a few states with more progressive political traditions, such as Wisconsin and New York, had genuine unemployment insurance programs (Katz, 2001; Moniz & Gorin, 2010; Patterson, 2001).

Although Western European nations had established and expanded these social welfare provisions between the 1880s and World War I, similar attempts in the United States failed for several reasons. With some notable exceptions, Americans generally lacked class consciousness and class-based political parties, particularly when compared with Europe and Latin America. Individually oriented explanations of people's problems remained popular; consequently, the public largely ignored the impact of structural and environmental factors on human well-being. In addition, the long-standing preference for states' rights combined with widespread corruption among local public officials undermined confidence in government as a potential problem solver. Finally, strong support for property rights, reflected in the judicial decisions of the period cited above, repeatedly challenged the constitutionality of reform legislation (Jansson, 2012; Reisch & Andrews, 2002). [*See Chapter 10 in this volume for further discussion of the role of the judiciary in social policy development.*]

As a result, despite the growing movement to establish social insurance programs (Lubove, 1968), there were few successful attempts during this period to use the government's power to regulate the market economy or address the nation's increasingly complex social problems. The most striking social welfare innovation during the 1920s was the expansion of corporate-sponsored social services, sometimes called "welfare capitalism" (Stoesz & Saunders, 1999). The policies that existed focused primarily on dependent populations and provided limited aid. Many Americans continued to associate relief with the "dole" and the poorhouse and stigmatized those who receive assistance. The popular press often associated social welfare reforms with socialism (Reisch & Andrews, 2002). It took the dual crises of the 1930s and 1940s—economic collapse and global war—to create a modern welfare state in the United States, but this occurred only through a socially and politically wrenching process (see Figure 2.19).

THE NEW DEAL AND THE FOUNDATION OF MODERN U.S. SOCIAL POLICY, 1933–1945

When the stock market crashed in October 1929, social policies in the United States reflected an uncoordinated mixture of local and state agencies and modestly resourced nonprofit social service organizations. Most major urban centers had public welfare departments, although 19th-century-style poorhouses still existed in smaller cities and rural areas. As discussed above, by this date nearly all states had enacted primitive forms of income support, called mothers', aid legislation and had created child welfare bureaus. Wide variations continued to exist within and among states, however, in the services provided. Even in local jurisdictions, there was little administrative coordination among agencies despite the efforts of the COS to "rationalize" the distribution of relief and the Community Chests to shape the nonprofit social service field (Patterson, 2001).

Most nonprofit organizations lacked the resources required to address the growing magnitude of individual and social problems adequately, particularly in crowded urban neighborhoods populated by recent immigrants from Southern and Eastern Europe and African Americans who had migrated from the rural South during the first two decades of the 20th century. Nevertheless, between 1910 and 1930 the number of both public and private sector agencies steadily increased, as did government expenditures for public relief, especially in large cities such as Chicago, New York, Philadelphia, and Detroit (Morris, 2009). These developments provided the foundation for the acceleration of relief spending that occurred during the New Deal (Brown, 1942).

Figure 2.21 Poorhouse.

Figure 2.22 Mary Church Terrell.

Figure 2.23 President Herbert Hoover.

Figure 2.24 Lange, Migrant Mother.

At the outset of the Great Depression, despite rising unemployment and the increased homelessness and impoverishment it created among working and middle class families, state and local government officials were reluctant to demand more funds for relief, in part because they assumed that the nation's need for cash assistance would be met through private charity. At the same time, these charities feared that the development of an extensive public welfare system would undermine their ability to raise funds. In combination, the self-interests of public and private officials produced a critical delay in providing help to millions of people (Reisch, 2004).

The economic realities of the Depression, however, could hardly be ignored. Eighteen months after the stock market crashed, nearly one sixth of all private-sector workers were unemployed, social and political unrest had intensified, and the pressure on government to intervene slowly became irresistible. Nevertheless, President Herbert Hoover proposed only modest policy initiatives. He and his advisers preferred to rely on the resiliency of the market economy and the benevolence of private charity to overcome the harsh conditions the Depression created.

By the inauguration of Franklin D. Roosevelt in March 1933, the economic crisis had reached unprecedented levels. Officially, 15 million people (25% of the workforce) were unemployed, and unofficial estimates of joblessness, especially in major cities, were estimated to be as high as 50–80%. Millions of Americans were working part-time or had given up looking for work. Average wages were about 40% lower in 1933 than they were just four years before. In Cleveland, Detroit, and New York, expenditures for relief had increased 400% to 500% in less than 3 years (Epstein, 1934). Many municipal governments faced fiscal insolvency and private nonprofit organizations could no longer keep pace with the growing demand for assistance (McElvaine, 1984; Morris, 2009; United Way of America, 1977). Conflicts

Figure 2.25 Harry Hopkins, director of the FERA and later the Works Progress Administration, testifying before Congress.

Figure 2.26a Family of James Strunk, farmer. Works for WPA (Works Progress Administration), earns forty-four dollars per month, drives twenty-six miles to work fourteen days per month. Car expense comes out of the forty-four dollars. Has eight children, four of them at home. Wheelock, North Dakota.

emerged between city officials, who were under increasing political pressure to take action against unemployment and poverty, and business leaders, who feared such actions would generate unfavorable publicity and stifle the economic recovery (McElvaine, 2000; Bird, 1966).

Between 1933 and 1942, through the creation of dozens of federally funded social policies, the Roosevelt Administration defused these explosive economic, political, and social crises. Influenced in part by the new economic ideas of John Maynard Keynes and infused with a spirit of pragmatism, Roosevelt pushed through legislative reforms that affected virtually every aspect of American life (McElvaine, 2008). [*See Chapter 1 in this volume for a brief explanation of Keynesian economics.*] These New Deal policies can be divided into two key phases.

Major developments in Phase I of the New Deal (1933–1936) included the establishment of the **Federal Emergency Relief Administration (FERA)** and the National Recovery Administration (NRA). Headed by a social worker, Harry Hopkins, FERA rapidly spent $500 million (~$9.2 billion in 2016 dollars) on relief for "any needy person" in an unprecedented effort to alleviate human suffering and create a floor on consumption to help revive the economy. To spend these funds as quickly as possible, Hopkins was compelled to use the staff of private social service agencies because a sizable public welfare workforce did not yet exist (Kurzman, 1974). His efforts throughout the 1930s led to a dramatic increase in the number

Figure 2.26b CCC (Civilian Conservation Corps) boys at work, Prince George's County, Maryland.

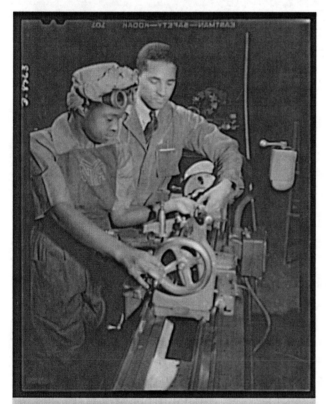

Figure 2.26c From National Youth Administration to Washington navy yard. Under the direction of Cicil M. Coles, NYA foreman, Miss Juanita E. Gray learns to operate a lathe machine at the Washington, D.C. National Youth Adminstration War Production and Training Center. This former domestic worker is one of the hundreds of Negro women trained at this center.

of social workers, particularly in government agencies, and a lasting realignment of government–nonprofit relations in the social welfare field (Hopkins, 2009; McJimsey, 1987).

The NRA was a sweeping attempt to implement wage, price, and production controls to revive the flagging U.S. economy. Despite an elaborate propaganda campaign to sell its policies to the American people, which included Hollywood newsreels and huge parades, Americans' opinions on the NRA were sharply divided and it was often attacked by opponents on both the left and the right. The controversy over the NRA was finally settled in 1934 when the Supreme Court declared that its provisions violated the Commerce Clause of the Constitution. [*See Chapter 10 in this volume for more discussion of the application of the Commerce Clause to the interpretation of social policy.*]

Consequently, during Phase I of the New Deal, state governments retained control of most social welfare programs, with the exception of FERA. They continued to provide small pensions to the elderly, widows, single mothers, and the blind. Private charities, whose resources were taxed by the demands of the Depression, also played a modest role in social provision. These long-standing structural conditions would soon be changed, however, by the policies developed by the Committee on Economic Security, chaired by Secretary of Labor and former settlement house worker Frances Perkins, whom President Roosevelt charged with drafting a comprehensive social security act (Downey, 2010).

The 1935 Social Security Act (SSA) the Committee produced was the centerpiece of Phase II of the New Deal (1936–1939) and has been the cornerstone of U.S. social policy ever since (Ball, 2009; Altman & Kingson, 2014). Unlike today, its most important components at the time were Old Age Assistance (now part of **Supplemental Security Income or SSI**) and unemployment compensation.

Table 2.2 The Great Depression and the New Deal: A Chronology.

November 1928: Herbert Hoover elected president. Five-year economic boom continues, fueled by stock market speculation and increased consumer spending, although unemployment in some sectors of the economy has been high since the mid-1920s.

October 1929: Stock market crashes; values fall 40% in a few weeks.

1929 to 1932: Unemployment soars as economy comes to a halt. Non-profit sector and local and state governments struggle to deal with the extent of social deprivation.

November 1932: Franklin Delano Roosevelt (FDR) elected president on platform of a balanced budget.

Winter of 1932–1933: Exceptionally cold winter; official unemployment is 25%—as high as 50% in cities such as Chicago and Detroit. National income is down by two thirds. State and local governments go broke trying to care for the unemployed.

March 1933: FDR inaugurated. Immediately declares a bank "holiday" to prevent run on assets. FDR enacts emergency legislation regulating banks and strengthening the Federal Reserve Board, and establishes the Civilian Conservation Corps (CCC).

May 1933: Congress passes the Federal Farm Loan Act and the Agricultural Adjustment Act, and creates the Farm Credit Administration, the Tennessee Valley Authority, and FERA, headed by social worker Harry Hopkins. FERA is given $500 million to provide relief for "any needy persons."

June 1933: Congress passes the Homeowners Loan Corporation and the NRA to regulate industry, and creates the Public Works Administration.

August 1933: The National Labor Relations Board is established.

June 1934: The Securities and Exchange Commission is created to regulate the stock market. Major strikes occur in the auto and textile industries. There is a general strike in San Francisco.

January 1935: The Works Progress Administration (WPA) is established to create public sector jobs.

July 1935: The Wagner Act is passed; unions gain the right to organize.

August 1935: The Social Security Act is passed.

1935: The Congress of Industrial Organizations is founded to organize workers who are ignored by the American Federation of Labor.

1934 to 1936: The Supreme Court declares the NRA, the Agricultural Adjustment Act, state minimum-wage laws, railroad labor legislation, and many other New Deal measures unconstitutional. End of first New Deal era.

November 1936: FDR is re-elected by a landslide. Second New Deal era begins.

1936 to 1937: The Congress of Industrial Organizations organizes 6 million workers.

February 1937: FDR's effort to "pack" the Supreme Court fails. However, the Court begins to shift its views on major New Deal legislation.

March 1937: the United Automobile Workers wins a recognition strike against General Motors.

May-June 1937: Major strike against Republic Steel. Memorial Day massacre occurs.

July 1937: Congress establishes the Farm Security Administration and passes the Fair Labor Standards Act, which regulates the number of work hours per week and establishes federal a minimum wage.

(Continued)

Winter 1937 to 1938: As the Roosevelt Administration begins to cut back on government social welfare programs, a new recession begins and unemployment starts to increase.

February 1938: Congress passes a revised Agricultural Adjustment Act.

November 1938: Republicans make gains in midterm elections. Second New Deal era ends.

1939: Prior to the start of World War II, unemployment in the United States is still at 14% to 15%.

Other key features of the legislation included retirement benefits, now referred to generically as "Social Security," maternal and child welfare grants, aid to the blind, and ADC—the antecedent of today's "welfare" program, Temporary Assistance for Needy Families (TANF) [*See Chapters 11, 12, and 13 in this volume for further discussion of Social Security, unemployment insurance and other welfare programs.*]

The following box summarizes the major legislation of the New Deal and the context in which it occurred:

In addition to the Social Security Act, other major policy initiatives during Phase II of the New Deal included government-funded and directed jobs programs (the Public Works Administration, the Works Progress Administration or WPA, and the Civilian Conservation Corps or CCC), the Agricultural Adjustment Act of 1937, and the Fair Labor Standards or Wagner Act. The latter established fair employment policies and the first federal minimum wage, created the National Labor Relations Board, and legalized collective bargaining by workers, providing a tremendous boost to the organizing efforts of industrial unions. The Social Security Act and the Agricultural Adjustment Act helped maintain a floor on consumption, while emergency public works and income support programs (FERA, WPA, and CCC) provided temporary assistance to the unemployed and diminished the possibility of widespread social and political conflict.

At the same time, however, New Deal policies reinforced traditional cultural values regarding work and self-reliance, stressed the temporary nature of public assistance—President Roosevelt wanted the federal government to end "this business of relief" as soon as possible—and maintained the institutional racism and sexism of previous public and private social welfare efforts. Discriminatory practices against women and African Americans in employment and relief distribution mounted (Rose, 1995, 2009). Despite the advocacy of Frances Perkins, the Social Security Act did not include health insurance because of the opposition of the American Medical Association and the Chamber of Commerce, who denounced it as "socialized medicine" (Starr, 1982). The Roosevelt Administration also balked at introducing much-needed civil rights legislation to appease the powerful Southern Democrats who controlled virtually all major Congressional committees and threatened to block the President's initiatives if they included federal attempts to alter racial conditions in that region (Hamilton & Hamilton, 1997; Lieberman, 1998). Nowhere are these patterns clearer than in the provisions of the 1935 Social Security Act [*See Chapter 11 in this volume.*]

The initial SSA excluded from coverage occupations in which African Americans, Latinos, and women predominated, such as farmworkers and domestic servants, and discriminated against women in calculating benefits (Poole, 2006). By giving states administrative control over ADC (welfare), the law abetted segregationist practices and produced huge disparities in welfare policy implementation within and among states. Other New Deal policies displayed similar characteristics.

Although the National Labor Relations Act established the right for workers to organize and bargain collectively, it contained no antidiscrimination clause, thereby allowing unions to discriminate on the basis of race, gender, and ethnicity (Hamilton & Hamilton, 1997). Both the WPA and the U.S. Employment Service regularly discriminated on the basis of race and gender in job placement and salaries (Rose, 2009), and the newly established Federal Housing Administration routinely sanctioned the practice of "red-lining" by banks, leading to the development of racially segregated urban ghettos after World War II (Sugrue, 2005, 2009). In sum, the New Deal created a two-channel social policy system in the United States that still exists today, which consisted of a social safety net for white, male industrial workers while sustaining racial and gender inequalities through its welfare, labor, and housing policies. Unfortunately, as discussed below and in other chapters of this volume, today even that safety net is beginning to unravel, leading to the social insecurity reflected in the 2016 election season.

Despite these serious and lasting shortcomings, the policies enacted during the Roosevelt Administration significantly expanded and improved standards of social welfare across the

Figure 2.27 Lester Granger (center) was an African American social welfare leader during the 1930s and 1940s who spoke out for civil rights as President of the National Conference of Social Work.

United States and provided recipients of aid with some sense of individual freedom and dignity. Above all, they established a regular, heretofore unprecedented role for the federal government as a source of aid and policy innovation. The New Deal made the provision of social welfare the obligation of every level of government and introduced the concept of legal entitlement to assistance into the American political vocabulary. Finally, it expanded the scope of social policies beyond financial aid to the poor to include housing, rural electrification, recreation and cultural activities, and social insurance in all its forms for Americans of all social classes.

FROM THE NEW DEAL TO THE REDISCOVERY OF POVERTY, 1945–1961

During the 1940s and 1950s, rapid economic growth, low unemployment, policies such as Social Security and the GI Bill, and a moderately progressive income tax created relative prosperity for many Americans (Patterson, 2001). Dramatic demographic shifts—the migration of more than 4 million African Americans and hundreds of thousands of Puerto Ricans to the nation's major industrial centers—accompanied these developments, although policymakers initially overlooked their long-term significance (Lemann, 1991). The Great Depression may have temporarily changed Americans' attitudes about poverty and unemployment, but it did not eliminate institutional racism or societal prejudices toward the poor, particularly toward those from racial or ethnic minority groups. U.S. social policy in the mid-20th century continued to reflect pre-New Deal myths about individuals and families who needed public assistance (Abramovitz, 1996; Lieberman, 1998; Stern & Axinn, 2012).

The "two-channel" system of social welfare created by the New Deal and the social policies implemented during the post-World War II "Fair Deal" era primarily benefitted middle-income white men. Aided by the GI Bill and the housing policies of the Truman Administration, white families began to leave cities for the burgeoning suburbs, driven equally by racially based fears of integration and a desire to achieve the "American dream" (Sugrue, 2005). The *de facto* racial and class segregation this produced in most metropolitan areas—what Massey and Denton (1993) called "American apartheid"—made poverty seem to disappear, a phenomenon abetted by the new medium of television (Danziger & Weinberg, 1994). The so-called "rediscovery of poverty" in the early 1960s must be understood in this context.

By the end of the Eisenhower Administration (1959–1960), the unique conditions that fueled the postwar recovery had begun to change. During the mid-1950s, the United States produced more than half of all manufactured goods in the world, largely because its industrial base had not been decimated by World War II as had those of virtually every other European and Asian nation. By the late 1950s, however, the impact of the Marshall Plan, the creation of the European Common Market, and the establishment of international financial institutions such as the World Bank and the International Monetary Fund had helped rebuild the economies of Western Europe and Japan. Their surging economies threatened American global hegemony.

As a result, unemployment among semiskilled industrial workers in the United States increased, and cities began to experience the first symptoms of the urban and welfare crises that would produce considerable controversy and conflict a decade later. Nevertheless, the isolation of urban ghettos and rural enclaves from more affluent suburbs and the images of universal material well-being fostered by advertising and television contributed to the invisibility of the millions of Americans who remained poor (Harrington, 1981). A generation after the New Deal had rescued the nation from the depth of the Depression, severe deprivation lurked below its prosperous surface.

At the same time, despite its comparative aggregate prosperity, the United States lagged considerably behind other Western industrialized nations in its social welfare provision. During the postwar period, in response to anti-Communist purges, Congressional efforts by Republicans and Southern Democrats to roll back New Deal policies, and increasing right-wing pressure from corporate-dominated boards and the media, both nonprofit and public sector agencies shifted the focus of their services from low-income to middle- and upper-income groups (Andrews & Reisch, 1997). Social activism declined, particularly within the social work profession, and the public's hostility toward welfare programs and "undeserving" welfare recipients increased (Reisch & Andrews, 2002). This growing resentment of the poor, particularly of African Americans, resulted in part from a shift in the racial composition of the welfare rolls that began in the late 1940s. The social conflict it created would soon undermine federal antipoverty efforts; it continues to fuel conflicts over welfare today (Bailey & Danziger, 2013; Edsall, 1991; Quadagno, 1994). [*See Chapters 12 and 13 in this volume.*]

In the early 1960s, well-publicized exposés of poverty, such as Michael Harrington's (1962, 1981) *The Other America* and Harry Caudill's (1963) *Night Comes to the Cumberlands*, revealed that more than 40 million Americans and more than half of all African Americans had been bypassed by postwar economic and social progress (Katz, 2001; Patterson, 2001). Poverty was particularly severe among the elderly and children. The policy responses that ensued, however, continued to reflect misconceptions about the extent and nature of poverty in the United States and about the character of the poor (Lewis, 1965).

THE WAR ON POVERTY, THE GREAT SOCIETY, AND THEIR LEGACY, 1964–1975

Just 2 months after the assassination of President Kennedy in November 1963, President Lyndon Johnson used his first State of the Union Address to declare an "unconditional War on Poverty." The major policies and themes on which they focused are summarized in Table 2.3.

Many of the policies created during the War on Poverty were based on the popular **"culture of poverty" thesis**, which assumed that the poor, particularly the African American and Latino poor, had different cultural norms and, by implication, were somehow inferior to other Americans in terms of their values, skills, aspirations, and behavior. Proponents of this perspective further assumed that these qualities were transmitted from generation to generation. As a result, by defining people's needs as the products of individual or cultural deficiency, rather than institutional or structural deficiency, the conditions and consequences of poverty were viewed as "normal" for large segments of the U.S. population (Ryan, 1971). This rationalized the emphasis of the antipoverty policies of the period on changing individual behavior rather than reforming societal institutions (Bailey & Danziger, 2013). These tendencies persist today, as evidenced by the motives and outcomes of "welfare reform" (Edin & Shaefer, 2015; Center on Budget & Policy Priorities, 2015; Schram, Soss, & Fording, 2011; Abramovitz, 2005). [*See Chapters 5, 12, and 13 in this volume.*]

During the same period, however, new "structuralist" analyses of social problems emerged among social scientists and advocates that challenged the dominant perspective. Focusing on such issues as juvenile delinquency, urban decay, and inter-generational family conflict, these analyses stressed how systemic obstacles to opportunities, rather than individual or cultural pathology, contributed to long-term poverty and other social ills. These insights inspired the development of a new kind of social

Table 2.3 The War on Poverty.

Policy Goal	Social Policy Development
Grow the "economic pie"	Tax cuts to stimulate the economy
Promote full employment	Job training programs and hiring incentives for business
Rehabilitate depressed communities	Office of Economic Opportunity, Community Action Programs, Community Legal Services
Increase aid to disadvantaged populations	Social Security amendments, Medicaid and Medicare, Older Americans Act, Aid to Families with Dependent Children—Unemployed Parent
Expand educational and employment opportunities	Job Corps, Neighborhood for Youth, Youth Corps, Head Start, Foster Grandparents Program (Danziger, 1991; Gillette, 1996)

service organization that employed a comprehensive approach to solving the complex problems of urban poverty (Lemann, 1988, 1989). The most famous examples of this innovative approach were Mobilization for Youth in New York, the Ford Foundation's "Gray Areas Projects" in Chicago and Cleveland, and the **Community Action Programs** implemented by the Kennedy and Johnson administrations (Gillette, 1996).

Other important social policy developments during the early 1960s included the establishment of the Area Redevelopment Agency in 1961 to provide increased federal funding to economically depressed regions such as Appalachia; the Manpower Development and Training Act of 1962, which focused on job training for displaced or under-skilled workers; and various amendments to public welfare programs, which extended benefits to children of unemployed workers in two-parent families and increased federal support for social services linked to cash assistance. Presaging later efforts at "welfare reform," these policy initiatives also stressed moving clients from welfare to work through the provision of job training and supportive programs such as child care (Katz, 1989; Patterson, 2001). In the late 1960s, in response to the backlash against civil rights legislation and the expansion of social welfare programs, further amendments and regulatory changes made the receipt of welfare more restrictive through the implementation of various "workfare" requirements and the separation of cash assistance from social services (Gillette, 1996; Quadagno, 1994). This trend has continued to the present. [*See Chapters 12, 13, and 15 this volume.*]

Developments in the mental health field followed a similar pattern. The Community Mental Health Centers Act of 1963, the product of decades of advocacy, emphasized prevention over treatment and attempted to implement a community-based rather than institutionally-based approach to service delivery. Ironically, the deinstitutionalization movement that both spawned and flourished as a result of this policy shift inadvertently worsened the plight of the chronically mentally ill when lawmakers did not adequately fund the community-based services required to enable deinstitutionalization to succeed (Frank & Glied, 2006; Grob & Glodman, 2006). Along with deindustrialization and urban gentrification, this failure contributed to the growing problem of homelessness in the 1980s and 1990s (Blau, 1992).

Perhaps the most important policy achievement of the Johnson Administration was the enactment of Medicare and Medicaid in 1965 (Titles XVIII and XIX of the Social Security Act). These measures established a mandatory federally funded program of hospital insurance and an optional program of physician care for the elderly and the disabled (Medicare), and a joint federal/state health insurance program for low-income persons (Medicaid). In the same whirlwind year, Congress established the Department of Housing and Urban Development (HUD), created a wide range of social services for the elderly through the Older Americans Act, passed the Food Stamp Program (now called the Supplemental Nutritional Assistance Program or SNAP), and made the federal government a major player in the field of K–12 education for the first time through the Elementary and Secondary School Education Act (Matusow, 1984).

By the late 1960s, opposition to these initiatives emerged even among some Democrats. Conservatives in both parties attacked programs such as Head Start as "radical" and "socialistic," and big-city mayors objected to the challenges to their political dominance created by the Community Action Programs established under the Economic Opportunity Act (Quadagno, 1994). The rapidly increasing fiscal and human costs of the war in Southeast Asia also directed the attention of policymakers and the public away from domestic matters. President Johnson could no longer choose to fund *both* guns and butter.

Yet, despite their liberal appearance and the conservative backlash they produced, the programs of the War on Poverty and Great Society did not represent a fundamental redirection of U.S. social policy. Instead, they reflected long-standing American preferences for employment over welfare and work incentives over income support. Social services focused on self-care and self-support and reinforced traditional political values such as decentralization, long-standing cultural values such as individualism and self-reliance. Above all, the policies of the 1960s continued to assume that the key to eliminating poverty was the promotion of sustained economic growth rather than a redistribution of income and wealth or a restructuring of societal institutions (Reisch, 2008).

The backlash against the social and cultural movements of the decade further undermined the policies of the War on Poverty and Great Society (Kornbluh, 1997; Kotz & Kotz, 1977; West, 1981). Violent civil unrest in cities such as Detroit, Los Angeles, and Newark and the rapid expansion of the welfare rolls changed popular attitudes about social welfare programs which had largely been favorable in the early 1960s (Nadasen, 2012). In November 1968, this backlash helped Richard Nixon win the presidency by a narrow majority on the vague promises of ending the war in Southeast Asia, restoring "law and order," and heeding the voices of the so-called "silent majority." These themes reverberate in American politics down to the rhetoric of the 2016 Presidential campaign (Cohen, 2016).

To this day, debates persist among historians, policy analysts, and media pundits over whether the War on Poverty was a success or a failure (Bailey & Danziger, 2013; Murray, 1984). In hindsight, its record was mixed. On the positive side, by recognizing and responding to poverty as a national issue, the policies

Figure 2.28–2.29 Dorothy Height and Whitney Young were African American leaders in the struggle for civil rights and the expansion of social welfare.

Figure 2.30 Impact of Social Security and Medicare on Elderly Poverty.

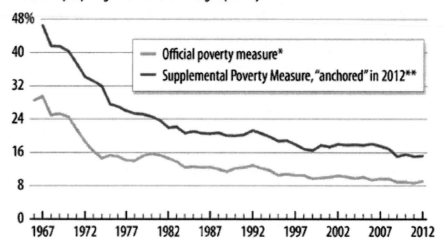

Elderly Poverty Rate Has Fallen Substantially

Percent of people aged 65 and older living in poverty

*Counts cash income only and uses the official poverty line

**Counts cash income plus non-cash benefits, reflects the net impact of the tax system, subtracts certain
expenses from income, and uses a poverty line based on today's cost of certain necessities adjusted back
for inflation

Source: Christopher Wimer et al., "Trends in Poverty with an Anchored Supplemental Poverty Measure,"
Columbia Population Research Center, December 2013.

Center on Budget and Policy Priorities | cbpp.org

emerging from the War on Poverty significantly reduced poverty among the elderly and African Americans. The passage of Medicare, Medicaid, Head Start, and the Older Americans Act were clearly major advances in U.S. social welfare (see Figure 2.30).

Yet the War on Poverty failed to develop an effective response to the "welfare crisis." It neither reformed welfare nor established a guaranteed annual income, despite the best efforts of the National Welfare Rights Organization and advocates in the Legal Services (Nadasen, 2012; Bussiere, 1997). The Community Action Programs, founded on the promise of "maximum feasible participation" for the poor, collapsed in the late 1960s under political and fiscal pressures (U.S. Congress, 1975; Rose, 1972). The well-intentioned deinstitutionalization movement inadvertently contributed to the emergence of homelessness as a major national problem. Above all, the War on Poverty did little to reshape U.S. perspectives on social policy and the welfare state. Because it did not achieve its grandiose goals, Americans were soon vulnerable to conservative arguments that welfare programs promoted rather than eliminated poverty and dependency and that government was the source of these problems, not the means by which they could be solved (Frank, 2005; Danziger, 1991).

FROM THE WAR ON POVERTY TO THE WAR ON WELFARE, 1969–1996

In the late 1960s and 1970s, dramatic changes in the distribution of political and economic power in the United States accompanied the retreat from the ambitious goals of the War on Poverty—precursors to the major policy shifts that have occurred during the past four decades. Primarily as a result of the growth of the energy and defense industries, the decline of American manufacturing (e.g., in automobile and steel production), and large-scale internal migration, the "Sunbelt" states of the South and West became increasingly powerful at the expense of the "Rust Belt" states of the East and Midwest. This "power shift" (Sale, 1976) had several important consequences.

Conservative lawmakers from the Sunbelt introduced anti-social welfare and anti-labor legislation and promoted fiscal policies at the state and federal levels that intensified income disparities within and across regions. The decline in union membership and the diminished influence of social movements, particularly in the area of civil rights, left a political vacuum that conservative, anti-government, and anti-tax forces quickly filled. At the same time, the rapidly deteriorating economic base of many urban centers—a by-product of "white flight" and deindustrialization—led to the fiscal crises that cities such as Cleveland and New York experienced in the mid-1970s (Abramson, Tobin, & Vandergoot, 1995; Massey & Denton, 1993; O'Connor, 1973).

The retreat from the ambitious goals of the War on Poverty, however, was neither rapid nor total. In 1970, a Republican President, Richard Nixon, proposed a Family Assistance Program (FAP) that would have replaced Aid to Families with Dependent Children (AFDC) with a guaranteed annual income (Moynihan, 1973). Although an unusual liberal–conservative coalition defeated this initiative, other major social policy reforms were adopted during the early 1970s, including the Comprehensive Employment and Training Act (CETA) in 1973 and the 1972 Social Security Amendments. These amendments created the Supplemental Security Income (SSI) program, which centralized and standardized aid to the disabled and low-income elderly and indexed Social Security retirement benefits to inflation, a policy innovation that proved particularly significant in the late 1970s when inflation reached double digits. [*See Chapter 11 in this volume for further discussion of the evolution of the Social Security program.*]

In contrast with these policy advances and the promotion of major environmental initiatives, such as the Clean Air and Clean Water Acts, the Nixon Administration cut domestic spending in other important areas. A major strategy, consistent with the Republican Party's states' rights philosophy, was to transfer administrative responsibility for antipoverty programs to state and local governments. Although between 1968 and 1972, this initially led to expanded federal support for such programs, the strategy relied on the control of these funds by elected officials rather than community-based organizations or community residents. In 1972, Congress institutionalized this strategy through the State and Local Fiscal Assistance Act. This legislation established the concept of "revenue sharing," which ultimately led to the dismantling of the Office of Economic Opportunity and the ambitious social policy agenda of the 1960s (Katz, 1989).

President Nixon resigned in August 1974 due to the Watergate scandal and the threat of impeachment. The major social policy accomplishment during the limited term of Nixon's successor, Gerald Ford, was **Title XX** of the Social Security Act, the so-called Social Services Amendment, which shifted the direction of public and nonprofit social services in several important ways. It attempted to slow the growth of government spending on social welfare by using revenue sharing to give states maximum flexibility in social service design and delivery in return for increased fiscal accountability and responsibility. It also tried to change the focus of services for low-income persons by emphasizing: (a) the prevention, reduction, or elimination of welfare dependency; (b) the prevention or remediation of abuse, neglect, or exploitation of children and vulnerable adults; (c) the substitution of alternative forms of assistance for institutional care, where appropriate; and (d) the requirement that a minimum of 50% of government funds on the social services target low-income persons (Bixby, 1990; Derthick, 1975).

During the Carter Administration (1977–1981), it became clear that Title XX had not achieved these goals. Its implementation suffered from a variety of administrative shortcomings, including fiscal inefficiency, program redundancy, uneven regulations and standards, and the lack of interagency coordination (Gilbert, 1977). By the late 1970s, a combination of double-digit inflation, slow economic growth, and high unemployment—a phenomenon referred to as "stagflation"—made it impossible for the federal government or the states to fund rapidly increasing social service expenditures or promote innovative program ideas. Representatives from politically conservative, largely white suburban districts took control of many state legislatures and used their power to direct a disproportionate amount of Title XX funds away from the legislation's intended beneficiaries and toward middle-income households (Edsall, 1991; Katz, 1989).

In hindsight, the policies of the Nixon, Ford, and Carter administrations failed to address the needs of the most vulnerable populations left behind in rapidly declining older industrial cities—racial and ethnic minorities, new immigrants, and the elderly poor—and were unsuccessful in promoting racial and class integration in the suburbs (Bonastia, 2008; Freund, 2007; Lamb, 2005; Massey & Denton, 1993; Blau, 1992). Although poverty continued to decline among the elderly, largely because of the effects of Medicare, Medicaid, food stamps, and the indexing of Social Security benefits to the cost of living, a virtual freeze on AFDC benefits, wage stagnation, and high inflation produced a steady increase in poverty among children—particularly African American and Latino children—reversing the trend from 1959 to 1973 that the combined effects of economic growth and antipoverty policies had produced (Danziger & Gottschalk, 2004; Patterson, 2001).

Other developments in the late 1970s would create future havoc for needy populations and chronic fiscal challenges for state and local governments and nonprofit social service agencies. The tax structure of the United States became increasingly regressive (i.e., it placed a disproportionate burden on lower income households) as states, confronted with cuts in federal spending, relied more and more on sales taxes to fund vital services. Anti-tax movements passed ballot initiatives, such as Proposition 13 in California, which limited the state's ability to tax residential and business properties even as their assessed value rapidly increased. Primarily as a consequence of Proposition 13, the quality of California's systems of K–12 education, higher education, mental health, and social services, which had been ranked at or near the top nationally during the 1950s and 1960s, declined precipitously within a few decades, as the state perpetually struggled to balance its budget (Rosenberg & Rosenberg, 2006).

Another significant policy development in the 1970s was the creation of **block grants** by the Carter Administration. Block grants combined numerous categorical programs (which focused on a specific problem or service) into broad programmatic areas and established a ceiling on total state social service expenditures in return for giving states greater control of spending. This development was particularly significant for struggling nonprofit organizations, especially those that had come to rely heavily on government grants and contracts for funding since the 1960s. Due to funding cuts at the federal and state levels during the 1970s and 1980s, nonprofit community-based organizations that had long served low-income neighborhoods experienced a precipitous drop in revenues (Blau, 1992). As a result, they were not prepared in the 1980s for unpredictable calamities such as the HIV/AIDS crisis, the crack cocaine epidemic, and the surge in homelessness. Nor were they ready for the even more dramatic cuts in social welfare spending implemented by the Reagan Administration.

THE REAGAN–BUSH WAR ON WELFARE, 1981–1993

The massive reductions in social welfare spending by the Reagan Administration were supported by a well-orchestrated political and ideological attack on government as a potential vehicle to solve the nation's economic and social problems. This attack had two primary purposes: to transfer the social costs of the economic changes produced by deindustrialization and globalization on to the most vulnerable segments of the population and to promote exclusive reliance on private-sector (largely market-oriented) policy solutions for complex social problems (Abramovitz, 1992; Ferguson, Lavalette, & Whitmore, 2005; Kapp, 1972). They represented the fulfillment of conservatives' promises to dismantle the social welfare system created by the New Deal and the War on Poverty.

Supporters of the rollback of social policies during the Reagan–Bush years justified their position by arguing that recent government attempts to reduce poverty had failed. Conservative analysts such as Charles Murray (1984), George Gilder (1981), and Lawrence Mead (1986) asserted that the expansion of social welfare had, instead, increased dependency and encouraged other forms of undesirable, even antisocial behavior, such as out-of-wedlock pregnancies and crime. Proponents of cutbacks, however, ignored dramatic the effects of dramatic economic and political transformations that had occurred in the United States since 1960. These included increasing monopoly control over key industries such as energy and banking; the growing power of multinational and transnational corporations (which presaged the advent of globalization); the transition from a goods-producing to a service economy; the growing gaps in income and wealth these trends produced; and the social consequences of these developments at the community level (Wilson, 1996).

Supporters of so-called "Reaganomics" held a view of social policy and social welfare markedly different from the consensus perspective that had existed in the United States since the 1930s. They often spoke of government as if it was incapable of responding effectively to the nation's problems. In fact, Reagan and his allies frequently portrayed government as the source of these problems or, at a minimum, that government intervention only made these problems worse by interfering with the self-correcting mechanisms of the market system and violating the sanctity of private property rights. Finally, they argued that the expansion of public policies undermined "traditional values," such as the sanctity of the family, was fiscally wasteful, and reduced individual freedom (Friedman & Friedman, 1980; Gilder, 1981; Murray, 1984).

The Reagan and Bush administrations also attacked the concepts of statutory entitlement and the value of mutual social obligation that lay at the heart of U.S. social policy since the New Deal. They sought to reduce the scope of government-funded policies and services, cut benefit levels, and shift as much responsibility as possible for addressing the nation's problems to the private sector, including for-profit enterprises. From President Reagan's first budget, innocently titled the "Omnibus Budget and Reconciliation Act of 1981," until the inauguration of President Bill Clinton in January 1993, entire social welfare programs were eliminated, drastically reduced, or significantly revised (Blau, 1999). The effects of these cutbacks continue to be felt well into the 21st century.

For example, expenditures on public housing were reduced by over 80%, the minimum wage was frozen for more than a decade, and because of benefit cuts, freezes, or regulatory changes, the purchasing power of households who depended on AFDC for economic survival declined by one third between the mid-1970s and mid-1990s. On the positive side, through bipartisan compromise, a looming crisis in the funding of Social Security and Medicare was temporarily forestalled in 1983 by a combination of modest tax increases and benefit reductions (Marmor, 2000). [*See Chapter 11 in this volume for further details of this compromise.*]

In the area of social services, block grants to states continued to consolidate categorical programs in such areas as child welfare, mental health, and community development, and to give state and local governments more authority and responsibility for their design and implementation. During the 1980s, however, these grants were often financed at levels about 25% below the combined funding of the categorical grants they replaced. Since the legal obligation to provide these services remained, the "unfunded mandates" this budget maneuver created presented a huge fiscal problem for state governments (Rosenberg & Rosenberg, 2006).

At the same time, ballooning federal deficits—largely caused by a combination of tax cuts, which primarily benefited wealthy Americans, and massive increases in military spending—precluded the passage of any major new social policy initiatives. Consequently, even during the relatively prosperous years of the mid- and late 1980s, poverty rates soared, particularly among children (to nearly 25%), young families, and persons of color (Children's Defense Fund, 1996). At the end of the 1980s, the percentage of urban householders who worked steadily and earned a living wage in the nation's 15 largest cities was lower than at any other time since World War II. By the early 1990s, the number of people officially listed as "poor" rose to 36 million, higher than it had been in a decade. As the chart below indicates, over the course of

Table 2.4 Changes in Real After-Tax Income in the U.S., 1979–2005.

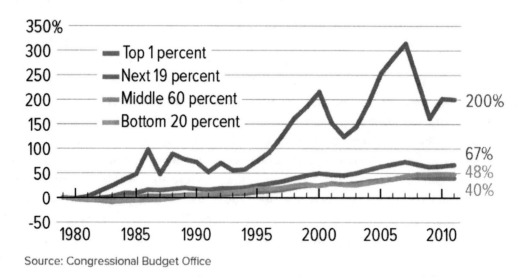

Income Gains at the Top Dwarf Those of Low- and Middle-Income Households

Percent change in real after-tax income since 1979

Source: Congressional Budget Office

CENTER ON BUDGET AND POLICY PRIORITIES | CBPP.ORG

3 decades the United States became more economically and socially unequal than any industrialized nation and more socially stratified than at any other time since the Great Depression (Bowles, Gintis, & Groves, 2005; Campbell, Haveman, Sandefur, & Wolfe, 2005; Center on Budget and Policy Priorities, 2006; U.S. Census Bureau, 1995).

In addition, increasing ideological resistance among fiscal and cultural conservatives during this period blocked or slowed action on emerging social problems such as the HIV/AIDS epidemic, homelessness, the scourge of crack cocaine, and the needs of immigrants and refugees from Central America and Southeast Asia. The same ideological forces, particularly at the state level, frequently attempted to restrict women's reproductive rights through the passage of anti-abortion legislation, expand the use of imprisonment for victimless crimes such as possession of illegal drugs, and oppose civil rights legislation on behalf of LGBTQ (lesbian, gay, bisexual, transgender, and queer) persons and individuals with disabilities. They exerted growing influence in the media, particularly "talk radio," and on Americans' perceptions of social issues such as poverty (Clawson & Trice, 2000).

There was some modest progress in the social policy area, however, during President Reagan's second term (1985–1989) and during the administration of George H. W. Bush (1989–1993). The passage of the Ryan White Act marked the first major federal effort to address the HIV/AIDS epidemic. The Americans with Disabilities Act (ADA) was a significant advance in the area of civil rights. A major federal attempt to overhaul the nation's ailing welfare system, the Family Support Act of 1988, however, was never adequately funded. It was left to the states and the Clinton Administration to tackle this persistent policy issue.

THE CLINTON YEARS, 1993–2001

Public dissatisfaction over the recession of the early 1990s and the presence of a third party candidate, the billionaire H. Ross Perot, led to the election of Bill Clinton as president in November 1992. Clinton, the former governor of Arkansas and a co-founder of the centrist New Democratic Coalition, campaigned as a "New Democrat" who would reform the nation's welfare system while reinvesting in human capital development—an approach compatible with the emerging ideology known as "neoliberalism." From the outset, however, the Clinton Administration's policy options were severely constrained by the huge budget deficits Republican presidents had created over the previous 12 years. Clinton was unable, therefore, to pass an ambitious domestic policy agenda and focused, instead, on budgetary restraint—including an unpopular tax increase—and the promotion of economic growth. Although most economists attribute the resurgent prosperity of the mid- and late 1990s to this policy shift (Blau, 2010), the failure of Clinton's legislative centerpiece—a comprehensive national health insurance program—and opposition to the tax increases required to reduce the federal deficit contributed to the Republican landslide in the 1994 Congressional elections.

Clinton attempted to recover from this political defeat and avoid political irrelevance by engaging in a strategy of "triangulation"—that is, borrowing some of the Republicans' ideas about social policy and thereby undercutting their agenda. After considerable debate within his administration and among his allies and after vetoing two earlier, harsher versions, he signed a Republican-sponsored welfare reform bill in 1996—the Personal Responsibility and Work Opportunity Reconciliation Act (PRWORA). This legislation marked a significant turning point in U.S. social policy. It replaced the 60-year-old entitlement to public assistance for needy children and their caretakers (AFDC) with block grants to states that included time limits and stringent conditions—particularly work requirements—on the receipt of cash assistance, now called TANF (Temporary Assistance to Needy Families). PRWORA also devolved responsibility for welfare program development to the states and increased the roles of private sector, nonprofit and for-profit, and faith-based organizations in program implementation. (The latter trends had begun during the Reagan and Bush administrations.) In addition, within a short period welfare reform made a range of educational, employment training, child care, health, mental health, transportation, housing, nutrition, and other social services more critical to people's well-being and more complicated for them to access while increasing the strain on small and mid-sized programs to deliver these essential services particularly in emergencies (Abramovitz, 2005; Albelda & Withorn, 2002; Bloom, 1997; Borjas, 2002; Fink & Widom, 2001; Piven, Acker, Hallock, & Morgen, 2002). These problems have become even more acute today as states have reduced the funds they provide for cash assistance (Floyd, et al, 2015; Edin & Shaefer, 2015). [*See Chapter 13 in this volume for further discussion of welfare reform.*]

Perhaps the most significant and effective social policy advance against poverty during the 1990s was the expansion of the **Earned Income Tax Credit (EITC)**. This program, which had considerable bipartisan support, provided additional income in an efficient, non-stigmatizing way to millions of low-income working families (Holt, 2011). [*See Chapter 12 in this volume for further discussion of the EITC.*] During the late 1990s, in combination with the lowest unemployment rate in two generations, an increase in the minimum wage, and near-zero inflation, this policy helped reduce the number of Americans living in poverty and raised the real income of working people for the first time in decades (Children's Defense Fund, 2006). Nevertheless, the gap between rich and poor Americans continued to widen, as the effects of aggregate economic prosperity were not equitably distributed (Blau, 1999; Boushey, Brocht, Gundersen, & Bernstein, 2001; Cancian & Reed, 2001; Cauthen & Lu, 2003; Corcoran, 2001; Gershoff, 2003; Glennerster, 2002; Iceland, 2003; Wilson, 1996). Stereotypes of the poor in the media and within policymaking circles continued to create obstacles to policy solutions (Clawson & Trice, 2000).

President Clinton left office in January 2001 with the dual legacy of a strong economy and the transformation of the huge federal budget deficit he had inherited into a surplus. [*See Chapter 7 in this volume for a discussion of the federal budget.*] Yet several major social policy issues remained unresolved. While his administration made some progress in providing health care for children in low-income families through the establishment of the State Children's Health Insurance Program (S-CHIP) in 1997, by the early 21st century more than 43 million Americans still lacked any coverage (Case, Fertig, & Paxson, 2005; Hofrichter, 2003; Wallace, Green, & Jaros, 2003). The soaring cost of prescription medications posed a particular threat to the economic well-being of elderly Americans (Caputo, 2005; Hudson, 2005). Proposals to provide this benefit through Medicare and to prevent a future crisis in funding for the Social Security retirement program and Medicare when the "baby boomer" generation retired made little progress in the 1990s because of political gridlock (Diamond & Orszag, 2005; Marmor, 2000; Morone & Jacobs, 2005; Skocpol, 1997). Nor was substantial progress made in addressing the spread of the HIV/AIDS epidemic, especially within the African American community, or the persistent problems of homelessness and substance abuse.

Finally, looming on the near horizon were the potentially catastrophic social consequences of enforcing the lifetime cap on TANF recipients during a period of economic slowdown (Chow, Osterling, & Xu, 2005) and the imminent demographic and fiscal "time bomb" of the Social Security and Medicare funding crises (Ozawa, 1997). President Clinton's successors, George W. Bush and Barack Obama, addressed these issues in very different ways. [*See Chapters 11 and 14 in this volume for further discussion of the funding crises in Social Security and in the U.S. health care system, respectively.*]

SOCIAL POLICY DURING THE G. W. BUSH YEARS, 2001–2009

Social policy development during the administration of President George W. Bush was shaped both by new political–economic realities and the unanticipated consequences of external events, such as war, global terrorism, and worldwide financial crises. The September 11 terrorist attacks produced a slowdown in the U.S. economy and led to major increases in military and national security spending, particularly for the wars in Afghanistan and Iraq. Combined with tax cuts that largely benefited the wealthiest U.S. households, the budget surplus that President Bush inherited quickly became a massive deficit. The presence of this deficit rationalized cuts in discretionary domestic spending, efforts to privatize social services, and the drive to reform entitlement programs. While the trend toward privatization continued, particularly in the areas of health and mental health care and criminal justice, Congress was unable to solve the long-term funding problems of Social Security and Medicare or to address their built-in gender and racial biases (Families USA, 2009; Favreau, Sammertino, & Steuerle, 2002; James, Edwards, & Wong, 2008).

The Bush Administration did, however, accomplish several important social policy goals. The passage of Medicare Part D provided the elderly with a much-needed benefit for costly prescription medications. Failure to fund this new entitlement adequately, however, further exacerbated the financing crisis of Medicare and added to the federal deficit. [*See Chapter 14 in this volume.*] Other social policy changes during this period included a reauthorization of PRWORA with more stringent work requirements; an expansion of the nation's food stamp program, now called the Supplemental Nutritional Assistance Program; additional funding for the State Children's Health Program; passage of the No Child Left Behind Act, a controversial measure to reform K–12 education; and significant increases in funding for HIV/AIDS programs, particularly in developing nations (Stern & Axinn, 2012). Reduced government regulation of the financial and housing industries, however, which had begun during the Clinton Administration, led to the near catastrophic financial crisis of 2007 to 2009 that almost produced a major global depression from which the nation is still struggling to recover. [*See Chapter 3 in this volume.*]

THE OBAMA ADMINISTRATION, 2009–2016

From the outset of the Obama Administration in January 2009, these fiscal and economic crises, coupled with heightened political resistance from Congressional Republicans, sharply constrained the President's social policy agenda. Shortly after his inauguration, in response to the severe recession, President Obama and the Democratic Congress passed an $800 billion economic stimulus package, the American Reinvestment and Recovery Act (ARRA), and negotiated a bailout of the moribund auto industry. Although ARRA was criticized both by conservatives, who opposed intervention in the market and decried alleged government inefficiencies, and by liberals, who asserted it was funded at an insufficient level, most economists credit the legislation with preventing a major depression and saving at least 1 million jobs. The stimulus funds it provided expired in late 2011, however, leaving many states struggling to replace lost revenues and rehire hundreds of thousands of public sector employees, including teachers, nurses, fire fighters, and social workers, who were laid off due to fiscal cutbacks. These trends have continued even as economic conditions have improved during the past five years (Leachman, et al, 2016; Johnson, Oliff, & Williams, 2011).

During his first term, when the Democrats briefly controlled both houses of Congress, President Obama was also able to push through his major domestic policy accomplishment, the Patient Protection and

Affordable Care Act (ACA), a sweeping attempt to reform the nation's health care system. In late 2010, the ACA began to go into effect and it survives, as of this writing, despite repeated court challenges to its constitutionality and dozens of attempts to repeal it by Congressional Republicans. In a major decision in late June 2012, the Supreme Court upheld the constitutionality of one of the act's major provision—the individual mandate to purchase health insurance—but in the same decision the Court invalidated the provision requiring states to expand Medicaid coverage. Consequently, the legislation has had a mixed impact to date. It has significantly reduced the number of uninsured Americans from 50 million to approximately 32 million and has slowed the rate of growth of health care costs. The ACA has also enabled children to remain on their parents' health plans until the age of 26, prevented individuals with pre-existing conditions from being denied coverage, and promoted primary care and prevention services, particularly among the elderly. On the downside, because over one third of the states refused to expand Medicaid, tens of millions of the neediest Americans still lack health insurance coverage. In addition, the continued reliance on private health insurance threatens to raise insurance premiums in the near future (Kaiser Family Foundation, 2016). Finally, the survival of the entire ACA and some of its provisions continues to be threatened by ongoing political and judicial challenges—for example, to the requirement that employment-based health plans provide contraceptive coverage—and the stated intention of Republicans to repeal the ACA if they retain control of Congress and gain the White House in 2016. [*See Chapter 14 in this volume for further discussion of the ACA.*]

Other important domestic policy developments during the Obama Administration have included the extension of the Bush tax cuts and the passage of temporary reductions in the payroll (Social Security) tax in an effort to promote economic growth; the replacement of the No Child Left Behind Act with the "Race to the Top" program in an attempt to improve the quality of public education; significant expansion of food assistance programs; and increased spending for job training, child care, and violence prevention. Like his predecessors, however, President Obama has been unsuccessful in solving the long-term financial crisis facing Social Security or the more immediate funding crisis of the nation's health care system, particularly Medicare and Medicaid. In the summer of 2011, an attempt to reach a "Grand Bargain" with the Republican opposition that would combine an overhaul of the tax code, additional spending on social infrastructure and human capital development, and entitlement reform failed due to partisan political divisions that intensified as the 2012 elections neared (Abel & Chaudry, 2010; Edelman, Golden, & Holzer, 2010; Mishel, Bivens, Eisenbrey, & Fieldhouse, 2011; Heinrich & Scholz, 2009). [*See Chapters 7, 9, 12, and 15 in this volume.*] This political standoff resulted in a freeze on spending for crucial domestic programs due to a process referred to as "sequestration." It also led to the Obama Administration using its executive authority to initiate changes in immigration, environmental, and labor policies, many of which have been opposed by Republicans on the grounds that they violated the president's constitutional authority. Recently, courts have upheld Presidential actions in the area of labor policy, but have overturned efforts by the Obama administration in the areas of immigration and environmental policy. [*The chapters in Part III of this volume discuss recent policy developments by the Obama Administration in considerable detail.*]

SOCIAL AND ECONOMIC CONSEQUENCES

The failure of the Bush and Obama administrations to make sustained investments in solving the problems created by globalization and the severe recession of 2007 to 2009 has produced serious and lasting social consequences (Cancian, Meyer, & Reed, 2010; Diez-Roux & Mair, 2010). In 2014, the official U.S. poverty rate was 14.8%, 2.3% higher than prior to the Great Recession (U.S. Census Bureau, 2015). This means that nearly 47 million Americans are now classified as poor; those with incomes just above the poverty line—the

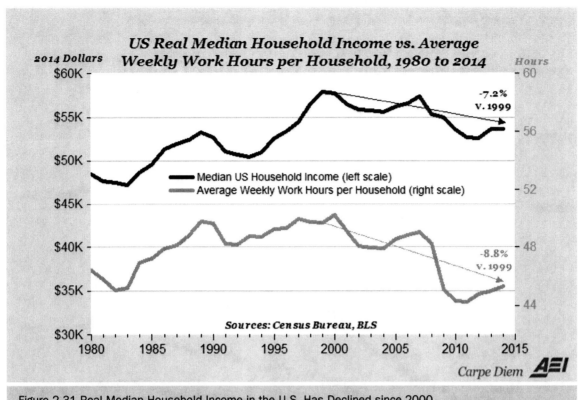

Figure 2.31 Real Median Household Income in the U.S. Has Declined since 2000.

"near poor"—number in the tens of millions more. Using the revised Supplemental Poverty Measure, nearly 16 percent of Americans were officially poor. More than 25% of African Americans and Latinos live below the poverty line; they are 2 1/2 to 3 times more likely to be poor than are whites (see Chapter 1, Figure 1.1b). Nearly 12% of African Americans and more than 10% of Latinos experience "deep poverty," living on incomes below 50% of the federal poverty line (Acs & Nichols, 2010; Buss, 2010), and 4 million Americans, including 3 million children attempt to survive on $2/day of cash assistance or less (Edin & Shaefer, 2015). This is the United Nations' definition of "extreme poverty." Although at present the official unemployment rate (~5 percent) is well below the level during the Great Recession, many Americans still experience economic insecurity because of tepid economic growth and wage stagnation (Bureau of Labor Statistics, 2015, 2016). These trends in the United States reflect broader economic developments worldwide (World Bank, 2015).

Children and women, particularly elderly women and single parents, remain the Americans most likely to be poor (Jiang, Okono, & Skinner, 2016; National Women's Law Center, 2015). In fact, the United States has the highest rate of child and female poverty among industrialized nations (Annie E. Casey Foundation, 2012; Buss, 2010; Twill & Fisher, 2010). In addition, many analysts assert that official measures of poverty significantly underestimate the number of Americans who are poor (Boushey et al., 2011; Brooks, 2011) and fail to account for the long-term impact of an extended spell of poverty, which a majority of Americans will experience in their lifetimes (Rank, 2004). Some projections indicate that poverty will likely increase in the future due to the lingering effects of the Great Recession (Monea & Sawhill, 2010).

As discussed in Chapters 1 and 3, perhaps a more ominous indicator is the widening class and racial gaps in income, wealth, education, skills, and health status (Stone, Trisi, Sherman, & Debot, 2015; Auerbach

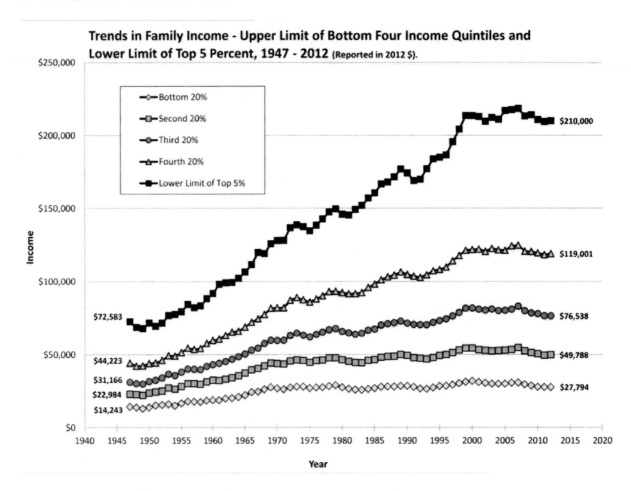

RSF *Russell Sage Foundation - Chartbook of Social Inequality*

Trends in Family Income - Upper Limit of Bottom Four Income Quintiles and Lower Limit of Top 5 Percent, 1947 - 2012 (Reported in 2012 $).

Data Source: U.S. Census Bureau. Table F-1. Income Limits for Each Fifth and Top 5 Percent of Families, from Historical Income Tables [http://www.census.gov/hhes/www/income/data/historical/index.html].

& Kellermann, 2011; Autor, 2010; Braveman et al., 2011; Bureau of Labor Statistics, 2010, 2011; Economic Policy Institute, 2012; Galea, Tracy, Hoggatt, DiMaggio, & Karpati, 2011; Koh, Graham, & Glied, 2011; Reiman & Leighton, 2010). Even before the recent recession, the top 1% of all households had as much discretionary income as the bottom 40%, the largest share of after-tax income since 1979 (U.S. Census Bureau, 2010). In 1979, these households earned 22 times as much as the bottom 20%. Today, they earn 70 times as much (Center on Budget and Policy Priorities, 2011).

The share of national assets owned by the richest 1% of Americans has also grown—from one fifth to more than one third of all private wealth—the most unequal distribution since 1928 (Lui, Robles, & Leondar-Wright, 2006; Palley, 2012; Wolff, 2010). Inequality has increased for several reasons, including the decline in unions, outsourcing of jobs, stagnation of wages, a decrease in the value of public assistance benefits, the persistence of institutional racism and sexism, and changes in the nation's occupational structure and corporate culture (Lin & Harris, 2008; Mishel & Shierholz, 2011; Navarro, 2007; Sherman & Stone, 2010). These conditions are disturbingly similar to those that existed just prior to the Great

Depression, as the charts in Figures 2.30, 2.31, and 2.32 demonstrate. The support for the Presidential candidacies of Donald Trump and Bernie Sanders reflects, in part, the depth of insecurity generated by the current status of the economy and the enduring perception of government's failure to make it work for many Americans.

The depth of this crisis is also reflected in the growing demand for food assistance. The Supplemental Nutrition Assistance Program now aids more than 45 million people, up 50% since December 2007 (Food Nutrition Service, 2011; U.S. Department of Agriculture, 2012). More than 30 million children participate in the National School Lunch Program, an increase of 20% since the start of the recession. Medicaid, the program that provides health care to low-income persons, now serves more than 50 million people (Pavetti & Rosenbaum, 2010). This increase has created an enormous fiscal burden on state governments, which are already reeling from the effects of declining revenues and growing demand for social services (Turner, Oliff, & Williams, 2010).

Wide variations among states exist in benefit levels and coverage for programs such as TANF and Medicaid because they are a joint responsibility of federal and state governments and states have considerable discretion in establishing eligibility requirements and the level of benefits. In the past 2 years, some states have lowered the amount of time families could receive TANF benefits, tightened mandatory work requirements, and cut families from their Medicaid rolls. It is forecast that TANF will assist even fewer families in the future and that, without massive federal assistance, states will no longer be able to sustain existing levels of Medicaid coverage (U.S. Department of Health and Human Services, 2012). Without this frayed safety net, as well as that provided by unemployment insurance, EITC, SSI, and Social Security, millions more Americans would be counted as poor (Lim, Coulton, & Lalich, 2009; Pavetti & Rosenbaum, 2010. [*See Chapter 12 in this volume.*]

At the same time, like many other industrialized nations, during the past 40 years the United States has undergone several major demographic and cultural transformations that are altering the character of American society, producing new forms of individual and social problems, and creating the need for innovative social policy solutions (Carlson, 1994; Muller, 1993; Portes, 1990; Waldinger, 2001; Yang, 1995). The substantial increase in the number of elderly Americans, particularly over the age of 85, already places enormous social and psychological burdens on their families and threatens the fiscal solvency of Social Security and Medicare (Kingson, Cornman, & Torre-Norton, 2009). The retirement of so-called "baby boomers" (individuals born between 1945 and 1964) will intensify these crises. By the mid-21st century, there will be no racial/ethnic majority population in the United States, although the elderly population will still be 2/3 white. Unless the inter-generational compact is reaffirmed—that is, elderly Americans agree to pay taxes to support young, working families, and younger adults are willing to pay taxes to maintain the viability of Social Security and Medicare—the nation faces a demographic/political time bomb that could make today's political deadlock look insignificant by comparison. Despite the recent focus on fiscal deficits and persistent attacks on government's role in the nation's social welfare system, large majorities of Americans support the preservation of existing entitlement programs and a majority supports raising taxes to increase Social Security retirement benefits (Gallup Organization, 2016) and adopting a single payer health care system (Altman, 2016).

Other important demographic changes that will affect social policy development include a rise in the number of single-person households, a decrease in the marriage and birth rates among most racial and ethnic groups, and a sharp decline in the rural population. Major cultural changes include increases in the rate of interracial, interethnic, and interreligious marriages; growing acceptance of LGBTQ and transgendered persons, including the right of same-sex couples to marry and adopt children; new perspectives on the meaning of aging, retirement, and old age; and a transformation of traditional gender roles.

Yet, while new problems have emerged and some long-standing problems have intensified, our major political parties have yet to respond with comprehensive or lasting solutions. In fact, increased political polarization has diminished the possibility of bipartisan compromise when it is more essential than ever. One area in which the effect of these changes has been especially dramatic is public support for antipoverty policies. In the United States, the needs of the poor are increasingly supplanted by the market imperatives of globalization. It may be that the nation's failure to respond effectively to the challenges created by globalization is due to the anachronistic nature of our political institutions. They often seem incapable of responding with sufficient speed to economic and social crises or taking action to address complex global forces, such as climate change, civil wars, and financial collapse.

SUMMARY: THE TRANSFORMATION OF U.S. SOCIAL POLICY

During middle decades of the 20th century, a political consensus about the relationship between government and social welfare gradually emerged in the United States. Leaders of both major political parties and most Americans believed that government intervention was necessary to develop effective responses to problems such as unemployment and poverty. They also regarded the establishment of legal entitlements to social welfare benefits as a means to strengthen the rights of citizenship (Foner, 2002; Katz, 2001). Finally, they assumed that both markets and social welfare provision operated primarily within national boundaries.

Over the past four decades, however, the emergence of a new political–economic reality has challenged many of these assumptions (Piketty, 2014; Klein, 2007, 2014; Smith, Stenning, & Willis, 2008). [*See Chapter 3 in this volume.*] The pressures of **economic globalization** and the ascendancy of market-oriented mechanisms have altered the underlying values, stated goals, and consequences of U.S. social policy in both the public and nonprofit sectors, and even threatened the future of the planet itself (Klein, 2014; Alperovitz, 2011; Bartik & Houseman, 2008; Baruah, 2010; Burtless & Looney, 2012; Collins & Mayer, 2010; Reisch, 2010). The impact of welfare reform, recent initiatives to privatize Social Security and Medicare, efforts to dramatically reduce spending on social programs, and proposed market-based solutions to poverty are stark illustrations of this phenomenon (Cooney & Shanks, 2010). During the past decade, spending cuts and the presence of structural deficits at the state and local level have exacerbated this situation (Williams, 2016; Turner et al., 2010).

For more than two centuries, with varying levels of commitment, U.S. social policies have focused primarily on the problem of poverty, rather than on socioeconomic inequality (Stiglitz, 2013; Baynton, 2001). This focus is most compatible with the American cultural value of individualism and an approach to human needs based on charity rather than justice. For legislative and regulatory purposes, it is also easier to quantify poverty, although there remain serious disagreements about how it should be defined and measured (Glennerster, 2002). An emphasis on poverty rather than inequality also rationalizes avoidance of the structural roots of the nation's economic problems and the relationship between poverty and social, physical, and psychological development (Drennan, 2015; Frankfurt, 2015; Rank, Hirschl, & Foster, 2014; Jones, 1992).

According to a classic article by Gans (1971), poverty in the United States helps preserve the economic, social, and political status quo in several ways. Economically, poverty ensures that society's dirty work gets done and subsidizes a variety of activities that exclusively benefit the affluent. Socially, by labeling low-income people as deviant and stigmatizing them if they receive social welfare benefits, poverty upholds dominant cultural values and reinforces prevailing social, racial, and gender hierarchies. Politically, because low-income groups lack power, they can be compelled to absorb the bulk of the social costs of growth and change in the society. Ideologically, the maintenance of conventional norms about poverty contributes to the development of social policies that support prevailing views about work and personal responsibility.

As a result, for the past century, poverty in the United States has been more widespread than in any other industrialized nation, particularly among children, women, and racial minorities (Watson, 2015; Allard, 2009). Ironically, in a society that exalts the myths of upward social mobility and opportunity, inequalities in income and wealth not only persist, they are increasing more rapidly in recent years due to the nation's wage structure, tax system, intergenerational distribution of assets, and long-standing occupational hierarchies (Stiglitz, 2012). The U.S. also lacks a political party or powerful social movement that advocates for social democratic or socialist alternatives. (As of this writing, it remains to be seen if the presidential campaign of Senator Bernie Sanders, an avowed democratic socialist, will have any lasting impact on our political system or social policies.) As Jerome H. Schiele suggests in Chapter 5 of this volume, a third reason for the failure of U.S. social policies to address poverty is the legacy of slavery and persistent institutional racism (Bates & Swan, 2010; Ward, 2005) which have produced wide inequities in the areas of education, employment, health care, and housing, and increasing use of "disciplinary regimes" in the nation's welfare, criminal justice, and educational systems (Soss et al., 2011; Wacquant, 2009). [*See Chapters 13 and 14 in this volume.*]

Finally, poverty persists in the United States because of the prevailing ideology of individual responsibility and the denial of our collective responsibility for human well-being it produces. Even in the midst of a lingering economic crisis largely precipitated by irresponsible and arguably criminal behavior by the nation's major financial institutions and housing industry, many Americans continue to have greater faith in the market than in government to solve our problems. Even when more favorably disposed towards government, they often prefer limited government intervention—preferably at the local level—and support only those government programs from which they personally benefit while opposing those programs they believe are funded solely by *their* taxes to assist undeserving others (Leonhardt, 2012). This perception is most visible in the attitudes expressed by members of the "Tea Party" and primary voters who have supported the presidential candidacy of Donald Trump. These attitudes have changed dramatically since the mid-20th century, when most Americans believed that government could be trusted all or most of the time to be an effective problem-solving agent.

CONCLUSION: U.S. SOCIAL POLICY IN A TURBULENT ENVIRONMENT

It is important to point out, however, that Americans possess significantly different attitudes about poverty, inequality, and social welfare based on their class, gender, race, religion, education level, generation, and geographic region. On a range of issues, such as the preservation of Social Security and Medicare, increased aid to public education, and the protection of the environment, Americans maintain "liberal" positions regardless of their personal party affiliations or ideological labels (Pew Research Center, 2011).

For most of the 20th century, social policies in the United States reflected this broad ideological consensus around a wide range of issues. Since the 1980s, however, the dominance of a conservative, anti-welfare, anti-government ideology, whose goals are to facilitate aggregate economic growth rather than distribute its benefits equitably, has dramatically altered the character of U.S. social policy. As discussed in subsequent chapters in this volume, these trends are reflected in attempts to discredit or repeal the Affordable Care Act; privatize Social Security and health care; tighten eligibility restrictions for the receipt of public assistance, housing support, or nutrition aid; and block tax increases for wealthy Americans (Reich, 2013; Aaron, 2011).

Thus, while there is some agreement in the United States today on the broader goals of social policy, there is less agreement on the means to achieve those goals. For example, broader workforce participation is widely recognized as an essential ingredient in the elimination of poverty, the stabilization of families and communities, and individual psychological well-being. Yet there is considerable resistance to the policies needed to increase employment opportunities and provide a living wage, particularly for people of color, women, and individuals with physical and mental disabilities, such as increased funding for public education, the creation of worker training programs, and the provision of adequate health care, child care, and transportation (Stiglitz, 2013; Reich, 2013; Alperovitz, 2011). [*See Chapters 12, 14, and 15 in this volume.*]

In the future, the urgency of the nation's social, economic, and environmental crises may produce a new social policy synthesis, in which the federal government is the primary source of financing, and local governments and the private sector assume responsibility for policy implementation. If this occurs, community-based organizations using innovative service models could perform an important role in ensuring the equitable distribution of societal resources and promoting greater participation in the design and delivery of policies and services. While it is clear that U.S. social policy is at a crossroads, it is not clear at this point which path the nation will take in the years ahead (Reisch, 2013; Reisch & Jani, 2012).

Discussion Questions

1. How have social policies in the United States reflected the contradictory impulses of aiding and stigmatizing individuals in need?
2. In what ways have economic, social, and cultural changes influenced the direction of social policy in U.S. history?
3. How has poverty been explained in U.S. history? How have the explanations for poverty changed, and how are these explanations reflected in past and current social policies?
4. What obstacles to the expansion of social welfare provision exist in the United States today? What are the sources of these obstacles, and how might they be overcome?
5. What are the main differences between charitable and social justice perspectives on social policy and social welfare? How have these differences been reflected in the history of U.S. social policy? How are they reflected today?

GOVERNMENT

CIA World Factbook: www.cia.gov/library/publications/the-world-factbook/

Congressional Budget Office: www.cbo.gov

The Library of Congress (Thomas): thomas.loc.gov/home/thomas.php

National Association of Counties: www.naco.org

National Conference of State Legislatures: www.ncsl.org

National Institutes of Health: www.nih.gov

National League of Cities: www.nlc.org

Poverty Statistics at the U.S. Census Bureau: www.census.gov/hhes/www/poverty.html

Social Security Administration: www.ssa.gov

Statistical Abstract of the United States: www.census.gov/prod/www/abs/statab.html

United States Conference of Mayors: www.usmayors.org

U.S. Supreme Court Decisions: www.fedworld.gov/supcourt/index.htm

POLICY RESEARCH AND ADVOCACY ORGANIZATIONS

American Enterprise Institute: www.aei.org

American Public Health Association: www.apha.org

Brookings Institution: www.brook.edu

Cato Institute: www.cato.org

Center on Budget and Policy Priorities: www.cbpp.org

Center for Law and Social Policy: www.clasp.org/

Child Trends: www.childtrends.org

Child Welfare League of America: www.cwla.org

Children's Defense Fund: www.childrensdefense.org

Economic Policy Institute: www.epinet.org

Families USA: www.familiesusa.org/

Heritage Foundation: www.heritage.org

Hudson Institute: www.hudson.org/hudson

Independent Sector: www.independentsector.org

Institute for Women's Policy Research: www.iwpr.org

National Association of Social Workers: www.naswdc.org

National Center for Children in Poverty: www.nccp.org/

Urban Institute: www.urban.org

Suggestions for Further Reading

Abramovitz, M. (1996). *Regulating the lives of women: Social policy from colonial times to the present* (Rev. ed.). Boston: South End Press.

Edin, K., & Shaefer, L. (2015). *$2 a day: Living on almost nothing in America*. Boston: Houghton Mifflin.

Jansson, B.S. (2012). *The reluctant welfare state: Engaging history to advance social work practice in contemporary society*, (7th ed.) Pacific Grove, CA: Brooks/Cole Cengage Learning.

Katz, M. B. (1996). *In the shadow of the poorhouse: A social history of welfare in America* (Rev. ed.). New York: Basic Books.

Katz, M. B. (2001). *The price of citizenship: Redefining the American welfare state*. New York: Henry Holt.

Mandler, P. (Ed.). (1990). *The uses of charity: The poor on relief in the nineteenth century metropolis*. Philadelphia: University of Pennsylvania Press.

Patterson, J. (2001). *America's struggle against poverty in the 20th century*. Cambridge: Harvard University Press.

Piven, F. F., & Cloward, R. A. (1993). *Regulating the poor: The functions of public welfare* (Rev. ed.). New York: Vintage Books.

Quadagno, J. (1994). *The color of welfare: How racism undermined the War on Poverty.* New York: Oxford University Press.

Reisch, M., & Andrews, J. L. (2002). *The road not taken: A history of radical social work in the United States.* Philadelphia: Brunner-Routledge.

Stern, M., & Axinn, J. (2012). *Social welfare: A history of the American response to need,* (8th ed.) Boston: Allyn & Bacon.

References

Aaron, H. J. (2011, April 28). How not to reform Medicare. *New England Journal of Medicine, 364*(17), 1588–1589.

Abel, L., & Chaudry, A. (2010, April). *Low-income children, their families, and the Great Recession: What next in policy?* Paper prepared for the Georgetown University and Urban Institute Conference on Reducing Poverty and Economic Distress after ARRA, Washington, DC.

Abramovitz, M. (1992). The Reagan legacy: Undoing race, class, and gender accords. In J. Midgley (Ed.), The Reagan legacy and the American welfare state [Special issue]. *Journal of Sociology and Social Welfare, 22*(4), 91–110.

Abramovitz, M. (1996). *Regulating the lives of women: Social policy from colonial times to the present* (Rev. ed.). Boston: South End Press.

Abramovitz, M. (2005). The largely untold story of welfare reform and the human services. *Social Work, 50*(2), 175–186.

Abramovitz, M. (2006). Welfare reform in the United States: Gender, race and class matter. *Critical Social Policy, 26,* 336–364.

Abramson, A., Tobin, M., & Vandergoot, M. (1995). The changing geography of metropolitan opportunity: The segregation of the poor in U.S. metropolitan areas, 1970–1990. *Housing Policy Debate, 6*(1), 45–72.

Acs, G., & Nichols, A. (2010, February). *Changes in the economic security of American families* (Low Income Families Paper 16). Washington, DC: Urban Institute.

Addams, J. (1895). The settlement as a factor in the labor movement. In *Hull House maps and papers, by residents of Hull House* (pp. 183–204). New York: Crowell.

Addams, J. (1910). *Twenty years at Hull House.* New York: MacMillan.

Albelda, R., & Withorn, A. (Eds.). (2002). *Lost ground: Welfare reform, poverty and beyond.* Cambridge, MA: South End Press.

Alexander, J. (1999). The impact of devolution on nonprofits: A multiphase study of social service organizations. *Nonprofit Management and Leadership, 10*(1), 57–70.

Alexander, M. (2010). *The new Jim Crow: Mass incarceration in the age of colorblindness.* New York: The New Press.

Allard, S. (2009). *Out of reach: Place, poverty, and the new American welfare state.* New Haven, CT: Yale University Press.

Alperovitz, G. (2011). *America beyond capitalism: Reclaiming our wealth, our liberty, and our democracy.* Boston, MA: Democracy Collaborative Press.

Altman, D. (2016, May 24). Why today's poll numbers on health programs are bound to change. *Wall Street Journal Think Tank Column*. Retrieved from http://blogs.wsj.com/washwire/2016/05/24/why-todays-poll-numbers-on-health-proposals-are-bound-to-change/

Altman, N.J., & Kingson, E.R. (2014). *Social Security works! Why Social Security isn't going broke and how expanding it will help us all*. New York: The New Press.

Andrews, J., & Reisch, M. (1997). Anti-communism and social work: An historical analysis. *Journal of Progressive Human Services, 8*(2), 29–49.

Annie E. Casey Foundation. (2012). *City KIDS COUNT: Data on the well-being of children in large cities.* Baltimore, MD: Author.

Association for the Improvement of the Condition of the Poor. (1853). *Report on tenement housing.* New York: Author.

Auerbach, D., & Kellermann, A. (2011, September). A decade of health care cost growth has wiped out real income gains for an average U.S. family. *Health Affairs, 39*(9), 1630–1636.

Autor, D. (2010). *The polarization of job opportunities in the U.S. labor market: Implications for employment and earnings.* Washington, DC: Center for American Progress and the Hamilton Project, Brookings Institution.

Axinn, J., & Stern, M. (1988). *Dependency and poverty: Old problems in a new world.* Lexington, MA: Lexington Books.

Badawi, J. (1995). *Gender equity in Islam.* Burr Ridge,IL: American Trust Publications.

Bailey, M.J., & Danziger, S. (Eds.) (2013). *Legacies of the War on Poverty.* New York: Russell Sage Foundation.

Ball, R. M. (2009). The nine guiding principles of Social Security; Social insurance and the right to assistance. In L. Rogne, C.L. Estes, B.R. Grossman, B.A. Hollister, & E. Solway (Eds.), *Social insurance and social justice: Social Security, Medicare, and the campaign against entitlements* (pp. 9–24). New York: Springer Publishing Company.

Bartik, T. J., & Houseman, S. N. (Eds.). (2008). *A future of good jobs? America's challenge in the global economy.* Kalamazoo, MI: W. E. Upjohn Institute for Employment Research.

Baruah, B. (2010). Gender and globalization. *Labor Studies Journal, 35*(2), 198–221.

Bates, K. A., & Swan, R. S. (Eds.). (2010). *Through the eyes of Katrina: Social justice in the United States* (2nd ed.). Durham, NC: Carolina Academic Press.

Baynton, D. C. (2001). Disability and the justification of inequality in American history. In P. K. Longmore & L. Umansky (Eds.), *The new disability history: American perspectives* (pp. 33–57). New York: New York University Press.

Bender, T. (1978). *Community and social change in America.* Baltimore, MD: Johns Hopkins University Press.

Bird, C. (1966). *The invisible scar.* New York: D. McKay.

Bixby, A. K. (1990). Public social welfare expenditures, fiscal years 1965–1987. *Social Security Bulletin, 53*(2), 10–26.

Blau, J. (1992). *The visible poor: Homelessness in the United States.* New York: Oxford University Press.

Blau, J. (1999). *Illusions of prosperity: America's working families in an age of economic insecurity.* New York: Oxford University Press.

Blau, J. (with Abramovitz, M.). (2014). *The dynamics of social welfare policy,* (4th ed.) New York: Oxford University Press.

Bloom, D. (1997). *After AFDC: Welfare-to-work choices and challenges for states.* New York: Manpower Demonstration Research Corporation.

Bonastia, C. (2008). *Knocking on the door: The federal government's attempt to desegregate the suburbs.* Princeton, NJ: Princeton University Press.

Borjas, G. (2002). *The impact of welfare reform on immigrant welfare use.* Washington, DC: Center for Immigrant Studies.

Boushey, H., Brocht, C., Gundersen, B., & Bernstein, J. (2001). *Hardship in America: The real story of working families.* Washington, DC: Economic Policy Institute.

Bowles, S., Gintis, H., & Groves, M. (Eds.). (2005). *Unequal chances: Family background and economic success.* Princeton, NJ: Princeton University Press.

Boyer, P. (1978). *Urban masses and moral order in America, 1820–1920.* Cambridge, MA: Harvard University Press.

Brace, C. L. (1872). *The dangerous classes of New York and twenty years work among them.* New York: Wynkoop & Hallenbeck.

Braveman, P. A., Kumanyika, S., Fielding, J., LaVeist, T., Borrell, L. N., Manderscheid, R., et al. (2011). Health disparities and health equity: The issue is justice. *American Journal of Public Health, 101,* 149–156.

Brooks, R. (2011, November 7). Official poverty measure (again) underestimates a growing crisis. *Policy Shop: The Demos Weblog.* Retrieved October 27, 2012, from http://www.policyshop.net/home/2011/11/7/official-poverty-measure-again-underestimates-a-growing-cris.html

Brown, E. L. (1942). *Social work as a profession,* (4th ed.) New York: Russell Sage Foundation.

Brown, T. J. (1998). *Dorothea Dix, New England reformer.* Cambridge, MA: Harvard University Press.

Bureau of Labor Statistics. (2015). *Unemployment rates by age, sex, race, and Hispanic or Latino ethnicity.* Washington, DC: Author.

Bureau of Labor Statistics. (2016). *The employment situation—May 2016.* Washington, DC: U.S. Government Printing Office.

Burtless, G., & Looney, A. (2012, January 13). *The immediate jobs crisis and our long-run labor market problem.* Washington, DC: Brookings Institution.

Buss, J. A. (2010). Have the poor gotten poorer? The American experience from 1987–2007. *Journal of Poverty, 14*(2), 183–196.

Bussiere, E. (1997). *(Dis)entitling the poor: The Warren court, welfare rights, and the American political tradition.*

Campbell, M., Haveman, R., Sandefur, G., & Wolfe, B. (2005). Economic inequality and educational attainment across a generation. *Focus, 23*(3), 11–15.

Cancian, M., Meyer, D. R., & Reed, D. (2010). Promising antipoverty strategies for families. *Poverty & Public Policy, 2*(3), 151–169.

Cancian, M., & Reed, D. (2001). Changes in family structure: Implications for poverty and related policy. In S. Danziger & R. Haveman (Eds.), *Understanding poverty* (pp. 69–96). Cambridge, MA: Harvard University Press.

Caputo, R. K. (Ed.). (2005). *Challenges of aging in U.S. families: Policy and practice implications.* New York: Haworth.

Carey, M. (1833). *An appeal to the wealthy of the land on the situation and prospects of those whose sole dependence for subsistence is one the labour of their hands.* Philadelphia: Stereotyped by L. Johnson.

Carlson, A. W. (1994). America's new immigration: Characteristics, destinations, and impact, 1970–1989. *Social Science Journal, 31*(3), 213–236.

Carson, M. J. (1990). *Settlement folk: Social thought and the American settlement movement, 1885–1930.* Chicago: University of Chicago Press.

Case, A., Fertig, A., & Paxson, C. (2005). The lasting impact of childhood health and circumstance. *Journal of Health Economics, 24*(2), 365–389.

Caudill, H. (1963). *Night comes to the Cumberlands: A biography of a depressed area.* Boston: Little, Brown.

Cauthen, N., & Lu, H. (2003). *Employment alone is not enough for America's low-income children and families living at the edge* (Research Brief No. 1). New York: National Center for Children in Poverty.

Center on Budget and Policy Priorities. (2015, June 15). *An introduction to TANF.* Washington, DC: Author. Retrieved online at http://www.cbpp.org/sites/default/files/atoms/files/7-22-10tanf2.pdf

Center on Budget and Policy Priorities. (2006, January 26). *Income inequality grew across the country over the past two decades.* Washington, DC: Author.

Center on Budget and Policy Priorities. (2011, November 28). *A guide to statistics in historical trends in income inequality.* Washington, DC: Author.

Chambers, C. (1967). *Seedtime of reform: American social service and social action, 1918–1933.* Ann Arbor: University of Michigan Press.

Chew, L. (2000). Reflections on Buddhism, gender and human rights. In K. M. Tsomo (Ed.), *Buddhist women and social justice: Ideals, challenges and achievements.* Albany: State University of New York Press.

Children's Defense Fund. (1996). *Statistics on child poverty in the United States.* Washington, DC: Author.

Children's Defense Fund. (2006). *Statistics on child poverty in the United States.* Washington, DC: Author.

Chow, J. C., Osterling, K. L., & Xu, Q. (2005). The risk of timing out: Welfare-to-work services to Asian immigrants and refugees. *AAPI Nexus, 3*(2), 85–104.

Cimbala, P. A., & Miller, R. M. (Ed.). (1999). *The Freedmen's Bureau and Reconstruction: Reconsiderations.* New York: Fordham University Press.

Clawson, R., & Trice, R. (2000). Poverty as we know it: Media portrayals of the poor. *Public Opinion Quarterly, 64*(4), 53–64.

Cohen, M.A. (2016). *Maelstrom: The 1968 election and the politics of division.* New York: Oxford University Press.

Collins, J. L., & Mayer, V. (2010). *Welfare reform and the race to the bottom in the low-wage labor market.* Chicago: University of Chicago Press.

Cooney, K., & Shanks, T. R. W. (2010). New approaches to old problems: Market-based strategies for poverty alleviation. *Social Service Review, 84*(1), 29–55.

Corcoran, M. (2001). Mobility, persistence, and the consequences of child poverty for children: Child and adult outcomes. In S. Danziger & R. Haveman (Eds.), *Understanding poverty* (pp. 127–161). Cambridge, MA: Harvard University Press.

Costin, L. B. (1983). *Two sisters for social justice: A biography of Grace and Edith Abbott.* Urbana: University of Illinois Press.

Danziger, S. (1991, September–October). Relearning lessons of the War on Poverty. *Challenge,* 53–54.

Danziger, S., & Gottschalk, P. (2004). *Diverging fortunes: Trends in poverty and inequality.* New York: Russell Sage Foundation.

Danziger, S., & Weinberg, D. H. (1994). The historical record: Trends in family income, inequality and poverty. In S. H. Danziger, G. D. Sandefur, & D. H. Weinberg (Eds.), *Confronting poverty: Prescriptions for change* (pp. 18–50). Cambridge: Harvard University Press.

Davis, A. F. (1984). *Spearheads for reform: The social settlements and the progressive movement, 1890-1914.* New Brunswick, NJ: Rutgers University Press.

Derthick, M. (1975). *Uncontrollable spending for social services grants.* Washington, DC: Brookings Institution.

Diamond, P. A., & Orszag, P. A. (2005). *Saving Social Security: A balanced approach* (Rev. ed.). Washington, DC: Brookings Institution.

Diez-Roux, A., & Mair, C. (2010). Neighborhoods and health. *Annals of the New York Academy of Science, 1186*, 125–145.

Downey, K. (2010). *The woman behind the New Deal: The life and legacy of Frances Perkins, Social Security, unemployment insurance, and the minimum wage.* New York: Anchor Books.

Drennan, M.P. (2015). *Income inequality: Why it matters and why most economists didn't notice.* New Haven, CT: Yale University Press.

Economic Policy Institute. (2012). *The state of working America.* Washington, DC: Author.

Edelman, P., Golden, O., & Holzer, H. (2010). *Reducing poverty and economic distress after ARRA: Next steps for short-term recovery and long-term economic security.* Washington, DC: Urban Institute.

Edin, K.J., & Shaefer, H.L. (2015). Welfare is dead. In *$2.00 a day: Living on almost nothing in America* (pp. 1–33). Boston: Houghton Mifflin.

Edsall, T. (1991). *Chain reaction: The impact of race, rights, and taxes on American politics.* New York: W. W. Norton.

Epstein, A. (1934). Social Security: Fiction or fact? *American Mercury, 33*(130), 129–138.

Families USA. (2009, September). *Health coverage in communities of color: Talking about the new census numbers* (Fact sheet from Minority Health Initiatives). Washington, DC: Families USA. Retrieved March 18, 2012, from http://www.familiesusa.org/assets/pdfs/minority-health-census-sept-2009.pdf

Faust, D. G. (2009). *This republic of suffering: Death and the American Civil War.* New York: Vintage Books.

Favreau, M. M., Sammertino, F. J., & Steuerle, C. E. (Eds.). (2002). *Social Security and the family: Addressing unmet needs in an underfunded system.* Washington, DC: Urban Institute Press.

Ferguson, I., Lavalette, M., & E. Whitmore (Eds.). (2005). *Globalisation, global justice and social work.* London: Routledge.

Fink, B., & Widom, R. (2001). *Social service organizations and welfare reform.* New York: Manpower Demonstration Research Organization.

Floyd, E., et al. (2015, June 16). *TANF continues to weaken as a safety net.* Washington, DC: Center on Budget & Policy Priorities.

Foner, E. (1988). *Reconstruction: America's unfinished revolution, 1863–1877.* New York: Harper & Row.

Foner, E. (2002). Who is an American? In *Who owns history? Rethinking the past in a changing world* (pp. 149–166). New York: Hill & Wang.

Foner, E. (2010). *The fiery trial: Abraham Lincoln and American slavery.* New York: W. W. Norton.

Food Nutrition Service. (2011, September 1). *SNAP monthly data.* Retrieved April 2, 2011, from http://www.fns.usda.gov/pd/34SNAPmonthly.htm

Frank, R. G., & Glied, S. A. (2006). *Better but not well: Mental health policy in the U.S. since 1950.* Baltimore, MD: Johns Hopkins University Press.

Frank, T. (2005). *What's the matter with Kansas?: How conservatives won the heart of America.* New York: Picador.

Frankfort, H.G. (2015). *On inequality.* Princeton, NJ: Princeton University Press.

Franklin, B. (1766). *An essay on the Corn Laws.* Philadelphia: Author.

Freund, D.M.P. (2007). *Colored property: State policy and white racial politics in suburban America.* Chicago: University of Chicago Press.

Friedman, M., & Friedman, R. (1980). *Free to choose: A personal statement.* New York: Harcourt, Brace, Jovanovich.

Galea, S., Tracy, M., Hoggatt, K. J., DiMaggio, C., & Karpati, A. (2011). Estimated deaths attributed to social factors in the United States. *American Journal of Public Health, 101*(8), 1456–1465.

Gallup Organization (2016). *Historic trends.* Retrieved from http://www.gallup.com/poll/1693/social-security.aspx

Gans, H. (1971, May–June). The uses of poverty: The poor pay all. *Social Policy, 2,* 20–24.

Gershoff, E. (2003). *Low income and hardship among America's kindergartners.* New York: National Center for Children in Poverty.

Gibbons, J. C. (1891). Wealth and its obligations. *North American Review, 152,* 385–395.

Gilbert, N. (1977). The transformation of social services. *Social Service Review, 53*(3), 75–91.

Gilbert, N. (2002). *Transformation of the welfare state: The silent surrender of public responsibility.* New York: Oxford University Press.

Gilder, G. (1981). *Wealth and poverty.* New York: Basic Books.

Gillette, M. (1996). *Launching the War on Poverty: An oral history.* New York: Twayne.

Ginzberg, E., & Solow, R. M. (Eds.). (1974). *The Great Society: Lessons for the future.* New York: Basic Books.

Glennerster, H. (2002). United States poverty studies and poverty measurement: The past twenty-five years. *Social Service Review, 79*(1), 83–107.

Grob, G. N., & Goldman, H. H. (2006). *The dilemma of federal mental health policy: Radical reform or incremental change?* New Brunswick, NJ: Rutgers University Press.

Gutman, H. G. (1976). *Work, culture, and society in industrializing America: Essays in American working-class and social history.* New York: Knopf.

Hall, P. D. (1992). *Inventing the nonprofit sector and other essays on philanthropy, voluntarism, and nonprofit organizations.* Baltimore, MD: Johns Hopkins University Press.

Hamilton, D. C., & Hamilton, C. V. (1997). *The dual agenda: Race and social welfare policies of civil rights organizations.* New York: Columbia University Press.

Harrington, M. (1981). *The other America: Poverty in the United States* (Rev. ed.). New York: MacMillan.

Heinrich, C. J., & Scholz, J. K. (Eds). (2009). *Making the work-based safety net work better: Forward-looking policies to help low-income families.* New York: Russell Sage Foundation.

Hofrichter, R. (Ed.). (2003). *Health and social justice: Politics, ideology and inequity in the distribution of disease—A public health reader.* San Francisco: Jossey-Bass.

Hofstadter, R. (1992). *Social Darwinism in American thought* (Rev. ed.). Boston: Beacon Press.

Holt, S. (2011). *Ten years of the EITC movement: Making work pay then and now.* Washington, DC: Brookings Institution.

Hopkins, J. (2009). *Harry Hopkins: Sudden hero, brash reformer.* New York: Palgrave/MacMillan.

Hudson, R. B. (Ed.). (2005). *The new politics of old age policy.* Baltimore, MD: Johns Hopkins University Press.

Iceland, J. (2003). Why poverty remains high: The role of income growth, economic inequality, and changes in family structure, 1949–1999. *Demography, 40*(3), 499–519.

Iglehart, A. P., & Becerra, R. (2011). *Social services and the ethnic community: History and analysis* (2nd ed.). Long Grove, IL: Waveland Press.

James, E., Edwards, A. C., & Wong, R. (2008). *The gender impact of Social Security reform.* Chicago: University of Chicago Press.

Jansson, B.S. (2012). *The reluctant welfare state: Engaging history to advance social work practice in contemporary society,* (7th ed.) Pacific Grove, CA: Brooks/Cole Cengage Learning.

Jiang, Y., Okono, M., & Skinner, C. (2016, February). *Basic facts about low income children—Children under 18 years of age, 2014.* New York: National Center for Children in Poverty.

Johnson, N., Oliff, P., & Williams, E. (2011, February 9). *An update on state budgets.* Washington, DC: Center on Budget and Policy Priorities.

Jones, J. (1992). *The dispossessed: America's underclasses from the Civil War to the present.* New York: Basic Books.

Kapp, J. W. (1972). *The social costs of private enterprise.* New York: Schocken.

Kasson, J. F. (1980). *Civilizing the machine: Technology and republican values in America, 1776–1900.* New York: Penguin Books.

Katz, M. B. (1986). *In the shadow of the poorhouse: A social history of welfare in America.* New York: Basic Books.

Katz, M. B. (1989). *The undeserving poor: From the War on Poverty to the war on welfare.* New York: Pantheon Books.

Katz, M. B. (1996). *In the shadow of the poorhouse: A social history of welfare in America* (Rev. ed.). New York: Basic Books.

Katz, M. B. (2001). *The price of citizenship: Redefining the American welfare state.* New York: Henry Holt.

Keisling, P. (1984, December). Lessons of the Great Society. *The Washington Monthly,* 50–53.

Kingson, E. R., Cornman, J. M., & Torre-Norton, A. L. (2009). The future of social insurance: Values and generational interdependence. In L. Rogne, C.L. Estes, B. R. Grossman, B.A. Hollister, & E. Solway (Eds.), *Social insurance and social justice: Social Security, Medicare, and the campaign against entitlements* (pp. 95–108). New York: Springer.

Klein, N. (2007). *The shock doctrine: The rise of disaster capitalism.* New York: Henry Holt.

Klein, N. (2014). *This changes everything: Capitalism vs. the climate.* New York: Simon & Schuster.

Knight, L. W. (2005). *Citizen: Jane Addams and the struggle for democracy.* Chicago: University of Chicago Press.

Koh, H. K., Graham, G., & Glied, S. A. (2011). Reducing racial and ethnic disparities: The action plan from the Department of Health and Human Services. *Health Affairs, 30*(10), 1822–1829.

Kornbluh, F. (1997). To fulfill their 'rightly needs': Consumerism and the nation welfare rights movement. *Radical History Review, 69,* 76–113.

Kotz, N., & Kotz, M. (1977). *A passion for equality: George Wiley and the movement.* New York: Vintage.

Kurzman, P. A. (1974). *Harry Hopkins and the New Deal.* Fair Lawn, NJ: R. E. Burdick.

Lamb, C.M. (2005). *Housing segregation in suburban America since 1960: Presidential and judicial politics.* New York: Cambridge University Press.

Lasch-Quinn. E. (1993). *Black neighbors: Race and the limits of reform in the American Settlement House Movement, 1890–1945.* Chapel Hill: University of North Carolina Press.

Leachman, M., Albares, N., Masterson, K., & Wallace, M. (2016, January 25). Most states have cut school funding, and some continue cutting. Washington, DC: Center on Budget & Policy Priorities.

Lemann, N. (1988, December). The unfinished war, Part I. *Atlantic Monthly,* 37–56.

Lemann, N. (1989, January). The unfinished war, Part II. *Atlantic Monthly,* 53–68.

Lemann, N. (1991). *The promised land: The great black migration and how it changed America.* New York: A. A. Knopf.

Leonhardt, D. (2012, October 24). Living standards in the shadows as a election issue. *New York Times*, pp. A1, A15.

Lewis, O. (1965). *Five families: Mexican case studies in the culture of poverty.* New York: New American Library.

Lieberman, R. (1998). *Shifting the color line: Race and the American welfare state.* Cambridge, MA: Harvard University Press.

Lim, Y., Coulton, C. J., & Lalich, N. (2009). State TANF policies and employment outcomes among welfare leavers. *Social Service Review, 83*(4), 525–555.

Lin, A. C., & Harris, D. R. (2008). *The colors of poverty: Why racial and ethnic disparities exist* (National Poverty Center Series on Poverty and Public Policy). New York: Russell Sage Foundation.

Lorenz, W. (2006). *Perspectives on European social work: From the birth of the nation state to the impact of globalisation.* Opladen, Germany: Budrich.

Lowell, J. S. (1890). The economic and moral effects of public outdoor relief. In the *Proceedings of National Conference of Charities and Corrections* (pp. 81–91). Madison, WI: Midland.

Lubove, R. (1968). *The struggle for Social Security, 1900–1935.* Cambridge, MA: Harvard University Press.

Luhby, T. (2011, November 7). Poverty rate rises under alternate Census measure. *CNNMoney.* Retrieved March 7, 2012, from http://money.cnn.com/2011/11/07/news/economy/poverty_rate/index.htm

Lui, M., Robles, B., & Leondar-Wright, B. (2006). *The color of wealth: The story behind the U.S. racial wealth divide.* New York: New Press.

Macpherson, C.B. (1985). *The political theory of possessive individualism: Hobbes to Locke,* (10th ed.) New York: Oxford University Press.

Mandler, P. (1990). Poverty and charity in the nineteenth century metropolis. In P. Mandler (Ed.), *The uses of charity: The poor on relief in the nineteenth century metropolis* (pp. 1–37). Philadelphia: University of Pennsylvania Press.

Margolin, L. (1997). *Under the cover of kindness: The invention of social work.* Charlottesville, VA: University of Virginia Press.

Marmor, T. (2000). *The politics of Medicare.* Hawthorne, NY: Aldine de Gruyter.

Massey, D. S., & Denton, N. A. (1993). *American apartheid: Segregation and the making of the underclass.* Cambridge, MA: Harvard University Press.

Matusow, A. J. (1984). *The unraveling of America: A history of liberalism in the 1960s.* New York: Harper & Row.

McElvaine, R.S. (Ed.) (2008). *Down and out in the Great Depression: Letters from the forgotten man* (25th anniversary edition). Chapel Hill, NC: University of North Carolina Press.

McElvaine, R. S. (1984). *The Great Depression, America 1929–1941.* New York: Times Books.

McElvaine, R.S. (2000). *The Great Depression: A history in documents.* New York: Oxford University Press.

McJimsey, G. T. (1987). *Harry Hopkins: Ally of the poor and defender of democracy.* Cambridge, MA: Harvard University Press.

Mead, L. M. (1986). *Beyond entitlement: The social obligations of citizenship.* New York: Free Press.

Mishel, L., Bivens, J., Eisenbrey, R., & Fieldhouse, A. (2011, September 2). *Putting America back to work: Policies for job creation and stronger economic growth.* Washington, DC: Economic Policy Institute.

Mishel, L., & Shierholz, H. (2011, March 14). *The sad but true story of wages in America* (Issue Brief No. 297). Washington, DC: Economic Policy Institute.

Monea, E., & Sawhill, I. (2010). *A simulation on future poverty in the United States.* Washington, DC: Urban Institute.

Moniz, C., & Gorin, S. (2010). *Health and mental health care policy: A bio-psychosocial perspective* (3rd ed.). Boston: Allyn & Bacon.

Morone, J. A., & Jacobs, L. R. (Eds.). (2005). *Healthy, wealthy, and fair: Health care and the good society*. New York: Oxford University Press.

Morris, A. J. F. (2009). *The limits of voluntarism: Charity and welfare from the New Deal through the Great Society*. Cambridge, MA: Harvard University Press.

Moynihan, D. P. (1973). *The politics of a guaranteed income: The Nixon Administration and the Family Assistance Plan*. New York: Random House.

Muller, T. (1993). *Immigrants and the American city*. New York: New York University Press.

Murray, C. (1984). *Losing ground: American social policy, 1950–1980*. New York: Basic Books.

Nadasen, P. (2012). *Rethinking the welfare rights movement*. New York: Routledge.

National Women's Law Center (2015). Poverty among women, 2014. Washington, DC: Author. Retrieved from http://nwlc.org/resources/nwlc-analysis-2014-census-poverty-data/

Navarro, V. (2007). *Neoliberalism, globalization and inequalities: Consequences for health and quality of life*. Amityville, NY: Baywood.

O'Connor, J. (1973). *The fiscal crisis of the state*. New York: St. Martin's Press.

Ozawa, M. (1997). Demographic changes and social welfare. In M. Reisch & E. Gambrill (Eds.), *Social work in the 21st century* (pp. 8–27). Thousand Oaks, CA: Pine Forge Press.

Paine, R. T. (1893). Pauperism in great cities: Its four chief causes. In *Proceedings, International Congress of Charities, Correction, and Philanthropy* (Sect. II; pp. 23–52). Baltimore, MD: Johns Hopkins University Press.

Palley, T. I. (2012). *From financial crisis to stagnation: The destruction of shared prosperity and the role of economics*. New York: Cambridge University Press.

Park, Y., & Kemp, S. P. (2006). 'Little alien colonies': Representations of immigrants and their neighborhoods in social work discourse, 1875–1924. *Social Service Review*, 80(4), 705–734.

Patterson, J. (2001). *America's struggle against poverty in the 20th century*. Cambridge, MA: Harvard University Press.

Pavetti, L., & Rosenbaum, D. (2010, February 25). *Creating a safety net that works when the economy doesn't: The role of the Food Stamp and TANF programs*. Washington, DC: Center on Budget and Policy Priorities.

PBS Online (2001). People & events: Anthony Comstock's "chastity" laws. Retrieved May 06, 2016, from http://www.pbs.org/wgbh/amex/pill/peopleevents/e_comstock.html

Pew Research Center for People and the Press. (2011, July 7). *Public wants changes in entitlements, not changes in benefits*. Washington, DC: Author.

Pierce, F. (1854). President Franklin Pierce's veto of the bill resulting from Miss Dix's efforts. *Congressional Globe*. Thirty-third Congress, 1st session, May 3 (pp. 1061–1063).

Piketty, T. (2014). *Capitalism in the twenty-first century*. Cambridge, MA: Belknap Press of Harvard University Press.

Piven, F. F., Acker, J., Hallock, M., & Morgen, S. (Eds.). (2002). *Work, welfare and politics: Confronting poverty in the wake of welfare reform*. Eugene: University of Oregon Press.

Piven, F. F., & Cloward, R. A. (1995). *Regulating the poor: The functions of public welfare* (Rev. ed.). New York: Vintage Books.

Poole, H. (2006). *The segregated origins of Social Security: African Americans and the welfare state*. Chapel Hill: University of North Carolina Press.

Portes, A. (1990). *Immigrant America: A portrait*. Berkeley: University of California Press.

Poynter, J. R. (1969). *Society and pauperism: English ideas on poor relief, 1795–1834*. London: Routledge & Kegan Paul.

Pumphrey, R. (1959). Compassion and protection: Dual motivations in social welfare. *Social Service Review, 33*(1), 21–29.

Quadagno, J. (1994). *The color of welfare: How racism undermined the War on Poverty*. New York: Oxford University Press.

Quincy, J. (1822). *Remarks on some of the provisions of the laws of Massachusetts affecting poverty, vice, and crime*. Cambridge, MA: Harvard University Press.

Rank, M. R. (2004). *One nation underprivileged: Why American poverty affects us all*. New York: Oxford University Press.

Rank, M.R., Hirschl, T.A., & Foster, K.A. (2014). *Chasing the American dream: Understanding what shapes our fortunes*. New York: Oxford University Press.

Reich, R.B. (2013). *Aftershock: The next economy and America's future*. New York: Vintage Books.

Reiman, J., & Leighton, P. (2010). *The rich get richer and the poor get prison: Ideology, class, and criminal justice*, (9th ed.) Boston: Allyn & Bacon.

Reisch, M. (2005). American exceptionalism and critical social work: A retrospective and prospective analysis. In I. Ferguson, M. Lavalette, & E. Whitmore (Eds.), *Globalisation, global justice and social work* (pp. 157–171). London: Routledge.

Reisch, M. (2004). Charity. In R. McElvaine (Ed.), *The encyclopedia of the Great Depression* (pp. 159–161). New York: Oxford University Press.

Reisch, M. (2008a). From melting pot to multiculturalism: The impact of racial and ethnic diversity on social work and social justice in the U.S. *British Journal of Social Work, 38*(4), 788–804.

Reisch, M. (2008b). Social policy and the Great Society. In J. Midgley & M. Livermore (Eds.), *Handbook of social policy* (Rev. ed., pp. 151–168). Newbury Park, CA: Sage.

Reisch, M. (2010). United States social welfare policy and privatization in post-industrial society. In J. L. Powell & J. Hendricks (Eds.), *The welfare state in post-industrial society: A global perspective* (pp. 253–270). New York: Springer.

Reisch, M., & Andrews, J. L. (2002). *The road not taken: A history of radical social work in the United States*. Philadelphia: Brunner-Routledge.

Reisch, M., & Jani, J. S. (2012). The new politics of social work: Understanding context to promote change. *British Journal of Social Work, 42*(5), 1–19.

Reisch, M. (2013). What is the future of social work? *Critical and Radical Social Work, 1*(1), 67–85.

Rose, N. E. (1995). *Workfare or fair work: Women, welfare, and government work programs*. New Brunswick, NJ: Rutgers University Press.

Rose, N. E. (2009). *Put to work: The WPA and public employment in the Great Depression* (2nd ed.). New York: Monthly Review Press.

Rose, S.M. (1972). *The betrayal of the poor: The transformation of community action*. Cambridge, MA: Schenkman.

Rosenberg, J., & Rosenberg, S. (Eds.). (2006). *Community mental health: Challenges for the 21st century*. New York: Routledge.

Rothman, D. J. (2002a). *Conscience and convenience: The asylum and its alternatives in progressive America* (Rev. ed.). New York: Aldine de Gruyter.

Rothman, D. J. (2002b). *The discovery of the asylum: Social order and disorder in the new republic* (Rev. ed.). New York: Aldine de Gruyter.

Russell, J.W. (2015). *Double standard: Social policy in Europe and the United States* (3rd ed.). New York: Rowman & Littlefield.

Ryan, W. (1971). *Blaming the victim.* New York: Vintage Books.

Sale, K. (1976). *Power shift: The rise of the Southern rim and the challenge to the Eastern establishment.* New York: Random House.

Schram, S. F., Soss, J., & Fording, R. C. (Eds.). (2003). *Race and the politics of welfare reform.* Ann Arbor: University of Michigan Press.

Sherman, A., & Stone, C. (2010, June 25). *Income gaps between very rich and everyone else more than tripled in last three decades, data show.* Washington, DC: Center on Budget and Policy Priorities.

Skocpol, T. (1997). *Boomerang: Health care reform and the turn against government.* New York: W. W. Norton.

Skocpol, T. (1992). *Protecting soldiers and mothers: The political origins of social policy in the United States.* Cambridge, MA: Belknap Press of Harvard University Press.

Skocpol, T., Liazos, A., & Ganz, M. (2006). *What a mighty power we can be: African American fraternal groups and the struggle for racial equality.* Princeton, NJ: Princeton University Press.

Smith, A., Stenning, A., & Willis, K. (Eds.). (2008). *Social justice and neoliberalism: Global perspectives.* New York: Palgrave MacMillan.

Sorensen, J. (Ed.). (2008). *The Grace Abbott reader.* Lincoln: University of Nebraska Press.

Soss, J., Fording, R. C., & Schram, S. F. (2011). *Disciplining the poor: Neoliberal paternalism and the persistent power of race.* Chicago: University of Chicago Press.

Starr, P. (1982). *The social transformation of American medicine.* New York: Basic Books.

Stern, M., & Axinn, J. (2012). *Social welfare: A history of the American response to need,* (8th ed.) Boston: Allyn & Bacon.

Stiglitz, J. (2012, October 26). Some are more unequal than others. *New York Times.* Retrieved October 28, 2012, from http://campaignstops.blogs.nytimes.com/2012/10/26/stiglitz-some-are-more-unequal-than

Stiglitz, J. (2013). *The price of inequality: How today's divided society endangers our future.* New York: W.W. Norton.

Stoesz, D., & Saunders, D. (1999). Welfare capitalism: A new approach to poverty policy?. *Social Service Review, 73*(3), 380–400.

Stone, C., Trisi, D., Sherman, A., & Debot, B. (2015, October 26). *A guide to historical trends on income inequality.* Washington, DC: Center on Budget and Policy Priorities. Retrieved from http://www.cbpp.org/research/poverty-and-inequality/a-guide-to-statistics-on-historical-trends-in-income-inequality

Sugrue, T. J. (2005). *The origins of the urban crisis: Race and inequality in postwar Detroit.* Princeton, NJ: Princeton University Press.

Sugrue, T. J. (2009). *Sweet land of liberty: The forgotten struggle for civil rights in the North.* New York: Random House.

Sumner, W. G. (1883). *What social classes owe to each other.* New York: Harper & Brothers.

Takaki, R. (1994). *From distant shores: Perspectives on race and ethnicity in America.* New York: Oxford University Press.

Telushkin, J. (1994). Let the law cut through the mountain: Jewish principles of justice. In *Jewish wisdom: Ethical, spiritual, and historical lessons from the great works and thinkers.* New York: William Morrow & Co.

Thakur, S. (1996). *Religion and social justice.* New York: St. Martin's Press.

Thompson, E.F. (2014). Social justice in the Middle East. In M. Reisch (Ed.), *The Routledge international handbook of social justice* (pp. 61–73). London: Routledge.

Tocqueville, A. D. (1835). *Democracy in America* (H. Reeve, Trans.). New York: G. Adlard.

Turner, M. A., Oliff, P., & Williams, E. (2010, May 25). *An update on state budget cuts: At least 45 states have imposed cuts that hurt vulnerable residents and the economy.* Washington, DC: Center on Budget and Policy Priorities.

Twill, S., & Fisher, S. (2010). Economic human rights violations experienced by women and children in the United States. *Families in Society: The Journal of Contemporary Social Services, 91*(4), 356–362.

United Way of America. (1977). *People and events: A history of the United Way.* Alexandria, VA: Author.

U.S. Census Bureau. (1995). *Poverty in the United States.* Washington, DC: U.S. Government Printing Office.

U.S. Census Bureau. (2010). Table H-2: Share of aggregate income received by each fifth and top 5 percent of households. Retrieved March 29, 2012, from http://www.census.gov/hhes/www/income/data/historical/household/index.html

U.S. Census Bureau. (2016). *Poverty in the United States.* Washington, DC: U.S. Government Printing Office.

U.S. Congress (1975, October 16). Examination of the effectiveness of community action programs in alleviating conditions of poverty in our nation. Hearing before the Subcommittee on Employment, Poverty, and Migratory Labor of the Committee on Labor and Public Welfare, United States Senate, Ninety-fourth Congress, first session. Washington, DC: U.S. Government Printing Office. HHHHh

U.S. Department of Agriculture. (2012). *Participation in the Supplemental Nutrition Assistance Program.* Washington, DC: U.S. Government Printing Office.

U.S. Department of Health and Human Services. (2012). *TANF recipients and their families.* Washington, DC: U.S. Government Printing Office.

Vroman, W. (2010, July). *The Great Recession, unemployment insurance, and poverty: Summary.* Washington, DC: Urban Institute.

Wacquant, L. (2009). *Punishing the poor: The neoliberal government of social insecurity.* Durham, NC: Duke University Press.

Wagner, D. (2005). *The poorhouse: America's forgotten institution.* Lanham, MD: Rowman & Littlefield.

Wald, L. P. (1909). The immigrant young girl. In *Proceedings of the National Conference of Social Work* (pp. 261–265). Chicago: University of Chicago Press.

Waldinger, R. (Ed.). (2001). *Strangers at the gate: New immigrants in urban America.* Berkeley: University of California Press.

Wallace, H. M., Green, G., & Jaros, K. J. (with Morris, N.). (Eds.). (2003). *Health and welfare for families in the 21st century.* Boston: Jones and Bartlett.

Ward, D. E. (2005). *The white welfare state: The racialization of U.S. welfare policy.* Ann Arbor: University of Michigan Press.

Watson, W. (2015). *The inequality trap: Fighting capitalism instead of poverty.* Toronto: University of Toronto Press.

Wenocur, S., & Reisch, M. (1989). *From charity to enterprise: The development of American social work in a market economy.* Urbana: University of Illinois Press.

West, G. (1981). *The national welfare rights movement: The social protest of poor women.* New York: Praeger.

Wiebe, R. H. (1967). *The search for order, 1877–1920.* New York: Hill & Wang.

Williams, E. (2016, April 13). *A fiscal policy agenda for stronger state economies.* Washington, DC: Center on Budget and Policy Priorities. Retrieved from http://www.cbpp.org/research/state-budget-and-tax/a-fiscal-policy-agenda-for-stronger-state-economies

Wilson, W. J. (1996). *When work disappears: The world of the new urban poor*. New York: Knopf.

Wolff, E. (2010, March). *Recent trends in household wealth in the United States* (Levy Economics Institute Paper No. 589). Annandale-on-the-Hudson, NY: Bard College.

World Bank. (2010). *Global monitoring report 2015*. Washington, DC: Author.

Yang, P. (1995). *Post 1965 immigration to the United States*. Westport, CT: Praeger.

Credits

3

THE POLITICAL ECONOMY OF U.S. SOCIAL POLICY

Joel Blau, DSW

In the United States, and other industrialized nations, the role of social policy is to distribute benefits and services. In some popular current interpretations of this process in both the media and aspects of our political discourse, the rich are taxed to benefit the poor, government intervention subverts the marketplace's inherent productivity, and the economy would flourish if we could dispense with social welfare. Those who believe these ideas, however, misunderstand the nature of the modern American economy and its complex impact on U.S. social policy. Despite the enormous role that government intervention plays in U.S. society—from funding schools to providing Social Security benefits, from paying for Medicaid, Medicare, and the military, to bailing out banks and the auto industry—the myth of the self-regulating marketplace is alive and well.

This myth is deeply rooted in our political culture. In one revealing study, researchers asked 1,400 Americans whether they had benefited from any of 21 different federal social programs. Although 57 percent of respondents said that they had not, in fact, 94% of them had used at least one program; the average respondent had used four (Mettler, 2011). Americans may live in a 21st century society, but many still seem to have internalized a 19th century conception of the marketplace as an economy based on small businesses, competitive capitalism, and very few social welfare programs.

Of course, even in the 19th century, American capitalism relied upon a wide range of government interventions: the construction of the Erie Canal, which opened transportation routes to the Midwest; the development of land grant colleges, which seeded institutions of higher education throughout the nation; and the provision of great swathes of land to the railroads as they built tracks across the continent. Nevertheless, except for the distribution of Civil War pensions later in the century, the nation's political economy did not include social welfare as conventionally defined (Skocpol, 1992). It is no wonder, then, that to understand the current role of social welfare in U.S. society we first have to identify what makes our contemporary economy so different and then explain why these differences require social welfare spending.

THE MODERN POLITICAL ECONOMY

Five features distinguish the contemporary political economy of the U.S.: its dominance by large corporations, especially those engaged in global commerce; the rise of finance capitalism; a pattern of boom and bust; the growth of socio-economic inequality and the consequent tendency toward under-consumption; and the increase in social costs that create a need for social policy intervention. In order to clarify the relationship of social welfare to the modern economy, we need to examine each of these features closely.

THE LARGE CORPORATION

Despite frequent paeans to small businesses as the nation's primary job and wealth creators, large multinational corporations constitute the chief characteristic of the modern U.S. economy; they distinguish contemporary capitalism from its small business, 19th century version. The size, scale, and reach of the modern corporation are astounding. In 2014, Wal-Mart, first on the *Fortune 500* list of the largest corporations, had $485 billion in revenues, greater than the Gross Domestic Product (GDP) of Austria and just

Figure 3.1 Wal-Mart store in Quanzhou, China.

below Norway. Standing alone, Wal-Mart is the 28th largest economy in the world. But Wal-Mart, however, is not unique. In 2012, many other major American corporations also had revenues exceeding the GDP of entire nations. Exxon Mobil's revenues surpassed the GDP of South Africa, Chevron's were bigger than Portugal's, and AT&T earned more than Hungary's GDP (Snyder, 2015; Make Wealth History, 2014).

Before the rise of monopolies like railroads, Standard Oil, and U.S. Steel over a century ago, the typical nineteenth century business was often family-owned and employed just a few people. Today, by comparison, Wal-Mart employs 1.3 million workers, or almost one percent of the U.S. labor force and through overseas contracts employs hundreds of thousands more), Its reach is global; it has stores in seventy-two different countries (Wal-Mart, 2016); and its market leverage allows it to get the lowest possible price from suppliers. While it is true that 99 percent of all firms in the U.S. gross under $25 million a year, and firms with fewer than twenty workers employ nearly 1 in 6 workers, it would be wrong to generalize about the contemporary U.S. economy from these figures. The payrolls of the more than 18,000 firms with more than 500 workers now surpass those of the 5.7 million companies which employ fewer than 500 workers (Bureau of the Census, 2016). In sum, despite the persistent myth, small businesses are no longer the prime "drivers" of the U.S. economy.

These facts have enormous implications for our contemporary social welfare system. Whatever problems 19th century competitive capitalism created—low wages, poor working conditions, and the lack of social provision—the scale of its enterprise, its leverage over the workforce, and the social consequences of production pale besides its modern counterpart. Nineteenth century businesses rarely moved across state lines and to other nations; twenty-first century businesses can and do. Workers cannot stop them, communities have little leverage over corporate decisions, and corporations have fewer incentives to support the communities in which they are housed. Because of this enormous power differential, both workers and communities are dependent upon the good will of corporations to remain where they are and pay decent wages. The frequent failure of modern corporations to do so creates a need for government-funded social welfare programs and for the continued existence of non-profit social service agencies.

FINANCE CAPITALISM

The centrality of **finance capitalism** is the second distinctive characteristic of the modern U.S. economy. In recent decades, the growth of finance capitalism means that instead of making consumer goods, like steel, cars, and appliances, as the U.S. industrial machine did in the mid-20th century, the core of the U.S. economy has shifted to what is often described as '**paper entrepreneurialism**'—speculation in stocks, bonds, complex financial instruments, and real estate. In the period immediately after World War II, the financial sector accounted for just 7 % of total corporate profits. By 2013, however, that share had soared to almost 30 percent (Weissmann, 2013)

This shift in the nature of the U.S. economy dramatically changed its relationship to the nation's social welfare system. Finance capitalism in the 21st century is far more mobile than mid-20th century industrial capitalism. Through the use of computers, its impact is felt globally and almost instantaneously. Companies can speculate on stocks and currency from anywhere in the world and transfer billions of dollars in assets in a second. The people the financial sector employs have different skills; they are more educated, less dependent on physical labor, and less likely to be unionized. Because finance capitalism concentrates its benefits, individuals with these skills are often well rewarded. Those who lack these skills, however, must compete within a hollowed out economy. This population consists of people of all races and all regions of the country—from small and mid-sized industrial towns in the so-called "rust belt" like Youngstown, Ohio to once great manufacturing cities like Detroit and Baltimore to long-neglected rural areas in Appalachia and the Mississippi Delta. Residents of these communities are more likely to need social welfare programs in order to survive.

Yet, for hard practical reasons, finance capitalism is not very hospitable towards social welfare. Unlike the great industrial enterprises of the mid-20th century, international financial institutions (IFIs) do not need a healthy, well-educated, and well-trained American workforce to prosper. If their needs cannot be met here for whatever they are willing to pay in taxes, they can always relocate to another country where conditions—lower taxes and wages, fewer environmental regulations—may be more favorable. This development fosters a paradox: finance capitalism is much more resistant to address the very need for social welfare that it creates. It is no wonder, therefore, that the rise of financial capitalism has paralleled the emphasis in the United States on tax cuts, restrictions on unions, rollback of environmental and occupational safety regulations, and cuts in social welfare spending. Ironically, as a consequence of their antipathy to government and their preference for market solutions, through their political choices Americans have chosen an economic system that is less responsive to the very conditions the new global economy has both created and requires.

THE TENDENCY TO BOOM AND BUST

The recession of 2007 produced a prolonged economic contraction whose effects have lingered for nearly a decade. After reaching a high of 10 percent in 2010, it required another five years for the official unemployment rate to return to its 2007 level of five percent (Bureau of Labor Statistics, 2016a) A broader measure of unemployment that includes discouraged and the involuntary part-time reached 17%, or more than one of every 6 U.S. worker (Bureau of Labor Statistics, 2016b). This statistic underlies the sense of growing insecurity fueling the anti-establishment sentiments of the electorate. Most media accounts of the Great Recession treated it as an unusual event—the most severe economic crisis America faced since the Great Depression of the 1930s. In one sense, this picture is true; unemployment was briefly higher in 1983, but otherwise, the U.S. had not experienced a comparable contraction in seventy years. In another sense, however, these analyses overlook the many occasions during the past forty years when financial speculation pushed the nation to a similar brink.

In 1970, for example, only the intervention of the Federal Reserve Bank prevented the bankruptcy of the Penn Central Railroad from bringing down First National City, the predecessor of CitiBank. Likewise, in 1982–83, indiscriminate bank lending to Latin America resulted in a serious debt crisis that national governments had to allay. This was soon followed by the savings and loan crisis of the late 1980s, which stemmed from the loan-financed overbuilding of commercial real estate. Only "off budget" Congressional intervention of nearly $750 billion prevented the collapse of these lending institutions. Although none of these earlier crises triggered a recession comparable to the 2008 contraction, their frequency suggests that a pattern of boom and bust is deeply embedded in the rise of finance capitalism (Krugman & Wells, 2011).

There are several plausible explanations for this phenomenon. One is that American corporations increasingly tend to outsource the production of goods, sending jobs overseas while banking huge profits. Flush with cash but faced with diminished purchasing power in the U.S., corporations naturally gravitate to perilous speculative ventures, e.g., lending money to people who should not be borrowing and investing in businesses on the assumption they will steadily increase in paper value. From the perspective of corporate CEOs, these risks are clearly worth taking because money does not earn very much today sitting in a bank given historically low interest rates on savings.

The upside of this strategy is that the right investment may spur the growth of a new sector of the economy (such as computers) and increase corporate profits considerably. If these investments sour, however, through a failed Internet company or a vacant Las Vegas housing development, the boom can turn into a bust in an instant, leaving thousands of people without jobs or homes, and in need of social welfare.

Put even more bluntly, during the past four decades the U.S. economy seems to be ever more dependent on economic bubbles to sustain it. The less our nation produces real consumer goods that can compete in the global marketplace, the more we look to "the next new thing" to inflate the economy and keep it going. This produces a recurrent cycle of boom and bust, bust and boom.

In the late 1990s, the Dot.Com bubble drove the stock market to its all-time high, but in the aftermath of its collapse, there was too little real economic activity to propel the economy. Consequently, the Federal Reserve Bank dropped the prime interest rate—the rate

Figure 3.2 Home in foreclosure.

that banks use to determine what they charge for mortgages—to an all-time low. This created the housing bubble that kept the economy afloat from 2001 to 2007: at their peak in 2006, housing prices were 70 percent above the normal trend line. When housing sales slowed and the bubble began to deflate, banks were caught with many complex financial instruments such as credit default swaps that were all based on worthless mortgages. By fall 2008, the entire financial sector teetered on the brink of collapse. (These developments were vividly captured in the recent film, "The Big Short.")

In response, the Bush Administration passed the Toxic Assets Relief Program (TARP) that saved many banks deemed "too big to fail." Six months later, President Obama's $787 billion economic stimulus package (officially named the "American Reinvestment and Recovery Act" or ARRA), with its mixture of tax cuts, job creation, and extended unemployment benefits, prevented the economy from plummeting further. In spite of these measures, the economic recovery was tepid: wage growth remains slow, and labor's share of corporate income still has not recovered (Economic Policy Institute, 2016). Although in recent years the U.S. economy has rebounded more than its European counterparts, its persistent softness suggests that the nation has still not found either a sound path to sustained economic health, or the next new bubble.

This persistent pattern of boom and bust accentuates the economic and social dislocation it creates. Today, unlike workers in the idealized economy of the post-World War II era, workers' jobs, prospects for future occupational or salary advancement, and expectations of financial stability can vanish in seconds. Until recently, in these circumstances American workers had a fair chance of obtaining some help from the nation's social welfare system. They could get job training, unemployment insurance, or a student loan. Now, however, the volatility of the U.S. economy, and the growing tendency for the wealthy few to garner most of its benefits, have shredded the safety net and brought about a crackdown on social welfare programs at both the federal and state level. The hallmarks of this new age are economic dislocation without a safety net and greater economic insecurity with less social security. Low taxes, fiscal austerity, and deregulation constitute the model business agenda, all designed to reduce the cost of labor and bend the government to the will of the large corporations and financial institutions that now dominate the economy.

Figure 3.3 Occupy Oakland General Strike in November 2011.

INEQUALITY AND UNDER-CONSUMPTION

In contrast with the pattern described above, economic gains in the U.S. during the three decades after World War II were widely shared. From 1945–1975, the income of the bottom 90% actually increased more rapidly than the income of the top 1%. Since the mid-1970s, this trend has reversed. Economic globalization, the increasing prominence of the finance sector, and the hyper-mobility of large businesses have combined to concentrate the benefits of economic growth. As a result, **income inequality** has risen in the United States to levels that have not been seen since the 1920s.

Income data are usually collected in **quintiles**—by fifths of the population. In 1976, the top quintile, the 20% of households with the most earnings, received 43.7 % of all income. By 2015, however, its share of income had risen to 51.3 %. Even more dramatically, during the same period, the income share of the top 5% rose from 16.6 to 21.9 %, while at the other end of the income spectrum, the share of the bottom quintile dropped from 4.3 to 3.1 percent (U.S. Bureau of the Census, 2015). The success of the top 1%—families earning more than $389,000/year—highlights a revealing undercurrent in these trends (CNNMoney, 2014). Between 1979–2011, for example, the after-tax income of this group increased two hundred percent (Center on Budget and Policy Priorities, 2015) Much of this spike occurred during the economic expansion of 2001 to 2007, when this small group reaped two-thirds of all income gains—about $521,000 per household compared to households in the bottom 90% which gained only $1,200/year (Center on Budget and Policy Priorities, 2009). The Bush Administration's changes in the nation's tax policies sharply exacerbated these trends. (See the Figure 3.4 below for trends in income inequality in the U.S. during the past 70 years.)

Inevitably, inequality of income distribution leads to inequality of wealth. The top quintile in the U.S. now possesses about 89% of all wealth, up from 81 percent in 1983. The top 1% owns 37% of this wealth (Wolff, 2014). Most Americans, however, are unaware of these developments. In a path-breaking study, Norton and Ariely (2011) asked Americans to choose between three models of wealth distribution: the actual American distribution, perfect equality, and the distribution of wealth in Sweden, where the top 20% has 36% of the nation's assets. By a 92–8 margin, Americans in the study preferred the Swedish model and offered 32%, a proportion below the Swedish figure, as their ideal. Even more significantly, when asked to estimate the actual distribution of wealth in the U.S., respondents said that the top quintile owned 59% of all wealth, more than 25 percent below the actual proportion (Norton & Ariely, 2011). As with so many other features of our economy, Americans have a sharply different conception of how they would like the marketplace to function from the way it actually does. These faulty assumptions are reflected in how the electorate responds to contemporary political discourse.

This shift toward greater income and wealth inequality has enormous implications for the nation's social welfare system. The steady upward shift of income has shortchanged families who are not in the higher

Figure 3.4 Income Inequality in the U.S.

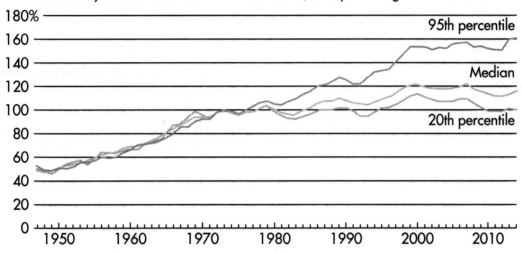

Income Gains Widely Shared in Early Postwar Decades – But Not Since Then

Real family income between 1947 and 2014, as a percentage of 1973 level

Note: In 2014 Census split its sample of survey respondents into two groups to test a set of redesigned income questions. In 2015 (reporting on 2014 income using the new questions), Census released two estimates of 2013 incomes, one based on the old questions and one on the new. The chart uses the estimate based on the old questions, based on CBPP's Judgement that, due in part to sample size, it is likely more accurate for 2013.

Source: CBPP calculations based on U.S. Census Bureau Data

income brackets. To compensate for their families' loss of income, women nearly doubled their paid work outside the home, from 32 percent in 1948 to 59 percent in 2000 (Kochhar, 2012). Families have also come to rely increasingly on credit card debt and home equity loans to maintain previous levels of consumption including the purchase of many services such as meal preparation and childcare that an at-home mother used to provide. Neither of these strategies, however, has been sufficient to overcome the increasingly persistent tendency to under-consumption in the American economy.

This is perhaps the fundamental paradox of modern American capitalism today. The benefits which accrue to one cost-cutting corporation lead to economic stagnation if every company follows its example. In other words, if businesses do not pay their employees adequate wages, these workers cannot buy enough to keep the economy going. This is particularly significant in the U.S. because domestic consumption accounts for about 70% of all economic activity.

This income-induced shortfall is both ominous and unrelenting. By upsetting the delicate balance between a desirable level of profits and a sufficient level of wages, the present pattern has put the U.S. economy in a precarious position in which speculative bubbles are required to boost demand, yet even this demand is not widespread enough to ensure an adequate level of consumption by many American households. It is no surprise, therefore, that the 2001–2007 expansion was the weakest of the ten expansions since

1948, and that the subsequent recession was the most serious economic debacle since the Great Depression of the 1930s (Henwood, 2010).

SOCIAL COSTS & SOCIAL WELFARE

Economic debacles of this nature have large social costs, such as unemployment and increased poverty. Since the 1930s, an increase in social costs has typically elicited greater social welfare spending. The most recent recession, however, produced enormous social costs, but the nation's social policy response has been, at best, timid and begrudging. Three specific indices illustrate this point: unemployment statistics, the record level of food stamp usage, and the link between rising inequality and health.

The most common index of unemployment is the Bureau of Labor Statistics (BLS) official unemployment rate, which broke the 10 percent barrier in late 2009 and only recently has dipped to 5%. Since the jobless rate bottomed out at 4.2 percent in 2001, this—the simplest measure of unemployment—demonstrates that we still have not returned to pre-recession levels (Bureau of Labor Statistics, 2016a).

The Bureau of Labor Statistics also tracks a fuller measure of the unemployment rate. This measure compensates for omissions in the official unemployment figures, which exclude workers who have stopped looking for a job (the BLS refers to them as "**discouraged workers**"), have never entered the workforce, and are incarcerated, homeless, or in the military, and designates as employed people, such as some Wal-Mart employees, who are involuntarily working part-time. If these categories are included, the unemployment rate rose to over 17 percent during the recession, meaning that more than one of every six Americans was either un- or underemployed. Since this measure is usually slightly less than twice the official unemployment rate, that number has now dipped below 10 percent. Another index, the **employment-population ratio**, also follows the same pattern: it reveals that while 64 percent of the adult population was working in 2001, only 58 percent were employed at the depths of the recession, and nearly 60 percent have jobs today (Bureau of Labor Statistics, 2011b; 2016b; 2016c).

Why has so little been done to address persistent unemployment? One explanation is that unemployment is concentrated among less educated workers who lack political or economic clout. In addition, regardless of the human suffering unemployment has caused, corporations remain well positioned to take advantage of overseas markets, and as a result, corporate profits are at an all-time high. Finally, the focus on reducing fiscal deficits and the nation's debt has impeded the formation of any coalition that would promote a full employment policy (Folbre, 2011). In comparison with the nation's response to other recessions, policymakers have devoted relatively little energy to addressing unemployment. [*See Chapter 12 this volume for further discussion of employment policy.*]

The recession has also brought about a sharp spike in the number of food stamp recipients. Now called **SNAP** (Supplemental Nutrition Assistance Program), participation in the Food Stamp program increased from 32 million persons in 2009 to 46 million in 2016. Some 22.6 million households now avail themselves of this benefit (Food Nutrition Service, 2016a; 2016b). The number of recipients of food assistance has tripled since 2000. Like most other social welfare programs, however, SNAP possesses a dual economic role: it reduces hunger among low-income people while it cushions the effect of the recession on farming communities. If SNAP benefits were counted as income, 4.7 million fewer people would be counted as poor.

A final indicator of the recession's long-term effects is reflected in the relationship between inequality and health. The recession clearly sharpened income disparities and pushed more people into poverty. These trends have significant health implications, because in recent years researchers have identified a close correlation between poverty and health. In one study, 119,000 deaths were attributed to income inequality and 133,000 additional deaths were attributed to poverty. Combined, these "excess deaths" equal a greater number than the 193,000 people a year who die from heart attacks (Galea et al, 2011). Another study projected that about one-third of all deaths in the U.S. could be attributed to inequality (Inequality.org, 2011).

In comparison with 21 other developed nations, the U.S. places next to last in income inequality and life expectancy, below every other country except Singapore. Since poverty statistics are merely a snapshot, and a full accounting of their lifetime impact suggests that nearly 59% of all Americans will be officially poor at some point in their adult life (Rank, 2004), these data surely underestimate the true impact of poverty and inequality. Although programs like Medicaid and Medicare attempt to reduce the effects of this inequality, they only mitigate the overall effects to some extent, effects which are not merely restricted to people's economic well-being.

These five factors—the growth of large multi-national corporations, the rise of finance capitalism, a persistent pattern of boom and bust, the growth of income and asset inequality and the consequent tendency toward under-consumption, and the increase in social costs—highlight the contrast between Americans' beliefs about the nation's economy and the way it actually functions. They also explode many related myths about the economy's relationship to social welfare. Although the recent focus on deficit reduction has increased calls to cut social welfare spending, such cuts risk producing prolonged stagnation, an even more severe downturn, and a further increase in social costs. Yet, since a few deeply rooted ideologically-based myths continue to fuel the focus on deficit reduction, they must be addressed before we can explore the true economic role of social welfare policy.

THREE CONSERVATIVE MYTHS ABOUT SOCIAL WELFARE AND THE ECONOMY

Perhaps the most enduring conservative myth behind recurrent efforts to cut social welfare spending is the belief that social welfare programs create dependency. As a corollary of the notion that without social welfare, the economy would boom, this belief makes a lot of sense. The problem is that this corollary seriously misunderstands the role of poverty and dependency in the U.S.

Poverty and people who are poor often get a lot of bad press. Typically, poverty is associated with crime, dangerous neighborhoods, poor schools, and much wasted human potential. Costly social programs to combat poverty are frequently cited as futile efforts that make these problems worse. This appealing argument has one fatal flaw: it fails to acknowledge the critical role that poverty plays in the U.S. economy.

In reality, while we may upbraid poor people for their behavior, we also have an acute need for them (Gans, 1995). When employers fight unions, they reduce the bargaining power of working people and create poverty. When businesses resist wage increases, their resistance creates poverty. Cutbacks in social welfare programs put more people at risk of poverty and exacerbate the poverty of those who are already poor. The real crisis of poverty is not merely that it is such a terrible condition; the real crisis of poverty is that it is a terrible condition, *and* that powerful economic interests reject doing anything about it because poverty plays an essential role in maintaining the current functioning of the U.S. economy.

Social welfare programs do maintain people in poverty. They maintain people in poverty, however, because if they offered a standard of living above the poverty level, they would violate the long-established principle of **less eligibility**, which requires recipients of public assistance to have a lower standard of living than the lowest paid worker. [*See Chapter 2 this volume for a discussion of less eligibility*]. It is hardly surprising, therefore, that as the federal minimum wage, whose current inflation-adjusted value from its peak in 1968 would equal about $11/hour, has stagnated at $7.25/hour (Oregon State, 2015) overall social welfare benefits have been pushed down. It is true that twenty-nine states—including two with a planned minimum wage increase to $15 an hour—have now responded to this decline by enacting a higher state minimum (National Conference of State Legislatures, 2016). Cities like San Francisco and Seattle have also

Figure 3.5 Historical Trends in the Minimum Wage.

Federal Minimum Wage, 1938–2014

Shown in nominal (not adjusted for inflation) dollars and 2014 (inflation-adjusted) dollars

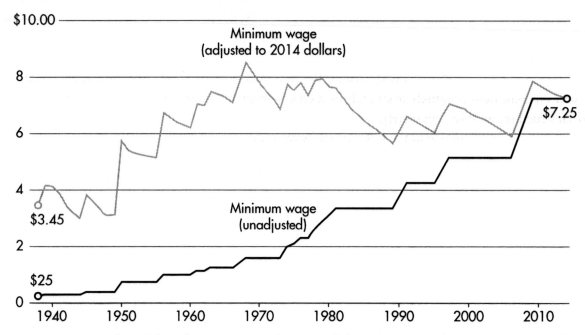

Note: Wage rates adjusted for inflation using implicit price deflator for personal consumption expenditures.
Sources: Bureau of Labor Statistics, Bureau of Economic Analysis, Pew Research Center analysis
Pew Research Center

taken steps to increase the minimum wage and "living wage" campaigns have had some modest success at the local level in cities such as Ann Arbor and Baltimore. Legislation to require paid sick leave has also been introduced in states such as Maryland. Nevertheless, despite this limited progress social welfare programs cannot be too generous if the principle of less eligibility is to be maintained.

This ceiling on the generosity of social welfare programs underscores a critical attribute of the relationship between social welfare and poverty/dependency. Contrary to myth, social welfare programs do not create dependency. [*See Chapters 12 and 13 this volume for a discussion of the relationship among poverty, welfare, and dependency.*] Instead, modern American capitalism requires a certain level of poverty and dependency, the costs of which it then transfers to the publically-funded social welfare system.

Conservative policymakers who favor market-oriented solutions also promote a second myth: that conservatives prefer smaller government and a noninterventionist approach to economic policy, especially with regard to social programs. Although it is true that most conservatives prefer to cut social programs or, if this is not possible, make their benefits more market-like and conditioned on work (Katz, 2001), this preference has little to do with a desire for smaller government. The administrations of conservative presidents, from Ronald Reagan to George W. Bush, have either maintained or expanded the government's role in the economy. Despite their public image, conservative policymakers remain steadfast in their commitment to government intervention in the economy, whether it is through tax cuts for wealthy individuals, military spending, or direct subsidies to corporations. These interventions, however, largely benefit a tiny portion of the U.S. population. From this perspective, ideological debates are not really over the size of the government or its role in the nation's economy and society, but rather the ends which government spending serves (Baker, 2006).

A final misconception about the relationship between social welfare and the economy involves the issue of taxes. Broadly **libertarian** in its outlook, proponents of lower taxes contend that because any money people earn is "their money," it is not to be taxed away, especially to support "unproductive people" who benefit from social programs. Individualism is the core value underlying this perspective. It assumes that people's income derives entirely from their own efforts, independent of any of the political, economic, or social structures in American society.

In truth, however, no one in the U.S. earns a living in this manner. Certainly, many people work hard, but even before they entered the workforce, most of them probably received a public education. Once they started a job, they worked with, or hired, people whose publicly funded education enabled them to function as a more productive team. As either an employee or as an employer, they are able to work because federally-funded drug research and government spending on health care protects them. People commute to work on publicly funded roads or via publicly funded mass transportation. It is highly likely that either the government is involved in the chain of purchases that enable businesses to sell their products or services, or that they would sell much less of these products or services if the government did not subsidize the income of some consumers.

In sum, however hard people work, their earnings are inseparable from American political, economic, and social institutions and the government funds that sustain them. One hundred fifty ago, if a frontiersman stood on his land, rejected the premise that it had been taken by force from Native Americans, and minimized the role of the U.S. army in ensuring his safety, he might have had a plausible argument that what his family earned was relatively independent of the marketplace and hence was solely the product of the sweat of his family's labor. In the contemporary U.S. economy, however, this contention has lost whatever shred of credibility it ever possessed.

THE INTERACTION OF SOCIAL POLICY AND THE ECONOMY

If we acknowledge that the U.S. economy today is significantly different from what it was 150 years ago, we can move beyond the folklore of an earlier era about the relationship between the economy and social policy. The path is now cleared to analyze what that relationship actually entails. This analysis, however, nonetheless comes with one significant qualification: under the new austerity regime where even a moderately liberal president like Barack Obama once expressed a willingness to cut **entitlement programs** like Social Security, the relationship between the economy and social policy is being modified once again. Although these changes may not be sustained—there is a long tradition in the U.S. of promising to slash social welfare programs and then backing down when their political and economic utility is "rediscovered"—it is noteworthy that some of social welfare's most established economic functions are under attack today and can no longer be considered inviolable. A complete list of these functions is, therefore, central to understanding the relationship between social policy and social justice under 21st century American capitalism.

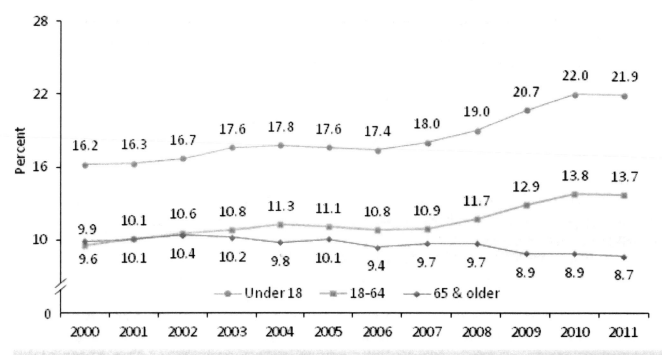

Figure 3.6 Poverty Rates of All Persons by Age, 2000-2011.

At the simplest level, the function of social welfare policy with the longest economic standing is *to cushion the effects of poverty*. This is especially true in the U.S., where most income support programs operate on a **selective** and **residual**, rather than an **institutional** and **universal** model. Eligibility for Temporary Assistance to Needy Families (TANF), Supplemental Security Income (SSI), the Supplemental Nutrition Assistance Program (SNAP, formerly food stamps), Medicaid, housing programs such as Section 8, now renamed **Housing Choice,** and training programs like Job Corps is determined by a **means test**. Even Social Security, a universal program that does not specifically target low-income people, provides at least 90% of the income for 47%, and more than 50% of the income for 74%, of its unmarried beneficiaries (Social Security Administration, 2015). [*See Chapter 11 this volume for further discussion of Social Security.*]

Even many Social Security recipients teeter on the edge of the **official poverty line,** which is currently $24,250 for four people. In a city such as Tupelo, Mississippi, this income might permit a family to scrape by. In larger and more expensive metropolitan regions such as New York, however, where the cost of living is almost two and half times greater, that amount does not permit families to satisfy their basic human needs (U.S. Bureau of the Census, 2015). In other words, most social welfare programs designed to assist low-income families are not very generous. They either maintain people in poverty, or in the case of training programs like Job Corps, rarely provide an escape route. Nevertheless, if we imagine how people would live without these programs, it is clear that they perform absolutely essential social and economic functions.

The economic functions of social programs, however, are hardly restricted to the poor. They also *increase consumer spending at all times, and act counter cyclically during recessions*—that is, they maintain a floor on consumption when the economy causes it to decrease. Whether people are poor and rely on welfare benefits for subsistence or are better off and use their monthly Social Security benefits to pay for discretionary purchases, social welfare programs give people extra money to spend. In an economy with strong tendencies toward under-consumption, one that consistently produces more than people can buy solely with their earned income (salaries), these supplements to wages perform a vital role. Through what economists call the multiplier effect, people's purchases circulate throughout the marketplace to the sellers of goods and services. This function is particularly important during an economic recession, when widespread inability to buy goods and services reduces the income of many people and threatens to trigger a downward spiral. During such circumstances, programs like Unemployment Insurance offset some lost income and prevent more severe economic consequences from occurring.

When government policies attempt to counter the effects of an economic downturn, social programs are often blamed for increasing fiscal deficits. Yet, in 2016, a year when the federal government is projected to spend $534 billion more than it receives, it is somewhat arbitrary to specify which federal expenditures, including the hundreds of billions spent on the military, pushed the budget into the red (Congressional Budget Office, 2016). Although wealthy individuals and institutions benefit from the deficit by earning interest on the money they lend to the government, their opposition to social welfare spending often stems from an ideological preference for a smaller welfare state, if not actually for a smaller government. Drawing on the reservoir of wariness about the size of the federal government, they see the growth of social programs during a recession as an inviting target, although their growth at that time is exactly what policymakers intended.

In U.S. social policy, however, a critical qualifier accompanies most social welfare programs. As discussed above, the principle commonly known as "less eligibility,"—the notion that program benefits cannot be more generous than the wage of the lowest paid worker—enforces the work ethic and is the fallback position of those who are concerned about the generosity of social welfare. What is truly important about the application of the concept of less eligibility today, however, is the way the social welfare system in the U.S. relies on it: most contemporary social programs for adults of pre-retirement age reinforce, rather than disrupt, labor market conditions. Prior to the 1960s, for example, some Southern states provided welfare benefits in the winter and then effectively stopped the program for African Americans during the growing season to compel them to accept agricultural employment at less than subsistence wages (Katznelson, 2005). Today this same principle underlies TANF, the nation's major welfare program. TANF benefits pay less than minimum wage work, and force low-income women to work outside the home rather than getting paid to take care of their children.

Of course, adding conditions to the receipt of a benefit reduces its value. Between 1979 and 2013, the real hourly wages of median income workers grew 6%; the real hourly wages of workers at the 10th percentile (those closest to the bottom) declined by 5 percent (Economic Policy Institute, 2015). If wages had stagnated, as they did from the mid-1970s to the mid-1990s, and welfare benefits had continued to rise as they did during the 1960s, welfare would have soon paid more than work. During an era when globalization intensified competition, the power of trade unions declined, and jobs were shipped overseas, a decrease in the value of welfare benefits was the only way to ensure the transition from an industrial to a service economy on terms favorable to employers. Quite apart from the new enforcement of work requirements, this explains the 47% drop in the median value of welfare benefits between 1970 and 2000 (House Ways and Means Committee, 2000). The declining value of welfare reinforced the declining value of work; they were complementary features of the same policy strategy that accompanied changes in the U.S. political economy.

Another dimension of the relationship between the economy and social policy revolves around efforts to *stabilize the marketplace.* This dimension takes two basic forms. In one form, social welfare systems include programs such as workers' compensation to protect individuals from work-related injuries. Funded by insurance that employers purchase, workers' compensation serves a dual function. By shielding employers from the huge costs of lawsuits, it reduces uncertainty. At the same time, by providing workers with another source of income, it shields them (and the economy) from the economically devastating consequences of an injury. Thus, in two ways, workers' compensation helps stabilize the marketplace.

Yet, the protection that social welfare offers to workers is even broader and more encompassing. In another critical function, *social welfare programs offer recipients some independence from the discipline of the marketplace.* If social welfare programs provide workers with an alternate source of income, they are not compelled to accept whatever wages employers offer. For example, if workers are receiving unemployment benefits, they can hold out for a job that is more suited to their talents, or one with better pay. From one perspective, a better match of talents and salary is an economic boon. From another perspective, however, the independence that social welfare provides helps explain why some employers criticize it so sharply.

Like many other dimensions of the relationship between social policy and the economy, this argument is curiously paradoxical. The paradox stems from the *role social welfare plays in raising business profits.* Social welfare programs raise profits by putting money in the hands of people who would otherwise be unable to sell a business or service. Just imagine hospital and doctors without Medicaid or Medicare; the lower rungs of the housing market without Housing Choice (Section 8 housing); or the food industry without the Supplemental Nutrition Assistance Program. In each instance, unless the government enhanced the purchasing capacity of recipients through these programs, the health care, housing, and agricultural sectors would all shrink to a fraction of their current size. Given this substantial economic benefit, how can we explain the apparent opposition of so many business people to these programs?

One answer to this question is that the beneficiaries of programs in one sector oppose benefits for the beneficiaries of programs in another. Real estate entrepreneurs might favor Housing Choice, but be concerned about the rise in health care costs, because increased spending in this area does not increase the profitability of their property. Hence, some opposition to social welfare spending within the business community is merely the result of inter-sectoral rivalry.

Yet, there is also a broader and more general reason. Although many business conservatives oppose social welfare for the independence it offers workers from the pressures of the marketplace, they relent when a program is designed to fit their specifications. In particular, they favor specifications that limit programs' generosity and ensure that whatever benefits they provide funnels greater profits to the business community. While some conservatives favor `small government' for philosophical reasons and do not have an immediate financial interest in this conflict, much of the current debate about social welfare spending is really a debate over the issue of whether a program will guarantee a sufficient profit to the provider of a benefit or service. In practice, this means that businesses will provide services as long as the government gives them enough money so that sellers do not distinguish too sharply between consumers who earned their money in the marketplace and consumers who can only purchase certain products because they receive social welfare.

A third explanation, which is more difficult to measure, reflects a desire to maintain certain class, gender, or race-based privileges, hierarchies, and social roles. The manufactured perception that the primary beneficiaries of the nation's social welfare policies are somehow "other" reinforces this desire. As discussed above, this perception exists even among many Americans who fail to acknowledge their own receipt of social welfare benefits, yet continue to believe that their taxes pay for programs only these "others" receive. [*See Chapters 4 and 5 this volume for further discussion of the role of race and gender in U.S. social policies.*]

TAX EXPENDITURES

The use of social welfare policies to increase profitability extends far beyond those who are the direct beneficiaries of these programs. When it is properly defined, a nation's social welfare system consists either of giving money or services to people, or allowing them to keep more of their income through provisions in the tax code. Called **tax expenditures**, these provisions are especially critical in the housing market. In 2016, deductions for local property taxes and the interest on home mortgages amounted to $112 billion, more than twice the $49.3 billion budget of the federal Department of Housing and Urban Development (Joint Committee on Taxation, 2015; HUD, 2016).

Because tax expenditures are less visible than direct social welfare expenditures such as rent subsidies, many beneficiaries think of them as their own money. Yet, if the interest on a homeowner's mortgage plus local property taxes comes to $10,000 annually, and if this family is in the 30 percent tax bracket, it will pay $3,000 less in taxes. The availability of this $250 a month subsidy could easily make the difference in deciding whether to own or rent a home.

Tax expenditures have been called the mansion subsidy because they are heavily biased towards wealthy people; households earning $250,000 get an average tax deduction of $5,460, while those with incomes of less than $40,000 get $91 annually (Sirota, 2012). Nevertheless, whether you own a mansion, or are struggling to make monthly mortgage payments, you are receiving a subsidy much like a direct welfare payment, and are benefiting from the boost social welfare provides to the overall economy. Critics of social welfare spending largely overlook this benefit or take it for granted as something they "deserve."

SPENDING ON PUBLIC INFRASTRUCTURE

Although *spending on public infrastructure* is even further removed from direct payments to individuals, it also belongs in any comprehensive list of social welfare functions. Admittedly, projects like dams, bridges, tunnels, and roadways are arguably not directly part of a nation's social welfare system, but many other forms of public infrastructure, such as parks, schools, libraries, and public housing projects, clearly are. In fact, legislation such as the 1937 Housing Act, the law that authorized the development of public housing projects, was specifically enacted to stimulate the construction industry. In this instance, housing was provided to workers who were temporarily unemployed on the condition that their construction helped to lift another important economic sector out of its doldrums.

Despite all the aid that is provided, it is indisputable that one of the main political and economic functions of social welfare is to *socialize the cost of maintaining the poor in poverty by distributing the expense among taxpayers.* As noted above, it is widely believed that social welfare programs cannot provide too much help, because if they did, they would erode the work ethic and violate the principle of less eligibility. Inevitably, the persistence of these beliefs determines how well social welfare recipients can be treated. If the conditions attached to these benefits create impediments to escaping poverty, then society must decide who will support people while they remain poor.

In this instance, the burden falls on taxpayers, who share the cost of keeping poor people in poverty. But unlike other economic functions of social welfare that either increase the productivity of the workforce (employment training programs, for example) or aid in **social reproduction** (such as health care) which helps to ensure the next generation of trained and healthy workers, this function is a pure social expense (Gough, 1979). When most poor people will not rise out of poverty, as research indicates increasingly is the case (Rank, Hirschl, & Foster, 2014), taxpayers bear the cost of insuring that they do not starve.

Ultimately, all of these economic functions have political consequences. A commitment to social provision offers an opportunity for constituency-building that often ties social welfare recipients to a particular political party—the Labor Party in Great Britain or, since the New Deal, the Democratic Party in the U.S. In addition, as Piven and Cloward (1971, 1995) famously argued, social provision has frequently been employed to induce political quiescence in times of social upheaval through a well-established pattern.

When poor people protest their conditions, policymakers expand social welfare provision until order is restored, when it is cut back again. This pattern occurred in the U.S. in the 1960s in response to urban unrest and welfare rights advocacy. Initially, welfare programs expanded, only to be attacked as the civil rights movement declined, and the perception grew that Great Society social programs were mostly intended to benefit poor African Americans. [*See Chapter 2 this volume for further discussion of this issue.*]

Over the past four decades, the primary political function of social welfare has been to provide a scapegoat for people who wanted to define themselves and their social position in opposition to the poor. Although wages have stagnated and the middle class has become increasingly economically vulnerable and insecure, many Americans continued to reassure themselves that despite their downward mobility, they were not poor. The maintenance of this illusion has helped conservatives increase their political power and influence, and prompted millions of Americans to vote against their economic interests as the results to date in the 2016 electoral process illustrate (Frank, 2004).

THE POLITICAL ECONOMY OF U.S. SOCIAL POLICY

The key to understanding the political economy of social policy in the United States is to dispose of the central myth that rationalizes it: that social welfare is inconsequential. Some proponents of this myth want simply to hack away at social welfare programs while others contend that any cutbacks demand a little more surgical precision. But by viewing social welfare programs solely as expenses that promote undesirable behaviors and attitudes, proponents of both positions accept the premise that the nation's social welfare system merely subtracts from the economy's overall health.

While social welfare programs constitute a major fiscal expense, the paradox is that they are a *necessary expense*, which simultaneously burdens and sustains the market economy. It constitutes a burden because it requires taxes to maintain poor people in poverty. Although the possibility of dispensing with these costs is always alluring, these expenditures are mostly a `pass-through' which help sustain the economy by ensuring profits in the sectors that transform common human needs such as food, housing, and health care into marketable commodities. In the absence of another mechanism to prop up these sectors, policymakers have been forced to piece together scarce resources in order to keep the economy afloat.

Most conventional analyses of the political economy of social welfare, however, ignore this dimension of its functions. In their view, the economic role of social welfare policy is simply to give money to poor people. This is an accurate, but incomplete explanation of its broader function. In the modern U.S. political economy, we only give money to poor people when the funds increase profit and reinforce the work ethic. Because this form of social welfare is so market-affirming, policymakers seem determined to override the multiple and conflicting functions of social welfare described above. One of these primary functions is social welfare's role in providing some independence from the marketplace. In today's environment, this leads to the following underlying principle: if money must be given to people in need, policies must be designed to ensure that it will be barely enough to help them survive.

SOCIAL JUSTICE AND THE POLITICAL ECONOMY OF U.S. SOCIAL POLICY

What constitutes social justice in the social policy arena is certainly a contentious topic (Reisch, 2010). Although some commentators might defend the current drift of social policy as a matter of economic or fiscal necessity, few would contend that the pursuit of social justice consists of defining bare and declining minimums. The difficulty is that determining what constitutes social justice is neither self-evident nor readily obtainable. In retrospect, it is clear that the apogee of the welfare state during the 1960s and early 1970s in the U.S. and Europe was but a moment in time, the product of a strong labor movement, unprecedented social activism, and a relatively stable industrial system. That moment will likely never return; if it does, it will come back in an entirely new form.

But what forms of social welfare will replace it? During the past three decades, social policies have been based on a **neoliberal** paradigm that prizes lower taxes, privatization, deregulation, and a focus on individual human capital development. This paradigm tries to resolve the tensions inherent in the provision of assistance by lopping off those elements of policy that conflict with the marketplace. Yet that marketplace, with all its hierarchy, inequality, and human costs, cannot possibly offer a path to the attainment of any plausible conception of social justice (Kotz, 2016). The success of recent social activism, such as the Black Lives Matter Movement and Senator Bernie Sanders' surprisingly strong showing in the 2016 Democratic Presidential nomination process, suggests that a growing number of Americans may well be allying themselves with this critique. They understand that the only plausible path towards greater social justice requires the creation of a welfare state with social policies that enhance democratic control over the economy and provide social supports irrespective of income. Rejecting the dominant neoliberal ideology, they see this political-economic model of social policy as the only one that would truly be worth replicating.

Discussion Questions

1. Choose a sector of the economy such as housing, food, or health care. How do social programs boost the profits in that sector, and what would happen to profits in that sector if those programs did not exist?
2. The text refers to the increasing dominance of finance capitalism. What are the characteristics of this form of capitalism and why is it so resistant to social welfare spending?
3. List three expenses or costs of social welfare policy. List three benefits of social welfare policy? How are they related. How do they conflict?
4. Do you think benefits should be targeted to poor people, or should they go to everyone irrespective of income? What are the advantages and disadvantages of these respective approaches?
5. Sketch out your vision of a just society. What specific role would social welfare policy play in achieving your vision?

Class Exercise

Designate one day to make a list of everything that you encounter that involves a social welfare component: the food you or clients bought, the road or bridge you drove on to get to school, the student loan that enables you to attend school, the housing you or your clients live in, etc. Combine your list with the lists that other students prepare. What would the U.S. economy look like if the items on your master list were simply taken away?

Recommended Readings

Alexander, M. (2010). *The new Jim Crow: Mass incarceration in the age of colorblindness*. New York: The New Press.

Baker, D. (2006). *The conservative nanny state*. Washington, DC: Center for Economic and Policy Research.

Blau, J. (2008). Income distribution. In T. Mizrahi and L. Davis (eds.) *Encyclopedia of social work*, (20th ed.), vol. 2 (pp. 455–459). New York: Oxford University Press.

Blau, J. (1989). Theories of the welfare state. *Social Service Review 63*(1), 26–38.

Collins, J. L., & Mayer, V. (2010). *Welfare reform and the race to the bottom in the low-wage labor market*. Chicago: University of Chicago Press.

Economic Policy Institute (2012). *The state of working America, 2012*. Washington, DC: Author. http://www.stateofworkingamerica.org/pages/about

Gough, I. (1979). *The political economy of social welfare*. London: Macmillan.

Henwood, D. *Left Business Observer* [periodical].

Mettler, S. (2011). *The submerged state: How invisible government programs undermine democracy*. Chicago: University of Chicago Press.

Piketty, T. (2014). *Capitalism in the twenty-first century*. Cambridge, MA: Belknap Press of Harvard University Press.

Soss, J., Fording; R. C.; & Schram, S. (2011). *Disciplining the poor: Neoliberal paternalism and the persistent power of race*. Chicago: University of Chicago Press.

Stiglitz, J. E. (2012) *The price of inequality: How today's divided society endangers our future*. New York: W.W. Norton.

Audio/Video Resources

Ferguson, C. (2010). *Inside job* (the 2010 Academic Award Winning Documentary on the financial meltdown).

McKay, A. (2015). *The big short*. http://www.imdb.com/title/tt1596363/ (Oscar-winning movie about the real estate collapse and subsequent financial melt-down

Moore, M. *Capitalism: A love story*. http://topdocumentaryfilms.com/capitalism-love-story/

Wolff, R. *Capitalism hits the fan*. http://www.capitalismhitsthefan.com/.

Websites

Bureau of the Census, http://census.gov

Center on Budget and Policy Priorities, http://www.cbpp.org/

Dollars & Sense, http://www.dollarsandsense.org/

Economic Policy Institute, http://www.epi.org/

United for a Fair Economy, http://www.faireconomy.org/

U.S. Bureau of Labor Statistics, http://bls.gov

References

Blau, J., with Abramovitz, M. (2014). *The dynamics of social welfare policy,* (4th ed.) New York: Oxford University Press.

Baker, D. (2006). *The conservative nanny state.* Washington, DC: Center for Economic and Policy Research.

Bureau of the Census (2016, February 29). *Statistics of U.S. business, all industries,* https://www.census.gov/econ/susb/index.html. Accessed April 4, 2016.

Bureau of the Census (2015, September). *Income, poverty, and health insurance, 2014.* https://www.census.gov/content/dam/Census/library/publications/2015/demo/p60-252.pdf. Accessed April 23, 2016.

Bureau of the Census (2015). *Historical income tables: Income inequality.* https://www.census.gov/hhes/www/income/data/historical/inequality. Accessed April 17, 2016.

Bureau of Labor Statistics (2011a), *Unemployment rate.* http//data.bls.gov/timeseries LNS14000000. Accessed August 29, 2011.

Bureau of Labor Statistics (2016a). *Unemployment rate.* http://data.bls.gov/timeseries/LNS14000000. Accessed April 4, 2016.

Bureau of Labor Statistics (2016b). *Total unemployed.* http://data.bls.gov/timeseries/LNS13327709. Accessed April 4, 2016.

Bureau of Labor Statistics (2016c, April 18). *Labor force statistics from the Current Population Survey.* http://data.bls.gov/timeseries/LNS12300000. Accessed April 118, 2016.

Center on Budget and Policy Priorities (2009, September 8). *Top 1 percent reaped two-thirds of income gains in last economic expansion.* http://www.cbpp.org/cms/index.cfm?fa=view&id=2908. Accessed August 27, 2011.

Center on Budget and Policy Priorities (2015, October 26). *A guide to statistics on historical trends in income inequality.* http://www.cbpp.org/research/poverty-and-inequality/a-guide-to-statistics-on-historical-trends-in-income-inequality. Accessed April 17, 2016.

CNNMoney (2014, April 4). The top 1% and what they pay. http://money.cnn.com/2014/04/04/pf/taxes/top-1-taxes/. Accessed April 17, 2016.

Congressional Budget Office (2016, March). *Budget.* https://www.cbo.gov/topics/budget. Accessed April 5, 2016.

Economic Policy Institute (2015). *Wage stagnation in nine charts.* http://www.epi.org/publication/charting-wage-stagnation/. Accessed April 23, 2016.

Economic Policy Institute (2016, April 1). Nominal wage tracker.http://www.epi.org/nominal-wage-tracker/#chart1. Accessed April 17, 2016.

Food Nutrition Service (2016a, April 8). *Supplemental Nutrition Action Programs, Number of persons participating.* http://www.fns.usda.gov/sites/default/files/pd/29SNAPcurrPP.pdf. Accessed April 18, 2016.

Food Nutrition Service (2016b, April 8). *Supplemental Nutrition Assistance Programs, Number of households participating.* http://www.fns.usda.gov/sites/default/files/pd/30SNAPcurrHH.pdf. Accessed April 18, 2016.

Frank, T. (2004). *What's the matter with Kansas.* New York: Metropolitan Books.

Galea, S. Tracy, M. Hoggatt, K. J., DiMaggio, C., & Karpati, A. (2011). Estimated deaths attributed to social factors in the United States. *American Journal of Public Health, 101* (8), 1456–1465.

Gans, H. (1995). *The war against the poor: The underclass and antipoverty policy.* New York: Basic Books.

Gough, I. (1979). *The political economy of social welfare.* London: Macmillan.

Henwood, D. (2010, November 24). What a damn mess. *Left Business Observer,* #130, 3.

House Ways and Means Committee (2000). *The 2000 Green Book.* Washington, DC: U.S. Government Printing Office, 390.

Inequality.Org. (nd). *Inequality and health.* http://inequality.org/inequality- health/. Accessed August 28, 2011.

HUD.GOV (2016, February 2). HUD releases proposed 2016 budget, http://portal.hud.gov/hudportal/HUD?src=/press/press_releases_media_advisories/2015/HUDNo_15-013. Accessed April 23, 2016.

Joint Committee on Taxation, Congress of the United States (2015, December 7). *Estimates of Federal tax expenditures for fiscal years 2015–2019.*https://www.jct.gov/publications.html?func=startdown&id=4857. Accessed April 23, 2016.

Katz, M. B. (2001). *The price of citizenship.* New York: Henry Holt.

Katznelson, I. (2005). *When Affirmative Action was white.* New York: W.W. Norton.

Kochhar, R. (2012, February 13). Labor force slows, Hispanic share grows. Washington, DC: Pew Research Center. http://www.pewsocialtrends.org/2012/02/13/labor-force-growth-slows-hispanic-share-grows-2/. Accessed February 13, 2012.

Kotz, D. M. (2016, January-February). All the king's horses: Neoliberal capitalism, its crisis, and what comes next. *Dollars and Sense* No. 322, 9–13.

Krugman, P., & Wells, R. (2011, July 14). The bust keeps getting bigger: Why? *New York Review of Books.* http://www.nybooks.com/articles/archives/2011/jul/14/busts-keep-getting-bigger-why/?pagination=false. Accessed February 11, 2012.

Make Wealth History (2014). *The corporations bigger than nations.* http://makewealthhistory.org/2014/02/03/the-corporations-bigger-than-nations/. Accessed March 13, 2016.

Mettler, S. (2011, September 20). Our hidden government benefits. *The New York Times,* A31.

National Conference of State Legislatures (2016, April 14). *State minimum wage chart.*http://www.ncsl.org/research/labor-and-employment/state-minimum-wage-chart.aspx. Accessed April 25, 2016.

Norton, M. I., & Ariely, D (2011). Building a better America: One wealth quintile at a time. *Perspectives on Psychological Science 6* (1), 9–12.

Oregon State (2015, June 19). *Minimum wage history.* http://oregonstate.edu/instruct/anth484/minwage.html. Accessed May 1, 2016.

Piven, F. F., & Cloward, R. (1971, 1995). *Regulating the poor: The functions of social welfare.* New York: Vintage.

Rank, M. R. (2004). *One nation, underprivileged: Why American poverty affects us all.* New York: Oxford University Press.

Rank, M.R., Hirschl, T.A., & Foster, K.A. (2014). *Chasing the American dream: Understanding what shapes our fortune.* New York: Oxford University Press.

Reisch, M. (2010). Defining social justice in a socially unjust world. In Birkenmaier, J., Cruce, A., Wilson, R. J., Curley, J., Burkemper, E., & Stretch, J. (Eds.). *Educating for social justice: Transformative experiential learning* (pp. 11–28). Chicago: Lyceum Books.

Sirota, D. (2012, December 14) End the mansion subsidy. *In These Times*. http://inthesetimes.com/article/14307/homeownership_support_shouldnt_be_a_mansion_subsidy, December 14, 2012. Accessed April 23, 2016.

Social Security Administration (2015, June). *Social Security fact sheet 2015*. https://www.ssa.gov/news/press/factsheets/basicfact-alt.pdf. Accessed April 23, 2016.

Skocpol, T. (1993). *Protecting soldiers and mothers: The political origins of social policy in the United States.* Cambridge, MA: Harvard University Press.

Snyder, B. (2015, June 6). 9 facts about Walmart that will surprise you. http://fortune.com/2015/06/06/walmart-facts/. Accessed March 13, 2016

Wal-Mart (February 29, 2016). Our story. http://corporate.walmart.com/our-story/our-locations. Accessed April 4, 2016.

Weissmann, J. (2013, March 5). How Wall Street devoured America. *The Atlantic.* http://www.theatlantic.com/business/archive/2013/03/how-wall-street-devoured-corporate-america/273732/. Accessed April 4, 2016.

Wolff, E. N. (2014, December). Household wealth trends in the United States, 1962–2013: What happened in the Great Recession? National Bureau of Economic Research, http://papers.nber.org/tmp/12906-w20733.pdf. Accessed April 17, 2016.

Suggested Graphics

http://billmoyers.com/2015/01/05/top-10-charts-2014/ ten charts on income inequality

http://www.americanprogress.org/issues/2011/01/te_012611.html on the mortgage deduction

http://www.fns.usda.gov/ops/snap-community-characteristics, on SNAP usage by Congressional district

http://www.pewsocialtrends.org/2009/09/03/recession-turns-a-graying-office-grayer/2/ [rising female workforce participation/gender changes in the U.S. labor market]

http://www.cbpp.org/research/economy/chart-book-the-legacy-of-the-great-recession, a book of charts illustrating the economic effects of the Great Recession

Credits

4

SOCIAL POLICY AND THE RACIAL REGULATION OF PEOPLE OF COLOR

Jerome H. Schiele, DSW

INTRODUCTION

A consistent observation in the social policy literature is that social policies often exert a social control function. From this perspective, social policies have regulatory intentions and consequences that seek to monitor and influence the behavior of those deemed socially deviant or politically threatening (Abramovitz, 1999; Day, 2006; Piven & Cloward, 1995; Reisch & Andrews, 2002). They are viewed as mechanisms to impose the cultural norms and mores of the dominant group or groups onto those who engage in nonconformity. This nonconformity can be expressed in both subtle and overt ways that challenge the cultural oppression of ruling elites and those who endorse this orthodoxy. Although the benevolent or social treatment aspect of social policies are also acknowledged, several writers believe that policymakers' concern over regulating the lives of deviant individuals and groups often takes priority (Blau with Abramovitz, 2014; Day, 2006; Gil, 1998; Quadagno, 1994). [*See also Chapter 13 in this volume.*]

The focus on the social control or regulatory functions of social policies tends to highlight social class and gender domination as the primary forms of inequality in the United States (Neubeck & Cazenave, 2001; Schiele, 2011; Ward, 2005). Social class inequality receives attention primarily because of the heavy influence of conflict-oriented theories in social policy research that take their lead from Marx and Engels' critique of the political-economy of capitalism. From this perspective, the poor are exploited for their labor, marginalized for their conspicuous deviation from cultural norms, and punished for their seeming rejection of the Protestant work ethic.

Gender inequality is considered important because of the enormous success of feminist thinkers in demonstrating patriarchy's role in suppressing the power and potential of women. The traditional public/private division of work roles places women at risk of being economically dependent on men and vulnerable to additional social and political consequences in a society that privileges men (Abramovitz, 1999; bell hooks, 2000). The inordinate attention to social class and gender inequality has led some to suggest that social policy analysis and research is guided considerably by a class and gender-based interpretative framework (Neubeck & Cazenave, 2001; Quadagno, 1994; Schiele, 2011; Ward, 2005). [*See also Chapter 5 in this volume.*]

Although the attention devoted to social class and gender is legitimate, race and racism appear to garner less consideration. The principal shortcoming of the social policy literature is not that it ignores racism but rather that racial inequality is usually understood through the prism of a class-centered or gender-centered perspective (Neubeck & Cazenave, 2001; Schiele, 2011). Too often in social policy circles, racism is conceived as a consequence of the political economy of capitalism or as a corresponding injustice with other forms of oppression such as gender. For example, in their book, *The Dynamics of Social Welfare Policy*, Blau with Abramovitz (2014) conceive racism and racial inequality as being subsumed under what they refer to as "three longstanding opposing political traditions—conservatism, liberalism, and radicalism" (p.122), and a fourth tradition of feminism. Throughout their text, racism is explained within the context of these broader class-based and gender-based ideologies. They give racism considerable attention, but do not present it as a stand alone ideology equal to the four political traditions they discuss.

When racism is not explained through a class or gender-based framework, its treatment is still overshadowed by other issues or perspectives. In Karger and Stoesz's *American Social Welfare Policy* (2013), the coverage of racism is primarily confined to two of their 18 chapters, a chapter on discrimination and one on poverty. Their approach to social policy is a "pluralistic" one in which an examination of the voluntary nonprofit, governmental, and corporate sectors of social welfare services is given foremost attention. However, little effort is aimed at applying this pluralistic approach to the problem of racism.

What is often missing, therefore, from the social policy literature is a racism-centered framework that places race at the center of its social policy analysis. A racism-centered perspective allows a more in-depth focus of the role race has played in the formulation and consequences of social policies, and it helps explain why people of color relative to non-Hispanic whites have disproportionately experienced injustices in the U.S. It furthers allows a more specific application of the social control model of social policy analysis to people of color so that the racial regulatory features of social policies can be more thoroughly investigated.

This chapter applies a racism-centered perspective of social policy analysis to demonstrate why and how these policies have racially regulated people of color. It examines two forms of racism—old style and new style—and uses these methods to highlight racism's role in the social policy regulation of people of color. Finally, the chapter offers some ideas to speculate about the future of racism's effects on social policy development.

WHITE SUPREMACY AND RACIAL REGULATION

Critical to an understanding of a racism-centered perspective is that white supremacy (i.e., white racial domination) is a chief motive of social policy development and implementation. Neubeck and Cazenave (2001) conceptualize this form of oppression as "European Americans' systematic exercise of domination over racially subordinate groups" (p. 23). They further contend that from a racism-centered perspective, the state becomes a racialized state and "...is the political arm of white racial hegemony" (p.23). Here, the state is assumed to protect and promote the political, economic, and cultural interests of whites relative to people of color. Walters (2003) refers to this white bias in state affairs as "white nationalism," and argues that a major outcome of this form of nationalism is "policy racism" (p. 250). Policy racism, according to Walters (2003), produces a racialized ideology that institutionalizes racism within all branches of government.

Schiele (2011) contends that the practice of white supremacy is guided by characterizations that marginalize and deny the human worth and dignity of people of color. Rooted in the historical conquest, domination, or enslavement of people of color, these characterizations essentially had the intent of dehumanizing people of color to achieve perpetual racial subjugation. The characterizations are as follows: (1) the notion that people of color were dominated by their emotions and that reasoning was beyond their ability; thus, people of color were thought to be intellectually inferior to whites; (2) because they were assumed to be dominated by their emotions, people of color were characterized as sub-human and immoral; and (3) these characterizations of intellectual and moral inferiority were also extended to describe the culture of people of color as "uncivilized" (for more elaboration of these beliefs, see Jefferson, 1998/1782; Gould, 1981; Guthrie, 1998; Jackson, 1830; Thomas & Sillen, 1972).

These characterizations provided the political and intellectual justification for the mistreatment and discrimination of people of color by many of the formative social policies in the U.S. In other words, they helped justify the "social control" or regulation of people of color through social policies. Moreover, this social control paradigm conceives people of color as deviants and threats to the cultural, economic, and political order. As deviant groups, they are believed to threaten the social order in five important ways: (1) by not successfully adopting what are considered essential American cultural values and norms; (2) by being an economic drain on society because of their excessive dependence on the public dole; (3) by engaging disproportionately in criminal acts, especially violent street crimes; (4) by their anger and resentment toward the broader society, which could proliferate into organized resistance efforts; and (5) by their reproductive behavior and birth rates, which could generate undesirable demographic shifts and political dislocations. Thus, socially controlling the behavior of people of color would help guarantee that they would not jeopardize the political, economic, and cultural domination whites had over the American landscape (Feagin, 2000; Zinn, 2000). The social control feature of social policies as they pertain to people of color can be understood as *racial regulation*.

Racial regulation, which is the material outcome of white supremacy, seeks to ensure that people of color continue to disproportionately experience stigmatization and subjugation. Racial regulation also is manifested externally and internally. Examples of external regulation are controlling people of color's mobility, civil rights, employment, family structure, education, reproductive capacities, and health care.

Internal regulation results from the ineffectiveness of social welfare policies in significantly reducing and eliminating the disproportional stigmatization and subjugation that people of color experience. This ineffectiveness fosters a kind of internal regulation of human aspirations and possibility that places people of color at risk of accepting marginalized self-definitions, or what some refer to as *internalized oppression* (Alleyne, 2005; Padilla, 2004; Young, 1990).

Racial regulation, therefore, is the primary concern of a racism-centered social policy analysis. This racism-centered framework speaks to the high-risk status of people of color who disproportionately experience the pain of injustice and inequality. It helps explain why people of color have been historically over-represented among the nation's poor and vulnerable, and it asserts that regardless of social class and gender, people of color collectively remain vulnerable relative to whites or European-Americans.

A racism-centered framework, however, also acknowledges the differential vulnerability that occurs *within* racial groups based on social class, gender, religion, and other forms of social distinction. Nonetheless, it posits that racism's legacy in the United States has been so extensive, entrenched, and normalized that within-racial group vulnerabilities are often overshadowed and even aggravated by the persistent production of between-racial group inequality. It is this between-racial group inequality—specifically inequality in how the state fosters differential treatment by race—that constitutes the thrust of a racism-centered perspective of social policy analysis. The system of white supremacy, therefore, essentially shields whites from the racial harassment promoted by social policies that too often prevent people of color from expressing their vast positive potential and diminish their overall life experience and well-being.

SOCIAL POLICIES AND RACIAL REGULATION

White supremacy has exerted subtle and overt manifestations in the history of the United States, and social policy development and implementation have not been immune from these expressions. Both overt and concealed racism are ways in which social policies have racially regulated the lives of people of color. Overt racism tended to be more popular in the past while concealed racism appears to describe the contemporary social scene more accurately.

Old style or overt racism was a system of racial oppression expressed in highly explicit and conspicuous forms (Bobo, Kluegel, & Smith, 1997; Bonilla-Silva, 2001). In this system, racism was legal and people of color were regulated through overt and often hostile means of racial control. People of color were formally barred from the rights and privileges of citizenship, and they frequently were victims of both mob and state-sponsored violence. Additionally, justifications to explain racial inequality and oppression were grounded specifically in messages of white superiority. People of color were openly represented as biogenetically, intellectually, and morally inferior to whites. For example, in responding to a query as to whether enslaved Africans should be emancipated, Thomas Jefferson (1998/1782) advanced the explicit notion of black inferiority:

> I advance it therefore as a suspicion only, that the blacks, whether originally a distinct race, or made distinct by time and circumstances, are inferior to the whites in the endowments both of body and mind. It is not against experience for men to possess different qualifications. Will not a lover of natural history then, one suppose, that different species of the same genus, or

varieties of the same species, who views the gradations in all the races of animals with the eye of philosophy, excuse an effort to keep those in the department of man as distinct as nature has formed them? This unfortunate difference of colour, and perhaps of faculty, is a powerful obstacle to the emancipation of these people.

This presumed inferiority gave whites the right, indeed the obligation, to regulate and subordinate people of color without equivocation. Because the consequence of this old style racism was overt racial injustice, the period in which it was applied may be characterized as the era of "oppression by terror."

Social policies in this era clearly intended to control and/or restrict the freedom of people of color, and were unapologetic in protecting the sociocultural, political, and economic interests of whites. Their interpretation of race and racial distinctions was fixed and hierarchical. As whites were considered at the zenith of this racial hierarchy, these policies reinforced Jefferson's (1998/1782) vision of the U.S. as an exceptional nation established for the advancement of a superior, white civilization.

OLD-STYLE RACIAL REGULATION

There are several examples of how old style or overt forms of racial regulation shaped social policy development and implementation. One example was the practice of creating boarding schools for Native Americans, especially Native American children. These schools were the product of the 1819 Indian Civilization Act that appropriated $10,000 a year for Native American education (Evans-Campbell & Campbell, 2011). The purpose of these schools was to re-socialize Native American children to enable them to assimilate successfully into mainstream society and incorporate the values and attitudes of European American culture. To achieve this goal, Indian children were forcibly removed from their homes and relocated, often far away, and placed in an environment where there were few or no Native American adult role models (Evans-Campbell & Campbell, 2011). The schools' curriculum was predicated on the notion that the values and practices of Native Americans were uncivilized and antithetical to the progress and manifest destiny of the white race (Adams, 1995). It emphasized learning English and internalizing the precepts of European American culture. The intent to extinguish Native American language and customs was so intense that at one boarding school the motto was "Kill the Indian and save the man" (Limb & Baxter, 2011).

Although funding for the Indian Civilization Act was discontinued in 1873, the sentiment behind efforts to extinguish Native customs and adopt European American culture did not disappear (Evans-Campbell & Campbell, 2011). Indeed, funds to support Native American re-education exceeded 3 million dollars by 1900 (Coleman, 2007), and, by 1930, almost half of Native American children had entered boarding or industrial schools (U.S. Department of Health and Human Services, 2001).

A second example of overt racial regulation of people of color through social policy development was the forced incarceration of Japanese Americans brought about by President Franklin Delano Roosevelt's Executive Order 9066. After the Japanese bombed and destroyed the U.S. base at Pearl Harbor, Hawaii in December 1941, many Americans, including leaders of the federal government, believed that Japanese Americans were a threat to homeland security (Takahashi, 2011). Succumbing to this belief, President Roosevelt issued Executive Order 9066 in 1942. This order mandated that Japanese Americans on the entire West Coast of the United States be restricted in their mobility. Its stated objective was to prevent a threat to the U.S. military and homeland security. As a result, the majority of Japanese Americans in this

Figure 4.1 The Carlisle Indian Industrial School (1879–1918) was a boarding school for American Indians.

region were forcefully removed from their homes and imprisoned in camps operated by the U.S. military (Takahashi, 2011). In a controversial 1944 decision, *Korematsu v. United States*, the Supreme Court upheld the constitutionality of Roosevelt's executive order.

There was also, however, an unspoken economic motive for this removal that focused on the concern many whites on the West Coast had about the growing economic power and prowess Japanese Americans had achieved in California and other Western states. Japanese and other Asian Pacific Islander Americans (from China, Korea, and the Philippines) had made significant economic inroads in such areas as farming, fishing, and small business ownership. Their growing economic influence was accompanied by an increase in their population; by the early 1940s, almost 100,000 Japanese Americans lived in California alone (Takahashi, 2011).

During the late 19th and early 20th centuries, concerns about what many political leaders called the "yellow peril" led to the passage of a number of discriminatory laws which restricted immigration from Asia and seriously diminished the mobility and civil rights of Japanese and other Asian Americans (Takahashi, 2011). One of the most significant policies was the Chinese Exclusion Act of 1882, the first major piece of legislation that restricted immigration into the United States. The Japanese attack on Pearl

Figure 4.2 Japanese American child enroute from Los Angeles with his parents to Owens Valley concentration camp under U.S. Army war emergency order.

Harbor provided a convenient rationale to further restrict the civil rights of Japanese Americans by forcing them into concentration camps. The racism underlying these policies is illustrated by contrasting the treatment of Japanese Americans with the treatment of other ethnic groups at the time. No other group at war with the U. S., including German and Italian citizens, was compelled to relocate to military concentration camps, although their numbers in the U.S. were considerably larger and the influence of German Bund organizations had grown since the mid-1930s, particularly on the East Coast.

The racial segregation laws of the Jim Crow South, which created an American form of apartheid, are another example of the overt regulatory features of U.S. social policy. These laws were instituted in the late 19th century after the emancipation of African American slaves in the 1860s and the collapse of post-Civil War Reconstruction during the mid-1870s (Foner, 1988). Their objective was to eliminate the political, economic, and social power African Americans had obtained in the period immediately following the Civil War.

Through the passage of the 1866 Civil Rights Act and the 13th, 14th, and 15th amendments to the U.S. Constitution, African Americans had gained civil rights protections and political power in the South that had been unheard of during their long period of enslavement. However, the Hayes-Tilden compromise of 1877, in which Northern leaders agreed to remove the federal troops who occupied the South and provided military protection for African Americans since 1865 in return for Southern support of the election of Rutherford Hayes as President (Woodward, 2001), ended this short-lived era of Black progress. The 1896

Plessy v. Ferguson Supreme Court ruling which upheld the "separate but equal" doctrine dealt the final legal blow to African American equality (Moss & Franklin, 2000; Woodward, 2001).

This landmark case originated in 1892 when Homer Plessy, who was biracial, took a seat in a "whites only" train car in Louisiana. After refusing to move to a car reserved for African Americans, Plessy was arrested for violating an 1890 Louisiana law that mandated segregated railroad accommodations. His lawsuit was a planned test case sponsored by a citizens' organization seeking to overturn the law (Hoffer, 2012).

The Louisiana judge who presided over the case, John H. Ferguson, ruled against Plessy contending that the railroad accommodations law was reasonable given the state's customs and traditions. Plessy and the citizens' organization appealed the ruling to the U.S. Supreme Court, which, in 1896, upheld the lower court's decision. In its majority opinion, the Court ruled that the lower court ruling did not violate the Equal Protection Clause of the 14th amendment and that separate accommodations were constitutional as long as they were equal in quality (Hoffer, 2012). Through the "separate but equal" doctrine, racial segregation between blacks and whites was affirmed and its practice was extended, leading to the disenfranchisement, marginalization, and racial harassment of Black Southerners. The decision also sanctioned racial injustice by legally prohibiting African Americans from receiving and benefiting from public services that were largely paid by their taxes. [*See Chapter 10 in this volume for further discussion of the impact of the Equal Protection Clause of the 14*th *amendment on social policy development.*]

The Jim Crow laws sanctioned by the *Plessy v. Ferguson* case were essentially formal structures of racial exclusion and separation. African Americans were separated from whites in many areas of social and economic life, including "courtrooms and cemeteries, in depots and trains, in hospitals and streetcars" (Carlton-LaNey, 2011, p.44). African Americans also were excluded from colleges and universities, hotels, restaurants, neighborhoods, restrooms, parks, charitable organizations, health care facilities, and many other public and private accommodations (Moss & Franklin, 2000; Woodward, 2001).

In addition, they were barred from participation in publically-sponsored social welfare organizations, including those established in Northern cities. For example, in Chicago, African American dependent children were restricted from orphanages that served white children (O'Donnell, 1994) and were not allowed to participate in settlement houses, such as Hull House (Lasch-Quinn, 1994). Such restrictions compelled African American reformers and community organizers to establish Black social welfare institutions that were based on the philosophy of Black self-help and racial uplift (Carlton-LaNey, 2001; Schiele, Jackson, & Fairfax, 2005). However, when African American reformers in Chicago attempted to establish Black-operated child welfare institutions, white social reformers worked to undermine them by maintaining that African Americans could not properly manage programs and money (O'Donnell, 1994), reflecting attitudes that reinforced the belief in Black intellectual inferiority.

Besides exclusion and segregation, the *Plessy* decision also provided the legal rationale underlining the racial terrorism of the Ku Klux Klan, which peaked in the early to mid-1920s (Moss & Franklin, 2000; Woodward, 2001). The Jim Crow laws sanctioned by the *Plessy* decision created a hostile social milieu that allowed mob and state-sponsored violence against African Americans to be condoned and even tolerated. The Rosewood Florida massacre of 1923 is just one example of this form of racial terrorism. In this massacre, a mob of white men burned every home in Rosewood, an all-Black town, in an attempt to locate a Black man who allegedly had raped a white woman. Although public safety officials were aware of the mob's intentions, they did not attempt to stop the violence or arrest the perpetrators (D'Orso, 1996). The Rosewood incident is significant today because in May 1994, nine survivors of the massacre were collectively awarded $2.1 million by the Florida State Legislature to compensate for damages they suffered (see Anonymous, 1994, 1995; Florida House of Representatives, 1994; Jerome & Sider, 1995).

The *Plessy* decision also had long-term deleterious consequences for African American economic development and public health conditions. Because of the restrictions placed on their employment, African Americans often held the lowest paid, least skilled, and most dangerous jobs (Moss & Franklin, 2000). Receiving less compensation for more perilous work conditions produced numerous labor injustices for African American workers and exacerbated the extreme poverty of African American families, which the post-Civil War system of sharecropping played a significant role in creating.

Consequently, as late as 1959, one of the last years of legal racial segregation, over half (54.9%) of African American families lived in poverty (U.S. Census Bureau, 2010). Perilous working conditions and extensive entrenched poverty also contributed to public health disparities that have only recently received public attention (Hoffman, 2001). For example, in 1900 in Richmond, Virginia, the death rate from diseases such as typhoid fever and tuberculosis among Blacks was about twice that of whites and Black children were nearly twice as likely to die in infancy as white babies (Hoffman, 2001).

A final example of the overt racial regulatory character of social policies affecting people of color was the white westward expansion into Texas, which was once a part of Mexico. This expansion demonstrated disregard for the Mexican people who had lived there for generations and for their land laws. The following remarks by Stephen F. Austin, who is considered the founder of Anglo-American Texas and after whom the state's capital, Austin, is named, demonstrate that this disregard was unequivocally motivated by the belief in white superiority: "[My] sole and only desire," Austin proclaimed, was to "redeem [Texas] from the wilderness—to settle it with an intelligent, honorable and enterprising people" (cited in Takaki, 1993, p.174). Austin also urged whites to settle Texas "each man with his rifle," "passports or no passports," so that the "mongrel Spanish-Indian and Negro race" could be subjugated (cited in Takaki, 1993, p.174).

Once whites had conquered Texas, they enacted several laws that discriminated against Mexicans (McWilliams & Meier, 1990; Takaki, 1993). These included poll taxes that limited their political participation; new land tax systems that placed Mexicans at risk of losing their property; and a caste labor system that placed whites in management and foreman roles and Mexicans in hazardous laborer positions (McWilliams & Meier, 1990; Takaki, 1993). These policies placed the Mexican population at risk of harm, humiliation, and impoverishment.

Indeed, after the Anglo-Texans defeated the Mexican army under General Santa Anna in 1836 and established Texas as an independent territory, many Mexicans who remained experienced overt hostility and consistent threats of violence (Vogel, 2004). The 1848 Treaty of Guadalupe Hidalgo that ended hostilities between Mexico and the United States required Mexico to relinquish over half of its territory (what is now present-day Arizona, California, New Mexico, and parts of Colorado, Nevada, and Utah) and for the U.S. to provide fifteen million dollars in compensation for war-related damage to Mexican property (Griswold del Castillo, 1992). The Treaty also guaranteed protection of the civil and property rights for Mexicans who chose to remain in the new acquired U.S. territory.

Most of the treaty's provisions, however, were ignored by the United States government (Griswold del Castillo, 1992). The rights of Mexicans living in these territories were not protected and much of their land was taken from them by either deceptive legal strategies or outright theft. Moreover, the violence against Mexicans and the exploitation of their labor that existed prior to the treaty continued (Griswold del Castillo, 1992). As in the 1877 Haynes-Tilden compromise noted above, the subtext of the Treaty of Guadalupe Hidalgo was the protection and advancement of white supremacy.

NEW-STYLE RACIAL REGULATION

Since the passage of major civil rights legislation in the 1960s, overt strategies to control and manipulate people of color, which spawned unambiguous messages of marginalization and inferiority, have been increasingly rivaled by subtle, insidious, and diffused schemes of subjugation (Bobo, Kluegel, & Smith, 1997; Collins, 1998; Kambon, 1998; Marable, 1996). The new civil rights legislation and the social changes it produced rendered old forms of overt racial subjugation antiquated. Although concealed, these new methods continue the control white Americans have over U.S. society's political, economic, and cultural institutions (Bobo, Kluegel, & Smith, 1997; Kambon, 1998; Marable, 1996).

In response, many people today use the concept of "color-blind racism" to characterize the concealed racism in contemporary society. Bonilla-Silva (2001, 2003) defines this term as "racism without racists." In this new age, racism is denied and those who benefit from its continuation boldly plead "not guilty." Although many of the institutional structures that support racism remain, the inequality these institutions produce is explained by other, seemingly non-racial factors. The high homicide rate among young African American males, for example, is explained as a problem created by too many absent and irresponsible Black fathers. Latino unemployment is thought to be the result of Hispanic indolence and the failure of persons of color to be promoted in places of employment is explained by the lack of a strong work ethic.

Color-blind racism also restricts society's understanding of racism to overt forms of aggression and discrimination (Bonilla-Silver, 2001, 2003). In this formulation, racism is never subtle or institutional; it occurs only through explicitly legal and state-sponsored methods of terror. Once these formal expressions of hate have been publically denounced and legally prohibited, proponents of color-blind racism refuse to acknowledge racism's relics, long-term effects, or its ability to mutate. Because people of color and whites can now legally engage in social integration, there is no longer the need to acknowledge and rely upon the old racial distinctions of the past. The need to identify and speak of people of color in racial or color terms is obsolete, for to do so is now labeled "racist." The reliance on color-blindness in this era of concealed racism suggests that "oppression by denial" is its *modus operandi*.

New style racism's role in social policy formulation is reflected in three recent developments: (a) welfare reform in the 1990s; (b) immigration policy since the 1990s and the proposals from 2016 presidential candidate, Donald Trump; and (c) the 2013 Supreme Court ruling on voting rights.

THE CONTRACT WITH AMERICA AND WELFARE REFORM

The 1994 Congressional election that propelled Republicans into the majority in the U.S. House of Representatives was a significant political victory. A primary reason for Republicans' ability to take over the House was the creation and successful marketing of their "Contract with America," developed by new Speaker, Newt Gingrich (R-GA) and other Congressional leaders.

A chief component of the Contract was the Personal Responsibility Act, which originally sought, among other things, to eliminate Aid to Families with Dependent Children (AFDC) that had been established by the 1935 Social Security Act, turn welfare responsibilities over to the states in the form of block grants, deny teenage mothers assistance, and place time limits on the receipt of assistance. The Personal Responsibility Act went through several Congressional revisions and was vetoed twice by President Bill Clinton until a compromise bill was developed. On August 22, 1996, under political pressure to demonstrate his commitment to welfare reform in order to enhance his chances for re-election (Reuter, 1996), President Clinton signed the revised Act, the Personal Responsibility and Work Opportunity Reconciliation Act (PRWORA), into law. The Act's prominent features included the elimination of the Aid to Families with Dependent Children (AFDC) and the Job Opportunity and Basic Skills Training (JOBS) programs, the replacement of these programs with block grants to states with federally approved Temporary Assistance Programs for indigent families with minor children, and its five-year restriction on assistance.

One way to understand the effects of racism on welfare reform is to examine the racially disproportionate representation among AFDC recipients before the program was eliminated and how the politics of racial imaging contributed to its demise. Before the passage of PRWORA, African Americans and whites constituted about the same percentage of AFDC recipients. In spite of arguments that suggested the difference between Black and white enrollments in AFDC was negligible, African Americans were overrepresented as AFDC recipients and whites were underrepresented in terms of their respective proportions of the population. Although African Americans represented only 11.8% of the overall U.S. population in 1993 (U.S. Bureau of the Census, 1994), they represented over three times (39.0%) that percentage among AFDC recipients in the same year (U.S. House Committee on Ways & Means, 1993). In comparison, while whites of non-Hispanic origin represented about three-fourths (74.8%) of the overall U.S. population in 1993 (U.S. Bureau of the Census, 1994), they only constituted about two-fifths (38.1%) of AFDC recipients in that year (U.S. House Committee on Ways & Means, 1993).

The point here is not to belittle the experiences of white Americans who suffered economic deprivation, but rather to demonstrate the lack of parity between African Americans and whites as AFDC recipients and thereby highlight the significance of race in U.S. society and social policy. In 1994, several explanations were advanced to explain the disproportionate representation of African Americans in the AFDC rolls, but the arguments used to justify PRWORA focused on the high rate of out-of-wedlock births among African American women, especially teenagers (Personal Responsibility and Work Opportunity Reconciliation Act of 1996). [*See Chapter 13 this volume for further discussion of welfare reform.*]

As noted above, in absolute numbers, former AFDC recipients were as likely to be white than Black. The question, therefore, is what were the reasons that African American families were more frequently portrayed in the media as recipients of AFDC? A racism-centered perspective would contend that since race is one of the defining attributes through which resources and power have been distributed historically in the United States (Schram, Soss, & Fording, 2003; Jansson, 2012), vested interests have developed that are predicated on the belief that the provision of more resources to African American families poses a threat to the economic and political status of European American families (Bell, 1992; Quadagno, 1994). The politics of race can best survive if there is an apparatus through which attitudes that support racial fear and conflict can be maintained. Probably one of the most effective instruments to achieve this goal is television imagery. Because television has multi-perceptual appeal, when compared to other media, it may have the greatest potential to shape images necessary to continue public attitudes, perceptions, and behaviors that foster economic and racial disparities (Kellner, 1990).

In this light, the image of African Americans as the primary recipients of AFDC can be construed as a media strategy targeted at maintaining and strengthening racial fear and hostility in an era of increasing racial scapegoating and anti-tax sentiments. By the middle 1990s, these anti-tax sentiments had been fueled in part by the Reagan Administration's effectiveness at disparaging "big" government and increased spending on social programs, and the ripple effects of California's Proposition 13 that reduced property tax rates on homes, businesses, and farms (Jansson, 2012). Furthermore, since the majority of Americans are non-Hispanic whites, and because the economic security of many of these families has been intensified by recent trends of fallen wages, the deindustrialization of the U.S. economy, and the relocation of American companies overseas to reduce production costs, racial scapegoating is one way that European Americans can explain their plight and justify reductions in their income taxes (Cohen, 1996; Hacker, 1992). [*See Chapter 3 this volume for further discussion of these issues.*]

Another political factor underlying welfare reform is that many of its leading proponents were Southern Republicans—the House Speaker, the Chairman of the House Ways & Means Committee, and the House Majority Leader. Before the modern civil rights movement changed the political landscape of the South, they probably would have been Southern Democrats, often called Dixiecrats. Consistent with the Dixiecratic slogan of *states' rights*, the push for welfare reform, especially by Southern Republicans, can be seen as an attempt to return to the days when state and local authorities dominated African Americans more autonomously by limiting "outside" federal scrutiny of their health, welfare, and educational policies and institutions.

IMMIGRATION POLICY AND DONALD TRUMP'S PROPOSALS

Another prominent example of racial regulation through social policy in the era of color-blind racism is the focus on immigration policy. Because the largest number of these immigrants is Latino/a, much of the discourse on immigration policy has centered on this population. In a comprehensive assessment of how immigration policy serves as racial regulation, León and Ortega (2011) demonstrated how three policies passed in 1996—the Illegal Immigration and Reform and Responsibility Act, the Antiterrorism and Effective Death Penalty Act, and the Personal Responsibility and Work Opportunity Reconciliation Act—created a combative and unwelcoming political, economic, and social milieu for Hispanic immigrants. The first two policies created several impediments that made immigration generally and undocumented immigration specifically more arduous in the United States. León and Ortega assert

> The intent [of this immigration legislation] was to strengthen border enforcement, make it more difficult to gain asylum, establish income requirements for sponsors of legal immigrants, streamline deportation procedures, remove procedural legal protections for migrants who lacked documents, and raise penalties for people who aid or employ people who lack documents (pp. 240–241).

The Personal Responsibility and Work Opportunity Reconciliation (PRWORA) of 1996, discussed above, also denied unauthorized immigrants important social and health services and it rendered legal aliens ineligible for most means-tested public benefits for their first five years of residence.

León and Ortega contend that in combination these policies produced the following consequences: (1) the exploitation of Hispanic labor; (2) the regulation of Hispanic individual and group liberty; and (3) increased risk of Hispanics being victimized by hate crimes. They maintain that the fear of deportation these policies created combined with the pressure to meet the economic needs of their families place many undocumented Hispanic workers at risk of being exploited in the workplace, primarily through unfair employment practices, very low wages, and long hours. Many employers use the fear of deportation to maintain workplace control and maximize their profits. If workers complain, employers can rely on a large reserve of unemployed, undocumented workers who would easily replace disgruntled employees (White, 2012).

Hispanic workers are also exploited by exposure to deleterious work conditions because they tend to be employed in jobs that demand considerable physical labor and are hazardous to their health, such as the construction industry. A survey conducted by the Southern Poverty Law Center (2009) revealed that 32 percent of Hispanic workers reported being injured on-the-job, but only 37 percent of those injured

Figure 4.3 Many undocumented workers are paid less than the minimum wage for their labor and endure unhealthy working conditions.

reported receiving proper medical treatment. León and Ortega (2011) cite a study that found that 80 percent of Mexicans are more likely to die in the workplace than other U.S. residents (see Pritchard, 2004).

In addition, León and Ortega point out that the individual and group liberties of Hispanics are restricted by increased racial profiling and incarceration. Racial profiling is "any police-initiated action that relies on the race, ethnicity, or national origin rather than the behavior of an individual or information that leads the police to a particular individual who has been identified as being, or having been, engaged in criminal activity" (Ramirez, McDevitt, & Farrell, 2000, p. 3). León and Ortega contend that the racial profiling of Hispanics has been enhanced by the increasing use of local police officials to enforce federal immigration laws.

A particularly controversial law is Arizona's SB-1070, which was signed by Governor Jan Brewer in April 2010. The law gives police broad discretion to detain and arrest individuals who are suspected of being undocumented immigrants (Archibold, 2010). Law enforcement officials are required to determine the immigration status of these individuals and can arrest suspected undocumented immigrants when they have probable cause that they have engaged in a criminal activity. Additionally, the law makes it a crime for immigrants to fail to register with U.S. immigration officials and prohibits undocumented immigrants from working.

In 2011, however, the 9th U.S. Circuit Court of Appeals ruled that there was sufficient evidence to believe provisions of SB 1070 were an unconstitutional breach of the exclusive authority of the federal government to regulate immigration (Liptak, 2011). The U.S. Supreme Court heard arguments about this case and, in June 2012, ruled to eliminate several provisions of the law (Barnes, 2012). However, the court upheld the provision allowing the police to verify the immigration status of those detained and suspected of entering the U.S. illegally (Barnes, 2012).

Prior to these developments, Maricopa County Arizona Sheriff, Joe Arpaio, used his law enforcement discretion to have his officers detain individuals thought to be illegal immigrants (Magaña, 2011). He justified this practice by relying on a provision of the 1996 Illegal Immigration and Reform and Responsibility Act that permitted local police officials to collaborate with the federal Immigration and Customs Enforcement agency to investigate violent and organized crimes committed by immigrants (Magaña, 2011). Magaña (2011) posits that this practice created enormous fear among many Latino residents of Maricopa County that they would be targeted for criminal arrest and deportation. As a result, innocent individuals were frequently arrested or detained and their lives disrupted by racial regulation. In 2012, similar anti-immigration laws were passed in other states, especially in the South (Lohr, 2012). As in Arizona, these laws attempt to restrict illegal immigration by providing law enforcement officials with more discretion in their power to arrest and detain persons suspected of being undocumented immigrants.

Finally, León and Ortega also contend that these tough immigration policies have fostered increased antagonism against Hispanics and produced more hate crimes directed against them. The Federal Bureau of Investigation (FBI), which collects data on hate crimes, uses the U.S. Congress' definition of such crimes as a "criminal offense against a person or property motivated in whole or in part by an offender's bias against a race, religion, disability, ethnic origin or sexual orientation." According to the FBI, of the 1,040 single-bias incidents reported in 2010 that were based on the perpetrator's perceptions of the victim's ethnicity, nearly two-thirds (65.5%) of the victims were Hispanic (U.S. Department of Justice, 2011). León and Ortega note that many Hispanics fear reporting these crimes because of the possibility of deportation. In addition, when these cases are adjudicated, anti-immigration public attitudes frequently preclude Hispanic victims from receiving full justice. Thus, the protection of Hispanic victims' human and civil rights is not ensured, and the physical safety and security of their communities is compromised (León & Ortega, 2011).

The political conflict surrounding immigration policy reached a new apex during the Presidential election campaign of Donald J. Trump, the Republican nominee. On June 16, 2015, in a speech officially launching his 2016 Presidential campaign, the billionaire businessman introduced his campaign slogan, "Make America Great Again." He lamented that the nation is on a downward social, cultural, and economic spiral that he attributed in large part to "the U.S. [becoming] a dumping ground for everybody else's problems" (*Time Magazine*, 2015). In this regard, he singled out Mexico and Mexicans, stating "They're bringing drugs. They're bringing crime. They're rapists" (*Ibid*, 2015). Part of his proposed remedy for this problem is to construct a large wall between Mexico and the United States the costs of which would be paid by Mexico (Trump, 2016). Later during the primary campaign, Trump extended his anti-immigration message to Muslims by advocating a "total and complete ban" on them as a way to protect America and prevent terrorist attacks (Johnson & Weigel, 2015).

Although some might view Trump's comments as an example of overt or old-style racism, which his rhetoric often suggests, they, nonetheless, conform to the norms of new style racism in that Trump and his supporters are the first to deny that the comments are racist or have a racial bias. Indeed, they contend that in the case of Mexican and Central American immigrants their concern is "illegal" immigration, and that "national security" underlies their call to ban non-American Muslims from entering the country. Both illegal immigration and national insecurity, they assert, pose a social, economic, and physical threat to all American citizens, regardless of their race, ethnicity, or religion (Trump, 2016). On his website, Trump cites the extremely high unemployment data for Black and Hispanic teenagers and the decline of adult labor force participation to suggest that American families, especially those in the middle-class, have been economically injured by ineffective and "disastrous" immigration policies and trade negotiations (Trump, 2016). Thus, to "make America great again," requires serious reconsideration of who is allowed to immigrate to the nation (and by what means) in order that current citizens are not disadvantaged and can regain their confidence in the nation's future.

Donald Trump's comments and proposals and the other immigration policy examples cited above represent a form of contemporary racial nativism that stigmatizes and marginalizes non-native groups ostensibly under the banner of curbing illegal immigration and enhancing national security. Central to this racial nativism, however, is fear (Galindo & Vigil, 2006). Galindo and Vigil (2006) contend this fear is expressed in three important ways. First, there is fear of linguistic diversity and that English will be eclipsed as the dominant U.S. language. Second, there is fear that the rising support for multicultural policies, such as Affirmative Action, will lead to people of color being favored over non-Hispanic whites in employment and college admissions, thereby causing white Americans to lose their political and economic dominance. A third fear is that new immigrants are a drain on social welfare spending since many are indigent and end up on public assistance paid for by American taxpayers. Although not discussed by Galindo and Vigil (2006), A final fear behind racial nativism, is the anxiety produced by the demographic transformation of the U.S. population, which has major implications for the future political and economic landscape (Craig & Richeson, 2014). The implications of this transformation will be discussed in more detail below. [*See also Chapter 1 this volume.*]

VOTING RIGHTS

In June 2013, in a 5 to 4 ruling, the U.S. Supreme court concluded that Section 4 of the 1965 Voting Rights Act was unconstitutional (Liptak, 2013). This section required several states, mostly in the South, to receive approval from the Justice Department before they could make both minor and major revisions to their voting procedures. This provision included in the 1965 legislation to ensure federal oversight of changes in voting procedures that might disadvantage those who had been previously denied the right to vote, especially African Americans in the South.

Consistent with new style racism, in his majority opinion Chief Justice John Roberts acknowledged that racial discrimination is wrong but argued that current conditions did not justify the continuation of Section 4 of the law. He based his decision on contemporary data indicating that the gap between Black and white voter registration in many of the affected states had been reduced significantly; for example, that the Black registration rate in Mississippi is now four percentage points higher than that of whites (Liptak, 2013). The Chief Justice used these data to suggest that the impact of racism on voter registration had been eliminated and, therefore, that federal oversight of certain states' voting practices was no longer needed. In his opinion, he essentially placed his faith in these states to "do the right thing" and not to implement changes in voting procedures that disadvantaged one group relative to another.

Since that ruling, however, 17 states have enacted new voting restrictions in Presidential elections (Brennan Center for Justice, 2016), such as strict photo ID requirements and reductions or elimination of early voting. Supporters of these new policies maintain that they guarantee integrity and prevent voter fraud. Opponents contend that there is scant evidence of voter fraud and that these policies are designed to suppress the vote among traditional Democratic Party constituents such as people of color, young people, and the elderly. Studies have shown that these groups tend to lack many of the required state-issued photo IDs more often than non-Hispanic whites (Morrison, 2016). Proponents of the laws assert that this is not a problem and that potential and eligible voters only need to acquire these new forms of identification. However, acquiring these new forms of identification, even when states say they will offer them for free, can generate hidden costs associated with traveling, missing time at work, and obtaining essential documentation that may no longer exist, such as a birth certificate (Morrison, 2016).

Consistent with new style racism, these policies appear to be non-discriminatory on the surface because they require universal application and adherence. However, their consequences would have a particularly discriminatory impact on people of color who tend to vote for Democratic candidates. One of the primary factors that catapulted President Obama to victory in both the 2008 and 2012 Presidential elections was the increasing proportion of voters of color as a percentage of the overall voting population. Indeed, it is projected that in the 2016 election almost one third (31%) of the electorate will be voters of color, up from 29% in the 2012 election (Krogstad, 2016). Critics of new style racism would contend that such trends are potent motivating forces behind the enactment of social policies that can have disparate and discriminatory effects on people of color. From this perspective, the ultimate goal of restrictions on voting is to maintain white racial supremacy and to increase the likelihood of electing government officials who ostensibly say they are for equal justice but who silently support a racist platform and agenda. Recent decisions by several appellate courts acknowledged this intention and invalidated new state election laws in North Carolina, Texas, and Wisconsin.

A LOOK INTO THE FUTURE

The previous analysis has demonstrated a consistent pattern of racial regulation by U.S. social policies. Two questions this raises are: How might this pattern look in the future? And how might people of color react? There are two possibilities. First, one of the consistent observations among many contemporary scholars and commentators who study racial oppression is that this form of oppression has mutated and appears now in more complex and diffused ways (Bonilla-Silva, 2003). Although there continue to be overt expressions of racial oppression, new style racial oppression, as discussed in this chapter, relies more on subtle and insidious mechanisms of subjugation. Proponents of these mechanisms increasingly imply that racism has either been eliminated or substantively diminished; they point to the election of President Barack Obama as a sign that the United States has entered a post-racial (and post-racism) era.

A major goal of this new form of racial oppression is to induce people of color to believe that the U.S. is race-neutral in its political and economic institutions. It is true that since the 1960s people of color have been afforded greater opportunities to be incorporated into the main fabric of U.S. society. This is largely due to the success of the Civil Rights movement in compelling President Lyndon Johnson and the Congress to enact anti-discrimination legislation, in particular the 1964 Civil Rights Act and the 1965 Voting Rights Act.

The elimination of overt, legal forms of discrimination, however, has made it less popular for people of color to rely exclusively on collectivistic strategies to promote racial equality. With newfound freedoms and opportunities, the value of individualism became much more appealing, and, perhaps even appropriate, for people of color. Although relics of the racial caste system remained, the civil rights laws passed during the 1960s gave individuals of color greater opportunities to demonstrate their personal skills and talents, which were increasingly being recognized and rewarded in newly integrated workplace environments. The professional advancement and increased visibility of people of color in these once racially segregated environments has led some to conclude that with hard work and perseverance, progress was possible for people of color in white America (see, e.g., Connerly, 2000; McWhorter, 2003).

The personal opportunities afforded by the 1960s civil rights thrust has placed people of color in jeopardy of abandoning their collective critical consciousness. Gil (1998) conceives critical consciousness as awareness and reflection that challenges existing social patterns and ideas, especially those that create and sustain oppression. If people of color increasingly abandon their critical consciousness, questions about the racial regulatory features of social policies may be reduced. In this sense, the kind of critical lens needed to analyze a policy's potential to foster racial regulation may be more difficult to develop. The ability of social policies to sustain racial oppression may gradually go undetected if greater numbers of people of color and whites are seduced into affirming the narrative of American race-neutrality. Any racial characteristics or consequences of social policies that appear to disadvantage people of color may be interpreted as unintentional and serendipitous. Moreover, these policies may be justified by people of color if the values of self-reliance and individualism increasingly define their worldview. Together, these trends would reduce the resistance efforts of people of color and solidify the achievements of the new era of racial oppression by incorporation.

A second scenario might illustrate the restoration of racial oppression by terror, or the more overt and explicit forms of racism. In this situation, domination by terror will be motivated primarily by the dwindling birth rates of white or European Americans. Low birth rates among European Americans and Europeans globally are currently reducing their proportion of the population, and projections indicate

Figure 4.4 Civil Rights March on Washington, D.C.

that this trend will continue (Buchanan, 2002; U.S. Census Bureau, 2009). At the same time, the population of all people of color has increased significantly. For example, in 2010, the U.S. Census Bureau (2011) reported that people of color represented almost 35% of the total U.S. population. This percentage represents an extraordinary increase since the early 1980s, when people of color represented only about 17 percent of the total U.S. population (U.S. Census Bureau, 1981). In states like California and major cities like New York and Los Angeles, there is no longer a "majority" population. It is currently projected that by the 2040s there will be no racial majority in the U.S. (U.S. Census Bureau, 2011).

A major implication of these demographic trends is the increased social visibility of people of color, which has been shown to create concerns and fears among majority group members (Bonilla-Silva, 2003; Hacker, 1992). This trepidation is based on the belief that the increased population of people of color poses a threat to the maintenance of the cultural, political, and economic control of European Americans. In combination, this demographic shift and its association with perceptions of dwindling European American power may bring about more drastic social policy measures to protect and defend white domination.

It is important to note that not all members of the majority racial group are anxious about the increased population of people of color. Many in this group have embraced and affirmed societal diversity through their political and personal behavior and will continue to do so. However, as Bell (1992) observed, much of

Figure 4.5 Black Lives Matter Protest.

contemporary racism is less about racial antagonism and more about racial nepotism. Although intermarriage between people of color and whites has dramatically increased in recent years, the dominant pattern continues to be racial endogamy (Wang, 2012). It remains to be seen whether this pattern will be reversed and, if so, whether it would engender more favorable race relations and social policies that are free of racism.

Despite the increased tolerance for racial difference and diversity among some Americans, there are still major signs of racial intolerance, especially in locations where people of color are now the majority or where their population has dramatically increased in recent years. For example, Magaña (2011) suggests that the rapid increase of the Mexican population was a primary motive for the enactment of Arizona's anti-immigration law. Moreover, throughout U.S. history, some of the harshest policies against people of color have been implemented in regions where people of color have represented a large segment of the population, such as Southern counties where African Americans either were in the majority or were a significant minority. A particularly egregious response to demographic panic occurred in the 1960s, when Georgia's Senator Richard Russell Jr., a diehard segregationist, proposed that the African American population be dispersed throughout the nation so they would not exceed five percent in any state (Fite, 1991).

In addition to the enactment of discriminatory policies, the growing proportion of people of color in major metropolitan areas has produced dramatic increases in arrests and hyper-incarceration rates among African Americans and Latinos, prompting Alexander (2010) to conclude that these developments represent the advent of a new era of Jim Crow. Indeed, African American men now have the highest incarceration rate of any racial or gender group in the U.S., 3,059 per 100,000 in 2010 (Guerino, Harrison, & Sabol, 2011). If demographic projections suggesting that people of color will be the majority in the United States before mid-century are correct (see U.S. Census Bureau, 2009), more drastic and desperate social policies that seek to sustain Eurocentric domination might become more apparent. The Black Lives Matter Movement has drawn increased attention to the most extreme consequences of such policies—the disproportionate number of African Americans who are victims of police violence.

If social policies become more blatantly racist and terroristic, people of color may respond with more intense and perhaps even violent resistance activities. The frustration aggression school of psychology contends that overt forms of injustice can lead to deep frustration that can produce aggressive actions against self and others (Muller & Weede, 1994). Thus, more overtly racist forms of social policy regulation might lead to greater feelings of alienation, despair, and frustration that generate resistance that is direct and antagonistic.

SUMMARY AND CONCLUSION

U.S. social policies have regulated the lives of many groups, and racial regulation has been a prominent feature of this control. In this regard, a racism-centered perspective of social policy analysis was used in this chapter to examine why and how U.S. social policies have regulated the lives of people of color. Drawing on the assumption that American social policies seek to reinforce and sustain white supremacy, this chapter examined how these policies achieve this goal under conditions of both old and new style racism. Whether expressed through overt or subtle forms of racial regulation, U.S. social policies have endeavored to suppress the vast potential people of color have to exercise freedom and advance themselves politically and economically. This suppression of human potential not only hurts people of color but our nation and world at large. For as King, Jr. (1964) reminded the sustainers of oppression in his day, "We are caught in an inescapable network of mutuality, tied in a single garment of destiny" (p. x).

The two scenarios discussed in the chapter's final section forecast a social policy future whereby the greater internalization of race-neutrality or the return to the overt expression of racism dominates. Both of these scenarios could be avoided. First, greater internalization of race-neutrality is a good thing if the aim of this neutrality is to preclude discrimination and further racial equality. Since the 1960s, however, race neutrality often has been used to justify racial inequality by underscoring the significance of personal responsibility and merit as the primary avenues for advancement. The negative consequences of race-neutrality as they relate to social policy could be avoided if greater attention was given to the importance of race in furthering the goals of cultural diversity.

Too often in the U.S., however, negative race consciousness pervades. Negative race consciousness is the view that a focus on racial differences can only have detrimental consequences and that the only solution is the practice of race neutrality or colorblindness (Crenshaw, Gotanda, Peller, & Thomas, 1996). To achieve a more racially just society, however, there needs to be more of a balanced approach when acknowledging racial differences that includes both negative and positive race consciousness. Positive race consciousness accentuates the favorable side of racial differences that underscore how diverse cultural perspectives emerge from these distinctions. Thus, racial distinctions are understood broadly to include various groups' cultural traditions and worldviews. Yet, positive race consciousness also acknowledges inequality in the affirmation of these cultural differences and assumes that the problem to be resolved is that of cultural oppression (Schiele, 2000).

From this line of thinking, the solution to this problem is the institutionalization of cultural pluralism, which rests on the assumption that intergroup antagonism is not a necessary outcome of intergroup differences (Lum, 2011). Rather, social cohesion can be achieved among people sharing a particular time and space but that cultural uniformity is not essential (Schiele, 2000). For social policy development, this means that divergent cultural perspectives, especially emanating from those for whom the policy is being formulated, should be integrated in the policy decision-making and implementation processes (Chapin, 1995). Therefore, a focus on addressing concerns of material inequality is significantly linked to an emphasis on addressing matters of cultural or symbolic inequality.

The focus on cultural diversity and pluralism also has implications for avoiding the return to overt and terroristic forms of racial regulation. The reduction of a dominant group's population and that group's demographic eclipse by minority groups should not be viewed negatively but rather as an opportunity to embrace culturally pluralistic thinking. Culturally pluralistic thinking underscores the importance of applying diverse values and strategies to solve problems that diminish human potential (Lum, 2011). From this perspective, dominant values and strategies are eschewed and contributions from divergent cultural/ethnic groups are encouraged in the process of addressing common human needs. This form of cultural and intergroup collaboration would help to reduce skepticism and distrust among groups because people who historically have been excluded will have a greater opportunity to demonstrate their talents and positive potential for society as a whole. The paucity of this demonstration, in part, contributes to continued stigmatization and disparagement that provide the psychographic foundation for justifying oppression (Schiele, 2000). Thus, if internalized and reinforced, culturally pluralistic thinking and practice might, over time, supersede culturally oppressive thinking and practice. If so, the return to overt strategies of racial regulation through social policy formation would be unnecessary.

Although only time will tell whether the two projected scenarios occur or are avoided, it is the actions of people, "as manufacturers of our world" that ultimately make the difference in either sustaining or eliminating societal practices and structures. A racism-centered framework of social policy analysis seeks to unseat the orthodoxy and consequences of negative race consciousness and replace it with a social vision where cultural and racial oppression become obsolete. In this way, social policy's exoneration from racial regulation could help foster a more inclusive society that could elicit the positive potential of a greater number of people.

References

Abramovitz, M. (1999). *Regulating the lives of women: Social welfare policy from colonial times to the present.* Boston, MA: South End Press.

Adams, D.W. (1995). *Education for extinction: American Indians and the boarding school experience.* Lawrence, KS: University Press of Kansas.

Alexander, M. (2010). *The new Jim Crow: Mass incarceration in the age of colorblindness.* New York: The New Press.

Alleyne, A. (2005). Invisible injuries and silent witnesses: The shadow of racial oppression in workplace contexts. *Psychodynamic Practice, 11*(3), 283–299.

Anonymous (1994, April 25). Florida legislature to pay $2.1 million to victims of 1923 racist massacre in Rosewood. *Jet Magazine,* 12.

Anonymous (1995, January 16). State of Florida to award each Rosewood massacre survivors $100,000 more. *Jet Magazine,* 18.

Archibold, R.C. (2010, April 23). Arizona enacts stringent law on immigration. *The New York Times.* Available: http://www.nytimes.com/2010/04/24/us/politics/24immig.html.

Barnes, R. (2012, June 25). Supreme Court upholds key part of Arizona law for now, strikes down other provisions. *The Washington Post.* Available: http://www.washingtonpost.com/politics/supreme-court-rules-on-arizona-immigration-law/2012/06/25/gJQA0Nrm1V_story.html.

Bell, D. (1992). *Faces at the bottom of the well.* New York: Basic Books.

Blau, J., with Abramovitz, M. (2014). *The dynamics of social welfare policy,* (4th ed.) New York: Oxford University Press.

Bobo, L., Kluegel, J.R., & Smith, R.A. (1997). Laissez-faire racism: The crystallization of a kinder, gentler, antiblack ideology. In S.A. Tuch & J.K. Martin (Eds.), *Racial attitudes in the 1990s: Continuity and change* (pp. 15–41). Westport, CT: Praeger Publishers.

Bonilla-Silva, E. (2001). *White supremacy and racism in the post-civil rights era.* Boulder, CO: Lynne Rienner.

Bonilla-Silva, E. (2003). *Racism without racists: Color-blind racism and the persistence of racial inequality in the United States.* Lanham, MD: Rowman and Littlefield.

Buchanan, P.J. (2002). *The death of the west: How dying populations and immigrant invasions imperil our country and civilization.* New York: St. Martin's Press.

Carlton-LaNey, I. (Ed.) (2001), *African American leadership: An empowerment tradition in social welfare history.* Washington, DC: NASW Press.

Carlton-LaNey, I. (2011). African American club women's resistance to oppressive public policy in the early 20th century. In J.H. Schiele (Ed.), *Social welfare policy: Regulation and resistance among people of color* (pp. 43–62). Los Angeles, CA: Sage Publications.

Chapin, R.K. (1995). Social policy development: The strengths perspective. *Social Work, 40* (4), 506–514.

Cohen, G. (1996). Toward a spirituality based on justice and ecology. *Social Policy, 26*(3), 6–18.

Coleman, M.C. (2007). *American Indians, the Irish, and Government Schooling: A comparative study.* Lincoln, NB: University of Nebraska Press.

Collins, P.H. (1998). *Fighting words: Black women and the search for justice.* Minneapolis, MN: University of Minnesota Press.

Connerly, W. (2000). *Creating equal: My fight against race preferences.* San Francisco: Encounter Books.

Crenshaw, K, Gotanda, N., Peller, G., & Thomas, K. (1996). *Critical race theory: The key writings that formed the movement.* New York: The New Press.

Day, P.J. (2006). *A new history of social welfare,* (5th ed.) Boston: Allyn & Bacon.

D'Orso, M. (1996). *Like judgment day: The ruin and redemption of a town called Rosewood.* New York: Putnam.

Evans-Campbell, T., & Campbell, C. (2011). Indigenist oppression and resistance in Indian child welfare: Reclaiming our children. In J.H. Schiele (Ed.), S*ocial welfare policy: Regulation and resistance among people of color* (pp. 295–314). Los Angeles, CA: Sage Publications.

Feagin, J.R. (2000). *Racist America: Roots, current realities and future reparations.* New York: Routledge.

Fite, G.C. (1991). *Richard B. Russell, Jr., Senator from Georgia.* Chapel Hill, NC: University of North Carolina Press.

Florida House of Representatives (1994). *Special master's final report on Rosewood case.* Tallahassee, FL: State of Florida Printing Office.

Foner, E. (1988). *Reconstruction: America's unfinished revolution, 1863–1877.* New York: Harper & Row.

Gil, D.G. (1998). *Confronting injustice and oppression: Concepts and strategies for social workers.* New York: Columbia University Press.

Gould, S.J. (1981). *The mismeasure of man.* New York: W.W. Norton & Company.

Griswold del Castillo, R. (1992). *The treaty of Guadalupe Hidalgo: A legacy of conflict.* Norman, OK: The University of Oklahoma Press.

Guerino, P., Harrison, P.M., & Sabol, W. (2011). *Prisoners in 2010.* Washington, DC: Bureau of Justice Statistics.

Guthrie, R.V. (1998). *Even the rat was white: A historical view of psychology,* (2nd ed.) Boston: Allyn & Bacon.

Hacker, A. (1992). *Two nations: Black and white, separate, hostile, unequal.* New York: Charles Scribner's Sons.

Hoffer, W.H. (2011). *Plessy v. Ferguson: Race and inequality in Jim Crow America.* Lawrence, KS: University Press of Kansas.

Hoffman, S.J. (2001). Progressive public health administration in the Jim Crow south: A case study of Richmond, Virginia, 1907–1920. *Journal of Social History, 35*(1), 175–194.

hooks, b. (2000). *Feminist theory: From margin to center.* Cambridge, MA: South End Press.

Jackson, A. (1830, December 8th). *Case for the Indian Removal Act.* First annual message to Congress. [Online]. Available: www.mtholyoke.edu/acad/intrel/andrew.htm

Jansson, B.S. (2012). *The reluctant welfare state: Engaging history to advance social work practice in contemporary society,* (7th ed.) Belmont, CA: Brooks/Cole.

Jefferson, T. (1998/1782). *Notes on the state of Virginia.* New York: Penguin Classics.

Jerome, R., & Sider, D., (1995, January 16). A measure of justice. *People Weekly,* 46–49.

Kambon, K.K. (1998). *African/Black psychology in the American context: An African-centered approach.* Tallahassee, FL: Nubian Nation Publications.

Karger, H.J., & Stoesz, D. (2013). *American social welfare policy: A pluralist approach,* (7th ed.) Boston: Allyn & Bacon.

Kellner, D. (1990). *Television and the crisis of democracy.* Boulder, CO: Westview Press.

King, Jr., M.L. (1964). *Why we can't wait.* New York: Harper and Row.

Lasch-Quinn, E. (1994). *Black neighbors: Race and the limits of reform in the American settlement house movement,* 1890–1945. Chapel Hill, NC: University of North Carolina Press.

León, A.L., & Ortega, D.M. (2011). Immigration, dehumanization, and resistance to U.S. immigration policies: Pushing against the boundary. In J.H. Schiele (Ed.), *Social welfare policy: Regulation and resistance among people of color* (pp. 237–253). Los Angeles, CA: Sage Publications.

Limb, G.E., & Baxter, A. (2011). American Indian child welfare: The impact of federal regulation and tribal resistance on policies and practice. In J.H. Schiele (Ed.), *Social welfare policy: Regulation and resistance among people of color* (pp. 315–327). Los Angeles, CA: Sage Publications.

Liptak, A. (2011, December 12). Court to weigh Arizona statute on immigration. *The New York Times,* Available: http://www.nytimes.com/2011/12/13/us/supreme-court-to-rule-on-immigration-law-in-arizona .html?pagewanted=all.

Lohr, K. (2012, March 28). In Southern states, immigration law battle rages on. *National Public Radio,* Available: http://www.npr.org/2012/03/28/149468058/in-southern-states-immigration-law-battle-rages-on.

Lum, D. (Ed.) (2011). Editor). *Culturally competent practice: A framework for understanding diverse groups and justice issues,* (4th ed.) Belmont, CA: Thompson Brooks/Cole.

Magaña, L. (2011). Fear of calling the police: Regulation and resistance around immigration enforcement activities. In J.H. Schiele (Ed.), *Social welfare policy: Regulation and resistance among people of color* (pp. 255–269). Los Angeles, CA: Sage Publications.

Marable, M. (1996). *Speaking truth to power: Essays on race, resistance, and radicalism.* Boulder, CO: Westview Press.

McWhorter, J. (2003). Authentically black: Essays for the black silent majority. New York: Gotham Books.

McWilliams, C., & Meier, M.S. (1990). *North from Mexico: The Spanish-speaking people of the United States,* updated (ed.). New York: Praeger.

Moss, A.A., & Franklin, J.H. (2000). *From slavery to freedom: A history of African Americans,* (8th ed.) New York: Alfred A. Knopf.

Muller, E. N., & Weede, E. (1994). Theories of rebellion: Relative deprivation and power contention. *Rationality and Society, 6,* 40–57.

Neubeck, K.J., & Cazenave, N.A. (2001). *Welfare racism: Playing the race card against America's poor.* New York: Routledge.

O'Donnell, S.M. (1994). The care of dependent African-American children in Chicago: The struggle between black self-help and professionalism. *Journal of Social History, 27*(4), 763–776.

Padilla, L.M. (2004). Internalized oppression and Latino/as. *The Diversity Factor, 12*(3), 15–21.

Piven, F.F., & Cloward, R.A. (1995). *Regulating the poor: The functions of public welfare,* revised (ed.). New York: Random House.

Pritchard, J. (2004). AP investigation: Mexican worker deaths rise sharply even as overall U.S. job safety improves. Associated Press. Retrieved April 18, 2009, from http://fmmac2.mm.ap.org/polk_awards_ dying_to_work_html/DyingtoWork.html

Quadagno, J. (1994). *The color of welfare: How racism undermined the War on Poverty*. New York: Oxford University Press.

Ramirez, D., McDevitt, J., & Farrell, A. (2000). *A resource guide on racial profiling data collection systems: Promising practices and lessons learned*. Washington, DC: U.S. Department of Justice.

Reisch, M., & Andrews, J. (2002). *The road not taken: A history of radical social work in the United States*. New York: Brunner-Routledge.

Reuter (1996). Amid mixed reviews, Clinton signs welfare bill. Available at: www.yahoo.com/headlines/special/welfare_reform.

Schiele, J. H. (2000). *Human services and the Afrocentric paradigm*. New York: Routledge.

Schiele, J.H., Jackson, M.S., & Fairfax, C.N. (2005). Maggie Lena Walker and African American community development. *Affilia: Journal of Women and Social Work, 20*(1), 21–37.

Schiele, J.H. (2011). Introduction. In J.H. Schiele (Ed.), *Social welfare policy: Regulation and resistance among people of color* (pp. 1–21). Los Angeles, CA: Sage Publications.

Schram, S.F., Soss, J., & Fording, R.C. (Eds.) (2003). *Race and the politics of welfare reform*. Ann Arbor, MI: University of Michigan Press.

Southern Poverty Law Center. (2009). Under siege: Life for low-income Latinos in the South. Retrieved May 1, 2009 from http://www.splcenter.org/legal/undersiege/UnderSiege.pdf

Stefancic, J., & Delgado, R. (1996). *No mercy: How conservative think tanks and foundations changed America's social agenda*. Philadelphia, PA: Temple University Press.

Takaki, R. (1993). *A different mirror: A history of multicultural America*. New York: Little, Brown and Company.

Takahashi, R. (2011). Japanese American resistance to World War II: Executive, legislative, and judicial policies. In J.H. Schiele (Ed.), *Social welfare policy: Regulation and resistance among people of color* (pp. 135–163). Los Angeles, CA: Sage Publications.

Thomas, A., & Sillen, D. (1972). *Racism and psychiatry*. Secaucus, NY: Citadel Press.

United States Bureau of the Census (1981). *Statistical abstract of the United States: 1981*. Washington, DC: U.S. Government Printing Office.

U. S. Bureau of the Census (1994). *Current population survey: March 1994*. Washington, DC: U.S. Government Printing Office.

United States Bureau of the Census (2009). *Population projections of the United States: 2008*. Washington, DC: U.S. Government Printing Office.

U.S. Bureau of the Census (2010). *Current population survey, Annual social and economic supplements*. Washington, DC: U.S. Government Printing Office.

U.S. Bureau of the Census (2011). *Overview of race and Hispanic origin: 2010 census brief*. Washington, DC: U.S. Government Printing Office.

U.S. Congress (1996, August 22). *Personal Responsibility and Work Opportunity Reconciliation Act of 1996*, Pub. L. No. 104–193. Washington, DC: U.S. Government Printing Office.

U.S. Department of Health and Human Services (DHHS; 2001), Administration on Children, Youth and Families. *Child maltreatment: 1999*. Washington, DC: U.S. Government Printing Office; 2001.

U.S. Department of Justice, Federal Bureau of Investigation (2011). *Hate crime statistics, 2010*. Washington, DC: U.S. Government Printing Office.

U.S. House of Representatives Committee on Ways & Means (1993). The green book. Washington, DC: U.S. Government Printing Office.

Vogel, R.D. (2004). *Stolen birthright: The U.S. conquest and exploitation of the Mexican people*. Houston, TX: Houston Institute for Culture.

Walters, R.W. (2003). *White nationalism, black interests: Conservative public policy and the black community*. Detroit, MI: Wayne State University Press.

Wang, W. (2012). *The rise of intermarriage: Rates, characteristic vary by race and gender*. Washington, DC: Pew Research Center.

Ward, D.E. (2005). *The white welfare state: The racialization of U.S. welfare policy*. Ann Arbor, MI: The University of Michigan Press.

Wessler, S.F. (2011). *Shattered families: The perilous intersection of immigration enforcement and the child welfare system*. Retrieved on May 25, 2012 from http://arc.org/shatteredfamilies.

White, D. (2012). Why the federal government cannot end illegal immigration. Retrieved May 25, 2012 from http://usliberals.about.com/od/immigration/a/IllegalImmi.htm.

Woodward, C.V. (2001). *The strange career of Jim Crow*. New York: Oxford University Press.

Young, I.M. (1990). *Justice and the politics of difference*. Princeton, NJ: Princeton University Press.

Zinn, H. (2000). *A people's history of the United States:1492-Present*. New York: Harper Perennial.

Credits

5

WOMEN AND SOCIAL POLICY

Susan J. Roll, PhD

Over the past century, the transformation of the American family has been the single most defining factor shaping social policies that affect women. Once an economic necessity, many of the family's functions have been replaced by labor-saving technology in the home and the development of a vast service industry that performs many traditional care-giving tasks, such as child care and support for the elderly, which were formerly the exclusive responsibility of women. In combination with major changes in the nation's economy and cultural norms, reflected in higher rates of divorce, the greater likelihood of single-parent households, and gradual acceptance of LGBTQ (lesbian, gay, bisexual, transgender, and queer) partnerships, this has produced dramatic changes in the structure of the family itself. As recent data indicate, long-term marriages combined with childbearing are no longer a given (DeParle & Tavernise, 2012). Consequently, over the past several decades, gender roles have become far less rigidly defined and families in the United States are now more diverse than ever (Boushey & O'Leary, 2009; Furstenberg, 2014).

This dramatic cultural and social transformation was initiated by changes in the labor market, which Goldin (2006) terms an evolution that was followed by a "quiet revolution." Initially, women began to work outside the home out of economic necessity. Gradually, as they acquired more control over their occupational and social choices, their workforce participation increased and cultural norms and expectations evolved to support new gender roles. Changes in U.S. culture and social policy provided women with greater freedom to choose if and when to have children and expanded the range of socially acceptable options regarding marriage and living arrangements with intimate partners. Yet, despite these significant gains, women still face discrimination at home and in the workplace, as public and private sector policies lag behind women's cultural progress.

To some extent, during the past several decades, the United States has adapted its social policies to meet these changing mores. Considerable barriers to gender equality still exist, however, necessitating further revision of many contemporary policies. As in the past, social workers must continue to guide and inform the development of policy based on their work with individuals, families, and communities to ensure that the nation's policies effectively address the needs of women in the changing economic and cultural environment.

This chapter begins with a brief discussion that frames the overall context of policy development regarding women.[1] This is followed by an overview of the historical evolution of the major social policies that have shaped the experiences of American women. The third section contains a discussion of the role of women in affecting social policy, through both formal and informal means. The final section outlines several significant policy issues affecting women today. These will help illustrate the processes by which social workers, as advocates, can influence the development and implementation of contemporary policies.

FRAMEWORK

A major component of social work practice is the understanding that there are reciprocal and influential relationships among social policy, the **sociopolitical** context, and the well-being of individuals, families, and communities. Nowhere is this more evident than in the relationship between social policy and women. During the past 150 years, changes in the patterns of work and family life have shaped social policy developments; in turn, these policies have transformed women's roles in the workplace, at home, and in their relationships with men. Changes in the social construction of women's roles as mothers, wives, daughters, workers, caregivers, politicians, and activists have occurred alongside changes in the nation's gender norms, cultural values, concepts of relationships, and power dynamics. These dramatic social and cultural changes have produced significant changes in social policies that affect women, children, and families.

Social policies are of fundamental importance to social workers in large part because they inform and play a major role in supporting or disrupting existing patterns of power and oppression. By understanding the relationship of women to social policy, social workers acquire new insights into how different demographic and cultural groups are influenced by the sociopolitical context, as well as how these groups can have an impact on that context. Engaging in a critical analysis of the environmental forces that shape social policies is an important step in the creation of new social policies and structural change.

Central to this analysis is the recognition that not every woman has the same experience in our society; in fact, differences among women are vast, reflecting the impact of class, race, ethnicity, religion, age, sexual orientation, ability status, occupation, and geography. However, by peeling apart these distinct layers of women's identity—as members of a single group, as members of other groups, and as distinct individual actors—we can obtain a clearer understanding of the subtle ways policies influence these roles and how women, through these different roles, can shape policies as well. Effective analyses of social policy thus require us to understand the impact of the intersection of the multiple identities women possess in society.

In the literature on **feminism**, these relationships have been termed **intersectionality**—that is, the traditional conceptions of oppression based on race, gender, and class, for example, do not exist independently of one another but are interrelated (McCall, 2005). These interrelated forms of oppression overlap and interact, contributing to systematic social inequality. To understand the social position of women, therefore, we must look through the multiple lenses of race, class, sexual orientation, citizenship status, age, differing abilities, and other characteristics, and not merely through the lens of gender.

What African American feminists have referred to as "triple jeopardy" is a vivid example of how these intersectionalities operate in U.S. society. Low-income African American women experience oppression in multiple ways based on a confluence of their race, class, and gender. This lens has helped uncover the unique impact on African American women of addiction, HIV/AIDS, and racial disparities in the distribution of

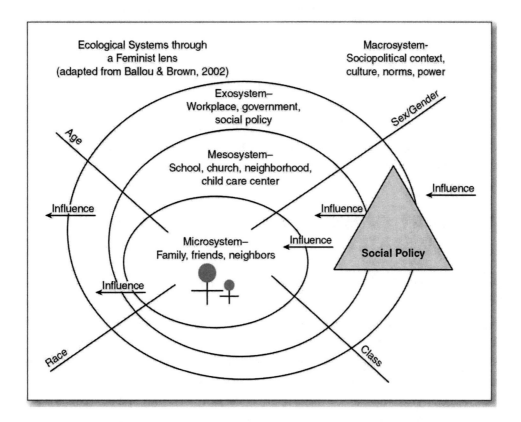

Source: Adapted from M. Ballou & L. S. Brown (eds.) (2002). *Rethinking mental health and disorder: Feminist perspectives.* New York: Guilford Press.

public benefits such as housing. A similar pattern of triple jeopardy is experienced by immigrant women, women with disabilities, and lesbian women. Because of this unique constellation of oppressive conditions, women can make progress in regard to one dimension of their identity (e.g., race), while the other aspects of their identity (e.g., gender or sexual orientation) remain oppressed. Recognition of this complex relationship between women and social policy provides the basis for a more in-depth understanding of women's role as activists. Sometimes, women activists will focus on gender politics; at other times, they may emphasize issues of race, immigration status, sexual orientation, religion, or social class. While these struggles often overlap, they can also conflict with one another.

One way to understand how these intersectionalities operate in the broader sociopolitical context is by combining ecological systems theory with a feminist analysis, as shown in Figure 5.1. Introduced by Bronfenbrenner (1979), ecological systems theory recognizes the multilayered environment in which people live and how these layers interrelate to create their lived experience. Building on the work of Bronfenbrenner, Ballou and Brown (2002) and Kemp (2001) outline a framework they call the Feminist Ecological Model. This model incorporates the multiple systems levels offered by Bronfenbrenner yet simultaneously considers the importance of gender, race, class, and age.

Recognizing the multilayered complexity of every social context is critical to understanding women's experiences. Because of their multiple identities, cultures, values, and beliefs, each woman will experience the world in a unique way. This will influence how she interacts with her family, friends, and neighbors.

Simultaneously, at the community level, women may or may not have access to critical resources such as jobs, child care, and social supports. At the institutional level, policies are developed that directly affect women and families—especially women who rely on government assistance. Each of these transactions occurs within a broad sociopolitical context that further shapes the environment in which women live and their ability to effect policy change.

Women's roles in shaping social policy have ranged from being central agents of change to being passive and, at times, unwilling recipients of changes initiated at all levels of government. Sometimes policies have changed as a result of concerted actions that were deliberate and intentional; at other times, they have been the unintended by-product of other social, economic, and cultural forces. In recent years, as global communications capacity grows and women around the world find common ground in their struggles, international movements are creating new possibilities for policy change.

A BRIEF HISTORY OF WOMEN AND SOCIAL POLICY IN THE UNITED STATES

Since the beginning of the 20th century, dramatic changes have occurred in women's roles in society and in the nation's political economy. In the spring of 1980, Donna Shalala, then Assistant Secretary for Policy Development and Research in the U.S. Department of Housing and Urban Development, acknowledged the implications of these changes and cautioned, "We need a new vision that helps women and communities to adjust to the overwhelming changes in the patterns of labor and living that have overtaken us in the past few decades" (Stimpson, 1981, p. S3).

As Shalala implied, since the start of industrialization in the United States, there has been ongoing tension in the social policy arena between the goal of gender equality and recognition of the gender differences between women and men. While some women, particularly white, middle- and upper-income women, have gained greater equality in the workplace, government, and education, there have been fewer changes in the nation's social and cultural norms regarding their roles in the domestic sphere. Women remain the primary caregivers of the family even as their workplace participation has soared.

Efforts to balance these gains with their ongoing care-giving responsibilities have placed women in a difficult position. While feminist activists have achieved some successes in their advocacy efforts on behalf of equal pay and antidiscrimination laws, the United States has still not constructed a policy framework that acknowledges the dual roles many women fulfill as workers and caregivers. While men are participating more than ever in domestic life, there remain vast gender disparities in the real and perceived share of their domestic labor (Parker & Wang, 2013).

Many scholars have attempted to explain how and why these gender distinctions arose, while recognizing that the experiences of women of color, lesbians, women with disabilities, and immigrant women have been vastly different. Much of the tension has been a result of the persistence of maternalist approaches to social policy that have both supported women in their dual roles of wage earner and caregiver and maintained their unequal socioeconomic status. While **maternalism**, or the support for women as the caregivers and nurturers of the family, was intended to improve and protect the lives of women in their unique role, it has also hampered women in their fight to be treated equally in the formal economy. A review of the development of U.S. social policies since the mid-19th century illustrates both the progress that has been made and the gaps that persist.

A CENTURY OF CHANGE

During the past century and a half, policy changes for women have occurred in two major waves. The first appeared in the second half of the 19th and early 20th centuries. In these years, American women fought to overturn legal obstacles to equality and establish their right to own property, vote, and have greater equality in marriage. The symbolic beginning of these efforts took place at the Seneca Falls Convention in the summer of 1848, organized by Elizabeth Cady Stanton and Lucretia Coffin Mott following their return from the World Anti-Slavery Convention. Other important white feminist leaders of the period included Lucy Stone, Susan B. Anthony, and Julia Sears. Each is known for her outspoken championship of women's rights and the abolition of slavery.

These **suffragettes,** as they were called, were soon joined by recently freed African American women who were fighting for both racial and gender equality. They included Sojourner Truth, Harriett Tubman, and Ida B. Wells, and white abolitionists such as Harriet Beecher Stowe, the author of *Uncle Tom's Cabin.* Despite their different backgrounds, women in these movements were closely aligned and often shared a common language and political strategy. Sojourner Truth (see the box below) spoke of this common struggle.

Despite such multiracial efforts, African American women were often excluded from the mainstream suffrage movement because of persistent racism and a fear among white women that the promotion of racial justice would undermine their cause. In response to their exclusion, African American women created alternative organizations such as Colored Women Voters to fight specifically for African American suffrage. This phase of feminist activism in the social policy arena ended in 1919 with the passage of the Nineteenth Amendment granting all women the right to vote.

During this first wave of women's activism, women's role in the formal economy slowly changed. It is important to note that in this period the workplace and home were not the separate entities they

Figure 5.2–5.4 African American women activists and reformers: Sojourner Truth, Ida B. Wells, and Harriett Tubman.

are today, although the split between private and public spheres had begun by the mid-19th century, particularly in urban America (Amott & Matthaei, 1991). While a clear gender division of labor existed, there was also a shared understanding that men and women both contributed to the economic needs of the family.

WORDS OF SOJOURNER TRUTH

Well, children, where there is so much racket there must be something out of kilter. I think that 'twixt the negroes of the South and the women at the North, all talking about rights, the white men will be in a fix pretty soon. But what's all this here talking about?

That man over there says that women need to be helped into carriages, and lifted over ditches, and to have the best place everywhere. Nobody ever helps me into carriages, or over mud-puddles, or gives me any best place! And ain't I a woman? Look at me! Look at my arm! I have ploughed and planted, and gathered into barns, and no man could head me! And ain't I a woman? I could work as much and eat as much as a man—when I could get it—and bear the lash as well! And ain't I a woman? I have borne thirteen children, and seen most all sold off to slavery, and when I cried out with my mother's grief, none but Jesus heard me! And ain't I a woman?

Then they talk about this thing in the head; what's this they call it? [member of audience whispers, "Intellect"] That's it, honey. What's that got to do with women's rights or negroes' rights? If my cup won't hold but a pint, and yours holds a quart, wouldn't you be mean not to let me have my little half measure full?

Then that little man in black there, he says women can't have as much rights as men, 'cause Christ wasn't a woman! Where did your Christ come from? Where did your Christ come from? From God and a woman! Man had nothing to do with Him.

If the first woman God ever made was strong enough to turn the world upside down all alone, these women together ought to be able to turn it back, and get it right side up again! And now they is asking to do it, the men better let them.

Obliged to you for hearing me, and now old Sojourner ain't got nothing more to say.

Sojourner Truth, 1851, Women's Convention, Akron, Ohio

Between the Civil War and World War I, however, as the United States was transformed into an industrialized nation, changes in the nature of work created distinctions between women and men and between women of color and white women (Amott & Matthaei, 1991). In the dominant culture, men maintained primary responsibility for paid work outside of the home, which was valued for its contribution to society.

Table 5.1 Proportion of U.S. Women in the Labor Force, Ages 16 and Over, 1870 to 1920.

	1870	1880	1890	1900	1910	1920
Percentage of women employed	14.8	16.0	19.0	20.6	24.0	24.2

Source: U.S. Department of Commerce, Bureau of Census, *Comparative Statistics for the United States, 1870–1940 (1943)*. Washington, DC: U.S. Government Printing Office.

White middle- and upper-class women were relegated to the home, where their labor had high cultural but little economic value. Regardless of class, paid work by married women was regarded as deviant, although it was clearly necessary for many working-class families to earn a "family wage." By the late 19th century, more than 1 million women worked outside the home, largely on farms, in factories, or as domestic servants (Kessler-Harris, 1981). Most of these women were young, single, and either white working class, immigrants, or African Americans. Table 5.1 shows the growth of women in the formal workforce from 1870 to 1920.

According to the 1900 Census, 41% of women of color were employed outside the home, compared with only 17% of white women. Of the latter, many were poor, recent immigrants (Chafe, 1972). Shortly later, however, expanded educational opportunities for white, middle-class women enabled them to obtain positions in newly emerging professions such as teaching, nursing, and social work. Yet even African American women with high school degrees were still not welcome in more prestigious jobs such as clerical work or teaching (Kleinberg, 1989). Along with recent immigrants, they worked primarily in factories and as domestic servants. When it was economically feasible, married women would drop out of the labor market altogether (Morales & Sheafor, 2001).

Racial disparities among working women persisted throughout the first half of the 20th century (Amott & Matthaei, 1991). In 1920, 43% of African American women over the age of 15 were employed, whether they were married or not. Twenty years later, at the start of World War II, more than twice as many African American women as whites worked outside the home (Amott & Matthaei, 1991).

During this period, an important court case framed the debate around U.S. social policy, reflecting a **maternalist perspective**. In *Muller v. Oregon* (1908), the U.S. Supreme Court upheld the constitutionality of a law limiting the maximum number of hours per day that women could work; yet it also decided that the same standard could not be applied to men based on "the difference between the sexes" (Koven & Michel, 1993). Although women were increasingly finding work alongside men and demanding equal treatment, the court unanimously ruled that women and men were not equal in this regard. This paradox continues to underlie much of U.S. social policy today.

Social policies providing cash assistance offer another example of U.S. society's conflicting values around the roles of women as mothers and as workers. While 43 states had passed so-called "mothers' pensions" by the early 1930s—largely to support widowed, white women—a federal system of public assistance, Aid to Dependent Children (ADC), first appeared as Title IV of the 1935 Social Security Act (Cauthen & Amenta, 1996). This policy not only established a legal entitlement to public assistance, but it recognized the needs of single mothers whose husbands had abandoned them and their children. Although initially ADC supported only 6% of female-headed households, by 1950 it aided one in four female-headed families (Amenta, 1998). Over the next several decades, this commitment to

Figure 5.5 Women Welders during World War II

Figure 5.6 First Lady Eleanor Roosevelt and Lorena Hickok, 1933

low-income families would change dramatically. [*See Chapters 12 and 13 in this volume for further discussion of this issue.*]

During and after World War II, employment opportunities for all women increased significantly, particularly in white-collar and clerical work. At that time, 58% of all white and African American women and 53% of Hispanic women were working in the paid marketplace. In addition, women in the workforce were now increasingly married and middle class (Kessler-Harris, 1981). Morales and Sheafor (2001, p. 246) outline eight social changes that made paid work more acceptable for women of all marital statuses and nearly equalized past racial disparities among women:

1. The introduction of more "labor-saving" devices in the home
2. The recruitment and expansion of employment opportunities for women during the war
3. Increased economic need for two wage earners, particularly when many returning servicemen took advantage of the GI Bill and went to college
4. Increased educational opportunities for women
5. Rising divorce rates and increasing numbers of female-headed households
6. Women's increasing control over contraception
7. New antidiscrimination laws in the areas of education and employment
8. Changing societal views of gender roles

Although the gender gap in occupational roles narrowed somewhat, vast gender-based pay disparities persisted. In 1940, the average female worker still earned less than half of what her male counterpart earned. This was partly due to the myth that women worked only to earn extra spending money, although 90% of working women reported to the Women's Bureau that they were working due to economic need (Chafe, 1972).

When World War II ended, an aggressive backlash against this surge of women into the workforce emerged to create employment opportunities for the 11 million returning veterans. A widespread media campaign, spearheaded by both government and the private sector, sought through persuasion and coercion to pressure women back into the home. Based on a revived "Cult of Domesticity" (Matthews, 1987), this campaign promoted a view of the ideal woman as pious, pure, submissive, and domestically engaged (Coontz, 2005). This backlash increased class and racial divides among working women and set the stage for a new era of significant policy change for women.

SECOND WAVE FEMINISM, 1960S TO 1990S

The second wave of political and policy change for women began in the early 1960s, largely in response to three developments: the approval of the birth control pill for contraception (see the box below); the establishment of the Presidential Commission on the Status of Women, chaired by former first lady Eleanor Roosevelt; and the publication of Betty Friedan's book *The Feminine Mystique*. The issues of gender equality and women's rights again took center stage in U.S. society. In 1962, 412 bills related to the status of women were introduced in Congress.

Two major pieces of legislation of particular importance to women and racial minorities were passed over the next several years: the Equal Pay Act of 1963, requiring equal pay for equal work, and the Civil Rights Act of 1964. Title IV of the Civil Rights Act specifically prohibited employment discrimination on the basis of race, color, religion, sex, or national origin. The Equal Employment Opportunity Commission

THE PILL: A DOCUMENTARY

The significance of the development and widespread use of the birth control pill as a means for women to make choices about contraception cannot be overstated. Its impact on women and U.S. social policy is detailed in a documentary by PBS titled *The Pill*. Here is a description:

> In May 1960, the FDA approved the sale of a pill that arguably would have a greater impact on American culture than any other drug in the nation's history. For women across the country, the contraceptive pill was liberating: it allowed them to pursue careers, fueled the feminist and pro-choice movements and encouraged more open attitudes towards sex.
>
> Among the key players in the development of the drug were two elderly female activists who demanded a contraceptive women could eat like aspirin and then paid for the scientific research; a devout Catholic gynecologist who believed a robust sex life made for a good marriage and argued tirelessly that the Pill was a natural form of birth control; and a brilliant biologist who bullied a pharmaceutical company into risking a possibly crippling boycott to develop this revolutionary contraceptive. In describing the obstacles they all hurdled, *The Pill* presents a compelling account of a society in transition.

Source: http://www.pbs.org/wgbh/amex/pill/filmmore/index.html

(EEOC) was created to implement Title IV, but it was largely ineffective in regard to gender issues, as evidenced in 1965 by its 3-to-2 ruling that sex segregation in job advertising was permissible.

In response, the newly formed National Organization for Women persuaded President Johnson to issue an executive order giving more teeth to the EEOC by requiring that all entities receiving federal contracts end discrimination in hiring. Soon after, Bernice Sandler, an activist and academic at the University of Maryland, filed a grievance with the Department of Labor's Office for Federal Fair Contracts Compliance. In 1972, her efforts led to the passage of Title IX of the Civil Rights Act forbidding discrimination in educational institutions.

In addition to a wide range of policy initiatives at the federal and state levels during this period, major judicial decisions reshaped the landscape for women and minorities of color. One of the most significant was the landmark 1973 Supreme Court ruling in *Roe v. Wade*. By establishing a right to privacy under the Due Process Clause of the Fourteenth Amendment, the court found that women had the right to choose to have an abortion. [See Chapter 10 in this volume for other important judicial decisions that shaped U.S. social policy.] Along with greater access to the birth control pill, this ruling significantly increased women's reproductive rights and freedom to make decisions about childbearing and marriage.

Concurrently, at the state level, the establishment of no-fault divorce laws altered the pattern of family formation in the United States. In the late 1960s, states began to allow couples to divorce based on "irreconcilable differences." The introduction of no-fault divorce initially produced an increase in the divorce rate, after which it leveled off (Wolfers, 2006). In addition, female suicide and domestic violence fell in states that adopted unilateral divorce, possibly due to a shift in women's bargaining power in their marriages (Stevenson & Wolfers, 2006).

RESTRUCTURING AND RETRENCHMENT, 1980 TO 2008

The next period of social policy change, from 1980 to 2008, was one of restructuring and retrenchment (Daguerre, 2011). During these three decades, programs that supported working families expanded while sharp cutbacks occurred in antipoverty programs. These changes had different consequences for women based on their race and social class, consequences that continue today.

Three pieces of federal legislation illustrate the impact on U.S. social policy of the changing sociopolitical discourse. The Family Medical Leave Act (1993) was a response to increased demands for workplace policies that supported women attempting to juggle family and work responsibilities. The Personal Responsibility and Work Opportunity Reconciliation Act (PRWORA, 1996) reflected hostility toward low-income women because of the perception that they were lazy and economically dependent on welfare. By eliminating the guarantee of support for mothers and state-sponsored alternatives to employment, the passage of PRWORA reflected a dramatic reversal of formerly maternalist policies.[2] Finally, in the same year, the Defense of Marriage Act (DOMA) reflected a reaction to rapid changes in family structure, the rise of the LGBTQ movement, and growing fears among conservatives about the demise of so-called traditional values. [*See Chapter 10 in this volume for an update on policy changes in this area.*]

The 1993 Family and Medical Leave Act (FMLA) provided up to 12 weeks of job-protected, unpaid leave during a 12-month period for the birth and care of a child, family member, or an individual's own serious health condition. While the legislation was widely applauded for its support of working women, there has been some debate about whether it enhanced gender equality in the home or reinforced women's obligations to attend to family responsibilities at the expense of their careers. It is telling that as of 2010, despite the gender-neutral language of the legislation, women made up 80% of the individuals who took leaves under the FMLA (Martin & Pyle, 2010).

In 1996, President Clinton signed the Personal Responsibility and Work Opportunity Reconciliation Act (PRWORA). This legislation fulfilled his 1992 campaign promise "to end welfare as we know it." By eliminating the 60-year-old entitlement to welfare, it signified a major shift in U.S. public assistance policy toward women, symbolized by the change in its name—from Aid to Families with Dependent Children to Temporary Assistance for Needy Families (TANF). The stated goals of PRWORA were to promote self-sufficiency and marriage, reduce the federal role, and decrease spending on public welfare programs. Over the past 16 years, however, the effects of PRWORA have been decidedly mixed, and assessments of its effectiveness continue to be debated (Schott, 2011).

During the late 1990s, a strong economy enabled many women who received public assistance to find and maintain a formal attachment to the workplace; this significantly reduced welfare rolls, particularly among white women (Abramovitz, 2006). Welfare reform, however, did nothing to change marriage trends among low-income families (Murray, 2012), and since 2007, welfare rolls have increased due to the recession and persistent economic stagnation. Because of its different impact on women of color, many social workers assert that TANF no longer functions as a public safety net; it only serves to perpetuate racism in the nation's welfare system (Abramovitz, 2006). [See Chapter 13 in this volume for more on welfare and welfare reform.]

In 2008, the United States and many other countries across the globe fell into a deep economic recession. The recession in the US affected men differently from women in that men actually lost more jobs than women. In large part this occurred because men are more likely to work in goods production and manufacturing while women more often work in health care, retail, and service industries (U.S. Department of Labor, 2011). The unemployment rate peaked in October 2009 at 11.4 percent for men and 8.8 percent for women. However, in this same year in households headed by a single woman, the unemployment rate was 13 percent (U.S. Department of Labor, 2011). [*See Chapter 3 this volume for additional discussion of the impact of the 2008 recession.*]

Also in 2008, President Obama was elected to the Presidency with the support of an historic proportion of the female electorate. His 14 percentage point advantage among women over his Republican opponent, Senator John McCain, was in large part a function of his campaign promises in favor of women's rights. These included the promotion of pay equity, investment in women-owned businesses, support of reproductive rights, efforts to combat violence against women, expansion of women's educational opportunities, and protection of women's health (Treuthart, 2016).

In January 2009, one of Obama's first acts as President was to sign the Lilly Ledbetter Fair Pay Restoration Act, which made it easier for women to sue their employers over pay discrimination. One month later, in February 2009, the President signed the American Recovery and Reinvestment Act (ARRA) which allocated $787 billion dollars in emergency funds for critical safety net programs, the expansion of unemployment benefits, and direct federal spending on infrastructure, education, health, and energy. A mandate of the ARRA was for states to provide unemployment insurance benefits to people seeking part-time work—the majority of whom are women. There were also provisions to support workers who leave their jobs to care for a sick family member and for those looking to leave violent relationships. [*See Chapter 3 this volume for further discussion of ARRA.*]

Due to a combination of economic and policy shifts, the U.S. economy began to emerge from the recession by late 2009. Since that time the unemployment rates for men and women have almost evened out. However, the gender wage gap remains; it not only has a significant impact on women's ability to make ends meet while in the formal labor market but also has implications for their retirement and future Social Security benefits. [*See Chapter 11 this volume for details about Social Security.*] Women are more likely to be employed part-time and in workplaces without benefits such as health insurance and are more likely than men to live in poverty. In 2014, 16 percent (25.9 million) of the nation's women and girls were living in poverty compared to 13.4% of men (U.S. Census Bureau, 2016).

This brief synopsis of some major historical antecedents to today's policies affecting women just scratches the surface of all that has changed for American women during the past 150 years. A central theme of policy advocacy on behalf of women during this period has been their desire to be treated as equals to men—when it comes to voting and property rights; employment practices such as pay equity; and physical safety at home, on the job, and in the streets. Parallel movements by people of color, new immigrants, LGBTQ individuals, and people with disabilities have also emphasized the theme of fair and equal treatment under the law. In sum, although women have made significant gains, particularly in the formal economy, the cultural expectation that women play the primary role of caregiver at home persists. Creating true gender equality will require more work in the policy arena.

CHANGING POLICY

Most often, social policy evolves in response to changing cultural trends and shifting social and economic priorities. As family and gender roles evolve and new ways of living and working become the norm, social policies adapt to meet the needs these changes create. For women, some policy developments reflect positive responses to their new social roles. Examples include the establishment of voting rights, the passage of laws prohibiting workplace discrimination, and legislation mandating gender parity in health care. Not all women, however, have benefited equally from these policy changes, and the needs of some women continue to be ignored or underserved. Significant differences continue to exist in the treatment of women of color, low-income women (especially those on TANF), immigrant women, and lesbians.

Policy changes emerge in all three branches of government. For this reason, increasing the number of women in elected and appointed offices is critical to the promotion of policy change. During the past several decades, some limited progress has been made in this area.

Women can also influence policy change through individual and collective activism to pressure policymakers to respond to their needs. For example, the battered women's movement, which emerged in the 1970s, was largely responsible for the passage of the Violence Against Women Act. The next section outlines the formal and informal ways women and racial minorities have acquired power and used it to influence social policies that affect them.

WOMEN IN FORMAL POSITIONS OF POWER

For many years, women were denied any formal political power in the United States. In fact, women could not vote in federal elections until 1920, when the recently adopted Nineteenth Amendment went into effect. Three years later, in 1923, the Equal Rights Amendment (ERA), which would guarantee women and men equal rights under the Constitution, was introduced in Congress. After nearly 50 years, Congress finally passed the ERA in 1972. Only 35 of the required 38 states ratified the amendment, however, and it is still not part of the Constitution.

It is interesting to note that during the first few decades of the 20th century, the ERA was a contentious issue among feminists and social workers. For example, Florence Kelley, founder of the National Consumers League and an avowed socialist, opposed the ERA. She believed that its adoption would undermine efforts to advance legislation that reflected a maternalist approach to social policy, an approach that she regarded as a "wedge" to expand social welfare to both women and men of all races more generally (Reisch & Andrews, 2002). [*See Chapter 2 this volume for further discussion of the influence of a maternalist approach to social policy during the Progressive Era.*]

Figure 5.7 Mary McLeod Bethune, Director of the Negro Affairs Division of the National Youth Administration

While the movements for women's suffrage and equal rights were formidable battles that produced mixed results, women did not hold any elective office at the federal level until 1917, when Jeannette Rankin, a social worker, became the first woman elected to Congress. Since Rankin's election, women have made slow progress in obtaining positions of power at the national level (see the box below).

EXAMPLES OF WOMEN'S "FIRSTS" IN PUBLIC OFFICE

1925 Nellie Taylor Ross, first woman elected as governor (Wyoming), following the death of her husband, Governor William Ross

1925 Miriam Ferguson, elected Governor of Texas succeeding her husband, who had been impeached

1933 Frances Perkins, a former settlement house worker, first woman to hold a cabinet position as Franklin Roosevelt's Secretary of Labor

1933 Mary McLeod Bethune, appointed director of the Negro Affairs Division of the National Youth Administration

1969 Shirley Anita St. Hill Chisholm, the first African American woman to serve in Congress (New York)

1974 Ella Grasso, first female governor (Connecticut) elected in her own right

1981 Sandra Day O'Connor, appointed by President Ronald Reagan as the first woman U.S. Supreme Court justice

1984 Geraldine Ferraro, first woman from a major political party chosen as its vice presidential candidate

1986 Barbara A. Mikulski becomes the first woman elected to the U.S. Senate in her own right and to serve in both houses of Congress. She was also the first woman to chair the Senate Appropriations Committee and to hold a leadership position in the Senate. A former community organizer with an MSW, she is the longest serving woman in Congress in U.S. history. She will retire in December 2016

1999 Tammy Baldwin, first out lesbian elected to Congress (Wisconsin)

2007 Nancy Pelosi, first female speaker of the House of Representatives

2008 Hillary Rodham Clinton, first viable woman presidential candidate of a major party

2012 Tammy Baldwin, first out lesbian elected to the U.S. Senate (Wisconsin)

2016 Hillary Rodham Clinton, the 2016 Democratic candidate for President.

Despite these numerous "firsts," by 1989, 70 years after the passage of the Nineteenth Amendment and 200 years after the adoption of the U.S. Constitution, women held only 6% of seats in Congress and only 15% of seats in the nation's state legislatures (Freeman, 2008). During the past generation, women have made modest progress in this regard. In November 2014, more women were elected to Congress than at any time in U.S. history. In the 114th Congress which took office in January 2015, there were 20 women (20%) Senators, including Tammy Baldwin (D-Wisconsin), the first open lesbian in the Senate, and 84 women (19.3%) in the House of Representatives. Thirty-three of these women are women of color. In 2016, six states have women governors, down from a peak of nine in 2011. The number of women in state legislatures, however, has remained virtually constant.

WOMEN IN PUBLIC OFFICE

Several organizations have taken up the cause of training, supporting, and financing women to run for public office, such as EMILY's List, the White House Project, and Women's Campaign Forum. The Women's Campaign Forum Foundation produced a video in September 2010, described here:

WCF Foundation's Voices from the Ladder performance piece disturbs complacency about the abysmally low number of women in public office and why their political equality plays a crucial role in our country's strength and future.

Source: http://www.imdb.com/title/tt0079638/

While women are still greatly outnumbered by men in formal positions of power, throughout U.S. history they have been among the strongest advocates and activists in movements that have influenced social policy. From the Seneca Falls Convention in 1848 and the Underground Railroad in the 1850s and 1860s to the civil rights movement of the mid-20th century and the recent push for fair wages, women have held formal and informal positions of power within key movement organizations.

WOMEN WITH INFORMAL POWER: ORGANIZING FOR CHANGE

At times, women have fought to expand their political and legal rights through the suffrage movement, the battered women's movement, and the movement to pass the ERA. One organization that has been a staple in citizen involvement in the political process is the League of Women Voters. Founded in 1920 by Carrie Chapman Catt during the convention of the National American Woman Suffrage Association, the League of Women Voters was established to ensure women's ability to carry out their newly won right to vote. Although it is formerly a non-partisan organization, the League has taken progressive stands on legislation to limit climate change, and in favor of campaign finance reform, reproductive rights, and gun control (Schulte, 2009).

Figure 5.8

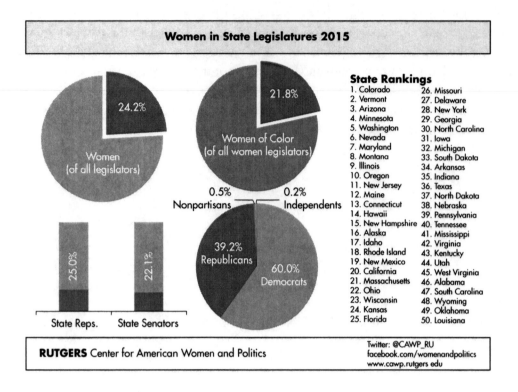

Women in State Legislatures 2015

24.2%

Women
(of all legislators)

21.8%

Women of Color
(of all women legislators)

25.0% 22.1%

State Reps. State Senators

0.5%
Nonpartisans

0.2%
Independents

39.2%
Republicans

60.0%
Democrats

State Rankings

1. Colorado	26. Missouri
2. Vermont	27. Delaware
3. Arizona	28. New York
4. Minnesota	29. Georgia
5. Washington	30. North Carolina
6. Nevada	31. Iowa
7. Maryland	32. Michigan
8. Montana	33. South Dakota
9. Illinois	34. Arkansas
10. Oregon	35. Indiana
11. New Jersey	36. Texas
12. Maine	37. North Dakota
13. Connecticut	38. Nebraska
14. Hawaii	39. Pennsylvania
15. New Hampshire	40. Tennessee
16. Alaska	41. Mississippi
17. Idaho	42. Virginia
18. Rhode Island	43. Kentucky
19. New Mexico	44. Utah
20. California	45. West Virginia
21. Massachusetts	46. Alabama
22. Ohio	47. South Carolina
23. Wisconsin	48. Wyoming
24. Kansas	49. Oklahoma
25. Florida	50. Louisiana

RUTGERS Center for American Women and Politics

Twitter: @CAWP_RU
facebook.com/womenandpolitics
www.cawp.rutgers.edu

At other times, women's movements have focused on women's social rights, such as Margaret Sanger's monumental struggle for reproductive rights and more recent efforts in support of LGBTQ rights and the rights of transgendered persons. Women have also played leadership roles in broader struggles on behalf of the rights of workers, immigrants, and people of color. In the mid-19th century, women such as Dorothea Dix, a teacher and activist, advocated on behalf of people with mental illness who were housed in county jails. [*See Chapter 2 this volume for further details about her work.*] At the turn of the 20th century, journalist and activist Ida B. Wells lead the fight to end the lynching of African Americans in the South and Midwest. In the mid-20th century, Dolores Huerta, co-founder and President of the United Farm Workers, worked in concert with Cesar Chavez to promote the rights of immigrant farmworkers. More recently, Asian American and African American women and Latinas have organized domestic care workers, hospital workers, and workers in the garment industry and the fast food industry, and have played leadership roles in the Occupy and Black Lives Matter movements. Thus, despite their frequent lack of formal positions of power both in the United States and abroad, women have often been the linchpins in many progressive struggles that have shaped social policy. Examples of these struggles are described below.

FAIR WAGES

The fight for fair wages in the United States spans many decades and occurred in many regions of the nation. It involved women and men, immigrants and native workers, whites and people of color. Some of the most notable struggles were led by unions such as the Industrial Workers of the World, which organized in such varying locales as the textile mills of Massachusetts and the mines and forests of the West. Modeled after trade unions, which had emerged in Great Britain during the Industrial Revolution, unions in the United States represented early examples of community organizing through which people with little power found ways to gain power with collective action.

The first organization of working women in the United States to fight for better working conditions and higher pay was the Lowell Female Labor Reform Association, established in 1844. Sarah Bagley, its first president, testified before the Massachusetts House of Representatives about the unsafe and desperate working conditions in the Lowell textile mills. While the association did not succeed in changing policy, its efforts marked the beginning of a movement that would last more than a century.

By the late 1940s, organizing campaigns on behalf of fair wages had spread across the country as a consequence of the massive increase in the domestic labor market that occurred after World War II. Although the Fair Labor Standards Act had been adopted in 1938, women and workers of color continued to experience wage discrimination, particularly when the nation's post-war political climate became more hostile to unions. In 1947 alone, 250 separate pieces of legislation were introduced in Congress to suppress union organizing, most notably the Taft-Hartley Act.

Figure 5.9 Dolores Huerta, one of the founders and leaders of the United Farm Workers.

FAIR WAGES

During the 19th and 20th centuries, as workers struggled to make ends meet and saw that their work was not being equally rewarded, they began to advocate for fair wages. Labor unions began to develop to protect the rights of workers. The legislation that passed limited who was covered and severely restricted the authority and activities of labor unions. In times of economic crisis, churches and social service agencies stepped in to help families meet basic needs and often allied with workers in their efforts to receive fair wages. Today, these struggles continue among both private- and public-sector workers.

Despite these conservative policies, mass advocacy for fair wages continued. By 1950, however, men still made up the overwhelming majority of the paid labor force (84.6%), resulting in few political gains by women. In the early 1950s, one labor struggle noteworthy for women's involvement occurred in Silver City, New Mexico. The local mine workers' union went on strike against the Empire Zinc Corporation and accused the company of discriminating against Mexican American miners in the areas of job safety, wages, and public sanitation in the company-supplied homes. The miners had been on strike for 9 months when a judge issued an injunction making it illegal for them to remain on the picket line. In response, their wives took their places on the picket line and eventually won the strike in January 1952. A powerful film about the strike, *Salt of the Earth*, was later blacklisted as Communist and anti-American.

In 2015, 11.1% of US workers belonged to labor unions (U.S. Department of Labor, 2016). Men were slightly more likely to be union members—11.5% compared to 10.6% for women. This gap has narrowed significantly over the past two decades (U.S. Department of Labor, 2016). Workers in the public sector have much higher rates of union membership (35.2%) compared to private sector workers (6.7%). Finally, union membership rates differ based on full or part-time employment. Approximately 1/8 of all full-time workers are union members (12.2%), while less than 6% of their part-time counterparts (5.9%) belong to unions (U.S. Department of Labor, 2016). While women are more likely to be employed in part-time jobs than men, women in unions make higher wages than women in non-union jobs. Union membership is, therefore, directly correlated with wages and explains some of the gender pay gap, although many other factors influence this outcome (Jones, Schmitt, & Woo 2014).

THE BATTERED WOMEN'S MOVEMENT

In the 1960s and 1970s, against the backdrop of the growing women's movement, a discussion emerged about women's physical safety that ultimately produced two separate but overlapping movements—one against sexual assault and one against domestic violence. Both began in large part from small-scale, private efforts to raise women's consciousness about their lives and experiences at the hands of men.

International developments also influenced these movements in the United States. In the mid-1970s, the first "Take Back the Night" rallies and marches in many European cities expressed the message that women around the world would no longer be silent about the violence inflicted on them. The first such rally is thought to have taken place in Belgium in March 1976, during the meeting of the International Tribunal on Crimes Against Women. Marches then took place in Germany, England, and Italy. The first such event in the United States was held in San Francisco in the fall of 1978. Marchers took to the streets of the city's red light district to protest rape and pornography. Over the past 40 years, annual "Take Back the Night" rallies have been particularly popular on college campuses.

The growing public concern about sexual assault and domestic violence produced two formal policy responses: the establishment of rape crisis centers and battered women's shelters, and the passage of state and federal laws designed to protect women. One of the most significant legislative reforms regarding sexual assault was the passage of state laws recognizing the existence of marital rape. States also adopted rape "shield laws," which disallowed court testimony on a victim's prior sexual history; these state laws eventually led to the 1975 federal Rape Control Act. In that same year, the National Institute of Mental Health established the National Center for the Prevention and Control of Rape. This produced increased government funding and more public awareness about the prevalence of this problem.

During this period, both state legislatures and Congress also passed legislation that expanded protections for women in the area of domestic violence, such as the 1984 Family Violence Prevention and Services Act. For a decade, this legislation provided the only dedicated federal funding to support battered women's shelters and other programs aiding victims of domestic violence. In 1993, however, the Senate Judiciary Committee, under the leadership of then-Senator Joseph Biden, initiated a multiyear study on the status of violence against women. Within a year, this led to the near unanimous passage of the Violence Against Women Act, which contained both criminal penalties for perpetrators of violence and federal and state grant programs to support victims of sexual assault, domestic violence, and stalking. The National Organization for Women described this legislation as the most significant development in the expansion of women's rights in nearly a generation.

The Violence Against Women Act (VAWA) has received high praise for its success in reducing the incidence rates of domestic violence in the U.S. (Catalano, 2012), Since its initial passage it has been reauthorized three times, most recently in 2013. Hoping to build on its success and bring this issue to the international stage, legislation was introduced in the 114th Congress (2015–2017), in both the Senate (S-713, Boxer) and the House of Representatives (H.R.1340, Schakowsky) entitled, the International Violence Against Women Act of 2015. This legislation is pending in committees in both houses of Congress as of this writing.

YOUNG WOMEN & SOCIAL MEDIA

The rapid increase in the use of the internet and social media has provided an unprecedented pathway for younger women to get involved in creating social change both locally and globally. Tools such as Facebook, Twitter, Instagram, and GoFundMe provide young women with access to people, groups, and power around the world that they never had before. A major example is the creation of the Black Lives Matter Movement, in the summer of 2013, by three women in three different cities in response to widely publicized incidences of violence against young Black men. Using the hashtag #BlackLivesMatter, this movement has acquired a voice on the national stage through non-violent protests at presidential campaign rallies and has focused increased public and media attention on racism within the criminal justice system and other

Figure 5.10 Black Lives Matter protest against Fox News and the New York Post, New York City, January 2, 2015.

societal institutions. Crediting the civil rights movement, the fight for LGBTQ rights, and Occupy Wall Street as its models, Black Lives Matters has demonstrated the access that young women have to get involved in social change.

MADRE: INTERNATIONAL ORGANIZING

During the past several decades, many American women have established connections with women in other nations and have focused their time and resources on international organizing and supporting women's social causes abroad. In 1983, at the invitation of Nicaragua's National Women's Association, a group of American women—including activists, poets, teachers, artists, and health professionals—traveled to Nicaragua to witness the impact of the U.S.-sponsored contra war against that nation's Sandinista government. They were shocked and horrified by what they saw, such as day-care centers, schools, and clinics that had been bombed by the contra rebels as part of a 10-year terrorist campaign; what they witnessed changed their lives. They returned to the United States with a mandate from the women of Nicaragua: Bring the stories of Nicaraguan women and children to the attention of the U.S. public, and mobilize people to demand a change in U.S. government policy. The outcome of their efforts was the creation of MADRE.

Today, MADRE is an international women's rights organization that works in partnership with women's community-based groups in conflict areas worldwide. Its programs address issues of sustainable development, community improvement, and women's health; violence and war; discrimination and racism; self-determination and collective rights; women's leadership development; and human rights education. MADRE provides resources and training to enable organizations to meet immediate needs in their communities and develop long-term solutions to crises. Since its creation in 1983, MADRE has provided more than $20 million worth of support to community-based women's groups in Sudan, Iraq, Nicaragua, Cuba, Haiti, Guatemala, Kenya, Peru, Colombia, Panama, Palestine, Afghanistan, Bolivia, and elsewhere. (For more information, visit http://www.madre.org.)

While the work of organizations such as MADRE may have only an indirect influence on U.S. social policy, its significance in this area should not be discounted. Through such international connections, American women learn other people's views regarding the effects of U.S. military and foreign policy, the inequalities that result from U.S. trade policy, and the impact on developing nations of multinational corporations, many based in the United States. This knowledge informs the organizing and advocacy efforts of women in groups such as farmworkers and the Coalition of Immokalee Workers around the issue of fair labor standards.

These examples of the many ways that women have organized to create change give a sense of the common struggles of women seeking equality, safety, and fair treatment under the law. Although organizing continues to be a powerful tool in creating social change, the nature of organizing is changing. By way of example, many women are finding success when they use the power of the Internet to reach more allies in more places. As former Secretary of State Hillary Clinton declared, "The spread of information networks is forming a 'new nervous system' for our planet" (Shahid & Silen, 2010).

ORGANIZING WOMEN AND YOUNG WORKERS: SOCIAL MEDIA AND FAMILY ISSUES

A recent report by the Cornell Labor Program specifically investigated how young organizers use social media to organize around work and family life issues. They found that 85% of women ages 18 to 29 go online several times each day, compared with 80% of men. Because of this, community and advocacy organizations are increasingly using the Internet to promote their causes, educate the public, raise their profiles, and direct traffic to their websites. When the researchers asked groups what issues they found most pressing for the current work/life dilemma that women are facing, they received the following responses:

Affordable housing

Discrimination against women

Early education and child care

Employee Free Choice Act

Equal Opportunity/Fair Pay Act

Equal pay

Family medical leave

Health care

Mitigating the media-constructed "mommy wars"

Paid parental leave

Paid sick days

Pay and hours

Pay equity

Social justice

Solidarity with striking workers

Unemployment insurance

Work–family balance

Workplace flexibility

Workplace standards

Source: http://www.ilr.cornell.edu/laborPrograms/

WOMEN AND SOCIAL POLICY IN THE 21ST CENTURY

Dramatic changes in the structure and composition of the modern American family have created the need for major social policy innovations with regard to women. Today, long-standing cultural expectations that women should marry and have children are not nearly as widespread as in the past. Women are now more able to make decisions about family and employment. Developments such as assisted fertility, the increased number of lesbian marriages, and the steady rise in both serial and step families have made the idealized nuclear family of the 1950s far less common (Coontz, 2005).

While many of these changes reflect progress toward women's equality, cultural and societal expectations of women to carry most of the household caregiving responsibilities for children and aging family members remain. During the past half century, U.S. social policies have begun to address some of these issues, through the passage of no-fault divorce laws, the Equal Pay Act (1963), the Civil Rights Act (1964), and the Family Medical Leave Act (1993). In many ways, however, the United States lags significantly behind other industrialized nations in creating policies that produce gender equality in the workplace, the health care system, and the area of marriage and divorce. An ongoing tension persists in U.S. society between policies that promote women's equality and those that recognize women's uniqueness.

FAMILIES IN THE 21ST CENTURY

In 2014, marriage rates in the United States were at their lowest levels in history, 6.9 per 1,000 Americans (National Center for Health Statistics, 2014). At the same time, divorce rates, which peaked in the late 1970s at almost 23 divorces for every 1,000 Americans have continued to decline to a new low of 3.2 per 1,000 in 2014 (National Center for Health Statistics, 2014). In addition, the rate of cohabitation among both heterosexual and gay couples has increased, with enormous implications for social policy in such areas as property rights, taxes, and eligibility for government and employment benefits.

The average size of U.S. households has also declined during this period from 3.4 people in 1960 to 2.6 people in 2010 (U.S. Census Bureau, 2010). Lundberg and Pollack (2007) attribute this decline to three trends: a decrease in fertility rates, an increase in single-parent households, and a decrease in three-generation households. Indeed, the U.S. birth rate fell from 118 per 1,000 people in 1960 to 60 per 1,000 in 1980 and has remained stable over the past several decades, except among certain segments of the population such as immigrants, Latinos, evangelicals, and women over 30. The birth rates for women under age 25 and for white, African American, Asian American, and Native American women have all fallen (U.S. Census Bureau, 2010). A final factor influencing birth rates is educational levels (Martinez, Daniels, & Chandra, 2012). Women with lower levels of education are most likely to have more children. This continues to be an important determinant of population growth and decline in the United States and globally.

An additional change has been an increase in single parenthood. Single-parent households are more common and socially acceptable today than ever before. In 2014, 35% of children were living in single-parent households (Annie E. Casey Foundation, 2015). Eighty percent of these households are made up of women with children. While 59% of mothers of all ages in 2009 were married when they had children, a majority of mothers under 30, who bear nearly two-thirds of all children in the United States, gave birth outside of marriage, particularly among lower income and working class women. According to Furstenberg, "marriage has become a luxury good" (quoted in DeParle & Tavernise, 2012, p. A-1).

It is difficult to determine the number and make-up of lesbian households in these various family constellations. It was not until the 1990 census that couples were able to identify as "unrelated adults." Black,

Sanders, and Taylor (2007) estimate that lesbian couples mirror heterosexual couples in terms of family formation. They partner at a rate of 63%, compared with 59% of heterosexual households; are similarly educated; and partner at about the same age. However, because of both legal and biological reasons, lesbian couples face different challenges in the workplace and in the areas of childbearing, family management, and access to government-funded social protections. In response, lesbians and their allies are increasingly demanding access to benefits, health care coverage, and legal protections equal to those of heterosexual women.

WOMEN, EMPLOYMENT, AND SOCIAL CLASS

Each of these trends contains important social policy implications for women with regard to education, health care, income support, child care, and employment. For the reasons outlined in this chapter, while race remains an important distinction among women today, in many ways social class is gaining in importance. The majority of women with means and education are marrying later and delaying childbearing. Some of these women are choosing to do neither, while others are choosing to marry and not have children or to have children but not marry. These increased options for affluent, better educated women enable them to compete more successfully in the formal economy because they are less burdened by traditional household chores and caregiving roles. Without major social policy changes, however, even these women will continue to face the challenges of balancing work and family life.

By contrast, women with fewer means and education are also delaying marriage but are not delaying childbearing as often as their middle- and upper-class counterparts. They are often single mothers who, as a consequence of childbearing and decreased government support, have more difficulty managing the dual demands of work and family. In recent years, the economic downturn has further exacerbated their plight. As a consequence of the severe recession of 2007, financially vulnerable families are at greater risk of wage and benefit cuts and are likely to experience reduced work hours and less flexible employment conditions. These all create higher levels of debt and affect families' child care arrangements and costs. If these trends continue, women in poverty will have even fewer opportunities to become financially stable and the nation's class divisions will widen (McCall, 2009).

WOMEN AND SOCIAL POLICY: WHERE DO WE GO FROM HERE?

It is impossible to discuss women and social policy without recognizing the broad effects that family formation and function have had on laws governing both the workplace and the personal lives of women. As families in the United States continue to change, social policies will need to adapt to the emerging needs of women in the home and workplace. How society constructs new social norms, values, gender roles, and relationships, and distributes power and resources in the private and public spheres will be a central component of this process. Until societal norms and expectations about men's participation in care-giving and domestic labor shift, the nation's social policies will need to respond to women's multiple roles in such areas as child care funding, workplace flexibility, and the provision of health care.

Child care, for example, has long been a critical social policy issue for women. Both quality of care and access to care are important factors in families' decision making, particularly in households with children ages 0 to 5 (Chaudry, Henly, & Meyers, 2010). Yet low-income women often face barriers to obtaining adequate child care, such as nonstandard work schedules, fluctuating hours, transportation challenges, and limited financial support through government or employment-based subsidies. Although child care subsidies are available to women on TANF and, to some extent, to other low-income families, funding is limited and varies considerably among the states. In addition, there are often long waiting lists, and administrative obstacles substantially reduce participation rates (Adams, Snyder, & Banghart, 2008).

The National Study of Child Care of Low-Income Families 1997–2007 revealed that less than 5% of employers had either on-site or subsidized care for their employees' children; that child care problems were a significant disruption to parents' work schedules; and that transporting children before and after work added 1 to 1 1/2 hours to a mother's workday. Many of these same challenges plague middle-class workers as well. While child care is universally available to families regardless of income in many European countries, the lack of affordable child care in the United States continues to place substantial stress on women, particularly on those with lower socioeconomic status.

One partial solution, the adoption of flexible work schedules, would require policy changes of a different nature. Emlen (2010) argues that families make solid, logical, financially sound choices based in large part on the degree of flexibility provided by their jobs, social support networks, and child care providers. He contends that universal child care is only one possible solution and suggests that policies should be informed by an expanded understanding of what parents need to be successful, including basic benefits, improved working conditions, tax incentives, higher wages, and expanded economic development at the local level. He argues that "instead of a relentless pursuit of cheap labor, we need policies that support the economic strength of families" (Emlen, 2008, p. 2). [See Chapters 3 and 12 in this volume.]

Finally, an important policy issue for women in the future will be the availability of affordable health care, the distribution of which, like many other issues discussed in this chapter, is often associated with race and social class. According to a Kaiser Women's Health Survey (Kaiser Family Foundation, 2008) low-income women were 3 times as likely to rate their overall health as fair or poor. However, only 45% of this population have paid sick leave, compared with 69% of higher income women. Low-income women are also far less likely to have employer-sponsored health insurance benefits. As a result, more than one-sixth of women ages 18 to 64 are uninsured.

The relationship between work and social policy will continue to be one of the most important issues facing women in the United States in the years ahead. Of particular significance will be the quality and types of jobs available to low-income women, not only in regard to wage levels and benefits but also concerning work schedules and access to child care. Without substantial changes in both the economy and social policy, these women and their children will have few opportunities to escape poverty.

In addition to these critical economic issues, persistent legislative and judicial challenges threaten to erode the gains women have made in the areas of reproductive and LGBTQ rights. Although the Supreme Court's historic 2015 decision legalized same sex marriage and declared the Defense of Marriage Act (DOMA) unconstitutional, using the justification of protecting "religious freedom," a number of states such as Indiana have taken steps that effectively sanction ongoing discrimination in the provision of goods or services to gays and lesbians. Employing a similar rationale, some states have supported efforts by some private companies and sectarian organizations to resist providing contraceptive coverage to their employees as required by the Affordable Care Act. In addition, legislatures in states like North Carolina have overturned municipal antidiscrimination ordinances that protected people based on their gender identity and, as of this writing, have required transgendered individuals to use restrooms based on the sex stated on their birth certificates.

Finally, according to research conducted by the Guttmacher Institute in 2015, states have enacted as many restrictions on women's access to abortions during the last five years as in the previous 15 years combined. During the 2015 legislative session alone, state lawmakers introduced over 500 measures that sought to restrict access to abortion services. In its next term, the Supreme Court will hear two potentially landmark cases regarding reproductive rights. These efforts have occurred concurrently with attempts in both Congress and numerous state legislatures to defund Planned Parenthood clinics which, if successful, would serious affect women's access to critical health care services (Nash, et al, 2015; Raymond, 2016). [*See Chapter 10 in this volume for further discussion of judicial decisions on these issues.*]

CONCLUSION

Social policies affecting women in the United States have changed dramatically over the past century as changes in the family, economy, and society have transformed women's roles and status in the home and workplace and enabled them to gain some equality in relation to men. Both formal and informal change processes helped produce this progress.

Yet women in the United States today still earn only 78% of what men do for comparable employment. They hold only a fraction of U.S. elected and appointed political offices and management and executive positions in the private sector. Women are also overrepresented in low-wage employment, where benefits such as sick leave, health insurance, and retirement pensions are frequently limited or entirely unavailable. At the same time, women remain the primary caregivers of children, elders, and those who are ill. These conditions are neither accidental nor inevitable. They reflect the norms, cultural values, relationships, power distribution, and social constructs that shape social policy in U.S. society.

Current and projected economic and social trends have created greater class and racial divides between American women. Women with higher levels of education and more resources are becoming better able to resolve some of their work–life balance issues, although they still have responsibilities that are not expected of men. The lives of women with lower levels of education and limited opportunities in the workplace, however, are being strained more than ever due to the lack of effective social policies that could support their complex economic and family needs. Unless these policies are changed, in this next century the class and racial divide between women will grow. Social workers, therefore, need to advocate for policy changes that address the needs of *all women*, particularly those who are most vulnerable.

Discussion Questions

1. In your family of origin, what role did women play? How did this shape how you understand women's roles in our culture today?
2. Write a definition of "family." Given Americans' varying ideas on what it means to be a "family," how can social policies affecting families be created and carried out so no one group or category of individuals is left out?
3. Some of the impacts of a maternalist approach to social policy were mentioned in this chapter. In what other social policies is there evidence of this "special" regard for women as caregivers and nurturers?

4. The chapter outlines the importance of understanding the "intersectionality" of identities. Think of some examples of social policies that affect women of different races and classes differently. What are some examples of when class and race overlap, and when can you see evidence of them acting against each other?
5. Think ahead 20 to 30 years. If current trends continue, from the traditional family of a married-for-life heterosexual couple toward more diverse family compositions, what will be some of the consequences for social policy and society as a whole?

Suggested Websites

California Women's Law Center: http://www.cwlc.org/

Center for American Progress: http://www.americanprogress.org/

Center on Budget and Policy Priorities: http://www.cbpp.org/

Emily's List: http://emilyslist.org/

Equal Rights Advocates: http://www.equalrights.org/

Feminist Majority Foundation: http://feminist.org/

Feministing: http://feministing.com/

Gender Spectrum: http://www.genderspectrum.org/

Human Rights Campaign: http://www.hrc.org/

Institute for Women's Policy Research: http://www.iwpr.org/

National Organization for Women: http://www.now.org/

Our Bodies, Ourselves: http://www.ourbodiesourselves.org/

RH Reality Check: http://www.rhrealitycheck.org/

Transgender Law Center: http://transgenderlawcenter.org/

Women's Law Project: http://www.womenslawproject.org/

Women's Media Center: http://www.womensmediacenter.com/

Suggestions for Further Reading

Albelda, R., & Tilly, C. (1997). *Glass ceilings and bottomless pits: Women's work, women's poverty.* Boston: South End Press.

Boushey, H., & O'Leary, A. (Eds.), (2009). *The Shriver Report: A woman's nation changes everything.* Washington, DC: Center for American Progress.

Butler, J. (2004). *Undoing gender.* New York: Routledge.

Currah, P., Jung, R., & Price Minter, S. (Eds.). (2006). *Transgender rights.* Minneapolis: University of Minnesota Press.

Holmstrom, N. (2003). *The socialist feminist project: A contemporary reader in theory and politics.* New York: Monthly Review Press.

hooks, b. (2000). *Where we stand: Class matters.* New York: Routledge.

Nestle, J., & Wilchins, R. (Eds.). (2002). *GenderQueer: Voices from beyond the sexual binary.* New York: Alyson Books.

Stryker, S., & Whittle, S. (Eds.). (2006). *The transgender studies reader.* New York: Routledge.

Williams, J., & Boushey, H. (2010). *The three faces of work–family conflict: The poor, the professionals, and the missing middle.* Washington, DC: Center for WorkLife Law & Center for American Progress. Retrieved from http://www.worklifelaw.org/pubs/ThreeFacesofWork-FamilyConflict.pdf

References

Abramovitz, M. (1996). *Regulating the lives of women: U.S. social policy from colonial times to the present* (Rev. ed.). Boston: South End Press.

Abramovitz, M. (2006). Welfare reform in the United States: Gender, race and class matter. *Critical Social Policy, 26,* 336–364.

Adams, G., Snyder, K., & Banghart, P. (2008). *Designing subsidy systems to meet the needs of families: An overview of policy research findings.* Washington, DC: Urban Institute.

Amenta, E. (1998). *Bold relief: Institutional politics and the origins of modern American social policy.* Princeton, NJ: Princeton University Press.

Amott, T., & Matthaei, J. (1991). *Race, gender, and work: A multicultural economic history of women in the United States.* Boston: South End Press.

Annie E. Casey Foundation (2015). *KidsCount 2015.* Baltimore, MD: Author.

Ballou, M., & Brown, L. (2002). *Rethinking mental health and disorder: Feminist perspectives.* New York: Guilford Press.

Black, D. A., Sanders, S. G., & Taylor, L. J. (2007). The economics of lesbian and gay families. *Journal of Economic Perspectives, 21*(2), 53–70.

Boushey, H., & O'Leary, A. (Eds.) (2009, January). *The Shriver report: A woman's nation changes everything.* Washington, DC: Center for American Progress. Retrieved August 12, 2011, from http://www.americanprogress.org/issues/2009/10/pdf/awn/a_womans_nation.pdf

Bronfenbrenner, U. (1979). *The ecology of human development: Experiments in nature and design.* Cambridge, MA: Harvard University Press.

Catalano, S.M. (2012). *The latest information from the Bureau of Justice Statistics (BJS) on Intimate Partner Violence, 1993–2010*. NCJ # 239203. U.S. Dept. of Justice, Bureau of Justice Statistics. Available from: http://www.bjs.gov/index.cfm?ty=pbdetail&iid=4536.

Cauthen, N., & Amenta, E. (1996). Not for widows only: Institutional politics and the formative years of Aid to Dependent Children. *American Sociological Review, 61*, 427–448.

Chafe, W. (1972). *The American woman: Her changing social, economic, and political roles, 1920–1970.* New York: Oxford University Press.

Chaudry, A., Henly, J., & Meyers, M. (2010). *Conceptual frameworks for child care decision-making* (ACF-OPRE White Paper). Washington, DC: Office of Planning, Research and Evaluation, Administration for Children and Families.

Coontz, S. (2005). *Marriage, a history: From obedience to intimacy, or how love conquered marriage.* New York: Viking.

Daguerre, A. (2011). U.S. social policy in the 21st century: The difficulties of comprehensive social reform. *Social Policy & Administration, 45*(4), 389–407.

DeParle, J., & Tavernise, S. (2012, February 18). Unwed mothers now a majority in births in 20s. *New York Times,* p. A-1.

Emlen, A. (2008). Solving the flexibility puzzle: Few communities, or companies, or even households are organized to provide working mothers with all the flexibility they need. *The Mothers Movement Online.* Retrieved November 6, 2012, from http://www.mothersmovement.org/features/08/05/emlen_1.html

Emlen, A. (2010). *Solving the childcare and flexibility puzzle: How working parents make the best feasible choices and what that means for public policy.* Boca Raton, FL: Universal.

Freeman, J. (2008). *We will be heard: Women's struggles for political power in the United States.* Lanham, MD: Rowman & Littlefield.

Furstenberg, F. F. (2014). Fifty years of family change: From consensus to complexity. *The Annals of the American Academy of Political and Social Science, 654*, 12–30.

Goldin, C. (2006). The quiet revolution that transformed women's employment, education, and family. *American Economic Review, 96*(2), 1–21.

Jones, J., Schmitt, J. & Woo, N. (2014). Women, working families, and unions. *Center for Economic and Policy Research.* Washington, DC.

Kaiser Family Foundation. (2008). *Kaiser women's health survey.* Menlo Park, CA: Author.

Kemp. S. (2001). Environment through a gendered lens: From person-in-environment to woman-in-environment. *Affilia: Journal of Women & Social Work, 16*(1), 7–30.

Kessler-Harris, A. (1981). *Women have always worked: A historical overview.* Old Westbury, NY: Feminist Press.

Kleinberg, S. J. (1989). *The shadow of the mills: Working-class families in Pittsburgh, 1870–1907.* Pittsburgh, PA: University of Pittsburgh Press.

Koven, S., & Michel, S. (Eds.) (1993). *Mothers of a new world: Maternalist politics and the origins of the welfare state.* New York: Routledge.

Lundberg, S., & Pollack, R. (2007). The American family and family economics. *Journal of Economic Perspectives, 21*(2), 3–26.

Martin, E., & Pyle, B. (2010, May). *Judicial gender perspectives in resolving FMLA conflicts.* Paper presented at the annual meeting of the Law and Society Association, Chicago.

Martinez, G. M., Daniels, K., & Chandra, A. (2012). Fertility of men and women aged 15–44 years in the United States: National Survey of Family Growth, 2006–2010. *National Health Statistics Report, 51.* Hyattsville, MD: National Center for Health Statistics.

Matthews, G. (1987). *Just a housewife: The rise and fall of domesticity in America.* New York: Oxford University Press.

McCall, L. (2005). The complexity of intersectionality. *Signs: Journal of Women, Culture and Society, 30*(3), 1771–1800.

McCall, L. (2009). Increasing class disparities among women and the politics of gender and equity. In D. Cobble (Ed.), *The sex of class: Women and America's labor movement* (pp. 15–34). Ithaca, NY: Cornell University Press.

Morales, A. T., & Sheafor, B. W. (2001). *Social work: A profession of many faces.* Boston: Allyn & Bacon.

Muller v. Oregon (1908). 208 US 412.

Murray, C. (2012). *Coming apart: The state of white America, 1960–2010.* New York: Crown.

Nash, E, et al. (2016, April 10). Laws affecting reproductive health and rights: *2015 State Policy Review.* Retrieved April 27, 2016, from https://www.guttmacher.org/laws-affecting-reproductive -health-and-rights-2015-state-policy-review

National Center for Health Statistics (2014). *National marriage and divorce rate trends.* Retrieved from: http://www.cdc.gov/nchs/nvss/marriage_divorce_tables.htm.

Parker, K., and Wang, W. (2013). *Modern parenthood: Roles of moms and dads converge as they balance work and family.* Washington, DC: Pew Research Center.

Raymond, L. (2016, April 19). Obama Administration warns states that defunding Planned Parenthood is probably illegal. Retrieved April 27, 2016, from http://thinkprogress.org/health/2016/04/19/3770825/ obama-administration-sends-states-strongest-warning-yet-not-to-defund-planned-parenthood/

Reisch, M., & Andrews, J. L. (2002). *The road not taken: A history of radical social work in the United States.* Philadelphia: Brunner-Routledge.

Schott, L. (2011, July 6). *An introduction to TANF.* Washington, DC: Center on Budget and Policy Priorities.

Shahid, S., & Silen, A. (2010, January 21). Clinton urges global Internet freedom. *Newseum.* Retrieved from http://www.newseum.org/news/2010/01/clinton-urges-global-internet-freedom.html

Schulte, T. (2009). Citizen experts: The League of Women Voters and environmental conservation. *Frontiers: A Journal of Women Studies, 30*(3): 1–29.

Stevenson, B., & Wolfers, J. (2006). Bargaining in the shadow of the law: Divorce laws and family distress. *Quarterly Journal of Economics, 121*(1), 267–288.

Stevenson, B., & Wolfers, J. (2007). Marriage and divorce: Changes and their driving forces. *Journal of Economic Perspectives, 21*(2), 27–52.

Stimpson, C. (1981). *Women and the American city.* Chicago: University of Chicago Press.

Treuthart, M. (2016). Feminist-in-Chief? Examining President Obama's executive orders on women's rights issues, 91 *Chi.-Kent. L. Rev. 171.*

U.S. Census Bureau. (2006). *Households by size: 1960 to present.* Retrieved from http://www.census.gov/ population/socdemo/hh-fam/hh4.pdf

U.S. Census Bureau. (2010). *2010 Census.* Retrieved August 12, 2011, from http://2010.census. gov/2010census

U.S. Census Bureau. (2016). *Historical Poverty Tables—Families.* Retrieved from: https://www.census.gov/ hhes/www/poverty/data/historical/families.html

U.S. Department of Commerce, Bureau of the Census. (1943). *Comparative statistics for the United States, 1870–1940*. Washington, DC: U.S. Government Printing Office.

U.S. Department of Labor (2011). *Women's employment during the recovery*. Retrieved from: http://www.dol.gov/_sec/media/reports/FemaleLaborForce/FemaleLaborForce.pdf.

U.S. Department of Labor, Bureau of Labor Statistics. (2016). *Unions members summary*. Retrieved from http://www.bls.gov/news.release/union2.nr0.htm

Wolfers, J. (2006). Did unilateral divorce raise divorce rates? A reconciliation and new results. *American Economic Review, 96*(5), 1802–1820.

Notes

[1]This chapter focuses on the relationship between women and social policy. Because it is the only chapter in this volume with a *specific* focus on gender, it is important to recognize the policy implications of the current social construct of gender, which defines it in binary terms—that is, there are two recognized and accepted genders, female and male. In fact, many people do not identify as either female or male. Consequently, they often find themselves in situations in which existing policies conflict with their needs, constrain their access to public or private benefits, or fail to protect their rights, particularly in the areas of health and health care. For additional reading and information on this topic, please see the resources listed at the end of this chapter.

[2]It is important to note that PRWORA is not the only part of Social Security policy that discriminates against women. Because men have long been the primary wage earners, women who divorced, stayed at home, or worked in lower paying industries have not benefited as men have from this government retirement plan. Yet women are also less likely than men to have savings or pensions (Abramovitz, 1996). [*See Chapter 11 in this volume for further discussion of Social Security policy and Chapter 13 in this volume for further discussion of welfare policy and the effects of welfare reform.*]

Credits

PART II

POLICY PRACTICE

Michael Reisch, PhD

The five chapters in Part II focus on the process of social policy development and the skills required to effect changes in the conceptualization, formulation, and implementation of social policy through policy analysis, advocacy, and coalition building.

Chapter 6, by Richard K. Caputo, opens by presenting an actual piece of proposed legislation and then uses this case example to discuss the three major ways of understanding social policy: policy as product, process, and performance. It emphasizes the major concepts and methodological approaches, and the tools and techniques germane to each of these three distinct aspects of policy analysis. The chapter is divided into four subsections: The first subsection, "Policy Studies," provides background on the field of policy studies, the relationship between politics and policy, and the role of social science in policy analysis. It focuses on the issues of value neutrality and value relevance in social science, and on the relationship between theory, policy, politics, and social work practice. The next subsection, "Policy as Product," discusses social welfare legislation and programs in light of who gets what benefits, why they get them, how they get them, and how the programs are financed. This is followed by a subsection that addresses "Policy as Process"—that focuses on the theoretical and practical aspects of policymaking and implementation. The final subsection, "Policy as Performance," discusses several theoretical and methodological approaches to assessing policy outcomes, including impact analysis and realistic evaluation perspectives. Content on how social workers can research the underlying assumptions and evaluate the impact of social policies is also included.

Social policy scholars such as Diana DiNitto have argued that the federal budget is the single most important policy instrument in the United States. Chapter 7, by Karen M. Staller, provides a basic introduction to the structure and content of government budgets at the federal and state level and their implications for social policy development. It emphasizes the role of budgets in redistributing wealth and how the budget process often serves as a battleground in conflicts over social justice in the United States, particularly in today's hyper-partisan political environment.

The chapter begins with an outline of the basic structure of the federal budget, including the relationship between *revenues* (or receipts) and *expenditures* (or uses) and their implications for the bottom line (i.e., whether the budget is balanced or has a surplus or deficit). The discussion covers the significance of various revenue sources, such as the personal income tax (and related fiscal policies of significance, such as the Earned Income Tax Credit), Federal Insurance Contributions Act or FICA (the Social Security/Medicare or "payroll" tax) and its associated demographic concerns, and business or corporate taxes. On the expenditure side, it discusses the difference between the purchase of goods and services (e.g., salaries for federal employees and the funding of government contracts) and transfer payments (including domestic and foreign transfers, entitlements, and discretionary spending). Next, it clarifies the distinction between budget deficits and the national debt, and addresses the "balanced budget issue" by examining the consequences of deficits and deficit spending, the effects of borrowing through bonds and bills, the significance of federal debt, the impact of interest on the federal debt, and the implications of international borrowing for the global economy, including the status of the United States as a "debtor" nation in contrast to China's "creditor" nation status. The chapter also includes content on the recent crisis "fiscal cliff" crisis, the ideological differences that drive recurrent confrontations over the budget, and the consequences of sequestration that resulted from the failure of Congress to resolve its long-term budget conflicts.

The chapter then covers state budgets, including the extent to which they rely on unique revenue sources (e.g., property and sales taxes), pay for unique expenditures (e.g., education, health, public safety, parks), and are affected by the double-edged sword created by federal revenue sharing. It examines the social justice implications of various structural arrangements for generating state revenue, such as progressive and regressive systems of taxation, and their impact on low-income populations. It also notes legal restrictions on states' ability to borrow, such as the constitutional imperative to balance state budgets. These restrictions contribute substantially to the distinction between the federal and state budget process, and have major implications for the development of social policies, programs, and services, and for the political rhetoric that surrounds government policymaking.

As Chapter 7 indicates, advocates for low-income people and for programs that serve them face many challenges, not the least of which is the complexity of how funding decisions are made in policymaking circles. Chapters 8 and 9 discuss how advocates can be more effective at the federal and state levels, respectively. As the authors of Chapter 8, Monica Healy and Gene Sofer, point out, successful advocacy at the federal level, for example, requires policy advocates to play a combination of an "inside game" and an "outside game."

This chapter is an excellent complement to the discussion in Chapter 7 of the budget process in Congress. Through an in-depth case study of the creation and evolution of the Save AmeriCorps coalition, Healy and Sofer describe a successful multi-year policy advocacy strategy at the federal level. They provide additional details about the stages in the federal legislative and budget processes outlined in Chapter 7 and present valuable insights into how advocates approach challenging decisions and where they may be able to influence the outcome of the policy development process. This chapter also describes how advocates might assess their strengths and weaknesses and mobilize resources they might not even be aware of to achieve their policy aims. It includes content on the role of media and professional organizations in policy advocacy. Finally, it updates the case study and summarizes its lessons for future advocacy efforts at the federal level.

During the past four decades, as responsibility for social policy has been "pushed down" (or devolved) to state and even sub-state jurisdictions (county, parish, city, township and other local governmental and quasi-governmental bodies), the importance of advocacy at these levels has correspondingly increased. As the author of Chapter 9, Richard Hoefer, asserts successful advocacy practices at the national level do not always translate well to lower levels of government and may not, in fact, be equally effective in different jurisdictions. To address these emerging issues, this chapter explores the following questions:

- What is the context of state and local policy advocacy?
- What do we know about the nature and extent of state and local policy advocacy?
- What do we know about the best practices of state and local advocacy?
- What does the future seem to hold regarding state and local advocacy?
- How can advocacy groups use the media effectively to promote advocacy goals?

The chapter discusses the impact of changes in the financing of political campaigns, the decentralization of policymaking, and federal cuts in social spending on state level policy development. It explores the diverse political cultures of states and, through the use of specific case examples, illustrates the implications of these diverse cultures for policy advocacy. Finally, it analyzes the barriers facing policy advocates today, assesses the role of technology and social media in policy advocacy, and presents several recommendations to enhance advocacy efforts in the future.

As reflected by a number of recent Supreme Court decisions, including cases decided in June 2016, the judiciary plays an increasingly important role in shaping the parameters of U.S. social policy and the processes by which policy can be implemented. Chapter 10, by Vicki Lens, examines the role of the judiciary in shaping, changing, and creating social policy in the U.S. After a brief historical overview of the role of state and federal courts in the U.S., the chapter describes the structure of the contemporary judiciary system, including where and how cases involving social policy issues are brought to its attention. It then summarizes the different ways judges interpret the U.S. Constitution, and explains the process by which courts decide cases and create social policy; this includes making law when no legislation exists and interpreting laws and the Constitution. Landmark Supreme Court decisions arising from the constitutional clauses that most affect social welfare legislation and social justice, including the Equal Protection and Due Process Clauses of the Fourteenth Amendment and the Commerce Clause, are discussed. The advantages and disadvantages of the judiciary playing a key role in social policy development and implementation are explored. Finally, the chapter discusses the roles that social workers can play in the judicial policymaking process.

6

POLICY ANALYSIS

Richard K. Caputo, PhD

This chapter provides an overview of policy analysis, with a focus on its relationship to advocacy and social justice. It traces the historical roots of policy analysis as a discipline of study; discusses value neutrality, value relevance, and critical thinking in the social sciences and social work; examines the setting of policy agendas; and presents an analytic framework of policy analysis as product, process, and performance. Before we start, however, consider the following bill as introduced in its entirety into the House of Representatives of the U.S. Congress:

H.R. 3010—Preserving Welfare for Needs Not Weed Act (Introduced in the House—IH)
114th CONGRESS
1st Session
H.R. 3010

To prohibit assistance provided under the program of block grants to States for temporary assistance for needy families from being accessed through the use of an electronic benefit transfer card at any store that offers marijuana for sale.

IN THE HOUSE OF REPRESENTATIVES
July 9, 2015

Mr. REICHERT introduced the following bill; which was referred to the Committee on Ways and Means

A BILL

To prohibit assistance provided under the program of block grants to States for temporary assistance for needy families from being accessed through the use of an electronic benefit transfer card at any store that offers marijuana for sale.

Be it enacted by the Senate and House of Representatives of the United States of America in Congress assembled,

SECTION 1. SHORT TITLE.

This Act may be cited as the 'Preserving Welfare for Needs Not Weed Act'.

SEC. 2. PROHIBITION OF THE USE OF ELECTRONIC BENEFIT TRANSFER CARD TO ACCESS TANF ASSISTANCE AT ANY STORE THAT OFFERS MARIJUANA FOR SALE.

(a) PROHIBITION.—Section 408(a)(12)(A) of the Social Security Act is amended—by
    (1) by striking "or" at the end of clause (ii);
    (2) by striking the period at the end of the clause (iii) and inserting "; or" and
    (3) by adding at the end the following:
        "(iv) any establishment that offers marijuana (as defined in section 102(16) of the Controlled Substances Act) for sale.".
(b) EFFECTIVE DATE. The amendments made by subsection (a) shall take effect on the date that is 2 years after the date of the enactment of this Act.

Source: https://www.congress.gov/114/bills/hr3010/BILLS-114hr3010ih.pdf

If you were the staff person asked to analyze this policy, how would you go about it? What challenges would you face in assessing its merits and the likelihood of it being enacted by Congress and signed by the President? Who is likely to support the bill? Who is likely to oppose it? What would be the reasons for their positions? What underlying assumptions would influence their decision? Aside from self-interest, what public interest arguments might opponents and supporters advance to augment their respective positions? If the National Association of Social Workers were to back this bill, would you be inclined to advocate for or against its passage? Why? How would passage/defeat of this bill serve social justice? Given what you know about human behavior and the social environment, if the bill became law, what unforeseen or unintended consequences, if any, for better or worse, might be likely to result?

Welcome to the world of policy analysis, one that presents formidable challenges to social workers seeking to retain a sense of professional integrity as analysts while fulfilling the professional mandate to pursue social justice. Policy analysis invariably entails applying a set of conceptual and technical skills to shed light on three dimensions of any given policy:

1. The policy *product* itself—that is, the tangible embodiment of a policy such as a specific piece of legislation, bill, or procedure
2. Policy *processes* such as those involved in policymaking (i.e., the politics involved in getting policies passed by a legislative body) and policy implementation (i.e., how policies are carried out by the executive branch of government and its designees, who often include social workers as program administrators and line staff)
3. Policy *performance*—that is, the outcomes of policies that have been passed and implemented

Each of these dimensions of the policy process involves establishing *priorities* and coming to terms with contestable social values about the merit or worth of policy goals, the means to obtain them, and the unintended consequences that result from implementing them.

Policies are invariably value laden, so policy analysts must possess conceptual and technical skills to enable them to identify and assess the values that underlie policies in question and those that may be ignored or downplayed. Social justice is one such value that social workers use in their assessment of policy as product, process, and performance, and in determining societal priorities. Policy analysis may serve a variety of purposes, contingent on the context in which it is carried out. As such, its relation to policymakers and others who have a stake or an interest in the particulars of any given policy complicates the role of the policy analyst. One of the goals of this chapter is to show how policy analysis might be done in a way that enables social workers to retain professional integrity. As this chapter makes clear, value-related conflicts are an inherent part of policymaking, whether viewed from the vantage point of product, process, or performance. The integrity of policy analysts in general and of agenda-driven policy analysts in particular, including social workers guided by the professional mandate to seek social justice, may be severely tested unless safeguards are in place. Another goal of this chapter is to highlight those safeguards that enhance the integrity and legitimacy of the practice of policy analysis itself.

To help get a better understanding of the components of policy analysis and to meet these two goals, this chapter covers the following material. First, it reviews the historical roots and development of policy analysis as a discipline of study and professional practice. Particular attention is given to the emergence of policy studies in academia, social work's mandate for advocacy and policy analysis, and the role of think tanks in the late 20th century and first decades of the 21st century.

Second, the chapter addresses the issue of value neutrality in the practice of policy analysis. The fact/value dichotomy, objectivity, and the roles of critical thinking in general and scientific thinking in particular are highlighted. Three roles of policy analysts will be briefly highlighted: objective technician, client's advocate, and issue advocate.

Third, the chapter provides an analytic framework of policy analysis as product, process, and performance. It discusses the merits and limitations of a social constructivist approach to social problem formation and presents criteria for assessing the desirability of social policies and programs. Theoretical and practical considerations are also discussed.

HISTORICAL ROOTS AND DEVELOPMENT OF POLICY ANALYSIS AS A DISCIPLINE OF STUDY

Policy analysis in the United States has its roots in the social reform efforts that emerged at the end of the Civil War: the formation of the American Social Science Association (ASSA) in 1865; the professionalization of the social sciences and the helping professions, such as social work, in the latter part of the 19th century and during the Progressive Era of the early 20th century; and demands for human science experts in government agencies and private foundations to address social problems produced by both World Wars in the first half of the 20th century (Cravens, 1971; Furner, 2011; Smith, 1994). Since World War II, policy analysis has been shaped by the proliferation of issue-oriented think tanks and foundations that seek to influence economic and social policies at all levels of government by financially supporting the policy-related scholars whose work supports their views; by promoting the publication of related books, policy briefs, and position papers targeting policymakers; and by nurturing a cadre of policy experts to staff government committees (Coser, 1977; Fischer, 1991; Tevelow, 2005).

The 19th Century

Social reform efforts in the late 19th century fused natural law moralism with scientific methodology, especially the empirical inductive approach earlier espoused by Francis Bacon (1620/2012; Snyder, 2011) and advanced in the United States by natural and social philosophers such as Frank B. Sanborn, who became secretary to the first State Board of Charities in 1863 and an organizer of the first Conference of Boards of Public Charities, which initially met in New York in 1874 as a section of the ASSA (Haskell, 2000; Sanborn & Ayers, 1931).

Natural law moralism entails a set of unverifiable, universally binding, and knowable precepts of practical reason that serve as ethical guides to human action, helping one determine what constitutes right reason about what one ought to do in conformity with nature. Some philosophical and religious traditions regard this as a reflection of *a priori* divine law, while others accept as self-evident, practical truths that nature is a limit and its own precondition (Lee, 1928; McAniff, 1953; O'Scannlain, 2011). Bacon's empirical inductive approach, adopted by social philosophers such as Sanborn, was premised on the accumulation of observable evidence that could be subjected to verification, although it required no consciously articulated theory of causation or theoretical questions to guide research—not even hypotheses (Furner, 2011).

Not coincidentally, social work, which had strong roots in social reform—particularly among the settlement house workers—also developed during this period (Bricker-Jenkins & Joseph, 2008). As professionally emergent social workers and social scientists attempted to ground their efforts in less moralistic and more objective ways of thinking and practice (Bryson, 1932; Franklin, 1986), they became increasingly ensconced in university settings, distanced themselves from reform efforts and applied work, and narrowed their advocacy to areas within their expertise (Bannister, 1987). At the time, however, there was no contradiction between Bacon's approach and social reformers' intentions; this made it convenient for the largely upper-class amateurs or generalists who attended meetings of the Conference of Boards of Public Charities and filled the ranks of the ASSA.

The ASSA's departmental structure was designed to accommodate the classic professions, such as law and medicine, in an enterprise devoted as much to the pursuit of practical reform as to social investigation (Haskell, 2000). Although its model of social inquiry was eclipsed by university-based disciplines, the ASSA helped legitimate the authoritative pronouncements about social problems and remedies by increasingly specialized social science professionals. This complemented the goal of social work and other reformers who sought to create a more "scientific" philanthropy to solve indiscriminate almsgiving to destitute individuals and to introduce more objective approaches to the study of social problems and social welfare (Bremner, 1956; Franklin, 1986; Gettelman, 1969–1970; also see Chapter 2 in this volume).

By 1909, in its efforts to transcend a class-based or self-interest-based view of authority and to create a more impartial basis for policy analysis, ASSA sowed the seeds of its own demise. The Conference of Boards of Public Charities formed its own organization in 1879. The ASSA spawned the American Historical Association in 1884—from which the American Economic Association (AEA) splintered in 1885—and the American Political Science Association in 1904. The American Sociology Society separated from AEA in 1905.

Speaking at the National Conference of Charities and Correction in 1915, educator Abraham Flexner had raised doubts about the professional standing of social work in part due to its lack of discipline-specific knowledge. Impersonal neutrality and discipline-specific knowledge became hallmarks of professional development, as evidenced by the development of university-based academic disciplines, professional organizations, and credentialing bodies. Reflecting these developments, the National Social Workers Exchange was organized in 1917—the same year Mary Richmond's *Social Diagnosis*, a basic methodological text for social work education, was published. And in 1919, the 17 schools of social work in the United States and Canada formed the Association of Training Schools for Professional Social Work, which later became the Council on Social Work Education in 1951.

From the Progressive Era to World War II

Both inside and outside the academy, however, the tension between knowledge and reform remained. Universities invariably sought to jettison faculty who were deemed "politically incorrect" (e.g., see Gruber, 1972). As emerging professionals in the early decades of 20th century America, social scientists increasingly tempered both the form and substance of their advocacy, and the tension between reform and knowledge reappeared as a conflict between advocacy and **objectivity** (Furner, 2011). As a result, universities and colleges as institutions further distanced themselves from cause-related or political activities.

New institutional forms that brought together larger groups of researchers for long-term investigations took shape with the backing of new general-purpose philanthropic foundations that embodied objectivist ideals (Smith, 1991; Zunz, 2011). The Carnegie Corporation, founded in 1911, and the Rockefeller Foundation, founded in 1913, for example, brought unparalleled resources to social research; the Russell Sage Foundation, established in 1907, nurtured a "faculty of experts" who did original social scientific research in settings different from that of discipline-based faculties in the universities (Mafinezam, 2003). Although committed to public education and advocacy—social surveys, statistical research, and analyses of social conditions were viewed as means of raising awareness of social problems and rousing the public to intelligent action—these researchers thought of themselves as neutral scientific investigators. Exemplary was the Pittsburgh Survey—funded by the Russell Sage Foundation and directed by Paul U. Kellogg (1912)—which, by means of team research, was the first to examine the effects of industrialization on the entire social life of one city (Greenwald & Anderson, 1996).

In addition to such prominent figures in the history of the social work profession as Hull House's Jane Addams (1909, 1910; Addams & De Forest, 1902) and Franklin Delano Roosevelt's New Deal administrator Harry Hopkins (1934), another leading example is Mary van Kleeck, a 1904 graduate of Smith College. She began her career as a settlement house worker in New York, where she surveyed the conditions of working women. She was hired by the Russell Sage Foundation and became head of its Department of Industrial Studies in 1909. Her work and that of her colleagues (van Kleeck, 1910, 1919) paved the way for her participation in government research projects in the Department of Labor during and after World War I, projects that contributed, in part, to the creation of the U.S. Women's Bureau (Smith, 1991).

The Great Depression of the 1930s provided policy experts of all stripes with an unparalleled opportunity to promote solutions. In 1933, during the legislative rush that occurred at the beginning of the Roosevelt Administration, the demand for knowledgeable researchers was insatiable. Social scientists from the Russell Sage Foundation and elsewhere were lured to Washington to serve New Deal agencies. By 1938, roughly 7,800 social scientists were working in the federal government; more than 5,000 of them were economists (Smith, 1991). This influx of social scientists into government service raised some concerns about their integrity. J. H. Willits, the longtime head of the Rockefeller Foundation's social science division, admonished scholars drawn to Washington for sacrificing their independence (Smith, 1991). The knowledge they produced began to look less like a form of higher intellectual counsel than another instrument

Figure 6.1 President Lyndon B. Johnson visits the Family of Tom Fletcher in Martin County, Kentucky, April 1964

of political power. This prompted Robert Lynd (1939), professor of sociology at Columbia University, to ask the elemental question, "Knowledge for what?" in a book of that same title.

World War II and Afterward

The demands created by World War II provided a response to Lynd's inquiry. Despite the horrific uses to which science was put during the war, such as genocidal eugenics (Kenny, 2002) and weapons of mass destruction, World War II restored faith in scientific approaches to problem solving. By mid-1942, some 15,000 historians, geographers, linguists, anthropologists, economists, sociologists, and psychologists joined the physicists, mathematicians, and chemists in the war effort and served in the State Department, Office of War Information, and countless other wartime boards and agencies. They contributed economic analyses, public opinion surveys, intelligence testing, examinations of stress in combat, and explorations of group dynamics. Economics emerged from the wartime experience as the most tangible influence on the thinking of government officials and businessmen, giving rise to new research organizations in and out of government, such as the Committee for Economic Development, and shaping policy in ways other advisory relationships could not (Smith, 1991).

During the 1960s, as Halberstam (1972) chronicled, Presidents Kennedy and Johnson actively recruited academics to government service, including some social workers. At the time, it was assumed that policy analysis units would be established at the top of organizations, with chief executives and senior line staff as the clients. These clients were expected to define the perspective, values, and agenda for the analytic activity. The completed analysis was to become an additional resource for decision makers and thereby improve policymaking. Over the next several decades, the policy sciences developed as a formal branch of study and ideologically driven think tanks seeking to influence government policies proliferated.

POLICY STUDIES

The policy sciences thus emerged as an amalgamation of "the philosophies, procedures, techniques, and tools of the management and decision sciences—operations research, systems analysis, simulation, 'war' gaming, game theory, policy analysis, program budgeting, and linear programming" that had become accepted in business, industry, and defense between World War II and the Kennedy and Johnson administrations (Quade, 1970, p. 1). They proffered a way for universities to reverse what pundits (e.g., Ways, 1969) called the inward-looking discipline approach to specialized knowledge that had become "independent from the direct demands of life" (as cited in Ericson, 1970, p. 434).

Universities set up interdisciplinary centers for the study of public policy designed to produce hybrid PhDs or master's-level professionals as research scientists/practitioners who would assume a variety of roles, such as policy analysts, evaluation researchers, and consultants in policymaking organizations. These included the Public Policy Program of the Kennedy School of Government at Harvard University and the Policy Sciences Program at SUNY Buffalo, among others (Crecine, 1971). The 1980s push in social work for research practitioners was quite consistent with this earlier development in the policy sciences (Tripodi, Layalayants, & Zlotnik, 2008).

PROLIFERATION OF IDEOLOGICALLY DRIVEN THINK TANKS

The idea of **think tanks** as currently understood was less than secure in the 1960s—by one estimate, more than two thirds of some 200 think tanks that existed in the United States by the mid-1990s were founded after 1970 (Rich, 2000, pp. 64–65). Throughout the 1960s, policy analysts became increasingly aware of the many paradoxes that emerged from the optimistic marriage of social scientific knowledge with political action (Lyons, 1969). The War on Poverty, urban and race-related strife, antiwar protests, and the emergence of the modern feminist movement challenged many assumptions about the relationship between government and science. Horowitz (1970) showed how social scientists engaged in government were committed to advocacy models defined by politicians and how they legitimated preexisting policy decisions rather than developing or verifying them.

Figure 6.2 Members of the military police keep back protesters during their sit-in protesting the Vietnam War at the Mall Entrance to the Pentagon. U.S. Army

As scholars and policymakers alike highlighted the limitations of the social sciences in addressing social problems, policy experts in think tanks on both ends of the political spectrum became ascendant. This development, in part exacerbated by an influx of money from very wealthy families (e.g., Koch, Olin, Scaife, Soros) with more pronounced economic and/or socially driven ideological agendas (Mayer, 2016 & 2010), produced two significant consequences that resonate to the present. First, it created an ideological divide in the policy analysis field and promoted the rise of social scientists whose work made little pretense of objectivity. Second, it established organizational alternatives to universities for nurturing and promoting policy analysts and commentators who sought to shape public policy and social action (Fischer, 1991; Zunz, 2011).

For example, on the political left, the Institute for Policy Studies (IPS) opened in 1963 and the Urban Institute was created in 1968. Public scholars at IPS were dismissive of objectivity and suspicious of claims of a value-free social science that could direct policy. IPS cofounder Marcus Raskin (1971) criticized social science for reinforcing the "pyramidal structure" (p. xiii) of American society and government, contending that policy experts and their analytic tools were antithetical to ideals of participatory democracy (Smith, 1991).

On the political right, a group of conservative legislative aides founded the Heritage Foundation in 1973. Many of its domestic economic policy analysts focus on budget cutting and tax reform proposals and advocate for free-market approaches, especially about environmental issues. Members of Congress and their staff make up the foundation's primary clientele, but its 200-plus publications per year, from short policy briefs to full-length books, enable it to influence a broader market. In 1979, Bob Friedman, founded the Corporation for Enterprise Development (CFED), a multifaceted organization that works with government at all levels to create economic opportunity to alleviate poverty. The organization is single-minded in the means it employs—reliance on economically conservative, market-based principles and mechanisms—to achieve its socially desirable aims. CFED promotes social entrepreneurship (e.g., micro-finance) and asset building (e.g., children's savings accounts; individual development accounts or IDAs) as ways of increasing the participation of low-income persons in the capitalist economy. CFED employs experts who are knowledgeable in federal and state level policy and produces a variety of advocacy tools, reports, and research studies, including an annual asset and opportunity scorecard, and periodic newsletters and press releases for public consumption.

From time to time, ideologically diverse think tanks join efforts to explore solutions to commonly identified social problems. For example, experts from the economically conservative American Enterprise Institute for Public Policy Research and the more liberal or progressive Brookings Institution addressed the issue of poverty, which President Obama in his final State of the Union address identified as one area where both parties in Congress might find common ground and reach consensus on a variety of policy solutions, such as promoting work requirements for government programs and raising the minimum wage (AEI/Brookings Working Group on Poverty and Opportunity, 2015).

VALUE NEUTRALITY, VALUE RELEVANCE, AND CRITICAL THINKING IN THE SOCIAL SCIENCES AND SOCIAL WORK PRACTICE

The proliferation of ideologically driven think tanks highlights a main dilemma facing social workers as policy analysts: the conflict between professional mandates to advocate for and influence policies beneficial to clients or client populations and the requirement to produce objective analyses of social policies. Failure to produce objective assessments of policy outcomes or options risks making the profession appear more like a partisan, self-interested group with ideological baggage. This may appeal to segments of the population, but it produces a loss of legitimacy in the eyes of the public at large. To fulfill this tension-prone mandate, it is helpful to explore the role of values and critical thinking in the social sciences and in social work.

Since Weber (1949) first articulated the issue, there is general agreement that values enter into the selection of the problems investigators choose to examine—this is what is meant by **value relevance**. **Value neutrality** implies that once a *value-relevant* problem has been selected, social scientists and policy analysts must hold in abeyance the values that entered into that selection choice while following the guidelines the data reveal. A policy analyst may choose to focus on compensatory policy solutions to workplace discrimination practices on hiring or promotion decisions on the basis of race/ethnicity, gender, or sexual orientation (Caputo, 2002). This would be an appropriate value-relevant decision, motivated in part by one's sense of fairness or social justice, guiding the choice of topic to examine.

If, however, the results of a national sample study of working-age adults showed that those who reported experiencing workplace discrimination also demonstrated increased positive outcomes, such as investing more in themselves rather than less, as human capital theory would predict (it would not be rational for a person to get more education or job training knowing that discrimination would prevent him or her from being hired or getting promoted), the analyst would be obligated to report those results. Rather than manipulating the data to show the need for compensation, this analysis would suggest that the need for compensation might not be warranted. In this manner, the analyst would be taking a value-neutral approach to policy analysis (see, e.g., Caputo, 2007).

To understand the importance and purpose of distinguishing between value-relevant and value-neutral approaches to policy analysis and to distinguish these approaches from the role of critical thinking in policy analysis, it is helpful to keep in mind the impartial disposition that guides social work practice in general. Assuming an impartial disposition toward clients (e.g., a physically abused female welfare recipient) and vulnerable client groups (e.g., institutionalized frail elderly persons) is an essential component of social work practice. Much like the role disinterestedness plays in science as a social enterprise, impartiality is less a matter of individual motivation than an institutionalized pattern of professional control of a wide range of motives that characterize the behavior of social workers (Parsons, 1939). Impartiality is essential to the integrity of the profession, imparting normative authority to its practices.

This is not to claim that social workers somehow jettison their personal attitudes, beliefs, or preferences about what is the good life or what constitutes best practices that might most benefit vulnerable populations. Rather, as Levy (1976) notes when discussing possible tensions between personal and professional values, what practitioners must aim for is refraining from imposing personal values when they conflict with those of the profession. The use of self as a cornerstone of social work practice necessitates that social workers know themselves well enough to be able to identify likely value biases and preferences so they do not interfere with their duty to clients, their assessment of a client's situation, or their determination of an appropriate intervention (Yan & Wong, 2005).

Critical thinking is another attribute requisite to social work practice (Brown & Rutter, 2006). Among other things, critical thinking entails the application of standards of adequacy and accuracy to what we or others say, do, or write (Bailin, Case, Coombs, & Daniels, 1999). It includes cognitive activities such as logical reasoning and careful scrutiny of arguments unsupported by empirical evidence. Critical thinking also involves a willingness to examine and the capacity to acknowledge the assumptions underlying one's own beliefs and behaviors; justifying one's own ideas and actions; judging the rationality of these ideas and actions accordingly; comparing one's ideas with a range of varying interpretations and perspectives; thinking through, projecting, and anticipating the likely consequences of ideas and actions based on these justifications; and testing the accuracy and rationality of these justifications against some kind of objective analysis of the "real" world as we understand it (Brown & Rutter, 2006).

Creativity and engaging others in deliberation are also requisite components of critical thinking for several reasons. New interpretations and perspectives may be offered as a basis of comparison with existing ones; imagination is involved in anticipating possible consequences, generating original approaches, and identifying alternative perspectives; and thinking through likely consequences entails discussion and dialogue with others (Bailin et al., 1999). Even as they combine value neutrality or impartiality with critical thinking in a variety of policy-analyst roles, social workers are nonetheless professionally obligated to advocate and take appropriate actions that reflect value-relevant concerns such as those of social justice.

ROLES OF THE POLICY ANALYST

Behn (1985) contended that the key standard in the policy sciences for evaluating the merits of policy analysis is policy relevance—that is, helping a policymaking client do his or her job. This contrasted with the traditional standard of the social sciences of contributing to the advancement of their respective disciplines by producing general theory. To the extent social scientists care little about whether or not their generalizations can help policymakers resolve particular policy dilemmas posed by social problems, they will be less useful to policymakers as analysts and their efforts may be ignored. Policymakers invariably juggle important concerns beyond the development of theoretically relevant, scientifically reproducible, and statistically significant tests of propositions that relate policy actions to policy outcomes, a prime concern for disciplinary-oriented social scientists.

Policymakers' other concerns that policy analysts need to take into account to produce policy-relevant analysis include more contextual matters such as managing conflicts between interests, obtaining general agreement on a particular course of action, and determining how action on one issue affected other issues. The policy analyst must also be able to expose conflicting values that affect a policy choice, develop creative and viable options, specify uncertainties about possible consequences of policy options, develop outcome measures so actions can be evaluated and modified accordingly, and design strategies for political adoption and organizational implementation.

Over the past several decades, policy analysts have been classified along a variety of dimensions, some on a purely conceptual basis (e.g., Meltsner, 1976; Smith, 1991), others on the basis of survey-related research (e.g., Morçöl, 2001). Weimer and Vining (2011) provide three perspectives on the appropriate role of the policy analyst: objective technician, client's advocate, and issue advocate. As noted below, each role is shaped by three fundamental values: analytical integrity, responsibility to clients, and adherence to one's conception of the good.

Objective Technician

Analytical integrity is the fundamental value of objective technicians. Their analytic skills are the main source of legitimacy. They view their primary task as providing objective advice about the consequences of proposed policies. Objective technicians maintain some distance from their clients, whose political fortunes take second place to their preparation, communication, and uses of analyses. Objective technicians are more likely to be found, for example, working for the Congressional Budget Office (CBO), which responds to Congress as a whole and anticipates changes in partisan control, than for a member of Congress who must run for reelection every two or six years in the House of Representatives or Senate, respectively. Although objective technicians identify relevant values, the resolution of trade-offs among conflicting values is left to clients. In the long run, objective technicians see themselves as contributing to the good of society by consistently providing unbiased advice, even when clients select less personally favored options.

Client Advocate

Client advocates place primary emphasis on responsibility to their clients and see themselves as deriving legitimacy as participants in the formation of public policy from clients who hold elected or appointed office or who represent organized political interests. In return for access, client advocates adhere to the medical ethos of "do no harm" to clients and to the legal ethos of vigorously promoting their clients' interests. Analytical integrity remains important in much the same way as attorneys view their responsibility in an adversarial system. They do not mislead clients with false statements or omissions of relevant information. Having fully informed clients, such advocates have little or no qualms about interpreting their analyses in the best possible light for their clients. In doing so, however, analytical integrity prohibits lying but requires neither full disclosure of information nor public correction of misstatements by clients.

Issue Advocate

For issue advocates, analyses are instrumental for making progress toward their conception of the good society. When conducting analyses, they focus on the values inherent in policy outcomes rather than on values such as analytical integrity and responsibility to clients. Issue advocates see themselves as intrinsic players in the policy process, perhaps even as champions of groups such as poor persons, racial minorities, women, and children whom they believe suffer from underrepresentation in the political process or exploitation by economic, legal, or other structural arrangements or processes. As with client advocates, issue advocates have few qualms about taking advantage of analytical uncertainty. Faced with results that fail to support their policy preferences, issue advocates question simplifying assumptions that inevitably accompany complex issues and challenge the choice of criteria used to evaluate alternatives. They feel no necessity to point out such analytic shortcomings when findings support or corroborate their policy preferences—that burden falls on their opponents.

Formulation of Policy Agendas and Alternatives

Regardless of whether one adopts the role of objective technician, client advocate, or issue advocate, policy analysts are well advised to examine and understand the context in and processes by which social problems are formulated and specific policies proposed, debated, and disposed (adopted or rejected). In their classic constructivist formulation, Spector and Kituse (1987) view social problems as a function of claims-making activity, defining social problems as *"the activities of individuals or groups making assertions of grievances and claims with respect to some putative conditions"* (p. 75; italics in original). For social workers as policy analysts, this formulation has some merit because it underscores the importance of politics and values in problem formation. How a problem or issue is framed provides the justification for action (or inaction) and shapes the policy response that is subsequently debated and eventually adopted or rejected. Lens (2000) shows how the media helped frame debates over welfare reform in 1988 and 1996 by focusing on individual responsibility while downplaying the social or structural factors that contributed to the plight of low-income single mothers with young children. [see also Chapter 1 in this volume].

Yet Spector and Kituse's (1987) contention that the factual basis of assertions should fall outside the scope of sociological inquiry creates problems for social workers in general and policy analysts in particular given the professional mandate to pursue social justice on behalf of vulnerable populations or groups. Although definitions of and claims about what constitutes social justice vary and are subject to challenge (Reisch, 2002; Sterba, 1999), at a minimum, social justice involves attainment of better outcomes for people (Meenaghan, Kilty, & McNutt, 2004). A critical task for policy analysts centers on determining what those better outcomes are by assessing current conditions regarding a particular issue. Without an understanding of how things currently stand, we have no way of knowing if our policy-related efforts make conditions better or worse. In other words, failure to assess and reach agreement about the nature and extent of a social problem, however contested, makes it impossible to determine if social justice goals are being met or thwarted by policy actions.

Structuring problems is an important activity for policy analysts. This refers to the phase of policy inquiry in which analysts search among competing formulations of different stakeholders with the aim of *correctly* identifying and characterizing the problem that needs to be addressed (Dunn, 2008). In addition to structuring policy problems, the question, "What should be done?" raises several larger

Table 6.1 Things to Consider About What Is to Be Done.

Questions	Options
What is the type or form of benefit?	Cash, in-kind, voucher, specific service
Who are the beneficiaries?	Children, aging persons, low-income persons or families, mentally and/or physically challenged persons, everyone
Who provides the benefit?	Government, private nonprofit agencies, private for-profit agencies
Who pays for the benefit and at what cost?	Government, private nonprofit agencies, private for-profit agencies
What are the anticipated or desired results?	Poverty reduction, greater income equality, better nutrition, enhanced self-determination

questions that analysts address including: What type of provision or benefit is suited to address the problem or issue? To whose benefit? By whom? At what cost? With what expected results? The question, "What benefits?" prompts decisions about such concerns as the appropriateness of cash, direct services, in-kind services, or vouchers, and an assessment of the merits associated with each type of assistance (see Table 6.1).

Asking "To whose benefit?" prompts a series of related questions, such as these: What constitutes need, vulnerability, and oppression? Who are needy persons? How is risk determined? What constitutes a population-at-risk? The question "By whom?" leads, in turn, to such questions as these: By government? If so, at which level or levels of government should this be determined? Or, is the answer: by the private sector? If so, should it be the for-profit or nonprofit sector?

The issue of cost requires us to consider the following questions: What is the major source of revenue to fund the benefit? Should it be tax revenue? If so, from what type of tax: federal income or, payroll taxes; local property, or consumption (sales) taxes? Or, should it come from private, philanthropic contributions? How should the cost burdens be distributed? What level of aggregate direct expenditure or revenue is lost through the tax code? What is the cost per individual or family recipient? Questions about expected results raise issues about realistic versus desirable results, and short-term versus long-term consequences.

Ethical, political, practical, and technical dimensions accompany all these questions. To get a better handle on how to address them, it is helpful, as the social work saying goes, to partialize the problem. For our purposes, this requires a discussion of the three Ps of policy analysis: product, process, and performance (Gilbert & Terrell, 2010).

POLICY AS PRODUCT

Policy products include tangible documents such as legislation, bills, policy manuals, judicial decisions, executive orders, administrative guidelines, codified rules, and regulations. When examining policy products, analysts function at times like journalists, asking who, what, and why questions and providing a descriptive summary of the document's contents based on the answers to those questions. Analysts go beyond journalistic description, however, by defining selective criteria for evaluating a policy's merits and demonstrating to what extent the particular policy product under consideration meets these criteria.

Who Gets What?

One of the first tasks of the policy analyst is to identify who benefits from the policy under consideration, what type of benefits they get, and what if any criteria are used to determine eligibility for those benefits. **Universal benefits** are available to an entire population as a basic right and, for the most part, are not determined by a **means test.** They are provided regardless of the income level of recipients and their families or households. Examples in the United States include public education and the Old Age, Survivors, Disability, and Health Insurance program, commonly referred to as Social Security.

Selective benefits are available on the basis of individual need, usually determined by a means test. Examples in the United States include the Temporary Assistance for Needy Families (TANF) program (also known as welfare), Medicaid (health care for low-income families), and the Supplemental Nutrition Assistance Program (SNAP), commonly referred to as food stamps. Types of benefits include cash (Social Security, TANF, and Unemployment Insurance), vouchers (SNAP, the Housing Choice Voucher Program or Section 8 Housing), in-kind services such as Medicare's Program of All Inclusive Care for the Elderly, and opportunity (Affirmative Action). All social programs in the United States, even universal programs, have eligibility criteria

Figure 6.3 Social Security is a universal benefit— it helps people of all generations.

that are inherently exclusionary in some way. For example, Social Security benefits require an accumulated work history and payroll taxes from workers and employers and are provided solely to retirees when they reach an age established by legislation or to their dependent beneficiaries. Public education is free to everyone only through high school. A tax deduction for dependent children and the Earned Income Tax Credit (EITC) are available to all families with minor children, but only households that file a federal income tax return can receive the deduction and only working families with incomes below a certain threshold are eligible. Under the Affordable Care Act, financial assistance through a health insurance marketplace is available only if one's annual income is 400% of the poverty level or below, making it a financial burden for millions of those whose annual income exceeds 133% of the poverty level and, therefore, are ineligible for Medicaid.

How Is the Policy or Program Financed?

Taxes are the main source of revenues for government, with varying distributional or "burden" effects depending on the type of tax, the type and level of earned [wages, salaries, tips] or unearned [stocks, bonds] income, and the tax-filing status of the taxpayer (Caputo, 2005). Some taxes, such as the payroll tax used to fund Social Security, are "regressive"; that is, everyone pays the tax on their earned income at the same rate regardless of their income. In addition, individuals pay this tax only up to the capped limit ($118,500

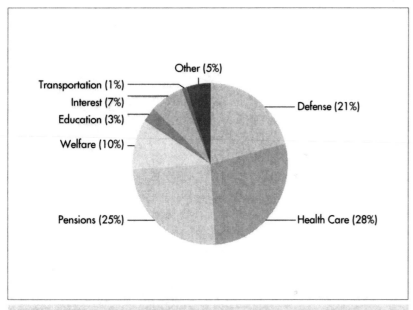

Figure 6.4 Total Spending: $4 trillion; Pensions: $1 trillion; Health Care (Medicare & Medicaid): $1.1 trillion; Education: $0.1 trillion; Defense: $0.9 trillion; Welfare: $0.4 trillion.

in 2016) and pay nothing in excess of that limit regardless of their total income. Consumption or sales taxes are also regressive, as everyone pays the same tax on an item regardless of income. As a percentage of total income, regressive taxes adversely affect low-income individuals and families more than affluent individuals and families.

Other taxes, such as the federal income tax, are "progressive" in the sense that individuals and families with higher incomes pay taxes at a higher rate than do lower wage workers. Property taxes are also progressive to the extent that property owners in more affluent neighborhoods are more likely to have higher incomes and pay higher taxes associated with the greater assessed value of their property. Overall, federal tax burdens have declined to historical lows for most income groups, particularly for middle-income families, since the George W. Bush Administration cut rates in 2001 and 2003. A family of four in the exact middle of the income spectrum now pays 4.7% of its income in federal taxes—the third lowest percentage in 50 years. Most of the drop is attributable to the pronounced decline in individual income tax burdens, with the sharpest drops among the highest income households. In 2010, when the 2001-to-2008 tax cuts were in full effect, 93% of the additional income in the United States went to the top 1%. Their income increased 11.6%. Thirty-seven percent of this additional income went to the top 0.01%, while the bottom 99% received an average increase of $80, adjusted for inflation (Brunet & Cox, 2009; Marr, 2012; see also Chapter 3 in this volume). In addition, as a result of policy changes since the 1980s, unearned income (e.g., dividends) is taxed at a much lower rate than is income from wages.

At the federal level, payroll and income taxes are the main sources of revenue that finance public programs; other sources include corporate and excise taxes. Payroll taxes are levied on employees and employers; each "contributes" 6.2% of salaries and wages into a Social Security Trust Fund from which payments are made to the current generation of retirees, and 1.45% to a trust fund that funds Medicare. In January 2013, a deal to avoid the so-called "fiscal cliff" raised the tax on Medicare for 2.35% for individuals earning above $200,000/year. Social Security and health care (Medicare, Medicaid, the State Children's Health Insurance Program, and Affordable Care Act marketplace subsidies), accounted for about 48% of all federal expenditures in fiscal year 2014 (Center on Budget and Policy Priorities, 2015). Income, corporate, and excise taxes are used to fund discretionary programs that include military-related expenses (about 21% of the federal budget), and all other social welfare programs, such as EITC, SNAP, Supplemental Security Income (SSI), housing assistance, and TANF (about 10%). (See Figure 6.4.)

Most states also collect income taxes to finance public programs. These are supplemented by property and sales taxes, which also finance municipal and county governments. Public education expenses are primarily borne by state and municipal governments and financed primarily through local property taxes, with many states implementing lottery systems to cover increasing costs and avoid raising property taxes.

[See Chapter 7 this volume for further discussion of the role of taxation in the creation of federal and state budgets.]

Select Criteria for Evaluating Policy Proposals

Kraft and Furlong (2010) identify eight criteria for evaluating public policy proposals: effectiveness, efficiency, equity, liberty/freedom, political feasibility, social acceptability, administrative feasibility, and technical feasibility. **Effectiveness** refers to the likelihood of a policy achieving its goals and objectives or its demonstrated achievement of them. Our ability to measure effectiveness is limited by our capacity to anticipate future events and their consequences. Determining a policy's **efficiency** entails an assessment of the relationship between the attainment of program goals or the provision of benefits and the policy's costs. It can be interpreted as either the least cost for a given benefit or the largest benefit for a given cost. Measuring all costs and benefits is not always possible, however—particularly those costs that are unforeseen, unintended, or determined by extrinsic factors—thereby limiting the use of this criterion.

Think of TANF and EITC, two anti-poverty programs designed to encourage labor force participation primarily among low-income individuals with children. TANF is a direct expenditure program that takes a "stick approach," penalizing recipients who withdraw from labor force participation by reducing or eliminating their cash benefits. By contrast, the EITC, which works through the tax system, takes a "carrot approach." It provides a tax credit to supplement the low wages of those who file tax returns. How would you assess which program is more efficient than the other?

Equity refers to fairness or justice in the distribution of a policy's costs, benefits, and risks. In policy debates, equity has two different meanings: **process equity**, often termed *procedural justice*, and **outcome equity**, often termed *social justice*. Process equity refers to the extent to which decision-making processes are voluntary, open, and fair. Proponents of process equity, such as Nozick (1974), contend that guaranteeing and protecting individual and property rights are the primary responsibility of government. They are likely to oppose government efforts to promote equality beyond assuring equal opportunity to participate in society's decisions.

By contrast, proponents of outcome equity, such as Rawls (1971), contend that equity or fairness refers to the fair distribution of societal goods such as wealth, income, or political power. They tend to favor government intervention to promote a more equitable distribution of society's resources than is possible through sole reliance on market forces, even under conditions of process equity. Measuring equity is also inherently problematic because reasonable persons can disagree about what makes up the "basket of social goods" that ought to be more equitably distributed and because of the technical challenges that invariably accompany efforts to distribute goods, particularly qualitative goods, more justly.

Affirmative Action programs highlight a tension between procedural and social justice. To the extent admissions criteria are transparent and applied in the same way to each applicant, advocates of procedural justice will deem the process as fair, regardless of the distributional effects or consequences of who gets admitted and who gets rejected. Noting disparate outcomes of admission policies by race/ethnicity for example, social justice advocates might point to structural factors that preclude the possibility of fair procedures (such as using standardized tests on which certain racial or ethnic groups perform either disproportionately worse or better than whites) or to historic injustices experienced by certain racial/ethnic groups that warrant interventions such as establishing racial/ethnic preferences in admissions designed to reduce long-standing disparities. Since 1978, in its *Regents of the University of California v. Bakke* decision, the U.S. Supreme Court has weighed in on this issue several times. As more recent cases demonstrate, however, it has yet to resolve the issue. [*See Chapter 10 this volume for further discussion of this issue completely.*]

Liberty, or freedom, refers to the extent to which public policy extends or restricts an individual's privacy, rights, and choices. Policies that provide cash benefits, such as TANF or SSI, maximize individual choice, whereas policies that employ food stamps or vouchers are more restrictive, since the benefits they provide must be used for a designated purpose. Public funds that support family planning or counseling organizations that include information about abortion services or provide such services affirm women's constitutional right to privacy about related decisions, ensuring more equitable access for low-income women than would otherwise be the case.

Political feasibility refers to the likelihood that a policy would be adopted; that is, the extent to which elected officials would support a policy proposal. It can be difficult to determine, contingent in part on perceptions of related issues, changing economic and political conditions, and the climate of opinion. A related concept is **social acceptability**, which refers to the extent to which the public will accept and support a policy proposal. This can also be difficult to determine, even when public support can be measured through opinion polls. Partisans of an issue may grab media headlines, giving the appearance of greater public support or opposition for their pet cause than is warranted. On many issues, ambivalence, uncertainty, or even indifference may be more the norm. Political feasibility is time sensitive, as conditions change so does public opinion. Think for examples, of the issues of same sex marriage and health care coverage. In 2004, Massachusetts became the first state to legalize same sex marriage. While some states followed suit, other banned it through legislation or ballot initiatives. On June 26, 2015, however, the Supreme Court ruled that states could not ban same-sex marriage. [*See Chapters 5 and 10 for further discussion of this issue.*] Similarly, prior to passage of the Affordable Care Act (ACA) in 2010 the prospect of Congress approving universal health insurance coverage was a political nonstarter since the failed attempt of the Clinton Administration in 1993, although Massachusetts had adopted a policy that presaged many of the features of the ACA. In other words, context and timing matter, and policy decisions are influenced by broader demographic and cultural trends, and social and political movements.

Administrative feasibility refers to the likelihood that a department or agency can implement the proposed policy or deliver its programs successfully. It entails an assessment of a department or agency's capacity, and a projection of available resources and agency staff behavior that may be difficult to estimate.

Finally, **technical feasibility** refers to the availability and reliability of the technology and information needed for effective policy implementation. It is often difficult to anticipate the technological changes that would affect feasibility. Technological advances in data collection, storage, and retrieval, for example, made it feasible for the federal government to require states to establish case registries to enhance the prospects of successful child support enforcement by enabling authorities to locate and track parents who were determined to owe such support.

POLICY AS PROCESS

Policy as process encompasses policymaking and implementation. In general, process studies are concerned with understanding how relationships and interactions among political, governmental, and interest groups affect policy formation and adoption (Gilbert & Terrell, 2010). Such studies examine how policies are adopted by legislative bodies. They are also concerned with understanding how adopted or proposed policies are or would be carried out. Such studies examine implementation processes.

MAKING POLICY

As social problems are formulated and recommended policies and programs are proposed, deliberative or legislative processes aimed at adopting appropriate responses are also set in motion. Legislative histories are a good source of information about the dynamics of legislative policy deliberation by national and state governments (e.g., Mendez, 2006). As Weimer and Vining (2011) demonstrate, the analysis of policy adoption entails consideration of what constitutes the "big picture"—that is, frameworks and theories, underlying assumptions, and practical approaches to assessing and influencing political feasibility.

CONCEPTUAL AND THEORETICAL CONSIDERATIONS

Relevant conceptual frameworks and theories about policymaking processes that have implications for policy analysis include interest group theory, institutional rational choice theory, *and* advocacy coalition and social construction frameworks (Sabatier, 1999; Weimer & Vining, 2011). **Interest group politics** entail those situations where both costs and benefits are concentrated, providing the relevant actors with incentives to participate in policymaking and policy analysts with a way of readily identifying and predicting their reactions to policy proposals. More diffuse interests require mobilization or the creation of representative organizations. They become effective by framing issues broadly or in terms of widely held values, or by creating sensational public events to attract attention. Analysts perform a valuable service by identifying those groups that would bear diffuse costs from policies if they are adopted. For example, failure to take into account diffuse costs associated with the Medicare Catastrophic Coverage Act passage in 1988, with support from both houses of Congress, resulted in its repeal in 1989, when strong opposition from wealthy elderly persons to progressive fees became apparent (Weimer & Vining, 2011). Early estimates by the Congressional Budget Office (2009) of the effects of the Affordable Care Act on health insurance premiums indicated that many of those without employment-related insurance, about 17% of the total market, would face higher premiums, up to 30% without subsidies, up to 13% when accounting for the subsidies anticipated for 2016. As noted above, a sizable percentage of those with incomes above 133% and below 400% of the federal poverty levels who were, therefore, ineligible for subsidies cannot afford premiums. The prospect of increased premiums is one of the factors contributing to continuing, but as yet unsuccessful efforts to repeal the ACA (Steinhauer, 2016). [*See Chapter 14 this volume for further discussion of the implementation of the ACA.*]

Analysts who rely on **institutional rational choice theory** focus on the role of institutions, defined roughly as "fairly stable sets of commonly recognized formal and informal rules that coordinate or constrain the behavior of individuals in social interactions" (Weimer, 1995; as cited in Weimer & Vining, 2011, p. 267). Three levels of operational rules are considered. At the first or *operational level*, operational rules shape the actions of individuals that usually initiate public policy. Such rules may be formal, such as the rules and regulations adopted by a state, or informal, such as conventions or norms about acceptable behavior.

Operational rules may also be set by rules generated at the *collective choice level* by government bodies according to their legislative and executive authorities. Finally, operational rules may also be set at the *constitutional level*, which sets rules about collective choice. At each level, policy analysts examine the processes by which a particular set of rules are decided on and how they get communicated to those to whom they apply, while remaining aware that modifications of rules can be a source of policy changes within or across levels. For example, in many states, those opposed to same-sex marriage have attempted to constrain their legislatures through constitutional bans via ballot initiatives, while proponents of marriage equality have often looked to the courts to pursue their policy goals.

Table 6.2 The Social Construction Framework of Target Populations

Social Construction	Political Power	
	+	−
+	Advantaged	Dependents
−	Contenders	Outsiders

The **advocacy coalition framework** assesses the learning that occurs by coalition members and its relationship to policy change within *policy subsystems* over time (Sabatier & Jenkins-Smith, 1999; Weimer & Vining, 2011). *Policy subsystems* are collections of individuals and organizations, such as advocacy or professional groups, that seek to influence public policy within a substantive domain such as health, education, or housing. Key elements of this framework include the policy subsystem as the unit of analysis, the focus on two or more relatively stable and opposed coalitions of actors within the subsystem, the belief systems of the coalitions, and the processes through which learning by the coalitions and policy change occur.

The **social construction framework** relies on the notion that interpretive frameworks used to interpret our observations of the world can to some extent be altered by arguments, thereby providing an avenue for changing the political support for various policies (Weimer & Vining, 2011). It applies this notion to the distribution of benefits and burdens among the groups that are targets of public policies. This framework identifies four target groups in reference to their social construction and political power, as can be seen in Table 6.2.

The *advantaged* are those groups with positive social constructions and strong political power, such as senior citizens, small-business owners, homeowners, and the military; policies targeting these groups are viewed as benefits, not burdens. *Dependents* include groups with positive social constructions but weak political power, such as children and mothers; policies targeting these groups tend to be viewed as benefits, but they are smaller and less secure than those provided to the advantaged. *Contenders*, such as big businesses and labor unions, have negative social constructions but strong political power relative to other groups; the benefits they receive are not always obvious to the public, and the burdens they bear (e.g., corporate taxes and linking wage increases to productivity gains, respectively) are often less severe than the rhetoric surrounding them would suggest. Finally, *outsiders*, such as welfare recipients and substance abusers, have negative social constructions and weak political power; they tend to be subject to burdens (e.g., least generous cash or in-kind benefits, stigma, social opprobrium) and have virtually no influence on the policymaking process.

PRACTICAL CONSIDERATIONS

Practical considerations to take into account when doing policy analysis include identifying the relevant actors, understanding their motivations and beliefs, assessing available resources, and identifying the arena or level at which rules governing the policymaking process occur (Weimer & Vining, 2011). Each arena or level has its own set of rules about how decisions are made. For example, legislatures have rules of order and agencies have administrative procedures. Unwritten traditions and standard practices about how decisions are made also need to be considered and understood. When choosing an arena, political strategies to consider include the use of cooptation, compromise, heresthetics (strategies that attempt to gain advantage through manipulation of the circumstances of political choice), and rhetoric. Assessing and influencing

Table 6.3 Theoretically Relevant "Black Box" Variables.

Tractability	Assessment of technical difficulties, the diversity of target group behaviors, the size of the target group in relation to the total population, and the extent of behavioral change required
Ability of statutes or other basic policy decisions to structure the implementation process favorably	Assessments of the clarity and consistency of purported objectives, incorporation of an adequate causal theory, initial allocation of financial resources required, hierarchical integration within and among implementing institutions, decision rules of implementing agencies, recruitment of implementing officials, and formal access by outsiders to control for partisan biases for/against the policy and to ensure impartial independent evaluation studies of performance
Non-statutory variables affecting implementation	Socioeconomic conditions and technology, public support, the attitudes and resources of constituency groups, support from sovereigns (i.e., those institutions that control the policy's legal and financial resources), and the commitment, leadership skill, and actions of implementing officials

political feasibility requires the ability and opportunity to use tools and techniques of data collection and analysis and to make appropriate inferences for recommending actions. This content is beyond the scope of this chapter. For the purposes of this chapter, the bottom line about the practical considerations for policy analysts charged with the responsibility of providing useful advice is to pay attention to the political environment and account for the interests of actors in the relevant political arenas.

IMPLEMENTING POLICY

The issue facing analysts once a policy has been enacted is what happens to it after it has been adopted (Patashnik, 2008). Policy analysis of implementation processes in part entails the identification and examination of indicators about the nature, quality, and quantity of the work of the agency, organization, or administrative body charged with the responsibility of carrying out adopted policies. From a system's perspective, implementation processes are viewed here as the "black box" between adopted policies and intended or actual outcomes. The role of the analyst is to assess what is taking place within that black box. This is important because the actions of administrators and other professionals responsible for implementing policies not only affect the likely outcomes but may also make policy in the process. Lipsky (2010) has shown how social workers and other professionals invariably create policy in their day-to-day work given the ambiguities associated with mandates that fail to cover the particular circumstances of their clients.

THEORETICAL CONSIDERATIONS

When conceptualizing the implementation process, the relevant "black box" variables that policy analysts need to consider fall into three broad categories (see Table 6.3). As can be seen in this table, these relate to the tractability or technical difficulties involved, how well the statute laid out the implementation process, and the net effect of factors that can influence intended outcomes (Mazmanian & Sabatier, 1989).

ADDRESSING UNPLANNED OR UNINTENDED CONSEQUENCES

During the course of implementation, adaptations or modifications to the original policy or program design invariably arise to meet unplanned or unintended consequences of the policy or program and/or changes in the environment in which policy or program development occurs (Browne & Wildavsky,

1984b). Purposive legislative actions are invariably accompanied by unplanned or unintended consequences that policy analysts who focus on implementation can highlight, account for, and incorporate into a feedback loop to those responsible for carrying out a policy or program. Program administrators, for example, usually have reporting requirements to monitor expenditures, revenues, and activity levels (types of clients served) built into program designs. Periodic reporting requirements of such routinely gathered information provide executive and legislative oversight to help spot anomalous performance and, perhaps, take corrective action (Weimer & Vining, 2011). Systematic analysis of side effects and changing circumstances over time and the accompanying greater awareness this produces enhance the prospects for evaluative assessment and social learning from implementation-related experiences among the public in general and policymakers and implementers in particular (Browne & Wildavsky, 1984a).

Sommerfeld and Reisch (2003), for example, documented the changes many family service agencies and other NGOs in Michigan experienced in light of the unanticipated burden that the work-first and other requirements of the 1996 welfare reform legislation place on them: increased caseloads, increased public assistance clients as a proportion of their total caseload, increased workloads, shifts in program priorities given greater need for food and shelter services, shifts in program objectives toward employment-related services, and the like. For another example, an official UK report on the efficacy of local welfare safety nets shows how increased spending resulted in funds being used to provide temporary shelter to those whom the Government did not intend the welfare reforms to affect (House of Commons Work and Pensions Committee, 2016).

THE ROLE OF STREET-LEVEL BUREAUCRATS

Street-level bureaucrats include police officers, teachers, social workers, nurses, doctors, lawyers, and other service providers such as lower court judges, corrections officers, and prison guards who occupy positions that have relatively high degrees of discretion and relative autonomy from organizational authority (Lipsky, 1969, 2010). They function in part as de facto policymakers, making policy decisions, so to speak, on the spot—at times varying from officially sanctioned guidelines and at other times creating policies when official guidelines are ambiguous or fail to cover the specific circumstances of their clients. For example, studies about the implementation of TANF highlight the role that discretion plays in creating a gap between officially expected actions and anticipated decisions by street-level bureaucrats and what they actually do in practice.

In one such study conducted in a suburban county in New York, Lens (2008) explored front-line workers' discretionary use of sanctions on TANF clients for failure to comply with work rules. Findings suggested that workers interpreted and applied sanction rules narrowly, failing to distinguish procedural violations from substantive ones. They also overlooked rules requiring them to show that a client's action was willful prior to imposing sanctions. These studies suggest that what goes on inside the "black box" of implementation influences the overall impact of policies and programs. They enable us to identify the extent of gaps between officially anticipated actions and performance outcomes, to be discussed below, and what contributes to the size of such gaps.

POLICY AS PERFORMANCE

Performance studies assess policy outcomes (Gilbert & Terrell, 2010). Performance is usually determined by collecting qualitative and quantitative data and applying a wide range of methodological tools from the academic disciplines. As taught in the academic disciplines and professional schools, research methodology provides the major technical and theoretical knowledge and requisite skills for undertaking performance-based studies. Fact determination is only one aspect of performance studies, which, as with any such study, have evaluative aspects.

Evaluations provide reliable and valid information about policy performance—that is, the extent to which needs, values, and opportunities have been realized through public action (Dunn, 2008). In addition, they entail efforts to determine the worth of a policy or program, focusing on judgments about its desirability or value. A goal such as diminished risk against destitution or better health in old age may be regarded as intrinsic or valuable in itself. It may also be viewed as extrinsically desirable because it leads to some other worthy end, such as the reduction of stress for adult children caretakers of elderly parents. As noted above, criteria for evaluation include effectiveness, efficiency, equity, liberty/freedom, political feasibility, social acceptability (appropriateness and responsiveness), administrative feasibility, and technical feasibility. The main approaches to evaluation include pseudo-evaluation, formal evaluation, and decision-theoretic evaluation (Dunn, 2008).

PSEUDO-EVALUATION

Pseudo-evaluations use descriptive methods to produce reliable and valid information about policy outcomes. A basic assumption is that measures of work or value are self-evident or uncontroversial; that is, any given outcome is taken for granted as an appropriate objective. In such evaluations, policy analysts typically use a variety of methods (e.g., quasi-experimental designs, questionnaires, random sampling, or statistical techniques) to explain variations in taken-for-granted policy outcomes in terms of policy input and process variables. Major techniques employed include graphic displays, tabular displays, interrupted time series, control-series analysis, and regression-discontinuity analysis. Pseudo-evaluations are suitable for monitoring program outcomes and include such forms as social experimentation, social auditing, and research and practice synthesis. For example, one might examine differences in educational outcomes across school districts or other geographical areas like cities or states by cross-classifying per pupil educational expenditures with input variables (e.g., teachers' salaries) and those intended to measure processes (e.g., class size as an indicator of the quality of student-teacher interaction). Outputs and impacts could also be cross-classified by types of preconditions (e.g., average income of community residents, ethic/racial composition of the area) and unforeseen disruptive events (e.g., frequency of strikes).

FORMAL EVALUATION

Formal evaluations use descriptive methods to produce reliable and valid information about policy outcomes that have been formally announced as policy or program objectives. A basic assumption is that formally announced or promulgated goals and objectives of policymakers and administrators are appropriate measures of worth or value. Policy analysts use legislation, program documents, and interviews with policymakers and administrators to identify, define, and specify formal goals and objectives. The appropriateness of the formally stated goals and objectives are taken as given, with effectiveness and efficiency used most frequently as evaluative criteria.

The two major types of formal evaluations are *summative* and *formative*. **Summative evaluations** involve an effort to monitor the accomplishment of formal goals and objectives after a policy or program has been in place for some period. They are designed to appraise products of stable and well-established public policies and programs. An experimental evaluation that involves monitoring and evaluation of outcomes under conditions of direct controls over policy inputs and processes is a form of *summative evaluation*.

Many studies by the Manpower Development Research Corporation (MDRC), such as a demonstration project assessing the effect of expanding the earned income tax credit to single working adults (Miller, Schultz, & Bernardi, 2015) take this form. **Formative evaluations** involve efforts to monitor continuously the accomplishment of formal goals and objectives. A developmental evaluation explicitly designed to serve the day-to-day needs of program staff is a form of *formative evaluation*. Mayer, Cullinan, Calmeyer, and Patterson (2015), for example, report findings of an experimental study that involved the continuous monitoring of providers and clients when applying behavioral economics to increase on-time renewals for child care subsidies.

DECISION-THEORETIC EVALUATION

Decision-theoretic evaluations use descriptive methods to produce reliable and valid information about policy outcomes that are explicitly valued by multiple stakeholders. A basic assumption is that formally announced as well as latent goals and objectives of stakeholders are appropriate measures of worth or value. Basic tasks of policy analysts doing decision-theoretic evaluations include identifying relevant policy or program stakeholders and uncovering and making explicit the latent goals and objectives of those stakeholders. Basic assumptions are that the goals and objectives of policies and programs cannot be satisfactorily established by focusing on the values of one or several parties (e.g., Congress, a dominant client group, or chief administrator) and that multiple stakeholders with conflicting goals and objectives are present in most situations involving evaluations. As part of its human resources toolkit, the World Health Organization provides a detailed set of guidelines for conducting such analyses of stakeholders (Schmeer, 2016).

Major forms of such evaluation include **evaluability assessment** and **multi-attribute utility analysis**, and major techniques for data acquisition include brainstorming, argumentation analysis, Delphi, and user-survey analysis. The particular tools and techniques of these forms and techniques go beyond the scope of this chapter but can be found in Dunn (2008). On the whole, however, to the extent policy analysts want to go beyond formally announced goals and objectives of policymakers and administrators and to take into account the values and interests of other parties that have a stake in the policy or program, the tools and techniques for decision-theoretic evaluation are most helpful.

CONCLUSION

This chapter traced the historical roots and development of policy analysis as a field of study; discussed the roles of value neutrality, value relevance, and critical thinking in the social sciences and in social work; examined what is entailed in the formation of policy agendas and alternatives; and presented an analytic framework of policy analysis as product, process, and performance. It sought to increase appreciation for and understanding of the challenges and complexities of undertaking policy analysis that meets professional obligations for integrity in the advocacy and pursuit of social justice. The chapter also sought to elevate the importance of policy analysis as an integral component of social work education and practice, to enhance the profession's capacity to contribute, on a more equal footing than is currently the case, to the field of policy analysis that economists, political scientists, sociologists, lawyers, and graduates of schools of public administration and policy science tend to dominate. To the extent this chapter has instilled a sense of how to think about policy analysis and what tools and techniques might be necessary to learn so policy analyses done by social workers can stand head-to-head with those of other policy-relevant disciplines and professions, it will have met its goal.

Discussion Questions

1. During the course of their development, what were the major issues confronting the policy sciences about advocacy and objectivity? In what ways are these issues still relevant today?
2. What implications for social justice flow from relying exclusively or primarily on a social constructivist framework to define or formulate social problems?
3. President Lyndon Johnson has been quoted as saying, "Our problem is not to do what is right. Our problem is to know what is right" (Dunn, 2008, p. 116). How would you know in advance which among policy options is the "right" one?
4. What criteria would you use to assess the merits of an adopted or proposed policy, and how would you weigh the importance of those criteria relative to one another?
5. What are the main theoretical and practical issues to consider when using the analytic distinctions of policy as product, process, and performance for purposes of policy analysis?
6. How might the goals and objectives of an adopted policy or program be affected while being carried out or implemented?
7. Given what you now know, how would you go about analyzing H.R. 3010, which opened this chapter?

Suggested Websites

Association for Policy Analysis and Management: http://www.appam.org/

Association for Research on Nonprofit Organizations and Voluntary Action: http://www.arnova.org/

Center for American Progress Experts: http://www.americanprogress.org

Congress: https://www.congress.gov/

Corporation for Enterprise Development (CFED): http://cfed.org/

Council on Social Work Education: http://www.cswe.org/

Information for Practice: http://ifp.nyu.edu/

Institute for Policy Studies: http://www.ips-dc.org/

National Association of Social Workers: http://socialworkers.org/

NIRA's World Directory of Think Tanks: http://www.nira.or.jp/past/ice/nwdtt/2005/index.html

Policy Experts: The Insider Guide to Public Policy Experts and Organizations: http://policy experts.org/

RAND Policy Experts: http://www.rand.org/about/people.html

Research Think Tanks: http://think-tanks.insidegov.com/

Social Work Policy Institute: http://www.socialworkpolicy.org/

U.S. Government Accountability Office: http://www.gao.gov/

Web Center for Social Research Methods: http://www.socialresearchmethods.net/

WWW Virtual Library: Evaluation: http://www.policy-evaluation.org/

Suggestions for Further Reading

Brown, K., & Rutter, L. (2006). *Critical thinking for social work*. Exeter, UK: Learning Matters.

Caputo, R.K. (2014). *Policy analysis for social workers*. Thousand Oaks, CA: Sage Publications.

Dunn, W. N. (2008). *Public policy analysis: An introduction*, (4th ed.) Upper Saddle River, NJ: Pearson/Prentice Hall.

Furner, M. O. (2011). *Advocacy and objectivity: A crisis in the professionalization of American social science, 1865–1905*. New Brunswick, NJ: Transaction.

Gilbert, N., & Terrell, P. (2010). *Dimensions of social welfare policy*, (7th ed.) Boston: Allyn & Bacon.

Kraft, M. E., & Furlong, S. R. (2010). *Public policy: Politics, analysis, and alternatives* (3rd ed.). Washington, DC: CQ Press.

Lipsky, M. (2010). *Street-level bureaucracy: Dilemmas of the individual in public service* (30th anniversary expanded edition. New York: Russell Sage Foundation.

Lynd, R. S. (1939). *Knowledge for what? The place of social science in American culture*. New York: Grove Press.

Lyons, G. M. (1969). *The uneasy partnership: Social science and the federal government in the twentieth century*. New York: Russell Sage Foundation.

Mafinezam, A. (2003). *For inquiry and reform: Think tanks of the Progressive Era*. Unpublished doctoral dissertation, Rutgers, The State University of New Jersey. Available from ProQuest Dissertations and Theses database (UMI No. 3077113).

Meenaghan, T. M., Kilty, K. M., & McNutt, J. G. (2004). *Social policy analysis and practice*. Chicago: Lyceum Books.

Smith, J. A. (1991). *The idea brokers: Think tanks and the rise of the new policy elite*. New York: Free Press.

Sterba, J. P. (1999). *Justice: Alternative political perspectives* (3rd ed.). Belmont, CA: Wadsworth.

Weber, M. (1949). *The methodology of the social sciences* (E. A. Shils & H. A. Finch, Trans. & Eds.). New York: Free Press.

Weimer, D. L., & Vining, A. R. (2011). *Policy analysis*, (5th ed.) Boston: Longman.

Addams, J. (1909). *The spirit of youth and the city streets.* New York: Macmillan.

Addams, J. (1910). *Twenty years at Hull House.* New York: Macmillan.

Addams, J., & De Forest, R. W. (1902). The housing problem in Chicago. *Annals of the American Academy of Political and Social Science, 20,* 99–107.

AEI/Brookings Working Group on Poverty and Opportunity. (2015). *Opportunity, responsibility, and security: A consensus plan for reducing poverty and restoring the American Dream.* Retrieved from http://www.brookings.edu/~/media/Research/Files/Reports/2015/12/aei-brookings-poverty-report/Full-Report.pdf?la=en

Bacon, F. (2012). *Novum organum* (Classic reprint ed.). [eBook]. Retrieved from http://www.forgotten-books.org/info/Novum_Organum_1000848298.php (Original work published in 1620)

Bailin, S., Case, R., Coombs, J. R., & Daniels, L. B. (1999). Conceptualizing critical thinking. *Journal of Curriculum Studies, 31,* 285–302.

Bannister, R. C. (1987). *Sociology and scientism: The American quest for objectivity, 1880–1940.* Chapel Hill: University of North Carolina Press.

Behn, R. D. (1985). Policy analysts, clients, and social scientists. *Journal of Policy Analysis and Management, 4,* 428–432.

Bremner, R. H. (1956). Scientific philanthropy, 1863–1893. *Social Service Review, 30,* 168–173.

Bricker-Jenkins, M., & Joseph, B. H.-R. (2008). Progressive social work. In T. Mizrahi & L. E. Davis (Eds.), *Encyclopedia of social work,* (20th ed.) Washington, DC, and Oxford, UK: National Association of Social Workers and Oxford University Press. Retrieved from http://www.oxfordreference.com/view/10.1093/acref/9780195306613.001.0001/acref-9780195306613

Brown, K., & Rutter, L. (2006). *Critical thinking for social work.* Exeter, UK: Learning Matters.

Browne, A., & Wildavsky, A. (1984a). Implementation as exploration. In J. F. Pressman & A. Wildavsky (Eds.), *Implementation,* (3rd ed. expanded) (pp. 232–256). Berkeley: University of California Press.

Browne, A., & Wildavsky, A. (1984b). Implementation as mutual adaptation. In J. F. Pressman & A. Wildavsky (Eds.), *Implementation,* (3rd ed. expanded), pp. 206–231). Berkeley: University of California Press.

Brunet, G., & Cox, K. (2009, April 14). *Federal tax burdens for most near their lowest levels in decades.* Washington, DC: Center on Budget and Policy Priorities. Retrieved from http://www.cbpp.org/cms/?fa=view&id=139

Bryson, G. (1932). The emergence of the social sciences from moral philosophy. *International Journal of Ethics, 42,* 304–323.

Caputo, R. K. (2002). Discrimination and human capital: A challenge to economic theory and social justice. *Journal of Sociology and Social Welfare, 29*(2), 105–124.

Caputo, R. K. (2005). Distribution of the federal tax burden, share of after-tax income, and after-tax income by presidential administration and household type, 1981–2000. *Journal of Sociology and Social Welfare, 32*(2), 3–18.

Caputo, R. K. (2007). Social theory and its relation to social problems: An essay about theory and research with social justice in mind. *Journal of Sociology and Social Welfare, 34*(1), 43–62.

Center on Budget and Policy Priorities (2015, March 15). *Policy basics: Where do our federal tax dollars go?* Washington, DC: Author. Retrieved from http://www.cbpp.org/research/policy-basics-where-do-our-federal-tax-dollars-go?fa=view&id=1258

Congressional Budget Office (2009). *An analysis of health insurance premiums under the Patient Protection and Affordable Care Act.* Washington, DC: Author. Retrieved from https://www.cbo.gov/sites/default/files/111th-congress-2009-2010/reports/11-30-premiums.pdf

Coser, L. A. (1977). *Masters of sociological thought: Ideas in historical and social context,* (2nd ed.) Fort Worth, TX: Harcourt Brace Jovanovich College Publishers.

Cravens, H. (1971). The abandonment of evolutionary social theory in America: The impact of professionalization upon American sociological theory, 1890–1920. *American Studies, 12*(2), 5–20.

Crecine, J. P. (1971). University centers for the study of public policy: Organizational viability. *Policy Sciences, 2,* 7–32.

Dunn, W. N. (2008). *Public policy analysis: An introduction,* (4th ed.) Upper Saddle River, NJ: Pearson/Prentice Hall.

Ericson, R. F. (1970). The policy analysis role of the contemporary university. *Policy Sciences, 1,* 429–442.

Fischer, F. (1991). American think tanks: Policy elites and the politicization of expertise. *Governance, 4,* 332–353.

Franklin, D. L. (1986). Mary Richmond and Jane Addams: From moral certainty to rational inquiry in social work practice. *Social Service Review, 60,* 504–525.

Furner, M. O. (2011). *Advocacy and objectivity: A crisis in the professionalization of American social science, 1865–1905.* New Brunswick, NJ: Transaction.

Gettelman, M. E. (1969–1970, Fall–Spring). John H. Finley and the academic origins of American social work, 1887–1892. *Studies in History and Society, 2,* 13–26.

Gilbert, N., & Terrell, P. (2010). *Dimensions of social welfare policy,* (7th ed.) Boston: Allyn & Bacon.

Greenwald, M. W., & Anderson, M. (Eds.). (1996). *Pittsburgh surveyed: Social science and social reform in the early twentieth century.* Pittsburgh, PA: University of Pittsburgh Press.

Gruber, C. S. (1972). Academic freedom at Columbia University, 1917–1918: The case of James McKeen Cattell. *AAUP Bulletin, 58,* 297–305.

Halberstam, D. (1972). *The best and the brightest.* New York: Random House.

Haskell, T. L. (2000). *The emergence of professional social science: The American social science association and the nineteenth-century crisis of authority.* Baltimore, MD: Johns Hopkins University Press.

Hopkins, H. (1934). Unemployment relief and the Public Works Administration. *Proceedings of the Academy of Political Science, 15*(4), 81–83.

Horowitz, I. L. (1970). Social science mandarins: Policymaking as a political formula. *Policy Sciences, 1,* 339–360.

House of Commons Work and Pensions Committee. (2016). *The local welfare safety net.* London: Author. Retrieved from http://www.publications.parliament.uk/pa/cm201516/cmselect/cmworpen/373/373.pdf

Kellogg, P. U. (1912). The spread of the survey idea. *Proceedings of the Academy of Political Science in the City of New York, 2*(4), 1–17.

Kenny, M. G. (2002). Toward a racial abyss: Eugenics, Wickliffe Draper, and the origins of the Pioneer Fund. *Journal of the History of the Behavioral Sciences, 38,* 259–283.

Kraft, M. E., & Furlong, S. R. (2010). *Public policy: Politics, analysis, and alternatives* (3rd ed.). Washington, DC: CQ Press.

Lee, H. N. (1928). Morals, morality, and ethics: Suggested terminology. *International Journal of Ethics, 38,* 450–466.

Lens, V. (2000). *Welfare reform and the media: A content analysis of two newspapers.* Unpublished doctoral dissertation, Yeshiva University. Available from ProQuest Dissertations and Theses database (UMI No. 9973140).

Lens, V. (2008). Welfare and work sanctions: Examining discretion on the front lines. *Social Service Review, 82,* 197–222.

Levy, C. S. (1976). Personal versus professional values: The practitioner's dilemmas. *Clinical Social Work Journal, 76,* 110–120.

Lipsky, M. (1969). *Toward a theory of street-level bureaucracy* (Institute for Research on Poverty Discussion Paper No. 48–69). Madison: University of Wisconsin.

Lipsky, M. (2010). *Street-level bureaucracy: Dilemmas of the individual in public service* (30th anniversary expanded edition). New York: Russell Sage Foundation.

Lynd, R. S. (1939). *Knowledge for what? The place of social science in American culture.* New York: Grove Press.

Lyons, G. M. (1969). *The uneasy partnership: Social science and the federal government in the twentieth century.* New York: Russell Sage Foundation.

Mafinezam, A. (2003). *For inquiry and reform: Think tanks of the Progressive Era.* Unpublished doctoral dissertation, Rutgers, The State University of New Jersey. Available from ProQuest Dissertations and Theses database (UMI No. 3077113).

Marr, C. (2012, April 2). *Federal income taxes on middle-income families remain near historic lows.* Washington, DC: Center on Budget and Policy Priorities. Retrieved from http://www.cbpp.org/cms/index.cfm?fa=view&id=3151

Mayer, A.K., Cullinan, D., Calmeyer, E., & Patterson, K. (2015). *Engaging providers and clients: Using behavioral economics to increase on-time child care subsidy renewals.* OPRE Report 2015–73. Washington DC: Office of Planning, Research and Evaluation, Administration for Children and Families, US Department of Health and Human Services. Retrieved from http://www.mdrc.org/sites/default/files/engaging_providers_and_clients_fr.pdf

Mayer, J. (2010, August 30). Covert operations. *The New Yorker.* Retrieved from http://www.newyorker.com/magazine/2010/08/30/covert-operations

Mayer, J. (2016). *Dark money: The hidden history of the billionaires behind the rise of the radical right.* New York: Doubleday.

Mazmanian, D. A., & Sabatier, P. A. (1989). *Implementation and public policy.* Lanham, MD: University Press of America.

McAniff, J. E. (1953). The natural law—Its nature, scope and sanction. *Fordham Law Review, 22,* 246–253.

Meenaghan, T. M., Kilty, K. M., & McNutt, J. G. (2004). *Social policy analysis and practice.* Chicago: Lyceum Books.

Meltsner, A. (1976). *Policy analysis in the bureaucracy.* Berkeley: University of California Press.

Mendez, J. P. (2006). *The history of the Pillsbury Doughboy: The essential elements of the Federal Pell Grant.* Unpublished doctoral dissertation, Indiana University. Available from ProQuest Dissertations and Theses database (UMI No. 3215185).

Miller, C., Schultz, C., & Bernardi, A. (2015). *Testing an expanded earned income tax credit for single adults.* New York: MDRC. Retrieved from http://www.mdrc.org/sites/default/files/Testing_an_Expanded_EITC_Brief.pdf

Morçöl, G. (2001). Positivist beliefs among policy professionals: An empirical investigation. *Policy Sciences, 34,* 381–401.

Nozick, R. (1974). *Anarchy, state, and utopia*. New York: Basic Books.

O'Scannlain, D. F. (2011). The natural law in the American tradition. *Fordham Law Review, 79*, 1513–1528.

Parsons, T. (1939). The professions and social structure. *Social Forces, 17*, 457–467.

Patashnik, E. M. (2008). *Reforms at risk: What happens after major policy changes are enacted?* Princeton, NJ: Princeton University Press.

Quade, E. S. (1970). Why policy sciences? *Policy Sciences, 1*, 1–2.

Raskin, M. G. (1971). *Being and doing*. Boston: Beacon Press.

Rawls, J. (1971). *A theory of justice*. Cambridge, MA: Harvard University Press.

Reisch, M. (2002). Defining social justice in a socially unjust world. *Families in Society, 83*, 343–354.

Rich, A. (2000). *Think tanks, public policy, and the politics of expertise*. Unpublished doctoral dissertation, Yale University. Available from ProQuest Dissertations and Theses database (UMI No. 9954357).

Sabatier, P. A. (Ed.). (1999). *Theories of the policy process*. Boulder, CO: Westview Press.

Sabatier, P. A., & Jenkins-Smith, H. C. (1999). The advocacy coalition framework: An assessment. In P. A. Sabatier (Ed.), *Theories of the policy process* (pp. 117–166). Boulder, CO: Westview Press.

Sanborn, F. B., & Ayers, J. (1931). The first public welfare association. *Social Service Review, 5*, 468–477.

Schmeer, K. (2016). Stakeholder analysis guidelines. In *The human resources for health toolkit*. Geneva: WHO, Global Health Workforce Alliance. Retrieved from http://www.who.int/workforcealliance/knowledge/toolkit/33.pdf

Schwabish, J., & Griffith, C. (2012). *The U.S. federal budget, fiscal year 2011*. Washington, DC: Congressional Budget Office. Retrieved from http://www.cbo.gov/ftpdocs/125xx/doc12577/budgetinfographic.pdf

Smith, J. A. (1991). *The idea brokers: Think tanks and the rise of the new policy elite*. New York: Free Press.

Smith, M. C. (1994). *Social science in the crucible: The American debate over objectivity and purpose, 1918–1941*. Durham, NC: Duke University Press.

Snyder, L. J. (2011). *The philosophical breakfast club: Four remarkable friends who transformed science and changed the world*. New York: Random House.

Sommerfeld, D., & Reisch, M. (2003). Unintended consequences: The impact of welfare reform in the United States on NGOs. *Voluntas: International Journal of Voluntary and Nonprofit Organizations, 14*, 299–320.

Spector, M., & Kituse, J. I. (1987). *Constructing social problems*. New York: Aldine de Gruyter.

Steinhauer, J. (2016, July 7). House votes to send bill to repeal health law to Obama's desk. *The New York Times*, p. A14. Retrieved from http://www.nytimes.com/2016/01/07/us/politics/house-votes-to-send-bill-to-repeal-health-law-to-obamas-desk.html?ref=todayspaper

Sterba, J. P. (1999). *Justice: Alternative political perspectives* (3rd ed.). Belmont, CA: Wadsworth.

Tevelow, A. A. (2005). *From corporate liberalism to neoliberalism: A history of American think tanks*. Unpublished doctoral dissertation, University of Pittsburgh. Retrieved from http://etd.library.pitt.edu/ETD/available/etd-08192005-162045/unrestricted/FinalTevelowETD.pdf

Tripodi, T., Layalayants, M., & Zlotnik, J. L. (2008). Research. In T. Mizrahi & L. E. Davis (Eds.), *Encyclopedia of social work*, (20th ed.) Washington, DC, and Oxford: National Association of Social Workers and Oxford University Press. Retrieved from http://www.oxfordreference.com/view/10.1093/acref/9780195306613.001.0001/acref-9780195306613

van Kleeck, M. (1910, March). Child labor in home industries. *Annals of the American Academy of Political and Social Science, 35*(Supplement), 145–149.

van Kleeck, M. (1919, January). Federal policies for women in industry. *Annals of the American Academy of Political and Social Science, 81*, 87–94.

Ways, M. (1969, January). The faculty is the heart of the trouble. *Fortune*, p. 95.

Weber, M. (1949). *The methodology of the social sciences* (E. A. Shils & H. A. Finch, Trans. & Eds.). New York: Free Press.

Weimer, D. L. (1995). *Institutional design*. Boston: Kluwer Academic.

Weimer, D. L., & Vining, A. R. (2011). *Policy analysis,* (5th ed.) Boston: Longman.

Yan, M. C., & Wong, Y.-L. R. (2005). Rethinking self-awareness in cultural competence: Toward a dialogic self in cross-cultural social work. *Families in Society, 86*, 181–188.

Zunz, O. (2011). *Philanthropy in America: A history*. Princeton, NJ: Princeton University Press.

Credits

7

FEDERAL AND STATE BUDGET BASICS FOR SOCIAL WORKERS

Karen M. Staller, PhD, JD

AUTHOR'S NOTE

Before ostensibly retiring in 2003, my father had been a professor of economics at Cornell University for more than 50 years. For nearly five decades, he taught the large, undergraduate course in macroeconomics, Econ 102. Each year, hundreds of undergraduate students crowded his amphitheater classroom. Yet, on the eve of his retirement, he remarked to me that he believed he had "finally learned how to teach Econ 102 right." Teaching basic material "right" is no easy matter.

When I first began teaching foundation classes in social welfare policy to social work students in the early 1990s, my father repeatedly sketched out for me, on disposable dinner napkins, restaurant placemats, and other readily available scraps of paper, an outline of one of his lectures on the structure of the federal budget. He believed it contained critical information for my instruction of budding social workers. I began experimenting with "Dad's lecture." Since then, I have taught the material every semester, at two additional universities, in every section of my foundation policy classes. Over the years, I disposed of the economic theory and models. Instead, I reinterpreted the information through a social work lens.

At first blush, students might think that federal and state budgets are of little interest to them, but, in fact, these budgets affect virtually every aspect of our lives and work and are rife with social justice issues. Increasingly, social work students will be graduating into a world where public and nonprofit social welfare resources are both scarce and shrinking. The outcome of current political debates over the budget is more critical now than it has been in a long time. It will directly affect students' career opportunities, the structure and delivery of social services, and the amount of resources available for our clients, programs, and agencies. Additionally, the outcome of these debates will reflect critical choices about the fundamental role of government and its relative responsibility in ensuring the welfare of the American people.

What follows is not meant as an economics lecture *per se*. It is meant to provide students with a framework with which they can process, understand, and interpret most current conversations in the media on issues concerning federal and state budgets. It provides a stable structure from which to make sense of arguments on contemporary controversies such as raising or lowering taxes, cutting or increasing spending, redistributing wealth, growing the economy, reducing deficit spending, fiscal responsibility, unfunded mandates, and other issues. Answering the question, "What should we do about this mess?" is beyond the scope of this chapter. However, answering the question, "How do I make sense of all these competing claims?" is not.

Over the past several decades, Republican and Democratic presidential administrations have come and gone. We have seen a fleeting budget surplus and a fluctuating federal deficit. There have been tax increases, tax cuts, and "rollbacks." There have been cost-of-living adjustments (COLA's) and increases for Social Security beneficiaries, large reductions in spending on discretionary social welfare programs, expenditure capping on social safety net programs, and the transformation of previously open-ended categorical programs into block grants. We have spent massive amounts on economic stimulus and jobs packages, created a new federal Department of Homeland Security, and enacted major health care legislation. We continue to fight a costly global "war on terror." By understanding the budget structure as presented in this chapter, students can make sense of these seemingly unrelated policy developments and how they affect their practice and the lives of their clients and constituents.

This chapter, therefore, will provide a basic overview of federal and state budgets, identify some of the controversies and issues that most directly dominate current budget debates, and provide students with a working skill set by which to recognize and organize the arguments they will hear from policymakers and in the media. Among other things, it offers a place to understand

- ideological differences between Republican and Democratic fiscal and welfare policy agendas;
- the role of the tax code and federal and state budgets in "redistributing wealth;"
- why entitlement programs (Social Security, Medicaid, and Medicare) are expenditure drivers at the federal and state levels that affect all government-funded social welfare programs;
- how our public priorities and commitments have changed over time;
- how different public funding mechanisms such as block grants and categorical grants work;
- how different constitutional interpretations about the role of government affect "the general welfare;"
- the relationship between federal and state responsibility for social welfare spending;
- how the Affordable Care Act of 2010 illustrates many of these discussion threads; and
- why discussions of fiscal policy and fiscal responsibility are so important for social workers.

Over the years, I have read untold numbers of students' policy papers that conclude with the general recommendation that we should increase funding for the student's favorite program. At the heart of this generic recommendation is that "someone" should pay for it. But who is that someone? At what cost should we fund one program over another favored by social workers? Facing the budget forces students to confront the more difficult questions of who pays, at what cost, for what things?

FEDERAL BUDGET: AN OVERVIEW

According to Diana M. DiNitto (2000), "The budget is the single most important policy statement of any government. The *expenditure* side of the budget tells us *who gets what* in public money, and the *revenue* side of the budget tells us *who pays the cost*" (p. 14; emphasis added). As a policy statement, the federal budget reflects the nation's social welfare priorities. To use a cliché, it is about "putting our money where our mouth is" and, therefore, reflects the concrete reality of who gets what and who bears the burden of paying for it.

To arrange these ideas, let's start with a T-table (see Figure 7.1). The "what goes in" side of the T-table may also be called **revenues** or **sources**. The "what goes out" side of the T-table may be called **expenditures** or **uses**. Not unlike the family checkbook, if the "what goes in" side equals the "what goes out" side, we have a **balanced** budget. Of course, at the federal level, this does not happen very often. The more likely alternative is a federal budget that is not balanced; in this case, there are two possibilities. If the "what goes in" side is greater than what gets spent, the government will have a **surplus**. In recent years, however, the more common occurrence is that we have spent more than we have taken in. In each year that we overspend, the government is said to run a **deficit**.

In every year that the U.S. government runs a deficit, it must take additional action to cover the cost of overspending. Although theoretically the government could just print more money, doing so would have detrimental inflationary consequences. [*See Chapter 3 in this volume for a fuller discussion of the political economy of social policy and social welfare.*] Therefore, the more common approach is to **borrow** money to cover the cost of **deficit spending**. Like any borrowing (e.g., a student loan, car loan, or home mortgage), the **principal** (the amount borrowed) must be paid back to the lenders along with **interest** payments charged for the privilege of borrowing the money in the first place. In brief, interest is "the fee a lender charges a borrower for the use of the lender's money" (Center on Budget and Policy Priorities [CBPP], 2009). We will see below that the annual interest payments the government pays on money previously borrowed make up a significant portion of our annual expenditures. It is listed, therefore, as a use on the T-table above (see Figure 7.1).

All our annual deficits added together—the total of all principal and interest owed to domestic and foreign creditors—is called the **federal debt.** It is important not to confuse the federal *deficit* (an annual shortfall) with the federal *debt* (the sum total of all our deficit spending over time). Debt, therefore, refers to the "cumulative amount of money the government has had to borrow" for *all* its past and current expenditures (CBPP, 2009).

To put this in perspective, for fiscal year (FY) 2015, the total U.S. federal revenue (the "what goes in") was ~$3.2 trillion. However, federal expenditures (the "what goes out") were ~$3.7 trillion. Therefore, the

Table 7.1 Federal Budget T-Table.

Expenditures/Uses	Revenue/Sources
1. Purchase of goods and services	1. Personal income tax
2. Transfer payments: a) Domestic transfers b) Foreign transfers	2. FICA (payroll taxes such as Social Security and Medicare withholdings)
3. Interest on the federal debt	3. Business tax
	4. Miscellaneous other taxes

remaining balance (approximately $438 billion) of federal expenditures was financed by borrowing (CBPP, 2016b). In future years, we will have to repay both the principal borrowed and the interest on that principal, all of which will be added to the existing federal debt.

The United States borrows this money by selling government **treasury securities** that can include **bills** (short-term loans) and **bonds** (longer term loans). For many years, the United States borrowed money exclusively from U.S. banks and U.S. citizens to cover deficit spending. By borrowing within the United States from banks, businesses, and citizens, we essentially "owned" our own debt. In other words, we owed money to ourselves. Increasingly, however, the U.S. government has been borrowing money from foreigners to cover our deficit spending. Chief among these foreign investors is China. In fact, given the global nature of the 21st century economy, the United States—along with many European nations—is now considered a "debtor nation," while China is called a "creditor nation."

The tensions between these political and economic realities were evident, for example, in the shifting public positions taken by Hillary Rodham Clinton. During her 2008 bid for the presidency, she argued "that reliance on Chinese bond purchases was making the U.S. dangerously dependent" and noted that "China's position as America's 'banker' was eroding the United States' leverage with Beijing" (Landler, 2009b; Richter, 2009). However, on her first state visit to China as the newly appointed Secretary of State in the Obama Administration, during a deepening economic crisis at home, Clinton admonished the Chinese to continue to invest in U.S. bonds for the economic well-being of both countries (Richter, 2009). "It's a good investment, it's a safe investment," she told the Chinese public (Landler, 2009a). Thus, during the early years of the Great Recession, Clinton argued that the United States needed to "be able to take on more debt" to "jolt the economy back to life" (Landler, 2009a). More recently, foreign governments, including China, Japan, Mexico, Turkey, and Belgium have been selling U.S. treasury debt in record numbers largely in efforts to stimulate their own economies (Egan, 2016; Gillespie, 2016). Even so, there is still considerable demand for U.S. treasuries because they are considered a "safe harbor" in the tumultuous global economy (Egan, 2016).

Theoretically, there are three ways to "balance" the budget or at least move to "reduce deficit spending" (which refers to reducing the *amount* of *annual* overspending). One way is to increase tax revenues, which for the federal government is primarily the income tax. A second option is to reduce expenditures. A third approach is to attempt to "grow the economy" through policy initiatives that stimulate the economy. The final option focuses on assuring that the burden of deficit spending *relative to the overall size of the economy*, as measured by the nation's Gross Domestic Product (GDP), is manageable. The acceptable ratio varies depending on the strength of the economy and the size of the deficit. For example, in 1992, the deficit was 4.7% of the nation's overall GDP. In 2015, although the deficit was larger in absolute dollars, it represented only 2.5% of the GDP.

To understand this relative size concept, think about two apple pies—a small one and a big one— representing the GDP. The deficit for any given year is a constant number, like 4 ounces of apple pie. A 4-ounce slice of the small pie might represent a large percentage of that whole pie. However, that same 4-ounce piece cut from a much bigger pie will represent a smaller slice of the overall pie. Economists argue about how much deficit spending is too much relative to the overall GDP (Leonhardt, 2008, p. 31). Using the pie analogy, they argue that the 4-ounce number is less important than its relative relationship to the total size of the pie. Some policymakers concentrate on initiatives that they believe will produce greater revenues, thus resulting in larger pies.

It is important to note that not all borrowing (or overspending) is bad. By analogy, consider the fact that you may have borrowed money to pay for school. This is a good investment because having a degree will increase your earning capacity in the future. By contrast, consider the consequences if—instead of borrowing for your education—you borrowed the same amount of money for an extravagant vacation. Despite its appeal, this expenditure would not increase your future earning potential and you would have to continue paying for the luxury well into the future. Similarly, in the midst of the Great Recession, President Obama argued for a "stimulus package" to "jump-start the economy". He based his position on the assumption that deficit spending was necessary to prevent a deeper recession and was a means to strengthen the U.S. economy in the future.

WHAT GOES IN AND WHAT GOES OUT

What Goes In: Revenues

Look at the basic structure of the T-table (Figure 7.1) and examine the "what goes in" side of the table. The government has four major sources of revenue: *personal income taxes, payroll taxes (based on the Federal Insurance Contributions Act, or FICA), business or corporate taxes*, and *miscellaneous other taxes*. The percentage contribution of each of these funding streams to overall federal revenues varies from year to year. However, in FY 2015, about 47% of total federal revenue came from personal income taxes, 33% from FICA taxes, and another 11% from corporate income taxes (CBPP, 2016a). The remainder came from miscellaneous sources (indirect business taxes, excise taxes, estate taxes, tariffs, duties, fines).

Although the relative percentages are not constant, the combined contributions of *income taxes* and *payroll taxes* have historically made up the lion's share of federal revenue. These two sources of revenue—income and payroll taxes—are the most important ones for social workers to know about, because the vast majority of federal revenue comes directly from the aggregate contributions of individual taxpayers (aka working Americans). Therefore, when students advocate that "someone should pay" for a public program or service, they should, in theory, be prepared to pay more taxes to fund it. The great jurist Oliver Wendell Holmes, Jr. famously said, "Taxes are what we pay for civilized society" (*Compania General De Tabacos De Filipinas v. Collector of Internal Revenue*, 1927). Thus, an assessment of U.S. tax policies may tell us something about how civilized we are as a nation.

Personal Income Tax: Redistribution and Equity

Each year, most working Americans file a personal income tax form in which a final accounting is made of their annual tax liability to the U.S. government. Although the idea may seem strange to social workers at first, the income tax code is where American income and wealth are primarily redistributed (or not). Therefore, as a social welfare policy instrument, the tax code is a critical tool to the attainment of social justice goals.

Some of the terms used on income tax forms—such as *exemptions, deductions, credits, allowances*, and *taxable income*—may be familiar. Although a thorough investigation of the meaning and implications of all these concepts is beyond the scope of this chapter, suffice it to say that each of these adjustments, as a matter of tax policy, allows some people to keep more money in their pockets while requiring others to pay more to Uncle Sam. In doing so, policy decisions are being made about who pays and who does not, thereby answering the question, "Who bears the burden?" In addition, the tax code can encourage or discourage certain economic and social behaviors. For example, the Earned Income Tax Credit, discussed below, provides a tax incentive for married couples who have one to three children to work. However, the tax benefit stays the same for families with three or more children, thereby greatly reducing its benefit the more children there are in the family. This type of policy arrangement favors certain types of family constellations.

The redistributive nature of the tax code can be thought of in four different ways. First, the tax code determines how much money overall will be collected and, therefore, is available to "redistribute" to the American public as expenditures on the other side of the T-table (see more below). Second, it determines the relative allocation of burdens between individual taxpayers and corporations or businesses. Third, it determines how much wealth is redistributed between different socioeconomic classes. In other words, it determines the relative burden paid by wealthy, middle-income, and lower income Americans. In this way, the tax code may offer a way of redistributing wealth *among* classes by asking some to pay a bigger share. Finally, it determines how wealth will be allocated between similarly situated taxpayers (those having the same incomes). I will briefly take up several of these issues next.

Tax Credits

To understand how wealth can be redistributed between similarly situated taxpayers, consider the role of credits, deductions, allowances, and other "tax breaks." For example, two individuals can have identical earnings but may bear different tax liabilities based on a set of conditions or behaviors, as well as the source of their incomes. Consider the case of two single women with identical annual incomes; one has a child, and the other does not. As a matter of tax policy, we allow only the woman with a child to take a "dependent care tax credit." There are good policy reasons for allowing a mother to keep a greater share of her earnings. Nonetheless, in terms of income redistribution, one woman is responsible for paying more money "into" the revenue side of the T-table than the other woman. If you think about the kinds of tax "breaks" available to various categories of taxpayers, you can begin to analyze the policy preferences that are in place. For example, the tax code favors people who own homes and have mortgages, those who place money in retirement accounts, those who make charitable contributions, and those whose income is derived from investments rather than employment. These various arrangements have important implications for social welfare and social justice.

One particular kind of tax credit, the Earned Income Tax Credit (EITC)—sometimes referred to as a *negative income tax*—deserves special attention from social workers because it is an excellent example of the redistributive features of the tax code. The EITC "is a federal tax credit for low- and moderate-income working people. It is designed to encourage and reward work as well as offset federal payroll and income taxes" (CBPP, 2011a). The EITC takes into account the number of children in a family (up to three). In doing so, it favors *working* families with one to three children. It is "refundable"; this means that if the maximum credit available to the family "exceeds a low-wage worker's income tax liability, the IRS will refund the balance" (CBPP, 2011a). In other words, the family actually gets a check from the government—hence the label "negative income tax."

Increasingly advocates have argued that the EITC is a more effective method of redistributing wealth to low-income working families than cash assistance programs, such as Temporary Assistance for Needy Families (TANF). Both EITC and TANF seek to redistribute benefits to low-income families. However, the former does it exclusively through the Internal Revenue Service (IRS), while the latter requires collecting revenue (on one side of the T-table) and then paying for a social welfare program as an expenditure (on the other side of the T-table). Under TANF, federal funds in the form of block grants are transferred to the states, which must develop and administer their own assistance programs. Opponents argue that this is expensive, inefficient, and discourages people from seeking employment. [*See Chapters 12 and 13 in this volume for a fuller discussion of TANF and antipoverty strategies.*]

Recent studies also point to the substantial long-term benefits of the EITC. The CBPP (2015) reports that a growing body of research shows that the EITC has been linked to "improved infant and maternal health," "better school performance," "greater college enrollment," and "increased work and earnings in the next generation" (p. 5).

Income Tax Burden and Income Inequality

Since the emergence of the Occupy Movement in 2007, there has been increased attention paid to income inequality in the United States. Although many inter-related factors affect the problem of income inequality, government tax policies (federal and state) are important contributing factors (CBPP, 2012). One such tax policy is the sharp cuts in the federal income tax rate paid by individuals with high incomes. Another is the dramatic decrease in tax rates on unearned income (income from investments or capital gains) introduced during several Republican administrations. Under the nation's current tax structure, wealthy Americans whose income is primarily derived from investments pay taxes at a lower rate than do middle-income Americans whose income is largely derived from employment. Unhappy about the *effective tax rate*, which measures "how much people pay in taxes as a percentage of their pretax incomes," President Obama expressed concern that the very wealthiest Americans pay a lower percentage of tax than middle-income Americans (Johnson, Rosenberg, & Williams, 2012). Politicians frequently debate these tradeoffs. For example, some Republicans have argued that it is important for the wealthy to receive tax breaks because they are the "job creators" and thus drive the rest of the economy. By contrast, scholars, like Robert Reich, President Clinton's Secretary of Labor, have strenuously argued that the real job creators are middle class consumers who buy things and, therefore, keep businesses producing. Under this line of argument, tax breaks for the middle or lower class are critical because if these people have more money in their pockets they will purchase more things, thereby driving the economy. [*See Chapter 3 in this volume for further discussion of this issue.*]

Payroll Taxes: FICA

The second largest source of federal revenue is derived from payroll tax deductions, better known as Social Security taxes authorized through the Federal Insurance Contribution Act (FICA). Leonhardt (2008) noted that the "income tax doesn't take the biggest bite out of most families' annual tax bill, the payroll tax does" (p. 34). When FICA is deducted from workers' paychecks, workers are metaphorically making a social insurance "contribution" to their future retirement in the form of Social Security and Medicare benefits—hence the name of the Act.

However, this notion of contributing directly to your retirement benefits is a fiction. These large entitlement programs are based on a "pay-as-you-go" system. This means that workers who are contributing to the system through payroll taxes today are actually funding current Social Security checks and Medicare for the elderly beneficiaries receiving them. (See the expenditure side of the T-table in Figure 7.1.) When the 1935 Social Security Act was signed into law by President Franklin Delano Roosevelt, policymakers were well aware of the inherent funding problems associated with the pay-as-you-go plan. As a result, Social Security was conceptualized, and structured, as an intergenerational social compact, with younger workers footing the bill for retirees who had contributed to the system during their own work lives. However, this

Figure 7.1 President Franklin D. Roosevelt Signing the 1935 Social Security Act. Frances Perkins, the Principal Author of the Act, is Behind Him.

framework does not account for the dramatic shifts in the ratio of workers to retirees that have occurred during the past 80+ years.

There are two substantial problems associated with the current Social Security funding scheme. The first has to do with the aging of a large group of individuals collectively referred to as the "baby boomers." The second relates to the way the baby boomers' "contributions" to Social Security were "banked" during their lifetime.

The **baby boomers** refer to a demographic group of individuals born immediately after World War II and extending roughly through 1964. (After 1964, birth rates began to fall.) During this period, a very large number of babies were born each year to the families formed by returning veterans of that war and the Korean War. Members of this large demographic group have made contributions (through payroll deductions) into the Social Security system for their entire working lives. Starting in 2008, however, the front edge of this baby boom cohort began receiving Social Security checks and became eligible for Medicare. Consequently, as the baby boomers continue to reach retirement age, there will be "an enormous rise in the government's Medicare and Social Security obligations" (Leonhardt, 2008, p. 30). Each year, for the next two decades, new waves of boomers will reach retirement age and begin drawing checks and receiving health care. As retirees, they will also stop contributing to the system in the form of payroll taxes. The impact of this dramatic shift from paying into the system to receiving benefits was as predictable as it is problematic.

Four aspects of this shift are worth considering at the moment. First, the baby boomers have paid *into* the Social Security system for their entire working lives with the promise of future benefits. Second, at the time of this writing, many baby boomers are still paying into the system and are doing so at their maximum earning capacity and, therefore, at the maximum tax rate. Third, as the boomers retire, they will expect, under the terms of the nation's existing social contract, to withdraw the benefits owed them. Finally, because average life expectancies have increased, the total number of years (or the duration of time) that baby boomers will be entitled to receive benefits has lengthened. The net effect is that less money will be going into the system and more money will be drawn out over a long period. Taken together, these factors will put a strain on the federal budget.

The second major problem has to do with the way Social Security revenues have been "banked." As baby boomers paid into the system during their entire working lives, the relative number of beneficiaries drawing out of the system was small. Theoretically, one might expect that the surplus being paid into the "insurance" system had been "saved" for the boomers' future retirements. This, however, has not been the case. In fact, we essentially spent this "extra" money on current annual expenditures. Berkowitz (1991) explains it this way:

> The government banked the money, but in a most unconventional way. The government invested its Social Security windfall in government securities or, to put it another way, in itself. In effect, the government loaned itself money and then promised to pay itself back in the future.

In this way, the government acted as both the owner and the customer of the bank. Much like a private citizen, the government bought U.S. saving bonds and then, unlike a private citizen turned around and spent the money. That meant that the Social Security money helped to finance the government's current operations such as welfare payments, public works, or the army's payroll. (p. 40.)

In short, one problem with this particular funding scheme is that we have been including FICA *surpluses* as part of our general *revenue* stream for decades. In doing so, we masked both the size of our annual deficits and failed to account for, and protect, the future liabilities of those paying into the system.

The Social Security system has been in danger before. In the early 1980s, "high inflation and slow wage growth placed increasing pressures on the Social Security financing system" (Apfel, 2008, p. 961). During the Reagan Administration, Congress is credited with "saving" Social Security (or at least postponing the day of reckoning) using several policy solutions. First, it raised the age of retirement, thereby keeping people in the workforce longer, paying FICA longer, and drawing benefits for fewer years. This has social justice implications given the dramatic disparities in life expectancies across demographic groups. For example, consider the plight of African American men who die, on average, much younger than Asian women (the demographic cohort with the longest average life expectancy). Is it fair that African American men get much lower returns, if any at all, than do Asian women, particularly if they have paid into the Social Security system for their entire working lives (Office of the Chief Actuary, 2012)?

Second, Congress increased payroll deductions, thus increasing FICA revenue. Third, it imposed a tax on Social Security benefits for higher income retirees. Of course, this makes little conceptual sense, since the benefits retirees received were supposedly a means of paying them back for taxes withheld in the first place. Note, however, that taxing Social Security benefits and treating them like income (albeit a second time) increases general revenues. In addition, since this tax applied only to higher income individuals it had additional redistributive effects.

Fourth, reforms to the Social Security system during the Reagan administration delayed COLA payments for retirees, a policy change that had first been implemented in 1973. Theoretically, a COLA is an automatic adjustment to the amount of a beneficiary's Social Security check, designed to keep pace with inflation. By delaying the COLA, less money was being expended from the federal budget. However, the burden was really born by retirees, because the purchasing power of their benefit checks did not keep pace with inflation. (For more, see http://www.ssa.gov/history/1983amend.html.) All these changes, while "politically unpopular," are credited with "saving Social Security." Since the program will be coming under increasing scrutiny as the baby boomers retire, you can anticipate hearing these same kinds of policy arguments in the future (Apfel, 2008, p. 961). [*See Chapter 11 in this volume for a more in-depth discussion of Social Security.*]

WHAT GOES OUT: EXPENDITURES, USES, OR OUTLAYS

Although we have introduced the topic of expenditures in the above discussion of Social Security benefits, we will now turn in earnest to the "what-goes-out" side of the T-table, also known as outlays or uses. Invariably, when I ask my students how the federal government spends its money, they list social welfare programs such as food stamps, welfare, Social Security, Medicaid, and Medicare. Usually they add military spending to the list. But are all these outlays the same *kind* of expenditure? No, not really. While there are many different ways of grouping federal expenditures, one schema consists of three major categories: the *purchase of goods and services, transfer payments,* and *interest payments on the federal debt* (See Table 7.1 above). What follows is a brief description of each.

Purchase of Goods and Services

The federal government is made up of many individuals who serve the people as federal employees. Their jobs range from President of the United States to security guards at the Smithsonian, park rangers, military personnel, postal carriers, federal court judges, in short, all the people who work for the legislative, executive, or judicial branches of the federal government. These employees must be paid for their *services* (including salaries and benefits). Furthermore, the government needs to supply them with the *goods* they need to do their jobs. This includes purchasing paper clips for FBI agents, fighter jets for the Air Force and computers for employees of the Department of Health and Human Services. In short, our tax dollars go, in part, to the outright purchase of *goods* for employees of the federal government and for the *services* they provide.

Transfer Payments

A second major conceptual category of federal expenditures are transfer payments. The idea embodied here is that money collected as revenue on the sources side of the T-table is then *transferred back* to taxpayers (or foreigners) as some form of benefit. In this manner, the government collects taxes from Americans with one hand and redistributes them through programs such as TANF, SNAP, Medicaid, or Medicare with the other. The United States also makes some transfer payments (albeit a relatively small amount) to foreigners. Foreign transfers include food aid, disaster relief, and other funds spent outside the United States.

What is important to understand is that most of the money for all these transfer payments comes from the payroll and income taxes we pay. While social work students would often like to see these kinds of federal programs (both domestic and foreign) expanded, they should remember that to do so requires finding additional revenue, cutting other expenditures, or being willing to increase overspending. An important question, therefore, is not *whether* it would be desirable to expand these programs but, rather, *how we should pay* for them and at what cost to whom.

Additionally, students often suggest that we decrease military spending to fund more domestic social welfare programs. This raises important ideological and constitutional questions about the primary function of the federal government. Democrats have tended to argue that the federal government should play an important role in ensuring the general welfare of the American people. Some Republicans have made constitutional arguments—based on the Tenth Amendment to the U.S. Constitution which is also known as the "reserve powers clause" because it reserves responsibilities not specifically delegated to the federal government to the "states" or "the people"—that social welfare policies ought to be the responsibility of the 50 states. They argue that the federal government should concentrate its efforts on the functions listed in the enumerated powers clause (Article 1 § 8). These enumerated powers, they argue, involve the kinds of things a centralized federal government ought to be doing, such as maintaining an army, providing uniform currency, and running a national postal system. These controversies reflect legitimate ideological differences over the role and responsibility of the federal government, which often surface in debates about the nation's funding priorities.

Interest on the Federal Debt

The final major category of federal expenditure is the interest the government pays annually on the national debt. In essence, this category reflects the price of our "overspending" or "deficit spending" from previous years. As noted above, when revenues are lower than expenditures, the government must borrow money to cover the difference. This money must be paid back, with interest, to our nation's creditors. As a result, each year there is a recurring federal expenditure on interest payments. For example, in FY 2015, approximately 6% of total federal outlays were on interest payments (CBPP, 2016b).

FEDERAL BUDGETING PROCESS

Figure 7.2 Social Security, which provides benefits to persons with disabilities, is an example of an entitlement or mandatory program.

Not all social welfare programs created by Congress through "authorizing" legislation (which specifies the limits of money that could be appropriated for them) are actually funded. They must be included in the federal budget to receive such funding. For example, the Federal Runaway and Homeless Act authorizes funding for runaway youth shelters, transitional living programs, street outreach activities, and a national toll-free crisis telephone line. However, whether federal money will be *appropriated* for these services in a given year depends on the outcome of debates over the federal budget itself.

Not surprisingly, the process of producing a federal budget is a complicated matter. It requires the action of both the President and Congress (CBPP, 2011b). Each year the President must send to Congress a detailed proposed five-year budget for the upcoming fiscal year (which starts on October 1) before the first Monday in February. In it, the President must make specific funding recommendations for all discretionary (or appropriated) programs. Discretionary programs require action each year to continue to receive funding; they include spending on the military, education, and other non-entitlement programs.

In addition, the President may make recommendations for changes in the *entitlement* (or *mandatory*) programs. As noted elsewhere, these programs include things such as Medicare, Medicaid, and Social Security. Third, the President's budget may include proposed changes to the tax code. These proposed changes affect the government's revenue projections for future years. Finally, the President's budget will also specify the suggested deficit or surplus. This "bottom line" takes into account an estimate of the rate at which the nation's economy will grow during this period, because the state of the economy will determine the amount of revenue the government will collect and the size of the expenditures it will incur. Taken together, the detailed budget is a statement of the President's policy priorities and objectives.

Next, Congress must work out a plan, known as a *budget resolution*, which "sets limits on how much each committee can spend" during the next fiscal year (CBPP, 2011b). This process starts in the House and Senate Budget Committees, with any differences in proposed budget resolutions needing to be resolved in a House–Senate Conference Report. The final Conference Report must be passed by both houses. The budget resolution is much less detailed than the President's statement. It identifies spending in 19 broad categorical areas, known as budget *functions*, and projects revenues for a minimum of five years.

Budget resolutions contain two different kinds of figures. They include the total amount to be allocated (known as *budget authority*) as well as the amount that actually "flows out of the treasury in a given year" (known as *outlays*) (CBPP, 2011b). Eventually, in each house of Congress, the Appropriations Committee will receive these reports and decide in more detail how this funding will be allocated among their 12 subcommittees. Subsequently, all appropriations bills must fit within these budget frameworks.

In addition to this budgeting process, students should be aware of a separate but important rule that applies to both House and Senate actions. It is known as the "Pay-As-You-Go" (PAYGO) Rule and requires that "all entitlement increases and tax cuts be fully offset" (CBPP, 2011b). Any such proposed bill (or enacted legislation) must be paid for over a specified number of years. For example, health care reform, enacted during the Obama Administration, necessarily included a plan to offset any increased costs. [*See Chapter 8 in this volume for further discussion of the federal legislative process and the role advocates can play.*]

IDEOLOGICAL DEBATES ON BUDGETS IN HISTORICAL PERSPECTIVE

To provide some idea of the ebb and flow of some of these budget debates over time, let's take a moment to look at the actions of several different presidential administrations. President Reagan famously called for reducing the size of federal government by lowering taxes and reigning in expenditures. Embedded in Reagan's economic message was a belief that federal social welfare expenditures had grown too large and that the cost of social welfare, in general, ought to be shifted to the states. In addition, Reagan believed that taxes on the wealthiest Americans were too high and that high taxes had created a disincentive either to expand or start new businesses. Indeed, when Reagan was elected in 1980, the "tax rates on top incomes were so high that even liberal economists now say the economy was suffering" (Leonhardt, 2008, p. 33).

In what was labeled in the popular press at the time as "trickle-down economics," Reagan persuaded Congress to reduce tax rates on the wealthiest taxpayers, anticipating that this would benefit the country as a whole. His 1981 tax cuts, however, are often blamed for the burgeoning federal deficits of the 1980s and for heralding an era of increasing socioeconomic inequality between the wealthiest Americans and everyone else. In his budgets, President Reagan also dramatically cut social welfare expenditures and slashed federal assistance to local governments. Taken together, these cuts to programs and governments increased poverty, including homelessness, and aggravated other social ills and hardships. At the same time, however, the Reagan Administration implemented substantial increases in military expenditures. Although publically promising to decrease the size of government—which he did only to a very limited extent—Reagan initiated a shift in the nation's relative funding priorities. [*See Chapter 2 for further discussion of the impact of Reaganomics.*]

President Obama has called Reagan's essential message of "low taxes, smaller government" both "simple" and "elegant" (Leonhardt, 2008, p. 54). He has admitted that "Reagan's central insight—that the liberal welfare state had grown complacent and overly bureaucratic, with Democratic policy makers more obsessed with slicing the economic pie than with growing that pie—contained a good deal of truth" (p. 31). In short, Reagan was able to package his economic message in a way that was readily understood by average Americans. That said, in reality, Reagan basically failed to reduce the size of government, although he did drastically reduce expenditures on social welfare programs.

Historically, Democrats have been accused by their political opponents of being the "tax-and-spend" party. In contrast to Reagan's message about small government and limited social welfare responsibility, Democrats have tended to favor a federally funded social welfare safety net. These stereotypical positions sometimes play out in political debates. For example, in the 2008 presidential campaign, Republican candidate John McCain repeatedly warned voters that Democratic candidate Barack Obama wanted to "spend *your* money." Embedded in this critique was the idea that Obama would increase taxes and spend the revenue on large federal programs that would benefit segments of the population other than those who were paying the taxes. Republican Presidential candidate, Mitt Romney, made similar charges during the 2012 campaign. Regardless of the political rhetoric that often obscures rather than clarifies policy differences between the two major parties, it is true that Democrats/liberals have generally favored redistributing societal benefits and burdens more equitably, while Republicans/conservatives have emphasized individual political and property rights and personal responsibility (Gilbert, 1995; Katz, 2001; Reisch & Staller, 2011).

Interestingly and seemingly contrary to popular stereotypes, however, it was a Democratic president, Bill Clinton, who first seriously tackled our deficit spending problem with his budget policies. Clinton sought to reduce deficit spending, and by the late 1990s, with the assistance of bipartisan Congressional support and a strong economy, he succeeded. When he left office in January 2001, the federal government had a budget surplus for the first time in memory, a surplus that at the time was projected to grow for the foreseeable future. Economist Alice Rivlin (2008) has noted,

> The transformation in the federal budget in the 1990s—from an escalating deficit to a large and growing surplus—occurred because there was strong bipartisan consensus that the budget should be balanced, and rules were in place to help achieve the goal. (p. 972)

The Budget Reform Act of 1990, passed during the presidency of George H. W. Bush, included two particularly useful process-oriented rules. The first placed caps on discretionary funding, which resulted in disputes over priorities needing to be resolved directly rather than ignored. The second, PAYGO, "kept both the executive and legislative branches from proposing tax cuts or entitlement increases that would increase the deficit" by requiring all proposals to be accompanied by "equal and opposite offsets over the budget period" (Rivlin, 2008, pp. 971–972).

The Budget Reform Act (and subsequent amendments) expired in 2002, eliminating many of the process-oriented safeguards. Furthermore, partisan political bickering and ideological intransigence have returned and created enormous barriers to Congressional budgetary compromises. In addition, in the early 21st century, the government quickly returned to deficit spending.

While President Clinton raised taxes on the wealthiest Americans to combat the budget deficit, his successor, George W. Bush, made the restoration of tax cuts a major campaign theme. Once in office, he fulfilled this campaign promise. In addition, following the September 11 terrorist attacks, Bush initiated a War on Terror, created a new cabinet-level Department of Homeland Security, pushed through a prescription drug benefit in the Medicare program (Part D) without creating a means to fund it, and launched two wars, in Afghanistan and Iraq, whose combined cost has been estimated in the trillions of dollars.

When President Obama took office in January 2009, he was confronted with the worst economic crisis the United States and the industrialized world had experienced since the Great Depression of the 1930s. This period (~2007–2010) has been dubbed the Great Recession. Obama immediately advocated for an economic stimulus program to prevent the crisis from deepening and to increase the nation's economic activity. In February 2009, just one month after his inauguration, he signed the American Recovery and Reinvestment Act into law. Among other things, this stimulus package cut taxes, contained incentives for job creation (using federal contracts, grants, and loans), and extended some safety-net benefits (such as

Figure 7.3 American Recovery and Reinvestment Act helped fund road, highway, and bridge projects.

unemployment insurance and health care). Although it cost nearly $800 billion and increased the size of the federal deficit, the President hoped these investments would jump-start the economy and ultimately increase federal revenues (McGinty, 2009).

In addition, in 2010, Obama signed a statutory PAYGO that resurrected some of the principles of the 1990 Budget Enforcement Act but applied them only to adjustments to entitlement programs and did not include discretionary spending. In 2011, partly as a compromise to resolve partisan divisions over fiscal policy, a bipartisan Congressional "super committee" made up of 12 House and Senate members, evenly divided between Democrats and Republicans, was charged with devising a plan to reduce the deficit by at least $1.5 trillion over a 10-year period. On the table was any mix of solutions that could be agreed on, including adjustments to taxes affecting revenues and cost-containment measures reducing expenditures or slowing spending growth. However, because of hyper-partisanship, this committee failed to reach a compromise in late 2011. The net result was that painful across-the-board budget cuts known as sequestration were imposed. As part of its ongoing responsibility the Congressional Budget Office (CBO) must report annually on this issue. In its final sequestration report for FY 2016, the Congressional Budget Office (CBO) estimated sequestration would not be necessary for 2016 (CBO, 2015).

In President Obama's final budget proposal for FY 2017, he proposed "major initiatives to increase economic opportunity, reduce poverty and boost investment in the infrastructure," while at the same time reducing the budget deficit (Greenstein, 2016). However, given the existing political climate, and Republican majorities in both houses of Congress it is unlikely this budget proposal for the future will survive the next steps in the process. For example, in March 2016, House Republicans proposed, and the House Budget Committee approved, a budget plan that would "secure 62 percent of its budget cuts from low-income programs even though they account for just 28 percent of total non-defense spending" (Kogan & Shapiro, 2016). Experts say that "if enacted, these proposals would constitute reductions in the safety net of unprecedented magnitude" (Kogan & Shapiro, 2016). The proposed cuts would include significant funding reductions in programs such as SNAP, Pell grants, and Medicaid.

In sum, each presidential administration has placed different emphases on the importance of taxing, spending, "growing the economy," and redistributing wealth. These assumptions, which are translated into policy through the federal budget, have disparate impacts on different segments of society and implicitly reflect different conceptions of social justice.

STATE BUDGETS

OVERVIEW AND BALANCED BUDGETS

The basic structure for understanding **state budgets** is similar to that of the federal budget. Yet, at the state level both the sources of revenue and the types of expenditures are different. For example, states do not generally incur military expenses, but they spend a great deal on education, which remains predominantly a state and local responsibility. More significantly, however, due to constitutional requirements *states must balance* their budgets each year, unlike the federal government. The only instances in which

Figure 7.4 States incur significant expenditures for education, which is predominantly a local responsibility.

states can borrow money are to fund specific, and often voter-approved, capital projects (roads, public buildings, bridges) through bonds. It is particularly difficult for state governments to comply with this balanced budget requirement when the economy is doing poorly. As unemployment increases, state revenues fall at the same time as people's social welfare needs increase. Consequently, in such circumstances, states are often forced to make painful program and services cuts to achieve a balanced budget.

STATE REVENUES

States differ in their relative sources of revenue. However, the options generally available include personal income taxes, corporate taxes, property taxes, sales taxes, and miscellaneous other sources such as licenses and fees (for such things as marriage, hunting, or driving; see Table 7.2). Finally, states also receive substantial transfer payments from the federal government. These transfer payments may be in the form of **categorical grants**, which fund specific, federally-approved programs, or **block grants**, which require funds to be spent in a general area but allow states freedom to design programs without requiring federal pre-approval.

The policy choices state legislators make about which configuration of revenue streams to rely on have serious social justice implications. In general, taxes are said to be either progressive or regressive. A *regressive tax* is one that is applied uniformly; that is, each individual or household pays the same percentage tax regardless of income. A sales tax is an example of a regressive tax, because any customer purchasing an item that is taxable in the state will pay the same amount of tax. Regressive taxes have a disproportionate impact on low-income individuals. For example, if the president of your university walked into a local bookstore and purchased a $45 textbook, she will pay the same sales tax as a poor student. As a result, that sales tax will take a much larger "bite" (percentage of overall income) from the student's income than it will from that of the university president.

By contrast, a *progressive tax* is one in which the tax rate graduates (becomes higher) according to income level. It increases as the individual's taxable income increases. Therefore, a progressive tax attempts

Table 7.2 Generic State Budget T-Table.

Expenditures/Uses	Revenue/Sources
1. State purchase of goods and services	1. Personal income tax
2. Education	2. Sales tax
3. Health care (Medicaid, State Children's Health Insurance Program)	3. Property tax
4. Other miscellaneous	4. Miscellaneous other (licenses)
	5. Transfer payments from the federal government

to make the tax burden more equitable, since rich people pay a larger percentage of tax relative to their incomes than do poor people.

Therefore, the way states collect revenue matters. If states collect revenue for their general fund by relying heavily on regressive taxes, such as a sales tax, they disproportionately place the tax burden on the poorest residents of the state. On the other hand, states that rely more heavily on progressive tax sources, such as property or income taxes, are more likely to spread the tax burden more equitably.

The Great Recession took its toll on state economies and put particular strain on state budgets. With more people unemployed for longer periods, state revenues fell while demands on state expenditures increased. Given states' constitutional imperative to balance their budgets, cuts to social services—particularly to public education and health care—followed and took their toll on the states' neediest residents. This situation was compounded by differences in states' political cultures, as some states have historically been more receptive to publically-funded social welfare policies than others. [*See Chapter 9 in this volume for further discussion of this issue.*]

STATE EXPENDITURES

Although states' total expenditures vary, all states incur most of their expenditures in two major categories, education and health (CBPP, 2015). Taken together more than half of all state revenues are spent in these two areas dwarfing expenditures in other areas such as the 5% spent on transportation (for maintaining roads and bridges), 4% on corrections (for prisons, juvenile justice programs, parole and other programs) and 1% on public assistance (for TANF and other small programs) (CBPP, 2015). Of course the relative percentage varies from state to state.

Education, including K–12, community colleges, and public universities is the largest item in state budgets. This is, in part, because primary responsibility for public education has historically rested with the individual states. During the Great Recession, many states sought to balance budgets, in part, by cutting education spending. Unfortunately, studies conducted in 2016 showed that many states have not reversed these trends even eight years after the worst of the recession was over. Compounding matters further, some states continue to cut education spending. The CBPP (2016) found that 31 states provided less funding per student in 2014 than in 2008 and in nearly half of these states the cuts exceeded 10% (p. 1). Two states, Arizona and Alabama, decreased their spending on education between 2008 and 2014 by over 20%, adjusted for inflation. On the positive side, some states have reinvested in education. For example, Vermont, Alaska, and Illinois have each increased education investments by over 10% (CBPP, 2016).

The second major expenditure for all states is health care for low-income residents (specifically Medicaid and the State Children's Health Insurance Program or S-CHIP). These entitlement programs are jointly funded by the federal government and the state. Although the federal government transfers some money to the states for these costly health care programs, states are also required to provide matching funds (according to complicated federal formulas) and to comply with regulatory requirements in order to "draw down" the federal dollars. Because the cost of health care is skyrocketing and these programs are mandatory entitlements, these expenditures are increasingly taking a larger chunk out of state budgets.

THE AFFORDABLE CARE ACT PROBLEM: AN EXAMPLE OF THESE INTERESTING DISCUSSIONS

The Affordable Care Act (ACA) of 2010 provides a particularly good example of many of the ideas discussed in this chapter. Among other things, the ACA mandated that every American have health insurance. To comply with the law, Americans had three basic options, (1) obtaining health insurance through their employers; (2) participating in large public insurance programs (VA, Medicare, Medicaid, S-CHIP); or (3) buying insurance privately in newly created "health exchanges" (either federal or state created). The original design of the ACA also relied heavily on the expansion of Medicaid for low-to-moderate–income Americans.

Prior to the passage of the ACA, Medicaid had been available only to low-income individuals who fell into several limited categorical groups. They were primarily the elderly, the blind, the disabled, and children. The ACA greatly expanded the Medicaid program by eliminating the categorical requirement (for example, making it available to working-aged individuals) and by slightly increasing the financial eligibility requirements. Since its passage, the ACA has engendered considerable political controversy, particularly among conservative Republicans who would like to see it repealed. It has also been battered by several important critical battles. Among the most important was the Supreme Court case *National Federation of Independent Business v. Sebelius*, which challenged the constitutionality of the ACA on two counts. The first was whether the ACA could require all Americans to purchase health insurance (the individual mandate). The second was whether the ACA could require states to expand their Medicaid programs. In a 5–4 decision, the Supreme Court ruled that while the ACA could impose individual mandates, it could not require states to expand their Medicaid programs. Important budget and social justice consequences followed.

As of 2016, 32 states have chosen to expand Medicaid, but 17 have decided not to expand Medicaid and two others continue to discuss the issue (Kaiser, 2016). Many of the states refusing to expand Medicaid are poor, Southern states, such as Alabama and Mississippi. Although there are ideological reasons these states have resisted expansion, politicians are also making financial arguments. Medicaid is a jointly funded federal-state program (states get federal transfer payments to help pay for the program. However, they must also come up with some of their own state revenue to cover some of the program's costs. In 2015—the first full year of Medicaid expansion—Medicaid enrollment increased 13.8% nationwide (Kaiser, 2015b). The federal government promised to cover 100% of the expansion costs imposed on state government initially. By 2020, however, the federal contribution to state funding will decrease to 90%. Therefore, states will need to allocate additional state revenue tax dollars to cover the remaining Medicaid liabilities. States refusing to expand Medicaid argue that even with 90% reimbursement from the federal government they cannot afford the additional costs. Furthermore, they argue that health care reform may impose a large "unfunded" or "underfunded" burden on the states in the future. Nonetheless, this refusal to expand Medicaid has serious social justice implications for poor people who are ineligible for Medicaid but—because of the ACA's individual mandate—must find a way to buy health insurance themselves or face a financial penalty.

[*See Chapter 10 in this volume for further discussion of judicial decisions regarding the ACA and Chapter 14 for more details about health policy.*]

CONCLUSION

This chapter has outlined the basic structure of federal and state budgets. In doing so, it has highlighted a number of recurring tensions and ideological debates that surround the difficult process of making budgeting decisions. In addition, given the ongoing retirement of the baby boomers and the drain placed on entitlement programs, arguments about how to be fiscally responsible and socially just will continue to occupy a central place in the nation's political discourse. The federal government is increasingly shifting social welfare responsibilities onto already stretched state budgets. Taken together, social work students should be well versed in the issues and trade-offs presented because of their effects on their clients and constituents and on the organizations in which they will work. To advocate effectively on behalf of their clients, they must understand how budget decisions shape the programs people need and limit the options available to create or expand them.

Discussion Questions

1. Visit the Committee for a Responsible Federal Budget website at http://crfb.org/stabilizethedebt/. Using the online simulation, how would you alter federal spending? What influence would this have on the federal debt?

2. Visit the Center for Budget and Policies Priorities at http://www.cbpp.org/.

   Using the "Policy Basics" link, examine the link on the "Earned Income Tax Credit" (EITC) at http://www.cbpp.org/cms/index.cfm?fa=view&id=2505. Examine the EITC graph, and do the following:

   a. Provide a brief descriptive narrative of the graph. How does the policy work?

   b. Assume you are a policymaker and would like to use the EITC mechanism to deliver cash assistance to working Americans. However, you would like to make the program more generous in nature. What policy amendments would you suggest?

3. Visit the websites of the following "think tanks": The Brookings Institution (http://www.brookings.edu/), Urban Institute (http://www.urban.org/), Center on Budget and Policy Priorities (http://www.cbpp.org/), and Heritage Foundation (http://www.heritage.org/). Examine the policy recommendations and economic analyses they provide. Which reflect conservative proposals? Which reflect liberal ones? Why?

4. Using the T-table structure provided in this chapter, explain where each of Ronald Reagan's adjustments that "saved Social Security" fit. What are the social justice implications of these decisions?

5. Locate current media stories on budgets, taxes, program spending, and the like. Using the T-table structure provided in this chapter, explain how the arguments made in the articles "fit" on the T-table. What are the social justice implications?

6. Debate the political and human rights implications of being reliant on China or other "creditor nations" in financing U.S. deficit spending.

7. Consider your home state. How is the tax burden allocated? Is it favorable or unfavorable to poor people? What are the social justice implications?

8. This chapter provides a very brief overview of the federal budget process but does not address the state budget process. Consider your home state and investigate how it produces its annual state budget.

Compare your results with those of classmates from different states. How do state budget processes differ (a) from each other and (b) from the federal budget process?

Suggested Websites

Brookings Institution (a center-left perspective): http://www.brookings.edu/

Cato Institute (a libertarian perspective): http://www.cato.org/

Center on Budget and Policy Priorities (a left liberal perspective): http://www.cbpp.org/

Heritage Foundation (a conservative perspective): http://www.heritage.org/

Urban Institute Economy and Taxes (a moderate liberal perspective): http://www.urban.org/economy/index.cfm

Suggestions for Further Reading

Ippolito, D. S. (2004). *Why budgets matter: Budget policy and American politics*. Princeton, NJ: Princeton University Press.

Schick, A., & Lostracco, F. (2007). *The federal budget: Politics, policy, process* (3rd ed.). Washington, DC: Brookings Institute.

TheCapitol.Net. (2010). *The federal budget process* (Government Series). Alexandria, VA: Author.

U.S. Government Accountability Office. (2009). *The federal government's financial health: A citizen's guide to the financial report of the United States government*. Retrieved from http://www.gao.gov/financial/fy2009/09guide.pdf

References

Apfel, K. (2008). Better information is needed to make better federal budget decisions. *Journal of Policy Analysis and Management, 27*(4), 960–962.

Berkowitz, E. D. (1991). *America's welfare state: From Roosevelt to Reagan*. Baltimore, MD: Johns Hopkins Press.

Center on Budget and Policy Priorities (2016, January 25). *Most states have cut school funding, and some continue cutting*. Washington, DC: Author.

Center on Budget and Policy Priorities (2016, March 4a). *Policy basics: Where do federal revenues come from?* Retrieved from:// http://www.cbpp.org/sites/default/files/atoms/files/PolicyBasics_WhereDoFederalTaxRevsComeFrom_08-20-12.pdf

Center on Budget and Policy Priorities. (2016, March 4b). *Policy basics: Where do our federal tax dollars go?* Retrieved from:// http://www.cbpp.org/sites/default/files/atoms/files/4-14-08tax.pdf

Center on Budget and Policy Priorities (2015, November 2). *Chart Book: The earned income tax credit and child tax credit*. Washington, DC: Author.

Center on Budget and Policy Priorities. (2015b, April 14). *Policy basics: Where do our state dollars go?* Washington, DC: Author.

Center on Budget and Policy Priorities (2009, March 19). *Policy basics: Deficit, debt and interest.* Retrieved from http://www.cbpp.org/cms/index.cfm?fa=view&id=2713

Center on Budget and Policy Priorities (2011a, September 6). *Policy basics: The Earned Income Tax Credit.* Retrieved from http://www.cbpp.org/cms/index.cfm?fa=view&id=2505

Center on Budget and Policy Priorities (2011b, January 3). *Policy basics: Introduction to the federal budget process.* Retrieved from http://www.cbpp.org/cms/index.cfm?fa=view&id=155

Compania General De Tabacos De Filipinas v. Collector of Internal Revenue, 275 U.S. 87, 100, dissenting; opinion (21 November 1927).

Congressional Budget Office (2015, December 28). *Final sequestration report for fiscal year 2016.* Washington, DC: Author.

DiNitto, D. M. (2000). *Social welfare: Politics and public policy,* (5th ed.) Boston: Allyn & Bacon.

Egan, M. (2016, March 17). Foreign governments dump U.S. debt at record rate. CNN Money. Retrieved from: http://money.cnn.com/2016/03/16/investing/us-debt-dumped-foreign-governments-china/

Gilbert, N. (1995). *Welfare justice: Restoring social equity.* New Haven, CT: Yale University Press.

Gillespie, P. (2016, February 17). China leads global U.S. debt dump. CNN Money. Retrieved from: http://money.cnn.com/2016/02/17/news/economy/china-us-debt-dump-central-banks/

Greenstein, R. (2016, February 9). *Greenstein; Obama's budget: More investment with more deficit reduction.* Washington, DC: Center on Budget and Policy Priorities.

Johnson, R., Rosenberg, J., & Williams, R. (2012, February 7). *Measuring effective tax rates.* Washington, DC: Urban-Brookings Tax Policy Center. Retrieved from http://www.taxpolicycenter.org/Uploaded PDF/412497-ETR.pdf

Kaiser Family Foundation (2016 February 24). Current status of state Medicaid expansion decisions. Retrieved//http://kff.org/health-reform/state-indicator/state-activity-around-expanding-medicaid-under-the-affordable-care-act/

Kaiser Family Foundation (2015, October). *Issue brief: Medicaid enrollment & spending growth:* FY 2015 & 2016.

Katz, M. B. (2001). *The price of citizenship: Redefining the American welfare state.* New York: Henry Holt.

Kogan, R., & Shapiro, I (2016, March 28). *House GOP budget gets 62 percent of budget cuts from low- and moderate-income programs: Slashes these programs by two-fifths in 2026.* Washington, D.C.: Center on Budget and Policy Priorities.

Landler, M. (2009a, February 23). A Clinton listening tour, but China gets an earful. *New York Times,* p. A8.

Landler, M. (2009b, February 22). Clinton paints China policy with new green hue. *New York Times,* p. A8.

Leonhardt, D. (2008, August 24). A free-market-loving, big-spending, fiscally conservative, wealth distributionist: Barack Obama has a lot to say about economics. How does he reduce it to a bumper sticker? *New York Times Magazine,* pp. 28–35, 52–54.

McGinty, J. C. (2009, February 13). That's what you call investing for the long term. *New York Times,* pp. A22–A23.

McNichol, E., Hall, D., Cooper, D., and Palacios, V. (2012, November 15). *Pulling apart: A state-by-state analysis of income trends.* Washington, D.C.: Center on Budget and Policy Priorities.

McNichol, E., Oliff, P., & Johnson, N. (2012, February 27). *States continue to feel recession's impact.* Washington, DC: Center on Budget and Policy Priorities. Retrieved from http://www.cbpp.org/cms/index.cfm?fa=view&id=711

Office of the Chief Actuary. (2012, March 20). *Trust Fund FAQs*. Retrieved from http://www.ssa.gov/OACT/ProgData/fundFAQ.html#n4

Penner, R. G. (2008). Federal budget decisions are bad because it is much harder to make good choices. *Journal of Policy Analysis and Management, 27*(4), 965–967.

Reisch, M., & Staller, K. M. (2011). Teaching social welfare history and social policy from a conflict perspective. *Journal of Teaching in Social Work, 31*(2), 131–144.

Richter, P. (2009, February 23). Clinton urges China to sustain U.S. economic support. *Los Angeles Times*. Retrieved from http://www.latimes.com/news/nationworld/world/la-fg-clinton-china23-2009feb23,0,476137.story

Rivlin, A. M. (2008). The federal budget: The erosion of bipartisan fiscal discipline. *Journal of Policy Analysis and Management, 27*(4), 970–972.

Credits

8

POLICY ADVOCACY AT THE FEDERAL LEVEL

A Case Study of AmeriCorps—How the Little Guys Won

Monica Healy and Gene Sofer, PhD

This chapter presents a case study of how advocates for the **AmeriCorps** national service program came together to achieve significant legislative victories during a 9-month period in 2003 and 2004. Against substantial odds, supporters of AmeriCorps were able to reverse deep funding cuts to grant programs in Fiscal Year 2003 funding by securing a substantial increase in funding for Fiscal Year 2004. It is particularly important to note that this battle took place while the Republican Party, important elements of which were not supportive of AmeriCorps, controlled the White House and both houses of Congress.

Told by two of the participants, this is a story of how an underfunded coalition marshaled its resources and mastered the legislative process to preserve AmeriCorps (Sofer & Spangenberg, 2010). Much of this story has not before been revealed. We believe that this episode holds important lessons for social justice advocates in the nonprofit sector who seek to affect the public policy debate. One lesson is that advocates must master the environment in which they work—in this case, the federal policymaking arena in which laws are enacted and programs funded.

It would be nice to report that as a result of the activities that took place almost a decade ago, Congress and the Bush and Obama Administrations reached a bipartisan consensus to continue to increase the size of the AmeriCorps program and fund it accordingly. Alas, that is not the case. AmeriCorps remains controversial. While the Congress actually increased funding for AmeriCorps in Fiscal Year 2016, the Republican majority on the House Budget Committee proposed the elimination of the Corporation for National and Community Service, the agency that administers the AmeriCorps program, in 2017. The continued controversy surrounding AmeriCorps makes the lessons we extract from this history as relevant today as they were at the time. We believe that the lessons of this case study, while unique in some ways, are generally applicable to the policy advocacy process at the federal level and that the strategies and techniques that we describe are also applicable for advocacy at any level of government.

THE LEGISLATIVE PROCESS IN CONGRESS

The legislative process can appear chaotic and confusing to the uninitiated, but in fact it's fairly simple, and savvy advocates for social justice know that it gives them many opportunities for shaping, changing, or even killing legislation. It's worth spending a little time to learn how. One key: The further along the process gets, the more difficult it becomes to effect change. If you think of the process as a pyramid, the higher you climb, the steeper it is. Jumping in the game earlier is *always* better than later.

Simply put, legislating is a two-step process. First, Congress creates or modifies a program (**authorization**), and then it provides money for it (**appropriation**). Typically, these two parts are entirely separate. Congress has many authorizing committees—the House Education and Workforce Committee, for example, or the Senate Health, Education, Labor, and Pensions Committee—with specific areas of jurisdiction or expertise. But in each chamber there's just one appropriations committee, although each has 12 subcommittees that more or less match up the respective authorizing committees. [*See Chapter 7 in this volume for further discussion of these processes.*]

The **authorizing process** provides at least *seven key entry points* for advocates to affect a law:

> The *first* comes when a bill is drafted by a member or members with input from advocates and constituency groups.
>
> Once the bill is drafted, it is introduced and referred to one or more authorizing committees. The authorizing committees have substantial expertise in the subjects they oversee, so other members tend to defer to them—it's unusual for the content of a bill to change significantly once the committee is finished with it, so it's important to get into the process at this stage. Typically, the full committee refers a bill to one of its subcommittees, which holds hearings and then meets to "mark up" the bill, which gives subcommittee members a chance to amend it. This is the *second* opportunity to change the bill.
>
> After mark-up, the subcommittee sends (or "reports") the bill to the full committee, which schedules its own mark-up—the *third* opportunity to change the bill. Once that's done, the full committee reports the bill to the full House or Senate for a floor vote.
>
> Before a bill gets to the floor, there must be rules for how it will be handled there—will there be unlimited amendments allowed or just a few, and if just a few, which ones? In the House, the Rules Committee sets those rules. In the more freewheeling Senate, amendments are usually the subject of negotiations between the majority and the minority. Amending the bill on the floor is the *fourth* opportunity to change it, but the process for getting an amendment considered starts long before the bill actually gets to the floor.
>
> Because the versions of the bill passed by the House and Senate almost always differ, a **House–Senate conference committee** usually hammers out a final bill. Influencing the conferees is the *fifth* opportunity to affect the bill.

Once there's a final bill, there's also a Conference Report that explains congressional intent, and getting "report language" into that report is the *sixth* opportunity to affect the process. Report language doesn't have the force of law, but it does guide the agencies and departments that implement the law and can even figure later in court decisions if the law is challenged.

At this point, the House and Senate pass the bill, which then goes to the president for his signature. It's the ultimate long shot, but a presidential veto is the *seventh* chance to affect the bill.

Once a law has been signed, the appropriations committee must decide whether or not to fund it and at what level. Unlike authorizations, which are in effect for many years or permanently, the appropriations process is usually good for only 1 year. The appropriations process follows an almost identical path from committee to subcommittee and back, then to the floor, conference committee, back to the floor, and finally to the president. It only sounds complicated.

By the middle of April, Congress is supposed to have approved a budget resolution that sets spending limits for the year. The appropriations committees take the total "discretionary" spending in the budget resolution and allocate it to their subcommittees.

Again, a great deal of deference is paid to the relevant subcommittee, because that's where the expertise resides. The goal is to complete work on each of the 12 bills by the end of the fiscal year, which is on September 30. This happens less and less frequently, and bills are often put together in huge omnibus packages to facilitate passage.

By deciding what to fund and what not to fund, appropriators wield considerable power over agencies and programs. Working the appropriations process is the eighth opportunity to affect policy.

Finally, each House operates more or less independently of the other. The same opportunities available in one House are likely to be available in the other. So, all told, there are as many as 15 points where advocates can try to affect the process. Again, the deeper into the process one gets, the more difficult it is to influence the result.

In short, if one's goal were to affect the content of the AmeriCorps program, one would focus on the authorizing committees. If the goal were to seek more funding for AmeriCorps, one would focus on the appropriations committees.

BACKGROUND

In 1993, President Bill Clinton signed the **National and Community Service Trust Act**, which built on the first National Service Act signed by President George H. W. Bush in 1990. The 1993 act established AmeriCorps, a network of national service programs that engage Americans in intensive service to meet the nation's critical needs in education, public safety, health, and the environment. The new law also consolidated several preexisting domestic community service programs such as Volunteers in Service to America (VISTA) in an independent agency in the Executive Branch called the **Corporation for National and Community Service** ("the Corporation"; Waldman, 1995).

AmeriCorps offered people, most of them young, the opportunity to do full- or part-time service, defined as 1,700 hours a year or less, in communities throughout the nation. The Corporation managed AmeriCorps and made grants directly to national nonprofits that operated in more than one state and to State Commissions appointed by governors, which in turn made grants to local nonprofit agencies. More than half of all AmeriCorps members received a **stipend** equal to a minimum-wage job (about an average of $9,300 plus health care benefits in 2002) or a prorated version of that stipend. AmeriCorps members who completed a full year of service were also eligible for an **education award** of $4,725,

Figure 8.1 AmeriCorps Volunteer in Denver, Colorado

which was deposited in a special trust fund, or a percentage of the award if they served fewer hours. The rest, enrolled in the so-called "Education Award Only" program, received only the voucher.

During the Clinton Administration, AmeriCorps grew in popularity, and tens of thousands of people enrolled, more than doubling the numbers between 1994 and 2001 from 25,000 to 59,000. Funding grew to keep pace, as Congress appropriated money for program administration and for stipends.

At the start of the Bush Administration in 2001 AmeriCorps appeared to be on sound footing. Although the program—a network of more than 2,000 service groups, all funded by a mix of public and private money—had its detractors, the United States had elected a Republican president who said he was a compassionate conservative, approved of service programs, and wanted to expand AmeriCorps from 50,000 to 75,000 members and increase its funding. President Bush may have been inclined to support AmeriCorps, but a little-known presidential tradition played a role as well.

At the height of the AmeriCorps debate, then Senator Hillary Clinton (D-NY) explained that when presidents left office, they asked their successors to take care of a few of their favorite programs and priorities. According to Senator Clinton, President Bush Sr. asked President Clinton to watch over the Points of Light Foundation, a service organization close to his heart. In turn, when President Clinton left office, he asked the younger President Bush to continue making service a priority by taking care of AmeriCorps.[1] The clearest demonstration of President Bush's interest came after the September 11 terrorist attacks, when he issued a call to all Americans to serve their country, tapping into the nation's resurgent patriotism. In his 2002 State of the Union Address, the president put national service at center stage:

> My call tonight is for every American to commit at least two years—4,000 hours over the rest of your lifetime—to the service of your neighbors and your nation.... We need more talented teachers in troubled schools. USA Freedom Corps will expand and improve the good efforts of AmeriCorps and Senior Corps to recruit more than 200,000 new volunteers.[2] ("State of the Union Transcript," 2002, p. 6)

Nor was President Bush alone. Senator John McCain (R-AZ) led a push to greatly expand the program from 50,000 to 250,000 members a year. McCain said AmeriCorps members "have begun to glimpse the glory of serving the cause of freedom" (Bovard, 2001). In fact, in an uncharacteristic "mea culpa," McCain (2001) wrote,

> Indeed, when [President] Clinton initiated AmeriCorps in 1994, most Republicans in Congress, myself included, opposed it. We feared it would be another "big government program" that

would undermine true volunteerism, waste money in "make-work" projects, or be diverted into political activism. We were wrong.

With support like this, the AmeriCorps was well positioned to grow. But then the roof fell in.

MISMANAGEMENT

In 2002, AmeriCorps' parent, the Corporation, made a huge blunder by allowing its network to sign up 40% more AmeriCorps members than it had money to support. The organization's budget had sufficient funds for only 50,000 members, but the Corporation's grantees enrolled 70,000 (U.S. General Accounting Office, 2004).[3] That fall, the Corporation belatedly realized that it did not have the funds to guarantee the $4,725 education vouchers to everyone who had signed up. Corporation officials abruptly stopped enrolling participants, but the damage was done.

The problem was that the methodology used to calculate the Corporation's budget request for the trust fund that held the education vouchers deposited in some of the previous years had been so badly flawed that Congress incorrectly thought the trust fund was running a surplus and had begun rescinding some of its funds (recapturing some of the money it had previously appropriated), a move that worsened the shortfall. This was obviously a serious problem, but after Corporation officials had intense talks with members and staff of the House and Senate **VA-HUD Appropriations Subcommittees** (which hold the purse strings for the Veterans Administration and the Department of Housing and Urban Development, among other disparate agencies), it seemed that an agreement had been reached to fix it. Before adjourning in the fall of 2002, Congress approved the Fiscal Year 2003 VA-HUD appropriations bill that funded the Corporation and, by extension, AmeriCorps.

All seemed well as 2003 began. But in June, the Corporation stunned the AmeriCorps community and its supporters by announcing that it could fund only 54 of 487 pending grant applications. Even those programs that received money would have to take an average cut of 60%, and some programs experienced cuts of 80%. The funding level that had been previously approved, however, was $100 million below what was needed to maintain AmeriCorps at its current levels.

This was a catastrophe for service groups that depended on AmeriCorps funding. A 60% cut meant that some programs would be hurt so badly they would have to shut down, and others would have to be drastically scaled back. Some might be able to stay alive by scrambling for funding from other sources.

In addition, the Corporation made some odd choices in targeting which programs to cut. For example, Teach for America, a pet program of First Lady Laura Bush that was highlighted in the FY 2004 budget the president had proposed earlier in the year, got the axe. All the programs in Alaska, the home state of Senate Appropriations Committee Chair Ted Stevens, suffered a similar fate.

THE COALITION GETS ACTIVATED

Many of the national organizations with multistate programs had banded together in 2002 to fight for their slice of AmeriCorps funding. Calling itself the Coalition for Effective National Service, this initial coalition included YouthBuild, the National Association of Service and Conservation Corps, City Year, Public Allies, Teach for America, Jump Start, and the National Association of Community Health Centers, among others. The **Save AmeriCorps Coalition**, an expansion of the existing one, began in a conversation that Gene Sofer initiated with more than a dozen leaders of some of the country's biggest AmeriCorps recipients. He expressed concerns that AmeriCorps funding was in for a tough slog: "It dawned on me and others that the threats facing AmeriCorps were sufficiently large that the individual nonprofits on their own would not be able to prevent it. We would have to work together" (as quoted in Beadle, 2003, pp. 1, 42). According to Sofer, the new, broader Coalition had two goals: "Grow AmeriCorps and fully fund the Trust" (p. 1). By mid-June, City Year assumed the de facto leadership of the coalition. DC-based lobbyists such as the authors of this chapter developed legislative strategies and took the lead in building support on Capitol Hill and within the executive branch.

The national service community went on red alert. The current situation was an emergency. Our small coalition quickly saw that we had to expand by involving additional groups from all over the country, such as the Red Cross, Habitat for Humanity, and Citizen Schools. We called the new, larger organization the Save AmeriCorps Coalition. Each brought its own board of directors, mailing lists, and other resources.

For the first time in a decade, the supporters of national service were galvanized into action. We began an all-out education and information campaign to inform those programs across the United States who had come to rely on AmeriCorps of what was about to happen. We understood that there would be power in numbers, so we reached out as broadly as we could, contacting governors whose commissions oversaw AmeriCorps at the state level, mayors whose constituents benefited from the service AmeriCorps members provided, directors of nonprofit organizations and members of their boards of directors who had integrated AmeriCorps into their service delivery, college presidents, business people and foundation executives, as well as thousands of AmeriCorps alumni. An association of AmeriCorps alumni that we reached out to through e-mail and phone contact was helpful in mobilizing former AmeriCorps members all around the country. Teach for America alumni were also extremely effective and helpful.

The Save AmeriCorps Coalition also called on the Bush Administration to help. Coincidentally, the administration had already launched an FY 2003 emergency **supplemental appropriations** bill for fire-fighting and other emergencies. Against this background, our coalition asked Congress to add $100 million to save AmeriCorps programs from closing.[4]

The coalition's efforts to build support had some initial success: 44 governors, led by Mitt Romney (R-MA) and Edward G. Rendell (D-PA), and 150 mayors, both Republicans and Democrats, supported our request. In our experience, that constituted an amazing amount of home-state political support. It helped us realize that quietly, and without fanfare, AmeriCorps had become a valued asset in communities throughout the nation. People from all around the country whose lives would be affected by these cuts began to lobby at home and in Washington. Capitol Hill offices were flooded with e-mails and letters. For example, during a five-day period in July 2003, just one organization, Teach for America, generated 2,000 letters to its supporters in Congress.

Media support was also critical to amplifying our efforts. Newspapers began writing stories about groups whose work would be ended or drastically cut back if AmeriCorps funding was reduced. In a short period, nearly 100 Save AmeriCorps editorials appeared in newspapers around the United States.

To help revive our effort, the Save AmeriCorps Coalition held an event in the Halls of Congress (during the day) and in a nearby office building called the Hall of States (at night) in late June with 100 straight hours of testimony spread over more than 4 days, from participants, program sponsors, community partners, business leaders, members of Congress, and other supporters. AmeriCorps programs from around the country once again weighed in to support the $100 million in funding. This talkathon kept the national service field energized. Whether or not it changed minds in Congress, it reminded the coalition's members what we were fighting for and instigated another wave of press coverage.

High-level networking also turned out to be a valuable tactic. Since the creation of AmeriCorps in 1993, many programs, especially those that received funding directly from the Corporation, had recruited high-powered board members with extensive political contacts. These organizations were now willing to put those contacts to work on behalf of AmeriCorps. For example, corporate chief executive officers (CEOs) and other top executives such as Jeffrey Swartz of Timberland; Don Fisher, founder and chair of the board of The Gap; and Orin Smith of Starbucks were actively involved. Fisher made a number of calls to the White House and Republican Congressional leaders to press them for more money. Starbucks paid for an ad in *The New York Times* signed by 250 business and philanthropic leaders who called on the president and Congress not to close AmeriCorps programs and to push for the additional $100 million in funding. Columnist E. J. Dionne, Jr. (2003) wrote in *The Washington Post*, "The biggest political surprise of the past few months is that a very small program could roar." Prospects for our request began to look very good.

SENATE ACTION

With prodding from Senators Barbara Mikulski (D-MD) and Hillary Clinton (D-NY), the Senate added the $100 million to its version of the supplemental appropriations bill. The legislation was controversial because the president and Congress almost always limit funding in emergency supplemental bills to crises such as hurricanes, floods, wildfires, and wars. The White House's position, shared by a number of Republican senators, was that the AmeriCorps crisis did not meet that standard. Alabama Senator Jeff Sessions (R-AL), who offered an amendment to strip the AmeriCorps money from the bill, summed up this position succinctly: "This is not an emergency," he said; "it's just one more typical bureaucratic failure" (Fram, 2003). But on July 11, in a surprising vote, 71 of 100 senators voted to retain the funds. Mikulski's position, "Who are we going to punish if we don't put out the money? Not the bureaucracy ... but the volunteers in our communities," won the day (Fram, 2003).

Many senior Republicans, however, including Senate Majority Leader Bill Frist (R-TN) and Appropriations Committee Chair Ted Stevens, also supported the emergency funding. Stevens had heard from constituents who were furious that the funds for all the AmeriCorps programs in Alaska had been eliminated. Senator Kit Bond (R-MO), chair of the Senate VA-HUD Appropriations Subcommittee, was also a key supporter. He was being pressured by many of his Senate colleagues who were being flooded with letters, e-mails, and phone calls about the adverse impact funding cuts would have on AmeriCorps programs in their states. But Senator Mikulski, a feisty former social worker and community activist who had been in the forefront of establishing the original national service programs, was clearly the driving force behind the Senate victory. Although she was in the minority party, she held great sway over her Republican counterpart Senator Bond, whose support was crucial to a successful vote in the Senate. That bipartisan vote constituted an overwhelming majority in the Senate, particularly on a controversial piece of legislation and when the president has a majority in Congress and does not support your cause—which was unfortunately true in this case.

In sum, this was a textbook example of how important it is for advocates to approach Congress from as many different directions as possible: employing grassroots activism and support from organizations that are affected by funding decisions, corporate CEOs, and local and state-elected officials. Media accounts also played a crucial role by spreading and amplifying the message that AmeriCorps was in trouble.

HOUSE ROADBLOCK

The Senate vote gave the bill a lot of momentum, and the coalition felt it was on a roll. We thought we were in good shape in the House of Representatives because a bipartisan majority, consisting of 233 members led by such AmeriCorps champions as Chris Shays (R-CT), Tom Osborne (R-NE), Harold Ford, Jr. (D-TN), and George Miller (D-CA), had already gone on record in support of the $100 million in a letter to the president.

But, unbeknownst to us, we had big problems. The fact that mismanagement at the Corporation and AmeriCorps had created the problem in the first place gave our congressional opponents a lot of ammunition to use against funding the program. Their argument was direct and effective: Why give these guys more money when they just blow it?

Our response, of course, was "Don't punish effective, well-run programs because of the ineptitude of the Corporation." In July, our supporters in Congress tried to lessen opposition and head off more drastic proposals by passing the Strengthen AmeriCorps Program Act, which improved internal controls, revised the formula the Corporation employed to estimate the needs of the education trust fund, and made other management improvements. Unfortunately, the act was not enough to appease AmeriCorps' powerful opponents, such as House Majority Leader Tom DeLay (R-TX), who simply did not like AmeriCorps. Fundamentally, our congressional opponents did not believe the federal government should spend taxpayer money for voluntary service. They also remembered that it was President Clinton who initiated the program, fought for it when he was president, and made it one of his most important priorities. The Corporation's mismanagement played right into the hands of these congressional Republicans.

That political animosity set the stage for the debate in the House. Although our coalition had strong support, DeLay managed to kill the $100 million in funding through skillful use of the congressional appropriations process.

Here's what he did: In the Senate, the emergency money had been attached to a larger bill that funded the operations of Congress, the so-called Legislative Branch Appropriations Bill. The House had already passed its version of that bill before the emergency money became an issue. Normally, the House and Senate would convene a conference committee to work out differences between the two bills. With strong support in both chambers for our $100 million, we thought keeping the money in the final bill would be easy. We received a warning of how tough things would be in the House, however, when Rep. Jim Walsh (R-NY), the chair of the House VA-HUD Appropriations Committee and a former Peace Corps volunteer who had supported AmeriCorps since its creation, announced his opposition to the Senate's action, arguing that no additional funds should be appropriated because of the Corporation's "poor management and weak financial oversight" (Fram, 2003).

Shortly before the August recess, DeLay made a clever move that completely out-maneuvered us. He reached into the bill, pulled out some popular emergency money—in this case, funds to pay for fighting forest fires raging out West—and offered those funds on the House floor as a stand-alone bill. In the process, he dropped the $100 million for AmeriCorps. There was little question that the House would pass an emergency firefighting bill. In addition, the House Republican leadership made it a test of party loyalty to block any attempts to change the bill, which would have provided the opportunity to reinsert the $100 million for AmeriCorps. Even our Republican supporters did not want to take the heat on that issue.

As a result, the House passed the emergency bill without the $100 million for AmeriCorps and sent it to the Senate on a take-it-or-leave-it basis. The House then quickly went home for its August break. The upshot was that even if the Senate had wanted to amend the bill to restore the $100 million, it would have to send the bill back to an empty House, where action on it would have to wait until September, and then the money to support firefighting would be held up all through August. Rep. DeLay had very cleverly put the Senate in a box, and the Senate passed the bill without our $100 million.

WHAT HAPPENED TO THE $100 MILLION IN EMERGENCY FUNDING?

In August, the Senate went on recess. Our coalition knew we were now on life support, but we did not think our cause was quite dead yet. The $100 million for AmeriCorps was still alive as part of the Legislative Branch Appropriations Bill, which was pending in a House–Senate conference committee. We knew that getting the money restored would be very difficult because we had lost a lot of the momentum we had before the August recess.

At this point, if President Bush had intervened in favor of the funding for AmeriCorps, the outcome might have been different. In fact, we thought the coalition had generated enough public pressure to make it hard for him not to act. But the White House stood on principle; it wanted to maintain the tradition of limiting supplemental appropriations bills to "real emergencies." The administration was concerned that if it supported the inclusion of AmeriCorps funding for a crisis it felt did not constitute a real emergency, it would lower the bar and provoke a flood of other requests from members of Congress. (It is not unprecedented for members to include their pet programs in emergency bills, but it is uncommon.)

At the time, we thought—wrongly, as it turned out—that the White House's hand would be forced anyway because the Bush Administration was losing the public relations battle. There were hundreds of news stories around the country about people who wanted to join AmeriCorps being denied the chance to serve, and of schools and local nonprofits that were cutting services to their communities because of mismanagement in Washington. Editorials lambasted the administration for not coming to the rescue of programs that meant so much to their communities. There were also numerous columns in national media outlets criticizing the president for breaking his promise to expand AmeriCorps.

For example, the influential *Washington Post* columnist David Broder covered the story, and Joe Klein, a well-known columnist for *Time* magazine and a regular on national TV shows, wrote a column in August that criticized the administration for defunding Teach for America, a program that had earned the support of First Lady Laura Bush and was a favorite of the president. Klein promoted the column when he appeared on NBC's *Meet the Press* the day before the magazine hit the streets. *Newsweek* columnist Jonathan Alter (2003) ripped the president and first lady in a column called "Lip Service vs. National Service" and said, "It's hard to believe that George and Laura Bush don't care about what happens to programs they trumpet. But the cuts are still coming." The story was also covered on *60 Minutes*.

Coalition leaders knew that Klein's column got the attention of White House officials, but we also heard that White House staff members were divided about how to respond. Some staff on the policy side thought supporting the emergency $100 million was the right thing to do, but the White House legislative and political staff opposed adding the money. Our members also heard, but could not confirm, that the first lady made some discreet phone calls to Capitol Hill expressing her concern about the impact the AmeriCorps funding shortfall was having on Teach for America.

In retrospect, we believe the president was so preoccupied with other priorities—this all happened in the summer of 2003, shortly after the start of the Iraq War—that he just did not focus on this particular issue. In the end, we lost the fight for the emergency money. But it turned out that all the momentum we had built in that struggle would help us in the very next round of appropriations. And in Washington, there is always a next round.

FY 2004 VA-HUD APPROPRIATIONS BILL

While we were trying to make AmeriCorps whole for FY 2003, we were also fighting for money on a separate track for FY 2004, which would begin on October 1, 2003. In their FY 2004 appropriations bills, the House and Senate had each provided roughly $340 million for AmeriCorps. While this was an increase over the previous year's funding, it was $100 million below the president's request for $440 million and what the coalition thought was needed to keep AmeriCorps growing.

The good news was that this was the first time since the Republicans took control of the House in 1995 that funds for AmeriCorps were even included in the House bill. In the past, members of the appropriations committees had not dared to include the funds because Republican conservatives had always threatened to take it out on the floor and make a mess of the bill. In 2003, however, the appropriators, led by Peace Corps veteran and moderate New York Republican Rep. James Walsh, took the risk. It worked.

In response, the coalition shifted our focus from the current-year emergency appropriations to the issue of obtaining sufficient funding for the coming year. Our goal was to get the extra $100 million added to the budget when the House and Senate met in a conference committee to resolve the differences between their respective bills. We had our work cut out for us. It is almost unprecedented to get significant extra money added in conference over and above what is already in bills when they pass. Usually the highest amount appropriated in either bill is considered the funding ceiling, not the floor. But at this time, all the work we had done over the summer in our vain attempt to save the emergency funding came to fruition.

DELAY REDUX

Appropriations bills often contain language that instructs the relevant agency about congressional expectations.[5] We were very worried that some language would be inserted in the appropriations bill that would force AmeriCorps in directions we felt would be harmful. For example, Congress could insert language designed to drastically reduce the federal share of program funding, which would make it hard for many AmeriCorps programs to function.

Our fears were certainly justified. At the time, a move was afoot by the conservative members of the House, led by DeLay, to add language that would have been even more detrimental to AmeriCorps programs. The conservatives wanted to reduce the federal share and "graduate" the programs that had been getting money from AmeriCorps; that is, they wanted nonprofits that had been getting grants for many years to gradually leave the AmeriCorps program so they would not become dependent on federal monies. They also wanted to reduce health care and child care benefits for AmeriCorps members. Thus, the coalition faced twin battles: trying to get an extra $100 million when the House and Senate conferees met and trying to fend off harmful policy changes by House conservatives.

FUNDING/APPROPRIATIONS BILL

Winning the money battle was a long shot. Most domestic programs were lucky to get even small funding increases, on average 2% to 3% above the previous year. In this situation, we were trying to justify a whopping 62% increase for AmeriCorps, a program that had badly mismanaged its funds. We also knew that the process was a zero-sum game: If the appropriators added the money for AmeriCorps, they would have to take it from other programs. We also assumed that even if we were successful regarding the funding, there would be an unpleasant price, most likely the unwelcome policy changes we found so onerous. At one point, some of the more prominent members of the coalition started to panic and were ready to abandon pursuit of the additional funds in exchange for getting a clean bill—that is, one with no policy changes. They were betting we would not "win" on all the issues and that the gamble was not worth the risks.

Figure 8.2. AmericaCorps National Civilian Corps Member Working at the Academy of Success Youth Development Center in Baltimore, Maryland.

THE WHITE HOUSE COMES THROUGH

Other members of the coalition, however, argued we should go for broke. Then we got some good news: Our allies in Congress told us that the White House had finally gotten involved in the process and was fighting for the extra money. Without the White House strong-arming the conservative Republicans in the House, our effort to get the money would have been doomed to the same fate as the money in the emergency supplemental bill. We had to have the administration's help to succeed; it seemed as though the pressure that had failed over the summer was finally working.

The White House was quietly working behind the scenes to get support to add the additional funds during the House–Senate conference on the omnibus spending bill that included all the spending bills that had not yet passed the House and the Senate.[6] When we first heard the rumors of White House support, we were skeptical. But we kept getting confirmation from the most curious sources, conservative Republicans in the House, the very people who had fought us tooth and nail over the emergency money. Reliable sources told us that David Hobbs, Director of Legislative Affairs for the White House, felt so bad about not serving the president well during the debate over the $100 million emergency money that he wanted to make up for it by pushing to get the extra $100 million included in the FY 2004 omnibus bill. We also heard that, when they were together on one of the president's trips, President Bush had cut a deal with Rep. DeLay to add the funds.

SENATE REACTION/FUNDING

When we reported this to our allies on the Senate Appropriations Committee, they gave us a reality check, reminding us that no extra money was available and asking how the funding for AmeriCorps was going to be paid for. Meanwhile, we continued to encourage supporters from around the country to contact members of Congress and ask them to approve the extra funds. In retrospect, we think the deal had already been sealed by late summer 2003. President Bush had pledged during his campaign to expand AmeriCorps, and now programs were being decimated on his watch. The White House simply could neither ignore the tremendous grassroots support for AmeriCorps nor the beating the president was taking in the media for breaking his campaign promise.

CREATING CONTROVERSY

We continued to work on two tracks: to secure the $100 million needed to prevent cuts in the AmeriCorps program and to prevent the unwanted policy changes from being included in the FY 2004 appropriations bill. On the funding side, we had the advantage of a clear message: Without enough money, good programs would be drastically scaled back and some would be shut down. On the policy front, our message was a tougher sell. It was much harder to capture the public's attention concerning complex policy language. As often occurs, some of the issues, while important, were hard to grasp for those who did not work in AmeriCorps programs.

These two advocacy tracks required two different strategies. While getting the $100 million in additional funding involved the mobilization of assets both in Washington and outside the Beltway, making sure bad policy language was not inserted in the final appropriations bill was an inside-the-Beltway effort. Because the language fight was so convoluted and arcane, it was much harder to generate grassroots support or get press. There was no obvious drama. Even so, we managed to create controversy. We exploited fiercely held congressional prerogatives by pitting congressional authorizers—those who create and oversee programs—against the appropriators that fund them. We went from office to office on Capitol Hill talking about how damaging the proposed language would be. We got the authorizers upset by warning them that the appropriators were trying to usurp their committee jurisdiction and policymaking authority. Members of Congress with responsibility for appropriations are technically forbidden from using appropriations bills to change policy, because that is not their responsibility. They do it anyway, but their colleagues with responsibility for authorizing programs resent it and fight such efforts whenever they can.

Our strategy began to pay off. Even members who might have agreed with the onerous appropriations language fought it on the grounds that it undercut their authority. Meanwhile, when we learned that the conservative House leadership was planning to insert their policy language in the bill, we brought it to the attention of the Republicans on the Senate Appropriations Committee. The Senate staff was concerned that the House was trying to use the bill in an inappropriate way to make policy changes in AmeriCorps. This was quite ironic, because the Senate had already made benign policy changes in its version of the bill. But the Senate staff had never intended for its language to open the door for even more changes, so they decided to push back.

Meanwhile, we also took our intelligence about the intentions of the conservative Republicans to the House Authorizing Committee, whose leaders decided to resist the proposed changes on jurisdictional grounds. In short, there were jurisdictional fights occurring everywhere. Our efforts had made AmeriCorps policy changes controversial. The White House and the Corporation also opposed the new controversial policy language for fear that it would cloud their positive message of adding more money for AmeriCorps.

To support our efforts, we argued that any policy changes should be made not through ad hoc, add-on language to an appropriations bill but through a fair and open process such as congressional reauthorization or executive rulemaking, which provides an opportunity for affected constituencies to give input. That message resonated.

In the end, we prevailed on both issues; we obtained the additional funding we requested and succeeded in getting the harmful language dropped from the House bill. Given how tough the battle was, and how painful the earlier loss of emergency funding was, our ultimate victory was a gratifying surprise. In retrospect, however, we did a lot of things right in ways that can be instructive for similar efforts in the future. Perhaps nobody summed up the effort better than Senator Kit Bond, the Missouri Republican, who played such a key role in the process. While chairing a Senate VA-HUD Appropriations Subcommittee hearing on the Corporation on April 8, 2004, Bond said:

> Some good did result from the painful experiences of the past year. The most notable result was the increased awareness and support for the program among members of Congress and the public, which led to a record budget for the AmeriCorps program. The numerous media reports raised the profile of AmeriCorps volunteers and their very positive impact on local communities

throughout the Nation. Prior to the well-publicized problems of AmeriCorps, only a handful of members expressed any serious concern or attention to the program. Now, the program has the attention of most, if not all, members of Congress (U.S. Senate, 2004, p. 382).

Bond's comment was certainly true at the time. It may be less true today in the aftermath of the Great Recession of 2008. Other initiatives, such as the enactment of the 2010 Affordable Care Act ("Obamacare"), the reauthorization of the Elementary and Secondary Education Act and the "Common Core" movement, and continued U.S. involvement in Afghanistan and Iraq, compete for the attention of members of Congress. Time does not heal all wounds but it may mitigate them. In 2016, a consensus has emerged, which pointedly does not include many Republican members of the House, that AmeriCorps provides substantial benefits to the communities it serves. This reputation has been greatly enhanced by AmeriCorps members' response to natural disasters—floods, tornadoes, and hurricanes— in areas that Republicans represent and to other activities at the local and county level that AmeriCorps members provided during the recession, when local governments severely cut back funding for social services.

As we suggested earlier, AmeriCorps has also been aided by expanding its advocacy strategy beyond the Beltway. Social media provide a way to reach and mobilize large numbers of people, and Voices for National Service has promoted the use of Facebook, Twitter, and Instagram as well as other platforms, to spread its message. It has also promoted the annual Mayor, County, and Tribal Recognition Day for National Service (sponsored by the Corporation for National and Community Service, the National League of Cities, and Cities of Service) in which 3,500 local elected officials expressed their support for AmeriCorps and other national service programs.

When writing this article we noted that persistence pays off. More than 10 years have elapsed since these events took place and the national service community has remained steadfast in its advocacy efforts. It may be, however, that our focus on the importance of traditional media is less important today than in 2004 because of the growth of cable news and alternative news sources. Nevertheless, getting earned media remains an important strategic goal.

Finally, we reiterate our prescriptions never to give up on those who have opposed you in the past or to take your friends for granted. The advocacy activities in the decade since the AmeriCorps funding crisis more than demonstrate that hard work, persistence, and results change minds and votes.

LESSONS LEARNED

1. *Politics is a process, and just about anyone can master it.* There are at least eight opportunities to affect the outcome as the legislative process proceeds through the House and Senate and, finally, (with luck) to the president's desk. Many people find the procedures arcane, but that is only true for those who never try to learn them. The process can be mastered, and that mastery is crucial to success, particularly for nonprofit advocates who must rely on knowledge to overcome other disadvantages, such as lack of funds.

2. *Winning requires both inside- and outside-the-Beltway strategies.* In our efforts, using one without the other would have failed—especially given our relative weakness inside the Beltway, where we lacked traditional lobbying tools such as political action committee money

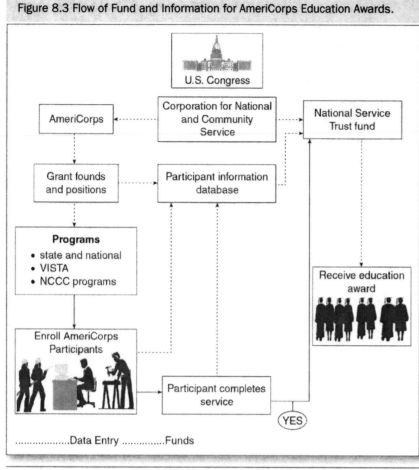

Figure 8.3 Flow of Fund and Information for AmeriCorps Education Awards.

Source: United States General Accounting Office (2004). *Corporation for National and Community Service: Better internal control and revised practices would improve the management of AmeriCorps and the National Service Trust.* Washington, DC: U.S. Government Printing Office.

and fundraising connections. Instead, we augmented our aggressive Washington-based lobbying campaign, led by organizations such as Teach for America, Public Allies, City Year, Jump Start, and the National Association of Service and Conservation Corps, with equally aggressive efforts to alert supporters and media outside the Beltway.

3. ***Successful campaigns require a lot of different skills.*** First, campaigns need a leader who is willing to be a tough taskmaster and keep pressure on people to make sure they are engaged and helpful. Second, they need lots of resources, money, and in-kind contributions—the work is very labor intensive. Third, advocacy coalitions need allied organizations to lend staff and provide other assistance. Fourth, none of these resources will matter unless there is a core group of members in the coalition who bring different strengths to it.

4. ***It helps to have villains.*** On our side, we had young people who wanted to give back to their community. On the other side, there was a seemingly incompetent government agency that was turning them away because the program that was supposed to provide them with minimal stipends and education vouchers had been badly mismanaged. In Congress, our chief adversary was Rep. Tom DeLay, the tough and powerful conservative Texas Republican who saw killing AmeriCorps as a way of getting even with former President Clinton. Our enemies gave us an emotional advantage: There was much more sympathy for the little guys who wanted to do good than for the villains.

5. ***There is strength in numbers.*** Hundreds of nonprofit groups from all over the country weighed in on behalf of AmeriCorps funding, and that clearly helped. They generated wide local media coverage and put effective pressure on members of Congress.

6. ***Persistence pays off.*** Over a 9-month period, we were relentless in keeping the heat on Congress and the Bush Administration. These efforts generated hundreds of editorials and news stories around the country. We contacted a majority of congressional offices either directly or through our grassroots effort.

7. ***It's crucial to target efforts in Congress, because not all members of Congress are equal.*** We identified key supporters, key opponents, and fence sitters in Congress. We identified key

congressional players who could influence the appropriations process, including leadership staff, authorizers, and appropriations committee members and staff. We took this targeted list and matched each congressional office with the organizations in the coalition that had contacts in these offices and/or programs in these members' districts or states. We also involved the extended AmeriCorps family (alumni, local board members, etc.). We assigned coalition members to contact friends and supporters.

8. ***Education is critical.*** Since Congress had not focused on the AmeriCorps authorization since 1993, there was a low level of awareness about what AmeriCorps programs actually did. A key to our success was educating members and staff about those programs. Capitol Hill traditionally has a large staff turnover, so there were very few staffers left who had been there when the original AmeriCorps legislation was debated. We educated the new staff about how AmeriCorps worked and how the programs it funded affected their communities and states.

9. ***It's crucial to bring disparate groups together to present a united front.*** We were able to bring the national nonprofits together with the state commissions appointed by the nation's governors to fight for a common cause. Before the crisis, these groups worked separately, sometimes at cross-purposes. The coalition succeeded because groups were willing to subsume their individual interests to the greater good, creating a powerful and effective partnership. We also had many influential business leaders in our coalition who had good connections with the White House and were willing to help. With some audiences, CEOs have credibility that other advocates do not.

10. ***Media coverage greatly influences the process.*** There were hundreds of news reports and editorials about the shutdown of local service programs. Our struggle had all the elements to capture press interest: A federal agency had mismanaged funds; programs were shut down, hurting communities all around the country; idealistic young people were denied the chance to help; and a group of hardcore conservatives in the House was bullying the groups and intimidating the Senate and the White House. There was also a political twist, which captured the attention of national columnists: "Bush Administration reneges on its promise to grow AmeriCorps."

11. ***White House support is incredibly helpful.*** Having White House support does not assure victory in funding battles, but not having it makes the challenge that much more difficult. We had a tough case to make: We were trying to get more money—lots more money, a bigger increase than almost any other federal program—for an agency that had mismanaged its funds. We could not have succeeded had the Bush Administration not fought for the money.

12. ***Work both sides of the political aisle, and never take your supporters for granted.*** Our hardest challenge was getting Republicans, not our natural allies for the most part, to support what we were trying to do. Many Republicans felt we were trying to save a softheaded and unnecessary Clinton-era program. We worked patiently to educate them about what the programs actually did and why they were valuable. And we built on the support we already had among key Republicans, such as Rep. Ralph Regula (R-OH) and Senator Bond (R-MO), who chaired appropriations subcommittees. While many Democrats supported AmeriCorps, some of their support was soft, and we worked hard to deepen it and get them to fight for our cause. To supplement our education efforts on the Hill, we made sure that they were hearing from their constituents who were being hurt by programs that were being cut.

13. ***Don't give up on members who have opposed your program in the past.*** Often, opposition to programs grows out of a lack of information about what the programs do and how important they are locally. For example, former Sen. Rick Santorum (R-PA), chair of the Senate Republican Study Conference, who had had serious concerns about AmeriCorps programs in the past, became one of our biggest allies. He was able to see firsthand how programs had a positive impact on communities in Pennsylvania.

14. ***Segment the market.*** It is important to be strategic and politically savvy about approaching members of Congress. For example, there were some programs that were more popular than others with Republicans. We were careful to highlight the popular programs when contacting GOP members. We made Teach for America and Habitat for Humanity, two programs that the Bush Administration liked, center stage when we contacted Republican offices. We also tried to get these kinds of programs highlighted by the national media. By the same token, it was important to downplay programs that had been closely associated with the Clinton Administration when we approached Republicans in Congress. Of course, when we met with Democrats, we would highlight programs they liked and remind them that AmeriCorps offered both educational opportunities and workforce training to disconnected youth.

15. ***Get people who directly benefit from the programs to help out.*** It was very helpful to involve people from communities around the nation who had directly benefited from AmeriCorps programs. For example, we brought in school principals and school administrators to talk about how important the tutors and teachers provided by the program were to them and their schools. We got governors whose programs had been cut back to weigh in with the White House and members of Congress.

16. ***Recognize and reward friends and supporters.*** This is critically important. The legislative process is not a one-way street. Members of Congress like to be recognized for their work. Doing that means there is a much better chance of getting a positive response when you come back again for more help. Not only did we send thank-you letters, we held an event at the botanical garden near the Capitol to honor members of Congress who were helpful. We even invited people who had been hard to win over. Everyone likes to be recognized.

Discussion Questions

1. Should the federal government "pay people to volunteer" or to serve in nonmilitary capacities?
2. How should we measure the effectiveness of AmeriCorps? Should the emphasis be on how it changes participants (i.e., makes them more civically engaged or more self-confident), or the community (e.g., fewer high school dropouts, more houses built), or both?
3. Using information you have gathered from the reading assignments, imagine that you are a congressional staff person who needs to write a short speech for your boss that explains why you support additional funding for AmeriCorps, or why you oppose such funding.
4. Put yourself in the shoes of a business leader. Why should the future of AmeriCorps be important to you? How might you communicate your position to policymakers?
5. The events described in this article predate the rise of social media. How would you use the tools available to you today to build the Save AmeriCorps Coalition? How would the result be different from what happened 10 years ago?

6. You are the director of a nonprofit organization that has AmeriCorps members. You have come to Washington to participate in a Hill advocacy day, meeting with Democratic and Republican members of Congress and their staffs. You need to segment your market. What are the five most important characteristics of liberal Democrats and conservative Republicans that you are targeting?

7. Should there be a federal mandate that every student after high school graduation enter national service, either military or civilian? Please provide a rationale for your response.

8. Given the current, even worse, budget constraints, if you were in Congress would you support funding for national service? Is it a good use of taxpayer's money as you compare it with pressing needs such as education, health care, and transportation?

9. This national debate was 10 years ago. Despite the initial strong opposition from prominent members of the Republican Party, after many members heard from their constituents about how it would hurt programs important to them, many of them changed their minds and supported the funding. Do you think, in today's polarized climate on Capitol Hill, with many more ideologues in Congress who don't believe the federal government should have a strong role, that this kind of grassroots energy would have the same impact?

Suggested Websites

Corporation for National and Community Service: www.cns.gov

ServiceNation: www.servicenation.org

Voices for National Service: www.voicesforservice.org

Suggestions for Further Reading

Beadle, A. D. (2003). Inside the fight to save AmeriCorps. *Youth Today, 12*(8), 1, 42.

Commission on National and Community Service (1993). *What you can do for your country.* Washington, DC: Author.

Eberly, D. J., & Gal, R. (2006). *Service without guns* [Ebook]. Lulu.com.

Frumkin, P., & Jastrzab, J. (2010). *Serving country and community: Who benefits from national service?* Cambridge, MA: Harvard University Press.

Lordeman, A., & Rudman, A. B. (2007, January 22). *The Corporation for National and Community Service: Overview of programs and FY 2007 funding.* Washington, DC: Congressional Research Service. Retrieved from http://www.voicesforservice.org/legis_update/CRSReport2007.pdf

Sagawa, S. (2010). *The American way to change: How national service and volunteers are transforming America.* San Francisco: Jossey-Bass.

ServiceNation (2008, September 11–12). *Strategies for becoming a nation of service.* Cambridge, MA: Author. Retrieved from http://s3.amazonaws.com/btcreal/856/SERVICENATION_POLICY_BOOK.pdf

Sofer, G., & Spangenberg, G. (2010, March 8). *Making and funding laws: Authorizations and appropriations in the U.S. Congress.* New York: Council for Advancement of Adult Literacy. Retrieved from www.caalusa.org/Making.pdf

Stengel, R. (2007, September 10). The case for national service. *Time.* Retrieved from http://www.time.com/time/specials/2007/article/0,28804,1657256_1657317,00.html

Time. (2008, September 22). 21 ways to fix up America [Special issue]. Retrieved from http://www.time.com/time/magazine/0,9263,7601080922,00.html

Waldman, S. (1995). *The bill: How the adventures of Clinton's National Service Bill reveal what is corrupt, comic, cynical—and noble—about Washington.* New York: Viking.

References

Alter, J. (2003, June 30). Lip service vs. national service. *Newsweek*. Retrieved from http://www.thedailybeast.com/newsweek/2003/06/29/lip-service-vs-national-service.html

Beadle, A. D. (2003). Inside the fight to save AmeriCorps. *Youth Today, 12*(8), 1, 42.

Bovard, J. (2001, November 19). Bloating AmeriCorps. *Mises Daily*. Retrieved from www.mises.org/daily/831

Dionne, E. J., Jr. (2003, June 27). Save AmeriCorps, Mr. President. *Washington Post*. Retrieved from http://www.voicesforservice.org/PressRoom/clippings/clippacWashPost6_27.htm

Fram, A. (2003, July 12). Senate Oks extra $100 million for AmeriCorps. *Associated Press*. Retrieved from http://www.voicesforservice.org/PressRoom/clippings/art_ap_7_12.htm

McCain, J. (2001, October). Putting the "national" in national service. *Washington Monthly*. Retrieved from www.washingtonmonthly.com/features/2001/0110.mccain.html

Sofer, G., & Spangenberg, G. (2010, March 8). *Making and funding laws: Authorizations and appropriations in the U.S. Congress.* New York: Council for Advancement of Adult Literacy. Retrieved from www.caalusa.org/Making.pdf

State of the Union transcript (2002, January 29). *ABC News*. Retrieved from http://abcnews.go.com/Politics/story?id=121228&page=1#.UKFzpoc8CSo

U.S. General Accounting Office (2004). *Corporation for National and Community Service: Better internal control and revised practices would improve the management of AmeriCorps and the National Service Trust.* Washington, DC: U.S. Government Printing Office. Retrieved from http://www.gao.gov/assets/250/241183.pdf

U.S. Senate (2004). *Senate hearings before the Committee on Appropriations: Departments of Veterans Affairs and Housing and Urban Development and independent agencies appropriations; Fiscal Year 2005, 108th Congress, Second Session, H.R. 5041/S.2825.* Washington, DC: U.S. Government Printing Office. Retrieved from http://www.gpo.gov/fdsys/pkg/CHRG-108shrg92167/pdf/CHRG-108shrg92167.pdf

Waldman, S. (1995). *The bill: How the adventures of Clinton's National Service Bill reveal what is corrupt, comic, cynical—and noble—about Washington.* New York: Viking.

Notes

[1]The Points of Light Foundation was a national, nonpartisan, nonprofit organization dedicated to engaging more people and resources more effectively in volunteer service to help solve serious social problems. Through more than 360 volunteer centers throughout the nation and more than 1,000 nonprofit, government, and business members, the Points of Light Foundation and Volunteer Center National Network provided leadership, knowledge, programs, and resources on a national and local scale to unify the national volunteering and service sector. In August 2007, the Points of Light Foundation and Volunteer Center National Network merged with the Atlanta-based Hands On Network to become the Points of Light Institute.

[2]The USA Freedom Corps was meant to connect Americans with more opportunities to serve their country and to foster a culture of citizenship, responsibility, and service (see georgewbush- whitehouse.archives. gov/infocus/bushrecord/factsheets/needs.html). The USA Freedom Corps was a White House office and fifth policy council within the White House. It described itself as a "Coordinating Council … working to strengthen our culture of service and help find opportunities for every American to start volunteering."

[3]"According to the Corporation's Trust database, AmeriCorps enrollments more than doubled between 1994 and 2000. Overall AmeriCorps enrollments increased from about 25,000 in 1994 to about 42,000 in 1999 to over 59,000 in 2001" (U.S. General Accounting Office, 2004, p. 9).

[4]Supplemental appropriations bills are used to provide additional funding when it has become clear that existing funding is inadequate. This is often the case with unforeseen events such as natural disasters. **Emergency appropriations** have the advantage of not being counted against appropriations ceilings; that is, they do not need to be offset by reductions in other programs.

[5]This guidance is usually included in reports that accompany the bills. Report language does not have the force of law, but agencies are very attentive to congressional intent.

[6]Congress traditionally does this when it doesn't have time—or doesn't want to take the time—to pass the bills separately. This tactic has become increasingly common since 2003.

Credits

9

STATE AND LOCAL POLICY ADVOCACY

Richard Hoefer, PhD

Advocacy is enshrined in the National Association of Social Workers' *Code of Ethics* (NASW, 2008) both on behalf of individuals (**case advocacy**) and on behalf of groups who are affected similarly by particular socioeconomic conditions (**cause advocacy**). While much discussion in the media focuses on events affecting policies at the national level, increasingly critical policy decisions are also being made at the state and local level on issues such as Medicaid, public assistance, education, and services for homeless persons. If states decrease funding for these programs, it could affect federal spending as well, and it will definitely have an adverse impact on program recipients.

While it is tempting to believe that advocacy at the state and local levels can be conducted "just the same" as at the national level, literature suggests that what appears to be the best advocacy practice at the national level does not always translate well to these lower levels of government. In fact, best advocacy practices are not even the same across different states and may not be the same from one local jurisdiction to the next. It is, therefore, vital for advocates to understand what contributes to effective advocacy at subnational levels of government (CQ-Roll Call, 2015a; Hoefer, 2000a).

In light of this need, this chapter explores the following questions:

- What is the current context of state and local policy advocacy?
- What structural factors affect state and local advocacy efforts?
- What are the best practices of state and local advocacy?
- What barriers inhibit social workers' participation in state and local policy advocacy?
- What does the future seem to hold regarding state and local advocacy?

THE CURRENT CONTEXT FOR STATE AND LOCAL ADVOCACY

While a host of factors are important in understanding the current context of state and local advocacy, this chapter focuses on four of the most important:

- The impact of unregulated funding for campaigns, which is often thought of as only a problem in national elections
- The decentralization of policymaking, a process often referred to as **policy devolution**
- The decrease in levels of state and local government funding
- The development of social networking and communications technology and software

UNREGULATED CAMPAIGN FUNDING AT STATE AND LOCAL LEVELS

The Supreme Court's 2010 decision in the Citizens United case prevents any government body from placing limits on the amount of its own money a corporation or private individual may spend to pay for supporting or attacking candidates in elections at any level. This decision allows corporations and a few wealthy persons to contribute staggering amounts of money to Super PACs (Political Action Committees) and other organizations in an attempt to affect the outcome of elections. This policy change has enhanced the ability of the economic elite (whether conservative or liberal) in the United States to control who is elected to public office and to influence them in particular policy directions (Kennedy, 2015). In the 2012 elections, so-called "dark money" (funding for campaigns that is given anonymously) totaled at least $300 million (Kennedy, 2015). Spending on state and local elections in the 2014 (non-presidential elections) was about $2.2 billion. Consequently, outcomes of elections at this level are increasingly being heavily influenced by large contributors (Kennedy, 2015).

If people with large amounts of money had the same policy preferences as other Americans, this would not necessarily skew the political landscape. Unfortunately, evidence shows that the wealthy are both extremely active politically and much more conservative than the American public as a whole with respect to important policies concerning taxation, economic regulation, and especially social welfare programs. Variation within this wealthy group suggests that the top one-tenth of 1 percent of wealth-holders (people with $40 million or more in net worth) may tend to hold still more conservative views that are even more distinct from those of the general public (Page, Bartels, & Seawright, 2013, p. 51).

Wealthy campaign contributors have had notable influence on state and local level races across the United States, but two remarkable examples stand out:

- In Missouri, Rex Sinquefield has spent $37 million on executive and judicial branch races at local and state levels. He supports the elimination of income and corporate taxes in favor of sales taxes which are more regressive. [See Chapter 7 in this volume for further discussion of tax policy.] He also favors privatizing public schools (McDermott, 2015).
- In North Carolina, Art Pope contributed millions to politicians who were elected. He was then named as the budget director for the state and, in this capacity, introduced cuts to education and social services. He was also instrumental in making voting more difficult through the establishment of voter ID laws, a policy that has subsequently been copied across the country. His money is credited with giving Republicans control of North Carolina's government for the first time in over 140 years (Mayer, 2011).

While a wealthy person of any political persuasion may have similar influence, the deck appears stacked in the direction of conservatives, such as the Koch brothers (who at one point indicated they were willing to spend nearly $900 million during the 2016 election cycle) and Sheldon Adelson, who spent $150 million in the 2012 elections (Kennedy, 2015).

DECENTRALIZATION OF POLICYMAKING

These developments in the area of campaign financing are increasingly significant because of the **decentralization of policymaking** from the national government to the state and local levels. This phenomenon, also known as policy devolution, began nearly 40 years ago with the "New Federalism" policies of the Nixon Administration, whose stated goal was to dismantle the programs developed during the War on Poverty of the mid-1960s (Ezell, 2001; Hoefer, 2005). Although the War on Poverty used several funding mechanisms, its policies usually relied on strong federal guidelines, if not outright federal control, of programs. [*Chapter 2 in this volume describes how this process of decentralization continued in the 1980s, through the development of block grants, in the 1990s, with the passage of welfare reform, and in the 21st century, in the areas of educational and health policy.*] While decentralization of social policy development and implementation is not a new phenomenon (it appeared, for example, in the welfare policies of the New Deal), it continues to be a theme of many, if not most, areas of U.S. social policy.

The Patient Protection and Affordable Care Act (P.L. 111-148) (ACA) and its companion law, the Health Care and Education Reconciliation Act of 2010 (P.L. 111–152) (often jointly referred to as "Obamacare") passed in 2010 represent a notable counter-example, but this legislation has subsequently been criticized harshly for "overreaching" constitutional limits, despite some decentralized features, and has barely survived judicial scrutiny. [*See Chapter 14 in this volume for further discussion of health care reform.*]

Despite this exception, the general direction of U.S. social policy has been to shift more decisions to states and localities. Even the ACA left it up to states to determine whether they wished to expand Medicaid (a joint Federal/State program to provide health care for low-income people). Social conservatives have introduced a large number of legislative efforts at the state level that would affect women's access to reproductive health care and the rights of LGBTQ and transgendered persons. Organizations such as the American Legislative Exchange Council (ALEC) write model bills and use their ability to lobby effectively to introduce and pass their proposals. Recent examples of ALEC-supported legislation are proposals to undermine public employee unions, privatize public schools, and prevent local governments from setting minimum wages higher than state levels or impose stiffer environmental protections within their limits (Graves, 2016).

The sudden influx of legislation at the state level regarding the regulation of public restroom use, which advocates for transgendered people argue are discriminatory, is an example of a law that has been passed in one state (North Carolina) and then introduced in many others, despite no evidence of a problem being given that would necessitate its adoption. Such laws, however, have the ability to make life much more difficult for some people, particularly those in excluded or marginalized populations. This demonstrates why social workers need to understand the importance of state- and local-level advocacy efforts.

DECREASE IN FEDERAL, STATE, AND LOCAL GOVERNMENT FUNDING

Much of the media coverage of social policy focuses on the problems of budgeting and taxes at the national level. However, at state and local levels, the effects of fiscal policy decisions are both more

Figure 9.1

Non-Defense Discretionary Spending Falling to Historic Lows

Spending as a percent of gross domestic product

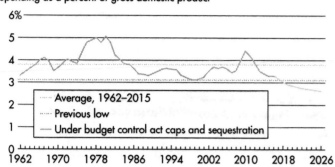

Note: Data available only back to 1962. Sequestration refers to budget cuts required under the 2011 Budget Control Act and includes modifications to it in te Bipartisan Budget Acts of 2013 and 2015.

Source: CBPP based on Office of Management and Budget and Congressional Budget Office data.

Center on Budget and Policy Priorities | cbpp.org

immediate and long-term. As indicated in Chapter 7 of this volume, unlike the federal government, states and localities are constitutionally obligated to produce balanced budgets. The sharp decline in the past decade in state spending contrasts sharply to trends during most of the latter half of the 20th century, a period in which state government spending increased from 4.5% of U.S. Gross Domestic Product in 1952 to 11.6% in 2006 (Baiker, Clemons, & Singhal, 2011). In recent years, states' ability to create budgets that stay out of the red has been dramatically challenged. They have experienced large-scale reductions in tax revenues due to lower receipts of sales and property taxes, and voluntary tax cuts. More recently, the decrease in the price of crude oil has affected some state budgets negatively as tax revenues from the sale of gasoline have fallen sharply. This loss of revenue has had a dramatic effect on social policy formulation at the state and local levels, even as social needs have increased as a consequence of ongoing economic stagnation.

At the same time, competition for the remaining federal funds and foundation resources has intensified. Consequently, many nongovernmental social service organizations are now struggling just to keep their doors open. The situation in some states is so precarious that nonprofits are shutting down simply because they have run out of money. State and local governments are delaying payment to nonprofits with which they have service contracts to such an extent that some organizations are exhausting their reserves, laying off or furloughing employees, and increasing the workloads of remaining staff. The results have been devastating to many agencies and their clients (Oliff, Mai, & Palacios, 2012).

Federal Funding

After reaching an all-time high in 2010, projected federal spending on "welfare" will decrease for at least the next several years. (The budget category "welfare" includes programs for families and children, including food and nutrition, unemployment insurance, workers compensation, housing, and other social protection programs [Chantrill, 2012].) While federal spending grew between 2008 and 2010, this increase was primarily due to greater spending on unemployment insurance and other programs whose benefits were triggered by the severe economic recession. In 2015, about 10 percent of the Federal budget (or $362 billion) was spent on "programs that provide aid (other than health insurance or Social Security benefits) … Spending on safety net programs declined in both nominal and real terms between 2014 and 2015 as the economy continued to improve" (Center on Budget and Policy Priorities, 2016). Analysts' projections call for further decreases over the next decade (see Figure 9.1). Because a portion of federal funds go to states and local governments for distribution to local service providers, decreases in this stream of nonprofit organizational revenue have a powerful impact on agencies and the people they serve (Gallup, 2011).

State Funding

In 2010, 2011, and 2012, virtually every state had serious problems balancing its budget. Although states are constitutionally prohibited from running a fiscal deficit, many state and local governments have built-in "structural deficits," which have required them to employ a combination of program cuts, new (often regressive) taxes, and creative accounting practices to balance their budgets. Many of these cuts occur at the expense of nonprofit agencies and the people they serve. Since 2012 the situation has improved somewhat; current estimates are that "only" 16 states were considered to be running deficits in Fiscal Year 2016 and/or Fiscal Year 2017 (Malm & Crosby, 2016). This number may increase, however, in the future depending on the outcome of the 2016 election and the state of the economy.

Data show that for over half of states "tax receipts have failed to match their peak from just before the start of the recession" that began in 2008. States face key financial problems in 2016 related to "underfunded pensions for state employees, low oil prices, political polarization, dwindling help from the federal government and the general sluggish growth" of recent years (CQ-Roll Call, 2016, Jan. 12). These fiscal issues will create limited options for states to expand spending. Many states continue to pass net tax and fee decreases further straining their capacity to fund additional priorities (CQ-Roll Call, 2016, Jan. 12).

LOCAL GOVERNMENT FUNDING

Tracking local government spending accurately in real time is very difficult. For example, it was not until January 2016 that the U.S. Census Bureau released its estimates of total local government funding for 2013. This time lag makes an appraisal of the extent of local government cuts challenging. Anecdotal evidence suggests, however, that cities and counties have been hit very hard since the onset of the Great Recession due to their reliance on state funding, property taxes, and sales tax revenues.

During the past few years, in states such as Michigan, some cities and towns have been taken over by state governments due to their fiscal plight sometimes with disastrous results. Flint, Michigan was one such city. The governor of Michigan appointed an emergency city manager who made the decision to shift the source of Flint's water supply to save money. This move, along with a decision not to add an anti-corrosion agent to preserve the pipes in the system, led to months of the city water supplies being tainted by high levels of lead, poisoning all of the residents of the city, and particularly harming the young and the elderly. Five years ago, in 2011, Jefferson County, Alabama filed for the largest bankruptcy in U.S. history. Other cities and counties are on the brink of similar fiscal calamity.

As noted above, even states in somewhat better financial condition have cut spending on many local government projects. Some cities have eliminated essential services, including libraries and fire protection, and have even reduced the hours of street lighting. While the national economy is showing some signs of improvement in recent years, many localities continue to have deteriorating situations. Even with higher levels of employment and low gasoline prices, consumers are handling uncertainty in the job market by cutting nonessential spending. This reduces states' sales tax revenues. Finally, due to the presence of powerful anti-tax sentiments among the electorate, it is difficult for government at any level to increase taxes to make up the shortfall.

BARRIERS AFFECTING STATE AND LOCAL ADVOCACY BY SOCIAL WORKERS

Although the NASW (2008) *Code of Ethics* states that advocacy is an ethical imperative of the profession, a number of barriers impede social workers' effective participation as advocates at all levels of government. Three problems in particular stand out: inadequate preparation, practical barriers, and negative attitudes. Today's students are inadequately prepared to be effective advocates because of a paucity of advocacy-related content in schools and departments of social work and a lack of advocacy-related continuing education opportunities (Rothman, 2013; Reisch, 2016). Although social workers are well trained to practice with individual clients, few receive training in how to make a difference in the political realm. While knowledge of policy processes is a required curriculum component in accredited social work programs (Council on Social Work Education, 2015), many social work students graduate without having participated in organized and effective advocacy efforts. Because their career goal is to engage in practice with individuals and families in a clinically therapeutic milieu, students often may not see the relevance of advocacy for their work.

In addition, much of the social work literature on advocacy is exhortatory rather than educational (Hoefer, 2005). Despite some recent improvements, it is seldom grounded in empirical research (Cochran, Montgomery, & Rubin, 2010; Hoefer, 2000a, 2000b, 2001, 2005, 2016; Hoefer & Ferguson, 2007; Teater, 2009). While practice experience and wisdom is useful, schools of social work are not currently providing students with either a theoretical understanding of political systems or evidence-based information on advocacy (Hoefer, 2005). Thus, future practitioners are urged to engage in more advocacy activities without being provided with the skills to do so.

Besides a lack of adequate educational preparation, there are practical barriers to participation. Practitioners lead harried lives, full of work obligations even after business hours, and they may not feel that there is room in their schedules for something as time-consuming as advocacy. Consequently, efforts to change policy often fall to volunteers, who are juggling other work and family responsibilities, or to staff members who find advocacy "yet another" task to squeeze into their overfilled schedules.

Lack of proximity to state capitals can also be a barrier to participation, particularly in large states such as California, Texas, and Florida. While this issue is less of a problem at the municipal level, county officials may also be located some distance away. Time spent away from running an organization or assisting clients can frequently feel like time wasted, especially because of the frequent delays involved in the policy advocacy process. As a result, advocacy is often depicted as a "Lone Ranger" sort of affair, with individual rather than organizational efforts being the implied norm (Ezell, 2001; Hoefer, 2005) because social work organizations rarely have the fiscal capacity to hire full-time advocacy personnel.

Because of misunderstandings about the law, social workers employed by governmental or nonprofit organizations are often unsure if they are allowed to advocate and, if so, how much time they can devote to advocacy activities (Smucker, 1999).Negative attitudes also can impede active involvement in advocacy. Social workers sometimes wish to avoid the political aspects of their practice. Politics is often viewed as a "dirty" world, full of ethical compromises, corruption, and greed. The reality is that some of these negative perceptions are true. The question for social workers is how to operate ethically in a situation that has these characteristics. To refuse to participate is to cede the policymaking arena to those who act without remorse to cut benefits, work against social justice, and aggrandize greed.

In a speech of interest to all current and potential advocates, Dave Meslin (2011), a community organizer in Toronto, Canada, discussed a number of barriers to local advocacy. In his view, these barriers include the following:

1. The way information is disseminated by both city hall and the media. Meslin suggested that if for-profit organizations advertised their products in a similar way, they would soon be out of business.
2. The control of public space and political messages by wealthy individuals and corporations.
3. The idea that heroes are "chosen" rather than the outcome being decided by people making a series of decisions to do the right thing.
4. The structure of political parties and elections, which are designed to decrease activism rather than encourage it.

In the end, Meslin argues that apathy is not an individual problem but a collective problem that can be decreased by changing key aspects of the system that make apathy seem like a realistic response.

STRUCTURAL VARIABLES AFFECTING STATE AND LOCAL ADVOCACY

States and localities also possess certain structural features that affect the viability of advocacy efforts by social workers and their allies. These include differences between advocacy at the national, state, and local levels; the variety of political cultures in the states; and the type of partisan control of states' political institutions. While all of these factors can be changed over time, in the short run they tend to be fairly fixed. As a result, they have a considerable impact on what policies are likely to be proposed, as well as on which advocacy tactics are most likely to be successful.

ADVOCACY AT THE NATIONAL LEVEL IS NOT THE SAME AS ADVOCACY AT STATE AND LOCAL LEVELS

Advocates at the state and local level must understand three key differences between their efforts and those of advocates at the national level. Unless they understand these differences, social work advocates may try uncritically to apply ideas based on advocacy at the national level to their work. This is often a serious mistake that leads to wasted effort and considerable frustration. Discussed below are the ways a state's economic base, its revenue-generating options, and its demographic composition constrain the policy solutions that advocates can realistically expect to be adopted.

Many states and most localities have a narrow base on which their entire economy rests. Michigan's economy, for example, was basically dependent on the automobile industry, despite the presence of tourism, natural resources, and other smaller industries. Once large American car manufacturers started having significant problems in the 1970s, so did the state of Michigan. Cities such as Flint that relied on one industry became virtual ghost towns and are not fiscally healthy to this day. By contrast, the United States as a whole usually has regions where the economy is doing well and other areas where the economy is not doing well during the same period.

States and localities are also more limited in the sources of revenue they can tap for spending purposes. A few states, for example, do not have an income tax. Nearly all states rely heavily on sales taxes, although tax rates and the proportion of state revenue derived from sales taxes vary from one state to another. Localities typically are heavily dependent on property taxes (particularly for school budgets) and sales taxes. By contrast, the primary source of revenue for the federal government is the income tax. And, as stated above, the national government can run a deficit—an option not constitutionally available to states. [*See Chapter 7 in this volume for further discussion of the relationship between taxes and budgets.*]

Just as states and localities are typically more dependent on one economic engine, they also tend to be demographically more homogeneous than the nation as a whole. An extreme example is Utah, which is nearly 80% non-Hispanic white (U.S. Census Bureau, 2011), with the population overwhelmingly belonging to just one religious denomination. In Utah, any person or organization advocating for policies that run counter to the wishes of the Church of Latter Day Saints (the Mormon Church) is going to face a strong uphill battle. The Roman Catholic Church holds a similar status in some states and localities. Smaller areas, such as counties or cities, sometimes have a similarly large preponderance of a single religious group, such as fundamentalist Baptists in parts of the South, Jews in parts of New York City and Los Angeles, and Muslims in Detroit suburbs such as Dearborn.

Demographic or cultural homogeneity can produce the same results. As a state, California is quite diverse—as are many of its cities—yet even communities that are statistically diverse like Oakland can be segregated along race, class, religious, or cultural lines. Some neighborhoods and voting areas are decidedly "Latino," "African American," "gay," or "elderly." This segregation means that, to be effective, advocates must thoroughly understand the cultural and economic enclaves in their localities and states.

The above differences underscore the importance of distinguishing ideas about subnational policy advocacy from those about policy advocacy at the national level. It is also important to understand the differences that exist among and even within states, counties, and cities.

STATE POLITICAL CULTURE

One of the most important aspects of understanding effective advocacy at the state and local level is the existence of different political cultures. A state's political culture refers to its residents' orientations toward important aspects of their state's political system, including the role of the individual in how state politics operates (Almond & Verba, 1965; Silver & Dowley, 2000). This culture is made up of a number of elements, including political views, the characteristics of its political processes, and the core values shared by state residents. Political culture affects not only individual behavior but also policymaking and implementation at the state level (Fisher & Pratt, 2006; Mead, 2004; Shock, 2008).

Daniel Elazar (1972) developed a theory of **state political culture** that can help advocates understand how it affects policy development and effective advocacy at the state and local levels. In brief, a state's political culture influences a variety of factors that arise in a number of different policy arenas. These include the range of problems human service delivery systems address (Bielefeld & Corbin, 1996); the stringency and frequency with which the death penalty is applied (Fisher & Pratt, 2006); the rigor of voter identification and ballot access laws (Hale & McNeal, 2010; Shock, 2008); the way political campaign ads are written (Joslyn, 1980); the overall amount of state and local spending (Koven & Mausolff, 2002); educational policy (Louis, Thomas, Gordon, & Febey, 2008); collective bargaining provisions affecting workers (McCurdy, 1998); the implementation of welfare reform (Mead, 2004); the extent of political corruption (Peters & Welch, 1978); the degree of prison privatization (Price & Riccucci, 2005); and the agenda-setting impact of media coverage (Tan & Weaver, 2009). Research also demonstrates the importance of a political culture's impact on policy down to the county level (Morgan & Anderson, 1991).

According to Elazar (1972) there are three types of political subcultures: moralistic, individualistic, and traditionalistic—each of which is characterized by different approaches to the role and reason for government. He posits that states' political cultures are related to the culture of the European country of origin of the early settlers in that state. For "moralistic states," the concept of "the commonwealth" is important. Being in a commonwealth entails the idea that citizens should participate in government as an act of civil society. In a commonwealth, society is made up of individuals who band together for the common good; what is best for all is more important than what is good for a small number. Government is seen as a force for good. If a problem exists that can be fixed, government (representing all the citizens of the community or state) should try to make the situation better (Elazar, 1972). States with a moralistic political culture include Michigan, Minnesota, Oregon, and Wisconsin.

Characteristics of a moralistic political culture include

- Being politically liberal and/or progressive in nature;
- Intolerance of political corruption;
- A tendency to seek innovative solutions to problems; and
- An activist orientation (Elazar, 1972; Joslyn, 1980; Morgan & Anderson, 1991).

The second ideal type of political culture, the individualistic, places much more emphasis on entrepreneurship in the private sector and conservative belief systems. Rather than being based on the commonwealth idea of the moralistic political culture, the individualistic culture is based on utilitarianism, or the greatest good for the greatest number. This approach can leave smaller, non-majority groups out in the political cold, with little influence on policy directed at their needs. Activity in the political sphere is limited to a specialized cadre of professionals; the general public is not expected to be interested in politics and is not encouraged to participate (Elazar, 1972).

Characteristics of the individualistic political culture include greater competition between parties (represented by professional politicians), a high respect for private party behavior being self-determined, and limited government action to interfere with private activity, particularly concerning property rights. There is a presupposition that government should be small. Thus, activities to support individuals with economic difficulties will be difficult to sustain. Examples of states with this culture are Illinois, Indiana, New York, and Pennsylvania.

The final type of political culture Elazar (1972) describes is traditionalistic. This type of culture is imbued with paternalism and an elitist political system. Government is indeed a positive force in the community, but its main goal is to maintain the system as it currently exists (because the current system is seen as a good way for society to be). In general, citizens are discouraged from attempting to be involved in the political system, as the local and state elites will "take care" of things for the masses. Traditionalistic states include Alabama, Georgia, Louisiana, and Virginia.

Despite this conception of three ideal types, empirical studies of states' political cultures have found that a number of hybrids, such as moralistic/individualistic or traditionalistic/individualistic exist, reflecting the influence of more than one stream of immigrants or, over time, a shift from one culture to another in a particular state. States with blended political cultures always have one dominant and one lesser culture, a situation that complicates matters for researchers and advocates.

Political culture is very slow to change. While it is possible to change partisan party control of governmental institutions every two years or so (depending on which institution one is looking at), the truth is that many states are effectively one-party states. The next section looks at this factor and its implications for advocacy.

PARTISAN CONTROL OF GOVERNMENTAL INSTITUTIONS

The term **governmental institutions** refer to the political governing bodies in states—that is, their legislative assemblies and governorships. Partisan control of these governmental institutions shapes the policies that emerge from the give and take of lawmaking. Partisan control sustains (and is sustained by) the state's political culture and values, which strongly influence the implementation of ideas relating to social justice (Alexander & Rolle, 2008). Fowler (2004) identifies two broad partisan ideologies, liberal and conservative, that influence the social, democratic, and economic values in U.S. politics. In general, the values supported by state government officials influence that state's policies in areas such as the human services. Thus, like any other social policy, human services policies reflect the social and political values of the society (Chambers & Wedel, 2009).

When analyzing U.S. politics, we need to examine the political ideologies of the two major political parties. Today, the Republican and Democratic parties are associated with conservative and liberal values, respectively, although differences within the parties persist as the 2016 election campaign reveals. In recent decades, the Democratic Party has been linked with liberalism and a progressive approach to social policy, with an emphasis on empowering working class and racial/ethnic minorities. This is connected to the party's view that government is potentially a force for good. Democrats believe, for example, that the federal government should intervene in the workings of the economy to ensure more equal outcomes and to protect the vulnerable. On the other hand, the Republican Party has been more frequently associated with laissez-faire economic policies, fiscal conservatism, and the promotion of personal responsibility over social welfare programs (Fowler, 2004). The nomination of Donald Trump as the Republican Party nominee for President has shown that the party is deeply split between "traditional" Republicans, and a populist segment that is angry at the Republican establishment. Trump's appeal to populist Republicans led him to victory in the primary race, beating many mainstream conservative leaders within the party.

Ideological polarization has increased markedly in recent years, reflected in people's relationship to the media, the Internet, and the political process itself. There are several reasons for this. Specialized media outlets now exist, such as Fox News (which is slanted toward conservative positions) and MSNBC (which is biased in a liberal way). People tend to watch one network or the other, but not both. They also tend to search websites that mirror their perspectives on specific issues. Receiving only one viewpoint from the media tends to reinforce viewers' current beliefs. The largest search engine, Google, links search results of an Internet query to what the user has viewed in the past, thus limiting the search query results that emerge. Redistricting efforts at the state level have increased the number of "safe seats" with less competition between the parties within a district. In addition, improved database-mining capabilities coupled with greater spending on elections and the rise of "super political action committees" (Super PACs) allow more targeted channeling of campaign messages to particular individuals. These messages are used to bring out supporters of a candidate and attempt to neutralize the participation of other candidates' supporters.

Whether a state or locality has conservative or liberal legal policies to address human services problems is, therefore, directly connected to which party is in the majority. For instance, Young, Farrell, Henderson, and Taxman (2009) reported that party affiliation of state governors was significantly associated with intensive treatment provisions for offenders in the adult and juvenile justice systems. Gershtenson, Mangun, and Smith (2004) found that state legislators with a Democratic Party affiliation supported pro-environment policies to a significantly higher extent than did their Republican counterparts (Crouch & Abbot, 2009). Lee and Donlan (2009) show that states with Democratic Party control of government bodies spend more funds on Medicaid. The refusal of most Republican governors to expand Medicaid provision after the passage of the Affordable Care Act is further evidence of this phenomenon.

While both major political parties are active in every state and partisan control of governmental institutions could change with every election, the reality is that political majorities are generally more stable than fluid. For example, some states vote so consistently for one party's presidential candidate that they are considered more or less permanently "Red" (Republican) or "Blue" (Democratic). In presidential elections, Southern, Plains, and Mountain states have been consistently "Red" in recent decades, while states along the Great Lakes, in the Northeastern part of the United States, and on the West Coast are more likely to vote for Democratic presidential candidates. The Presidential election of 2016 may cause some shifts in these historical patterns.

Voters, however, are often less consistent in state and local elections, particularly in **off-year elections** (those that do not include a presidential election), and during periods of considerable discontent. For example, in 2008 (the year President Obama was first elected) gubernatorial elections resulted in a redistribution of political party affiliation of just one governor's office. By contrast, the 2010 off-year elections were held at a time of considerable discontent over the economy and increased activism by conservative political forces such as the Tea Party movement. In that year, there was a significant shift in party control of governorships (Republicans gained five) and a dramatic shift in the balance of power in state legislatures. Republicans gained 680 seats at the state level, the largest switch in the number of seats gained since the Watergate-scandal–influenced election of 1974. This was significant both for policy development and for future political outcomes, as these reconstituted legislatures had the authority for redistricting based on the 2010 census.

These results were reinforced in 2014, another non-presidential election year. For state and local advocacy groups one of the lessons of this recent history is that off-year elections are much more likely to result in changes in partisan control of the legislature than are elections when the presidency is being decided. This is because only strongly motivated voters tend to participate in off-year elections, and they are usually people motivated by anti-incumbent sentiment.

BEST PRACTICES FOR STATE AND LOCAL ADVOCACY

Relatively little empirical literature provides guidance regarding the best practices for state and local advocacy. This section describes what advocacy activities are, in general, at the organizational and individual level, and then discusses the findings of recent research regarding legislative advocacy at the state level.

WHAT ARE ADVOCACY ACTIVITIES?

To be effective, one must know the gamut of possible advocacy activities that one can select to match the activity to the situation at hand. In their classic study of political participation, Verba and Nie (1972) used participation in activities such as voting, contacting elected officials, and participating in protests, as their measure of participation. With the advent of additional technology in the past 40 years, however, an expanded list of activities could be constructed, including sending an e-mail message to an elected or appointed official, making an online donation to an advocacy group, or posting a political message on one's Facebook page.

Hoefer (2016) presents a model of individual level advocacy. The variables that lead to greater levels of advocacy among social workers are higher levels of education, embrace of the values of social justice supporting advocacy, a greater sense of professional responsibility, higher levels of interest caused by self-interest

Figure 9.2 Anti-Abortion Activists at a "March for Life" in Washington, DC

or recruitment by others, participation in other organizations, the possession of more skills coming from education, training or experience in organizational politics, and more free time to devote to advocacy. Each of these variables can be increased or decreased by the conditions at one's workplace. If agency directors desire higher levels of advocacy among staff members, they can provide in-service training or request continuing education courses from a local provider. Administrators can also provide time during the workday to attend coalition meetings or use flex-time arrangements to free up morning or afternoon hours for advocacy purposes (Hoefer, 2016).

Plitt-Donaldson and Shield's (2009) Policy Advocacy Behavior Scale is designed to measure advocacy activities by individuals within an agency. Among other behaviors, they ask whether testimony has been provided at a public hearing, whether participation in work groups on a public policy issue has occurred, whether information about political issues has been distributed to clients, and whether media outlets have been engaged to discuss political issues. They found that the average score on the Policy Advocacy Behavior Scale among the agencies they contacted was 34.5 out of a possible 96 points (36%).

Walker (1991) outlines the following seven useful activities in which interest groups might engage:

- Work with members of the legislature
- Work with government agencies to formulate policy
- Develop consensus among experts
- Pursue issues in court
- Attempt to influence public opinion through the media
- Aid in the election of public officials
- Engage in public protests or demonstrations

The first three are considered "inside" tactics because they take place within well-established routines and affect the legislators and regulators directly. The final four are considered "outside" tactics because they work to influence legislators and regulators indirectly. For example, having a court make a decision about the implementation of a law affects the legislature and the bureaucracy indirectly by having the court dictate what they must do. Similarly, trying to influence public opinion through the media involves changing the way elected or appointed officials decide by getting the public to push for a particular viewpoint. These are advocacy tactics for organizations to pursue while trying to garner support for their views. To enhance advocacy behavior in social service agencies, human service nonprofits need to have supportive leadership, membership in coalitions, and the backing of their boards (Plitt-Donaldson, 2007).

Most research on advocacy conducted at the state level focuses only on one state (Cochran et al., 2010; Comerford, 2003; Teater, 2009; Thomas, 2010). Much of this research is descriptive in nature, rather than analytic. (Teater, 2009, is a notable exception.) Lee and Donlan (2009) conducted an analysis of variables affecting health policy for indigent individuals in all 50 states. Although their research did not assess models of lobbying effectiveness, it did examine how the context within a state affects policy.

Teater (2009) gathered data from state legislators in Ohio using qualitative methods. Based on her results, she developed a framework to understand legislators' (rather than advocates') views

Figure 9.3 Pro-Choice Proponents Protesting Against Proposed Funding Cuts for Planned Parenthood Clinics

of what produced effective advocacy. Five important findings emerged. First, the most effective groups were based locally and "bubbled up" from that level. According to respondents, legislators pay most attention to groups of local constituents who, even after successfully starting their organization, maintain contact with local citizens. In this way, effective interest groups report the concerns and issues affecting their members to elected officials, acting as messengers of their needs and desires.

Legislators also report that the groups they find most effective have clear plans, a focused mission, specific goals, and an involved membership. The leaders inform members of the larger context, and the members keep the leaders working on specified goals. This two-way communication and accountability is vital for legislators to accept the leaders' legitimacy. Groups must also "market" themselves to legislators so communication is established and relationships are built. As a result of relationship building, legislators begin to feel that the group is credible, understands and acts on the legislators' individual preferences for receiving information, and has a "presence" in the political world (Teater, 2009).

In a four-state study—Minnesota, Mississippi, Pennsylvania, and Texas—Hoefer (2005) developed and tested a model of interest group effectiveness using variables that were shown to be significant in differentiating more effective versus less effective interest groups at the national level (Hoefer, 2000a). When testing a full model of interest-group effectiveness at the state level, he used five variables: percentage of time used to influence policy (resources), use of inside strategy (strategy), level of cooperation with state government (relationships), degree of coordination with other organizations (coalitions), and desired level of social services (policy position).

Results indicated that the model was at best moderately successful in predicting interest-group effectiveness in the various states and that different variables were important in different states. In Minnesota and Mississippi, for example, the amount of resources devoted to advocacy and the policy position of the group were both significantly associated with effectiveness. In Texas, using an inside strategy was the only variable that reached statistical significance, and in Pennsylvania, none of the variables seemed important.

More effective groups were found to

- Be knowledgeable about and proactive in the policy process;
- Provide timely and policy-related information;
- Build a relationship with decision makers; and
- Build coalitions with other interest groups and policy actors (Hoefer, 2001, p. 3).

Based on these findings, Hoefer (2005) developed two implications for practice:

> First, despite the seeming reasonableness of believing that effective advocacy at the state level should be the same as effective advocacy at the national level, the evidence tells us otherwise. Second, because states are also different from each other, advocacy practice knowledge must be gathered on a state-by-state basis. Decentralization of policy making must lead to decentralization of knowledge gathering (p. 225).

FUTURE OF STATE AND LOCAL ADVOCACY

While it is hazardous to one's reputation to foretell events, it appears a few predictions are fairly safe: Advocates at the state and local levels will increase their use of electronic tools and social media, organizations will increasingly see the connections between advocacy efforts and fundraising, and social justice battles will intensify at the state and local levels.

DEVELOPMENT OF SOCIAL NETWORKING AND COMMUNICATIONS TECHNOLOGY

The nature and practice of cyber-based advocacy, or **cyber-activism**, is changing so rapidly that this section of the chapter may be out of date before it is published. Advocates now have a host of **social media** and communications technology available that have transformed the ways they can recruit, motivate, inform, and incite potential participants and followers (McNutt & Menon, 2008).

Easy access to the Internet and its tools has put 24-hour-per-day "advocates" onto a very large number of people's desks, at work and at home. The spread of mobile platforms has put the power of the Internet into small packages that people have with them all the time. Smart phones and tablet computers have expanded access to the Internet and its treasures of information, and calls to action proliferate wherever a wireless connection is available. In addition, social media software, such as Facebook, Instagram, and Twitter, has become a useful tool for technology-savvy advocates and leaders. New interactive features and components crop up frequently (Web 2.0 and Web 3.0) and keep the momentum flowing (Edwards & Hoefer, 2010).

In general, the Internet has had three main effects on advocacy. First, the use of the Internet is changing the way people actually find and use information. What might have taken days or months to find out about an issue (if it could be found at all) can now take less than a minute, although determining which websites can be trusted takes some additional time and effort. Increasingly large numbers of people are taking advantage of this ability and are receiving information nearly instantaneously. Second, communications technology such as I-phones and web-based presentations enable people to connect with like-minded individuals in their city, state, and nation, and across the world. Sharing strategy and information is becoming second nature and allows a movement to grow quickly at low cost.

A third benefit for advocates using social media strategies is the amount of publicity one can generate and receive quickly. The 2011 Arab Spring uprisings against well-entrenched government leaders would have been impossible without such technology. Occupy Wall Street is an example of an advocacy movement that created and spread information in real time. Black Lives Matter is the most recent example of this phenomenon. In the 1960s, at civil rights and antiwar protests, demonstrators depended on local and national news crews to film, record, and interview them to get the word out. Now, everyone with a cell phone with video capacity can quickly upload images and words to Facebook and other sites to circulate their unfiltered views throughout the world. Each person, with minimal equipment, is now potentially an entire news crew, and, through the power of interactive Web 4.0 tools, each person can also comment on others' views. For example, videos of police abusing members of the public have been instrumental in creating a movement to change the perception of the police in many locales.

Figure 9.4 Occupy Wall Street Demonstration in Zuccotti Park, New York City.

THE NEED FOR GREATER USE OF ELECTRONIC ADVOCACY AND SOCIAL MEDIA SOFTWARE

A small but growing literature indicates that advocacy by social workers must become more attuned to the electronic and social media facets that have emerged and will continue to become more important. Nearly two decades ago, McNutt and Boland (1999) began to map out the landscape for nonprofit use of electronic advocacy. More recently, McNutt and Menon (2008) are able to state convincingly:

Figure 9.5 Rev. Dr. William Barber speaking a Moral Monday rally in North Carolina protesting against actions of the North Carolina state legislature.

> The use of the Internet and related technologies offers advocates the promise of a new and exciting set of tools to promote causes, develop change efforts, and promote real change. While current campaigns and programs are impressive, the future holds much promise for newer and more exciting efforts (p. 37).

A similar theme is expressed by Dunlop and Fawcett (2008), who list a large number of software tools that have potential for advocates working for social justice issues. The use of social media and Web 4.0 software can be enormously powerful because they enable people to organize quickly and cheaply. Communicating through a Facebook page or text messaging with a smartphone enables the creation of nearly instantaneous plans. Because the technology and applications change so quickly, it requires considerable time and effort to stay abreast of new developments and how they can be used effectively.

Edwards and Hoefer (2010) show that social work advocates are not using social networking tools well on their websites, and they compare the practices of social work organizations unfavorably with those of other types of organizations. While better use of the Internet and interactive social media is not confined to state and local organizations, it may be most important at this level to use these tools to create more interactive and cohesive advocacy groups. State and local groups tend to have fewer monetary resources than national level groups, so their ability to leverage the power of technology is more vital to their success. This perspective complements Teater's (2009) observation that policymakers are looking to work with groups that have a well-defined constituency and clear goals.

MORE POWERFUL CONNECTIONS BETWEEN ADVOCACY AND FUNDING

While the information is not yet being reported in academic literature, nonprofit technology purveyor Blackbaud is finding that nonprofits can strategically use advocacy for fundraising purposes (Daigneault, Davis, & Sybrant, 2011). Using advanced technology to connect to their base of supporters, nonprofits are able to raise substantially more money and increase up to sevenfold the percentage of information provided to donors. Advocacy efforts motivate potential donors to see the value of the organization and provide an opportunity to strengthen their connection with them. Connected people give more to "their" organization. To achieve these impressive results, organizations must develop an advocacy center, where all relevant information on the "issue of the day" is available; e-mail communications to get information out quickly to targeted people; and a well-conceived social media program.

Much of the process Daigneault et al. (2011) outline is not new, although the use of Internet-based tools combined with more traditional resources and techniques presents a powerful solution to the typical twin problems of getting people to respond to calls for activism and the need to raise funds. For example, Daigneault et al. describe who the best targets are for a call to action, followed by a fundraising appeal. As one would surmise, a good candidate is someone who has taken one advocacy action on behalf of the organization in the previous 12 months.

More appropriate targets are, however, first-time activists who have done something in the past day, repeat activists who have done something in the past week, lapsed donors who have done something in the past month, or "basic activists" who have been active two to five times in the past year. Finally, the best candidates for a new appeal are repeat activists who have done something in the past day, current donors who have been active within the past month, and "super activists" who have participated in six or more actions during the past year (Daigneault et al., 2011). This type of segmentation of a group's members is not new; what is useful information to add is the way to connect past activity rates with what advocacy groups can expect of their members through the use of new technologies such as "donate now" buttons on information-based websites, targeted e-mails, and follow-up information based on auto-responder software.

SOCIAL JUSTICE BATTLES WILL INTENSIFY AT THE STATE AND LOCAL LEVELS

As state and local governments confront increased fiscal pressures, some are making cuts to many social programs. On the current and future chopping blocks are programs that affect housing, education, nutritional services, energy assistance, environmental conditions, and welfare. Because aid recipients are often poorly organized and usually unable to coalesce into a powerful political presence, they frequently will be the ones affected by the deepest cuts (Postmus & Hahn, 2007).

Medicaid is a good example of the impact of forces currently at work. Because of the fiscal stimulus bill passed by Congress in 2009, states received, on average, $2.68 for each dollar they spent on the program. This funding allowed states to respond to the increasing numbers of recipients who were enrolling due to the financial problems they experienced during the prolonged recession. Once the stimulus funds ran out in July 2011, however, reimbursement rates returned to pre-stimulus levels. (This involves a $1.60 match from the federal government for each dollar spent by the states.)

Still hurting from weakened economies, states began to look for ways to reduce their Medicaid spending. They have increased copayments for recipients and cut reimbursement rates for providers. Lower rates lead to fewer doctors and other health professionals who are willing to accept Medicaid patients, creating a downward spiral of health care accessibility. When people do not seek treatment with family care providers, illnesses often get worse, leading to more extensive use of public hospital emergency rooms, which then leads to higher costs (Luhby, 2011). Nursing-home providers also experienced substantial rate cuts. In Texas, for example, rate reductions caused potential problems for at least 45,000 elderly residents (Luhby, 2011).

These problems are not confined to the Medicaid program. In Washington State, 5,000 families were cut from the Temporary Assistance for Needy Families (TANF) rolls in a single day. Those remaining on TANF had their benefits reduced by 15% (Jenkins, 2011). Arizona cut 1,600 families (including 2,700 children) off the program in May, 2015 (Roberts, 2015).

Due to a new law, food aid recipients in Michigan face the loss of benefits if they have more than $5,000 in assets (Barber, 2011). According to National Public Radio (NPR), many states are reducing the budgets of programs to prevent child abuse (Fessler, 2010). County and local officials trying to save money in Topeka, Kansas, temporarily stopped prosecuting domestic violence cases (Curry, 2011).

In each of these cases, the underlying debate is about the proper role of government and who should pay taxes to support programs aimed at the common good. All too frequently, people whose conception of justice is individual rather than social and who prefer policies that lower taxes and allow those in need to do without are winning the political battles. As state and local governments continue to look for ways to save money, they may turn increasingly to contracting out the administration of services to the private sector. As Squillace (2010) warns, however, turning public administration over to private bodies decreases accountability and transparency. In the future, advocates may need to adopt additional practices and develop skills as monitors of the regulatory process to respond to changes in the way services are administered.

HOW CAN YOU BECOME A SOCIAL JUSTICE ADVOCATE AT THE STATE AND LOCAL LEVEL?

The information shared in this chapter might have the unintended outcome of leading you to think there is little you can do to affect policy at the state and local level. You may even believe that social justice advocacy just sounds too lonely or too difficult. That is not the intention at all—in fact, it is only when you know the facts about the situation that you can truly prepare yourself to participate in effective advocacy efforts. Now that you have more information about state and local advocacy, here are some practical steps you can take to become an advocate for social justice as a social worker.

First, choose a policy arena you are interested in now and believe you can stick with for the long haul. It takes a while to get to know the background and the ins and outs of any policy area, whether you're interested in stopping sex trafficking, ending poverty, preventing child abuse and neglect, changing laws around interpersonal violence, or any other of the vital areas where social workers advocate. You will have more impact if you can become an acknowledged expert in a topic than if you know a little bit about a lot of things.

Second, find one or more existing organizations you agree with that are active in that policy arena. Link with their efforts—there is always strength in numbers. Knowing you have the support of others who are interested in the same topic can help keep you motivated as well, and you can keep others going, too.

In these groups you will find policy practice mentors who can discuss strategic and tactical options that lead to achieving short- and long-term goals. Mentors can speed up your learning process greatly and also guide you around common "rookie errors." You need them for your learning, and they need you and others to keep advocacy fresh. You will often have perspectives that are different and important to share, as well as greater sophistication in the use of new technology or the various avenues that could be used to approach different generations effectively.

Third, recognize and celebrate every small victory. Policy advocacy at the state and local level is not always easy. It is a marathon, not a sprint. You and your colleagues may lose often. But you will also win, at least sometimes, and celebrating those wins sustains you as you grow stronger in knowledge, skill, and influence. Every step towards greater social justice is an important one.

SUMMARY AND CONCLUSION

State and local advocacy always occurs in a particular context, which social workers need to understand before seeking to effect policy changes. Some of the critical contextual factors today are the impact of unregulated funding for political campaigns, continued decentralization of policymaking, decreases in government funding, and the development of social networking and communications technology and software. For social workers, these underlying factors are also affected by obstacles to advocacy such as inadequate preparation, practical barriers, and negative attitudes about politics.

Finally, there are structural variables that affect state and local advocacy. These include the differences between state and local advocacy and advocacy at the national level; variations in states' political cultures; and the extent of partisan control of state and local government institutions. What constitutes "best practices" in advocacy, therefore, differs considerably from one state to the next and from one local area to another. This requires advocates to understand their state, city, county, or school district in depth. Only then can social workers determine which of a variety of advocacy techniques would be the best particular combination in their community.

To be effective in the future, advocates at the state and local level will have to assimilate a great deal of information in a very short time. Yet the compelling need to do so may spur them to take on this challenge. Only by understanding the political context, mastering the tools available, and maintaining a desire to promote social justice for all can social workers live up to the high demands of the NASW *Code of Ethics* (2008) and play a key role in the policy struggles that lie ahead. Those struggles will not be solely in Washington, DC. They will be in every state capital, in every county courthouse, and in every city hall throughout America.

Discussion Questions and Exercises

1. Take a quick poll among your friends. How many of them know who their local- and state-level elected officials are (governor, state senators, state representatives, mayor, city council member)? How many

know who their federal-level elected officials are (senators, representatives, president)? If there is a difference in knowledge, why do you think it exists?

2. What are some social policy issues that are much more common at the state or local level than at the federal level? What are issues that are much more prominent at the federal level? Which have more immediate impact on you and your friends? Explain why.

3. Locate information on political donations to members of your state and local government (governor and state legislators, as well as judges and elected officials at the local level). Can you find in patterns the information? Are contributions spread across many people or do they seem to be concentrated in the hands of relatively few people?

4. Look up information on your state's political culture as defined by Elazar (1972). What effect, if any, do you see on your state's social policies that may be linked to its political culture?

5. Choose a social policy issue that is important in your locality or state. Who, specifically, is making the decisions about that issue? How could you contact that person or persons?

6. Having identified a particular person you could contact regarding this issue, make an appointment to talk with that person, or write a letter, send an e-mail, or make a phone call stating your view on the issue.

7. Do you believe that social workers you know fully fulfill the NASW *Code of Ethics* (2008) mandate to perform advocacy? Why or why not?

Suggested Websites

Find the websites for your state's legislative bodies and governor.

Look up the websites of municipal and county governments in your area.

Explore the website for your state chapter of the National Association of Social Workers.

American Psychological Association. (2012). Resources for grassroots and state-level advocacy. Retrieved from http://www.apa.org/pi/lgbt/resources/policy/state-advocacy.aspx

California Youth Empowerment Network. (2012). State level advocacy. Retrieved from http://ca-yen.org/policy-advocacy/

Influencing State Policy: http://www.statepolicy.org/

National Conference of State Legislatures: http://www.ncsl.org/

National Governors Association: http://www.nga.org/cms/home.html

The Henry J. Kaiser Family Foundation State Health Facts: http://kff.org/statedata//

U.S. Census Bureau: State and County QuickFacts: http://www.census.gov/quickfacts/table/PST045215/00

Suggestions for Further Reading

Graves, L. (2016, May 5). ALEC's 2016 agenda moving in the states: A snapshot. The Center for Media and Democracy's PR Watch. Retrieved from http://www.prwatch.org/news/2016/05/13099/alec%27s-2016-agenda-snapshot

Hoefer, R. (2016). *Advocacy practice for social justice* (3rd ed.). Chicago: Lyceum.

McNutt, J., & Menon, G. (2008). The rise of cyberactivism: Implications for the future of advocacy in the human services. *Families in Society, 89*(1), 33–38. doi: 10.1606/1044-3894.3706

Squillace, J. (2010). The effect of privatization on advocacy: Social work state-level advocacy with the executive branch. *Families in Society, 91*(1), 25–30. doi: 10.1606/1044-3894.3951

Tan, Y., & Weaver, D. (2009). Local media, public opinion and state legislative policies: Agenda setting at the state level. *International Journal of Press/Politics, 14*(4), 454–476.

Teater, B. (2009). Influencing state legislators: A framework for developing effective social work interest groups. *Journal of Policy Practice, 8*(1), 69–86.

References

Alexander, N. A., & Rolle, A. (2008). *Translation of values into dollars: A look at policy values and spending.* Paper presented at the annual meeting of the Midwest Political Science Association, Chicago, IL.

Almond, G., & Verba, S. (1965). *The civic culture: Political attitudes and democracy in five nations.* Boston: Little, Brown.

Baiker, K., Clemons, J., & Singhal, M. (2011). The rise of the states: Fiscal decentralization in the postwar period. Harvard Kennedy School. Retrieved from https://surveys.udmercy.edu/limesurvey/index.php?sid=32841&lang=en

Barber, B. (2011, October 13). State cuts could mean hundreds face loss of welfare food assistance in Great Lakes Bay region. *Saginaw News.* Retrieved from http://www.mlive.com/news/saginaw/index.ssf/2011/10/state_cuts_mean_hundreds_face.html

Bielefeld, W., & Corbin, J. (1996). The institutionalization of nonprofit human service delivery: The role of political culture. *Administration and Society, 28*(3), 362–389.

Center for Budget Priorities and Public Policy (2016, March 4). Policy basics: Where do our Federal tax dollars go? Retrieved from http://www.cbpp.org/research/federal-budget/policy-basics-where-do-our-federal-tax-dollars-go

Chambers, D. E., & Wedel, K. R. (2009). *Social policy and social programs: A method for the practical public policy analyst,* (5th ed.) Boston: Pearson Education.

Chantrill, C. (2012). US federal government FY10 budget. Retrieved from http://www.usgovernmentspending.com/federal_budget_fy10bs12011n_4041#usgs302

Cochran, G., Montgomery, K., & Rubin, A. (2010). Does evidence-based practice influence state legislators' decision-making process? An exploratory study. *Journal of Policy Practice, 9*(3–4), 263–283.

Comerford, S. (2003). Confronting power: Undergraduates engage the legislative process in Vermont. *Social Policy Journal, 2*(2–3), 123–143.

Council on Social Work Education. (2008, 2015). *Educational policy and accreditation standards.* Alexandria, VA: Author. Retrieved from http://www.cswe.org/File.aspx?id=13780

CQ-Roll Call (2015a). *How to track state legislation.* Washington DC: Congressional Quarterly.

CQ-Roll Call (2016, Jan. 12). Thank your lucky stars you're not a state legislator in 2016: Here's why. Retrieved from http://cqrollcall.com/statetrackers/thank-your-lucky-stars-youre-not-a-state-legislator-in-2016-heres-why/

Crouch, R. C., & Abbot, D. (2009). Is green education blue or red? State-level environmental education program development through the lens of red- and blue-state politics. *Journal of Environmental Education, 40*(3), 52–62.

Curry, C. (2011, October 12). Topeka DA will again prosecute domestic violence after all. *ABC News.* Retrieved from http://abcnews.go.com/US/topeka-kansas-repeals-domestic-violence-law-amid-budget/story?id=14720962

Daigneault, S., Davis, M., & Sybrant, M. (2011, June). *Connecting online advocacy and fundraising.* Charleston, SC: Blackbaud. Retrieved from http://www.blackbaud.com/files/resources/downloads/WhitePaper_ConnectingOnlineAdvocacyAndFundraising.pdf

Dunlop, J., & Fawcett, G. (2008). Technology-based approaches to social work and social justice. *Journal of Policy Practice, 7*(2–3), 140–154.

Edwards, H., & Hoefer, R. (2010). Are social work advocacy groups using Web 2.0 effectively? *Journal of Policy Practice, 9*(3–4), 220–239.

Elazar, D. E. (1972). *American federalism: A view from the states.* New York: Thomas Y. Crowell.

Ezell, M. (2001). *Advocacy in the human services.* Belmont, CA: Brooks/Cole.

Fessler, P. (2010, March 2). State budget cuts threaten child welfare programs. *NPR.* Retrieved from http://www.npr.org/templates/story/story.php?storyId=124127356

Fisher, P., & Pratt, T. (2006). Political culture and the death penalty. *Criminal Justice Policy Review, 17*(1), 48–60.

Fowler, F. C. (2004). *Policy studies for educational leaders: An introduction.* Upper Saddle River, NJ: Pearson, Prentice Merrill Hall.

Gallup. (2011, April 29). *Americans pick spending cuts over taxes to reduce deficit.* Retrieved from http://www.gallup.com/video/147320/Video-Deficit-Ryan-Obama.aspx

Gershtenson, J., Mangun, W. R., & Smith, B. W. (2004). *The Republican revolution and the dynamics of environmental policy voting.* Paper presented at the annual meeting of the Midwest Political Science Association, Chicago, IL.

Graves, L. (2016, May 5). ALEC's 2016 agenda moving in the states: A snapshot. The Center for Media and Democracy's PR Watch. Retrieved from http://www.prwatch.org/news/2016/05/13099/alec%27s-2016-agenda-snapshot

Hale, K., & McNeal, R. (2010). Election administration reform and state choice: Voter identification requirements and the HAVA. *Policy Studies Journal, 38*(2), 281–302.

Hoefer, R. (2000a). Human services interest groups in four states: Lessons for effective advocacy. *Journal of Community Practice, 7*(4), 77–94.

Hoefer, R. (2000b). Making a difference: Human service interest groups influence on social welfare program regulations. *Journal of Sociology and Social Welfare, 27*(3), 21–38.

Hoefer, R. (2001). Highly effective human service interest groups: Seven key practices. *Journal of Community Practice, 9*(2), 1–13.

Hoefer, R. (2005). Altering state policy: Interest group effectiveness among state-level advocacy groups. *Social Work, 50*(1), 219–227.

Hoefer, R. (2016). *Advocacy practice for social justice* (3rd ed.). Chicago: Lyceum.

Hoefer, R., & Ferguson, K. (2007). Moving the levers of power: How advocacy organizations affect the regulation-writing process. *Journal of Sociology and Social Welfare, 34*(1), 83–108.

Jenkins, A. (2011, February 2). States cut benefits to welfare families. Retrieved from http://kplu.org/post/state-cuts-benefits-welfare-families

Joslyn, R. A. (1980). Manifestations of Elazar's political subcultures: State public opinion and the content of political campaign advertising. *Publius, 10*(2), 37–58.

Kennedy, L. (2015). Top 5 ways *Citizen's United* harms democracy and top 5 ways we're fighting to take democracy back. *Demos.* Retrieved from http://www.demos.org/publication/top-5-ways-citizens-united-harms-democracy-top-5-ways-we%E2%80%99re-fighting-take-democracy-back

Koven, S., & Mausolff, C. (2002). The influence of political culture on state budgets: Another look at Elazar's formulation. *American Review of Public Administration, 32*(1), 66–77.

Lee, J., & Donlan, W. (2009). Cultural, political, and social influences on state-level indigent health care policy formulation. *Journal of Policy Practice, 8*(2), 129–146.

Louis, K., Thomas, E., Gordon, M., & Febey, K. (2008). State leadership for school improvement: An analysis of three states. *Educational Administration Quarterly, 44*(4), 562–592.

Luhby, T. (2011, March 28). Shrinking Medicaid funds pummel states. *CNNMoney.* Retrieved from http://money.cnn.com/2011/03/28/news/economy/medicaid_states/index.htm

Malm, L. & Crosby, J. (2016, February 23). Which states have state budget deficits or shortfalls? That question is harder to answer than you'd think. Retrieved from https://www.multistate.com/insider/2016/02/which-states-have-a-budget-deficit-that-question-is-harder-to-answer-than-youd-think/

Mayer, J. (2011, October 10). State for sale. *The New Yorker.* Retrieved from http://www.newyorker.com/magazine/2011/10/10/state-for-sale;

McCurdy, A. H. (1998). The case of collective bargaining provisions and a test of Elazar's and Lieske's measures of political culture. *Review of Public Personnel Administration, 18*(1), 23–38.

McDermott, K. (2015, January 19), At $37 million and counting, mega-donor Sinquefield says he's not going anywhere. *St. Louis Post Dispatch.* Retrieved from http://www.stltoday.com/news/local/metro/at-million-and-counting-mega-donor-sinquefield-says-he-s/article_9f75ba07-618d-56ff-bd47-2a35ee-2a2e5e.html

McNutt, J., & Boland, K. (1999). Electronic advocacy by non-profit organizations in social welfare policy. *Non-Profit and Voluntary Sector Quarterly, 28*(4), 432–451.

McNutt, J., & Menon, G. (2008). The rise of cyberactivism: Implications for the future of advocacy in the human services. *Families in Society, 89*(1), 33–38. DOI: 10.1606/1044–3894.3706

Mead, L. M. (2004). State political culture and welfare reform. *Policy Studies Journal, 32*(2), 271–296.

Meslin, D. (2011, April 12). *The antidote to apathy.* Retrieved from http://www.ted.com/talks/dave_meslin_the_antidote_to_apathy.html

Morgan, D. R., & Anderson, S. K. (1991). Assessing the effects of political culture: Religious affiliation and county political behavior. *Social Science Journal, 28*(2), 163–174.

National Association of Social Workers. (NASW) (2008). *Code of ethics.* Washington, DC: Author. Retrieved from https://www.socialworkers.org/pubs/code/code.asp

Oliff, P., Mai, C., & Palacios, V. (2012, June 27). *States continue to feel recession's impact.* Washington, DC: Center for Budget and Policy Priorities. Retrieved from http://www.cbpp.org/cms/?fa=view&id=711

Page, B., Bartels, L., & Seawright, J. (2013). Democracy and the policy preferences of wealthy Americans. *Perspectives on Politics, 11*(1), 51–73. DOI: http://dx.doi.org/10.1017/S153759271200360X

Peters, J., & Welch, S. (1978). Politics, corruption, and political culture: A view from the state legislature. *American Politics Research, 6*(3), 345–356.

Plitt-Donaldson, L. (2007). Advocacy by nonprofit human service agencies. *Journal of Community Practice, 15*(3), 139–158.

Plitt-Donaldson, L., & Shields, J. (2009). Development of the Policy Advocacy Behavior Scale: Initial reliability and validity. *Research on Social Work Practice, 19*(1), 83–92.

Postmus, J., & Hahn, S. (2007). The collaboration between welfare and advocacy organizations: Learning from the experiences of domestic violence survivors. *Families in Society, 88*(3), 475–484. doi: 10.1606/1044-3894.3658

Price, B., & Riccucci, N. (2005). Exploring the determinants of decisions to privatize state prisons. *American Review of Public Administration, 35*(3), 223–235.

Reisch, M. (2016). Why macro practice matters. *Journal of Social Work Education, 52*(3), 1–11.

Roberts, L. (2015, May 20). Arizona's leaders cut off help to 2,700 kids. *The Arizona Republic.* Retrieved from http://www.azcentral.com/story/laurieroberts/2015/05/19/tanf-benefits-cut-in-arizona/27610523/

Rothman, J.R. (2013). *Education for macro intervention: A survey of problems and prospects.* Los Angeles: Association of Community Organization and Social Administration. Available online at www.acosa.org.

Shock, D. R. (2008). Securing a line on the ballot: Measuring and explaining the restrictiveness of ballot access laws for non-major party candidates in the United States. *Social Science Journal, 45*(1), 48–60.

Silver, B. D., & Dowley, K. M. (2000). Measuring political culture in multiethnic societies: Reaggregating the world values survey. *Comparative Political Studies, 33*(4), 517–550.

Smucker, B. (1999). *The nonprofit lobbying guide* (2nd ed.). Washington, DC: Independent Sector.

Squillace, J. (2010). The effect of privatization on advocacy: Social work state-level advocacy with the executive branch. *Families in Society, 91*(1), 25–30. doi: 10.1606/1044-3894.3951

Tan, Y., & Weaver, D. (2009). Local media, public opinion and state legislative policies: Agenda setting at the state level. *International Journal of Press/Politics, 14*(4), 454–476.

Teater, B. (2009). Influencing state legislators: A framework for developing effective social work interest groups. *Journal of Policy Practice, 8*(1), 69–86.

Thomas, L. (2010). The variations and strategies of faith-based advocacy organizations in Virginia. *Journal of Policy Practice, 9*(3–4), 240–262.

U.S. Census Bureau. (2011, March). Table 11: Non-Hispanic white alone population and the minority population for the United States, regions, states, and for Puerto Rico: 2000 and 2010. In *Overview of race and Hispanic origin: 2010.* Retrieved from http://www.census.gov/prod/cen2010/briefs/c2010br-02.pdf

Verba, S., & Nie, N. (1972). *Participation in America: Political democracy and social equality.* New York: Harper.

Walker, J., Jr. (1991). *Mobilizing interest groups in America: Patrons, professions and social movements.* Ann Arbor: University of Michigan Press.

Young, D. W., Farrell, J. L., Henderson, C. E., & Taxman, F. S. (2009). Filling service gaps: Providing intensive treatment services for offenders. *Drug and Alcohol Dependence, 103*(1), S33–S42.

Credits

Fig. 9.1: Copyright © 2016 by The Center on Budget and Policy Priorities.

Fig. 9.2: Copyright © 2013 by Miss.Monica.Elizabeth, (CC BY-SA 3.0) at https://commons.wikimedia.org/wiki/File%3AStudents_at_the_March_for_Life_DC_2013.JPG.

Fig. 9.3: Copyright © 2012 by Fibonacci Blue, (CC BY 2.0) at https://commons.wikimedia.org/wiki/File%3ARally_to_support_Planned_Parenthood.jpg.

Fig. 9.4: sookietex / Copyright in the Public Domain.

Fig. 9.5: Copyright © twbuckner (CC by 2.0) at https://commons.wikimedia.org/wiki/File%3AWilliam_Barber_at_Moral_Mondays_rally.jpg.

10

THE JUDICIARY AND SOCIAL POLICY

Vicki Lens, PhD, JD

What do the right of women to have abortions, the racial integration of schools, the invalidation of laws prohibiting sodomy, the abolition of the death penalty for juveniles, and the right to have one's ethnicity considered in an application for law school all have in common? They are just a few of the results of decisions made by the U.S. Supreme Court, a powerful actor in the nation's social policy arena. This chapter examines the role of the judiciary in shaping, changing, and creating social policy. After a brief historical overview, the structure of the judiciary system is described, including where and how cases involving social welfare issues are brought to its attention. Next, the process by which courts decide cases and create social policy is explained; this includes making law when no legislation exists and interpreting laws and the Constitution. Landmark Supreme Court decisions arising from the constitutional clauses that most affect social welfare legislation and social justice, including the Equal Protection and Due Process Clauses of the Fourteenth Amendment and the Commerce Clause, are discussed. The advantages and disadvantages of the judiciary playing a key role in social policy development and implementation are explored. Finally, the role of social workers in the judicial policymaking process is discussed.

HISTORICAL OVERVIEW

Throughout U.S. history, the judiciary, particularly the Supreme Court, has often decided the nation's policy debates, determining what can or cannot be done to address pressing social problems or issues. During the Progressive Era, as the philosophy of laissez-faire government was replaced with a more interventionist approach, legislative disputes turned into legal ones as the losers in the legislative arena challenged newly enacted laws in the courts. In the early

20th century, when New York State legislators sought to improve the working conditions of the working poor by passing legislation limiting the number of hours a baker could work to 10 hours a day, the Supreme Court invalidated the law. In *Lochner v. New York* (1905) it held that the law constituted an "unreasonable, unnecessary and arbitrary interference with the right and liberty of the individual to contract" (p. 56) under the Due Process Clause of the Constitution. Only three years later, in *Muller v. Oregon* (1908), the same court upheld an Oregon law restricting the number of hours a woman could work to 10 daily. The court rationalized these rulings based on the difference between the sexes, and by framing the protection of women's health as an issue of public concern:

> That woman's physical structure and the performance of maternal functions place her at a disadvantage in the struggle for subsistence is obvious ... by abundant testimony of the medical fraternity continuance for a long time on her feet at work, repeating this from day to day, tends to injurious effects upon the body, and as healthy mothers are essential to vigorous offspring, the physical well-being of woman becomes an object of public interest and care in order to preserve the strength and vigor of the race (p. 412).

The *Muller* and *Lochner* cases illustrate several basic principles about the role of the judiciary in social policy that resonate in the present day: that courts can act as a deterrent or catalyst for social change; that the path they will choose is often hard to predict and can shift over time; and that its decisions, while based in law and legal reasoning, are also influenced by the social, political, and cultural milieu of the day. Notwithstanding such uncertainties and extra-legal influences, specific principles and procedures guide the judiciary and distinguish its activities from legislative and executive policymaking. These include the ways policy issues come to the judiciary's attention and its decision-making process.

TYPES OF POLICY DISPUTES BEFORE THE JUDICIARY

One of the most significant differences between the judiciary and the other branches of government is that, unlike the executive and legislative branches, it cannot initiate a policy dispute. Courts must wait until a dispute is brought before them in the form of a lawsuit filed by one party against another. However, in virtually every domain of interest to social workers, including mental health, child welfare, education, health care, and public assistance, disputes have emerged that required court intervention and resulted in court decisions with significant implications for social policy.

Frequently, such disputes involve government programs, benefits, or practices. For example, a landmark Supreme Court case, *Goldberg v. Kelly* (1970), prevented government officials from terminating welfare benefits without giving recipients an opportunity to challenge the cut-off at a hearing. A court decision in *Thurman v. the City of Torrington* (1984) shaped domestic violence policy. The case involved police officers who stood by and refused to intervene as Tracy Thurman's estranged husband beat her, resulting in severe injuries. By holding that police officers have an affirmative duty to assist victims of domestic violence disputes, the Court significantly altered the ways police departments responded to such complaints.

Disputes between private parties can also shape social policy. An example is the case of *In re Baby M* (1988), involving a surrogacy agreement between a married couple and a young woman who agreed to be artificially inseminated with the husband's sperm and relinquish her rights to the baby for adoption by the couple. When the surrogate mother refused to turn over the baby upon its birth, the couple asked the New Jersey state court to resolve the dispute. The court invalidated the surrogacy agreement but required the young woman to give the child to the couple because it was in the "best interests" of the child. The court thus set social policy on the practice of surrogacy and determined the standard for deciding future custody disputes involving surrogates.

THE STRUCTURE OF THE COURT SYSTEM

Cases enter the judiciary through one of two paths: state or federal. Each state has its own independent court system, and a federal court system operates throughout the nation. The two systems are parallel; one does not have authority over the other. A decision by the U.S. Supreme Court, however, can overrule a decision made by state courts. The state court system has jurisdiction over disputes involving state constitutions and state laws, while the federal court system hears disputes involving federal law and the U.S. Constitution. Some common types of state laws involving social welfare include statutes regarding criminal and juvenile delinquency, family situations—including divorce, custody, and adoption—child welfare, health and mental health, education, and public assistance. While federal and state laws can overlap—for example, in the provision of education, child welfare, and public welfare benefits—there are also some distinct areas. For example, immigration and national defense are exclusively under the jurisdiction of the federal government, and family law is primarily the province of the states.

In the examples above, both *Kelly* and *Thurman* were decided in the federal court system because they involved issues of U.S. constitutional law. In *Kelly*, the issue was whether the Due Process Clause of the U.S. Constitution required a hearing before benefits were discontinued. In *Thurman*, the plaintiff claimed that the Equal Protection Clause of the U.S. Constitution required that police treat victims of domestic violence the same way they treat violence between persons not in a personal relationship. (Both of these clauses are discussed further below.) The case of *Baby M* was heard in state court because it involved issues of contract law and family law, both of which fall within the authority of state courts. A case involving a federal program such as Social Security disability benefits would be heard in federal court, while a case involving state aid to the needy would be heard in state court.

If a case involves both state and federal law, the parties can choose in which court, state or federal, the case will be heard. However, if the state law is of more importance in the case, or should be decided before the federal claim is heard, a federal court may "abstain" from hearing the case until a state court decides the state law issue. For example, an anti-abortion counseling agency being prosecuted by the state in a state court for deceptive business practices, because it advertised as an abortion clinic to lure pregnant women to its premises, sued the state in federal court alleging a violation of its First Amendment rights to free speech under the U.S. Constitution. The federal court refused to hear the case until the state court decided whether the agency was engaged in deceptive business practices under state law, thus possibly obviating the need for the federal lawsuit if the state court determined it was not engaging in deceptive business practices and, hence, was free to continue advertising.

Other cases may involve a conflict between state and federal law; in such cases, a decision will be made by the court as to whether the federal law is supreme and preempts the state law, or whether the state is allowed to legislate in that area notwithstanding the existence of federal law on the same subject. For example, in *Gonzales v. Raich* (2005), the Supreme Court held that a state law that allows the use of marijuana for medical purposes was preempted by a federal law that considers marijuana an illegal substance and is intended as the definitive policy on drug use for all purposes.

Both federal and state courts share the same basic structure, containing both a trial court, where cases are first heard, and appellate courts, where the decision of the trial, or lower court, is reviewed and either upheld or reversed. In both federal and state courts, there are two levels of appellate courts. In the state courts, the names of the various trial and appellate courts may vary from state to state. For example, an appellate court may be called the Supreme Court in one state, while in another state the trial court is referred to as the Supreme Court. The federal courts, which are divided into 13 circuits, with each circuit encompassing several states, are more uniform. The lower court is called the U.S. District Court, the appellate court is called the U.S. Court of Appeals, and the highest court is the Supreme Court of the United States.

How far-reaching policy consequences will be depends on which court—federal or state, trial or appellate—decides a case. A decision by an appellate court is more authoritative than one by a trial court. Decisions are also limited geographically; the one exception is the U.S. Supreme Court. Its decisions apply in every state and in every federal circuit. In all other state and federal courts, decisions apply only to the state, or federal circuit, of the court making the decision.

Thus, the decision by the New Jersey state court in the *Baby M* case above applied only in that state. The decision in *Kelly* applied to all 50 states because it was decided by the U.S. Supreme Court, despite its origin in a single state. In contrast, *Thurman* applied only to the federal circuit in which the case was heard, because it was decided by a federal district court. (Recall that federal circuits are made up of several states.) In such circumstances, however, other states or federal circuits may voluntarily choose to apply the legal rules of that case, especially when an issue is one of "first impression"—that is, the first time *any court* has decided the issue. Such cases may become influential beyond their borders, because people assume courts in other states or federal circuits may decide the same way. This is what happened in the *Thurman* case, which influenced how police departments handled domestic violence cases in other states.

HOW COURTS DECIDE CASES

Courts make law in three ways: (a) by deciding a case where there is no legislation or regulation addressing the issue; (b) by interpreting laws passed by legislatures; and (c) by interpreting and applying the Constitution. In each of these cases, the courts' decisions can shape social policy.

MAKING LAW WHERE NONE EXISTS

In some cases, a dispute that has not been addressed by the legislature comes before a court. The *Baby M* case is an example of this; at the time, surrogacy contracts were a new way for infertile couples to have a child. Thus, no legislatures (or courts) had decided whether or not such contracts were valid and should be enforceable. In such cases, the court must make new law to resolve the dispute. To do this, the court looks back to previous court cases where similar issues have been decided, applying and extending the principles of those cases to the dispute before it. These cases are called **precedents**, and the body of cases and legal principles that emerge from this process are called the **common law**. *Stare decisis* is the legal principle that existing precedents—decisions in previous cases—are to be followed by the court unless the prior principle is overturned or modified.

Another example of particular relevance to social workers is the case of *Tarasoff v. Regents of the University of California* (1976) decided by California's highest court. Tarasoff was the father of a young woman, Tatiana, who was murdered by Prosenjit Poddar, a student at the University of California, Berkeley, whom she had dated. Prior to the murder, Poddar had confided to the campus therapist he was seeing that he wanted to kill Tatiana. The therapist notified campus police, who briefly detained Poddar but then released him when he appeared rational. No one warned Tatiana of the threat to her life. After she was murdered, her father sued the University of California, claiming it acted negligently when it failed to warn Tatiana of the danger she was in. In response, the university claimed that it did not have a duty of care to Tatiana or her parents, did not act negligently, and was not responsible for her death.

At the time, there were no laws requiring therapists to protect individuals who are specifically being threatened by a therapy client. While ethics, a concern for doing what is right and not merely what the law requires, may have led the therapist to warn Tatiana, a court decision must be based solely on the law. The court thus turned to prior case law (or precedents) where courts had enunciated the principle that no person owed a duty to control the conduct of another, or to warn those endangered by such conduct, except where there was a special relationship to the person whose conduct needed to be controlled. The court found that a special relationship existed between Poddar and his therapist and that it extended to third parties such as Tatiana, requiring the therapist to break confidentiality with his client and help Tatiana by taking steps to protect her life. Noting that "the protective privilege [of confidentiality] ends where the public peril begins" (p. 347), the court held that "when a therapist determines, or pursuant to the standards of his profession should determine, that his patient presents a serious danger of violence to another, he incurs an obligation to use reasonable care to protect the intended victim against such danger" (p. 340).

This case marked the first time that therapists were found to have duties that extended beyond the therapeutic relationship to people who may be harmed by their clients, thus constituting a major change in social policy. After the decision, many states adopted "duty to warn" legislation. Thus, this case is an example of how a single state court decision by the California Supreme Court influenced public policy across the country.

In sum, when there is no existing law that will resolve a dispute, courts create new law, in the form of court decisions that elucidate new principles or standards. The court's decision applies only to the case before it, but as noted above, depending on the level of the court (appellate or trial court) and its geographic boundaries, the court's decision will influence how other similar disputes are resolved. It may also serve as a template and trigger for legislation on the social issue being addressed.

INTERPRETING LAWS

Another way that courts make social policy is by interpreting laws passed by the legislative branch. As anyone who has observed the legislative process knows, it is often a confusing and cantankerous process. The compromises necessary to get a law passed often result in vague and unclear language that can be interpreted in different ways. Laws are also intentionally written with broad strokes because they are meant for general application and because lawmakers cannot anticipate every situation that may arise. The details are added later, by the executive agency in charge of implementing the law, in the form of regulations and guidelines. Disputes arising under the law are also heard by the courts, which further clarify and interpret the law in the context of these disputes. Using a variety of sources, including the intent and purpose of the law (often derived from its legislative history and floor debates), the common meaning of words, the way certain terms have been used and interpreted in other similar laws, and (more controversially) the judges' assessments of which policies make sense, courts will decide how the law will be applied and what situations it will cover.

An illustrative example involves Title VII of the Civil Rights Act, which outlawed discrimination. The legislative language states:

> It shall be an unlawful employment practice for an employer to fail or refuse to hire or to discharge any individual, or otherwise to discriminate against any individual with respect to

his compensation, conditions, or privileges of employment, because of such individual's race, color, religion, sex or national origin (*Civil Rights Act of 1964*, U.S. Public Law 88–352, 78 Stat. 241).

This law, like many others, is written in broad, general terms. It does not define key phrases. For example, what is meant by "conditions" of employment? Does it include the work environment itself and the ways people behave toward one another at work? Does it include such things as racial or sexual harassment? What if that racial or sexual harassment does not result in economic harm such as a lost job or reduced pay, or even psychological harm? Does the law still prevent it?

Executive agencies, as noted above, provide some of the answers as they implement regulations. In this instance, the Equal Opportunity Employment Commission, the agency charged with enforcing the law, issued a regulation providing that harassing conduct violates the law if "it has the purpose or effect of unreasonably interfering with an individual's work performance or creating an intimidating, hostile, or offensive work environment." But it is the court that decides whether such regulations are consistent with the law, while also further clarifying and elaborating what the law means.

This is what the Supreme Court did in the case of *Harris v. Forklift* (1993), which involved a supervisor at an equipment rental company who harassed his female employees with verbal insults and gestures. He made sexual innuendos and once asked several female employees to fish coins out of his front pants pocket. The employees suffered neither economic nor psychological harm. The court found that such conduct constituted sexual harassment and created a hostile work environment. It further found that the women affected did not have to prove psychological harm. The court explained: "Title VII comes into play before the harassing conduct leads to a nervous breakdown" (p. 22). It recognized that such conduct "can and often will detract from employees' job performance, discourage employees from remaining on the job, or keep them from advancing in their careers" (p. 22).

By holding that sexual harassment was a form of sexual discrimination, and that women need not be economically or psychologically harmed before suing, the court expanded the reach of the Civil Rights Act, making it possible for more people to sue for violations of the law. The court's decision also transformed the ways workplaces across the nation handled such complaints and monitored the work environment. It is, therefore, a prime example of how courts shape social policy.

Both state and federal courts have many such opportunities to expand, narrow, and fill in the gaps of laws passed by legislative bodies. It is often in the courts where such phrases as "danger to oneself or others" allowing forcible commitment to a mental institution, the "best interests of the child" in child welfare law, or the requirement that "reasonable accommodations" be made in the workplace for disabled people under the Americans With Disabilities Act, to name just a few examples, are given form and meaning.

Statutory interpretation may also change over time, diluting and even eviscerating laws previously upheld by the courts. This is what occurred in *Shelby v. Alabama* in 2013 when the Supreme Court invalidated a key provision of the 1965 Voting Rights Act, which required that certain states with a history of voter suppression obtain clearance from the Justice Department or the courts when changing their voting procedures. The court claimed that the clearance provision no longer applied to such states because it did not reflect current conditions, and was based on decades old data on voter suppression practices, such as literacy tests, which had since been eliminated. This change in statutory interpretation not only let states off the hook from federal supervision, but made challenging newer forms of voter suppression, such as voter I.D. requirements, reductions in early voting hours, elimination of same day voter registration, and cuts in the number of polling places, more difficult to regulate.

Perhaps the most notable and visible way the courts, and in particular the Supreme Court, shape policy is when they interpret the Constitution. Unlike legislation, which legislators can amend if they do not agree with the court's interpretation of the law, the Supreme Court has the final say as to what the words of the Constitution mean. Those words, similar to statutes, are also broad and vague. They also reflect inspirational and ideological notions of what our democracy should look like. Thus, phrases such as "no State shall deny to any person within its jurisdiction the equal protection of the law" (Fourteenth Amendment, Sec. 1) or that no state shall deprive any person "of life, liberty, or property without due process of law" (Fourteenth Amendment, Sec. 1) can have dissimilar meanings for different people.

It is the Supreme Court that decides these conflicts, reshaping the social welfare landscape with its decisions and often seesawing between liberal or conservative interpretations of these phrases as the composition of the court changes. The court is composed of nine justices, who serve for life. They are appointed by the president, with the consent of the Senate. Thus, which party is in power—Republican or Democrat—when a Supreme Court vacancy occurs can affect the ideological composition of the court. Changing social mores and expectations can also influence who is appointed to the court. For example, prior to 1967, when Thurgood Marshall was appointed, no African Americans had served on the court. Sandra Day O'Connor, appointed in 1981, was the first woman to serve on the court. The court's present composition includes three women, including the first Latina to serve on the court, Sonia Sotomayor, and one African American man, Clarence Thomas (see Table 10.1).

Ideological distinctions are reflected in the different philosophical approaches to interpreting the Constitution, which include textualists, originalists, doctrinalists, and developmentalists (or proponents of the "living Constitution").

Textualists rely only on the words of the U.S. Constitution, seeking their ordinary meaning without relying on other texts or outside sources, such as the legislative history of an act. For example, in interpreting the Sixth Amendment, which says the accused has the right "to be confronted with the witnesses against

Table 10.1 Characteristics of Current Supreme Court Justices.

Justice	Date of Birth	Appointed By	Religion	Ethnicity
Anthony Kennedy	1936	Ronald Reagan (1988)	Roman Catholic	White
Clarence Thomas	1948	George H. W. Bush (1991)	Roman Catholic	African American
Ruth Bader Ginsburg	1933	Bill Clinton (1993)	Jewish	White
Stephen Breyer	1938	Bill Clinton (1994)	Jewish	White
John G. Roberts	1955	George W. Bush (2005)	Roman Catholic	White
Samuel A. Alito, Jr.	1950	George W. Bush (2006)	Roman Catholic	White
Sonia Sotomayor	1954	Barack Obama (2009)	Roman Catholic	Latina
Elena Kagan	1960	Barack Obama (2010)	Jewish	White

Figure 10.1 Comparing the Supreme Court Justices in 1966 to the Supreme Court Justices in 2010 shows how the gender and ethnic makeup of the court has evolved.

Figure 10.2 Comparing the Supreme Court Justices in 1966 to the Supreme Court Justices in 2010 shows how the gender and ethnic makeup of the court has evolved.

him," a textualist would argue that the clause requires face-to-face confrontations. Under this interpretation, the use of screens shielding testifying victims or witnesses (as in cases against organized crime figures) or the use of closed-circuit televisions for testimony (where victims of sexual abuse are minors) would violate this clause because the word *confronted* means a physical encounter.

Originalists look at the text but also analyze the original meaning of the clause based on what the framers intended, or what people at the time understood the words in the clause to mean. They rely not just on the literal meanings of the words, as a textualist would, but also on the values and principles underlying the words as written at that time. For example, in interpreting the First Amendment provision that "Congress shall make no law respecting an establishment of religion, or prohibiting the free exercise thereof," originalists would argue that the purpose of the clause at the time was to prohibit the federal government from establishing a national church (as in England) or inter-fering with an individual state's ability to establish religion. They would conclude that it was not intended to prohibit all forms of religious expression, such as nonsectarian prayers at public schools, or in a more extreme interpretation, to prohibit individual states from establishing their own churches. Both textualists and originalists argue that by preserving the original meaning of the founding documents, the bedrock principles of our democracy are preserved and protected against arbitrary changes by unelected judges. Change should occur only through amendments to the Constitution, thus ensuring the people's will.

Doctrinalists believe that the Constitution means what past courts have said it means; reflecting the accumulation of rules and principles decided by the U.S. Supreme Court over time. This approach relies heavily on precedent (previous rulings of the court) and the principle of *stare decisis*, which states that judges are required to respect and follow those previous rulings. Thus, in the example above regarding the First Amendment and religion, the court would look to previous cases deciding the meaning of the clause and would apply the principles of those cases to the facts before it.

Developmentalists believe in what they call a "living Constitution"; they view the Constitution as a foundational but flexible document able to change and grow with society. To developmentalists, past practices and meanings are relevant but not controlling; present interpretations should reflect present contexts. In their view, the genius of the Constitution is in its breadth and flexibility, allowing words from the past to retain meaning in the future. Thus, the Sixth Amendment right of a defendant "to be confronted with the witnesses against him" can be interpreted in light of new technology that allows for different types of confrontation, while still preserving the principle behind the amendment. Evolving social mores, such as a growing acceptance of same-sex relationships or a refusal to execute juveniles, can be integrated into the Constitution's foundational principles regarding liberty or due process.

These different approaches to constitutional interpretation have implications for social change and social justice today, as illustrated by the example of the right to an abortion. A textualist would not find such a right, as it is not mentioned in the text of the Constitution. An originalist would argue that it was never the intent of the framers to cover such practices as abortion in the Constitution. Both would argue that it is up to the legislative branch, not the courts, to decide if abortion should be legal. A doctrinalist would look to past court precedents, which developed the right to privacy in the areas of family, marriage, and procreation. For a developmentalist, who believes in a living Constitution, as abortion became more acceptable and control over reproductive decisions was considered necessary for women to participate equally in society, the Constitution would be interpreted to support a woman's right to an abortion.

Several actual constitutional cases involving abortion are discussed next, along with other seminal cases involving social change and social justice under the Due Process and Equal Protection Clauses and the Commerce Clause. As the discussion of these cases will demonstrate, the different philosophical approaches to constitutional interpretation are woven into these decisions—sometimes directly, other times more subtly.

DUE PROCESS CLAUSE

The **Due Process Clause** has generated some of the most controversial Supreme Court decisions during the past half century because it seeks to define the parameters of core American values such as liberty and the right to privacy. The cases decided under it intrude on the personal and the private. For example, can government control when we have children by outlawing abortion? Can it restrict with whom we have sexual relationships? The court answered no to the first question, and yes and then no to the second.

In its landmark *Roe v. Wade* (1973) decision, the court upheld a woman's right to choose between abortion and childbearing, striking down a Texas state law that criminalized abortion except to save the woman's life. The court located that right in the Due Process Clause of the Fourteenth Amendment, which, as noted above, provides that no state shall deprive any person "of life, liberty, or property without due process of law." It interpreted the clause as requiring more than "due process" before the government takes "life, liberty, or property" away (referred to as procedural due process) but also as including certain substantive rights (referred to as substantive due process)—in this case, the right to an abortion. The court also relied on what it called the "penumbra of rights" flowing from the sum of several provisions of the Bill of Rights and establishing a right to privacy. This interpretation was widely criticized by the conservative dissenting justices on the court, who argued for a strict adherence to the text of the Constitution, noting that the word *privacy* does not appear anywhere in it.

This conservative position was rejected again in *Planned Parenthood v. Casey* (1992), which was a challenge to a law restricting access to, although not prohibiting, abortion. These restrictions included the requirements that women be provided certain information at least 24 hours before an abortion (thus requiring two visits before an abortion was provided), that minors obtain the consent of a parent (with an option to ask a judge for the consent), and that married women notify their husbands of intent to seek an abortion. The law also established various reporting requirements for facilities providing abortions. With the exception of the spousal notification requirement, all these restrictions were upheld. The court, however, reaffirmed the right to an abortion, locating it definitively in the Due Process Clause of the Fourteenth Amendment and, in particular, in the word *liberty*. It relied heavily on the importance of following Supreme Court precedents, noting that "an entire generation has come of age assuming abortions are available and organizing their intimate relationships around it" (p. 860). It also acknowledged what was at stake for women, noting that the "ability of women to participate equally in the economic and social life of the nation has been facilitated by their ability to control their reproductive lives" (p. 856).

However, despite these sentiments, the court also made it easier for states to restrict abortions. It replaced the unfettered right to an abortion in the first 3 months of a pregnancy provided for in *Roe* with a new test allowing the state to elevate its interest in potential life and favor childbirth over abortion. Specifically, it allowed states to regulate abortions as long as they did not impose an "undue burden" or "place a substantial obstacle in the path of a woman" (p. 877). The battleground thus shifted from seeking to outlaw abortions to restricting them, with the test interpreted very broadly, beginning with *Casey*, to allow many such restrictions. In June 2016, in *Whole Woman's Health v. Cole*, a decision as significant as *Casey*, the court reversed this trend when it invalidated a Texas law which required all physicians who perform abortions to have admitting privileges at a hospital and all abortion facilities to meet the same requirements as ambulatory surgical centers. The law would have shut down most abortion facilities throughout the state, making it extremely difficult for women to obtain abortions. The court held that such restrictions constituted an undue burden and a substantial obstacle, while providing few, if any, health benefits.

The court also delved into another very private area of domestic life when it decided whether state laws criminalizing sodomy violated the Due Process Clause. In *Bowers v. Hardwick*, decided in 1986, the court refused to extend "a fundamental right to homosexuals to engage in acts of consensual sodomy" (p. 192). It rejected the idea that homosexual activity was similar to the liberty interests involved in family, marriage, or procreation. Yet, 17 years later (a short time in Supreme Court history), the court reversed itself in *Lawrence v. Texas* (2003), finding that the *Bowers* court failed "to appreciate the extent of the liberty at stake" (p. 513). As the court explained:

> Although the laws involved in Bowers and here purport to do more than prohibit a particular sexual act, their penalties and purposes have more far-reaching consequences, touching upon the most private human conduct, sexual behavior, and in the most private of places, the home.... The liberty protected by the Constitution allows homosexual persons the right to choose to enter upon relationships in the confines of their homes and their own private lives and still retain their dignity as free persons (p. 513).

In another advance for the cause of gay rights, in 2013 the court in *United States v. Windsor* struck down the Defense of Marriage Act (DOMA), which defined marriage for the purposes of federal law as between one man and one woman. Two years later, the court went even further, holding in *Obergefell v. Hodges* (2015) that both the Due Process Clause and the Equal Protection Clause protects the fundamental right of same sex couples to marry. The Court's stirring language, at the end of the decision, demonstrated just how far the court had come in understanding the dignity and rights of gay people:

> In forming a marital union, two people become something greater than they once were. As some of the petitioners in these cases demonstrate, marriage embodies a love that may endure even past death. It would misunderstand these men and women to say they disrespect the idea of marriage. Their plea is that they do respect it, respect it so deeply that they seek to find its fulfillment for themselves. Their hope is not to be condemned to live in loneliness, excluded from one of civilization's oldest institutions. They ask for equal dignity in the eyes of the law. The Constitution grants them that right (p. 28).

These cases under the Due Process Clause illustrate several principles about the court's role in social policy. They demonstrate the fluidity of concepts such as due process and the tremendous power of the court, as the final arbiter of the Constitution, to decide in any given generation what those words mean. They also demonstrate the court's ability to respond to changing social norms when interpreting the Constitution's foundational precepts. Finally, these cases demonstrate the role of precedent in Supreme Court decision making—specifically, that the court often honors precedent, but not always.

The Due Process Clause has also been used to establish important protections for vulnerable populations, such as individuals with mental illness. In *O'Connor v. Donaldson* (1975), the Supreme Court established the principle that the confinement of mentally ill persons who were not dangerous to themselves or others in state institutions violated the Due Process Clause because it unlawfully deprived them of their liberty. The case of *Wyatt v. Aderholt* (1974) elucidated what the Due Process Clause required when the state confined such persons.

Wyatt involved a state mental institution in Alabama that was failing to provide even a minimum standard of care to its residents, among them mentally ill children, who lived in overcrowded wards with no privacy or even the basic rudiments, such as furniture to put clothes away, eating utensils, and access to clean toilet facilities. In lieu of treatment, the residents were placed in seclusion or restraints. A federal court found that such conditions violated the Due Process Clause of the Constitution because it deprived individuals of their liberty without due process of law.

The court-ordered agreements that resulted set basic standards for people with mental illness or developmental disabilities who resided in institutional settings, which have served as a model for other states. These standards, known as the "Wyatt Standards," include the provision of a humane psychological and physical environment, adequate staffing, individualized treatment plans, and minimum restrictions on patient freedom. *Wyatt*, a decision of a federal court below the Supreme Court, is an example of how cases involving the U.S. Constitution do not have to reach the Supreme Court for the judiciary to act as a catalyst for nationwide change. It also demonstrates the judiciary's ability to reshape and restructure our social welfare institutions.

EQUAL PROTECTION CLAUSE

The **Equal Protection Clause** of the Fourteenth Amendment requires the government to treat equally situated people in the same way, reflecting the concept of equity or justice. Many laws classify people; for example, a law prohibiting driving until age 18 classifies people by age based on the assumption that a certain maturity level is necessary to drive a motor vehicle safely. The Equal Protection Clause focuses on the accuracy and reasonableness of these classifications, with certain classifications— specifically those involving race, gender, national origin, or religion—more scrutinized than others. It does not prevent all classifications but requires the government to have a good and valid reason for making classifications when it does.

Over time, through case law, the Supreme Court has elucidated three levels of scrutiny. The underlying rationale among these three standards is that unless certain protected groups are involved, legislatures should be relatively free to decide what laws and policies work best in a given area. The highest level of scrutiny, called strict scrutiny, applies to what the Supreme Court calls a "suspect class," defined as a group that has experienced historical discrimination, is politically less powerful or unrepresented, and has immutable characteristics that are not subject to change or are difficult to change. The court has placed the following characteristics in this category: race, national origin, religion, and alienage (the legal term for the status of a foreigner). Any law that classifies people by these characteristics, either on its face or as applied, must be shown to serve a compelling governmental interest and be narrowly tailored. The practical application of this standard is that very few laws can pass this test; its application has been described as "strict in theory, but fatal in fact" (*Adarand Constructors, Inc. v. Pena*, 1995, p. 237).

The next level of scrutiny is referred to as intermediate scrutiny and applies to "quasi-suspect" classes, which has been defined by the court to include gender and out-of-wedlock children. The standard for judging laws in this category is that they must serve important governmental objectives and be substantially related to achieving those objectives, or must have an exceedingly persuasive justification. This standard is difficult, but not impossible, to meet.

The lowest level of scrutiny, called rational basis, is applied to all classifications that do not fall within the other categories. These include laws regulating business and social welfare. Such laws must be rationally related to a legitimate state interest. Practically, this standard is easy to satisfy. As the court explained in *Dandridge v. Williams* (1970), where it upheld a state law capping the amount of public assistance a family could receive, thus discriminating against large families:

> In the area of commerce and social welfare, a state does not violate the Equal Protection Clause merely because the classifications made by its laws are imperfect. If the classification has some reasonable basis it does not offend the Constitution simply because the classification is not made with mathematical nicety or because in practice it results in some inequality. (p. 485)

The application of these standards is best understood in the context of individual cases. A key case involving gender is *United States v. Virginia* (1996), which challenged the exclusion of women from the Virginia Military Institute (VMI), an all-male public military college in Virginia. In response to earlier court rulings, Virginia proposed a women's military college that used a more cooperative form of learning designed to increase self-esteem and that had fewer resources and less prestige, including fewer PhDs on the faculty and a narrower choice of majors. The issue before the court was whether women's exclusion from VMI and the creation of a parallel program violated the Equal Protection Clause. In deciding which standard to apply, the court noted that "supposed 'inherent differences' are no longer accepted as a ground for race or national origin classifications" (p. 533) but that "physical differences between men and women, however, are enduring" (p. 533) and, thus, the highest level of scrutiny was not required. Nonetheless, it found that Virginia did not have an "exceedingly persuasive justification" for excluding women from VMI. As the court stated:

> "Inherent differences" between men and women, we have come to appreciate, remain cause for celebration, but not for denigration of the members of either sex or for artificial constraints

on an individual's opportunity. Sex classifications may be used to compensate women "for particular economic disabilities [they have] suffered," to "promot[e] equal employment opportunity," to advance full development of the talent and capacities of our Nation's people. But such classifications may not be used, as they once were, to create or perpetuate the legal, social, and economic inferiority of women (pp. 533–534).

The court further noted that women who had "the will and capacity" (*United States v. Virginia,* 1996, p. 542) to withstand VMI's adversative methods should not be excluded. The court found that such exclusion relied on "overbroad generalizations about the different talents, capacities, or preferences of males and females" (p. 533). As the court explained, "generalizations about 'the way women are,' estimates of what is appropriate for *most women,* no longer justify denying opportunity to women whose talent and capacity place them outside the average description" (p. 550). The court also found that the parallel women's program violated the Equal Protection Clause because it was only a "pale shadow" (p. 553) of VMI in multiple ways, including its curriculum, faculty, funding, and prestige.

As noted above, laws that implicate race receive the highest scrutiny from the court. Throughout our history, these decisions have arguably provoked the most debate reflecting the unease and tension underlying the legacy of slavery and racial relations in the United States. Two Supreme Court decisions in particular, *Plessy v. Ferguson* (1896) and *Brown v. Board of Education* (1954), serve as bookends to the evolution of those relationships. *Plessy* upheld a state law requiring railroad companies to provide equal but separate accommodations for African American passengers. The court interpreted the Equal Protection Clause as requiring civil and political equality but not social equality, placing who sat with whom on a train in the latter category. As the court stated, "If one race be inferior to the other socially, the constitution of the US cannot put them on the same plane" (p. 552).

This "separate but equal" doctrine was reversed more than 50 years later in the case of *Brown v. Board of Education* (1954), perhaps one of the best-known Supreme Court cases, which ended the practice of separate schools for black and white children. The court specifically rejected the notion that the Constitution cannot address the social consequences of racial discrimination. Instead, the court made it the centerpiece of its decision by noting that "to separate them [children] from others of similar age and qualifications solely because of their race generates a feeling of inferiority as to their status in the community that may affect their hearts and minds in a way unlikely ever to be undone " (p. 494).

Figure 10.3 Rally in Little Rock, Arkansas, protesting the integration of Central High School in August 1959, five years after the Supreme Court's ruling in Brown v. Board of Education.

Since *Brown,* the court has been a central player as the United States grapples with the legacy of racial discrimination in its present forms. In virtually every area of American life, from education to the workplace to marriage, the court's decisions have determined social policy. Many of its recent decisions have addressed what measures are appropriate to address the harm caused by racial discrimination, such as Affirmative Action programs, which require that race or ethnicity be taken into account to ensure minority participation and to compensate for past wrongs. The use of this standard has, in turn, raised new issues: Can this remedial action itself be a violation of the Equal Protection Clause because it considers race? Can a clause intended to help the disenfranchised also be used to protect the privileged? Is the Equal Protection Clause color-blind?

The Supreme Court has consistently upheld the use of Affirmative Action as a remedy for prior discrimination, although such plans are subject to the same level of scrutiny—strict scrutiny—as any race-based law (see *Adarand Constructors, Inc. v. Pena,* 1995). In other words, whether the intent is malicious or benign, the standard is the same. Whether race-based remedies can go beyond remedial actions and be used primarily to promote diversity has been addressed in the context of education, and specifically in the cases *Grutter v. Bollinger* (2003) and *Gratz v. Bollinger* (2003). *Grutter* and *Gratz* involved, respectively, challenges to the undergraduate and law school admissions process at the University of Michigan. The undergraduate program gave underrepresented ethnic groups an automatic 20-point "diversity" bonus on the point scale used to determine admissions. The law school also used race as a factor but did not give it a specific weight, considering it as one factor among many (e.g., geography, special talents, or demonstration of overcoming adversity).

For the first time, a majority of the court recognized that "student body diversity is a compelling state interest that can justify the use of race in university admissions" (*Grutter v. Bollinger, 2003*, p. 325), noting the "educational benefits that flow from student body diversity" (p. 330), both in learning outcomes and preparing students to participate in a diverse workforce. As noted above, strict scrutiny requires, in addition to a compelling interest, that the methods used are narrowly tailored, meaning that there are no other workable alternatives that do not rely so heavily on race. The court found that the use of race in undergraduate admissions failed to meet this standard because it relied on a mechanical and rigid use of race. In contrast, it upheld the law school's use of race because it was but one factor in a holistic and flexible assessment of the candidate. Thus, while rigid race-conscious formulas or a quota system are not appropriate, the court allowed universities "to consider race or ethnicity more flexibly as a 'plus' factor in the context of individualized consideration" (p. 341).

However, in *Fisher v. University of Texas* (2012, 2016), the court signaled that such plans- even holistic ones- will be closely scrutinized. The University of Texas admitted undergraduate students on two tracks. Students who graduated in the top 10% of their class were automatically admitted. A much smaller number were admitted under a holistic review program that considered race along with many other factors. Although the holistic review plan was upheld by the lower courts, the Supreme Court sent it back to the Court of Appeals for a second look, claiming that the court had failed to scrutinize the plan strictly, and had deferred too much to the state's argument that the plan was narrowly tailored to meet diversity goals. The Court of Appeals again upheld the plan and upon appeal, it returned once again to the Supreme Court. This time, however, as a result of the death of Justice Scalia, a consistent opponent of Affirmative Action, the balance on the court shifted. It upheld the University's admission plan and reaffirmed the value of diversity. The court determined that the University's goals—to end stereotypes, promote cross-racial understanding and to prepare students for a diverse workforce—constituted a compelling state interest and that there were no other workable race neutral alternatives.

Race-conscious plans, however, have not fared so well in secondary public schools. In 2007, the court curtailed the use of such remedies in *Parents Involved in Community Schools (PICS) v. Seattle*. The *PICS* case involved a plan in Seattle that used race to determine the composition of the city's public high schools. Specifically, the school district allowed incoming ninth-graders to choose from among any of the district's high schools, ranking however many schools they wished in order of preference. If too many students listed the same school as their first choice, the district employed a series of "tiebreakers" to determine who would fill the open slots at the oversubscribed school. One of the tiebreakers depended on the racial composition of the particular school and the race of the individual student. If an oversubscribed school was not within 10 percentage points of the district's overall white/nonwhite racial balance (41% white, 59% all other groups), the district selected for assignment students whose race brought the school into balance.

The court determined that the plan violated both prongs of strict scrutiny; it did not serve a compelling state interest, nor was it narrowly tailored. It noted that the plan was not required to remedy past racial discrimination by the Seattle schools, which would have justified the use of race-conscious remedies. Nor, according to the court, was it designed to achieve the compelling state interest of diversity, as in *Grutter v. Bollinger* (2003). Rather, the court viewed the determinative role that race played at certain stages in the application process as an unconstitutional form of racial balancing:

> Accepting racial balancing as a compelling state interest would justify the imposition of racial proportionality throughout American society, contrary to our repeated recognition that [a]t the heart of the Constitution's guarantee of equal protection lies the simple command that the Government must treat citizens as individuals, not as simply components of a racial, religious, sexual or national class (p. 730).

Both the majority and dissent in *PICS* claimed the mantle of *Brown*. To the majority, honoring the *Brown* decision meant making no distinction between the beneficent uses of race to remedy past discrimination or achieve diversity and more malevolent uses of race. Both were equally abhorrent. Or, as Justice Kennedy summed it up in his concurrence, "The way to stop discrimination on the basis of race is to stop discrimination on the basis of race" (*PICS v. Seattle*, 2007, p. 748). The dissenters saw the majority's decision as a repudiation of *Brown*, and of the Equal Protection Clause itself, noting "the legal and practical difference between the use of race-conscious criteria in defiance of that purpose, namely to keep the races apart, and the use of race-conscious criteria to further that purpose, namely to bring the races together" (p. 592). The dissenters feared that the majority's decision called into question the many federal and state laws that voluntarily employ racial classifications to ensure inclusiveness.

Whether the decision in *PICS* undermines these laws remains to be seen. Unlike legislation or executive orders that can cover wide swaths of people and issues, Supreme Court decisions are limited to the dispute before the court. And, as we have seen above, precedents can be overturned or fine-tuned based on the context and facts of each case. Like the Due Process Clause, the Equal Protection Clause is also subject to multiple and conflicting interpretations. While the Supreme Court has the final say in determining what the Constitution means, these meanings can change over time in response to changing social conditions, the emergence of new problems, and the development of new policy solutions. Consequently, the larger ramifications of *PICS* will not be clear until the court decides additional cases.

COMMERCE CLAUSE

Unlike the Due Process and Equal Protection Clauses, the relevance of the **Commerce Clause** to social welfare policy and social justice issues is not readily apparent. This clause gives the federal government the power "to regulate commerce with foreign nations, and among the several states, and with Indian Tribes." Significantly, at its founding, the federal government was not granted the inherent right to promote the general welfare of its citizens; its actions must be anchored to a specific power granted to it in the Constitution. The clause that comes closest to granting the federal government a generalized power to promote the general welfare is the Commerce Clause. Because economic and social issues are often intertwined, Congress has been able to use this clause to pass laws addressing such widely divergent issues as discrimination, violence against women, and health care.

The Commerce Clause goes to the very foundation of the U.S. system of government, which is characterized by a centralized national government of limited powers existing alongside 50 autonomous state governments, in a system referred to as federalism. Which level of government—state or federal—has the authority to make policy around certain issues is the central question of federalism. It is also a question that has defined the policy positions of both liberals and conservatives, with conservatives advocating for "states' rights" and limited federal government intervention, and liberals arguing for broader national powers to protect the rights of all citizens in such crucial areas as civil rights.

Prior to the New Deal, the Supreme Court hewed to a narrow interpretation of the Commerce Clause, limiting it to activities that affected economic activity between the states only directly. However, as the nation grew and developed, the Commerce Clause grew with it, and the Court broadly interpreted the word *commerce* to include not just economic activity but any activity that had a substantial effect on interstate commerce. This more expansive interpretation of the word *commerce* supported the liberal view of federalism and allowed Congress to address a multitude of issues such as labor relations, environmental regulations, consumer protection, and workplace safety.

During the 1960s, Congress and the Court significantly expanded the use of the Commerce Clause, with Congress relying on it to pass the Civil Rights Act of 1964, which, among other things, prohibited discrimination in employment and public accommodations (e.g., hotels, restaurants, theaters, and stores). Unable to address such discrimination under the Equal Protection or Due Process Clause (which applies only to government and not private entities, such as businesses), Congress justified its actions through the use of the Commerce Clause. In a key Supreme Court case of this era, *Katzenbach v. McClung* (1964), the court affirmed Congress's ability to extend its reach deep into individual states and private businesses, holding that a small, family-owned restaurant that never served out-of state travelers was nevertheless subject to antidiscrimination laws because it purchased meat from a local supplier who received it from an out-of-state source, thus affecting interstate commerce. In *Heart of Atlanta Motel Inc. v. United States* (1967), the Court made clear it would not second-guess Congress on the proof needed to establish the connection between a regulated activity and commerce. It permitted Congress to rely on anecdotal evidence, and not formalized findings, that racial discrimination by motels and restaurants affected commerce.

With these cases firmly establishing the Commerce Clause as a legitimate basis for combating discrimination, the clause became an instrument for remedying both economic and social problems, as long as Congress could show some connection between them. This was not difficult to do, because most social problems have economic consequences and the Supreme Court lowered the bar for establishing the relationship between a particular problem and the national economy.

However, this expansive interpretation of the Commerce Clause came to an end in 1995, when for the first time in 58 years the Supreme Court struck down a federal law based on the Commerce Clause. The case, *United States v. Lopez* (1995), involved a challenge to the federally enacted Gun Free School Zones Act, which made it a federal crime to knowingly possess a firearm in a school zone. The Court found that there was no connection between illegally possessing a gun and interstate commerce. It rejected arguments that guns cause violent crimes that affect economic activity by increasing insurance costs, by making people hesitant to engage in business in unsafe areas, and by interfering with the educational process and thereby reducing the productivity and efficiency of workers. Although the Supreme Court did not expressly over-rule its previous precedents on the Commerce Clause, it criticized these earlier decisions, indicating that the Court had too easily deferred to Congress's judgment in the past. The Court found that to continue to do so would obliterate the "distinction between what is truly national and what is truly local," thus allowing the federal government to intrude into areas traditionally regulated by the states (p. 567).

The *Lopez* decision was followed by the decision in *United States v. Morrison* (2000), in which the Court similarly limited the reach of the Commerce Clause. *Morrison* involved a challenge to the Violence Against Women Act, which was designed to address the escalating problem of violence against women by providing a new avenue of redress for victims, among other provisions. Recognizing that both the criminal justice system and the state court civil system often failed to fully compensate victims of gender-based violence, Congress provided a new remedy, permitting victims to sue their attackers in federal court for money dam-ages. Congress developed this remedy after 4 years of extensive investigation and voluminous testimony on the extent of violence against women and how this violence affects women's economic opportunities, including lost careers, decreased productivity, and shrinking employment choices, and monetary losses to employers because of absenteeism related to domestic violence. Despite this ample evidence, the Supreme Court invalidated part of the act, holding that "gender-motivated crimes of violence are not, in any sense of the phrase, economic activity" and, hence, cannot be regulated under the Commerce Clause (p. 613). The Court reasserted its concern that Congress might use the Commerce Clause to intrude in areas that should properly be left to the states, including such traditional areas of state concern as marriage, divorce, and child rearing. To prevent such legislation, the Court again distinguished between commerce and noncom-mercial activities that might affect commerce.

The dissenters noted that before *Lopez* in 1995, the Supreme Court would have upheld the act. Why, the dissenters asked, is it valid to use the Commerce Clause to prohibit racial discrimination (see *Heart of Atlanta* and *Katzenbach*) but not to provide a remedy for gender-based violence? The dissent noted that "the voluminous nature of the legislative record here is far more voluminous than the record compiled by Congress and found sufficient in two prior cases upholding Title VII of the Civil Rights Act" (*United States v. Morrison,* 2000, p. 635). The dissent also noted that

> gender-based violence in the 1990s was shown to operate in a manner similar to racial dis-crimination in the 1960s in reducing the mobility of employees and their production and consumption of goods [which] shaped interstate commerce. Like racial discrimination, gen-der-based violence bars its most likely target—women—from full participation in the national economy (pp. 635–636).

Morrison and *Lopez* illustrate the power of the Supreme Court to change the rules of the game, rein-terpreting constitutional clauses in ways that affect Congress's ability, for better or worse, to address social problems. They also illustrate another lesson: that it is often hard to read the tea leaves of Supreme Court decisions and determine how they will rule in future cases. At the time of *Lopez* and *Morrison,* many commentators thought that the use of the Commerce Clause as an instrument for implementing social policy had been severely curtailed. However, subsequent decisions have modified this assessment, with the court upholding the right of Congress to require the states to comply with the Family and Medical Leave Act (*Nevada Department of Human Resources v. Hibbs,* 2003) and to regulate drug policy, even when it involves the noncommercial medicinal use of drug substances such as marijuana (*Gonzales v. Raich,* 2005). This latter case in particular suggests a more expansive interpretation of when noncommercial and local activities can be considered as affecting interstate commerce.

However, the most recent Supreme Court case interpreting the Commerce Clause, decided in June 2012, involving the recently enacted reform of the health care system, the Patient Protection and Affordable Health Care Act of 2010, calls into question this broader interpretation. [See Chapter 14 in this volume for more discussion of this act.] The case involved whether Congress has the authority under the Commerce Clause to require individuals to purchase private health insurance. The Court had to decide whether a decision not to purchase something—in this instance, health insurance—is economic in nature, and whether the aggregate of such individual decisions substantially affects interstate commerce—in this instance, the national health insurance market. While the Court upheld the insurance mandate under Congress's power to levy taxes, it invalidated it under the Commerce Clause on the grounds that the mandate "does not regulate existing commercial activity. Instead it compels individuals to *become* active in commerce" (*National Federation of Independent Business v. Sebelius,* 2012, p. 3). Thus, the Court again appeared to reign in the use of the Commerce Clause in ways that will not become apparent until future Commerce Clause cases are decided. The court's decision on this landmark legislation illustrates once more its critical role in shaping social policy, the difficulty of forecasting its decisions, and the potential consequences of its occasionally unpredictable and surprising actions.

THE ROLE OF SOCIAL WORKERS IN THE JUDICIAL POLICYMAKING PROCESS

Social workers are less visible in the judiciary process than in other advocacy venues. Unlike the policymaking processes in the executive and legislative branches, where there are structured opportunities for input, such as the notice and comment period for regulations and legislative lobbying, the judiciary is primarily the province of lawyers. However, there are still several important roles that social workers could play.

Social workers can identify policy issues that are ripe for judicial intervention. Typically, these are issues that have proven unsolvable in other government venues or where more conciliatory approaches have failed. Social workers are especially suited for identifying such issues because their daily work exposes them to the gaps and weaknesses in our institutions and social safety net. For example, it was social workers within the welfare system who first identified the high rate of wrongful terminations of public assistance, leading to the Supreme Court case *Goldberg v. Kelly* (1970), which required hearings before the termination of cash assistance. Legal advocates who bring such cases often seek plaintiffs whose stories can effectively illustrate the need for judicial intervention. Because social workers are likely to be aware of people who are affected by poorly constructed policies or practices, they can be instrumental in identifying these plaintiffs.

Social workers can also provide evidence in court. While cases are decided based on law, many cases involving social policy also rely on social science evidence. In fact, the first use of such evidence in a Supreme Court case occurred in *Muller v. Oregon* (1908), which employed research gathered by settlement house workers in New York City. In a more recent example, the Supreme Court's decision in *Brown v.*

Board of Education (1954) prohibiting segregation in public schools relied on social science research that determined that segregation caused African American children psychological damage. In sum, by identifying both potential plaintiffs and problems that require judicial intervention and by providing social science evidence, social workers can influence judicial policymaking.

THE JUDICIARY'S ROLE AS SOCIAL CHANGE AGENT: HELP OR HINDRANCE?

As the cases described in this chapter demonstrate, nearly all social and political questions in the United States become legal issues, with the Supreme Court often acting as the final arbiter. We also often turn to the courts when our institutions fail, asking the judiciary to reform practices and rehabilitate our child welfare system, mental hospitals, schools, and prisons. In addition, when legislative and other policy advocacy strategies fall short, we ask the courts to intervene. For example, when state legislatures refused to sanction same-sex marriage, advocates turned to the state courts to establish this right.[1]

Whether the judiciary is an appropriate vehicle for social change has long been debated. One view is that the judiciary has too much power and is ill suited to solving social problems. The judiciary is the only branch of government whose power is virtually unchecked. Many judges, Supreme Court justices in particular, cannot be voted out of office and are not held accountable for their decisions in the same way as legislators or executives are. This presents what is called the counter-majoritarian dilemma, where unelected judges can invalidate laws passed by democratically elected legislatures. When those laws involve complex questions of social policy, the judiciary's deficiencies become even more apparent. Judges are trained in the law; they are not psychiatrists, social workers, penologists, educators, or trained in any of the other disciplines whose expertise is needed to address controversial social problems.

The search for solutions to policy dilemmas also requires reconciling conflicting interests and seeking consensus and cooperation; the adversarial nature of our legal system, however, emphasizes conflict over agreement, winning over compromising. Courts cannot hold hearings and weigh testimony, nor can they negotiate and compromise with different interest groups to decide how best to address a problem or which issue to prioritize when there are limited resources. Because they are restricted to deciding the cases before them, courts also cannot consider the interconnectedness of social problems or impose holistic solutions. Court-mandated policy changes do not come with a blueprint or map of how they will be implemented, including how the changes will be funded or absorbed into existing institutional structures. The next steps after a court decision has been issued are often unclear and subject to the interpretation and practical concerns of administrators and other policy implementers. Consequently, policy changes may become diluted or distorted when actually applied. Finally, the judiciary's top-down approach, where unelected judges frequently impose policy solutions, can also wreak havoc on grassroots, community-based efforts to solve problems, thereby disenfranchising citizens.

Advocates for judicial intervention contend that the judiciary advances, rather than impedes, the democratic ideal because it protects the rights and interests of minorities. Whereas one needs power and connections for access to legislators, access to the court is guaranteed to all. Thus, rather than disenfranchising citizens, courts enfranchise them, especially those citizens who lack a voice in the legislative process. Most courts are also less susceptible to outside pressure, which allows them to do what is right rather than what is popular. The adversarial system, with its emphasis on facts and garnering evidence, can also be more thorough than the legislative process. It is also more transparent; unlike legislators, a court is required to issue written opinions that explain the basis for its decisions. For this reason, it cannot ignore or obfuscate claims and arguments as readily as other government institutions, or base its decisions on public opinion or political expediency. It also cannot avoid issues. Unlike legislators, who can decline to consider legislation, the judiciary cannot refuse to hear a case. A single court case can also propel intransigent institutions to the bargaining table, or dramatize an issue and spur action for change in other venues. For example, when several state courts determined that the prohibition of same-sex marriage violated the Equal Protection Clause of their respective state constitutions, it spurred legislatures to pass laws legalizing same-sex unions.

Regardless of one's views on the issues, it is clear that the judiciary will continue to play a crucial role in shaping social policy in the years ahead; at times, it will obstruct and at other times advance the causes of social change and social justice. As several of the above cases demonstrate, it is not always possible to predict which effect the courts will have. When to use or avoid the judiciary is, therefore, a strategic decision for policy advocates. Factors that should be considered include the strength of past precedents, the current ideological composition of the court, the likelihood of success, and the risks or downside of any negative decision. However, the structure of our government and the judiciary's defining role in disputes involving the Constitution ensure that it will inevitably play a role in social policy development and implementation as long as people disagree about the best solutions to the nation's social problems.

Discussion Questions

1. What are some of the advantages of having the judiciary make social policy? What are some of the disadvantages? Can you give an example from your field placement or elsewhere of a social problem where court intervention would be helpful? Where it would be harmful?

2. Which approach to interpreting the Constitution (textualist, originalist, doctrinalist, or living Constitution) is more consistent with social work values and social justice? Why?

3. What are some of the advantages of a textualist or originalist approach to interpreting the Constitution? How might it deter a judge from imposing his or her own personal values or ideology when deciding a case?

4. Which of the following oaths would you prefer a judge to take and why?
   a. I solemnly swear that I will administer justice without respect to persons and do equal right to the poor and the rich, and that I will faithfully and impartially discharge and perform all duties incumbent on me according to the best of my ability and understanding, agreeably to the Constitution of the United States.
   b. I solemnly swear that I will administer justice with respect to ethnic, cultural, gender, and class differences between individuals and groups, and favor those groups or individuals who are oppressed over those who are privileged, and that I will faithfully perform all duties incumbent on me according to the best of my ability and understanding, agreeably to the Constitution of the United States.

5. Is it possible for a judge to decide a case without considering his or her own ideology or values? Do you think ideology should play a role in our selection of judges? Overall, what characteristics are important in a judge?

6. In *Lawrence v. Texas (2003),* the court reversed its earlier decision upholding the right to prosecute individuals engaged in same-sex sexual relations, in part because of changing social norms. Do you think the court should consider changing social norms and practices when deciding cases? If so, how should the court decide when a social norm or practice has changed? What measurements/evidence should it rely on? What if the changing social norm or practice is one that disadvantages disenfranchised groups?

7. How would you resolve, if at all, the counter-majoritarian dilemma?

Suggested Websites

Chicago-Kent College of Law, multimedia archive of the Supreme Court: http://www.oyez.org/

Cornell University Law School, Legal Information Institute: http://www.law.cornell.edu/supct/

Legal information and resources: http://www.findlaw.com

U.S. Supreme Court: http://www.supremecourt.gov

Suggestions for Further Reading

Baker, T. E. (2004). Constitutional theory in a nutshell. *William and Mary Bill of Rights Journal 13*, 57–123.

Barber, S., & Fleming, J. (2007). *Constitutional interpretation: The basic questions.* New York: Oxford University Press.

Baum, L. (2009). *The Supreme Court* (10th ed.) Washington, DC: CQ Press.

Carp, R., Stidham, R., & Manning, K. (2010). *Judicial process in America* (8th ed.) Washington, DC: CQ Press.

Epstein, L., & Walker, T. (2009). *Constitutional law for a changing America: Rights, liberties, and justice.* Washington, DC: CQ Press.

Galowitz, P. (1999). Collaboration between lawyers and social workers: Reexamining the nature and potential of the relationship. *Fordham Law Review, 67*, 2123–2154.

Howard, R., & Steigerwalt, A. (2011). *Judging law and policy: Courts and policymaking in the American political system.* New York: Routledge.

Pollack, D. (2003). *Social work and the courts: A casebook.* New York: Routledge.

Rosenberg, G. (1991). *The hollow hope: Can courts bring about social change?* Chicago: University of Chicago Press.

Stein, T. (2004). *The role of law in social work practice and administration.* New York: Columbia University Press.

Toobin, J. (2007). *The nine: Inside the secret world of the Supreme Court.* New York: Doubleday.

Court Cases Cited

Adarand Constructors, Inc. v. Pena, 515 U.S. 200 (1995)

Bowers v. Hardwick, 478 U.S. 186 (1986)

Brown v. Board of Education, 347 US *483 (1954)*

Dandridge v. Williams, 397 U.S. 471 (1970)

Fisher v. University of Texas at Austin, 570 U.S. ___ (2012)

Fisher v. University of Texas at Austin, 593 U.S. ___ (2016)

Goldberg v. Kelly, 397 U.S. 254 (1970)

Gonzales v. Raich, 545 U.S. 1 (2005)

Gratz v. Bollinger, 539 U.S. 244 (2003)

Grutter v. Bollinger, 539 U.S. 306 (2003)

Harris v. Forklift, 510 US 17 (1993)

Heart of Atlanta Motel Inc. v. United States, 379 U.S. 241 (1967)

In re Baby M, 537 A.2d 1227 (N.J. 1988)

Katzenbach v. McClung, 379 U.S. 294 (1964)

Lawrence v. Texas, 539 U.S. 558 (2003)

Lochner v. New York, 198 U.S. 45 (1905)

Muller v. Oregon, 208 U.S. 412 (1908)

National Federation of Independent Business v. Sebelius, 567 U.S. _____ (2012)

Nevada Department of Human Resources v. Hibbs, 538 U.S. 721 (2003)

Obergefell v. Hodges 576 U.S. _____ (2015)

O'Connor v. Donaldson, 422 U.S. 563 (1975)

Parents Involved in Community Schools (PICS) v. Seattle, 551 U.S. 701 (2007)

Planned Parenthood v. Casey, 505 U.S. 833 (1992)

Plessy v. Ferguson, 163 US 537 (1896)

Roe v. Wade, 410 U.S. 113 (1973)

Shelby v. U.S. 570 U.S. _____ (2013)

Tarasoff v. Regents of the University of California, 551 P.2d 334 (Cal. 1976)

Thurman v. the City of Torrington, 595 F. Supp. 1521 (1984)

United States v. Lopez, 514 U.S. 549 (1995)

United States v. Morrison, 529 U.S. 598 (2000)

United States v. Virginia, 518 U.S. 515 (1996)

United States v. Windsor 570 U.S. ___ (2013)

Whole Woman's Health v. Cole, 593 U.S. ___ (2016)

Wyatt v. Aderholt, 503 F.2d 1305 (1974)

Credits

KEY AREAS OF SOCIAL POLICY

Michael Reisch, PhD

Part III of the book contains in-depth analyses of five major areas of contemporary U.S. social policy. These chapters reflect themes identified earlier in the book and connect recent policy developments with the historical forces that shaped them. They assess the prospects for socially just policy development in a rapidly changing environment.

Since its passage in 1935, the Social Security Act has been the cornerstone of U.S. social policy. For a half century, Social Security received bipartisan political support that enabled it to expand through a variety of incremental steps and become a near-universal policy with modestly redistributive results. During the past three decades, however—and particularly since the 1990s—the financial viability of the system has been questioned and the underlying assumptions of Social Security have been challenged. There is considerable uncertainty, therefore, about the future structure of the system's programs even as the need for the benefits it provides becomes more urgent.

Chapter 11, by Benjamin W. Veghte and Elliott Schreur, traces the evolution of Social Security in the United States, from its origins in European social insurance policies to the present. It examines the underlying philosophical assumptions of the system, its structure and financing mechanisms, and the economic, demographic, and political forces that have shaped its development. It includes current statistics on how benefits are calculated, an analysis of Social Security's effectiveness in lifting elderly persons out of poverty, and a discussion of the role of Social Security in an increasingly diverse society. Finally, it analyzes the realities behind the current "crisis" in the Social Security system, assesses the various solutions to this crisis that have been proposed, including the motivations and strategies of their proponents, and explores the potential consequences of these proposals for the system's future and U.S. society.

The values underlying the Social Security system in the United States are also reflected in the nation's policies regarding poverty and employment. "Opportunity is available for those who seek it," "Success comes to those who play by the rules," and "Hard work pays off" are popular examples of rhetoric that conveys a set of historic beliefs about the *causes* of economic success in the United States. Such beliefs, which are predominantly individualistic and meritocratic, have similarly informed many of the *policies* pertaining to economic success, however defined. In contrast, other rhetorical statements signify a set of alternative beliefs that predominantly emphasize the importance of mutuality and social justice. These include "Children are innocent bystanders of their parents' actions" and "A just society provides a safety net for those who need it."

In Chapter 12, Roberta Rehner Iversen illustrates how long-standing beliefs influence U.S. policies about poverty, workforce development, and employment. The chapter focuses on four main themes: (1) the ongoing debate about the nature of poverty, how poverty should be measured, and the relationship of poverty to work and welfare; (2) current debates about the role of education and job training/workforce development in enhancing people's economic well-being; (3) the changing characteristics of employment today; and (4) the effectiveness of recent policies in the areas of employment assistance, child care, and transportation in responding to the changing nature of work. The chapter assesses current efforts to change policy in this area, for example, by increasing the minimum wage, requiring the provision of a "living wage," or expanding funding for supportive services such as child care, housing, education, and job training. It concludes with a discussion of future policy directions and their implications for social justice.

As the chapters in Part I indicate, during the past several decades there has been a dramatic shift in the underlying logic that informs U.S. social policy, particularly in the area of cash assistance. Starting in the 1970s, a concerted campaign emerged that sought to delegitimize government interventions associated with the Keynesian philosophy that informed the New Deal and the post–World War II social contract between capital and labor. These policies, designed to counteract the inequities produced by the market, eventually lost support in the face of well-organized attacks mounted by business interests and right-wing cultural ideologues working in coalition as the "New Right." Yet the New Right's strategy did not produce a return to laissez-faire economics; instead, it led to the development of a post-Keynesian welfare state.

This new welfare regime no longer emphasizes redistributive policies that decommodify labor and support families who are unable to provide for themselves through employment at a minimally decent level; rather, it emphasizes policies that focus on disciplining the poor so they are more socially compliant and market-rational actors willing to fit into the bottom rungs of the emerging low-wage occupational structure of the globalizing economy. These disciplinary approaches have transformed the goals of U.S. social policy from economic redistribution to punishment, from reflecting values of social welfare to being more aligned with the philosophy of criminal justice, and from protecting citizens from the vicissitudes of the market to monitoring and penalizing them—especially the poor—for alleged misbehavior.

Consequently, from zero-tolerance policies for public housing tenants to work requirements for welfare recipients, contemporary social policies reflect the underlying logic of a new regime of poverty governance, based on neoliberal and paternalist political orientations. In addition to an overview of contemporary welfare policies and how they evolved, Chapter 13, by Sanford F. Schram, Joe Soss, and Richard C. Fording, describes how this new regime operates and assesses its consequences for welfare recipients and U.S. social policy as a whole.

No domestic policy issue has attracted more attention during the past decade than health care. This is not surprising since the U.S. health care system constitutes more than one-sixth of the nation's gross domestic product and health care touches virtually every aspect of all people's lives. Chapter 14, by Stephen Gorin and Cynthia Moniz, focuses on the current state of health and mental health policy in the United States. It begins with a concise historical overview of the politics of health care policy from 1912 to the present and the evolution of the significant policy developments in this field. It then summarizes and analyzes the key features of major health-related policies in the United States, such as Medicare, Medicaid, and the State Children's Health Insurance Program. Next, it discusses the main goals and major provisions of the Patient

Protection and Affordable Care Act (ACA) of 2010. It addresses the ongoing judicial and legislative battles over the ACA and analyzes the achievements and limitations of this landmark legislation to date with a particular focus on the central goals of the legislation: expanding health insurance coverage; reducing or slowing the growth of health care costs; and enhancing the quality of health care provision. The chapter concludes with a concise assessment of the challenges facing the Medicare program and its prospects for the future.

During the 19th and 20th centuries, in response to a wide range of individual, family, and community problems, the United States established a complex and multifaceted social service delivery system. Under the auspices of public, nonprofit, and private for-profit organizations, and mutual aid societies, an extensive array of social services are now provided to address such diverse community needs as poverty, health, mental health, substance abuse, domestic violence, and child welfare. Although many of these services are readily available to the general public, they are being used differently by people based on their demographic background, socioeconomic status, and other characteristics, such as culture, age, immigration status, and geography. In fact, there is considerable evidence that only a small proportion of those who are in need of a given service actually receive it.

This disparity between the existence of complex, multiple human needs and the lack of programs to address them is particularly acute among racial and ethnic minority populations, including immigrants. Research indicates that multiple sources of disparities in social services utilization exist at the policy, organizational, and individual levels. The dynamic interaction of contextual factors between service agencies and users' locations could also play an important role. Beginning with the question: "Who uses what types of services?" Chapter 15, by Julian Chun-Chung Chow, Catherine M. Vu, and Isabel Garcia, outlines the major in-kind social services provided by the U.S. social welfare system, including Head Start, nutritional assistance, and child care. It addresses the different barriers—administrative, structural, cultural, and linguistic—that cause disparities in social service access and utilization by racial and ethnic minorities and immigrants, and presents several successful strategies to reduce these disparities and improve the quality of services delivery to these populations.

11

SOCIAL SECURITY
Past, Present, and Future

Benjamin W. Veghte, PhD and Elliot Schreur

Social Security is a fund to which Americans contribute when they are gainfully employed in order to cushion themselves and their families against loss of income if they become unable to work due to retirement, disability, or death. It redistributes income across the life cycle, from times when one can afford to contribute to times when an individual or one's family is in need. It is a **social insurance program**, not a welfare program. This means that only families whose earners contribute to the system while working are eligible to receive benefits when those earners are no longer employed. The program was introduced in the Social Security Act of 1935 and covers over 90% of all workers today.

WHY DO WE HAVE SOCIAL SECURITY?

In recent decades, Social Security is often portrayed in the media and in public policy debates primarily as a budgetary issue—so much so that many see the program itself as a problem rather than a solution to a problem. This begs the questions: Do we really need Social Security? If so, why do we have it? What social needs does it address?

Over the course of their lives, all persons have phases during which they are more or less productive. Children are not capable of providing for themselves. Adults are, except when they are sick or injured or need to care for family members. Elders either have accumulated sufficient savings on which to retire or are dependent on the support of others.

In preindustrial communities, during phases of partial or full interdependence, people tended to have their needs met by family members or by their community, often through religious institutions. As a consequence of the industrial revolution of the 19th century, when the United States went through a transformation from a largely rural and agricultural to an urban, wage-based economy, these networks of social support attenuated. Families became more geographically dispersed and communities more fluid and anonymous. In our contemporary

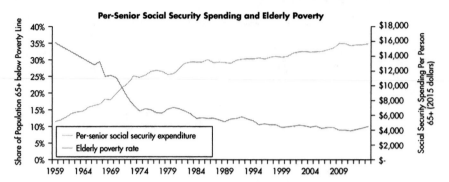

Per-Senior Social Security Spending and Elderly Poverty

Note: No formal data on the percentage of elderly persons living in poverty exists for the years 1960 to 1965. The dotted line denotes a linear extrapolation between the earliest data point (1959) and the beginning of the complete series (1966).

Sources: Authors' analysis of U.S. Census Bureau. 2015. Poverty Data. Table 3: Poverty Status of People, by Age, Race, and Hispanic Origin: 1959 to 2014. http://www.census.gov/hhes/www/poverty/data/historical/people.html. • Bureau of Labor Statistics. 2015. CPI Detailed Report Data for August 2015. Table 24. Historical Consumer Price Index for All Urban Consumers (CPI-U): U. S. city average, all items. http://www.bls.gov/cpi/. • SSA. 2015. Old-Age and Survivors Insurance Trust Fund, 1937-2014. http://www.ssa.gov/OACT/STATS/table4a1.html. • U.S. Census Bureau. Various dates. Population Estimates. Historical Data. http://www.census.gov/popest/data/historical/index.html.

society, during the phases in the life course when people cannot provide for themselves, many no longer have families or community charities to which they can turn for aid. [*See Chapter 2 in this volume.*]

This absence of financial assistance became particularly apparent during the Great Depression of the 1930s, when poverty among the elderly reached an estimated 50% (Altman, 2005). Largely due to the Social Security program, this poverty rate dropped steadily over the ensuing half century. By 1959, 35% of elders were poor. During the 1960s and 1970s, poverty among older Americans declined further for the same reasons that their median incomes rose: More of them had worked long enough in covered jobs to qualify for Social Security benefits, and Congress had increased the level of these benefits. The elderly poverty rate dropped to 25% in 1970 and 15% in 1975. It then gradually declined to about 10% in 2000, where it has hovered since. Engelhardt and Gruber (2006) find that the increase in Social Security benefits between 1967 and 2000 can explain 100% of the decline in elderly poverty during this period. They conclude further that higher benefits have led many elderly to live independently rather than with family members and that the effect of Social Security in reducing poverty would have been even more dramatic in the absence of these changes in living arrangements.

THE HISTORICAL ROOTS OF SOCIAL SECURITY

Social Security's roots go back several centuries before the passage of the 1935 act. The model for Social Security, as for all social insurance programs, was the sickness, survivors, and old-age funds established by medieval European guilds. These forms of cooperative self-help migrated across the Atlantic with European immigrants to the United States and were widespread in 19th and early 20th century America in the form of the mutual aid societies organized by the working classes. [*See Chapter 2 in this volume.*]

These institutions did not cover a majority of the workforce, however, and were far more widespread among skilled than unskilled workers. They excluded African Americans and were typically ethnically homogeneous.

In light of this fragmented and piecemeal landscape of insurance against the critical risks of the life course, unemployed workers experienced widespread suffering during the Great Depression. President Franklin Delano Roosevelt recognized that the crisis of the Great Depression was not merely short-term in nature. It also exposed structural gaps in the economic security of individuals and families in modern industrial society—not just in old age but throughout the life course. To cope with these risks, he introduced, among other pieces of New Deal legislation, the Social Security Act of 1935. [*See Chapter 2 in this volume.*]

This landmark legislation included a combination of welfare and social insurance programs designed to cushion the effects of income loss due to various social and biological risks workers face in modern industrial society. It created social insurance programs to provide a modest measure of income security in retirement (what we now refer to as Social Security) and unemployment (Unemployment Insurance). But social insurance programs pay benefits only to those who are eligible for benefits through their work and contribution history. To help those who did not qualify for these social insurance programs, the Social Security Act also introduced a nationwide, federal–state welfare program—Aid to Dependent Children (ADC), which later became Aid to Families with Dependent Children (AFDC), and was replaced in 1996 by Temporary Assistance for Needy Families (TANF). This welfare program helped Americans survive the immediate crisis of the Great Depression, while the Social Security Act's social insurance programs ensured that the nation would build up sufficient financial reserves to cushion the social impact of future crises. [*See Chapters 2, 12, and 13 in this volume.*]

THE EVOLUTION OF SOCIAL SECURITY

EXPANSIONS IN COVERAGE

The retirement benefits in the 1935 Social Security Act were originally scheduled to begin in 1942 after workers had contributed to the program for several years. Modeled after a private insurance plan, its designers assumed that the program had to build up its reserves. In 1939, several important amendments were introduced. The Social Security program was expanded to include survivors' benefits for spouses and dependent children. The start date for distributing benefits was moved up from 1942 to 1940. Perhaps of greatest long-term significance, the financing of the program was changed from full reserve to a "pay-as-you-go" system. This means that the taxes paid by current workers contribute to the benefits received by current recipients. The unanticipated implications of this change for the program's financial viability will be discussed below.

Social Security has expanded considerably since its inception both in terms of the types of workers it covers and the kinds of risks against which it insures contributors. At the time of its passage, Social Security covered only about 60% of the workforce. It did not cover the self-employed, domestic workers, or agricultural workers. As discussed in Chapter 2, these latter two exclusions disqualified the vast majority of African Americans from participation in the program.

During the 1950s, the Social Security program began to cover most self-employed persons, household and farm employees, the majority of state and local government employees, and those serving in the military. In 1956, Social Security added a benefit for disabled workers aged 50 to 65, as well as for the disabled adult children of deceased or retired insured workers. This was expanded in 1960 to cover all disabled workers.

In 1965, the Social Security Act was amended to include Medicare and Medicaid, which provide health insurance to the aged and the poor, respectively. Medicare, which offered hospital (Part A) and medical (Part B) insurance for the aged, became Title XVIII of the Social Security Act. Subsequently, Congress added an optional supplemental medical insurance program (Part C) and, during the Bush Administration, an optional prescription drug plan (Part D) to Medicare. Medicaid, which requires states to offer health insurance to those at or near the poverty level and provides federal matching funding for this purpose, became Title XIX of the act. The 2010 Affordable Care Act attempted to expand Medicaid coverage with limited success. [*See Chapter 14 in this volume.*]

In 1972, Congress created another federal program, Supplemental Security Income (SSI), to provide a minimal level of welfare assistance to those elderly disabled who do not qualify for Social Security. The program, which went into effect in 1974 as part of Title XVI of the Social Security Act, replaced a web of previously existing state programs and consolidated programs for the elderly poor, the blind, and the disabled established by the original legislation. Today, SSI provides average monthly benefits to 2.3 million elderly and 6.9 million disabled Americans (U.S. Social Security Administration, 2015a).

INCREASES IN CONTRIBUTION LEVELS

To keep pace with expansions in coverage, contribution levels have also increased over the program's history. When Social Security was introduced, the payroll tax that funded its programs (often referred to as FICA, or the Federal Insurance Contribution Act) was a mere 1% for employers and employees, respectively. At the time, little revenue was needed since workers across the age spectrum were paying into the program and very few people were collecting benefits. (The ratio of workers to retirees was then 7:1.) As contributors aged and became beneficiaries, Social Security required higher contribution rates to maintain the program's solvency. These rates increased to 3% in 1960, 4.2% by 1970, and since 1990 the rate has remained 6.2%.[1] In most advanced industrial countries, however, payroll taxes are much higher than in the U.S., and they insure against more types of risks (U.S. Social Security Administration, 2012).

The changes in coverage and contribution levels for Social Security over time make one point abundantly clear: Social Security is a flexible policy instrument for coping with diverse risks of income loss in modern societies. It can be used for as few or as many types of risks as policymakers deem appropriate. Some policymakers, for example, advocate using the program to mitigate the economic risks associated with having and raising children by offering paid family leave through Social Security, or by providing caregiver credits to parents who withdraw from the workforce for an episode of full-time child care (Boushey & Glynn, 2012; O'Leary, 2012).

Social Security is not the only form of payroll tax Americans pay. Employers pay unemployment insurance payroll taxes for their workers, at rates that vary by state, industry, and the firm's history of layoffs. When Medicare was introduced in 1965, the hospital insurance portion of the program (Part A) was financed through payroll taxes that both employers and employees pay. (Most workers pay 1.45%.) While these are not popularly considered "Social Security taxes," they are technically taxes authorized through FICA, the same law that finances Social Security old-age retirement, disability, and survivors' benefits.[2]

HOW SOCIAL SECURITY WORKS

FINANCING MECHANISMS

Since Social Security is self-financed through payroll taxes, it is not part of the regular federal budget. (It is legally "off-budget.") Its funding originates primarily from payroll taxes. When revenues from payroll taxes exceed benefits paid in a given year, these excess revenues are invested—by law—in U.S. Treasury bonds and thereby saved up for payment of future benefits. These investments are collectively known as the Social Security Trust Fund.[3] Interest earned on these amounts held in the trust fund is a second source of income for the program. A third source of funding comes from income taxes collected on Social Security benefit payments made to high-income beneficiaries. When benefits are paid to higher income beneficiaries, a portion of these benefits is taxable if the beneficiary's income from other sources, plus half of their Social Security benefits, exceeds $25,000 for an individual or $32,000 for a married couple filing jointly. Some of these tax revenues flow back into Social Security's finances (Reno & Lavery, 2009).

Payroll contributions are taxes that employers and employees pay on workers' wages up to a certain income level, known as the **Social Security wage base**. In 2016, the taxable wage base is capped at $118,500. As stated above, since 1990, the Social Security payroll tax rate has been 6.2% for employers and employees, respectively. However, to stimulate the economy during the recovery from the Great Recession, President Obama and Congress agreed to a temporary "payroll tax holiday," which cut the employee rate down to 4.2%. This 2 percentage point cut in workers' contributions to the Social Security Trust Fund was counterbalanced by an equivalent transfer of funds from general federal revenues to the trust fund. In other words, the payroll tax cut was intended to stimulate the economy without having a negative effect on Social Security's finances. This stimulus measure was extended for 2011 and 2012, and expired at the end of 2012.

In 2015, 85% of Social Security's revenues came directly from payroll taxes, 11% came from interest on investments, and 3% came from taxation of benefits paid to upper-income beneficiaries (Board of Trustees, 2015; percentages do not total to 100% because of rounding).

ELIGIBILITY FOR SOCIAL SECURITY

Each type of Social Security benefit has its own eligibility criteria. A *retired worker* is eligible for Social Security if she or he is 62 years of age or older and has earned at least $1,260 (in 2016) in employment covered by Social Security[4] for at least 40 quarters—a total of 10 years—over the course of her or his working life.[5] A *spouse of a retired worker* is eligible for spousal retirement benefits if (1) she or he is 62 or older (this applies to a divorced spouse as well, if the marriage lasted at least 10 years), or (2) she or he has a child under 16 or is caring for a disabled child. A *disabled worker* is eligible for Social Security Disability Insurance (SSDI) benefits if she or he meets both medical and employment-related criteria. The medical criteria depend on the specific physical or mental disability, but to qualify, the disabled worker must have a medical condition that is expected to render one unable to work for at least a year, or to end in death.

The employment criteria for disabled-worker benefits entail a "duration of work" test and a "recent work" test. First, a person must have worked and paid into the system for a minimum period that varies by age. For example, individuals disabled at ages 21 to 24 require only 6 quarters/credits of covered

MORE SECURITY FOR THE AMERICAN FAMILY

WHEN AN INSURED WORKER DIES, LEAVING DEPENDENT CHILDREN AND A WIDOW, BOTH MOTHER AND CHILDREN RECEIVE MONTHLY BENEFITS UNTIL THE LATTER REACH 18.

FOR INFORMATION WRITE OR CALL AT THE NEAREST FIELD OFFICE OF THE
SOCIAL SECURITY BOARD

Figure 11.2 Social Security Poster from the 1940s.

employment; those disabled at ages 31 to 42 require 20 Social Security credits; and those retired at age 62 or older require at least 40 credits. Second, a person must have recently worked. For example, those disabled at ages 21 to 24 must have earned 6 work credits in the 3 years before disability onset, those disabled at ages 24 to 31 must have worked at least half the time since turning 21 (i.e., earned half the credits attainable during that period), and those 31 or older must have worked at least 5 out of the previous 10 years.

Disabled children are not eligible for SSDI *per se*, because they have not paid into the system. They are eligible only as dependents of qualified workers who are themselves either disabled or deceased. However, a child who has a disability that began before age 22, and who was eligible for Social Security benefits as a dependent child on the basis of a disabled or deceased parent's earnings record, may remain eligible for benefits into adulthood.

A *child* is eligible for Social Security benefits only if a parent is eligible and the child is unmarried and under age 18 (19 if in high school full-time), or over 18 and disabled from a disability that occurred before age 22. A *spouse* of a Social Security beneficiary is eligible for Social Security retirement benefits if he or she is at least age 62 or is caring for a child who is either under age 16 or receiving SSDI benefits. The spouse is eligible for dependent benefits on the basis of the retired worker's earnings record.

Anyone who has not paid into Social Security long enough to qualify for benefits, including children born with a disability, can apply for Supplemental Security Income (SSI) instead. SSI is categorically different from Social Security retirement or SSDI. It is a welfare program and thus is a **means-tested program**. To qualify for SSI, applicants must not only be aged or disabled but also have little or no income or assets (less than $2,000 for an individual or $3,000 for a couple). (For more information on the SSI program, see Center on Budget and Policy Priorities, 2015.)

CALCULATION OF BENEFITS

Because Social Security is a social insurance program and not a welfare program, its benefits are based on contributions that, in turn, are based on career earnings. We will discuss retirement, disability, and survivors' benefits separately below.

The Social Security Administration (SSA) computes retirement benefits based on the average monthly earnings over one's 35 highest-earning years. From this average, SSA computes the retiree's benefit based on the following formula. For ease of comparison with annual incomes, annual earnings are used here instead of monthly earnings.

- 90% of the worker's first $10,272 (inflation adjusted) in average annual earnings;
- 32% of average annual earnings between $10,272 and $61,884; and
- 15% of average annual earnings over $61,884.

The thresholds of $9,204 and $55,448—known officially as **bend points**—change over time based on inflation. The purpose of this tiered formula is to improve the progressivity of Social Security benefits, so that they provide the most help to those most in need.

To see how this formula works, let's consider an example. Let's assume that before retiring at age 66, Jane Doe had worked for a total of 28 years over her lifetime. Let's further assume that she was unable to pursue gainful employment during other years in her adult life because she attended an institution of higher education and/or raised a family full-time. In addition, let's assume that, on average, she earned the equivalent of $54,000 per year in today's dollars in those years she did work. To calculate her Social Security retirement benefits, we first need to calculate her average annual earnings over her top 35 earnings years. Twenty-eight years of $54,000 plus 7 years of $0 yields average annual earnings of $43,200.

Her annual benefit would be the sum of the following:

- 90% of her first $10,272 in average annual earnings ($9,244.80)
- 32% of her average annual earnings between $10,272 and $43,200 ($10,536.96)

Her resulting base benefit amount, called the **primary insurance amount (PIA)**, is $19,781.76 per year ($1,648.48 per month).

Adjustments in Retirement Benefits for Early Retirement

There is another dimension to this benefit calculation. The formula above determines one's PIA, which in this example is $1,648.48 per month. This is the amount Jane would receive if she retired at the **normal (or full-benefit) retirement age**, which for those attaining age 66 in 2016 is 66. As part of the cost-saving reforms contained in the Social Security Amendments of 1983, a series of gradual increases in the full retirement age from 65 to 67 were scheduled for the first quarter of the 21st century. These are in the process of taking effect (see Table 11.1).

People who retire before their birth cohort's full retirement age suffer a permanent reduction in benefits equal to about 6.67% for each of the first 3 years of early retirement, plus 5% for the fourth and/or fifth year(s). Those who delay retirement receive a **delayed retirement credit** of 8% for each of the 1, 2, 3, or 4 years of delay, up to a maximum retirement age of 70.

The earliest one can retire and claim Social Security benefits is age 62, often referred to as the **earliest eligibility age**. In the above example, if Jane Doe were to retire at age 62 instead of her birth cohort's full

Table 11.1 Full Retirement Age and Year, by Birth Year.

Year of Birth	Age 66 Attained In...	Age of Full Retirement
1943–1954	2009–2020	66
1955	2021	66 and 2 months
1956	2022	66 and 4 months
1957	2023	66 and 6 months
1958	2024	66 and 8 months
1959	2025	66 and 10 months
1960 and later	2026 and later	67

Source: U.S. Social Security Administration (2016a). *Normal retirement* age. Retrieved from http://www.ssa.gov/oact/ProgData/nra.html

benefit age of 66, her benefits would be reduced by (6.67% × 3) + 5% (i.e., 25%). Table 11.2 shows the percentage of one's PIA received at different ages of retirement.

As Table 11.2 makes abundantly clear, there is a tremendous financial incentive for Jane to retire as late as possible. Recall that if she were to retire at her full retirement age of 66, her lifetime monthly benefit would be $1,648.48. If she retired at age 62, her benefit would be reduced by 25% (i.e., it would be $1,236.36). If she were to delay her retirement until age 70, however, her lifetime monthly benefit would be $2,176. In other words, if Jane could delay her retirement until age 70, she would receive a benefit that is 76% greater than if she were to take early retirement at age 62.

It is important to note that the adjustments to benefit levels based on the age of retirement are all calculated to be actuarially neutral. In other words, based on life expectancy tables for the entire population, the Social Security Administration estimates that on average, it will pay the same total amount of lifetime benefits to people who retire late as to those who retire early or at the full retirement age. Consequently, the decision as to when to retire may be based on a variety of factors, including one's health, family history, dependent care responsibilities, and other sources of retirement income.

Adjustments in Retirement Benefits for Family Status

A worker's retirement benefit is adjusted for family status as well. Eligible spouses receive a spousal benefit amounting to half the PIA of the retired worker, if the spouse waits until his or her own full retirement age to claim spousal benefits. If the spouse claims benefits earlier, the spousal benefit is reduced, unless the spouse is caring for a child who is under 16 or disabled. If the spouse has independently earned a retirement benefit larger than the spousal benefit, then that amount is paid instead.

For each dependent child, a worker's retirement benefit is supplemented by an amount equal to half the worker's PIA, up to a **family maximum benefit**. The amount of a worker's family maximum is related to his or her PIA, as well as to the number of family members who qualify on his or her work record. The maximum family benefit typically ranges from about 150% to 180% of a worker's retirement benefit (U.S. Social Security Administration, 2016c, 2016d).

Table 11.2 Percentage of PIA due at Different Ages of Retirement

Year of Birth	Full Retirement Age (FRA)	Credit for Each Year of Delayed Retirement after FRA (Percentage)	Benefit, as a Percentage of PIA, Beginning at Age						
			62	63	64	65	66	67	70
1943–1954	66	8	75	80	86 2/3	93 1/3	100	108	132
1955	66, 2 mo.	8	74 1/6	79 1/6	85 5/9	92 2/9	98 8/9	106 2/3	130 2/3
1956	66, 4 mo.	8	73 1/3	78 1/3	84 4/9	91 1/9	97 7/9	105 1/3	129 1/3
1957	66, 6 mo.	8	72 1/2	77 1/2	83 1/3	90	96 2/3	104	128
1958	66, 8 mo.	8	71 2/3	76 2/3	82 2/9	88 8/9	95 5/9	102 2/3	126 2/3
1959	66, 10 mo.	8	70 5/6	75 5/6	81 1/9	87 7/9	94 4/9	101 1/3	125 1/3
1960 and later	67	8	70	75	80	86 2/3	93 1/3	100	124

Source: U.S. Social Security Administration (2016b). *Effect of early or delayed retirement on retirement benefits.* Retrieved from http://www.ssa.gov/oact/ProgData/ar_drc.html

Cost-of-Living Adjustments

For the first few decades of the program's existence, Congress adjusted benefit levels periodically to maintain their real value against inflation. In the wake of higher-than-average levels of inflation in the late 1960s and early 1970s, as well as controversy over the politicization of Congressional decisions about benefit increases, an automatic formula for adjusting benefits to inflation was introduced in 1972. This automatic **cost-of-living adjustment (COLA)** increases benefits by the percentage change in consumer prices, as measured by the Consumer Price Index for Urban Wage Earners and Clerical Workers (CPI-W), from the third quarter of one year to the same quarter the following year, effective the following January. If there is no increase in prices, then there is no COLA, as was the case in 2010, 2011, and 2016. The introduction of this COLA helped reduce poverty among the elderly and enabled their incomes to keep pace with inflation for the remainder of the 20th century, in sharp contrast to the effects that wage stagnation and declining welfare benefits had on average workers and welfare-dependent households.

Disability Benefits

As with retirement benefits, SSDI benefits vary with age and earnings/contribution history, and benefits are supplemented for spouses and/or children. The maximum family disability benefit a worker can receive, however, is limited to between 150% and 180% of the disabled worker's individual disability benefit (U.S. Social Security Administration, 2016e).

Survivors' Benefits

If a spouse or divorced spouse (if the marriage lasted at least 10 years) of a qualified deceased worker has reached his or her own full retirement age, she or he receives a survivors' benefit in the amount of the deceased worker's retirement benefit. This benefit is actuarially reduced if the surviving spouse retires early, and it may be claimed as early as age 60. Surviving spouses younger than age 60 can claim these benefits only if they are disabled or caring for a disabled child (U.S. Social Security Administration, 2016d).

Children receive survivors' benefits in the amount of up to half the deceased parent's full retirement (or disability) benefit. Any one family's survivors' benefits cannot exceed the family maximum of 150% to 180% of the deceased worker's full benefit amount (U.S. Social Security Administration, 2016d).

WHO RECEIVES SOCIAL SECURITY TODAY?

As of 2015, 43 million retired Americans and their dependents received old-age benefits from Social Security, 10.8 million Americans collected disability benefits, and 6.1 million collected survivors' benefits (U.S. Social Security Administration, 2016f; see Table 11.3).

Retirement beneficiaries make up 72% of all Social Security beneficiaries. About 18% of beneficiaries are disabled, and about 10% are survivors of deceased spouses or parents. Moreover, 8.5 million children, or between 11 and 12 percent of all American children, receive Social Security, most often because they live in households that rely on Social Security payments for at least part of their household income. Of these children, about 3.2 million receive direct benefits from Social Security through their late teens because they are children of deceased, disabled, or retired workers (Gabe, 2015).

BENEFITS LEVELS

What benefits do contributors to Social Security receive when they become old or disabled, and what benefits do their survivors receive upon their death? Table 11.4 shows average benefit levels for various types of beneficiaries in April 2012.

Table 11.3 Who Receives Social Security?

Type of Beneficiary	Number (in Thousands)	Percentage
Retirement benefits	43,073	71.8
Disability benefits	10,806	18.0
Survivors benefits	6,084	10.2
Total	59,963	100.0

Source: U.S. Social Security Administration (2016).

Table 11.4 Average Social Security Benefits Paid to Families in January 2016, by Type of Beneficiary Family.

Type of Beneficiary Family	Benefit Amount
All beneficiaries	$1,228
Retirement benefits	
Retired workers	$1,332
Retired worker with aged spouse	$2,219
Survivors benefits	
Widow(er)	$1,286
Widow(er) and child	$2,214
Disability benefits	
Disabled worker	$1,148
Disabled worker with spouse and child	$1,977

Source: U.S. Social Security Administration (2015); U.S. Social Security Administration (2016g).

SOCIAL SECURITY AND ECONOMIC SECURITY IN RETIREMENT

As discussed in Chapters 1 and 6, social policies should be assessed in terms of their effectiveness in achieving their goals. The goal of Social Security is to enable—indeed, to mandate—sufficient savings by Americans during their working lives so that when they are unable to work due to old age, disability, or death, their families have sufficient income to make ends meet.[7] The next section focuses on retirement security. Progressives and conservatives disagree about the extent to which this goal should be pursued through Social Security or through tax-favored private savings.[8] Both progressives and conservatives agree, however, that the government should create a public policy framework that enables the elderly to have sufficient income to meet their basic needs.

HOW MUCH INCOME DO RETIREES NEED TO LIVE WITH DIGNITY?

In evaluating a social program such as Social Security, the second step after defining the policy goal is to develop relevant metrics for measuring key dimensions of the program's performance. One possible metric

Table 11.5 Effect of Social Security on Poverty.

Age Group	Percentage in Poverty Excluding Social Security	Number Lifted Out of Poverty by Social Security Including Social Security	
Children under 18	22.6	21.1	1,106,000
Adults 18–64	16.5	13.5	5,832,000
Elderly 65 and over	41.5	10.0	14,488,000
Total, all ages	**21.6**	**14.8**	**21,426,000**

Source: Kathleen Romig (2015). *Social Security lifts 21 million Americans out of poverty.* Washington, DC: Center on Budget and Policy Priorities.

is the **poverty line**, which can tell us how many elderly are lifted out of poverty by Social Security benefits, and how many remain in poverty despite receiving Social Security. Table 11.5 shows that about 21 million Americans are lifted out of poverty by Social Security. This makes it by far the most effective antipoverty program in the United States, and it is entirely self-financed. In other words, because of the mandatory nature of contributions, the program fights poverty without burdening the federal budget, simply by forcing workers to save for a rainy day.

The antipoverty performance of Social Security for the elderly is dramatic—about four out of ten seniors would live in poverty without Social Security, while, thanks to the existence of the program, only ~10% suffer poverty. Still, even with Social Security, about 4.6 million elderly Americans live in poverty (U.S. Census Bureau, 2015b). These are people who either did not work long enough (40 quarters, or 10 years) in covered employment to qualify for benefits or who worked in low-wage jobs for an insufficient number of years to qualify for a benefit sizable enough to lift them out of poverty. About 1 million of these elderly poor—a large number of whom are immigrants—receive SSI (U.S. Social Security Administration, 2015b). Because the official poverty level is extremely low (only $11,880 per year, or $990 per month for an aged person living alone in 2016), another useful metric is the percentage of people who are **poor or near poor**. This is defined as living on less than 125% of the poverty line, or less than $14,850 per year. Table 11.6 shows how various demographic groups of elderly are faring—including Social Security benefits—using this metric.

Even with Social Security, racial minorities suffer very high rates of deprivation: one quarter of elderly African Americans are poor or near poor, as are over a quarter of elderly Latinos. Many unmarried women—mostly widows—are also in dire straits, more than a quarter of them having to get by on less than $14,850 a year.

The discussion thus far has been based on the official poverty measure. Experts agree, however, that this measure is not only unrealistically low but deeply flawed methodologically. [*See Chapter 12 of this volume.*] It was created in 1963 by Mollie Orshansky, a Social Security Administration researcher, who defined the poverty line by extrapolating as best as possible from the inadequate data available at the time. The 1955 Household Food Consumption Survey revealed that the average family of three or more spent one-third of its after-tax income on food. Orshansky created a set of poverty thresholds—that differed based on household size and composition—that defined poverty as 3 times a subsistence food budget. The measure is applied to a household's pre-tax cash income.

Table 11.6 Percentage of Elders Poor or Near Poor.

Characteristics	Percentage	
	Poor	Poor or Near Poor
All persons 65 and older	9.5	15.1
Married	4.7	7.4
Unmarried men	11.9	19
Unmarried women	17.6	28
White	8.4	13.7
Black	17.6	25.6
Hispanic	19.8	28.4

Source: U.S. Social Security Administration (2015c).

By 1969, this had become the official poverty measure for all U.S. programs, and it is still used today. While it has been updated for inflation, the core assumption of the measure has never been updated—that poor families spend one-third of their income on food. Hence, according to the logic of the measure, if you know how much a family spends on food and triple it, you know how much money it needs to make ends meet. When Ruggles (1990) and Schwarz (2005) replicated Orshansky's methods with more recent data on expenditure patterns, each found that the poverty line today should be about 70% higher.

In the early 1990s, the National Academy of Sciences (NAS) created a panel to develop a better approach to measuring poverty, which issued a set of recommendations in 1995 (Citro & Michael, 1995). Because the NAS measure yielded higher poverty thresholds for most types of households than did the official measure, it was opposed by those who resist increases in government spending on antipoverty programs. Consequently, to this day, the government continues to base eligibility for means-tested social programs on the antiquated Orshansky measure.

But in 2010, the U.S. Census Bureau began collecting data for a more realistic measure, the Supplemental Poverty Measure (SPM), largely following the NAS recommendations. It differs from the official poverty measure both in terms of what it counts as income and how it calculates the poverty threshold. To calculate household income, it adds the sum of cash income and any federal government in-kind benefits that families can use to meet their food, clothing, shelter, and utility needs (including the Earned Income Tax Credit). Then, it subtracts taxes paid, work-related expenses (on commuting and child care), and out-of-pocket expenditures for health care, and is adjusted for differences in housing costs across the nation (U.S. Census Bureau, 2010). It also sets the poverty threshold at the 33rd percentile of Americans' spending on food, clothing, shelter, and utilities. This makes it a relative—rather than an absolute—poverty measure.

The SPM is a far more useful metric for evaluating the performance of government programs, because it measures the cost of living of various demographic groups with far greater accuracy and takes into consideration major non-cash benefit programs, such as the Earned Income Tax Credit and SNAP (food stamps) that help households meet their needs. (Both the current official poverty measure and the SPM count Social Security and other cash benefits.) Using this more data-driven measure, the child poverty rate would drop from 21.5% to 16.7%, while the poverty rate for seniors would increase from 10% to 14.4% (Short, 2015). This increase in the poverty rate for the elderly is due primarily to the fact that the SPM takes into account out-of-pocket health care costs, which are a major expense for elderly households.

A final metric useful in assessing the performance of Social Security is the Elderly Economic Security Index (Elder Index), developed by Wider Opportunities for Women in collaboration with the Gerontology Institute at the University of Massachusetts, Boston. Unlike the other two indices, it does not measure poverty by comparing income to a threshold. Rather, it estimates the minimum amount of income seniors need to make ends meet, given the cost of living where they live, the characteristics of their household (i.e., household size), their housing status (homeownership or renter), means of transportation, and health status. While the most recent Elder Index data are a few years old, they are still illustrative. Table 11.7 estimates how much money these various types of elderly households need to meet their basic needs.

From Table 11.7, we see that an elderly couple that has not yet finished paying off their mortgage needed $28,860 in 2011 to make ends meet, while a senior living alone and renting needed $22,848.

We have discussed the three primary metrics available to assess the adequacy of Social Security retirement benefits. All three report worrisome rates of economic deprivation among the elderly. According to the official poverty line, 14% are poor or near poor, while the SPM reports that 16% are poor. The Elder Index, meanwhile, indicates that an elderly couple still paying off a mortgage receives Social Security

Table 11.7 The Elder Economic Security Standard Index for the United States, 2011.

Monthly Expenses for Selected Household Types

Expenses: Monthly and Yearly Totals	Elder Person (Age 65+)			Elder Couple (Both Age 65+)		
	Owner w/o mortgage	Renter, one bedroom	Owner w/o mortgage	Owner w/o mortgage	Renter, one bedroom	Owner w/o mortgage
Housing (incl. utilities, taxes, and insurance)	$457	$769	$1,270	$457	$769	$1,270
Food	$243	$243	$243	$446	$446	$446
Transportation	$246	$246	$246	$380	$380	$380
Health care (good health)	$381	$381	$381	$762	$762	$762
Miscellaneous	$265	$265	$265	$409	$409	$409
Elder Index per month	$1,592	$1,904	$2,405	$2,454	$2,766	$3,267
Elder Index per year	$19,104	$22,848	$28,860	$29,448	$33,192	$39,204

Source: Wider Opportunities for Women (2013).

benefits that typically amount to only 56% of the income they need to be economically secure, while the Social Security benefits of an elderly renter living alone typically cover only 65% of what he or she needs to meet basic needs. In sum, Social Security reduces elderly poverty from around 42%, to between 10% and 16%, depending on the measure. Yet regardless, the lesson is that today's benefits are still not adequate to meet many seniors' basic needs. In the following section, we will examine the extent to which other sources of retirement income make up the difference.

SOCIAL SECURITY, PENSIONS, AND SAVINGS

In the United States, Social Security is the foundation of retiree income security, in terms of both coverage (the percentage of people receiving benefits) and the amount of income provided. Yet, it was not designed to cover 100% of an elderly person's income needs in retirement. Rather, it was intended to be part of a "three-legged stool" of retirement income, consisting of Social Security benefits, savings, and private pensions.

However, while nearly all older Americans today—9 in 10—receive Social Security income[9] only 3 in 10 have a **defined benefit pension** or assets in a **defined contribution plan** (Wu, 2013). In a defined-benefit pension, a worker's employer promises to pay a lifetime annuity after retirement (or, in some cases, provides the option of an equivalent amount as a lump sum at retirement). In a defined contribution plan, a worker contributes her own income pre-tax and the employer has the option to contribute as well. The reason why so few Americans have access to a defined benefit employer pension is because they are eligible only if they worked in a company that offered one, and only if they worked at the same company long enough to become "vested" in the plan (i.e., eligible to receive pension benefits).

Unlike Social Security, the distributional dynamics of these private sources of retirement income are extremely skewed toward the top quintile of the income spectrum. The average annual tax benefit from defined benefit and defined contribution plans (taken together) for the highest income quintile (the top 20%) is 180 times as large as that of the lowest quintile: those in the top quintile received about $3,851 in tax benefits in 2013, while those in the lowest quintile received about $21 (Harris et al., 2014). Income received in retirement from these sources is similarly skewed: an analysis by the Employee Benefit Research Institute revealed that the average annual benefit (defined benefit and defined contribution combined) for the highest income quintile was 150 times as large as that of the lowest quintile for the years 2004 to 2006. Those in the top quintile received about $16,000 per year, while those in the lowest quintile received about $100 per year (Employee Benefit Research Institute, 2010). Three-fifths of retirees across the income spectrum received less than $142/month in employer-based pension benefits. Based on similar findings, Baily and Kirkegaard (2009) conclude that the

> seeming inability of the voluntary U.S. employment-based pension system to expand much beyond the top income echelons is a powerful reminder that there are few if any effective voluntary replacements for the Social Security system to provide retirement income to the majority of Americans (p. 436).

Employer-based pensions in the United States thus do not substantially alleviate the problem of the low income replacement rates of Social Security.

Figure 11.3 Reliance on Social Security Benefits by Income Quintile

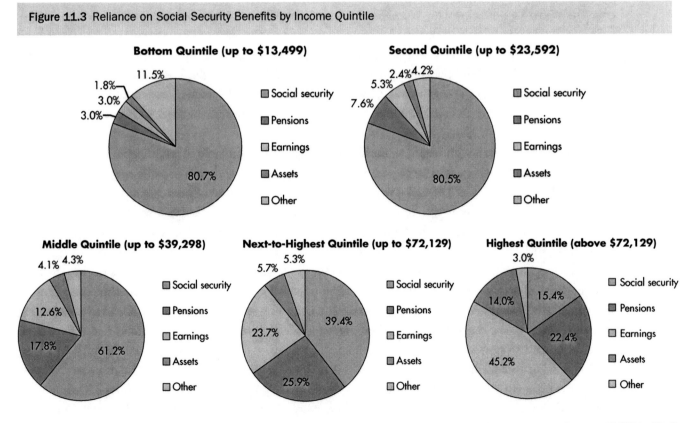

Source: U.S. Social Security Administration (2016h, Table 10.5). Author's analysis of U.S. Census Data. Data are from here: https://www.ssa.gov/policy/docs/statcomps/income_pop55/2012/sect10.pdf

The Social Security Administration provides information on the percentage share of household income of elderly households by income source (see Figure 11.3 above). These data confirm that only the highest earning fifth of seniors receive a significant share of their income from assets.

The first three pie charts in Figure 11.3 show that three in five retirees get at least 61% of their income from Social Security. This demonstrates that Social Security remains the bedrock of economic security for most elderly households. Pensions and savings (income from assets) provide only about 22% of retirement income for middle-income retirees and 10% or less for the bottom 40% of aged households. This suggests that for three in five households, Social Security is about all they can rely on in retirement, especially as they age into their 70s and 80s and become less and less able to supplement their Social Security benefits with earnings, spend down their savings, and see the value of their pensions (if they have one) eroded by inflation. For this majority of senior households, even small reductions in Social Security benefits could have a significant impact on their standard of living. In addition, it should be noted that even Americans in the top quintile in Figure 11.1 rely to a significant extent on Social Security as they age, become less capable of working, and spend down their savings.

THE IMPORTANCE OF SOCIAL SECURITY IN A DIVERSE SOCIETY

Social Security is particularly important to certain demographic subgroups of Americans. Almost 50 percent of elderly women, for example, would live in poverty without the program (Van de Water, Sherman, & Ruffing 2013). As noted above, even if they receive Social Security benefits, 25% of elderly unmarried women, 27% of elderly Latinas, and 29% of elderly African American women live in poverty or near poverty. The Wider Opportunities for Women (2013) Economic Security Index reports that

> older adults of color are at significantly greater risk for economic insecurity than are white elders. Forty-nine percent of households headed by white adults report household incomes that fall short of economic security, compared to 76% of Hispanic-headed households, 74% of African American-headed homes and 65% of Asian American-headed households (p. 1).

Of particular concern with regard to the financial well-being of people of color in the U.S. is their lack of household wealth, which is in large part a product of decades—and, in a broader sense, centuries—of public policy (Lui, Robles, & Leondar-Wright, 2006). The typical African American and Latino household has a mere $5 and $6 of net worth, respectively, for every $100 in assets held by the typical non-Hispanic white household (Meschede, Shapiro, Sullivan, & Wheary, 2010). This is all the more disconcerting for two reasons. According to the U.S. Census Bureau (2008), America's racial minorities will become a majority of the U.S. population by 2042. In addition, unless the government adopts policy reforms during the next three decades, shortly before these segments of the population with extremely limited lifetime savings enter retirement, the Social Security program will experience funding shortfalls, which could lead to benefit cuts. This development could produce the highest rates of elderly poverty the United States has experienced since the Great Depression.

Social Security reform options to forestall this crisis of retirement security will be discussed further below. The problem is too large, however, to be solved through Social Security reforms alone. Unless more is invested in public education to ensure that a majority of children coming of age during the next few

Figure 11.4–11.6 A vulnerable population who need Social Security.

decades have the skills needed to succeed in a globalized economy, they will not be able to earn enough—and, hence, save enough—to retire with economic security.

While Social Security's retirement benefits are extremely important to racial minority communities, its disability and survivors benefits are equally vital, if not more so. While 74% of white Americans who receive Social Security benefits receive retirement benefits, nearly half (45%) of African American beneficiaries and a majority (58%) of persons of "other" (neither white nor black) racial and ethnic groups rely on Social Security for its survivor and disability benefits (Rockeymoore & Lui, 2011). This is due to myriad factors—most notably, African Americans (and Native Americans) die younger, on average, than white Americans and, consequently, either do not collect their Social Security retirement benefits or receive them for fewer years, compared with whites. People of color also tend to suffer higher rates of poverty, disability, and morbidity than whites, in part because they tend to work in more physically challenging and dangerous jobs (Bucknor & Baker, 2016).

THE OUTLOOK FOR THE FUTURE

Since the 1970s, real wages of all but the top 1% of U.S. households have stagnated, even as more and more women have joined the workforce (Piketty & Saez, 2007). From 1979 until the eve of the Great Recession in 2007, the top 1% received almost two-fifths of all gains in household income (Hacker & Pierson, 2010). The vast majority of Americans who will be retiring in the coming decades have been treading water economically during most of their working lives, struggling to pay off student loans, pay down a mortgage, pay rising tuition costs for their children, and pay down credit card debt that they accumulated in an attempt to maintain their tenuous standard of living. The Great Recession of 2007 to 2009, combined with the persistence of high unemployment and underemployment since the recession officially ended, have further undermined workers' savings and net worth, through lost wages for the unemployed, declining home values, and the need to cash out or borrow from 401(k) plans. Rosnick and Baker (2009) find that the "loss of wealth due to the collapse of the housing bubble and the plunge in the stock market [during 2008 to 2009] will make baby boomers far more dependent on Social Security and Medicare than prior generations"(p.2). Using data from the Federal Reserve Board's Survey of Consumer Finances, the Center for Retirement Research at Boston College calculated that as of 2011, Americans had an aggregate "retirement income deficit"—the gap between what they should have saved for retirement and what they actually have saved through Social Security, employer pensions, 401(k)'s, other forms of saving, and home equity—of $6.6 trillion (Retirement USA, 2012).

THE IMPACT OF SOCIAL SECURITY BENEFIT CUTS

As noted above, pensions and savings currently provide a significant share of income to only the top 30% to 40% of elderly households. But what do data on access to employment-based pension plans and retirement savings of today's workforce portend for the future of retirement income security? In the next section, we will discuss policy options for reforming Social Security. Many policymakers propose cuts to retirement benefits. To assess the advisability of such cuts, it is important to know how many Americans have pension plans and how much Americans have accumulated in retirement savings.

Traditionally, retirement income security was understood as a three-legged stool consisting of Social Security, a sizable occupational defined benefit pension, and individual savings. Over the past several decades, however, it became increasingly rare for a worker to remain with the same employer for life. At the same time, increasing international competition forced companies to cut costs, pushing most to trim their pension contributions. As a result, fewer and fewer employers have contributed substantially to their employees' retirement income security through a defined-benefit pension.

Consequently, the Federal Reserve Board's Report on the Economic Well-Being of U.S. Households found that only 47% of households own any assets in a 401(k) or other employment-related retirement account. About 2 in 10 are vested in a defined benefit pension (Federal Reserve Board, 2015). For the past 30+ years, employers have been transitioning from defined-benefit pensions, where they were obligated to pay a fixed annuity for life, to defined contribution plans, where they are obligated only to match workers' contributions—if they so choose and up to the level they choose. This development is part of a broader trend in the American political economy since the 1970s of privatizing risk (Hacker, 2006) [*See Chapter 3 in this volume.*]

Many policymakers regard defined contribution plans as a policy alternative to Social Security. But compared to Social Security, these plans have major drawbacks—drawbacks that are mostly shared by Individual Retirement Accounts (IRAs) as well. These include the following:

- *Coverage in defined contribution plans is nowhere near as universal as Social Security.* Only about half of households have 401(k)-style accounts (29% have IRA-style accounts), and coverage correlates strongly with income, education, and race (Federal Reserve Board, 2015).
- *Contributions are voluntary for employers and employees.* Since median wages have been stagnating since the mid-1970s, and in recent years there has been a severe economic downturn and high unemployment, most workers have lacked sufficient disposable income to contribute significant amounts to their retirement accounts, meaning that their account balances upon retirement will be low.
- *401(k) plans and IRAs contribute to the federal deficit.* Employees do not pay income tax on amounts contributed to 401(k)'s, whether the amounts are contributed by themselves or by their

employers. In the case of IRAs, individual contributions are also tax deductible. In 2015, for example, the present value of the costs of the subsidy provided by the federal government for defined contribution plans and IRAs was about $78 billion (U.S. Office of Management and Budget, 2015, Table 14.4).

- *Tax expenditures on 401(k)'s are highly regressive.* According to the Urban Institute-Brookings Tax Policy Center, roughly 70% of tax subsidies (a form of fiscal welfare) go to the top 20% of the income distribution, and half go to just the top 10% (Harris et al., 2014).

- *Much of the money that is contributed to these plans "leaks" out before a worker ever reaches retirement.* This is because workers can cash out their 401(k) balances (subject to a penalty) whenever they change jobs, and can borrow from them without penalty for a range of purposes, limiting the extent to which their contributions grow. IRAs are prone to similar leakage prior to retirement.

- *Up to 30% of the money contributed to 401(k)'s does not benefit the worker at all but goes to the investment firms managing the plan in the form of profits; administrative, marketing, and investment management fees; and trading costs* (Hiltonsmith, 2012). By contrast, no profit is deducted from a worker's contributions to Social Security, and the program's administrative expenses are less than 1%.

- *Individual accounts—whether defined contribution or IRA—are subject to the volatility of the stock and bond markets.* This was particularly evident in the recent economic downturn that began in 2008, when the average 401(k) balance dropped by a third. Such market downswings cause major problems for workers when they occur in the years leading up to when they need to—or had planned to—retire. This problem is compounded because the ability to delay retirement until the market recovers is limited by the poor employment outlook during such economic downturns, when many employers are looking to shed higher-earning older workers. Social Security benefits, by contrast, are predictable, and one's retirement age can be planned independently of market swings.

- *For purposes of income security, what retirees most need is a lifetime inflation-adjusted annuity such as that provided by Social Security*—that is, a steady, risk-free, monthly stream of income to mitigate the risk of living longer than expected (outliving one's savings), of inflation eating up one's savings, and of spending down one's assets quickly rather than budgeting carefully for one's later retirement years. Yet few retirees convert their 401(k) or IRA accounts into annuities, thereby leaving themselves exposed to these risks (Topoleski, 2011).

In light of these numerous, serious weaknesses of defined contribution plans and IRAs as retirement savings vehicles, it is not surprising that among the roughly half of American households that had balances in such accounts in 2013, their median value was a mere $59,000 (Federal Reserve Board, 2014). The median for households approaching retirement (aged 55 to 64) was about $100,000. Even the $100,000 accumulated for retirement will not go very far. Purcell (2009) estimates that with $100,000 in retirement savings, a 65-year-old man could buy a life annuity of about $700 a month, based on interest rates current in April 2009. In other words, individual accounts have clearly failed as a vehicle of retirement income security.

Given how few Americans have been able to accumulate significant savings in 401(k)'s or IRAs despite 30 years of public policy efforts to encourage such saving, how regressive federal tax expenditures on these accounts are as a form of social policy, and that tax expenditures on such private, individual savings vehicles contribute significantly to the federal deficit, it is puzzling that so many elected representatives and members of Washington think tanks argue that 401(k)'s and IRAs are a functionally equivalent policy alternative to Social Security (i.e., that cuts to Social Security benefits could be compensated for by increased tax expenditures on these optional, individualized solutions). That said, in recent years, some serious efforts have been made to develop modified versions of existing individual accounts that would make them more closely resemble Social Security by making participation automatic, contributions mandatory, and leakage less common (Ghilarducci, 2008).

THE DEMOGRAPHIC CHALLENGE, RETIREMENT BENEFITS, AND INTERNATIONAL COMPETITIVENESS

All over the world, populations are aging due to some combination of three factors: increasing longevity, declining fertility, and the aging of the "baby boom" generation. How does the U.S. demographic challenge compare to that of other industrialized nations? While the number of older Americans is growing, the share of the future U.S. population over age 65 will not be as large as in many other nations, because the number of younger Americans is also growing due to higher fertility rates and more net immigration than is experienced elsewhere. The share of Americans aged 65 and older is projected to increase from 14.5% of the population today to about 21% by 2050. In contrast, Germany and Japan are already coping with aging populations of 21% and 26%, respectively. By 2050, seniors are projected to make up 26% of the population in Canada, 33% in Germany, and 39% in Japan (Organization for Economic Cooperation and Development [OECD], 2013; OECD, 2015).

Despite the comparatively favorable demographic outlook in the United States, the growing number of older Americans still poses a challenge to the U.S. Social Security system. The severity of this challenge for Social Security is mitigated, however, by three factors. First, even though the full benefit age for Social Security is scheduled to be about average in the OECD, reaching 67 for those attaining age 65 by 2025, the effective retirement age—when people actually retire—is higher in the United States than in all but four (for men) or five (for women) OECD countries (Baily & Kirkegaard, 2009). The later onset of retirement in the U.S. diminishes the amount of benefits that need to be available for retired workers and their spouses. Second, as already noted, Social Security benefits in the United States are modest by international standards, and, as discussed earlier, U.S. replacement rates will decline in the future as the age for full-benefit receipt rises to 67. Most important, as will be detailed below, the Social Security system has saved $2.8 trillion for the retirement of the baby boom generation (Board of Trustees, 2015). No other OECD country has saved anywhere close to this amount for these cohorts' retirement. Together, these factors mean that the economic competitiveness of the United States is less threatened by an aging society.

SOCIAL SECURITY'S FINANCIAL OUTLOOK

According to the most recent actuarial calculations, Social Security can pay all scheduled benefits for the next 20 years and more than three quarters of promised benefits for the 55 years thereafter (Board of Trustees, 2015; Buffin, 2002). The retirement of the baby boom generation beginning in 2010, often depicted as a threat to Social Security's financial stability, was actually anticipated for a half century by Social Security's actuaries, who are required by law to plan 75 years in advance. To prepare for this wave of retirees, Congress enacted reforms in 1983 that increased Social Security's revenue stream and cut benefits, both over the short and long terms. As a result, the program has been running surpluses for the past three decades and, thereby, largely prefunded the retirement of the baby boom generation. After being able to pay 100% of scheduled benefits over the next two decades; however, the program will likely have a funding shortfall of about 25% per annum starting in 2034 (Board of Trustees, 2015).

OPTIONS FOR SOCIAL SECURITY REFORM

Experts of all political ideologies agree that to mitigate this long-term shortfall, some combination of revenue increases or spending cuts is needed. Others highlight the retirement income deficit and argue that benefits need to be increased. Hence, the policy reforms currently under discussion fall into three categories: reforms that would cut the program's costs (i.e., cut benefits), reforms that would increase Social Security's revenues, and reforms that would improve benefit adequacy (increase benefits).

OPTIONS TO CUT BENEFITS
A range of policy reforms have been proposed in recent years to cut Social Security benefits with the goal of reducing the program's expenditures. The two most prominently discussed options are described and assessed below.

    1.   Increase the retirement age.

The primary benefit cut advocated by those seeking to reduce Social Security expenditures is to raise the full benefit age gradually to age 70 (increasing by 36/47 of a month every year). This could eliminate about a quarter of the 75-year shortfall in Social Security's finances (U.S. Social Security Administration, Office of the Chief Actuary, 2015).

Advocates of raising the retirement age say that it does not really constitute a cut, because workers could still receive full benefits, just at a later age. They also argue that this would be one of the most equitable ways to control program costs, because in contrast to other options, such as reducing the COLA, raising the retirement age would give individuals who would be affected time to adjust their savings behavior and planned retirement age. Moreover, proponents claim, the vast majority of Americans are able to work longer than in previous generations, because longevity has increased and work today is less physically demanding than it used to be. From this perspective, raising the retirement age would merely incentivize people to work longer. Let us consider each of these arguments in turn.

First, opponents of raising the retirement age point out that any increase in the full-benefit age has the effect of an across-the-board cut in retirement benefits at any age benefits are claimed (Gregory, Bethell, Reno, & Veghte, 2010). This is because if people retire at the same age in the wake of the reform as they would have prior to the reform, their monthly benefit will be lower for the rest of their lives. Workers could escape this monthly benefit cut only if they retired later. Yet, past experience shows that about half of all workers claim Social Security at the earliest age of eligibility, despite the resulting benefit cut. Even still, retiring later to attain equal benefits as before the benefit-age increase means that retirees' total lifetime benefits would be lower.

Second, while it is true that, on average, Americans are living longer today than in the 1930s, the increase in longevity is not as substantial as is often claimed. Most of the increase in life expectancy since the 1930s is not due to increased longevity but to a decrease in child mortality. A more relevant metric for setting the retirement age is life expectancy at age 65. Since 1940, this has increased by about 6 years, while the

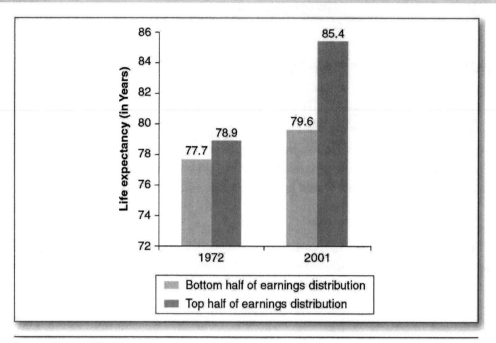

Figure 11.7 Life Expectancy at Age 60 for Male Social Security-Covered Workers, by Socioeconomic Status, 1972 and 2001.

Source: Waldron (2007).

retirement age itself has increased by 1 year and, by 2026, will have increased by 2 years, to a full-benefit age of 67 for those who turn 66 that year (U.S. Social Security Administration, 2015d).

A case can certainly be made that workers today should not be able to be retired any longer on average than their great grandparents could be in the 1940s. Interestingly, though, when one analyzes the data further, one discovers an equity issue: The increase in longevity has not been evenly distributed across demographic groups. As Figure 11.7 shows, almost all the gains in life expectancy since the early 1970s have gone to the top half of the income spectrum.

Men in the upper half of the earnings distribution saw an increase of 5.8 years, while those in the bottom half experienced a gain of only 1.2 years. In addition, African Americans, particularly men, continue to die at a younger age than whites, and better educated individuals have a greater life expectancy at 65 than do those with less education.

A third claim made by proponents of raising the retirement age is that the shift from an industrial to a service economy has made work less physically demanding, allowing workers to work later in life. While it is hard to compare today's work to the work performed several decades ago by different workers under different conditions in a different societal context, there is research available on the demands placed on the older workforce today. A study by the Center for Economic and Policy Research found that 34% of workers aged 62 to 65 and 33% of workers aged 66 to 69 work in physically demanding jobs or under difficult conditions—for example, as janitors, home health care workers, and cooks (Bucknor & Baker, 2016). Workers in these jobs often have difficulty continuing to work into their late 60s.

In addition, decisions about when to retire are shaped largely by factors other than the full-benefit age. A representative survey conducted in 2011 found that 42% of workers retire early due to poor health, care responsibilities, job loss, or other negative reasons (Kingson & Morrisey, 2012). Under current arrangements, such workers are already suffering a sizable lifetime benefit reduction due to early retirement.[10] Additional increases to the retirement age would cut their benefits even further and—if the past is a guide—are unlikely to result in a large percentage of seniors retiring later. Moreover, the current system already incentivizes later retirement, as benefits are increased if one delays retirement.

In short, raising the retirement age is a method of cutting benefits that hits disadvantaged socioeconomic and demographic groups the hardest. Opponents argue that if benefits need to be cut, more equitable types of cuts—such as reducing spousal benefits or reducing COLAs—are preferable.[11]

2. Reduce the COLA.

The second most widely proposed benefit cut is reducing Social Security's COLA by adopting the chained Consumer Price Index (CPI). This would reduce the program's long-term shortfall by about 21% (U.S. Social Security Administration, Office of the Chief Actuary, 2015).

When Congress enacted automatic Social Security COLAs in 1972, the Bureau of Labor Statistics (BLS) produced only one CPI. It measured inflation experienced by urban wage

Figure 11.8 Social Security promotes well-being.

earners and clerical workers (about 32% of the population). The 1972 Social Security amendments used this CPI as the measure of inflation, and it remains the basis for determining Social Security COLAs today.

In 1978, BLS expanded the CPI to cover all urban residents (about 87% of the population, including most retirees) and named it the CPI-U (the original CPI was renamed the CPI-W). The CPI-U is used to index personal income tax brackets and poverty thresholds, but is not used to determine Social Security COLAs. In 1988, the BLS launched a third, experimental index, the CPI-E, which reflects the spending patterns of persons age 62 and older (about 18% of the population). All these indexes measure changes over time in the price of a representative market basket of goods and services purchased by their respective populations.

In 1999, the BLS slowed the growth of all the indexes by accounting for consumer substitution among similar items, such as different varieties of apples. Experts agreed that through substitution—buying fewer items that rose more in price (e.g., Granny Smith apples) and more of those whose prices rose less or fell (e.g., Golden Delicious apples)—consumers could lessen the increase in their cost of living caused by inflation. In 1999, BLS began tracking a "chained" version of the CPI-U that reflects the extent to which consumers make changes in their purchasing patterns across dissimilar categories of items—such as spending more on fuel and less on food—in response to relative price changes. Since 1999, the chained CPI-U has risen about 0.3 percentage points more slowly per year than the revised CPI-W.

Most of those in Washington seeking to cut Social Security benefits advocate switching to the chained CPI-U as the basis for determining Social Security's COLAs. Doing so would yield a Social Security COLA that is about 0.3 percentage points lower each year, which would result in a Social Security benefit that is about 8.4% lower by the time a retiree reaches age 92. Similarly, an individual who begins receiving disability benefits at age 35 would receive a benefit that is about 8.4% lower by age 65.

Proponents of this benefit cut claim that it is merely a technical correction, but in fact there is no evidence to support the claim that seniors change consumption patterns across dissimilar categories of items in response to price changes—such as spending more on fuel and less on food—to maintain their standard of living. More often, seniors have to respond to increases in the price of health care by cutting back in other areas, and it is hard to believe that they maintain their standard of living in doing so. Still, compared with raising the retirement age, this option has the merit of affecting all demographic groups equally, although it could be argued that its effects would be more significant for racial and ethnic minorities who are more dependent on Social Security for their retirement income.

OPTIONS TO INCREASE REVENUES

A number of options have been proposed to increase Social Security's revenues. Two are presented here.

1. Eliminate the tax cap.

At present, payroll taxes are levied only on earned income (income from wages rather than investments) and only up to a **taxable maximum,** which is inflation-adjusted annually ($118,500 in 2016). In 1983, the taxable maximum captured 90% of wages in the economy. Since 1979, however, 40% of U.S. income growth has gone to the top 1% of earners. Because this income growth has been taking place disproportionately beyond the reach of Social Security's tax base, today the tax cap captures only 83% of aggregate wages in the economy (U.S. Social Security Administration, 2016i, Table 4.B1). Unequal income growth, therefore, limits Social Security's payroll tax base and robs it of considerable revenue. Eliminating the cap on earnings subject to Social Security contributions would reduce the long-term shortfall by about 71% (U.S. Social Security Administration, Office of the Chief Actuary, 2015).

The advantage of eliminating the tax cap is that it would raise revenue in progressive fashion by burdening only those who could afford it. Higher wage earners would also earn larger Social Security benefits in the process, making the reform reasonably fair. An argument against eliminating the tax cap is that many of the workers whose payroll taxes would be increased would have earnings below the income tiers which have experienced most of the income gains in recent decades, i.e. the top 1%—and particularly the top one-tenth of 1%. In addition, the latter group has experienced most of its income growth not in earned income but in investment income, which is not subject to the Social Security tax. Hence, incorporating investment income into the Social security tax base might be a better way of securing additional revenue for the Social Security system than marginally raising the tax cap.

2. Increase the payroll tax rate.

Payroll taxes are currently levied on 6.2% of earned income, with matching employee and employer contributions. Raising this rate to 7.6% for employers and employees would *completely eliminate* Social Security's 75-year shortfall. The principal merit to this proposed reform is that it would clearly retain Social Security's core principle of earned benefits—workers would fund their own future income security by saving more now. The downside to this reform is that it would reduce low- and moderate-income workers' disposable income in an era when many of these households are struggling to make ends meet and that it would make the payroll tax even more regressive.

Social Security benefits suffice in most cases to lift recipients out of poverty, but still leave one half to two thirds of elderly households with less than they need to make ends meet. Moreover, certain demographic groups—for example, widows, African Americans, and Latinos—are disproportionately economically insecure in retirement. In response, many experts call for increasing, rather than cutting, Social Security benefits. A wide range of options for doing so has been proposed (Reno & Lavery, 2009). We will focus next on two potential policy alternatives to achieve this goal.

1. Raise benefits for widowed spouses.

Widowed spouses (usually women) suffer the highest poverty rate (45%) of any demographic group among the elderly. Social Security pays widowed spouses 100% of their deceased partner's earned benefit. This provides good benefits to women whose husbands were the main wage earners in the household. When, however, both partners earned similar, modest amounts during their working lives, then the husband's earned benefit is roughly equal to his wife's. This is increasingly common in the 21st century. In such cases, the wife's benefit does not increase upon the death of her husband. A more equitable policy in such cases would be to add up both partners' earned benefits and pay the surviving spouse 75% of this amount. This would modernize Social Security by adapting it to the increase in gender equality and the transformation of gender roles that have occurred in recent decades. Doing so would cost an amount equal to only about 4% of Social Security's long-term shortfall (U.S. Social Security Administration, Office of the Chief Actuary, 2015).

2. Increase the COLA.

Experts acknowledge that the cost-of-living index on which Social Security's COLA is currently based, the CPI-W, and the index used by the proposed chained CPI fail to measure accurately the actual living costs of the elderly. (See the section on benefit cuts above.) Indeed, neither index even *attempts* to measure accurately the living costs of the elderly. This is because neither index is based on surveys of the specific goods and services the elderly consume and the prices they pay. The most glaring source of potential error in these indexes is the underestimation of health care costs; on average, the elderly spend a much greater share of their income on health care than do other Americans. In addition, health care inflation tends to rise much faster than inflation in general.

There is a cost-of-living index, however, that *is* based on the goods and services consumed by the elderly. It is called the CPI-E, or experimental CPI. The CPI-E is not yet perfected. While it reflects the spending of households age 62 and older, it is based on a relatively small sample. Those who advocate basing Social Security's COLA on the CPI-E have called on the BLS to survey a larger sample of households and to survey shopping outlets specifically used by the elderly. Given that roughly $800 billion flows into and out of the Social Security program every year, the few million dollars it would cost to generate more robust CPI-E estimates would surely be worth the expense.

How much would a CPI for the elderly improve benefit adequacy? The chief actuary of the Social Security Administration estimates that the CPI-E will rise about 0.2 percentage points faster than the CPI-W (Veghte, Reno, Bethell, & Walker, 2011). This would translate into a Social Security benefit that is about 6% higher by the time a retiree reaches age 92. For the program as a whole, this would increase expenditures by an amount equal to about 14% of the long-term shortfall (U.S. Social Security Administration, Office of the Chief Actuary, 2015).

THE POLITICS OF SOCIAL SECURITY TODAY

Public opinion polls consistently reveal that upwards of three quarters of Americans support Social Security, oppose benefit cuts, and would rather increase contributions than cut benefits, if forced to choose. Yet, since the 1980s, there has been a concerted effort by conservative think tanks and Wall Street campaign donors to undermine public confidence in the program. A possible impetus for this is that about $900 billion flows through the Social Security system each year. If Social Security were privatized, as President Bush attempted to do in 2005, and this money were to flow into private investment accounts, firms handling these accounts would stand to earn billions of dollars each year in additional revenues through fees and profits. Another motivation for well-funded campaigns promoting Social Security cuts is that if Social Security benefits were to be reduced significantly for future generations, the nearly $3 trillion that the federal government has borrowed from the Social Security Trust Fund might never have to be fully repaid. This would ease pressure on the federal budget and allow lower tax rates in the future.

THE "LENINIST STRATEGY"

The conceptual foundation for the Right's anti-Social Security strategy was laid out in a white paper written for the Cato Institute, titled "Achieving a Leninist Strategy" (Butler & Germanis, 1983). The authors argued that undermining public support for Social Security would require three things: (a) dividing the existing coalition supporting Social Security by telling older people their benefits would not be cut while telling younger people the program would go bankrupt long before they retired; (b) constructing a coalition of private investment firms who would stand to profit from privatizing Social Security; and (c) enacting legislative reforms to make private alternatives to Social Security—401(k)'s and IRAs—more attractive.

Over the past three decades, this strategy has been followed closely and with considerable success. The Peter G. Peterson Foundation, launched by a former hedge fund manager, has alone invested tens of millions of dollars in anti-Social Security messaging, giving substantial sums to think tank researchers, financing a press outlet (*The Fiscal Times*) that publishes articles in *The Washington Post*, creating college curricula and exercises that teach college students that Social Security is unsustainable and needs to be cut, and orchestrating a sophisticated public relations campaign involving a national tour of paid experts preaching this same message.

FIVE PERSISTENT MYTHS ABOUT SOCIAL SECURITY

This attack on Social Security has been accompanied by the repetition of persistent and pernicious myths about the program that have muddled the debate over the future of Social Security and created confusion and division among the public. The five major myths are as follows:

1. *Social Security contributes to the federal deficit.*

President Roosevelt designed Social Security to be separate from the federal budget to protect workers' retirement income from Washington's annual budget battles. For decades, this represented a consensus perspective in American politics, and today the program is still officially "off budget." In recent years, however, many politicians, journalists, and think tank researchers have stopped respecting the legally distinct status of the program's finances and have begun discussing Social Security cutbacks in the context of deficit reduction.

Yet, Social Security and the federal deficit are completely unrelated, because they refer to separate pools of money. Payroll taxes go into the Social Security Trust Fund, and benefits are paid from this fund. The trust funds cannot be spent on other programs. If the federal government borrows from the Social Security Trust Funds, which are required by law to be invested in U.S. Treasury Bills, it has to pay the money back—just as it has to pay back holders of other U.S. Treasury bonds. If Social Security itself ever lacks sufficient funds to pay scheduled benefits, these benefits will be automatically cut, but the program is legally not allowed to borrow. In short, Social Security was set up in such a way that it cannot contribute to the federal deficit. It never has, and it never will. [*See Budget Charts in Chapter 1 of this volume.*]

2. *Social Security drains money from programs for youth.*

One line of argument against Social Security, consistent with the Leninist strategy, pits the young against the old in an attempt to undermine the intergenerational compact at the heart of the program. This "generational conflict" strategy claims that the government spends so much on Social Security (and Medicare) that it does not have enough money left over to fund programs for youth, such as education. Interestingly, most people who put forward this argument favor cuts both to Social Security and to programs serving youth. Moreover, because Social Security is not part of the federal budget, it is simply false to argue that money spent on Social Security could have been spent on programs serving youth. Social Security is not funded by the government—it is funded primarily by workers' payroll contributions as discussed above.

3. *Social Security is going bankrupt.*

Think of an office birthday fund where everyone contributes what they can afford and gets a gift on their birthday. Just like an office pool cannot "go bankrupt," neither can Social Security. Social Security is nothing more than pooled worker savings for various rainy day purposes. The money is either there or it isn't. If it isn't, benefits for all retirees, disabled persons, and survivors will be reduced proportionally—to continue the metaphor, they will all receive more modest gifts. In short, the term *bankruptcy* has no relevance to Social Security. Moreover, many in Washington feign concern over the harm that a Social Security "bankruptcy" decades from now might do to America's elderly, while at the same time advocating cuts to the program that are even larger than the ones that would automatically take effect if no action were taken.

4. *Social Security is unsustainable.*

Analogous to the notion of environmental unsustainability, this myth implies that if the Social Security program has larger scheduled benefits than scheduled contributions over the long term, which is currently the case, then something bad will occur beyond a reduction in benefits. In reality, if the program's long-term funding shortfall is not eliminated through reforms, all that will occur is an automatic cut in benefits by about 20% from 2034 onward (Bethell, Arnold, & Schreur, 2015). There would be no negative impact on the federal budget or economy, other than the fact that beneficiaries would have less money to spend, something that could be prevented only by increasing benefits, not cutting them.

5. *Social Security's negative cash flow means the program is "in the red."*

In 2011, the Social Security system started paying out more in annual benefits than it collected in annual contributions. Yet it was not "in the red"; it had more than enough money to fund scheduled benefits. This is because annual payroll tax collections are only one source of its financing. The other two sources are interest on investments, and taxation of the Social Security benefits of affluent beneficiaries. Proponents of this myth ignore the existence of the Social Security Trust Fund—which is expected to grow to nearly $3 trillion by 2019—and focus on the program's annual "cash flows." The metric of annual cash flows, however, is not considered by experts to be a key metric indicating the financial health of a pension fund (Bethell, Arnold, & Schreur, 2015).

CONCLUSION

This chapter began with a discussion of Social Security's purpose and evolution since its creation in 1935. It then presented information on eligibility for Social Security retirement, disability, and survivors' benefits; average benefit levels; and the demographic composition of the Americans who rely on Social Security for their income security. The final section discussed the program's financial outlook and policy reform options to increase benefit adequacy, increase revenues, or cut spending.

In sum, we can conclude that Social Security's finances are in good shape overall. Although modest reforms are needed to restore 100% solvency for the next 75 years, these reforms are feasible, even if they seem difficult to enact in the current partisan political environment. Increasing the payroll tax for employers and employees from 6.2% to 7.6% would restore 75-year solvency, for example, while increasing the tax base to which these rates apply (e.g., including unearned income in the tax base, as do Medicare payroll taxes) would put a sizable dent in the long-term shortfall.

While solidifying the finances of the Social Security program is straightforward, achieving retirement income security for American households presents a far more difficult challenge. Making a sufficient dent in Americans' retirement income deficit of $6.6 trillion will require reforms to enhance the adequacy of Social Security benefits in targeted fashion, which will have to be funded by some combination of increasing Social Security revenues and cutting benefits. Such enhancements to Social Security should be accompanied by reforms to government subsidies to 401(k) plans and IRAs to make them more equitably distributed across the income spectrum.

Finally, beyond the need for modest reforms to the Social Security program to shore up its finances and enhance Americans' retirement income security, the United States must invest more in education and training so future generations of retirees are able to attain sufficient income to earn adequate Social Security benefits and supplement these benefits with private savings. In addition, policymakers would do well to modernize Social Security so it does justice to 21st century family structures, for example, by increasing the benefits of surviving spouses where partners had similar earnings and by providing caregiver credits and income replacement during family leave.

Discussion Questions

1. On a deeper level, the debate over the future of Social Security is a debate about the role of government in U.S. society. Do you think it is appropriate for government to force workers to save for their retirement, disability, and survivors benefits? Or should the decision to save or not save be voluntary?
2. Do you think the Social Security payroll contribution rate should be increased, left at current rates, or lowered? What are the advantages and disadvantages of each approach?
3. What is the relationship between Social Security and the federal deficit and debt?
4. Do you think Social Security should be converted from a social insurance program to a welfare program targeted to poor people? Why or why not?
5. How would you reform Social Security to make its eligibility and benefit structure better suited to today's labor market and family structure?

Class Exercise

Ask each student to talk to three elderly people of different socioeconomic and ethnic backgrounds and interview them each for 10 minutes about what Social Security means to them. They should ask these seniors, if they were entering the workforce today, what kinds of reforms to Social Security they would advocate: reforms that would increase benefits, cut benefits, or increase revenues. The students should collate the answers they received in three tables on the blackboard and then discuss their own opinions on the issue.

Suggested Websites

Center on Budget and Policy Priorities: http://www.cbpp.org

Center for Global Policy Solutions: http://globalpolicysolutions.org/

Center for Retirement Research: http://crr.bc.edu/

Economic Security Database: Elder Initiative (Wider Opportunities for Women): http://www.basiceconomicsecurity.org/EI/

National Academy of Social Insurance: www.nasi.org

Social Security Stories Project (Frances Perkins Center): http://socialsecuritystories.org/

Social Security Works: http://www.socialsecurityworks.org/

Strengthen Social Security Coalition: http://strengthensocialsecurity.org/

U.S. Social Security Administration, Office of Research, Statistics, and Policy Analysis: http://www.socialsecurity.gov/policy/

Suggestions for Further Reading

Altman, N. J. (2005). *The battle for Social Security: From FDR's vision to Bush's gamble*. Hoboken, NJ: John Wiley.

Butler, S., & Germanis, P. (1983). Achieving a Leninist strategy. *Cato Journal, 3*(2), 547–556.

Edwards, K.A., Turner, A., & Hertel-Fernandez, A. (2016). *A young person's guide to Social Security,* (3rd Ed.) Washington, DC: National Academy of Social Insurance.

Ghilarducci, T. (2008). *When I'm 64: The plot against pensions and the plan to save them*. Princeton, NJ: Princeton University Press.

Hacker, J. S. (2006). *The great risk shift: The assault on American jobs, families, health care, and retirement—and how you can fight back*. New York: Oxford University Press.

Laursen, E. (2012). *The people's pension: The struggle to defend Social Security since Reagan*. Oakland, CA: AK Press.

Lui, M., Robles, B., & Leondar-Wright, B. (2006). *The color of wealth: The story behind the U.S. racial wealth divide*. New York: W. W. Norton.

Oliver, M., & Shapiro, T.M. (2006). *Black wealth/White wealth: A new perspective on racial inequality*. New York: Routledge.

Rockeymoore, M. M., & Lui, M. (2011). *Plan for a new future: The impact of Social Security reform on people of color*. Washington, DC: Commission to Modernize Social Security.

Sullivan, L., et al. (2015). *The racial wealth gap: Why policy matters*. New York: Demos.

References

Altman, N. J. (2005). *The battle for Social Security: From FDR's vision to Bush's gamble*. Hoboken, NJ: John Wiley.

Baily, M. N., & Kirkegaard, J. F. (2009). *U.S. pension reform: Lessons from other countries*. Washington, DC: Peterson Institute for International Economics.

Bethell, T., Arnold, K., & Schreur, E. 2015. *Social Security finances: Findings of the 2015 trustees' report*. Washington, D.C.: National Academy of Social Insurance.

Board of Trustees (2015). *Annual report of the Board of Trustees of the Federal Old-Age and Survivors Insurance and Federal Disability Insurance Trust Funds*. Washington, DC: U.S. Social Security Administration.

Boushey, H., & Glynn, S. J. (2012). *Fast facts on our proposed Social Security Cares Program*. Washington, DC: Center for American Progress.

Bucknor, C., & Baker, D. (2016). Still working hard: An update on the share of older workers in physically demanding jobs. Washington, DC: Center for Economic and Policy Research.

Buffin, K. (2002). The U.S. Social Security system: Solvency and sustainability. *Benefits & Compensation International 34*(4), London, England: Pension Publications Limited.

Bureau of Labor Statistics. (2015). CPI detailed report data for August 2015. Table 24. Historical consumer Price Index for all urban consumers (CPI-U): U. S. city average, all items.

Butler, S., & Germanis, P. (1983). Achieving a Leninist strategy. *Cato Journal, 3*(2), 547–556.

Center on Budget and Policy Priorities. (2015). *Policy basics: Introduction to Supplemental Security Income*. Washington, DC: Author.

Citro, C. F., & Michael, R. T. (Eds.). (1995). *Measuring poverty: A new approach*. Washington, DC: National Academy Press.

Congressional Budget Office. (2011). *Trends in the distribution of household income between 1979 and 2007*. Washington, DC: U.S. Government Printing Office.

Employee Benefit Research Institute. (2010). *Databook on employee benefits*. Washington, DC: Author.

Engelhardt, G. V., & Gruber, J. (2006). Social Security and the evolution of elderly poverty. In A. J. Auerbach, D. E. Card, & J. M. Quigley (Eds.), *Public policy and income distribution* (pp. 259–287). New York: Russell Sage Foundation.

Federal Reserve Board. (2015). *Report on the economic well-being of U.S. households in 2014*. Washington, DC: U.S. Government Printing Office.

Federal Reserve Board (2014). *2013 survey of consumer finances*. Washington, DC: U.S. Government Printing Office.

Gabe, T. (2015). *Social Security's effect on child poverty*. CRS Report RL33289. Washington, DC: U.S. Government Printing Office.

Ghilarducci, T. (2008). *When I'm 64: The plot against pensions and the plan to save them*. Princeton, NJ: Princeton University Press.

Gregory, J. M., Bethell, T. N., Reno, V. P., & Veghte, B. W. (2010). *Strengthening Social Security for the long run*. Washington, DC: National Academy of Social Insurance.

Hacker, J. S. (2006). *The great risk shift: The assault on American jobs, families, health care, and retirement—and how you can fight back*. New York: Oxford University Press.

Hacker, J. S., & Pierson, P. (2010). *Winner-take-all-politics: How Washington made the rich richer—and turned its back on the middle class*. New York: Simon & Schuster.

Harris, B. et al. (2014). *Tax subsidies for asset development: An overview and distributional analysis*. Washington, DC: Urban Institute.

Hiltonsmith, R. (2012). Hidden fees are eating up your 401(k)'s. *CNN*.

Kingson, E., & Morrisey, M. (2012). *Can workers offset Social Security cuts by working longer?* Washington, DC: Economic Policy Institute.

Lui, M., Robles, B., & Leondar-Wright, B. (2006). *The color of wealth: The story behind the U.S. racial wealth divide*. New York: W. W. Norton.

Meschede, T., Shapiro, T. M., Sullivan, L., & Wheary, J. (2010). *Living longer on less: Severe financial insecurity among African-American and Latino seniors*. New York: Demos.

O'Leary, A. (2012). *Protecting workers and their families with paid family leave and caregiving credits.* Washington, DC: Center for American Progress.

Organization for Economic Cooperation and Development (OECD) (2015). Country statistical profiles. Geneva, Switzerland: Author.

Organization for Economic Cooperation and Development (OECD) (2013). Health at a glance, ageing and long-term care, 8.1. Demographic trends. Geneva, Switzerland: Author.

Piketty, T. & Saez, E. (2007). *Income and wage inequality* in the United States, 1913–2002. In Atkinson, A.B. Atkinson & T. Piketty (Eds.), *Top incomes over the twentieth century: A contrast between European and English-speaking countries.* Oxford: Oxford University Press.

Purcell, P. (2009). *Retirement savings and household wealth in 2007.* Washington, DC: Congressional Research Service.

Reno, V. P., & Lavery, J. (2009). *Fixing Social Security: Adequate benefits, adequate financing.* Washington, DC: National Academy of Social Insurance.

Retirement USA. (2012). *The retirement income deficit.* Retrieved from http://www.retirement-usa.org/retirement-income-deficit-0.

Rockeymoore, M. M., & Lui, M. (2011). *Plan for a new future: The impact of Social Security reform on people of color.* Washington, DC: Commission to Modernize Social Security.

Romig, K. (2015). *Social Security lifts 21 million Americans out of poverty.* Washington, DC: Center on Budget and Policy Priorities.

Rosnick, D., & Baker, D. (2009). *The wealth of the baby boom cohorts after the collapse of the housing bubble.* Washington, DC: Center for Economic Policy Research.

Ruggles, P. (1990). *Drawing the line: Alternative poverty measures and their implications for public policy.* Washington, DC: Urban Institute Press.

Schwarz, J. E. (2005). *Freedom reclaimed: Rediscovering the American vision.* Baltimore, MD: Johns Hopkins University Press.

Short, K. (2015, September). The Supplemental Poverty Measure: 2014. *Current Population Reports.* Washington, DC: U.S. Census Bureau.

Topoleski, J. (2011). *401(k) plans and retirement savings: Issues for Congress.* Washington, DC: Congressional Research Service.

U.S. Census Bureau (2015a). *Poverty Data. Table 3: Poverty status of people, by age, race, and Hispanic origin: 1959 to 2014.* Washington, DC: U.S. Government Printing Office.

U.S. Census Bureau (2015b). Income and poverty in the United States: 2014. *Current Population Reports.* Washington, DC: U.S. Government Printing Office.

U.S. Census Bureau (2010). *Observations from the interagency technical working group on developing a supplemental poverty measure.* Washington, DC: U.S. Government Printing Office.

U.S. Census Bureau (2008). *An older and more diverse nation by mid-century.* Washington, DC: U.S. Government Printing Office.

U.S. Office of Management and Budget. (2015). *Analytical perspectives, FY 2017 Budget.* Washington, DC: U.S. Government Printing Office.

U.S. Census Bureau (various dates). *Population estimates. Historical data.* Washington, DC: U.S. Government Printing Office.

U.S. Social Security Administration (2016a). *Normal retirement age.* Washington, DC: U.S. Government Printing Office.

U.S. Social Security Administration (2016b). *Effect of early or delayed retirement on retirement benefits.* *Social Security Online.* Retrieved from http://www.ssa.gov/oact/ProgData/ar_drc.html.

U.S. Social Security Administration (2016c). *Social Security retirement benefits.* Washington, DC: U.S. Government Printing Office.

U.S. Social Security Administration (2016d). *Social Security survivors' benefits.* Washington, DC: U.S. Government Printing Office.

U.S. Social Security Administration (2016e). *Disability planner: Family benefits.* Washington, DC: U.S. Government Printing Office.

U.S. Social Security Administration (2016f). *Social Security beneficiary statistics; Number of beneficiaries receiving benefits on December 31, 1970–2015.* Washington, DC: U.S. Government Printing Office.

U.S. Social Security Administration (2016g). *Family benefits in current payment status.* Washington, DC: U.S. Government Printing Office.

U.S. Social Security Administration (2016h). *Income of the population 55 or older, 2014.* Washington, DC: U.S. Government Printing Office.

U.S. Social Security Administration (2016i). *Annual statistical supplement, 2015.* Washington, DC: U.S. Government Printing Office.

U.S. Social Security Administration (2015a). *SSI annual statistical report, 2014.* Washington, DC: U.S. Government Printing Office.

U.S. Social Security Administration (2015b). *Annual report of the Supplemental Security Income Program.* Washington, DC: U.S. Government Printing Office.

U.S. Social Security Administration (2015c). *Fast facts and figures about Social Security, 2015.* Washington, DC: U.S. Government Printing Office.

U.S. Social Security Administration (2015d). *Cohort life expectancy (Table V.A4).* Washington, DC: U.S. Government Printing Office.

U.S. Social Security Administration (2015e). *Social Security trust fund data. Old-Age and Survivors Insurance Trust Fund, 1937–2014.* Washington, DC: U.S. Government Printing Office.

U.S. Social Security Administration, Office of the Chief Actuary (2016). *Social Security benefits: Types of benefits.* Washington, DC: U.S. Government Printing Office.

U.S. Social Security Administration, Office of the Chief Actuary (2015). *Proposals affecting trust fund solvency.* Actuarial Publications. Washington, DC: U.S. Government Printing Office.

U.S. Social Security Administration, Office of Retirement and Disability Policy (2012). *Social Security programs throughout the world: Europe, 2012.* Washington, DC: U.S. Government Printing Office.

Van de Water, P. N., Sherman, A., & Ruffing, K. (2013). *Social Security keeps 22 million Americans out of poverty: A state-by-state analysis.* Washington, DC: Center on Budget and Policy Priorities.

Veghte, B. W., Reno, V. P., Bethell, T. N., & Walker, E. A. (2011). *Should Social Security's cost-of-living adjustment be changed?* Washington, DC: National Academy of Social Insurance.

Waldron, H. (2007) Trends in mortality differentials and life expectancy for male Social Security-covered workers, by socio-economic status. *Social Security Bulletin, 67*(3), 1–28.

Wider Opportunities for Women (2013). *Doing without: Economic insecurity and older Americans No. 3: Race and ethnicity.* Boston, MA: Gerontology Institute, University of Massachusetts.

Wu, K. B. 2013. *Sources of income for older Americans, 2012.* Washington, DC: AARP Public Policy Institute.

[1]The self-employed pay both the employer and employee contributions (i.e., 12.4% of income) but can deduct the employer contribution from their taxable income for income tax purposes.

[2]Initially, Medicare FICA taxes amounted to only 0.35% of the first $6,600 of income earned in a given year. In an attempt to keep pace with the high levels of inflation in the health care sector, Medicare payroll taxes have risen steadily over the program's history, much like premiums in the private health-insurance sector. In 1994, the upper wage limit on which Medicare contributions are levied was eliminated so that today Medicare taxes apply to all earned income, unlike Social Security taxes, which are levied only up to a taxable maximum ($118,500 in 2016). In 2012, the Medicare payroll tax was 1.45% for the employer and employee on all wages earned. The Affordable Care Act of 2010 increased Medicare payroll tax revenues considerably. It added a 0.9% surtax on earned income of more than $200,000 ($250,000 for married couples), and a 3.8% surtax on unearned (investment) income for such high-earning households.

[3]In fact, Social Security has two trust funds: Old-Age and Survivors Insurance (OASI) and Disability Insurance (DI), referred to together as the OASDI trust funds. The two trust funds function similarly, and in practice, policymakers have allowed the two funds to borrow from each other to meet obligations. For the sake of simplicity, the two are discussed here collectively as the Social Security Trust Fund.

[4]Over 90% of the workforce is in covered employment. Those not covered include most federal employees hired before 1984, railroad employees with more than 10 years of service, and employees in some state and local governments that chose not to participate in the Social Security program.

[5]The Social Security Administration is lenient in calculating earnings per quarter. For example, if someone earns at least 4 times the minimum amount required for one quarter of Social Security credit ($1,260 in 2016) in just one month of a given year, the Social Security Administration grants them the full four credits for that year.

[7]These worker "savings" are pooled collectively, not individually, but they may still be considered savings from an individual's standpoint.

[8]Other policies through which the federal government contributes to income security for the elderly are favorable income-tax treatment of employer contributions to pensions and 401(k)'s on the one hand and employee contributions to 401(k)'s and individual retirement accounts (IRAs) on the other. These will be discussed in more detail below.

[9]Those who do not qualify for Social Security because they did not contribute to the program during their working lives may apply for the means-tested SSI, the welfare program for the elderly.

[10]As global economic competition has put increasing pressure on companies to cut labor costs in recent decades, many have shed older, less productive and higher-earning workers, and many of these workers,

who might have been retained in an earlier era, have had either to claim Social Security retirement benefits early or—if they were significantly impaired—to apply for Social Security disability benefits.

[11]Proponents of raising the retirement age beyond 67—such as Alan Simpson and Erskine Bowles, chairs of the 2010 National Commission on Fiscal Responsibility and Reform—offer to soften the distributional inequity of the benefit cut by including "hardship exemptions" for workers in poor health and in physically demanding jobs. But studies of this issue suggest that the percentage of those in their late 60s who would qualify for such a hardship exemption is likely to be large, making the exemption expensive (Kingson & Morrisey, 2012). Moreover, the administrative costs of adjudicating such determinations on a case-by-case basis, with the right to appeal, would be considerable, as adjudication proceedings in the Social Security Disability program have shown. The costs of adjudicating and granting hardship exemptions might well exceed the cost savings generated by the benefit cut. From a public policy perspective, one must also ask whether workers' contributions to Social Security might be better spent on benefits than on such invasive and costly administrative procedures.

Credits

12

POVERTY AND UNEMPLOYMENT

Does a "Work First" Remedy Work?

Roberta Rehner Iversen, PhD

Americans are continuously bombarded with rhetoric that reinforces the value of individual effort in determining one's life chances: "Opportunity is available for those who seek it," "Success comes to those who play by the rules," and "Hard work pays off." Such beliefs also inform many social policies designed to help individuals achieve economic success, however defined.

In contrast, an alternative set of beliefs emphasizes mutuality, equity, and equality in the distribution of responsibilities and rewards. This is reflected in statements such as "Children are innocent bystanders of their parents' actions," and "A just society provides a safety net for those who need it." Throughout U.S. history, policies that address poverty and unemployment have contained both of these perspectives, provoking a "debate about the roots of poverty ... that is hardly matched in any other area of discussion in the social sciences" (Strier, 2009, pp. 1071–1072). These contrasting positions are based on different views, religious and secular, about human nature and the proper role of the state. They appear today in arguments about who are the "deserving" and "undeserving" poor and the "deserving" and "undeserving" unemployed. [*See Chapters 1 and 2 in this volume for a discussion of the historical roots of this issue.*]

Today, this debate is rooted in different theoretical perspectives about the relationship between social stratification and life chances (Weber, 1922/1978) and the importance of human, social, and cultural capital in determining them (Becker, 1993; Bourdieu, 2001; Coleman, 1990). Briefly, stratification refers to how ascribed individual characteristics such as race, gender, or family background affect education and economic attainment. Capital theories refer to how schooling, skills, and health (human capital); networks of relationships outside the family (bridging social capital); and cultural enrichment experiences fostered within the family and community, such as travel, art, and books (cultural capital), influence life outcomes. These theories also help identify the extent to which equality and social justice exist in a society or community.

This chapter first examines how poverty is defined and measured to serve as context for an analysis of the policies developed to address it. Then, after examining how employment is defined and measured, it provides a brief overview of today's labor market to provide some additional context for examining the main federal workforce policy in the United States, the Workforce Innovation and Opportunity Act of 2014 (WIOA; P.L. 113–128), which amended the Workforce Investment Act of 1998 (WIA; P.L. 105–220). After demonstrating that the WIA was seriously limited as a remedy to poverty and unemployment, especially for low-income participants (Cielinski & Socolow, 2015), and describing the intentions and hopes for WIOA, the chapter next examines other contemporary work-related policies, such as unemployment insurance, tax credits, government subsidies, and wage actions designed to moderate the effects of unemployment and poverty-level wages on millions of workers in the United States. Finally, the chapter raises a question that is often unexplored in the policymaking arena: Is work sufficient *by itself* to enable individuals and families to be economically self-sufficient? The chapter concludes with a few brief examples of creative anti-poverty, pro-employment, and economic development policies from the United States and abroad that embody principles of reciprocity, mutuality, and justice.

THE POVERTY CONTEXT: DEFINITION AND MEASUREMENT

In the United States, poverty is primarily defined in economic terms, as either an absolute or a relative condition. Living in absolute poverty implies a lack of resources to obtain food, shelter, and other basic necessities for oneself and one's family. In the United States, poverty is calculated in terms of a specific level of annual income, based on a formula initially developed a half century ago. In 2016, for example, the poverty line for a family of four was set at $24,300/year by the Office of Management and Budget. U.S. households in "deep poverty" have incomes below 50% of the official poverty line, while globally the World Bank (2016) defines extreme poverty as income of $1.90 a day or less. In a recent book examining extreme poverty in the U.S., Edin and Shaefer (2015) rounded this figure up to $2 per day.

By contrast, relative poverty uses a comparative and changing metric—for example, a percentage of median income. The choice of which standard to use in measuring poverty is determined by cultural and institutional values. In turn, the measurement choice determines what policy remedies are proposed, legislated, and implemented, and who is and is not eligible for the various remedies provided.

POVERTY MEASUREMENT: HISTORY

Because the United States uses an absolute measure, nearly every article on poverty in the United States refers to the percentage of persons who are *in poverty*, *below poverty*, or *above poverty*. This rhetoric gives the impression that persons who are "above poverty" are economically self-sufficient and that families living "above poverty" are able to feed, clothe, house, and educate their children adequately. The reality of what "above poverty" means, however, is far different, as history shows.

The **poverty thresholds** in the United States were originally developed in 1963 to 1964 by Mollie Orshansky, a research analyst in the Social Security Administration (Fisher, 1997), shortly after the publication of Michael Harrington's (1962) influential book *The Other America* and just before the federal government launched the War on Poverty. Orshansky calculated the poverty thresholds by multiplying the cost of the U.S. Department of Agriculture's economy food plan for families of three or more persons by a little more than three; this produced a figure that would satisfy a family's food needs in an emergency.

This multiple was based on a 1955 Department of Agriculture food consumption survey, which found that families of three or more persons spent about one-third of their after-tax money on food.

Consequently, the main poverty measure was and still is based *solely* on the cost of *one* aspect of a family's basic needs—food. Since the 1960s, the only aspect of this measure that has been updated is changes in food prices. Moreover, the 3x formula has never been changed, even though today the share of income spent on food is about one-third only for families with incomes in the lowest quintile. The share that all other families spend is below 20 percent (U.S. Department of Agriculture, 2016). Finally, although the poverty measure minimally accounted for family size and composition, it did not factor in the wide geographic variation in the cost of living in the United States. Ironically, Orshansky implied that her poverty thresholds were a measure of income *inadequacy*, not of income adequacy (Fisher, 1997). Nevertheless, with some minor adjustments, in 1969 the Bureau of the Budget (later the Office of Management and Budget) designated the poverty thresholds as the federal government's official *statistical* measure of poverty (Fisher, 1997).

POVERTY THRESHOLDS: POVERTY RATES AND THE POVERTY LINE

Today, the poverty thresholds are used to determine the number of Americans in poverty each year and how this number compares with previous years. For example, in fall 2015 the government announced that the poverty rate in 2014 was 14.8%—a rate that had not changed statistically since 2010. This calculation revealed that 46.7 million people in the U.S. were "officially" in poverty that year (U.S. Census Bureau, 2015a, 2015b). (It is important to note that the reported rates reflect data collected in the prior year.)

The poverty thresholds also establish the government's *official poverty line,* which designates the minimum level of income deemed necessary to achieve an adequate standard of living. In practice, the poverty line is an absolute figure that varies only by family size and age (< or > age 18) and is the same nationwide except for the states of Alaska and Hawaii.

POVERTY GUIDELINES: THE FEDERAL POVERTY LEVEL (FPL)

Each year, in the *Federal Register,* the Department of Health and Human Services issues the government's **poverty guidelines**, a simplified version of the federal poverty thresholds that is generally called the federal poverty level, or FPL. The guidelines are used for *administrative* purposes, such as determining financial eligibility for certain federal or state social programs. This eligibility level is usually set at 100% of the FPL, although occasionally eligibility is established at 125% or 150% FPL (see U.S. Department of Health and Human Services, 2016). The guidelines vary by family size, as do the thresholds. There is one set for the 48 contiguous states and the District of Columbia, one for Alaska, and one for Hawaii.

By design, the poverty thresholds and guidelines are intended to identify the extent of poverty and help determine eligibility for the nation's "safety net" programs. Within a decade after they were developed, however, critics challenged their effectiveness in determining the true extent of need in the United States. During the 1970s and 1980s, more and more groups argued for a new poverty metric, contending that too many people were being excluded from income support programs and that the existing measure sustained an inequitable status quo.

THE SUPPLEMENTAL POVERTY MEASURE: NEW IN 2011

Finally, in the mid-1990s, the National Science Foundation charged U.S. Census Bureau researchers with developing an alternative federal poverty measure that would take into account noncash benefits, such as housing vouchers, Medicaid, or food stamps (now called the Supplemental Nutrition Assistance Program,

For example, the "Smiths" are a Philadelphia, Pennsylvania family of four—two parents and two children under age 18—whose total family income in 2016 is $24,300. As the poverty threshold for a family of four in 2016 is $24,300 (U.S. Census Bureau, 2016), the Smith family is described as living *at the poverty line* or at *100% of poverty*. By this means, the threshold can also be used to identify who is *below poverty* (if the Smith family income were $24,000 in 2016) or *above poverty* (if the Smith family income were $25,050 in 2016). When the terms *below* or *above* poverty are used, they are always in reference to this official poverty line—the 100% figure. Thus, "above poverty" can mean anything from $1 above the official line to infinity, and "below poverty" can mean anything from the poverty line to zero income. Adding a little more perspective on the Smith family's poverty status, most social work and social welfare scholars, practitioners, and policymakers consider 200% of the poverty line (that is, two times the $24,300 income figure, or $48,600 in 2016 for a family of four) to be *bare self-sufficiency*, particularly in large metropolitan areas. Some analysts believe that even 200% of the poverty line is too low.

or SNAP), and common sources of income assistance such as the Earned Income Tax Credit (EITC). At the same time, the measure also had to account for household expenditures that did not exist earlier, such as the need many more women experienced for work clothing, transportation, and child care, and for higher medical costs (Center on Budget and Policy Priorities, 2010b).

In November 2011, the U.S. Census Bureau released its research on a new measure of poverty called the Supplemental Poverty Measure (SPM). In contrast to the previous measure whose principle criteria were food, family size, and family composition, the SPM includes selected expenditures and resources and adjusts for geographic differences in housing and health care costs (Short, 2011). The government expected the poverty rate to increase under the SPM, but although some analyses confirmed that outcome (Brooks, 2011; Luhby, 2011), others reported no change in poverty had occurred (Short, 2011). By 2014 the poverty rate for the total U.S. population according to the SPM was 15.3%, a significant difference from the official rate of 14.8% (Short, 2015, p.4). Importantly, SPM data suggest that anti-poverty programs reduced the percentage of the population with incomes below half of the poverty threshold, or "deep poverty" (Short, 2015, p. 7). Nevertheless, largely because of population increases, 48.4 million people were poor in 2014 according to the SPM, which is notably higher than the 46.7 million assessed by the official measure (Short, 2015, p.4).

Perhaps more important for the development of poverty reduction policies and programs, the two measures revealed significant differences in what proportion of various subgroups of the population—for example, the elderly, young, and immigrants—are in poverty. Both measures reveal large group differences in poverty according to race and ethnic origin. They each show that poverty rates for Blacks and Hispanics are twice as high as those for whites and Asians (Short, 2015, p. 5). Nevertheless, and despite the comment of Brookings Institution poverty expert Ron Haskins that "the lead story should be that government programs are effective in reducing poverty" (Luhby, 2011), the SPM is still used for *statistical* and *research* purposes only. Programs that have used the official poverty guidelines to assess eligibility remain tied to the old metric, at least until the programs, one by one, undergo Congressional reauthorization. Some states, however, have experimented with other, more equitable poverty measures such as the Self-Sufficiency Standard (Center for Women's Welfare, 2016) and the Economic Policy Institute's Family Budget Calculator

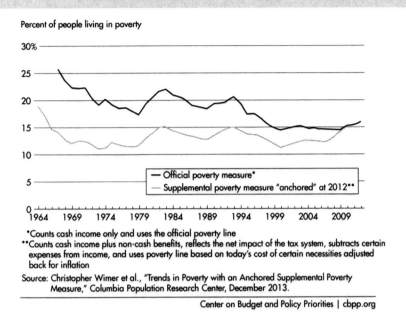

Figure 12.1 Poverty Has Fallen Significantly Since the 1960s Under the "Anchored" Supplemental Poverty Measures.

Percent of people living in poverty

— Official poverty measure*
···· Supplemental poverty measure "anchored" at 2012**

*Counts cash income only and uses the official poverty line
**Counts cash income plus non-cash benefits, reflects the net impact of the tax system, subtracts certain
   expenses from income, and uses poverty line based on today's cost of certain necessities adjusted
   back for inflation
Source: Christopher Wimer et al., "Trends in Poverty with an Anchored Supplemental Poverty
   Measure," Columbia Population Research Center, December 2013.

Center on Budget and Policy Priorities | cbpp.org

(2015). If the measure developed by the Budget Calculator was applied to the city of Philadelphia, the Smith family introduced earlier, whose annual income is just at the poverty line, would need an annual income of $76,393 to be considered economically self-sufficient.

Overall, using an absolute, universal poverty guideline is not conducive to achieving socially just outcomes. Having an income marginally above the poverty line is not substantially different from having an income marginally below it. Yet, this slight difference has major consequences in determining people's eligibility for a wide range of social and economic supports. In addition, the negative effects of poverty tend to be continuous rather than discrete, and the same level of income affects different people in different ways. Poverty statistics are a "snapshot" of a household's current economic status. They do not reveal the lingering effects of a long spell of poverty on a family or its individual members. It is thus critical to remember that the designation of an individual or family as "in poverty" or "not in poverty" often rests on miniscule differences and still signifies insufficient income overall.

THE EMPLOYMENT CONTEXT: DEFINITIONS AND MEASUREMENT

Employment statistics serve several functions. They are indicators of national economic performance and how many jobs exist in the U.S. economy, and they reflect individuals' status in relation to employment and unemployment (Whittaker, 2004). Like poverty statistics, employment data are derived from two main sources. First, a survey of payrolls in non-farm industries provides a job-based measure that yields information on how many persons are currently working, wage rates, and the number of salaried jobs created and lost in the economy (Whittaker, 2004). Second, longitudinal population surveys conducted by the U.S. Bureau of Labor Statistics (2015) of the U.S. Department of Labor among the civilian non-institutional population 16 years and older measure the number and percentage of people in the United States in several employment-related categories.

It might seem easy to determine whether a person is employed or unemployed, and the official U.S. definitions support this assumption. People with wage or salaried jobs, which includes self-employment, are considered *employed*, and people who are jobless, have actively looked for work in the four weeks prior to the survey, and are currently available for work are considered *unemployed* (U.S. Bureau of Labor Statistics, 2015). A third category, *not in the labor force*, is defined as persons who are neither employed nor unemployed: those who are neither working nor seeking work (U.S. Bureau of Labor Statistics, 2015). Examples are some (but not all) retired persons, persons providing family care, students, and disabled or ill persons who are unable to work.

However, because every worker (or would-be worker) does not fall into one of these three categories, the definitions are vulnerable to inequities. For example, the very notion of "working" itself is contested, as official definitions primarily count only wage work as "work." For decades, scholars and advocates have debated the monetary value of "housework" in a capitalist society, but this issue has not penetrated the calculus of the U.S. Bureau of Labor Statistics. There is, however, a little-known official category called "*unpaid family workers*" that includes "any person who worked without pay for 15 hours or more per week in a family-owned enterprise operated by a family member with whom they live" (U.S. Bureau of Labor Statistics, 2015).

A final "official" category consists of those "*marginally attached to the labor force*," defined as individuals without jobs who are not currently looking for work but who have looked for a job sometime in the prior 12 months, thereby demonstrating some degree of labor force attachment (U.S. Bureau of Labor Statistics, 2015). A subset of "marginally attached" workers includes the category of "*discouraged*" workers, individuals who have not looked for work during the previous 12 months or who have given up looking for work for the time being. If individuals in these two categories were considered "unemployed," the employment rate would increase significantly (Bronars, 2012). Also, when the U.S. Bureau of Labor Statistics examines employment trends, it only provides state data on how many workers are "*underemployed*," defined as those who are working part-time involuntarily, but it does not measure how many workers are working in positions that do not use their full array of skills and thus are earning wages below their level of competency. Underemployment is particularly rampant during recessions and tight labor markets.

Despite being incomplete, employment statistics reported monthly by the U.S. Bureau of Labor Statistics (2015) include the "total number of employed and unemployed persons in the United States for the previous month along with many characteristics of such persons." This enables us to make short- and long-term comparisons to assess the equity of current policies on the basis of such characteristics as gender, race/ethnicity, and age. In addition, although the monthly unemployment rate report is a frequent reminder of the nation's economic health and a useful tool in policy advocacy and development, its calculation must always be understood to be an undercount.

THE LABOR MARKET CONTEXT

Just as people in the United States hold competing views about poverty—that some deserve policy help and others do not—they also hold competing views about unemployment. Some analysts assert that jobs are available for any who want them (Mead, 1992), while others contend that jobs—particularly "good jobs" with wage and benefits sufficient to support a family adequately—have decreased continually for the past 30+ years in the United States (Schmitt & Jones, 2012). The views of those with the latter perspective were confirmed during the Great Recession of 2007 to 2009, considered by many to have been the worst economic downturn since the Great Depression. This recession negatively affected the incomes and employment situations of about 14 million Americans, nearly 10% of the working-age population, many of whom had previously been "middle income" (Iversen, Napolitano, & Furstenberg, 2011). Although the unemployment rate began to fall by 2012, it exceeded 9% on average nationally for 3½ years, with higher—sometimes much higher—rates in some parts of the country, especially for youth, racial and ethnic minorities, and those with less than 12 years of education (U.S. Bureau of Labor Statistics, 2010). Worse, although the unemployment rate fell to a more "normal" rate of 5% in 2016, there are still 7.9 million unemployed persons, one quarter (25.7%) of whom have been unemployed for 27 weeks or more (U.S. Bureau of Labor Statistics, 2016b).

The long view of the employment market for today's workers and potential workers remains pessimistic for several reasons: the transformation of the U.S. workforce since the 1970s from well-paid manufacturing jobs to generally lower paid jobs in the service economy; the ongoing transfer of jobs overseas to workers in other countries; and higher demand for high-school-and-beyond graduates with more demanding technological and technical skills. Many of the other aspects of the rapidly changing labor market that make it more difficult for workers to earn a family-sustaining wage are beyond the scope of this chapter, but the bottom line is that it has become, and likely will continue to be, harder for many workers to support their families consistently through employment alone, even when two parents are employed. [*See Chapter 3 in this volume for additional discussion of changing economic conditions in the United States.*] As a result, a number of employment-building and unemployment-moderating policies are now increasingly necessary to help working families make ends meet and avoid slipping into poverty. **Workforce development**, formerly known as education and job training, is now considered the main legislative remedy to under- and unemployment-based poverty. As the next section illustrates, this is much easier said than done.

WORKFORCE DEVELOPMENT

For more than two centuries, different types of job training programs have been viewed as the remedy to unemployment and poverty. In the 19th century, impoverished adults were indentured and children from poor families were farmed out as apprentices or placed in institutions such as almshouses or workhouses that would, theoretically, teach them employable skills and better work habits. In contrast to welfare programs, which have increasingly encouraged work but were originally established to enable poor mothers to care for their children at home (*see Chapter 12 in this volume*), public job training has always focused on helping individuals get jobs or obtain better jobs.

Today, programs in the public workforce development system focus variably on educational components, including office skills and computer literacy, or on training in soft skills, such as how to write a resumé, present oneself at an interview, and navigate office policies and procedures. The assumption underlying hard-skills training, whether in construction, manufacturing, or computer skills, is that such training is a good educational investment for the "deserving unemployed," whereas the assumption underlying a soft-skills focus is that it is compensatory for the individual failings of the "undeserving unemployed." The newest legislation also encourages systemic partnerships with community colleges and area businesses (U.S. Department of Labor, 2014a).

JOB TRAINING SINCE THE 1930S

Since the 1930s, federal programs, administered largely by the Department of Labor, have provided education and training to select groups of people. Until recent years, most of these programs were oriented to adult men (Rose, 1999)—particularly to those who were unemployed and displaced, and, to a lesser

Figure 12.2 A farmworker attending the Works Progress Administration apple-packing school at the Farm Security Administration family migratory labor camp in Yakima, Washington (1941).

degree, to those who were underemployed. This emphasis reflects the ongoing gender bias in U.S. policymaking, whereby welfare targets women and work-related programs focus on men. Since the 1960s, however, this pattern has changed somewhat, as women have entered the labor market in greater numbers.

The principal public job-training programs for adults and youth during the 1930s, the Works Progress Administration and the Civilian Conservation Corps, were inspired largely by the high levels of unemployment in the Great Depression and growing concerns about the social unrest mass unemployment would create. Workers in these job-creation programs made a major contribution to the construction and expansion of the nation's physical infrastructure—bridges, tunnels, roads, dams, and buildings. Despite these successes, many workers remained unemployed, particularly those of color, in part because of racial bias in the administration of these programs. Since the New Deal, however, job-creation proposals have not been seriously considered by Congress (Collins, 2016; Burtless & Looney, 2012; Eisenbrey, Mishel, Bivens, & Fieldhouse, 2011), perhaps because they conflict with the pervasive rhetoric of individualism and meritocracy in the United States.

After World War II, as the economy recovered and the New Deal work-related programs dissolved, Congress passed the G.I. Bill (officially titled the Servicemen's Readjustment Act of 1944, P.L. 78–346) to provide college or vocational education and one year of unemployment compensation for returning World War II veterans. This legislation enabled thousands of returning veterans, predominantly men, to obtain a college education or vocational training and helped spur the post-war economic boom. Yet, despite the prosperity of the post-war period, access and sustained attachment to the labor market remained a problem for many workers, particularly in the African American community and in rural areas. This led the Department of Labor to initiate a series of job-training initiatives that emphasized training individuals for private sector employment rather than creating jobs (Lafer, 2002).

The Manpower Development and Training Act of 1962 was the first of these policy initiatives. It spawned an array of remedial education, vocational training, on-the-job training, subsidized work experience, and job search programs for workers dislocated by technological advances (known as "dislocated workers") and economically disadvantaged job seekers. This act also produced the first wave of program evaluation research, mainly by the Manpower Demonstration Research Organization (now known simply as MDRC). The Job Corps, a specialized, primarily residential academic and job-training program for youth, was added in 1964 as part of the Johnson Administration's War on Poverty.

In 1973, Congress passed the Comprehensive Employment and Training Act in an effort to consolidate these various programs. For the first time, however, in line with the "New Federalism" philosophy of the Nixon Administration, the act decentralized program responsibilities to local governments—a pattern that persists today. [*See Chapter 2 in this volume for further discussion of the New Federalism.*] Decentralization resulted in a revival of public sector job creation as well as a continued focus on training individuals with little or no work experience for private sector employment.

Introduced at the height of the severe 1981 to 1982 recession, the Job Training Partnership Act of 1982 also focused on the needs of the chronically unemployed through a decentralized approach that emphasized public–private sector collaboration. This act created a system of Private Industry Councils (PICs) to synchronize training and job opportunities locally. At the same time, critiques that previous education and training programs resulted in ineffective rates of work attachment and limited ability to increase employment and earnings received substantial publicity (Bloom, Orr, Cave, Bell, & Doolittle, 1993). The most notable of these reports, written by neoconservative policy analysts Charles Murray (1984) and Lawrence

Figure 12.3 Many Works Progress Administration-staffed day nurseries, such as this one in Childersburg, Alabama, cared for low-income workers' children (1942).

Mead (1992), led to the widespread, rapidly accepted but erroneous notion that "job training doesn't pay." These critiques, combined with the growing public perception that men, especially low-skilled African American men, simply did not want to work, fueled the *work-first* and *work-only* focus of the WIA (P.L. 105–220), which deemphasized education and training and prioritized One-Stop Career Center job connection services. This shift was symbolically captured in legislative language: Rather than highlighting a job-training partnership, the act stressed investment in work. [*See Chapters 3 and 13 in this volume for further discussion of how this emphasis has shaped U.S. social policy in recent decades.*]

To some extent, the critiques of government-funded job-training programs were justified. Despite intentions to the contrary, the programs were often plagued by administrative fragmentation, outdated teaching philosophies and materials, and inadequate funding. Nevertheless, their emphasis on education enabled some participants to gain their General Education Development certificate (GED) and even post-secondary credentials, which improved their employability and wages. Although recent scholarship has challenged the "job training doesn't pay" conclusion and demonstrated that both male and female participants have benefited economically from job-training programs (Ganzglass, 2011; King & Heinrich, 2010), "work first" via the WIA became the employment law of the land.

WORKFORCE INVESTMENT ACT OF 1998

Under WIA, each state was required to develop a "one-stop" delivery system that makes an array of services, such as career counseling, job listings, training referrals, and other employment-related resources, available at a single location. Local Workforce Development Areas and local Workforce Investment Boards constituted the central clearinghouses for WIA and Temporary Assistance for Needy Families (TANF) job programs and funding. [*See Chapter 13 in this volume for a discussion of TANF.*] These local areas also served as the center for welfare and workforce development contracts with private employment programs. Overall, the purpose of WIA activities was to promote an increase in participants' employment, job retention, earnings, and occupational skills. These, in turn, were expected to improve the quality of the workforce, reduce poverty and welfare dependency, and improve the productivity and competitiveness of the nation through the creation of a cadre of workers who were "work ready" and trained according to local employers' needs.

Eligibility

Individuals who were eligible for services under WIA included job seekers, laid-off workers, youth, new entrants to the workforce, veterans, individuals with disabilities, employers, and incumbent workers. The latter refers to workers who are currently employed but could be laid off because of skill deficiencies or those who need new skills to remain employed or to be reemployed if/when they are laid off.

Income eligibility for One-Stop Center program services is based on the Lower Living Standard Income Level (LLSIL; U.S. Department of Labor, 2011), which is determined annually by the Secretary of Labor. States use the LLSIL to determine eligibility for a variety of services for youth and for the Work Opportunity Tax Credit (WOTC), a tax credit to businesses that hire eligible workers (discussed later in this chapter). Persons who are qualified are "low-income individuals," defined as those whose income for a 6-month period did not exceed the higher of the poverty line or 70% of the LLSIL. Unfortunately, the design of program services relegated low-income and low-skilled unemployed persons to the very back of the queue for the types of education and training services that could actually help them obtain and keep jobs, as the next sections show.

Program Services

One-Stop programs were designed to provide three tiers of services that had to be accessed in the following order:

- *Core services* included labor-market information, initial assessment of skill levels, and job-search and placement assistance.
- *Intensive services* were available to eligible unemployed individuals who had completed at least one core service but had not been able to obtain employment, or employed individuals needing additional services to obtain or keep employment that would lead to personal self-sufficiency.
- *Training services* were available to eligible individuals who had met the requirements for intensive services and had not been able to obtain or keep employment. Individual Training Accounts were established to finance training based on the individual's choice of selected training programs.

By making education and training a "last resort," services under WIA were clearly not designed to serve the lowest-income and lowest-skilled workers. Research underscores this inequity. For example, Sum, McLaughlin, Khatiwada, Beard, and Palma (2010) found in Massachusetts that while men and women were served about equally, youth (age 21 and under) were underserved and individuals who were older than 45 and those with post-secondary degrees were overserved relative to the group's share of unemployed persons in the study area. WIA services, therefore, seemed oriented more toward dislocated or underemployed workers or those who were working but poor "temporarily." This indicates that the focus of federal workforce development services, which in the past were directed to the hardest-to-serve ("undeserving") population, had shifted under WIA to more "deserving" workers. The recessions in the first decade of the

21st century—particularly the Great Recession (which ran officially from 2007–2009)—illuminated the major weakness of the federal workforce system, especially during an economic downturn. Recognition of this flaw paved the way for WIA reauthorization in the form of the Workforce Innovation and Opportunity Act of 2014.

To meet the needs produced by the economic recession, scholars and advocates strongly recommended that a reauthorization of WIA ease the rigid, lock-step tiers of the original legislation to facilitate greater engagement with post-secondary training and education (Ganzglass, 2009; 2011). Reauthorization proponents also contended that skill deficits were harmful to the nation's economic recovery, particularly in the context of increased global competition. Perhaps most important, state legislators emphasized the need for greater innovation in the workforce system for the 21st century (National Conference of State Legislatures, 2012). For these and other more administrative reasons, on July 22, 2014 the new federal workforce system legislation, the Workforce Innovation and Opportunity Act (WIOA) [P.L. 113–128], replaced the WIA. The new legislation retained some elements of WIA, but notably returned service attention to lower-income, lower-skilled adults as well as to in-school and out-of-school youth—the groups that suffered highest and most sustained levels of unemployment during and after the Great Recession. Although implementation of WIOA has just begun, the new legislative mandates are intended to make the public workforce system more administratively efficient and its services more personally effective (U.S. Department of Labor, 2014a).

For example, new administrative mandates include consolidation and alignment of multiple existing programs (e.g., YouthBuild, Americorps, and Job Corps) in order to consolidate strategic planning, and strengthening the governing bodies that establish state, regional, and local workforce investment priorities. In regard to service provision at the American Job Centers (the new name for One-Stop Centers), while state and local partnerships had been emphasized under WIA, the WIOA adds regional partners to the mix. In terms of new service emphases, WIOA importantly eliminates the original "sequence of services" and combines all services into a new "career services" category (National Skills Coalition, 2014). This means that services for those needing adult basic skills and English as a Second Language (ESL) education will be expanded, as will services for individuals with disabilities, low incomes, and low skills, who will now be able to start programs by addressing their education and training needs rather than engage with them as a "last resort," as was the case under WIA. In fact, successful pathway models to work and careers, such as Project Match in Chicago, form the template for the "career pathways" approach in WIOA, which is focused particularly on individuals who face significant barriers to employment, whatever their age (Lee, 2015). Finally, new WIOA services will also include greater attention to partnerships between the workforce system and community colleges and local businesses in order to tailor training to area employers' needs.

Implementation Concerns under WIOA

Despite the fact that WIA's "work first" focus was singularly unsuccessful in enhancing most low-income, low-skill individuals' economic mobility and self-sufficiency, WIOA's return to an education and training focus carries both a legacy perceived as unsuccessful, even though shown otherwise over time, and two potential policy implementation challenges. The first challenge is the common belief that education is the primary key to greater mobility and self-sufficiency. The second is that successful regional workforce partnerships can be replicated on a national scale without significant modifications.

The positive effects of workforce development programs have tended to be larger for women than for men. Women's earnings may increase as much as $2,400 a year, or by about 25% of average earnings, while men's might increase by around $1,700 or about 15% of average earnings (King & Heinrich, 2010, pp. 11–12). But these data can be misleading because the base wages of workers or potential workers in the national workforce development system may be very low. Table 12.1 shows the median weekly earnings in 2015 by educational attainment for full-time wage and salary earners age 25 and over (U.S. Bureau of Labor Statistics, 2015).

As the median annual earnings suggest (calculated as median weekly earnings multiplied by 50 weeks a year), only workers holding a bachelor's or advanced degree earned wages that exceeded 200% of the FPL for a family of four (two adults and two children). This figure was $48,072 in 2015, a wage that was considered adequate to support a family.

As in the past, real wage gains are produced by employer-sponsored on-the-job training programs, which disproportionately benefit middle- and upper-skilled workers. In 2015, employers spent $70.6 billion, or $702 per employee, on formal workplace learning (*Training Magazine*, 2015). In contrast, the 2015 U.S. Department of Labor budget request for discretionary spending on workforce development programs (which include programs for WIA, adult basic education, community and technical colleges, and incumbent work) was $11.8 billion—a mere 16% of employers' average expenditures.

Moreover, the funding issues still beg the question of whether education and training are enough to raise the wages of millions of today's workers to family-sustaining incomes. For example, policymakers have recently used a "skills mismatch" argument (Memmott, 2011) to justify all types of post-secondary education programs, based on the assumption that *education* is the primary cause of differences in income, rather than the *type of job and the wage it provides*. In contrast, some scholars find the skills argument "overblown and unpersuasive" (Burtless, 2014), as much, if not more a result of employers' unwillingness to offer on-the-job training as of applicants' under-education. In a similar vein, educational or training certificates may primarily be "signals" that reflect the reputation of the education or training provider and the fact that it had already "vetted" the participant, rather than indicators of a person's actual skills (Ehrenberg & Smith, 2003). Because of this ambiguity and the proliferation of relatively low-wage service sector jobs that offer little to no on-the-job training, the debate about the benefits of education and training for a large swath of workers in the United States likely to continue until more definitive research is conducted (Burtless, 2014).

Table 12.1 Weekly Earnings by Educational Attainment of Full-Time Earners Age 25 and Over.

Education Level	Median Weekly Earnings 2015	Median Annual Earnings
Less than a high school diploma	$493	$24,650
High school diploma	$678	$33,900
Some college no degree	$738	$36,900
Associates degree	$798	$39,900
Bachelor's degree only	$1,137	$56,850
Master's degree	$1,341	$67,050

Source: U.S. Bureau of Labor Statistics

In addition, although thoroughly crafted workforce development partnerships headed by workforce intermediaries and sector training strategies seem to be promising practices for both workforce development service users and employers (see e.g., Giloth, 2004; Meléndez, 2004), funding tied to work first rather than to work *and* skill enhancement means that workforce development can be only a partial remedy to unemployment and poverty. That reality suggests that increased attention needs to be given to the role that wage and income supplements play in remedying unemployment and poverty among low-earning families. In this vein, the next section briefly examines policies that directly address these issues, such as unemployment insurance, tax credits, subsidies for child care and housing, and wage efforts.

INCOME SUPPLEMENTS AND WORK SUBSIDY PROGRAMS

UNEMPLOYMENT INSURANCE PROGRAM

The unemployment insurance program is a federal–state social insurance program, established by the 1935 Social Security Act, designed to moderate spells of unemployment and keep workers and their families out of poverty. It is important to remember that the category "unemployed" is officially defined as a previously employed individual who is only temporarily unemployed and is looking for work. As such, the key features of unemployment insurance include the following (U.S. Department of Labor, 2015):

- Workers are eligible only if they become unemployed through no fault of their own (as determined by the law of the State in which they were employed) and meet certain other eligibility requirements established by the State.
- The benefits provided by unemployment insurance are intended to provide *temporary* financial assistance to unemployed workers who meet the requirements of State law.
- Each state (which includes the 50 states, plus the District of Columbia, Puerto Rico, and the U.S. Virgin Islands) administers a separate unemployment insurance program within guidelines established by Federal law.
- Benefits are funded primarily by a tax imposed on employers.
- Workers must meet State requirements for wages earned or time worked during an established period of time referred to as a "base period."

Historically, unemployment protection emerged at the end of the 1800s, initially in Europe, as industrial economies expanded during a period of frequent booms and busts. By the early 20th century, a few states and some large corporations had organized their own unemployment compensation funds. During the Great Depression of the 1930s, when unemployment on an unprecedented scale could no longer be attributed to an individual's choice or character, or the result of a temporary downswing in business productivity, it soon became apparent that efforts by local governments and the private sector were insufficient. [*See Chapter 2 in this volume for further discussion of this development.*] After considerable social turmoil and public debate, the Roosevelt Administration proposed a more inclusive unemployment insurance program as part of the Economic Security Act of 1935 (later called the Social Security Act). This program, however, was limited to businesses with more than eight employees and provided benefits only to those workers who had been employed at the business for at least 20 weeks (Katz, 2001). Consequently, most workers were excluded from this initial policy effort to address the problem of unemployment, particularly those "in small firms, agriculture, domestic service, the public and nonprofit sector, and seasonal workers … and [thus] most African Americans and women" (p. 225).

Over subsequent decades, the unemployment insurance program became more inclusive of new working populations, and offered the possibility in rough economic times of a 13-week extension of benefits to the base of 26 weeks. At the same time, however, the program still excluded some workers and became more restrictive by limiting eligibility criteria as described in the first bullet above. This proved to be problematic because unemployment insurance is based on a federal–state partnership. This produces the following effects that appear to contradict the initial purposes of the program:

During economic slowdowns or recessions, more workers lose their jobs and need the program. Because these unemployed workers are not paying income tax, state governments lose revenue at the same time that their expenditures increase in response to greater social needs. As a result, states often have greater budget shortfalls. As states are constitutionally prohibited from running a fiscal deficit [*see Chapter 7 this volume*], unless they receive emergency assistance from the federal government they tend to tighten eligibility restrictions and reduce benefits. A glaring example of such restrictions occurred in January 2012 when House Republicans proposed a bill (H.R. 3630) to subject workers who lost their jobs to mandatory drug tests, disqualify workers who did not complete high school, and allow states to experiment with new workfare-type requirements (National Employment Law Project, 2012, p. 1).

Restrictions notwithstanding, unemployment insurance usage has been limited, even in the recent economic downturn. For example, from late 2007 through 2009, during the Great Recession in which 15 million workers lost their jobs, only half of them received unemployment insurance benefits; one quarter of those who received benefits had exhausted their benefits by early 2010 (Government Accountability Office, 2012). More than half of the workers in the exhausted-benefits category (55%) had previously earned incomes above 200% of the FPL. Despite continuing economic distress and rates of unemployment in the 9% range after the recession "officially" ended in mid-2009, Congress barely approved an extension of unemployment insurance in December 2011, to as much as 99 weeks in certain states, because of divisive partisan conflict over the issue of the national debt. By this point, half of the 41% of unemployed respondents in a national random panel survey of American workers (2009–2011) had been unemployed for more than two years (Van Horn & Zukin, 2011).

Figure 12.4 People in their early 20s, as well as men and women in their 50s, were hardest hit by the Great Recession.

This demonstrates the program's lack of horizontal adequacy. Equally problematic is the program's lack of vertical adequacy. [*See Chapter 1 this volume.*] Over the 80-year history of the unemployment insurance program it has been generally accepted that the weekly benefit should replace half of a worker's wages. Yet today the national wage replacement rate is only 35.6% and in seven states it is below 30% (Wentworth, 2010).

Overall, as these examples show, the philosophy underlying the unemployment insurance program has historically been individualistic: "American workers must look out for themselves—government's responsibility remains limited and partial" (Katz, 2001, p. 223). As such, the program's moderating effects on poverty and unemployment, especially during hard economic times, must be augmented by income-enhancing tax policies.

TAX CREDIT POLICIES

In contrast to federal budget proposals, which are highly public and often hotly debated, expenditures implemented via the tax system—fiscal welfare—are a powerful but poorly understood tool of social policy (Howard, 1997, p. 3). As defined by Steuerle (2004), tax expenditures generally grant special tax relief to encourage certain kinds of behavior by taxpayers or to aid taxpayers in special circumstances. As discussed in Chapter 7, federal tax expenditures include tax credits, tax exemptions, and tax exclusions for such things as the home mortgage interest deduction, college savings accounts, childcare expenses, and business tax breaks. Tax credits are particularly important tools to address the issues of poverty and unemployment, especially if they have redistributive goals.

Briefly, **tax credits** are a dollar-for-dollar reduction in the tax owed by an individual or household, which thereby increases their income. In recent years, this approach has become a more politically palatable way of redistributing income than policies that provide direct cash assistance, although most tax credits target middle- and upper-income families

Figure 12.5 Older Workers Often Need Updated Skills to Re-Enter the Workforce

rather than those with lower incomes (Center on Budget & Policy Priorities (CBPP), 2016b). Two critical aspects of tax credits determine how useful they are to low-income households: their *refundability* and their eligibility requirements. A tax credit is refundable if the credit exceeds the amount of federal taxes a low-wage worker owes. In such cases, the Internal Revenue Service will return the excess as a refund check. A tax credit's eligibility criteria have a strong influence on overall **participation rates** and how inclusive the policy's coverage is. Lower-earning working families with children are generally eligible for two tax credits: the Earned Income Tax Credit (EITC) and the Child Tax Credit (CTC), in addition to the standard exemption for dependents. In addition, employers may be eligible for the Work Opportunity Tax Credit (WOTC) which indirectly helps unemployed persons in certain categories.

EARNED INCOME TAX CREDIT

Enacted initially in 1975, the EITC has been expanded several times, including as a (temporary) recession recovery measure in 2009; it is now considered the largest (unofficial) antipoverty program in the United States. The EITC-eligible population of low- and moderate-income working tax filers overlaps with but is

Table 12.2 EITC for 2016 Tax Year: Eligibility Criteria and Maximum Potential Benefit.

Earned Income and Number of Qualifying Children	Maximum Potential Benefit
$47,955—three or more children $53,505 married filing jointly)	$6,269
$44,648—two children $50,198 married filing jointly)	$5,572
$39,296—one child $44,846 married filing jointly)	$3,373
$14,880—no children ($20,430 married filing jointly)	$506

Source: Internal Revenue Service

distinct from the population defined as poor. Eligibility for the EITC and the amount received are determined by a person's income, marital status, and number of children (CBPP, 2016a). Thus, many households in poverty are either not eligible for the EITC or receive very small refunds because they do not meet the earned income or qualifying children criteria.

Here's how the EITC works: If a family is eligible for a $4,000 EITC but owes only $3,000 in taxes, it receives a $1,000 refund check. In this way, as a form of "negative income tax," the EITC considerably enhances the income of many working families. In 2013, for example, the poverty rate among children would have been 25% higher without the EITC (CBPP, 2016b). Widespread outreach efforts by local governments and nonprofit organizations have increased the participation rate of eligible persons nationally to 80%. Despite such efforts, one-fifth of all eligible families still do not benefit from the credit.

As Table 12.2 shows, the EITC is intended primarily for working parents with children. To be eligible for the EITC in 2016, the income of a single-parent family with one child could not exceed $39,296, which is just slightly below 200% of the federal poverty line. At the upper end, a married couple with three or more children reaches its eligibility limit at $53,505, which is about 150% of the poverty line (or less if they have more than three children). Individuals with no qualifying children are only eligible for a very small refund, and taxpayers with low earnings but substantial wealth, such as those with investment income greater than $3,400, are not eligible at all (Internal Revenue Service, 2016).

The American Recovery and Reinvestment Act of 2009 expanded the EITC in two ways: It added a third tier of benefits for families with three or more children and it expanded marriage penalty relief by allowing couples to receive larger benefits. Together, these changes assisted 7 million people and kept more than 3 million people out of poverty. Although these provisions were initially due to expire at the end of 2012, Congress extended them to 2017 as part of the compromise to avoid the so-called fiscal cliff. Twenty-four states and the District of Columbia have created refundable state EITCs to augment the federal program, but the credit amount they provide ranges widely, from 3.5% to 40% of the federal credit (CBPP, 2015a). Advocates hope that the EITC provisions will be made permanent in 2017 and that changes will be introduced that would dramatically increase coverage for "childless workers"—those without children and non-custodial parents. Advocates fear that without such changes millions of low-income working families will lose all or some of their credits (CBPP, 2015b).

CHILD TAX CREDIT

Created in 1997, the CTC was expanded after 2001 to make it available to more families with low and moderate incomes. The credit potentially reduces the federal income tax owed for each qualifying child under 17 by up to $1,000, in addition to the regular dependent credit which is available to all taxpayers. If in combination the regular dependent credit and the CTC reduce the claiming parents' federal tax liability to zero, the credit may be partially refundable. Eligibility criteria to received the CTC include a child's age, family income, relationship to the claiming parent, citizenship, and residence with the claiming parent for more than half the year of the claim. Parents with two children and annual incomes up to $110,000, and single parents or head-of-household filers with annual incomes up to $75,000, are eligible to file for the credit (CBPP, 2016c).

The initial orientation of the CTC favored higher—rather than lower-earning families. Parents were eligible to claim the CTC only if their earnings were $12,050 or higher. The 2009 Recovery Act (ARRA), however, made the credit available to tax filers with as little as $3,000 in annual earnings. This change extended coverage to 3 million additional children and expanded benefits for the 10 million children already eligible (Sherman, 2009, p. 1). In January 2013, Congress expanded and made permanent tax credit provisions relating to the dependent care tax credit and the child tax credit.

WORK OPPORTUNITY TAX CREDIT

A final form of tax credit aimed at enhancing the incomes of lower-earning new workers targets the workers indirectly through employers. The WOTC was passed in 1996 in the context of the newly enacted welfare reform legislation, as a successor to the Targeted Jobs Tax Credit, which existed between 1978 and 1994. [*See Chapter 13 in this volume for a discussion of welfare reform.*] As of 2016, the WOTC offers a federal tax credit to *employers* who hire individuals from particular target groups that have consistently faced difficulty gaining employment. These groups include TANF recipients, veterans, SNAP recipients aged 18 to 39, individuals aged 18 to 39 who live within an Empowerment Zone or Rural Renewal County, summer youth workers aged 16 to 17, vocational rehabilitation referrals, ex-felons, and Supplemental Security Income recipients (U.S. Department of Labor, 2016a). In 2016, the WOTC can offset target employee wages between $1,200 and $9,600 (U.S. Department of Labor, 2016b). The credit thus attempts "to incentivize workplace diversity and facilitate access to good jobs for American workers" (U.S. Department of Labor, 2016b).

Although businesses would appear to benefit from the WOTC, concern about time-consuming paperwork, greater visibility to tax auditors, and other reasons keep many from making use of the credit (Hamersma, 2005). Perversely, in terms of employer protection and equity, the WOTC application form has to be filled out on or before the date of hire, which means that the potential new hire must be willing to divulge his or her targeted category, which is a potential recipe for stereotype and stigma.

In sum, the three tax credit policies discussed here enhance (or have the potential to enhance) the incomes of unemployed and lower-earning workers. This helps keep them out of poverty technically, but rarely raises their incomes to the level of economic sufficiency. To achieve this goal, federal housing and child care assistance programs may provide additional help.

FEDERAL SUBSIDY PROGRAMS

Housing assistance in the United States is provided by the U.S. Department of Housing and Urban Development (HUD), which gives local housing agencies the funds to administer various programs. As of December 2015, about 10 million people, including nearly 4 million children, were helped by federal rental assistance programs (CBPP, 2015c). Overall, HUD provides rental assistance to more than 4.6 million households through at least 10 different programs (CBPP, 2015d). Given the post–Great Recession landscape of housing foreclosures, the provision of housing assistance is critical to helping families avoid poverty, contend with unemployment and low-wage jobs, and broaden national economic recovery. Rental assistance programs commonly take three forms (CBPP, 2015d, 2015e):

1. Government-constructed public housing projects, administered by local housing agencies.
2. Project-based rental assistance (PBRA), which is funded by a prior arrangement with public housing agencies (PHAs), not by HUD. Project-based vouchers are designated for specific units in a public apartment complex that have contracts with a government agency to provide rental assistance. The number of units in housing complexes dedicated to this program is limited.
3. Tenant-based rental assistance, commonly called Section 8 (having been established in Section 8 of the U.S. Housing Act of 1937), is now part of the HUD Housing Choice Voucher Program that is external to public projects. Tenant-based vouchers provide partial rent to private, market-based housing, giving renters a choice of location, type of housing, and price.

Eligibility for housing assistance is determined by the local public housing agency based on area median income as determined by HUD, rather than on the federal poverty measure. The eligibility ceiling for

Figure 12.6a–12.6b. Housing problems in urban areas

families is usually at or below 80% of the area median income. Starting in 2014, a share of new families each year must be designated "extremely low income," with incomes at or below 30% of the area median (CBPP, 2015d).

Housing project residents generally pay monthly rents of 0% to 30% of their monthly income, although very few public housing residents live for free. Rates change as residents' income changes, although calculating rent and income is complex (U.S. Department of Housing and Urban Development, 2016). HUD also reports that long waiting periods are common and that because of funding limitations, only one in four eligible households receives federal rental assistance (CBPP, 2015c). Further limiting housing assistance for the most needy, Congress cut funding to the Housing Choice Voucher and public housing programs after the 2012 elections, which negatively affected at least 85,000 households (CBPP, 2015c)

CHILD CARE ASSISTANCE

Although child care assistance is addressed elsewhere in this volume in relation to welfare (*see Chapter 13*), the receipt of a child care subsidy can also be a critical moderator of poverty and unemployment. For example, the very name of Philadelphia's subsidy program—"Child Care Works"—emphasizes that caring for children is integrally connected with employment, as well as with reducing poverty.

According to a large national survey (Child Care Aware of America, 2015), the average cost of 9-month child care (in both licensed center-based and licensed family care homes) for infants with single parents across *all* states exceeds one-quarter of the median income for single parent families. In the highest-cost states, such as Minnesota, Oregon, New York, Massachusetts, and Illinois, the cost of nine months of licensed child care for an infant with a single parent reaches over 50% of the state's median income. The cost is also high for infants with two parents: more than 12% of the state median income in Pennsylvania, for example, and around 15% of the median income in the highest-cost states. The cost of child care for one- and two-parent families for their four-year-olds is only about 10% lower on average. Shockingly, in all regions of the U.S., average center-based child care fees for an infant are higher than the average amount that families spend on food. In the Northeast, for example, the average child care cost of $22,415 for families with two children is twice as high as average college tuition ($11,622) and over three times higher than the family's food expenses (Child Care Aware of America, 2015, p. 31).

These costs, however, are only calculated for nine-month care and raise several problems: What happens to these parents—single and married alike—who have full-time, year-round jobs? Do parents have to send their children to lower-quality care part of the time? Do they simply shell out an even higher percentage of their incomes for those three months? Finally, how do cost disparities foster the national movement for all children to be able to access quality nursery and pre-k education, especially from the standpoint of those who believe that more education will be necessary for the 21st century workforce?

This narrative from the Child Care Aware of America report (2015) graphically illustrates the employment opportunity costs of child care, even for a middle-income family:

> My husband stays home with our three [year-old] and 15-month-old because he cannot earn enough to pay for care or break even. The first center I visited would have cost us $36,000 for the two young ones and not covering the costs for after school for my 6-year-old at $285 per month. He's struggling to find work worth the cost of child care and the lack of quality even available at a high cost. He has to make at least $50,000 to break even paying for child care and I have a PhD in family studies and make $80,000 per year. I can't imagine

this process for families with less resources and knowledge.—Married mother of three, Denver, CO (p. 29).

Other than the child care subsidies connected with post-1996 welfare reform [*see Chapter 13*], the Child and Dependent Care Tax Credit (CDCTC) is the nation's primary work-related child care assistance program. CDCTC provides families with a cash refund of a percentage of their child care expenses. The maximum refund is $3,000 for one qualifying person or $6,000 for two or more qualifying persons. The subsidy is paid directly to the care provider, which must be a licensed, official organization. A major problem with the CDCTC, however, is that families earning too little to pay federal income tax are not eligible for the credit. Thus, the program while somewhat redistributive is inequitable.

Some states' programs are particularly problematic for low earners because inadequate funding results in long waiting lists. In Pennsylvania, for example, waiting lists affected over 11,000 children in 2012 (Child Care Aware of America, 2012); in 2016, families experienced a wait of at least four months (Child Care Information Services, 2016). In addition, as TANF-related child care subsidy eligibility criteria epitomize, some states do not subsidize child care for unemployed parents who are looking for a job, while other states subsidize job search but cut off their child care subsidy as soon as the job seeker locates a job. As a whole, federal housing and child care subsidy efforts help boost the incomes of *some* low-earning workers but in the long run do much less to address the problems of poverty and insufficient incomes compared with what higher wages could do.

WAGE LEGISLATION AND WAGE MOVEMENTS

In addition to the useful but uneven income enhancement of tax credit policies and the federal subsidy programs just discussed, two wage-related policy options are potential moderators of poverty and unemployment. One of them, minimum wage legislation, has a relatively long history, while activities associated with the "living wage" movement are more recent.

MINIMUM WAGE LAWS

The Fair Labor Standards Act of 1938 (FLSA) established federal minimum wage provisions for workers in industries that, all told, made up about one-fifth of the labor force at the time (Grossman, 1978). Despite the initial act's narrow scope, the vigorous efforts of Labor Secretary Frances Perkins and subsequent labor activists and legislators resulted in much-expanded coverage by the 2000s. Today, most U.S. workers are protected by FLSA standards for minimum wage, overtime pay, record keeping, youth employment and child labor standards affecting full-time and part-time workers in the private sector and in federal, state, and local governments (Repa, 2016; U.S. Department of Labor, 2014b). Technical coverage alone, however, does not prevent the violations of FLSA that occur regularly in U.S. industries and businesses, particularly those employing low-earning workers (Bernhardt et al., 2009).

At the same time, because of the shift to low-paying jobs over the past few decades, 42% of U.S. workers currently earn less than $15 an hour (Sonn, 2016). In recent decades, the effectiveness of the minimum wage in combating poverty has been reduced because the inflation-adjusted value of the wage has dropped steadily. In 1938, the minimum wage was established at $0.25 an hour. Its value moved slowly upward until it peaked in 1968 at almost $10 an hour (in 2008 dollars). Since the late 1960s, however, the value of the minimum wage steadily declined. In 2009, after 10 years of no change, the federal minimum wage was finally increased to $7.25 an hour, which was still 7.8 percent less than its value in 1967 (in 2011 dollars)

(Mishel, 2013, p.1). No further increases in the federal minimum wage have been approved during the past decade. As a result, in 2016 a full-time worker earning the federal minimum wage would have an annual income of just over $15,000 (based on the standard metric of 208 workdays a year), slightly under the poverty level for a two-person family and considerably below the poverty level for a family of four ($24,300). Increasing the federal or state minimum wage to $15 an hour, which several states and cities have already adopted, would help to reduce wage inequality, but *only* if it is implemented quickly. For example, by the time California fully implements a $15 per hour wage in 2022, inflation and/or further erosion of the value of the wage may not help low earners very much.

LIVING WAGE MOVEMENT

One response to the limited effectiveness of the minimum wage is the emergence of the living wage movement. As economist and social worker Jared Bernstein (2002) describes it, "The living wage movement takes as its theme the reasonable position that no one who works for a living should be poor" (p. 2). At its core, the movement revolves around the following contradiction: Overall productivity in the United States (defined as goods produced per hour of labor) increased 62.5% from 1989 to 2010, but real hourly wages for both private sector and state and local government workers grew only 12% during the same period (Mishel & Shierholz, 2011, p. 1). Put another way, if the minimum wage had kept pace with worker productivity, it would be at least $14.65/hour—more than double the 2016 level of $7.25/hour (Brooks, 2007). [*See Chapter 3 in this volume for further discussion of changes in the U.S. economy and their policy implications.*]

Living wage proponents critique minimum wage legislation for its failure to reflect the cost of living in different family configurations and locales. The earliest proponents of a living wage pressed businesses with large city contracts to pay their workers wages that were a few dollars *above* the minimum wage. These advocacy efforts, in cities like Baltimore and Ann Arbor, Michigan, were led by large stakeholder coalitions, most notably faith-based organizations and labor unions. Such collaborations can be extremely powerful, but they can also splinter or dissipate as large groups tend to do, especially after achieving their original goal (Simmel, 1950). This diminishes the coalition's ability to protect hard-won wage gains or increase them in the future.

Despite these challenges, the living wage movement has produced 140 new living wage laws in cities, and the coalitions developed by the movement have promoted other economic justice issues in the areas of health insurance, immigrants' rights, expansion of states' EITC, and increases in the minimum wage (Brooks, 2007). More recently, living wage and minimum wage activists have coalesced around the "Fight for $15" campaign (Rotondaro, 2015) discussed in the previous section. At the same time, the movement faces strong odds in particular parts of the country, including regions that experienced severe economic distress. As Rotondaro notes, "today these [social justice] movements are taking place in a very fractured political economy" (p. 3).

The actual wage rate that living wage movements establish is typically between the minimum and self-sufficiency wage for the region. Even successful efforts, therefore, do not solve the problem of income insufficiency. In addition, living wage ordinances often pertain only to public sector jobs or apply to firms with government contracts. There is evidence, however, that living wage laws tend to "trickle up" and increase the wages of workers in lower wage positions who are not directly covered by the legislation.

In sum, four problems are particularly endemic to the income-enhancing policies and subsidy programs discussed in this chapter as "work first" poverty and unemployment remedies: (1) eligibility criteria are not high enough to ensure family income sufficiency; (2) access to benefits and support services is often cumbersome and difficult for employed parents; (3) policy and subsidy specifics are too minimal; and (4) outreach, other than for the EITC, is inadequate, as are overall coverage participation rates. Although these legislative and tax-based income supplements and work subsidies are well-intentioned, to date they have a mixed record in terms of providing greater equity. All the policies discussed in this chapter help *some* people in need to *some* extent, but even when several are combined, they are seldom adequate compensation for insufficient wages.

CONCLUSION: FUTURE POLICY POSSIBILITIES

Many political solutions to poverty and unemployment have been offered over the past half century, yet their enactment and maintenance inevitably depend on whether the nation has the political will to implement them and modify them in response to changing economic and social conditions (Iversen & Armstrong, 2006; Post, Raile, & Raile, 2010). The current political climate in the United States is particularly inhospitable to the use of public policy initiatives to achieve such social justice goals. The two suggestions below, however, might be able to gather traction, even in today's environment.

First, policymakers should continue to work through the tax system to avoid political stasis. For example, they might consider use of tax credits to firms that more equitably balance executive and employee compensation. Given the publicity around the Occupy Movements in 2011 and the energy that the 2016 Presidential campaign of Senator Bernie Sanders generated, people across the country could bring considerable pressure to bear on their local businesses to better equalize wages. Supporting the redistributive goal of such a tax credit, legislators could study successful wage compression efforts in Europe (Mourre, 2009) and related efforts in the United States (Johnston, 2014).

An analysis of executive pay in the United Kingdom, for example, suggests that the level of differential between executive and average worker pay matters: "Exceed around 14:1 between top and bottom and people feel that pay and reward is fundamentally 'unfair' … and 'felt fairness' matters to employee engagement," which in turn, is associated with customer engagement (Isles, 2006, p. 9). There may even be a role for government regulation of compensation levels, patterned after the Sarbanes-Oxley Act of 2002 (P.L. 107–204), which regulates auditing practices of publicly held firms and holds boards of directors and top executives fiscally responsible for the accuracy and completeness of the company's financial reports. Imagine holding a top executive fiscally responsible for making sure that no one in his or her firm earns more than 14 times the wages of any other employee in the firm!

Second, legislators and advocates could coalesce on behalf of job creation policies, which also produce economic growth (for different perspectives, see Bivens, 2013; Eisenbrey et al., 2011; Greszler, 2014). Proponents of job creation as an antidote to poverty and unemployment as well as a key to larger economic growth assert that the lack of job creation since the Great Recession is the reason economic recovery has lagged. Particularly challenging to the goal of job creation, though, is Bernstein's (2013) caution that "our economy has generated too few jobs for most of the last 30 years" (p. 1). Thus, it will be essential for stakeholders to coalesce jointly and actively around job creation and wage compression efforts.

Finally, it is critical to remember that changes such as those suggested here take time and must be collaborative and consultative of all stakeholders. As Robert Putnam (2000) reminds us, "Figuring out how to renew our stock of social capital is a task for a nation and a decade, not a single scholar, or even a single group" (p. 404).

1. What does it mean to be "in poverty," "above poverty," and "below poverty"?
2. What are the arguments for using the official poverty measure? What are the arguments for using the new Supplemental Poverty Measure? Which arguments do you find most compelling?
3. What does it mean to be officially "employed," "unemployed," and "out of the labor force"? What additional "official" employment categories are there, and why are they not used often?
4. Who gets omitted from the "official" employment categories such that they are not considered in policymaking and program design?
5. What does the term *workforce development* mean, and what is the main public workforce development program? How effective are workforce development programs in helping people out of poverty?
6. What services were offered at One-Stop Centers under the Workforce Investment Act of 1998? Who did the services help most? Who did they help least? What components of the newest workforce legislation, the Workforce Innovation and Opportunity Act of 2014 (WIOA), are likely to improve wages for low-earning workers? What components are likely to hinder wage improvement for those workers?
7. What new policies or programs might be more effective for poverty alleviation than education and job training/workforce development?
8. What is the minimum wage today? For whom does working full-time, full-year at minimum wage result in economic self-sufficiency (i.e., no use of social or cash support programs)? For whom does it not result in economic self-sufficiency? How helpful are minimum wage laws and laws produced by the living wage movement to low earners, and how much do the earners' incomes increase under these two different types of legislation? What contributes to the differences?
9. What are the main tax credit programs that are designed to boost the incomes of people who are unemployed or low earners? How effective are these tax credit programs, and for whom?
10. What federal subsidy programs are low-earning families eligible for, and what proportion of those who are eligible actually use the programs? How adequate are these programs in helping such families earn a family-sustaining income?

Suggestions for Further Reading

Bartik, T. J., & Houseman, S. N. (Eds.). (2008). *A future of good jobs? America's challenge in the global economy*. Kalamazoo, MI: W. E. Upjohn Institute for Employment Research.

Ehrenreich, B. (2001). *Nickel and dimed: On (not) getting by in America*. New York: Henry Holt.

Giloth, R. (Ed.). (2004). *Workforce intermediaries for the twenty-first century*. Philadelphia: Temple University Press, with American Assembly, Columbia University.

Heinrich, C. J., & Scholz, J. K. (Eds.). (2009). *Making the work-based safety net work better: Forward-looking policies to help low-income families*. New York: Russell Sage Foundation.

Iversen, R. R., & Armstrong, A. L. (2006). *Jobs aren't enough: Toward a new economic mobility for low-income families*. Philadelphia: Temple University Press.

Kalleberg, A.L. (2011). *Good jobs, bad jobs*. New York: Russell Sage Foundation.

Stiglitz, J.E. (2013). *The price of inequality: How today's divided society endangers our future*. New York: W.W. Norton.

Suggested Websites

American Enterprise Institute: www.aei.org

The Brookings Institution: www.brookings.edu

The Cato Institute: www.cato.org

Center on Budget and Policy Priorities: www.cbpp.org

Center for Law and Social Policy: www.clasp.org

Center on Poverty, Work and Opportunity: www.law.unc.edu/centers/poverty/default.aspx

Economic Policy Institute: www.epi.org

FactCheck.Org: A Project of the Annenberg Public Policy Center: www.factcheck.org

The Heritage Foundation: www.heritage.org

Institute for Research on Poverty: www.irp.wisc.edu

Institute for Women's Policy Research: www.iwpr.org

National Poverty Center: www.npc.umich.edu

Spotlight on Poverty and Opportunity: www.spotlightonpoverty.org

The Urban Institute: www.urban.org

U.S. Government Accountability Office: www.gao.gov

Waging a Living: Award-winning PBS documentary (2006) produced by Roger Weisberg, featuring five individuals who are working but still poor and their families: http://www.pbs.org/pov/wagingaliving/

The Working Poor Families Project: www.workingpoorfamilies.org

References

Becker, G. S. (1993). *Human capital*, (3rd ed.) Chicago: University of Chicago Press.

Bernhardt, A., Milkman, R., Theodore, N., Heckathorn, D., Auer, M., DeFilippis J., Gonzáles, A.L., Narro, V., Perelshteyn, J., Polson, D. & Spiller, M. (2009). *Broken laws, unprotected workers*. New York: National Employment Law Project.

Bernstein, J. (2002). *The living wage movement—Viewpoints/EPI*. Washington, DC: Economic Policy Institute.

Bivens, J. (2013). *Still a "perfect match"—Increasing tax fairness to finance job creation*. Washington, DC: Economic Policy Institute.

Bloom, H. S., Orr, L. L., Cave, G., Bell, S. H., & Doolittle, F. (1993). *The national JTPA study: Title II-A impacts on earnings and employment at 18 months*. Washington, DC: U.S. Department of Labor.

Bourdieu, P. (2001). The forms of capital. In M. Granovetter & R. Swedberg (Eds.), *The sociology of economic life* (pp. 96–111). Boulder, CO: Westview.

Brooks, F. (2007). The living wage movement: Potential implications for the working poor. *Families in Society, 88*(3), 437–442.

Brooks, R. (2011, November 7). Official poverty measure (again) underestimates a growing crisis. *The De-mos Weblog*. Retrieved from http://www.policyshop.net/home/2011/11/7/official-poverty-measure-again-underestimates-a-growing-cris.html

Burtless, G. (2014). *Unemployment and the 'skills mismatch' story: Overblown and unpersuasive*. Washington, DC: Brookings.

Burtless, G., & Looney, A. (2012, January 13). *The immediate jobs crisis and our long-run labor market problem*. Washington, DC: Brookings.

Center on Budget and Policy Priorities (2010, October 7). *Policy basics: Introduction to the food stamp program*. Washington, DC: Author.

Center on Budget and Policy Priorities (2015a) *Policy basics: State Earned Income Tax Credits*. Washington, DC: Author.

Center on Budget and Policy Priorities (2015b). *Chart book: The Earned Income Tax Credit and Child Tax Credit*. Washington, DC: Author.

Center on Budget and Policy Priorities (2015c). *Policy basics: Federal rental assistance*. Washington, DC: Author.

Center on Budget and Policy Priorities (2015d). *Federal rental assistance factsheets: Sources and methodology.* Washington, DC: Author.

Center on Budget and Policy Priorities (2016a). *Policy basics: Federal tax expenditures*. Washington, DC: Author.

Center on Budget and Policy Priorities (2016b). *Policy basics: The Earned Income Tax Credit*. Washington, DC: Author

Center on Budget and Policy Priorities (2016c). *Policy basics: The Child Tax Credit*. Washington, DC: Author

Child Care Aware of America (2015). *Parents and the high cost of child care*. Arlington, VA: Author.

Child Care Aware of America (2013). *Number of children on waiting lists for child care assistance*. Retrieved May 18, 2016, from www.naccrra.net

Child Care Information Services (2016). *Child Care Works subsidy program*. Retrieved May 18, 2016, from http://www.ccisinc.org

Coleman, J. S. (1990). *Foundations of social theory*. Cambridge, MA: The Belknap Press of Harvard University Press.

Collins, M. (2016). Where have all the good paying jobs gone? *Industry Week*, March 4, 2016.

Economic Policy Institute (2015). *Family budget calculator*. Washington, DC: Author.

Ehrenberg, R. G., & Smith, R. S. (2003). *Modern labor economics: Theory and public policy* (8th ed.). Boston: Addison-Wesley.

Eisenbrey, R., Mishel, L., Bivens, J., & Fieldhouse, A. (2011). *Putting America back to work: Policies for job creation and stronger economic growth* (Briefing Paper No. 325). Washington, DC: Economic Policy Institute.

Fisher, G. M. (1997). *The development and history of the U.S. poverty thresholds: A brief overview.* Retrieved from http://aspe.hhs.gov/poverty/papers/hptgssiv.htm

Ganzglass, E. (2009). *WIA reauthorization: Proposal to create career pathways state policy leadership grants program.* Washington, DC: Center for Law and Social Policy.

Ganzglass, E. (2011, May 11). *Hearing on removing inefficiencies in the nation's job training programs* (Testimony to the U.S. House of Representatives, Subcommittee on Higher Education and Workforce Training, Committee on Education and Workforce). Washington, DC: Center for Law and Social Policy.

Giloth, R. (Ed.) (2004). *Workforce intermediaries for the twenty-first century.* Philadelphia: Temple University Press, with American Assembly, Columbia University Press.

Government Accountability Office (2005). *Means-tested programs* (Report No. GAO-05–221). Washington, DC: Author.

Grossman, J. (1978). *Fair Labor Standards Act of 1938: Maximum struggle for a minimum wage.* Retrieved March 9, 2012, from http://www.dol.gov/oasam/programs/history/flsa1938.htm

Harrington, M. (1962). *The other America: Poverty in the United States.* New York: Macmillan.

Hamersma, S. (2005). *The Work Opportunity and Welfare-to-Work tax credits.* Washington, DC: Urban-Brookings Tax Policy Center.

Howard, C. (1997). *The hidden welfare state.* Princeton, NJ: Princeton University Press.

Internal Revenue Service (2016). *2016 EITC income limits, maximum credit amounts and tax law updates.* Retrieved May 17, 2016, from http://www.irs.gov/credits-deductions/individuals/earnedincome-tax-credit

Isles, N. (2006). The risk myth: CEOs and labour market risk. *Provocation Series, 2*(4), 1–16. London: The Work Foundation.

Iversen, R. R., & Armstrong, A. L. (2006). *Jobs aren't enough: Toward a new economic mobility for low-income families.* Philadelphia: Temple University Press.

Iversen, R. R., Napolitano, L., & Furstenberg, F. F., Jr. (2011). Middle-income families in the economic downturn: Challenges and management strategies over time. *Longitudinal and Live Course Studies, 2*(3), 286–300.

Johnston, K. (2014). Efforts to regulate CEO pay gain traction. *Boston Globe,* October 26.

Katz, M. B. (2001). *The price of citizenship: Redefining the American welfare state.* New York: Henry Holt.

King, C. T., & Heinrich, C. J. (2010). *How effective are workforce development programs? Implications for U.S. workforce policies in 2010 and beyond.* Retrieved from http://www.utexas.edu/research/cshr/pubs/pdf/Heinrich%20and%20King%20-%20How%20Effective%20Are%20Workforce%20Development%20Programs.pdf

Lafer, G. (2002). *The job training charade.* Ithaca, NY: Cornell University Press.

Luhby, T. (2011, November 7). Poverty rate rises under alternate Census measure. *CNN Money.* Retrieved March 7, 2012, from http://money.cnn.com/2011/11/07/news/economy/poverty_rate/index.htm

Mead, L. M. (1992). *The new politics of poverty.* New York: Basic Books.

Meléndez, E. (Ed.) (2004). *Communities and workforce development.* Kalamazoo, MI: W. E. Upjohn Institute for Employment Research.

Memmott, M. (2011, June 15). 2 million 'open jobs'? Yes, but U.S. has a skills mismatch. *NPR.* Retrieved from http://www.npr.org/blogs/thetwo-way/2011/06/15/137203549/two-million-open-jobs-yes-but-u-s-has-a-skills-mismatch

Mishel, L. (2013). *Declining value of the federal minimum wage is a major factor driving inequality.* Washington, DC: Economic Policy Institute.

Mishel, L., & Shierholz, H. (2011, March 14). *The sad but true story of wages in America* (Issue Brief No. 297). Washington, DC: Economic Policy Institute.

Mourre, G. (2009). *Wage compression in Europe: First evidence from the Structure of Earnings Survey 2002* (CEB Working Paper No. 09/051). Brussels: Solvay Brussels School of Economics and Management.

Murray, C. (1984). *Losing ground: American social policy, 1950–1980.* New York: Basic Books.

National Conference of State Legislatures (2012). *NCSL labor and economic development committee— Policy: Workforce Investment Act reauthorization and funding.* Retrieved from http://www.ncsl.org/ state-federal-committees/sclaborecon/workforce-investment-act-reauthorization-and-fundi.aspx

National Employment Law Project (2012, January 12). *Sticking to principles: Congress should oppose barriers to unemployment insurance and instead provide meaningful reemployment tools* (Legislative Update). New York: Author.

Post, L.A., Raile, A.N.W., & Raile, E.D. (2010). Defining political will. *Politics & Policy, 38*(4), 653–676.

Putnam, R. D. (2000). *Bowling alone: The collapse and revival of American community.* New York: Simon & Schuster.

Repa, B.K. (2016). Who is covered by the Fair Labor Standards Act? Retrieved May 18, 2016, from http:// www.nolo.com.

Rose, N. E. (1999). Jobs for whom? Employment policy in the United States and Western Europe. *Journal of Economic Issues, 33*(2), 453–460.

Rotondaro, V. (2015). US movements battle for living wage, economic equality. *National Catholic Reporter,* July 31.

Sherman, A. (2009, February 12). *Recovery agreement temporarily expands Child Tax Credit for large numbers of children in every state.* Washington, DC: Center on Budget and Policy Priorities.

Short, K. (2015, September). *The Supplemental Poverty Measure: 2014.* Washington, DC: U.S. Census Bureau Economics and Statistics Administration and U.S. Department of Commerce.

Short, K. (2011, November). *The research Supplemental Poverty Measure: 2010.* Washington, DC: U.S. Census Bureau Economics and Statistics Administration and U.S. Department of Commerce.

Simmel, G. (1950). *The sociology of Georg Simmel* (K. H. Wolff, Ed. & Trans.). New York: Free Press.

Sonn, P. (2016). How we got to $15, and where we go from here. *New York Daily News,* April 1.

Steuerle, C. E. (2004). *Contemporary U.S. tax policy.* Washington, DC: Urban Institute.

Strier, R. (2009). Community anti-poverty strategies: A conceptual framework for a critical discussion. *British Journal of Social Work, 39,* 1063–1081.

Sum, A., McLaughlin, J., Khatiwada, I., Beard, A., & Palma, S. (2010). *An overview and assessment of the operations and outcomes of the WIA One-Stop Career Centers in the Metro South/West WIA area.* Boston: Northeastern University, Center for Labor Market Studies.

U.S. Bureau of Labor Statistics (2016a). *Employment projections.* Washington, DC: Author.

U.S. Bureau of Labor Statistics (2016b). *The employment situation—April 2016.* Washington, DC: Author

U.S. Bureau of Labor Statistics (2015). *How the government measures unemployment.* Washington, DC: Author.

U.S. Census Bureau (2015a). *Income, poverty and health insurance coverage* in the United States: 2014. Retrieved May 14, 2016, from http://www.census.gov/newsroom/press-releases/2015/cb15–157.html

U.S. Census Bureau (2015b). *Poverty thresholds by size of family and number of children.* Retrieved May 14, 2016, from https://www.census.gov/hhes/www/poverty/data/threshold

U.S. Department of Agriculture, Economic Research Service (2016). *Food spending as a share of income declines as income rises.* Retrieved May 14, 2016, from http://www.ers.usda.gov/data-products/chart-gallery/detail.aspx?chart

U.S. Department of Health and Human Services (2016). *Poverty guidelines.* Retrieved May 14, 2016, from https://aspe.hhs.gov/poverty-guidelines

U.S. Department of Housing and Urban Development (2016). *HUD's public housing program.* Retrieved May 17, 2016, from http://portal.hud.gov/hudportal/HUD?src=/topics/rental_assistance/phprog

U.S. Department of Labor (2016a). *Work Opportunity Tax Credit target group eligibility.* Retrieved May 17, 2016, from http://www.doleta.gov/business/incentives/opptax/PDF/Target.Group_Eligibility.pdf

U.S. Department of Labor (2016b). *Help put America to work.* Retrieved May 17, 2016, from http://www.doleta.gov/business/incentives/opptax/eligible.cfm

U.S. Department of Labor (2015). *State unemployment insurance benefits.* Retrieved May 15, 2016,, from http://workforcesecurity.doleta.gov/unemploy/uifactsheet.asp

U.S. Department of Labor (2014a). *The Workforce Innovation and Opportunity Act—July 22, 2014.* Washington, DC: Author.

U.S. Department of Labor (2014b). *Handy reference guide to the Fair Labor Standards Act.* Washington, DC: Author, Wage and Hours Division.

U.S. Department of Labor (2011). Workforce Investment Act: Lower living standard level. *Federal Register, 76*(54), 15342–15348.

Van Horn, C. E., & Zukin, C. (2011). *The long-term unemployed and unemployment insurance: Evidence from a panel study of workers who lost a job during the Great Recession.* New Brunswick, NJ: Rutgers University, John J. Heldrich Center for Workforce Development.

Weber, M. (1978). *Economy and society* (G. Roth & C. Wittich, Eds.). Berkeley: University of California Press. (Original work published in 1922)

Wentworth, G. (2010). *Unemployment Insurance at 75*: Assessing benefit eligibility, adequacy and duration. Retrieved May 15, 2016, from www.nelp.org/content/uploads/UIat75Wentworth.pdf

Whittaker, J. M. (2004, October). *Employment statistics: Differences and similarities in job-based and person-based employment and unemployment estimates.* Retrieved August 19, 2011, from http://digital commons.ilr.cornell.edu/key_workplace/248

World Bank (2016). *Working for a world free of poverty.* Retrieved May 14, 2016, from http://www.world-bank.org

Credit

WELFARE, WELFARE REFORM, & NEOLIBERAL PATERNALISM

Sanford F. Schram, PhD; Joe Soss, PhD; and Richard C. Fording, PhD

For several decades, there has been a dramatic shift in the underlying logic of U.S. social welfare policy. Even if provided in limited amounts, welfare grants from the 1960s until the mid-1990s provided cash assistance to those who were eligible to buffer the effects of the economy when it failed to provide jobs or when recipients had legitimate reasons for being unable to work. But since the 1990s, the nation's welfare system increasingly failed to provide cash assistance even to the poorest of the poor. More than ever, it serves to discipline them to accept whatever limited opportunities the economy offers (Soss, Fording, & Schram, 2011).

This trend began in the 1970s, when economic elites and moral conservatives coalesced in a concerted campaign to roll back the welfare state. Continuing into the current period, this reactionary movement sought to delegitimize government-sponsored interventions that had been grounded in the thinking of the great Scottish economist John Maynard Keynes, whose work informed the social policies developed during the New Deal and continued to be influential until the mid-1970s. These policies, especially the Social Security Act of 1935, created the foundations of the modern U.S. welfare state, including, most prominently, retirement benefits for the elderly, unemployment insurance for workers, and public assistance for poor families. For years these programs have been under assault in an environment where the reigning philosophy is that the era of "big government is over" (Pierson, 1994). Today, persistent pressure to limit income redistribution to the poor has resulted in expanding the shift away from Keynesianism to what we call Neoliberal Paternalism.

During the 1960s, the Great Society and War on Poverty programs developed by President Lyndon B. Johnson added significantly to the welfare state by enacting legislation creating Medicare (health insurance for the elderly) and Medicaid (free health care for the poor). By the early 1970s, food stamps became a nationally uniform program available throughout the United States. Other policies such as housing assistance and employment training also began to grow at this time. [*See Chapter 2 in this volume for further discussion of these developments.*]

While limited compared with the social welfare states developed in Europe, the U.S. system was consistent with the Keynesian philosophy to counteract economic difficulties produced by market instability through increased government spending. A specific goal of U.S. social welfare policy was to provide a floor on consumption that could boost the economy. During the past several decades, however, this approach eventually lost support in the face of attacks mounted by business interests and right-wing cultural ideologues working in coalition as the "New Right." [*See Chapter 3 in this volume for further discussion of this development.*]

Yet, this campaign did not produce a return, as some had hoped, to 19th century laissez-faire, literally "hands-off" economics, where the government played little or no role in aiding those who were disadvantaged by economic problems. Instead, the New Right campaign led to the development of what can be called a "post-Keynesian welfare state." Proponents of the New Right philosophy were not able to roll back the welfare state entirely, so they shifted their strategy toward transforming it. The post-Keynesian welfare state they created moved away from redistributive policies that transferred income from the rich to the poor and toward disciplinary policies to compel the poor to fit into the bottom rungs of the emerging low-wage occupational structure of the globalizing economy (Barker, 2007).

As Saskia Sassen (2006) suggests, welfare policies in the United States today reflect a general shift away from a "national capitalist state" that focused on creating a national economy that benefited most citizens and toward a "global capitalist state" that is geared to maximizing economic gains from participation in the global economy, even if it means that the rich get richer and the poor get poorer. As a result, welfare policy has become ever more focused on getting the nonworking poor to increase their integration into the global economy and to accept docilely "the verdict of the marketplace" by taking whatever low-wage jobs are available (Mead, 1986, p. 87). [*See Chapter 3 in this volume for further discussion of the political economy of social policy.*]

This heightened emphasis on a disciplinary approach toward the nonworking poor that includes both incentives and penalties has fundamentally altered the nature of U.S. social welfare policy. Instead of reflecting the goal of economic redistribution, social welfare policies now more closely resemble criminal justice policies: They punish people, especially the poor, for misbehavior (Wacquant, 2009); focus on greater monitoring of their behavior; and promote greater discipline among them. This disciplinary shift is part and parcel of a wholesale transformation of poverty governance focused on enforcing market-compliant behavior among the poor. It is reflected in a wide variety of social welfare policies and practices, including zero-tolerance policies regarding drug use for public-housing tenants and mandatory work requirements for welfare recipients. In sum, the overall goal of these policies is to compel the poor to accept personal responsibility for their condition, engage in prosocial behavior, and become compliant members of society by taking the limited jobs the globalizing economy affords them.

The transformation of welfare policy toward a more disciplinary regime of poverty governance reflects the ideological orientations of **neoliberalism** and **paternalism**. Neoliberalism emerged during the 20th century initially as a relatively obscure idea among right-wing economists, particularly Friedrich Hayek (and his mentor Ludwig von Mises) and Milton Friedman (and his University of Chicago colleague, Gary Becker) (Peck, 2008). It eventually became the primary ideology used to justify economic globalization (Harvey, 2005). In terms of domestic policy, neoliberalism did not propose a return to laissez-faire economics but, instead, a change in the role of government so it operated in a manner more consonant with market principles in the name of promoting economically rational behavior (Brown, 2003). In effect, the goal of neoliberalism became the restructuring and repurposing of the state and its programs and services to mirror and support market-oriented principles. In social welfare policy, where much of neoliberal reform has been centered, this often led to the devolution of policymaking authority to states and localities, privatization of the administration of service programs, and the institution of performance management systems to ensure that contract agencies met program goals (Soss, Fording, & Schram, 2011).

The new welfare regime that emerged is neoliberal in the sense that it attempts to instill market logic from top to bottom in its operations (Brown, 2003), relying on incentives and penalties to enforce economic logic among all participants in the system, including governmental bodies, contract agencies, frontline workers, and clients (McDonald & Reisch, 2008). The neoliberal regime enforces market logic on the system so clients become themselves market compliant. Yet the new regime also exhibits paternalistic tendencies (Mead, 1986) to achieve the same ends in that it operates as a father with his child, instructing welfare recipients on how to think and act so they internalize market logic, behave in market-compliant ways, stop being dependent on public assistance, and develop a willingness to take jobs in the emerging low-wage labor markets of the globalizing economy. This new regime integrates welfare and criminal justice policies to intensify them as instruments of poverty management and the monitoring and disciplining of subordinate populations, especially as segregated along race and class lines, so that they pose less of a threat economically or politically to the broader populations. Further, limitations on the ability of immigrants to access benefits and a more carceral approach to illegal immigration or even the treatment of refugees extends the reach of this disciplinary regime (Theoharis & Marchevsky, 2016). This chapter discusses the history of U.S. welfare policy to illustrate how the neoliberal paternalist regime of poverty governance has emerged by focusing on what is commonly called welfare, i.e., the cash assistance program for the non-aged poor—a program that was created by the 1935 Social Security Act and ultimately transformed by the Personal Responsibility and Work Opportunity Reconciliation Act (PRWORA) of 1996, also known as welfare reform. The effects of the new disciplinary regime it reflects will be presented through an in-depth analysis of how this critical policy is administered today.

WELFARE POLICY AS LEGISLATIVE PRODUCT: A HISTORICAL PERSPECTIVE

An important debate regarding the history of U.S. social welfare policy is whether policies have been increasingly progressive, humanistic, and altruistic (Trattner, 1999), or whether policy changes continue to serve a social control function of disciplining the poor to fit into the existing political–economic order (Piven & Cloward, 1971/1993). Trattner argues that during the 19th and 20th centuries U.S. policy evolved from "poor law to welfare state"—that is, social welfare policy became less focused on disciplining the poor and more concerned with helping them deal with the social and economic adversities they confront. Piven and Cloward, however, argue that social welfare policy has historically operated as a secondary institution calibrated to serve the functions of the primary institutions of government and the market economy. In other words, they acknowledge that welfare policy is designed to help the poor but argue that this assistance is provided only in ways that are consistent with broader political and economic objectives.

Welfare policy in the United States, therefore, is designed to reinforce the work ethic and compel the poor to take whatever jobs the economy makes available, even if these jobs do not provide sufficient income to support them. This reflects the longstanding principle imported from Great Britain of **less eligibility**, which posits that welfare benefits should not be higher than wages from the lowest paying jobs. Welfare policies must be flexible enough, however, to liberalize benefits to mollify the poor and quell dissent when the poor become disruptive. In addition, Piven and Cloward (1971/1993) argue that welfare policy tends to operate cyclically, giving more emphasis to political or economic objectives as circumstances dictate. When the poor are quiescent, welfare policy focuses on its economic function and the principle of less eligibility

Figure 13.1

is more strongly enforced. When the poor are disruptive, as in the 1930s and 1960s, welfare policy is liberalized to quell dissent.

History can be far messier and more complex than these models suggest. Yet they have value because they help us think about the historical purposes of welfare policy and ask whether circumstances are better today than in the past (see Chapter 2 in this volume).

Michael Katz (1997) suggests that U.S. welfare policy has historically always been about "improving or uplifting the poor" by changing their behavior so they can better fit into the norms and expectations of the dominant culture regarding work and family values. As Piven and Cloward (1971/1993) suggest, this reflects the social control element in welfare policy that operates in a variety of ways, however liberal the intentions of policymakers and no matter how much aid welfare provides. Although this goal remains at the center of contemporary welfare policy, it is sometimes easier to recognize in policies from the past.

Early welfare policy in the United States reflected debates in England that lasted well into the late 19th century over whether to provide cash assistance to destitute families in their homes ("outdoor relief") or to deny such aid and insist that families in need enter the poorhouse or other institutions ("indoor relief") (Wagner, 2005). In the late 19th century, the Charity Organization Societies promoted the elimination of outdoor relief in the name of helping the poor avoid becoming passive dependents inured to a life of reliance on assistance (Boyer, 1978). Reformers sought to teach the poor to become self-sufficient (Lowell, 1911). Their campaign was quite successful in gaining repeal of assistance programs in ways that foreshadowed the passage of welfare reform a century later (Pimpare, 2004).

In the early 20th century, however, concern arose among other reformers about the growing number of children being placed in orphanages, many put there by living parents who could not afford to support them (Crenson, 1998). As a result, most states created mothers' pensions to enable poor mothers to stay home with their children and forego their placement in orphanages (Skocpol, 1992). By the early 1930s, 43 states had approved some form of mothers' pensions. [See Chapter 2 this volume *for further discussion of the evolution of welfare policy.*]

Yet, because states provided this aid, there was tremendous variation in benefits and widespread discrimination in determining eligibility, particularly to women of color (Gordon, 1995). In fact, the campaign to promote mothers' pensions was highly racialized from the outset. Proponents argued they were needed to promote white "Republican Motherhood" and to avoid "race death" for the country at the hands of growing numbers of African Americans and immigrants from Asia, Latin America, and Southern and Eastern Europe (Ward, 2005). Although aid was given to selected groups of immigrants in the hope that they could be Americanized, in most counties African Americans were systematically denied assistance (Ward, 2005).

Mothers' pensions, therefore, served as a policy vehicle for implementing racial agendas that emphasized civic incorporation. Reformers promoted mothers' pensions as a tool for "Americanizing" Polish, Irish, German, and Italian immigrant families—groups that were viewed as "nonwhite" at the time and eventually made up a disproportionate number of recipients. Indeed, by emphasizing the potential for social and civic assimilation, mothers' pension advocates made arguments that positioned them as the racial liberals of their time. While conservatives tended to view non-WASPs (White Anglo-Saxon Protestants) as irremediably inferior, liberals tended to regard them as inferior in culture but potentially responsive to a socialization process that could bring them "up" to "American" standards. Mothers' aid supporters frequently spoke of building citizenship qualities in both adult and child recipients as one of the program's goals (Gordon, 1995).

Reflecting this complex mixture of agendas, mothers' pensions were implemented in ways that varied greatly across communities and emphasized intrusive efforts to instill virtue and reform behavior. Yet their shared roots in the ideals of white Republican Motherhood also allowed these programs to serve as a foundation for more ambitious federal action during the New Deal.

By the mid-1930s, the effects of the Great Depression finally compelled the federal government to enact major policy changes in the system of public assistance for the poor through passage of the 1935 Social Security Act. The welfare program included in the legislation—titled Aid to Dependent Children (ADC) and later Aid to Families with Dependent Children (AFDC)—was a minor element of the original Social Security Act. This landmark legislation established a two-tier system of provision divided along class, race, and gender lines, in which "universal" social insurance programs were controlled at the national level and means-tested "selective" welfare programs for the poor were administered by states and localities.

Social insurance programs, particularly Social Security retirement benefits, primarily assisted the families of white male workers. Originally, they excluded from coverage many jobs held by large numbers of women and people of color, such as domestic, nonprofit, and agricultural employment (Lieberman, 1998; Mettler, 1998). Consequently, public assistance programs became the primary source of aid for poor, female-headed families and persons of color (Gordon, 1995). [*See Chapters 4, 5, and 11 in this volume.*]

The subsidiary status of the ADC program partly reflected the race and gender basis of prevailing civic hierarchies (Lieberman, 2005; Nelson, 1990). As Hugh Heclo (1995) explains, the 1935 law cemented a particular "settlement of the social question" by giving civic priority to "the male breadwinner and the family dependent on his earnings" and specifying "the nation-state as the appropriate arena" of social protection for these citizens in full standing (pp. 667–668). Exclusion from the national social insurance programs reflected and institutionalized the subordinate civic standing of women and racial minorities (Mettler, 1998).

The segregation of programs for the poor in a lower tier, however, reflected more than just a hierarchy of civic status. It emerged from material efforts to sustain the exploitation of cheap African American labor in the segregated South and unpaid women's household labor throughout the nation (Gordon, 1995). The racial dimensions of this agenda in particular were driven by Southern white agricultural interests and their representatives in government. As plans for national social programs emerged in the 1930s, these actors mobilized to make sure that new forms of federal aid for the poor would not disturb the sharecropping system that relied on poor African American families to work the fields (Lieberman, 1998). They demanded and won a separate stream of federally funded programs for the poor that allowed the states to retain substantial control over eligibility criteria, benefit levels, and program rules.

In the decades that followed, Southern officials worked to ensure that African American families had limited access to public relief, especially during planting and harvesting seasons. African American women had far more stringent expectations to work and confronted "suitable home" rules, "man in the house" provisions, and other "morals tests" that were administered in racially biased ways (Bell, 1965). The intricate rules provided a pretext for removing them from the welfare rolls and making sure they were not secretly sharing their benefits with African American men who were needed in the fields (Piven & Cloward, 1988). To augment these strategies, some Southern states created "employable mothers" rules "in areas where seasonal employment was almost exclusively performed by nonwhite families" (Bell, 1965, p. 46).

In all states, local welfare offices operated in discretionary, intrusive ways that contrasted sharply with the emphasis on rights and bureaucratic restraint found in the upper-tier social insurance programs. But because poor African American women were concentrated in the Southern political economy, they confronted variants of ADC that were stricter and more focused on labor regulation. In sum, the New Deal provided assistance to African American mothers primarily through state ADC programs that were segregated from national insurance, designed to support labor exploitation, and organized around rules that mothers in other parts of the country rarely encountered.

In the 1960s, the ADC program was renamed AFDC, and the patchwork quilt of local relief practices gave way to a more accessible and rule-based system. Once again, racial politics played a key role. During this period, the War on Poverty emerged from the tumultuous political struggles of the civil rights movement that allowed racial minorities to finally achieve meaningful citizenship in the United States (Quadagno, 1994). The legislative centerpiece of the War on Poverty, the Economic Opportunity Act of 1964, joined the Civil Rights Act of 1964 and the Voting Rights Act of 1965 to create a new system of civil, political, and social rights for racial minorities.

In the two decades prior to their passage, large numbers of African Americans had migrated from the rural South to urban centers around the nation, fleeing Southern segregation and seeking employment opportunities in Northern factories. In the North, they gained access to the ballot and became a more significant voting bloc within the Democratic Party. At the same time, disruptive social movements organized to push for civil rights, and later welfare rights, in ways that divided elites and put pressure on governments to take action (Piven & Cloward, 1977). Across the states, these pressures inspired sharp increases in rates of welfare participation and incarceration that tracked closely with levels of African American insurgency and electoral power (Fording, 1997, 2001; Schram & Turbett, 1983). During the 1960s, the War on Poverty became a key site for local political conflict that pivoted on issues of Black Power, white privilege, and competing visions of racial integration and justice in the new civic order (Quadagno, 1994).

By the end of the 1960s, the implementation of antipoverty policies had become more than a racialized field of practice; it was now a racialized object of political discourse and public perception as well (Kellstedt, 2003; Weaver, 2007). From the failed presidential campaigns of Richard Nixon (1960), Barry Goldwater (1964), and George Wallace (1968) through Nixon's election in 1968, the politics of poverty was reshaped by "law-and-order" calls to crack down on African American criminality, welfare dependence, and social dysfunction (Weaver, 2007). African Americans became the public face of welfare and crime policy, as their images increasingly prevailed in media coverage of poverty (Gilens, 1999). In the years that followed, the Democratic Party became closely associated with programs for the African American poor, and attitudes toward African Americans became a key predictor of white Americans' policy preferences, partisan loyalties, and voting behaviors (Carmines & Stimson, 1989; Edsall, 1991; Kinder & Sanders, 1996). Ironically, just as white racial attitudes were growing more tolerant (Schuman, Steeh, Bobo, & Krysan, 1997), "blackness" was becoming a more powerful frame for poverty politics (Winter, 2008).

WELFARE REFORM AS PROCESS: THE CAMPAIGN TO DISCIPLINE THE POOR

To explain these seemingly contradictory developments, one must understand the conservative resurgence in U.S. politics that reshaped public policy and drove economic inequality skyward after the 1970s. In the closing decades of the 20th century, well-organized political actors mobilized against the activist state that had developed from the New Deal through the Great Society (Pierson & Skocpol, 2007). Their grievances were not specific to poverty. They were a response to the major political victories of the preceding decades: expansions of the regulatory state, progressive taxation, and social protections (Pierson, 2007); civil rights achievements (Weaver, 2007); and revolutions in race, gender, and sexual relations (Luker, 1996). The successes of the counter-movements flowed from their deep resources and strategic creativity as well as from changes in the organization of U.S. politics. Their focus on poverty governance reflected the political utility of the "disorderly poor" as a vehicle for advancing their broader ambitions. Their outsized effects in this area reflected the political vulnerability of the poor as well as the weaknesses and strategic choices of their opponents.

By the end of the turbulent 1960s, social movements had combined with Democratic Party control to fundamentally reshape the United States. The old racial order was upended, gender relations were recast, and new sexual and reproductive freedoms were reshaping the social and cultural landscape (Davis, 1983). The regulatory powers of government expanded in both depth and breadth, reaching new heights in the areas of consumer protection, occupational health and safety, and environmental protection (Melnick, 2005).

Citizenship and governance were redefined by a sweeping rights revolution that spread outward from civil and voting rights to a wide variety of antidiscrimination laws (Skrentny, 2002). The two-tiered national welfare state designed in 1935 grew dramatically on both the social insurance and public assistance levels in coverage, protection, and cost (Noble, 1997). In the mid-20th century, business interests adopted a posture of pragmatic acceptance toward social protections, recognizing the stability they afforded and the political risks of attacking them. With most of the industrialized world still recovering from World War II, U.S. businesses could afford to be tolerant; they held a dominant position in global markets that generated sizable profit margins. Many firms also benefited directly from public programs that subsidized employee benefits and created markets for their goods.

By the end of the 1960s, however, this relatively peaceful settlement had fractured. Global markets became more competitive and profits declined (Noble, 1997). The burdens of regulation and social protection were more costly now, and they were expanding. Indeed, from 1969 to 1972 "virtually the entire American business community experienced a series of political setbacks without parallel in the post-war period" (Vogel, 1989, p. 59). The backdrop for a shift from a national capitalist state to a global capitalist state had emerged. The table was set for change. The political response from business was not long in coming.

The nascent political operations that business had developed in the early 1960s exploded into a fierce organizational offensive (Martin, 2004). Between 1974 and 1978, the number of corporate-sponsored political action committees (PACs) grew from 89 to 784, with an additional 500 PACs emerging to represent trade associations and business interests (Conway, 1986). Older organizations such as the Chamber of Commerce worked to increase their memberships and lobbying capacities, as new organizations such as the Business Roundtable were created to bring corporate leaders together as a more potent political force (Akard, 1992). Offices representing business proliferated in Washington, where they paired the pursuit of insider influence with strategies for mobilizing grassroots support for legislative efforts (Vogel, 1989).

Going on the offensive, business interests pushed a broad agenda (Akard, 1992; Ferguson & Rogers, 1986; Vogel, 1989). They fought to cut corporate tax burdens and shift them onto workers, deregulate financial markets, and weaken newly created environmental and workplace protections. They moved to curtail worker power by undercutting labor unions and pushing aid recipients into labor markets. They worked to lower the costs of existing social supports and block the creation of new protections against changing societal risks. Together, these efforts restructured the American political economy in ways that allowed "the rich to pull away from the rest" (Bartels, 2008). Their effects on poverty governance were amplified by the simultaneous rise of social conservatism as a potent political force. [*See Chapter 3 in this volume for further discussion of the changes that have occurred recently in the U.S. political economy.*]

THE RISE OF THE NEW RIGHT: NEO-CONS AND THEO-CONS

Until the mid-20th century, Christian fundamentalists generally disdained the worldly activity of political conflict. The first stirrings of change emerged in the early 1960s, in the form of outrage at the U.S. Supreme Court's ban on prayer in public schools. In the years that followed, anxieties rose steadily as women's rights and gay rights advanced; changes in cultural attitudes, particularly regarding sexuality and reproduction, took root; and abortion was legalized. A growing number of Christian leaders began to argue that the time had come "to get in there and fight" (Hodgson, 1989, p. 174).

In the 1980s, churches began to develop new capacities for local activism that would later be stitched together as a potent national network by Pat Robertson's 1988 presidential campaign and the drive to roll back abortion rights (Diamond, 1995). By the 1990s, "the Family Research Council had 300,000 subscriber members in its communication bank, the Eagle Forum had 80,000 members, and the Christian Coalition could marshal 1.7 million donors and activists" (Heclo, 2001, p. 181). Leaders such as Jerry Falwell and Ralph Reed moved aggressively to amass resources, build organizations, and, ultimately, remake state institutions and policies as instruments for the pursuit of moral purposes.

The social conservative movement drew the Christian Right together with other groups activated by perceptions of moral decline and social disorder. Neoconservatives, who began as disaffected liberals opposing communism, developed a broader agenda for using the American state to combat declining social order and moral restraint (Norton, 2004). Racial conservatives, galvanized by civil rights victories, began to pursue a "law-and-order" campaign that identified social protest, civil disobedience, urban riots, street crime, and deviant behaviors in poor neighborhoods as related parts of a single problem: the breakdown of social order (Simon, 2007; Weaver, 2007). Together, "neo-cons" and "theo-cons" formed a powerful coalition pushing an agenda rooted in order, discipline, personal responsibility, and a moral state.

As conservatives and business interests mobilized, they sought more than just immediate policy victories. Adopting a longer view, they invested in efforts to transform the intellectual and organizational landscape of American politics. Corporations and wealthy conservatives, such as Richard Mellon Scaife, poured millions of dollars into the creation of new organizations (think tanks, foundations, and academic societies) designed to shift the terms of political debate and discredit Keynesian ideas. In the legal arena, they funded the rise of the Federalist Society and the law and economics movement (Teles, 2008). More broadly, their investments produced a right-wing revolution in policy-focused think tanks (Rich, 2004). At organizations such as the Heritage Foundation, American Enterprise Institute, and Cato Institute, conservatives turned broad ideas into detailed proposals, churned out research to support their agendas, and spent lavishly to spread their arguments through books, periodicals, and public events (Rich, 2004). In the area of poverty governance, right-wing think tanks invested heavily in promoting welfare critics such as Charles Murray, Marvin Olasky, Lawrence Mead, and Robert Rector.

Conservative mobilization had equally profound effects on the party system. Opportunity came in the form of a fraying Democratic coalition. Support for civil rights in the 1960s badly weakened the party's hold on the formerly "Solid South" and on the loyalties of working-class white men throughout the United States. Capitalizing on this opening, business interests and conservatives did more than just increase their support for the Republican Party; they organized to push the party to the right. Conservative activists recruited far-right candidates and poured resources into their campaigns. New groups such as the Club for Growth targeted moderate Republicans for elimination and funded primary challenges by more conservative opponents (Hacker & Pierson, 2005). The result was a steep and asymmetric rise in party polarization that has recently intensified. As its conservative Southern members lost office, the Democratic Party's average ideological position moved slightly to the left. By contrast, the Republican Party shifted sharply to the right as it replaced its moderates with more aggressive advocates for free markets and traditional morality (McCarty, Poole, & Rosenthal, 2006; Theriault, 2006).

Conservative mobilization did little, however, to move public opinion to the right (Fiorina, 2004; Page & Jacobs, 2009) or to shift public attention from economic to cultural issues (Bartels, 2008; Stonecash, 2000). It drove political change by underwriting the Republican Party's rise to power, supplying it with organized networks of business leaders and social conservatives and, perhaps more important, providing unprecedented financial resources for political combat. Indeed, conservatives benefited greatly from the rising political importance of money in the late 20th century, as electoral campaigns and lobbying efforts became vastly more expensive.

In 1980 and again in 1994, Republicans rode a wave of business money as corporate interests abandoned their usual pragmatic strategy of investing in both major parties (Piven, 2007). As money became more central to elections, spiraling inequality concentrated this resource at the top of the income distribution. In 2000, 95% of the people who gave $1,000 or more to a campaign came from the one-eighth of U.S. households with incomes of more than $100,000 per year (APSA Task Force, 2004). Both major parties reorganized their operations to reflect their growing dependence on affluent donors (Campbell, 2007). For Republicans, this focus fit easily into a pro-business policy agenda. For Democrats, it created significant incentives to downplay questions of inequality, redistribution, and social protection.

This situation worsened for Democrats following the U.S. Supreme Court's ruling in *Citizens United v. Federal Election Commission,* 558 U.S. 08–205 (2010). In this decision, the court determined that corporations and unions were like individual citizens who had First Amendment rights to free speech under the U.S. Constitution and, therefore, that the government could not limit their independent expenditures promoting political causes. As the 2010, 2012, and 2014 campaigns reveal, this opened the floodgates of contributions from corporations and billionaires into the American electoral process.

THE DISCIPLINARY TURN IN POVERTY GOVERNANCE

The disciplinary turn in poverty governance was ultimately a product of these broad political developments. It would be a mistake, however, to think that the poor were simply swept up in this political wave, as one facet of change among many. From their inception, the rising conservative movements made the poor, and policies directed at the poor, a central focus of their political rhetoric and reform efforts. Indeed, the emphasis on poverty governance was no accident. It reflected the strategic utility of focusing on "the unruly poor" as a way to unite the emerging coalition and divide and discredit the opposition. By focusing on the poor, organized conservatives avoided the political obstacles they confronted in other policy domains and distracted attention from policy agendas that attracted far less public support.

Beginning in the late 1960s, the symbolic uses of the unruly poor became a prevalent feature of national politics. Although the "get-tough-with-the-poor" theme did not immediately produce victories in presidential campaigns, it succeeded in demonstrating how a focus on social disorder and cultural anxiety could link political protest and street crime, capitalize on racial resentments, and blame liberals for social unrest. The lessons were not lost on leading Republicans who kept hammering away on this point.

In 1968, by making law and order the centerpiece of his Southern Strategy for winning over disaffected white Democrats, Richard Nixon was narrowly elected president. In 1970, he followed up on his campaign rhetoric by declaring war on "the criminal elements which increasingly threaten our cities, our homes, and our lives" (as quoted in Western, 2006, p. 60).

By the 1980s, this approach had become widespread among conservatives, who elaborated a rich narrative of "the underclass" that drew attention away from the structural problems of deindustrialization and the compounding effects of racial segregation in American cities (Massey & Denton, 1993; Wilson, 1997). Instead, the narrative they adopted in books such as Charles Murray's (1984) *Losing Ground* blamed Great Society policies for a rising tide of irresponsibility, promiscuity, violence, and welfare dependence because, in their view, these policies coddled criminals and rewarded individuals' bad choices with handouts. As president, Ronald Reagan extended the war on crime to a war on drugs and made the image of the "welfare queen" into a powerful metaphor for the idea that hardworking, law-abiding Americans were being exploited by the lazy and criminal poor.

The prominence of these themes in the conservative rise to power is best understood as a tactical response to the political opportunities and obstacles the coalition confronted (Hinton, 2016). On the opportunity side, they offered a wedge issue almost uniquely well suited for exploiting post-1960s popular anxieties and divisions in the Democratic coalition. The race-coded themes of urban disorder, crime, and welfare were aimed at the newly contested white electorates (in the South and elsewhere) who felt abandoned by Democratic support for civil rights, desegregation, busing, and Affirmative Action. Criticisms of welfare, a program that was now equated with poor single mothers of color (Hancock, 2004), played on diverse anxieties surrounding changes in gender roles, sexuality, and family formation. As the real wages of U.S. workers stagnated, images of lazy welfare queens provided a scapegoat for economic fears, channeling popular anxieties into anger at government for taxing hardworking families to support the allegedly irresponsible poor.

At the same time, conservatives used their focus on the unruly poor as a way to put a populist face on their agenda, clothing it in anti-statist and anti-elitist rhetoric (Ehrenreich, 1987). Welfare, in this frame, was not a hard-won protection for poor workers and their families; it was the self-serving creation of a liberal "intelligentsia" who used big government to shower special benefits on the poor at the expense of workers' checkbooks and most cherished values.

Indeed, the image of a victimized "silent" and "moral" majority became a central trope of conservatism (Simon, 2007). According to this narrative, people who played by the rules were being abused by the "illegitimate takings" of welfare freeloaders and violent criminals and, later, undocumented immigrants. The earned and deserved rights of hardworking Americans were being ignored by liberal elites who cared more about the rights of the victimizers—the criminal defendants and welfare recipients of the urban underclass. The interests of such ordinary Americans, in this frame, were equated with efforts to promote victims' rights, taxpayers' rights, and a society based on personal responsibility (Simon, 2007).

The conservative emphasis on poverty and crime, however, was not simply a matter of seizing opportunities. It also reflected the challenges that confronted an emerging political coalition. Pro-market advocates and social conservatives have never been easy allies, as the 2012 election campaign demonstrated. Libertarian desires for free markets clash with the drive to create a moral-authoritarian state. Social conservatives recoil at the sight of corporations upending community traditions, promoting mass consumerism, and profiting from the sale of sex and sin. The growing alliance of the two movements depended on the suppression of divisive issues and the elevation of agendas valued by both wings. In this regard, poverty governance has offered an inviting alternative.

Reform in this area was a priority for two segments of the business community: low-wage employers eager to keep labor on the market and firms that stood to profit directly from privatization (Ehrenreich, 1997; Piven & Cloward, 1971/1993). It was equally important to social conservatives, who were eager to bring vice and violence under control and to change welfare programs that they saw as encouraging marital breakdown, sexual promiscuity, and moral irresponsibility (Ehrenreich, 1987; Gilder, 1981).

In addition, the conservative focus on poverty governance emerged as a tactical response to the barriers the coalition confronted in other areas as it tried to reform the activist state. Even as Republicans gained control of elected offices, conservatives found that the state's expanded capacity and reach could not be easily repealed (Pierson, 2007). The status quo bias of the U.S. political system, which had often thwarted efforts to expand the welfare state, now allowed retreating liberals to block efforts to dismantle it (Noble, 1997). Rising party polarization made it more difficult to build bipartisan coalitions for policy change (McCarty, 2007), and in many areas the activist state had produced policy constituencies that now mobilized to defend their programs (Campbell, 2003; Pierson, 1994). Repeatedly, conservatives found that Americans welcomed the rhetoric of personal responsibility more than policy changes that actually stripped them of protections and left them to fend for themselves on the market (Page & Jacobs, 2009).

As Jacob Hacker (2004, 2006) rightly notes, these and other obstacles channeled the assault on social protections toward strategies of "stealth" (reducing protections below the public radar) and "drift" (preventing policies from adapting to evolving risks and needs). Poverty governance was a notable exception to this rule. Dramatic changes for the poor were pursued in the most visible ways and achieved with great fanfare. This was most strikingly demonstrated by the passage of welfare reform in 1996, which was heralded far and wide as a major accomplishment by both Democrats and Republicans. Several factors explain the discrepancy.

First, the poor provided a weak and isolated political target, unable to push back as other groups could. Stigmatized and lacking resources, the poor are rarely able to defend themselves in the policy process by conventional means (Piven & Cloward, 1977). In addition, by the last decades of the 20th century, their organized allies were in short supply. Labor unions were in sharp decline and largely focused on their own problems (Goldfield, 1989). Foundation-supported nonprofits that focused on poverty, such as the Children's Defense Fund, had no grassroots networks or mass memberships to mobilize (Skocpol, 2003). The public interest organizations that proliferated on the left focused mainly on "quality-of-life" issues, devoting few resources to issues of economic distribution and protection (Berry, 1999). Even social justice organizations, formed to advocate for groups such as women or racial minorities, tended to pay little attention to welfare, treating it as a narrow subgroup issue with limited significance for their broader constituency (Strolovitch, 2008). These developments followed in the heels of the decline of the welfare rights movement, whose influence peaked in the late 1960s and early 1970s (Kornbluh, 2007).

Organizational weakness among welfare recipients was compounded by institutional isolation, especially for clients in the AFDC program. Over the course of the 20th century, successive legislative actions segregated poor single women and their children from bona fide social insurance contributors (1935), the surviving dependents of deceased social insurance contributors (1939), and people with certified disabilities (1972). [*See Chapter 11 this volume for further discussion of the different components of the Social Security Act.*] Thus, as attacks on AFDC moved into high gear, recipients could not seek political cover through alignment with other groups receiving government aid who were more powerful and viewed more favorably by the public. Poor women with children stood alone, denigrated as a lazy and licentious racial other and contrasted with more deserving beneficiaries (Hancock, 2004; Winter, 2008).

Another obstacle to the development of common cause was America's "hidden welfare state" of tax expenditures, which obscured the public supports given to non-poor families and made it appear that AFDC was unique in offering government-funded assistance to able-bodied parents (Hacker, 2002; Howard, 1997; Mettler, 2012). The creation of coalitions along gender lines was further undercut by the paucity of child care and other supports being offered to working women, which made it seem as though welfare clients received special treatment (Orloff, 2002). Finally, the design of the AFDC program itself kept recipients very poor, insecure, and mired in social crises. Since the early 1970s, the failure of AFDC to keep pace with inflation compounded this situation (Edin & Lein, 1997). In this policy context, calls for "welfare reform" came from across the political spectrum and few allies could be found to oppose the conservative vision of change.

With the poor isolated by institutions and by social and residential segregation, Americans were encouraged to think about changes in poverty governance as if they mattered only for deviant others. Yet this was far from the case. The assault on the poor served as a symbolic vehicle for mobilizing opposition to the welfare state more generally and discrediting the ideas of political liberals. It transformed iconic images of dependent African American single mothers and criminally violent men into the symbolic faces of social entitlement and government support. As Hacker (2006) points out, the themes sounded in the anti-welfare campaign were only the most visible part of a "Personal Responsibility Crusade" that sought to undermine a wide array of collectivizing policies so Americans would take greater ownership of their risks and choices. "By protecting us from the full consequences of our choices," in areas from health care to pensions to child care, reformers argued that government supports erode "our incentives to be economically productive and personally prudent" (p. 38).

The political spectacle constructed around the underclass served the broader effort, not just by using the deviant poor to legitimate its broad themes but also by distracting attention from policy changes that were shifting risks onto the backs of working Americans. The symbolic image of counterproductive handouts to the poor focused public attention and framed an argument with far wider implications. Former Republican Congressman Dick Armey (1995) stated this perspective succinctly: "Social responsibility is a euphemism for individual *irresponsibility*" (p. 317).

The conservative onslaught sowed division in the Democratic Party, not just in the electorate but also in the form of elite factions, such as the Democratic Leadership Council that organized in the 1980s to shift the party away from Great Society liberalism. Politically divided and outgunned, Democratic Party leaders fought back selectively as they engaged in a tactical retreat. On issues of greater concern to the affluent and well organized, Democrats worked aggressively to block or temper conservative legislation, sometimes less successfully than other times. Around other issues, such as financial services deregulation, Democrats joined with Republicans to push through banking modernization reform that later exposed U.S. citizens to highly questionable lending practices that produced the collapse of the mortgage market and the onset of the Great Recession [*See Chapter 3 in this volume*].

In the area of poverty governance, Democrats increasingly adopted a strategy of cooptation, seeking to evade the charge of being soft on crime and welfare by embracing milder versions of conservative proposals as their own (Hinton, 2016). Poor people, of course, had little ability to force the party to expend its dwindling political capital on their behalf. With images of the poor increasingly racialized, a vigorous counter-offensive would have risked deepening the racial divides that threatened the party's coalition (Frymer, 1999). Instead, leading Democrats began to argue that liberal positions on crime and welfare were costly political liabilities that undercut public support for party candidates and broader progressive agendas. By aligning themselves with efforts to transform poverty governance, they hoped to take the corrosive issues of race, crime, and welfare off the table, thereby freeing the party from the wedge issues that Republicans had used so effectively and clearing the way for less "distorted" debates over work and poverty (Soss & Schram, 2007).

Time and again, the same storyline played out on crime and welfare legislation. Leading Democrats attempted to counter the party's image as being weak in the wars against crime and drugs to overcome the damage inflicted by Republicans' law-and-order campaigns. For example, in the summer of 1986, when the death of basketball star Len Bias set off a moral panic over the growing abuse of crack cocaine, Speaker of the House Tip O'Neill moved quickly to ensure that Democrats established a strong anti-drug position before the upcoming elections. As a result, the Anti-Drug Abuse Act of 1986, which established mandatory minimum drug sentences, was passed with less than a month of public deliberation, just in time for the November elections.

"The grand strategic game of realigning the image of the Democratic Party" reached its high point in the 1990s, under the presidency of Bill Clinton (Weaver, 2002, p. 116). As a candidate in 1992, Clinton combined populist economic appeals with efforts to establish himself as a New Democrat who would not be beholden to labor unions, racial minorities, feminists, environmentalists, or other groups viewed as "special interests" of the Democratic Party (Williams, 2003). Clinton emphasized his credentials as a pro-death-penalty, tough-on-crime governor. The crowd-pleasing centerpiece of his campaign, however, was his pledge to "end welfare as we know it" and tell the welfare poor "two years and you're off."

Clinton's pledge would be put to the test 4 years later, after Republicans took over Congress in 1994 and introduced a "Contract with America" that promised to get tough with the poor. As Republicans seized control of the policy agenda, Clinton was forced to address welfare proposals that were far more stringent and included far fewer supports than the plans he and his advisor David Ellwood had envisioned (DeParle, 1996; Ellwood, 1988). After contesting some of the most extreme provisions successfully, Clinton ultimately came to the same conclusion Tip O'Neill reached in 1986. To shed an electoral liability and clear the path for new policy efforts, Democrats would need to position themselves out front in abolishing "the welfare mess."

Figure 13.2 President Clinton signing the Personal Responsibility and Work Opportunity Reconciliation Act in 1996.

As the 1996 election season moved into high gear, Clinton signed the Personal Responsibility and Work Opportunity Reconciliation Act, abolishing welfare as an entitlement and replacing it with a block grant to the states that emphasized work requirements, time limits, **sanctions** for noncompliance, and governing arrangements designed to promote privatization and performance-based contracting. For poor families in the new Temporary Assistance for Needy Families (TANF) program, the era of neoliberal paternalism was officially at hand.

WELFARE REFORM AND THE NEW DISCIPLINARY REGIME

The Personal Responsibility and Work Opportunity Reconciliation Act was the most visible legislative event in the recent history of U.S. poverty governance. It also produced one of the most stunning policy effects: Between 1994 and 2008, the number of AFDC/TANF recipients in the United States declined by about 72% (U.S. Department of Health and Human Services, 2008). While this decline had been widely trumpeted as a sign of the reform's success in ending welfare dependency by getting recipients to leave the welfare rolls for work, there is strong evidence that the reform law has greatly reduced access to assistance for families that need it (Schram & Soss, 2001). Between 1994 and 2005, the percentage of TANF-eligible families receiving TANF decreased from 84% to only 40% (U.S. Department of Health and Human Services, 2008). This figure became even lower since the onset of the Great Recession, due to the combination of increasing poverty rates and a lack of growth (and even a continued decline in many states) in the TANF rolls. In addition, there has been increasing concern over the growing population of "disconnected women," defined as the percentage of low-income women who report themselves neither as working nor on welfare. According to some estimates, the size of this population doubled between the mid-1990s and mid-2000s and now stands at 20% to 25% (depending on the precise definition) of all low-income women (Blank & Kovak, 2008).

Welfare reform abolished the 60-year-old entitlement to assistance and imposed time limits, work requirements, and other restrictions on access to aid. In fact, welfare reform shifted national policy away from cash assistance as the main form of aid and focused more of its expenditures on services designed to promote work. Because TANF was a block grant that states could use in a variety of ways, as Figure 13.3 demonstrates, by 2000 more than half the TANF block grants monies going to states was being spent on services other than cash assistance to the poor (Allard, 2009).

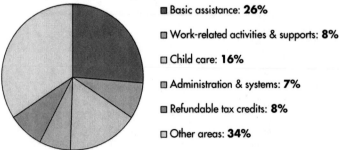

Figure 13.3 How States Spent Federal and State TANF Funds in 2014

How States Spent Federal and State TANF Funds in 2014

- Basic assistance: **26%**
- Work-related activities & supports: **8%**
- Child care: **16%**
- Administration & systems: **7%**
- Refundable tax credits: **8%**
- Other areas: **34%**

source: http://www.cbpp.org/how-states-spent-federal-and-state-tanf-funds-in-2014

Many observers have described these changes as a return to a laissez-faire approach to welfare provision, in which government retreats and the poor are left to fend for themselves in the market (Somers & Block, 2005). Others combine this narrative with a focus on rising correctional control. They assert that "as the state more completely sheds economic responsibility" it produces insecurity and disorder, which, in turn, "necessitates the grandeur of the penal state" (Wacquant, 2009, p. 19).

Yet the American state has not shed its economic responsibilities; instead, it has recast them. In this domain, as in many others, political challengers did not dismantle the activist state; they reorganized it and turned it to new purposes (Pierson & Skocpol,

2007). The approaches to governance they put in place operate according to the logics of neoliberal paternalism described earlier, and they rely on a strong activist state in *both* the social welfare and criminal justice fields. The key developments have not occurred along the quantitative dimension of more versus less state intervention. They have focused on *how* the state is intervening, for what purposes, and for whose benefit. Poverty governance has been reorganized to replace centralized state control with decentralized cross-sector collaborations and to serve as a site of profitable investment for corporations such as Lockheed Martin, Maximus, Affiliated Computer Systems, and Corrections Corporation of America.

Welfare investments that shield the poor from market pressures have, indeed, declined; the emphasis is now less on providing cash aid to families and more on compelling the heads of those families to take paid employment at prevailing wage rates. In other social welfare programs, there is a similar turn to a more disciplinary focus, with time limits and work requirements introduced even in housing programs. Program cuts mostly target working-age, nondisabled Americans. In some cases, efforts to curb such protections have been overt. In the 1980s, the Reagan Administration reduced federal investments in state unemployment insurance trust funds (Pierson, 1994) and many states terminated or restricted their General Assistance programs for single adults who did not qualify for other benefits (Gallagher, Uccello, Pierce, & Reidy, 1999).

Much of the erosion in assistance to the needy, however, was accomplished by simply blocking efforts to keep benefits aligned with inflation and coverage aligned with changes in labor markets (Hacker, 2004). Even before welfare reform, the value of the combined AFDC–food stamp package had dropped precipitously, largely because lawmakers allowed the real value of these benefits to decline by 42% between 1970 and 1996 (Pavetti, 2001). Unemployment insurance, which serves a more economically diverse group, declined as well. The unemployment insurance eligibility period and average replacement rate for wages held steady. But new policies restricted access by allowing employers to challenge their former workers'

Figure 13.4 How Welfare Reform Diminished Support for Needy Families and Children.

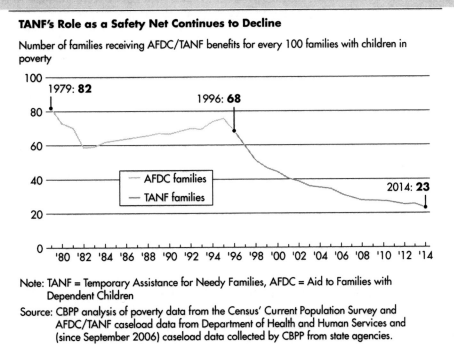

TANF's Role as a Safety Net Continues to Decline

Number of families receiving AFDC/TANF benefits for every 100 families with children in poverty

Note: TANF = Temporary Assistance for Needy Families, AFDC = Aid to Families with Dependent Children

Source: CBPP analysis of poverty data from the Census' Current Population Survey and AFDC/TANF caseload data from Department of Health and Human Services and (since September 2006) caseload data collected by CBPP from state agencies.

Center on Budget and Policy Priorities | cbpp.org

applications, and policy drift left workers unprotected in the fastest-growing sectors of the labor market (Fagnoni, 2007; U.S. General Accounting Office [GAO], 2000). Overall spending declined from $12,000 per unemployed worker in 1970 to less than $4,000 in 2000 (Massey, 2007), with most of the reductions coming from declining coverage of the lowest wage workers (GAO, 2000). By the 1990s, low-wage workers were twice as likely to be unemployed but, relative to other unemployed workers, were less than half as likely to receive unemployment insurance (GAO, 2000). [*See Chapter 12 in this volume for further discussion of employment policies.*]

As supports outside the market dwindled, equally significant changes occurred in policies that were designed to create incentives to seek employment and "make work pay." The crucial shift involved the decline of the minimum wage, which forces employers to bear the costs of increasing incomes, and the rise of the Earned Income Tax Credit (EITC), which puts this burden on taxpayers. The EITC has had positive effects in reducing poverty but at the expense of even greater declines in poverty that would have resulted if the minimum wage had kept up with the rising cost of living.

From 1968 to 2006, the real value of the minimum wage dropped from $9.30 to $5.15 per hour—that is, from 45% to 28% of the average wage and from 93% to 50% of the poverty line (Bartels, 2008; Massey, 2007). Faced with overwhelming public support for a minimum-wage increase (Bartels, 2008), business interests pushed hard for the alternative strategy of expanding the EITC (Herd, 2008). The EITC, however, offers no protection for the unemployed and puts no floor under wages. Instead, by using tax revenues to augment wages, it strengthens work incentives for the poor and relieves wage pressures on employers. From 1975 to 2006, federal EITC spending rose from $5 million to $45 million (Scholz, Moffitt, & Cowan, 2009). These investments substantially increased labor force participation among the poor (Grogger, 2003; Meyer, 2002) and led to reductions in market wages for low-skilled workers (Rothstein, 2009). [*See Chapter 12 in this volume for further discussion of this issue.*]

The EITC is aimed at working-age, nondisabled adults who are in the labor market. On one side of this group lie target populations such as the disabled and elderly. Major programs for these populations continue to provide more generous nonmarket protections, but they have been reformed in recent years to present modest but clear work incentives, as is the case for disability insurance and Supplemental Security Income, both of which provide cash assistance for those citizens technically deemed not able to work. On the other side, there are means-tested programs for the working-age, nondisabled poor who lack a clear attachment to the labor market. Here, the work push is stronger and more paternalistic.

In other words, the emphasis on work over welfare is not limited to TANF. For example, since the passage of the Quality Housing and Work Responsibility Act of 1998, the federal government has required recipients of public housing aid to work or volunteer each month and has made TANF sanctions a basis for denying rent reductions due to lost income. Similar changes have been made to food assistance policy. Today, recipients of the Supplemental Nutrition Assistance Program (SNAP, formerly known as food stamps) must register for work, accept suitable employment, and participate in work-promoting programs as a condition of aid. Working-age adults without children can receive SNAP for only 3 months in a 36-month period if they do not work or participate in a workfare program, a rule that parallels the strict work requirements imposed on adults without dependents in state General Assistance programs (Gallagher et al., 1999).

Similarly, since 1979, federal rules have promoted prison labor by allowing the sale, interstate commerce, and international export of goods made by prisoners. Between 1979 and 2005, "prison industries" contributed an estimated $97 million toward the costs of incarceration and $47 million in federal and state taxes (U.S. Department of Justice, 2009). Over the same period, cheap prison labor was increasingly contracted to for-profit firms, with private prison operators such as Correction Corporation of America also profiting directly by using prisoners as maintenance workers (Kang, 2009). The carceral turn in social policy and the resultant rise of mass incarceration in the latter part of the 20th century influenced welfare reform and helped integrate it into the new disciplinary regime. At the same time, the intensified focus in welfare policy on moving recipients into low-wage jobs affected changes in criminal justice policies, including especially re-entry programs. Funding for such policies as the Second Chance Act of 2008 focused on funneling ex-felons into low-wage employment upon leaving prison (Schram, 2015). As a result, the hard "right-hand" of the state (i.e., criminal justice policies) and the softer "left-hand" of the state (i.e., welfare policies) came to be more closely attuned (Wacquant, 2009).

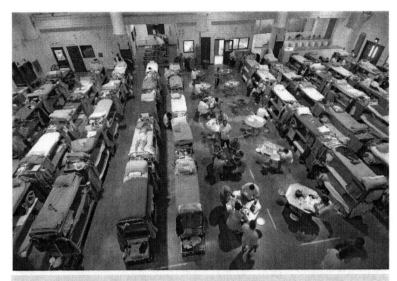

Figure 13.5 Overcrowding in a California state prison

Rationalized by paternalistic principles, work promotion has been accompanied by dramatic increases in procedures for monitoring and documenting poor people's behavior. Aid recipients have been increasingly subjected to drug testing, fingerprinting, and questioning regarding their sexual relations (to establish paternity and pursue child support). On the criminal justice side, the expansion of supervision has been greater still. Between 1970 and 2003, state and federal prison populations grew sevenfold, primarily consisting of perpetrators of victimless crimes, such as minor drug possession, with most of the growth occurring among poor, undereducated racial minorities (Western, 2006). Per capita corrections expenditure in the states rose from $23 in 1970 to $125 in 2001, from 1% to 3.5% of all budget outlays (Guetzkow & Western, 2007).

FROM POLICY PRODUCT TO PERFORMANCE OUTCOMES IN THE NEW DISCIPLINARY REGIME

In penal and welfare operations alike, the reach of state supervision has been growing beyond the limits of the official "participation spell" (i.e., the time during which a person is in prison or on welfare). In some states, new forms of "post-exit paternalism" specify that welfare leavers must remain in their jobs to continue to receive transitional supports. Similarly, parole supervision has become more vigilant and has been applied to an escalating percentage of the post-prison population. In 2003, 4.7 million Americans were under probation or parole supervision, and the number of individuals leaving prison each year stood at 630,000, quadruple the rate in 1978 (Travis, 2005). More than 80% of people leaving prison were being placed on parole, and the number being sent back for parole violation was 7 times higher than it had been 20 years earlier (Western, 2006). Drug offenders receive especially close scrutiny in private "recovery houses," where they are monitored daily and risk a return to prison if they relapse (Fairbanks, 2009). When prisoners finish "doing their time" today, they are typically released into "a closely monitored terrain, a supervised space, lacking much of the liberty that one associates with normal life" (Garland, 2002, p. 178).

Neoliberal paternalism has also guided equally important shifts in *how* poverty governance is organized and carried out. As the activist state has been turned to new purposes, it has been "rolled out" to diverse actors and locales through privatization and devolution (Peck & Tickell, 2002). Emphasizing efficiency and performance, reformers have "reinvented government" as a diffuse network of governing relationships rooted in market principles. Increasingly, poverty governance is structured by contractual relations, decentralized to facilitate entrepreneurial innovation, and evaluated on market terms rather than democratic values.

The introduction of contemporary poverty governance was driven by more than just ideology; it also served practical political purposes. Outside the elected offices of national government, the entrenched liberal state could not be easily purged of its established cultures, routines, and actors. Devolution and privatization shifted authority to sites with fewer barriers to establishing new governing logics. New performance systems facilitated outsourcing by establishing outcome-based logics of public accountability (distant from democratic control and transparency) that could be applied to both nonprofit and for-profit contractors as easily as to state agencies. As indicated by our research on welfare reform as implemented in the state of Florida, governance became more decentralized. These performance systems also provided mechanisms for disciplining the operations of far-flung agents to improve the odds that principals' goals would be achieved in ways that served the overriding objective to find the most cost-efficient ways to discipline clients to accept low-wage work (Soss, Fording & Schram, 2011).

Many of the developments associated with welfare reform across the states have been accompanied by rhetorical attacks on "big government" that celebrate market efficiencies, local knowledge, and the compassion of nonprofit and religious organizations. The political salience of such appeals has obscured a more basic fact: Neoliberal paternalism is not about weakening the state; it is about strengthening the state as a disciplinary authority. New approaches to governing the poor have extended the reach of government via contractual relationships with market and civil society organizations. State powers of surveillance and discipline have expanded dramatically, even as the public sector has been attacked and prevented from growing to meet new needs.

NEOLIBERAL PATERNALIST DISCIPLINARY WELFARE POLICY IN THE AGE OF MANUFACTURED AUSTERITY

Welfare policies across the states as administered in the new decentralized system continue to reflect the insistences of the racialized, neoliberal paternalist disciplinary regime (Schram & Soss, 2015). Yet, it seems things have gone from bad to worse during the first two decades of the 21st Century. At present, more than a quarter of poor women with children are, in all likelihood, "disconnected"—that is, they do not receive cash assistance of any kind or welfare (Blank & Kovack, 2008). Increasingly these women and their children are part of a burgeoning population of individuals and families living in deep poverty (i.e., below half the poverty line) or even extreme poverty (i.e., living on less than $2.00 per day per person—the international standard for extreme destitution). It is currently estimated that four million Americans live in extreme poverty, including three million children. Their numbers have grown each year post-welfare reform which is undoubtedly the major cause for this upsurge (Edin & Shaefer, 2015).

At the same time, the percentage of TANF-eligible families who actually received this benefit decreased dramatically from 1994 to 2008 from 84% to only 40% (U.S. Department of Health and Human Services, 2008), and declined further to 23% in 2014 (Pavetti, 2016). The states have continued to find new ways to restrict access to cash assistance and have joined with the federal government in making it more difficult to receive SNAP (formerly food stamps). Non-white citizens and immigrants disproportionately bear the brunt of the new restrictions. The need to demonize the poor seems now to be on automatic pilot long after welfare reform has essentially delivered on President Clinton's 1992 campaign promise to "end welfare as we know it" (something neither he nor his wife, Democratic Presidential nominee Hillary Rodham Clinton, will say in retrospect was a mistake). This demonstrates that the bipartisan commitment to the failure of neoliberal paternalist welfare reform persists (Theoharis & Marchevsky, 2016).The political response to the presidency of Barack Obama, the nation's first African American President, has exacerbated this trend (Tesler, 2016). The "Obama Effect," as Michael Tesler (2016) calls it, suggests that his presidency has intensified the racialization of government assistance to the poor and heightened conservative opposition on the grounds that welfare programs of any type encourage dependency and resistance to acting consistent with dominant cultural (i.e., "white") values about work and family. Ironically, the research of Kathryn Edin and Luke Shaefer (2015) and others has demonstrated that these values are increasingly difficult for all low-income families (white and non-white alike) to realize in practice. For example, states where Republicans dominate politically have been resistant to the expansion of Medicaid included in the Patient Protection and Affordable Care Act (ACA) of 2009. Low-income African Americans are the primary population that has been denied increased access to health insurance as a result of this resistance (Tesler, 2016, p. 118), but many low-income and working class white individuals and families have suffered as well. These facts, however, seem to have no impact on the increased racialization of welfare policy in our supposedly post-racial society, a society that has sadly proven to be anything but post-racial, as simmering racial tensions have not only increased, they have spilled over into electoral politics, media coverage of contemporary issues, and community life.

CONCLUSION

A new disciplinary regime of poverty governance has emerged in the United States during an age of globalization. It is designed currently to funnel people in poverty into the bottom rungs of low-wage markets and not rely on the decreasing amounts of public assistance that remain available under the manufactured austerity of the age. Welfare reform that transformed cash assistance to poor families with children lies at the center of this shift. Today, the focus of welfare policy is more about disciplining single mothers with children to become docile compliant workers willing to take whatever jobs the low-wage labor markets of the globalizing economy provide. With time limits, work requirements, and sanctions for failure to comply with program rules, cash aid has all but evaporated and been replaced by welfare-to-work services. By 2001, just 5 years after the passage of federal reform, the U.S. welfare system had reached the point where more than half of federal TANF block grants to the states were being spent on noncash services designed to promote and assist transitions to work. Thus, just as welfare recipients have become a dwindling percentage of the poor, so too has cash income support become a more meager component of welfare provision (Allard, 2009). Earlier conservative efforts to roll back the welfare state met with resistance and led to the development of a more market-oriented welfare system focused on serving employers of low-wage workers rather than families in need of aid.

Welfare programs today continue to serve the same basic functions that Piven and Cloward specified in 1971, but the operations that fulfill these functions have shifted in important ways. Like the policies of the Charity Organization Societies in the 19th century, welfare programs continue to play a key role in "regulating the poor" in precisely the ways Piven and Cloward suggested. Yet they are also organized to "discipline the poor" in ways that go beyond their landmark analysis. Welfare policy today is less associated with economic or other social policies and more associated with criminal justice policy. It is part of a larger system of managing the poverty population through disciplinary techniques such as conditioning aid by demonstrating compliance or suffering the imposition of financial penalties.

Our research in the state of Florida indicates that this shift in welfare policy is part of the development of a neoliberal–paternalist regime of poverty governance designed to discipline the poor to accept their plight on the bottom of the low-wage labor markets of a globalizing economy (Soss, Fording, & Schram, 2011). In the context of globalization, limitations on immigrants receiving assistance continue to be an important feature of this policy regime. These restrictions complement the racialization of welfare recipients by focusing on the disciplining of these "others" and compelling them to comply with supposed white, middle-class norms of work and family. The retreat from the more inclusive policies of the War on Poverty of the 1960s could not be more explicit.

Discussion Questions

1. Discuss the principle of less eligibility and how it affected the push for the 1996 welfare reform law.
2. Define **neoliberal paternalism** and indicate how welfare reform is reflective of this perspective.
3. What is meant by the "**medicalization** of welfare"? Provide examples of changes that reflect this shift in welfare policy implementation.
4. Provide examples of how **race** influences welfare policy implementation today. Compare its influence today with that of previous eras.
5. Contrast the treatment of low-income persons in previous years with the practice of disciplining the poor in the current era. Discuss how the implementation of welfare reform reflects this increased emphasis on discipline in an age of **neoliberal globalization**.

Suggested Websites

National Poverty Center: http://www.npc.umich.edu/

Poverty in America blog, *The Nation:* http://www.thenation.com/blogs/greg-kaufmann

Spotlight on Poverty and Opportunity: http://www.spotlightonpoverty.org/

Suggestions for Further Reading

Collins, J., & Mayer, V. (2010). *Both hands tied: Welfare reform and the race to the bottom of the low-wage labor market.* Chicago: University of Chicago Press.

Edin, K., & Shaefer, L. (2015). *$2.00 a day: Living on almost nothing in America.* New York: Houghton, Mifflin Harcourt.

Piven, F. F., & Cloward, R. A. (1993). *Regulating the poor: The functions of public welfare.* New York: Vintage. (Original work published in 1971)

Reese, E. (2010). *They say cut back, we say fight back! Welfare activism in an era of retrenchment.* New York: Russell Sage Foundation.

Wacquant, L. (2009). *Punishing the poor: The neoliberal government of social insecurity*. Durham, NC: Duke University Press.

Western, B. (2006). *Punishment and inequality in America*. New York: Russell Sage Foundation.

References

Akard, P. J. (1992). Corporate mobilization and political power: The transformation of U.S. economic policy in the 1970s. *American Sociological Review, 57*(5), 597–615.

Allard, S. (2009). *Out of reach: Place, poverty, and the new American welfare state*. New Haven, CT: Yale University Press.

APSA Task Force (2004). American democracy in an age of rising inequality. *Perspectives on Politics, 2*(4), 651–666.

Armey, R. (1995). *The freedom revolution: The new Republican house majority leader tells why big government failed, why freedom works, and how we will rebuild America*. New York: Regnery.

Barker, I. (2007). Citizen exceptions: Global capitalism, immigration, and welfare regime change. Unpublished paper available from the authors.

Bartels, L. (2008). *Unequal democracy: The political economy of the new gilded age*. Princeton, NJ: Princeton University Press.

Bell, W. (1965). *Aid to Families with Dependent Children*. New York: Columbia University Press.

Berry, J. M. (1999). *The new liberalism: The rising power of citizen groups*. Washington, DC: Brookings Institution Press.

Blank, R., & Kovak, B. (2008). *The growing problem of disconnected single mothers* (Working Paper No. 07–28). Ann Arbor, MI: National Poverty Center.

Boyer, P. (1978). *Urban masses and moral order, 1820–1920*. Cambridge, MA: Harvard University Press.

Brown, W. (2003). Neo-liberalism and the end of liberal democracy. *Theory and Event, 7*(1). Retrieved from http://muse.jhu.edu/journals/theory_and_event/

Campbell, A. L. (2003). *How policies make citizens: Senior political activism and the American welfare state*. Princeton, NJ: Princeton University Press.

Campbell, A. L. (2007). Parties, electoral participation, and shifting voting blocs. In P. Pierson & T. Skocpol (Eds.), *The transformation of American politics: Activist government and the rise of conservatism* (pp. 68–102). Princeton, NJ: Princeton University Press.

Carmines, E. G., & Stimson, J. A. (1989). *Issue evolution: Race and the transformation of American politics*. Princeton, NJ: Princeton University Press.

Conway, M. M. (1986). PACs and congressional elections in the 1980s. In A. Cigler & B. Loomis (Eds.), *Interest group politics* (pp. 70–90). Washington, DC: Congressional Quarterly.

Crenson, M. A. (1998). *Building the invisible orphanage: A prehistory of the American welfare state*. Cambridge, MA: Harvard University Press.

Davis, A. (1983). *Women, race, and class*. New York: Vintage Books.

DeParle, J. (1996, December 8). Mugged by reality. *New York Times Magazine*. Retrieved from http://www.nytimes.com/1996/12/08/magazine/mugged-by-reality.html?pagewanted=all&src=pm

Diamond, S. (1995). *Roads to dominion: Right-wing movements and political power in the United States*. New York: Guilford Press.

Edin, K., & Lein, L. (1997). *Making ends meet: How single mothers survive welfare and low-wage work*. New York: Russell Sage Foundation.

Edin, K., & Shaefer, L. (2015). *$2.00 a day: Living on almost nothing in America.* New York: Houghton, Mifflin Harcourt.

Edsall, T. B., with Edsall, M. D. (1991). *Chain reaction: The impact of race, rights, and taxes on American politics.* New York: Knopf.

Ehrenreich, B. (1987). The new right attack on social welfare. In F. F. Piven, R. A. Cloward, B. Ehrenreich, & F. Block (Eds.), *The mean season: The attack on the welfare state* (pp. 161–193). New York: Pantheon Books.

Ehrenreich, B. (1997). Spinning the poor into gold: How corporations seek to profit from welfare reform. *Harper's Magazine, 294*(1767), 44–52.

Ellwood, D. T. (1988). *Poor support: Poverty in the American family.* New York: Basic Books.

Fagnoni, C. (2007). *Unemployment insurance: Receipt of benefits has declined, with continued disparities for low-wage and part-time workers* (Testimony before the Subcommittee on Income Security and Family Support, U.S. House of Representatives, Committee on Ways and Means). Washington, DC: Government Accountability Office.

Fairbanks, R. P. (2009). *How it works: Recovering citizens in post-welfare Philadelphia.* Chicago: University of Chicago Press.

Ferguson, T., & Rogers, J. (1986). *Right turn: The decline of the Democrats and the future of American politics.* New York: Hill & Wang.

Fiorina, M. P. (2004). *Culture war? The myth of a polarized America.* New York: Longman.

Fording, R. C. (1997). The conditional effect of violence as a political tactic: Mass insurgency, welfare generosity, and electoral context in the American states. *American Journal of Political Science, 41,* 1–29.

Fording, R. C. (2001). The political response to black insurgency: A critical test of competing theories of the state. *American Political Science Review, 95*(1), 115–131.

Frymer, P. (1999). *Uneasy alliances: Race and party competition in America.* Princeton, NJ: Princeton University Press.

Gallagher, L. J., Uccello, C. E., Pierce, A. B., & Reidy, E. B. (1999). *State general assistance programs 1998.* Washington, DC: Urban Institute. Retrieved from http://www.urban.org/UploadedPDF/ga_main.pdf

Garland, D. (2002). *The culture of control: Crime and social order in contemporary society.* Chicago: University of Chicago Press.

Gilder, G. (1981). *Wealth and poverty.* New York: Basic Books.

Gilens, M. (1999). *Why Americans hate welfare: Race, media, and the politics of antipoverty policy.* Chicago: University of Chicago Press.

Goldfield, M. (1989). *The decline of organized labor in the United States.* Chicago: University of Chicago Press.

Gordon, L. (1995). *Pitied but not entitled: Single mothers and the history of welfare, 1890–1935.* New York: Free Press.

Grogger, J. (2003). The effects of time limits, the EITC, and other policy changes on welfare use, work, and income among female-headed families. *Review of Economics and Statistics, 85*(2), 394–408.

Guetzkow, J., & Western, B. (2007). The political consequences of mass imprisonment. In J. Soss, J. Hacker, & S. Mettler (Eds.), *Remaking America: Democracy and public policy in an age of inequality* (pp. 228–242). New York: Russell Sage Foundation.

Hacker, J. S. (2002). *The divided welfare state: The battle over public and private social benefits in the United States.* New York: Cambridge University Press.

Hacker, J. S. (2004, May). Privatizing risk without privatizing the welfare state: The hidden politics of social policy retrenchment in the United States. *American Political Science Review, 98,* 243–260.

Hacker, J. S. (2006). *The great risk shift: The assault on American jobs, families, health care and retirement—and how you can fight back.* New York: Oxford University Press.

Hacker, J. S., & Pierson, P. (2005). *Off center: The Republican revolution and the erosion of American democracy.* New Haven, CT: Yale University Press.

Hancock, A.-M. (2004). When multiplication doesn't equal quick addition: Examining intersectionality as a research paradigm. *Perspectives on Politics, 5,* 63–79.

Harvey, D. (2005). *A brief history of neoliberalism.* New York: Oxford University Press.

Heclo, H. (1995). The social question. In K. McFate, R. Lawson, & W. J. Wilson (Eds.), *Poverty, inequality, and the future of social policy* (pp. 665–691). New York: Russell Sage.

Heclo, H. (2001). The politics of welfare reform. In R. M. Blank & R. R. Haskins (Eds.), *The new world of welfare* (pp. 169–200). Washington, DC: Brookings Institution Press.

Herd, P. (2008). *The fourth way: Big states, big business, and the evolution of the Earned Income Tax Credit.* Paper presented at the annual meeting of the American Sociological Association, Boston.

Hinton, E. (2016). *From the war on poverty to the war on crime: The making of mass incarceration in America.* Cambridge: Harvard University Press.

Hodgson, G. (1989). *The world turned right side up: A history of the conservative ascendancy in America.* New York: Houghton Mifflin.

Howard, C. (1997). *The hidden welfare state: Tax expenditures and social policy in the United States.* Princeton, NJ: Princeton University Press.

Kang, S. (2009). Forcing prison labor: International labor standards, human rights and the privatization of prison labor in the contemporary United States. *New Political Science, 31*(2), 137–161.

Katz, M. B. (1997). *Improving poor people: The welfare state, the "underclass," and urban schools as history.* Princeton, NJ: Princeton University Press.

Kellstedt, P. M. (2003). *The mass media and the dynamics of American racial attitudes.* New York: Cambridge University Press.

Kinder, D., & Sanders, L. (1996). *Divided by color: Racial politics and democratic ideals.* Chicago: University of Chicago Press.

Kornbluh, F. (2007). *The battle for welfare rights: Poverty and politics in modern America.* Philadelphia: University of Pennsylvania Press.

Lieberman, R. C. (2005). *Shaping race policy: The United States in comparative perspective.* Princeton, NJ: Princeton University Press.

Lieberman, R. C. (1998). *Shifting the color line: Race and the American welfare state.* Cambridge, MA: Harvard University Press.

Lowell, J. S. (1911). The economic and moral effects of public outdoor relief. In W. R. Stewart (Ed.), *The philanthropic work of Josephine Shaw Lowell* (pp. 158–174). New York: Macmillan.

Luker, K. (1996). *Dubious conceptions: The politics of teenage pregnancy.* Cambridge, MA: Harvard University Press.

Martin, C. J. (2004). Reinventing welfare regimes. *World Politics, 57*(1), 39–69.

Massey, D. S. (2007). *Categorically unequal: The American stratification system.* New York: Russell Sage Foundation.

Massey, D. S., & Denton, M. (1993). *American apartheid: Segregation and the making of the underclass.* Cambridge, MA: Harvard University Press.

McCarty, N. (2007). The policy effects of political polarization. In P. Pierson & T. Skocpol (Eds.), *The transformation of American politics: Activist government and the rise of conservatism* (pp. 223–255). Princeton, NJ: Princeton University Press.

McCarty, N., Poole, K. T., & Rosenthal, H. (2006). *Polarized America: The dance of ideology and unequal riches.* Cambridge: MIT Press.

McDonald, C., & Reisch, M. (2008). Social work in the workfare regime: A comparison of the U.S. and Australia. *Journal of Sociology and Social Welfare, 35*(1), 43–74.

Mead, L. M. (1986). *Beyond entitlement: The social obligations of citizenship.* New York: Free Press.

Melnick, R. S. (2005). From tax-and-spend to mandate-and-sue: Liberalism after the Great Society. In S. M. Milkis (Ed.), *The Great Society and the high tide of liberalism* (pp. 387–410). Amherst, MA: University of Massachusetts Press.

Mettler, S. (1998). *Dividing citizens: Gender and federalism in New Deal public policy.* Ithaca, NY: Cornell University Press.

Meyer, B. (2002). Labor supply at the extensive and intensive margins: The EITC, welfare and hours worked. *American Economic Review, 92*(2), 373–379.

Murray, C. (1984). *Losing ground: American social policies, 1950–1980.* New York: Free Press.

Nelson, B. J. (1990). The origins of the two-channel welfare state: Workmen's compensation and mother's aid. In L. Gordon (Ed.), *Women, the state, and welfare* (pp. 123–151). Madison: University of Wisconsin Press.

Noble, C. (1997). *Welfare as we knew it: A political history of the American welfare state.* New York: Oxford University Press.

Norton, A. (2004). *Leo Strauss and the politics of American empire.* New Haven, CT: Yale University Press.

Orloff, A. S. (2002). Explaining U.S. welfare reform: Power, gender, race, and the U.S. policy legacy. *Critical Social Policy, 22*(1), 96–118.

Page, B. I., & Jacobs, L. R. (2009). *Class war? What Americans really think about economic inequality.* Chicago: University of Chicago Press.

Pavetti, L.A. (2016, January 11). *Let's improve TANF and hold states accountable for results.* Washington, DC: Center on Budget and Policy Priorities.

Pavetti, L. A. (2001). Welfare policy in transition: Redefining the social contract for poor citizen families with children and for immigrants. In S. Danziger & R. Haveman (Eds.), *Understanding poverty* (pp. 229–277). New York: Russell Sage Foundation.

Peck, J. (2008). Remaking laissez-faire. *Progress in Human Geography, 32*(1), 3–43.

Peck, J., & Tickell, A. (2002). Neoliberalizing space. *Antipode, 34*(3), 380–404.

Pierson, P. (1994). *Dismantling the welfare state? Reagan, Thatcher, and the politics of retrenchment.* New York: Cambridge University Press.

Pierson, P. (2007). The rise and reconfiguration of activist government. In P. Pierson & T. Skocpol (Eds.), *The transformation of American politics: Activist government and the rise of conservatism* (pp. 19–38). Princeton, NJ: Princeton University Press.

Pierson, P., & Skocpol, T. (Eds.). (2007). *The transformation of American politics: Activist government and the rise of conservatism.* Princeton, NJ: Princeton University Press.

Pimpare, S. (2004). *The new Victorians: Poverty, politics, and propaganda in two gilded ages.* New York: New Press.

Piven, F. F. (2007). Institutions and agents in the politics of welfare cutbacks. In J. Soss, J. S. Hacker, & S. Mettler (Eds.), *Remaking America: Democracy and public policy in an age of inequality* (pp. 141–156). New York: Russell Sage Foundation.

Piven, F. F., & Cloward, R. A. (1977). *Poor people's movements: Why they succeed, how they fail.* New York: Vintage.

Piven, F. F., & Cloward, R. A. (1988). *Why Americans don't vote.* New York: Pantheon.

Piven, F. F., & Cloward, R. A. (1993). *Regulating the poor: The public functions of welfare.* New York: Vintage. (Original work published in 1971)

Quadagno, J. (1994). *The color of welfare: How racism undermined the War on Poverty.* New York: Oxford University Press.

Rich, A. (2004). *Think tanks, public policy, and the politics of expertise.* New York: Cambridge University Press.

Rothstein, J. (2009). *Is the EITC equivalent to an NIT? Conditional cash transfers and tax incidence* (NBER Working Paper No. w14966). Cambridge, MA: National Bureau of Economic Research. Retrieved from http://papers.ssrn.com/sol3/papers.cfm?abstract_id=1405974

Sassen, S. (2006). *Territory, authority, rights: From medieval to global assemblages.* Princeton: Princeton University Press.

Scholz, J. K., Moffitt, R., & Cowan, B. (2009). Trends in income support. In M. Cancian & S. Danziger (Eds.), *Changing poverty* (pp. 203–241). New York: Russell Sage Foundation.

Schram, S. F. (2015). *The return of ordinary capitalism: Neoliberalism, precarity, occupy.* New York: Oxford University Press.

Schram, S. F., & Soss, J. (2015, September 3). Demonizing the poor. *Jacobin.* https://www.jacobinmag.com/2015/09/welfare-republicans-sam-brownback-race-corporations/.

Schram, S. F., & Soss, J. (2001, September). Success stories: Welfare reform, policy discourse, and the politics of research. *Annals of the American Academy of Political and Social Science, 557,* 49–65.

Schram, S. F., & Turbett, J. P. (1983). Civil disorder and the welfare explosion: A two-step process. *American Sociological Review, 48*(3), 408–414.

Schuman, H., Steeh, C., Bobo, L., & Krysan, M. (1997). *Racial attitudes in America: Trends and interpretations* (Rev. ed.). Cambridge, MA: Harvard University Press.

Simon, J. (2007). *Governing through crime: How the war on crime transformed American democracy and created a culture of fear.* New York: Oxford University Press.

Skocpol, T. (1992). *Protecting soldiers and mothers: The political origins of social policy in the United States.* Cambridge, MA: Belknap Press of Harvard University Press.

Skocpol, T. (2003). *Diminished democracy: From membership to management in American civic life.* Norman: University of Oklahoma Press.

Skrentny, J. D. (2002). *The minority rights revolution.* Cambridge, MA: Belknap Press, Harvard University Press.

Somers, M. R., & Block, F. (2005). From poverty to perversity: Ideas, markets, and institutions over 200 years of welfare debate. *American Sociological Review, 70*(2), 260–287.

Soss, J., Fording, R. C., & Schram, S. F. (2011). *Disciplining the poor: Neoliberal paternalism and the persistent power of race.* Chicago: University of Chicago Press.

Soss, J., & Schram, S. F. (2007). A public transformed? Welfare reform as policy feedback. *American Political Science Review, 101*(1), 111–127.

Stonecash, J. M. (2000). *Class and party in American politics.* Boulder, CO: Westview.

Strolovitch, D. Z. (2008). *Affirmative advocacy: Race, class, and gender in interest group politics.* Chicago: University of Chicago Press.

Teles, S. M. (2008). *The rise of the conservative legal movement: The battle for control of the law.* Princeton, NJ: Princeton University Press.

Telser, M. (2016). *Post-racial or most-racial: Race and politics in the Obama era.* Chicago: University of Chicago Press.

Theoharis, J., & Marchevsky, A. *(2016).* Why it matters that Hillary Clinton championed welfare reform. *The Nation,* March 1, 2016.

Theriault, S. M. (2006). Party polarization in the U.S. Congress: Member replacement and member adaptation. *Party Politics, 12*(4), 483–503.

Trattner, W. I. (1999). *From poor law to welfare state: A history of social welfare in America,* (6th ed.) New York: Simon & Shuster.

Travis, J. (2005). *But they all come back: Facing the challenges of prisoner reentry.* Washington, DC: Urban Institute Press.

U.S. Department of Health and Human Services, Administration for Children and Families (2008). *Temporary Assistance for Needy Families (TANF) program, tenth annual report to Congress.* Washington, DC: Government Printing Office.

U.S. Department of Justice (2009). *Prison Industry Enhancement Certification Program (PIECP).* Washington, DC: Bureau of Justice Assistance.

U.S. General Accounting Office (2000). *Welfare reform: State sanction policies and number of families affected* (GAO/HEHS-00–44). Washington, DC: Author.

Vogel, D. (1989). *Fluctuating fortunes: The political power of business in America.* New York: Basic Books.

Wacquant, L. (2009). *Punishing the poor: The neoliberal government of social insecurity.* Durham, NC: Duke University Press.

Wagner, D. (2005). *The poorhouse: America's forgotten institution.* Lanham, MD: Rowman & Littlefield.

Ward, D. E. (2005). *The white welfare state: The racialization of U.S. welfare policy.* Ann Arbor: University of Michigan Press.

Weaver, R. K. (2002). Polls, priming, and the politics of welfare reform. In J. Manza, F. L. Cook, & B. I. Page (Eds.), *Navigating public opinion* (pp. 106–123). New York: Oxford University Press.

Weaver, V. M. (2007). Frontlash: Race and the development of punitive crime policy. *Studies in American Political Development, 21,* 230–265.

Western, B. (2006). *Punishment and inequality in America.* New York: Russell Sage Foundation.

Williams, L. (2003). *The constraint of race: Legacies of white skin privilege in America.* State College: Pennsylvania State University Press.

Wilson, W. J. (1997). *When work disappears: The world of the new urban poor.* New York: Vintage.

Winter, N. J. G. (2008). *Dangerous frames: How ideas about race and gender shape public opinion.* Chicago: University of Chicago Press.

Credits

14

HEALTH AND MENTAL HEALTH POLICY

Stephen Gorin, PhD, and Cynthia Moniz, PhD

This chapter focuses on the history, background, and status of three primary dimensions of health care and health care reform: the coverage, cost, and quality of care in the United States. It examines the significance of an employer-based system of insurance and care, the importance of Medicare and Medicaid, and the impact of the 2010 **Affordable Care Act**. Essential features of the delivery of health and mental health services are included. The chapter concludes with a discussion of the impact of unequal **access** to health care because of race, gender, class, sexual orientation, or health inequities.

BACKGROUND: THE PROGRESSIVE ERA

Modern efforts to expand health care coverage in the United States began during the first two decades of the 20th century. In the 1912 presidential campaign, Theodore Roosevelt's Progressive Party—with support from settlement house leader Jane Addams—called for the "adoption of a system of social insurance," including the "protection of home life against the hazards of sickness" (as cited in Birn, Brown, Fee, & Lear, 2003). Much of the impetus for compulsory insurance, or National Health Insurance (NHI), came from the American Association for Labor Legislation (AALL), a coalition of social reformers that included Jane Addams, and labor and business leaders (Quadagno, 2005; Schlabach, 1969). The AALL developed legislation that would have provided medical and other benefits to workers, with costs to be shared by employers, employees, and the state (Starr, 1982). Although some labor leaders and physicians supported this effort, it faced strong opposition from local medical societies, organized labor (many of whose members opposed government involvement in negotiations between workers and management), and insurance companies. By the end of the decade, in the wake of World War I and the Russian Revolution, efforts for reform, including NHI, had waned and were frequently characterized as "Bolshevik" in nature.

Early health care reform campaigns often overlapped with efforts to expand **public health** measures, particularly between 1900 and 1930, a period described as a "golden age for public health" (Starr, 1982, p. 197). Public health issues came to the fore because the rise of urbanization and industrialization created health problems that were impossible to ignore. During the 1890s, many cities "instituted new public works sanitation projects (such as piped water, sewer systems, filtration and chlorination of water) and public health administration" (Haines, 1991, p. 105). By the turn of the century, research demonstrated that many diseases that plagued urban populations, in particular, were communicable in nature. With the development of vaccines against rabies and diphtheria, many communities, particularly in the East, required their residents to become immunized (Garrett, 2000).

It did not take long for public health advocates to run afoul of the same forces opposed to NHI. In 1920, Edward Amory Winslow, founder of the Yale School of Public Health and one of the nation's leading experts, defined public health as the

> science and art of preventing disease, prolonging life … promoting health and efficiency through organized community effort … and the development of the social machinery which will ensure to every individual in the community a standard of living adequate for the maintenance of health (As cited in Starr, 1982, p. 180).

As Starr noted, such an expansive definition was "an invitation to conflict" with property owners and others opposed to a strong role for government. Physicians, in particular, were concerned about anything that might infringe on what they viewed as their unique role. This led them to oppose "public treatment of the sick, requirements for reporting cases of tuberculosis, and the creation of public health centers" (Starr, 1982, p. 181).

In a sense, public health reform was also undermined by its own success. The discovery that microorganisms caused many diseases led researchers to shift their focus away from the environmental causes of epidemics. In 1916, the Rockefeller Foundation, which had played a central role in the development of medical education, argued that the "environmental and social" roots of disease were being overlooked and called for the establishment of "independent schools of public health" to "address 'the determinants of health and disease in populations'" (White, as cited in Gorin, 2001, p. 2). Unfortunately, this development "reinforced" a separation between "efforts to prevent disease and efforts to cure it" (Gorin, 2001, p. 2). Increasingly, physicians "focused on biomedical research and clinical practice," relegating public health measures to a "secondary status" (Starr, 1982, p. 197).

THE ROOSEVELT AND TRUMAN ERAS

In 1934, the newly elected President Franklin D. Roosevelt created a Committee on Economic Security, headed by Frances Perkins—the Secretary of Labor and a National Association of Social Workers (NASW, 2011) Social Work Pioneer—to address the economic crisis. The work of this committee eventually led to the enactment of the Social Security Act in 1935 [*See Chapters 2 and 11 in this volume.*] Although Perkins and others on the committee, as well as Roosevelt, had hoped to include health insurance as part of the new legislation, they recognized that this would be difficult due to fierce opposition from the American Medical Association (AMA). AMA members "bombarded members of Congress with letters, postcards, and phone calls decrying compulsory health insurance" (Quadagno, 2005, p. 23). Worried that NHI would doom the entire bill, Roosevelt "finally pulled the plug on it himself" (Downey, 2009, p. 243). Despite this, the legislation included funds for maternal and child health, public health, and "aid to crippled children," which Grace Abbott, director of the Children's Bureau and an NASW Social Work Pioneer, hoped would "become the 'entering wedge for medical care'" (p. 243).

During the late 1930s and 1940s, several health care bills were introduced in Congress with little success. In 1939, Senator Robert Wagner (D-NY) introduced a bill that would have provided funds to the states to address health care needs and begun "the development of a national health care system" (U.S. Congress, 1938). In 1943, Congress considered the Wagner-Murray-Dingell NHI bill, but like the original Wagner bill, it "died in committee" (Altmeyer, 1965). According to Starr (1982), this bill was intended to create "'cradle-to-grave' social insurance" (p. 280). In 1944, Roosevelt

Figure 14.1 Frances Perkins, head of the Committee on Economic Security established by President Roosevelt to draft what became the 1935 Social Security Act

called for an Economic Bill of Rights, which included "the right to adequate medical care and the opportunity to achieve and enjoy good health" (U.S. Social Security Administration, 1944).

Roosevelt's successor, Harry S. Truman, strongly supported NHI. In a special message to Congress in 1945, he recommended enactment of a "comprehensive and modern health program for the Nation," including "expansion of our existing compulsory social insurance system" to include health and dental care (Truman, 1945). When Truman was unexpectedly elected in 1948, it seemed that NHI might become a reality (Corning, 1969). This was not to be, of course. In hindsight, the election was less a mandate for NHI than a personal "victory" for Truman, who had fought courageously against seemingly insurmountable political odds (Corning, 1969).

In response to Truman's victory, the AMA and its allies, including a conservative coalition of Republicans and Southern Democrats, mobilized to defeat any effort to enact NHI (Doherty & Jenkins, 2009). At the AMA's 1949 convention, Clem Whitaker—a well-known public relations specialist hired by the association to mobilize opposition to NHI—depicted the battle against NHI as a defense of "individual liberty" against "government domination" (Quadagno, 2005, pp. 767–775). According to one author, Whitaker and Baxter, the AMA's public relations firm, mobilized a coalition that included more than a thousand organizations and distributed more than 25 million "pieces of literature to physicians and others" (McCuan, 2010). At the same time, organized labor, which had long led the pro-NHI forces, was now ambivalent, as many unions had succeeded in obtaining "private health insurance coverage directly from … employers, through collective bargaining" (Corning, 1969).

Truman initially tried to turn the 1950 elections into a referendum on NHI, but the military conflict in Korea soon deflected his attention. At the same time, the AMA and its allies engaged in a sophisticated propaganda campaign that their opponents could not come close to matching (Doherty & Jenkins, 2009; Quadagno, 2005). Pro-NHI forces spent less than $40,000 that year, while the AMA spent $2.25 million on a "national educational campaign" (Starr, 1982, p. 287). In the end, several leading supporters of NHI went down to defeat in the November 1950 elections, and Truman soon recognized he would be unable to enact NHI. He later described this as his most "bitter disappointment" (cited in Quadagno, 2005, p. 43).

Despite this failure, Truman's efforts likely set the stage for the eventual passage of Medicare. In 1947, he appointed Oscar Ewing to head the Federal Security Agency, which regulated the Social Security retirement program and other health and welfare services. A year later, in a report on *The Nation's Health*, Ewing called for "the institution of a prepaid system of Government [health] insurance" (U.S. Social Security Administration, 1948, p. 11). After the disastrous election of 1950, advocates of NHI moved to compromise, in the hope, as Ewing later put it, of getting "something instead of nothing" (Fuchs, 1969). In 1952, with Ewing's support, Senator James Murray and Representative John Dingell introduced legislation that would have provided health care benefits to individuals 65 and older (U.S. Social Security Administration, n.d.). Although this bill made no progress in Congress—even President Truman seemed ambivalent about it—President Lyndon Johnson may have had it mind when, in signing Medicare into law in 1965, he acknowledged Truman as "the real daddy of Medicare." However, the election in 1952 of Dwight D. Eisenhower, an opponent of NHI who advocated state efforts and subsidies to private insurers to cover people with low incomes, signaled an end to efforts for national reform at the time (Moniz, 1990).

THE "GREAT SOCIETY": MEDICARE AND MEDICAID

During the late 1950s, Representative Aime Forand (D-RI) introduced legislation to extend health insurance to Social Security beneficiaries (Moniz, 1990). If the nation failed to support universal coverage, he believed it could surely see the importance of providing coverage for older adults in their retirement. The Forand bill, however, faced strong opposition from the AMA and conservative forces in Congress and ultimately was defeated (Moniz, 1990). However, by focusing on older adults, "who felt the problem of hospital costs with unusual keenness" and who were seen as "both needy and deserving," liberals were able to "change the terms of debate" (Starr, 1982, p. 368).

Despite the failure of Forand's bill, which the NASW had supported, the issue of government coverage for older adults—or **Medicare**, as it was soon called—did not fade away. In January 1960, Senator John F. Kennedy (D-MA) introduced a Senate version of the Forand bill. He also "created the Senate Committee on Aging and formed the Senior Citizens for Kennedy organization to cultivate older voters" (Quadagno, 2005, p. 59). With polls showing broad support for the legislation, Republicans proposed voluntary, state-administered programs for low-income older adults as an alternative. As a compromise, Congress enacted the Kerr-Mills bill (1960), a means-tested, optional grant-in-aid program to the states for poor older adults. However, many states were slow to join the system, and only a few had systems in place to pay physician fees (Trattner, 1999). Clearly, a more expansive policy was needed.

After his election as president, Kennedy worked with Wilbur Cohen—another NASW Social Work Pioneer, who chaired his Task Force on Health and Social Security and later served as Secretary of the Department of Health, Education, and Welfare—to develop a program of hospital and nursing home coverage for older adults under the Social Security Act (Bernstein, 1991). The King-Anderson bill, a scaled-back version of the Forand bill, was introduced, but no action was taken on it until late 1963 when President Johnson took up the mantle of health care reform after Kennedy's assassination (Marmor, 1973).

Cohen is widely viewed as the key player in the development of Medicare. He negotiated the final version of Medicare with Representative Wilbur Mills (D-AK), the head of the powerful House Ways and Means Committee and a long-time opponent of Medicare. The turning point for Mills was Lyndon Johnson's landslide victory in the November 1964 election, which Mills believed had demonstrated strong support for the program (Transcript, 1987). In a surprising move, he proposed a "three-layered cake" approach, which created compulsory insurance for hospital, nursing home, and home health care for retirees (Medicare Part A), voluntary insurance for physicians' services for retirees (Medicare Part B), and a means-tested insurance plan for individuals with low incomes (Medicaid) (Starr, 1982, p. 369).

The enactment of Medicare and Medicaid in 1965 was, nonetheless, a compromise between those who favored and opposed universal coverage. For those seeking a universal comprehensive health plan, Medicare established the principle of non-means-tested universal coverage for a given population (older adults) with uniform benefits. It offered the promise of future expansions that

Figure 14.2 President Johnson signing the Medicare Program into law, July 30, 1965. Former President Harry S. Truman is on the right.

eventually could lead to coverage for everyone. Medicare and Medicaid also gave the federal government, for the first time, a stronger role in the regulation of hospital, physician, and nursing home policies and practices. This speeded up the desegregation of hospitals in the South and "contributed to dramatic improvement in the health of the elderly and disabled minority population" (Eichner & Vladeck, 2005, p. 365).

On the other hand, the passage of Medicare and Medicaid also slowed the momentum that had been building toward the adoption of universal national health coverage and helped preserve the existing system of private insurance and a fee-for-service model of health care provision (Anderson, 1968; Falk, 1973). If we fast-forward to the debates of the 1990s and the eventual passage of the Affordable Care Act in 2010, the same principle of preserving the private insurance industry continued to be a central issue in these most recent reform efforts.

THE NIXON ERA

During the 1960s, national health care spending increased rapidly, from $27.1 billion in 1960 to $74.3 billion in 1970 (Patel & Rushefsky, 1999). Although the passage of Medicare and Medicaid was often blamed for this development, this argument was somewhat disingenuous. As part of the price for enacting the legislation, the Johnson Administration basically agreed to relinquish control over what providers could charge (U.S. Social Security Administration, 2011a). Like private insurers, the new public programs reimbursed hospitals on a cost-plus basis and physicians on the basis of their "reasonable" and "customary" fees (Starr, 1982, p. 385). This amounted to a built-in inducement for charging whatever the market would bear and resulted in "rampant inflation in medical fees" (p. 385). Medicare and Medicaid thus "reinforced" an already existing, wasteful system of financing.

In 1971, in reaction to rising costs, and renewed pressure from Democrats for NHI, President Richard Nixon announced his own approach to address what he called "a breakdown in our medical system" (Starr, 1982, p. 381). Under his proposal, employers would be required to insure their workers or pay a tax to enable the government to cover those workers without insurance (Quadagno, 2005). The plan also included funds for the creation of prepaid group practices, or **health maintenance organizations (HMOs)**.

Interestingly, the AMA, which supported Nixon in 1968, had a long history of opposing prepaid group practices. However, Dr. Paul Ellwood, a proponent of prepaid plans, convinced Nixon that a "competitive market strategy" organized around HMOs, which would replace **fee-for-service medicine**, would rein in health care inflation (Patel & Rushefsky, 1999). In 1973, Congress, with broad support, enacted the Health Maintenance Organization Act. Nixon's proposal requiring employers to insure their employees was not enacted, but it did reappear years later in President Bill Clinton's ill-fated Health Security Act.

THE REAGAN ERA

After the election of Ronald Reagan in 1980, efforts for NHI took a back seat to market-oriented approaches to social issues (Stockman, 1981). In the area of health care, David Stockman, Reagan's director of the Office of Management and Budget, envisioned a largely unregulated system based primarily on consumer choice and provider competition. As a result, during the Reagan Administration, federal funding for "social programs" was "sharp[ly]" reduced (p. 209), and the federal government relinquished its role as "the unquestioning payer for health services" (Barr, Lee, Benjamin, & Estes, 2003, p. 209).

Despite Reagan's opposition to regulation, his administration did introduce the Medicare Prospective Payment System, under which reimbursement to providers is "made based on a predetermined, fixed amount" (Centers for Medicare and Medicaid Services, 2011a) for a range of medical conditions referred to as Diagnostically-Related Groups (DRGs). White (2008) found that the Prospective Payment System and related regulatory changes contributed to the "slowdown" in excess spending growth in Medicare between 1983 and 2005.

In 1988, Reagan signed the Medicare Catastrophic Coverage Act, the first significant expansion of benefits under the Medicare program since its inception in 1965 (Christensen, 1988). Yet, a year later, in the face of strong opposition from older adults who were responsible for paying the cost of the new legislation, the law was repealed (Rice, Desmond, & Gabel, 1990).

PRESIDENT CLINTON AND THE HEALTH SECURITY ACT

During the late 1980s, interest in NHI reemerged. In 1990, the U.S. Bipartisan Commission on Comprehensive Health Care—known as the Pepper Commission, after its first chair, Representative Claude Pepper (D-FL), a long-time supporter of NHI—issued its report, which depicted a "health care system ... approaching a breaking point" (Pepper Commission, 1990). The Commission recommended "legislation" [guaranteeing] "all Americans coverage for health and long term care within a system that both ensures quality and contains costs" (p. 1). The Commission report served as a rallying point for many activists seeking to renew interest in health care reform, which polls indicated had broad public support (Patel & Rushefsky, 1999).

In the run-up to the 1992 presidential election, all the Democratic candidates supported health care reform. During his campaign against President George H. W. Bush, Bill Clinton initially urged his staff to focus on the economy. However, he soon became convinced that health care reform, particularly bringing costs under control, was central to "fixing the economy." In a September 1992 speech, Clinton (2003) "outlined" a plan to control health care inflation, limit "paperwork" and "red tape," and ensure "that all Americans had health insurance" (p. 115).

As president, Clinton essentially sought a middle path between a Canadian-style **single-payer health care system**—in which, as in Medicare, the government serves as insurer—and the largely unregulated approaches advocated by conservatives. Clinton's **Health Security Act (1993)** was based on a "quasi-private" approach known as "managed competition," which had been developed by Alain Enthoven (1993) and others (Clinton, 2003). A key difference between Enthoven's approach and the Health Security Act was that under the latter the government would serve as an "emergency brake" to control "the growth of insurance premiums" if competition failed to work (Domestic Policy Council, 1993, p. 59). The act would have guaranteed "all citizens and legal residents … a defined, comprehensive package of health care benefits, comparable to those offered by most major corporations" (Zelman, 1994, p. 14).

The Health Security Act provoked opposition from both the left and the right. Many on the left supported a single-payer plan and criticized Clinton's bill for preserving the employer-based system of health care coverage and relying on private insurance companies. On the right, insurers and pharmaceutical companies, along with conservative interest groups, engaged in a massive campaign aimed at defeating the bill (Clinton, 2003). The administration's inability to respond effectively to this campaign resulted in widespread confusion. Polling showed that while the public supported specific elements of the Health Security Act, Americans strongly opposed what was called the Clinton Plan (Bok, 1998). As a result, although the Democrats controlled Congress, the Health Security Act died without coming to a vote.

With the failure of the Health Security Act, the Clinton Administration resorted to promoting a series of narrower, incremental changes. In 1996, Congress enacted the Health Insurance Portability and Accountability Act (HIPAA; PL 104–191), which aimed at preventing insurers from excluding individuals from coverage due to preexisting conditions (Moniz & Gorin, 2014). Although HIPAA closed some gaps in the small-group market, it did not prevent insurers from charging exorbitant prices or evading the intent of the law. It also failed to address significant problems in the individual insurance market, particularly high costs and exclusions and limitations in coverage due to preexisting conditions (Doty, Collins, Nicholson, & Rustgi, 2009; Quadagno, 2005). Although HIPAA also introduced measures to promote the growth of private long-term insurance and protect patients' rights, its impact in these areas has been unclear (Moniz & Gorin, 2014).

The Clinton Administration also attempted to address the issue of **mental health parity**. In 1996, Congress enacted the Mental Health Parity Act, which took a step toward parity; it prevented group health plans from imposing annual or lifetime dollar limits on mental health benefits that are lower than its limits for medical and surgical benefits. In practice, however, these efforts have been limited by the federal Employment Retirement Income Security Act (ERISA) of 1974, which prevents states from regulating plans financed by employers. In addition, the legislative effort to strengthen mental health parity through the Wellstone Equitable Mental Health Treatment Act was derailed when its sponsor, Senator Paul Wellstone (D-MN), died in a plane crash in 2002. New legislation, in Wellstone's memory, was not passed until 2008.

This legislation, the Paul Wellstone and Pete Domenici Mental Health Parity and Addiction Equity Act of 2008, built on the original parity bill by banning differences in copayments, deductibles, and other treatment limitations. However, the 2008 legislation did not cover everyone with insurance and offered little to those without insurance. Most recently, however, through the passage of President Obama's Affordable Care Act, parity has been expanded to a much wider population.

In 1997, as part of the Balanced Budget Amendment, Congress created Title XXI of the Social Security Act, the State Children's Health Insurance Program (S-CHIP). The aim of S-CHIP was to enable states "to initiate and expand the provision of child health assistance to uninsured, low-income children" (U.S. Social Security Administration, 2011b). S-CHIP amounted to "the largest single expansion of coverage to children since the enactment of Medicaid in 1965" (Kenney & Yee, 2007, p. 356). Although at the time of its enactment, S-CHIP was welcomed as proof that bipartisanship and incremental reform could work, S-CHIP was caught up in partisan battles over the role of government (Moniz & Gorin, 2014; Oberlander & Lyons, 2009) until it was reauthorized in 2009 as the Children's Health Insurance Program Reauthorization Act (CHIRPA). Although S-CHIP increased the number of children with health insurance, many continued to go without coverage (Quadagno, 2005). CHIRPA expanded coverage to an additional 4 million children by increasing the upper income limit (Kaiser Family Foundation, 2009). (Table 14.1 provides a summary of the benefits covered by Medicare, Medicaid, and S-CHIP.)

THE GEORGE W. BUSH ADMINISTRATION

Although concern about terrorism dominated the nation's political agenda during George W. Bush's presidency, health care did not completely disappear as an issue. In 2002, Bush appointed a New Freedom Commission on Mental Health to examine the nation's "mental health service delivery system, and ... make recommendations that would enable adults with serious mental illnesses and children with serious emotional disturbance to live, work, learn, and participate fully in their communities" (President's New Freedom Commission on Mental Health, 2003). In an interim report, the commission characterized our current mental health delivery system as being "fragmented and in disarray." In its final report, it recommended a fundamental transformation in "how mental health care is delivered in America" (President's New Freedom Commission on Mental Health, n.d.), including creation of a "highly individualized health management program," elimination of "disparities" in service delivery, and protection of patients' rights.

In 2003, with Bush's support, the Republican-controlled Congress enacted the Medicare Prescription Drug Improvement and Modernization Act of 2003 (MMA), which created a new Medicare Part D (Health Policy Alternatives, 2003). The passage of this legislation was ironic since Republicans had long opposed efforts to add prescription drug coverage to Medicare. Some observers have argued that electoral politics, and a desire to negate the Democrats' traditional advantage with older voters, played a critical role in this reversal (Oberlander, 2007).

The MMA contained several controversial provisions. To begin with, the legislation relied on "stand-alone" private plans to deliver the drug benefit, not traditional fee-for-service Medicare—an approach some critics argued would undermine the "social insurance nature" of Medicare (van de Water, 2011a). The bill also included an unusual coverage gap, known as the "donut hole." In 2016, after paying a $360 deductible, individuals are responsible for up to 25% of the costs they incur up to $3,310. They will then enter the so-called "donut hole," making them responsible for as much as 86% of costs up to $4,850. At this point, they will be responsible for only 5% of their subsequent costs (Medicare.gov, 2016).

In addition, the MMA created health savings accounts (HSAs), which enable individuals "covered by high-deductible health plans" to "receive tax-preferred treatment of money saved for medical expenses" (U.S. Department of the Treasury, 2011). Although conservatives have advocated HSAs as a way of bringing health care costs under control, the bulk of health care spending "occurs well above the deductibles," making it "unlikely" that these plans will "produce significant reductions in overall" spending (Feldman, Parente, Abraham, Christianson, & Taylor, 2005; Park, 2006). The MMA also set the stage for restructuring Medicare, beginning in 2010 (Berenson, 2004). In 1997, as part of the Balanced Budget Act, Congress created a network of private plans known as Medicare+Choice. Under the MMA, these plans, many of which had run into financial difficulty, now became Medicare Advantage plans, or Medicare Part C. Medicare Advantage plans include various types of private managed plans, such as HMOs or preferred provider organizations (PPOs).

Table 14.1 National Health Policies: Major Public Health Insurance Programs in the United States.

MEDICARE (enacted 1965)

National program administered by federal government that ensures access to health insurance for older adults over age 65 and younger adults with disabilities

<u>PART A (HOSPITAL INSURANCE)</u> Mandatory (covers hospital stays, skilled nursing facility care, home health and hospice care)

<u>PART B (SUPPLEMENTARY MEDICAL INSURANCE)</u> Voluntary (covers outpatient care, physician and provider services, including mental health, preventive services, diagnostic and laboratory tests, durable medical equipment, and home health)

<u>PART C (MEDICARE ADVANTAGE)</u> Optional (coverage through **managed care** plans provided by private companies approved by Medicare)

<u>PART D (PRESCRIPTION DRUGS)</u> Optional (Must have) Parts A and B—new as of January 1, 2006 (Prescription drug coverage through drug plans provided by private companies approved by Medicare)

Source: U.S. Centers for Medicare and Medicaid Services (2012).

MEDICAID (enacted 1965)

State and federal partnership program that provides coverage for individuals with low incomes, older adults, people with disabilities, and some families and children.

Medicaid is a means-tested program (income and asset limits).

Income standards vary by beneficiary group (and by state).

"Eligibility is complicated due to the combination of categorical and financial factors, the mixture of mandates and options, and the discretion afforded each state to select coverage categories, establish income and resource standards, and decide how income and resources are treated. As a consequence, eligibility varies considerably state-to-state" (U.S. Department of Health and Human Services, 2007).

States must provide inpatient and hospital care; outpatient hospital care; physician services; prenatal care; pediatric and family nurse practitioner services; vaccines for children; nurse midwife services (authorized by the state); laboratory and X-ray services; nursing facility and home health care for adults over age 21; early and periodic screening, diagnosis, and treatment for children and youth under age 21; family planning services and supplies; 60 days of postpartum services; rural health clinic services; federally qualified health center services (FQHCS) and ambulatory services of an FQHCS (U.S. Department of Health and Human Services, 2012b).

State Children's Health Insurance Program (S-CHIP) (enacted 1997)

Children's Health Insurance Program Reauthorization Act (CHIRPA) (enacted 2009)

Expansion of Medicaid program to cover children in families with incomes too high to be eligible for Medicaid yet unable to afford private insurance. Administered by states either by

1. expanding state Medicaid program by increasing the age of eligibility or the income level for eligibility, or both, on a statewide basis;

2. establishing a new state program or expanding the state-run health insurance program already available to children; or

3. providing some combination of both options by changing the state Medicaid program and establishing or expanding a state-run program.

The majority of states (46 plus the District of Columbia) cover children with incomes up to 200% of the federal poverty level (FPL) in Medicaid and S-CHIP; 24 of these states and the District of Columbia cover children up to 250% of the FPL.

Sources: U.S. Department of Health and Human Services (2010).

Figure 14.3 President Obama, Vice President Joe Biden, and senior staff in the Roosevelt Room of the White House reacting to the passage of the Affordable Care Act.

The MMA also created "regional PPO plans," which along with the older private plans, were heavily subsidized by the government "for the purpose of building an alternative infrastructure for head-to-head competition with, and ultimately replacement for, traditional Medicare" (Berenson, 2004, p. 542). The election of a Democratic president and Congress in 2008 and the enactment of the 2010 Affordable Care Act (ACA) prevented these changes, but the premium support and competition originally included in the MMA remain popular and could be reinstated depending on the outcome of current negotiations between the White House and Congress over the budget and entitlement reform.

PRESIDENT BARACK OBAMA AND THE AFFORDABLE CARE ACT

Although health care was not the focal point of the 2008 elections, the issue was "intertwined" with the nation's economic crisis, which was the central issue of the presidential campaign (Commonwealth Fund, 2008–2009). During the campaign, then Senator Barack Obama advocated an approach to health care that built "on the current system of mixed private and public group insurance" (Commonwealth Fund, 2008–2009). Following Obama's election and after more than a year of contentious debate, Congress enacted the Patient Protection and Affordable Care Act (ACA) in March 2010. Although progressives hoped the legislation would include a "public option," which would force private insurers to compete with a government-funded plan based on cost and quality, it was not included in the final version of the bill due to strenuous opposition from Republicans and some Democrats (Gorin, 2009). Despite this setback, and other limitations, the ACA marked an important step forward in the long struggle for NHI.

IMPACT OF THE ACA: COVERAGE, COST, AND QUALITY

COVERAGE

Historically, Americans have obtained health care coverage through a patchwork system of programs, including Medicare, Medicaid, S-CHIP, the Veterans Health Administration, the Indian Health Service, the Public Health Service, and community mental health centers. Unlike other major industrialized nations, the bulk of coverage in the U.S. is through employer-based insurance (EBI); in 2016, about 154 million people had EBI (Kaiser Family Foundation, 2016). Millions of individuals who are ineligible for these programs may lack insurance and access to health care services. Although 20 million more Americans have health insurance coverage since the passage of the ACA, in 2016, an estimated 33 million people are without coverage for all or part of the year; millions more are underinsured (Kaiser Family Foundation, 2016).

To address the issue of coverage, the ACA established an "individual mandate," that went into effect in 2014, which requires nearly all individuals not already covered by an employer or public insurance (e.g., Medicare or Medicaid) to buy an approved private insurance policy or pay a penalty (Kaiser Family Foundation, 2011b). In addition, the law also requires employers with 50 or more full-time-equivalent employees to cover their workers or pay a penalty (van de Water, 2010). The legislation includes subsidies to assist individuals and families with low incomes in buying the mandated coverage (Gruber, 2011). Further, the ACA increases funding for community health centers, "introduces important changes in health care delivery," and takes steps to "improve community and population health"(Kaiser Commission on Medicaid and the Uninsured, 2010, p. 1). With the introduction of the ACA, the number of uninsured dropped to 33 million in 2014 (U.S. Census Bureau, 2015) and has remained steady since.

While the ACA has achieved its target of expanding coverage to over 20 million enrolled individuals, enrollment has been lower than expected; some observers have also questioned whether the government will be able to continue to expand coverage. Several factors contribute to these concerns. First, although it was anticipated that employers would drop coverage to allow employees to take advantage of subsided premiums through the ACA; this has not occurred. Second, individuals are still purchasing their own private insurance (ACA-compliant plans, "grandfathered plans," and "transitional" plans); this is particularly true for those who are not eligible for premium subsidies. Third, and perhaps, most importantly, the cost of ACA marketplace plans is a "challenge." Individuals who have not purchased plans indicate that cost is the reason, although it remains unclear whether the plans are too expensive or there is insufficient awareness of the availability of premium subsidies. Individuals with incomes below 150 percent of the poverty line receive the largest subsidies but they still may be unable to afford their portion of the premium. Those with incomes up to 250% of the poverty level may not be able to afford the deductibles and co-pays, even with subsidized premiums. In addition, premium subsidies for individuals with incomes over 300 percent of the federal poverty level may provide too little incentive to enroll in ACA marketplace plans (Kaiser Family Foundation, 2016).

Finally, the anticipated gains in health insurance coverage have been stymied by the failure of nearly half the states to expand eligibility for Medicaid coverage, despite the ACA provision that the federal government would pay for 100% of the cost initially and 90% of the cost through the early 2020s. This opposition was bolstered by the Supreme Court's 2012 ruling that the Medicaid coverage mandate was an unconstitutional expansion of federal authority. Ironically, the states which have refused to expand Medicaid coverage are those with the poorest health outcomes and the highest proportion of residents who lack health insurance (Kaiser Family Foundation, 2016). (See below)

In addition to expanding coverage through subsidies, the ACA also banned exclusions for preexisting conditions for children and, beginning in 2014, for everyone; it also prohibits insurers from imposing lifetime limits on "most benefits" (U.S. Department of Health and Human Services, 2011a). In most cases, young adults are also eligible to remain on their parents' plan until age 26. According to the Congressional Budget Office (CBO), as a result of the ACA, an additional 34 million nonelderly individuals, or "95 percent

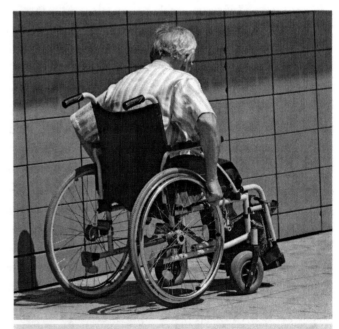

Figure 14.4 The preservation of Medicare and Medicaid and the expansion of health care coverage for individuals with chronic illness are critical components of health care reform.

of legal nonelderly residents," will have coverage in 2021; without the ACA, only 82% are projected to have coverage (Elmendorf, 2011).

The ACA also attempted to address the problem of racial, ethnic, and income disparities in health and health care provision (Gorin, Gehlert, & Washington, 2010). In 2010, 30.7% of Latinos were uninsured, compared with 20.8% of African Americans, 18.7% of Asian Americans, and 11.7% of whites (DeNavas-Walt, Proctor, & Smith, 2011). With the advent of the ACA, these rates have improved substantially; in 2014, 19.9% of Latinos, 11.8% of African Americans, 9.3% of Asian Americans, and 7.6% of whites were uninsured (U.S. Census Bureau, 2015). EBI contributes to and compounds these disparities. People of color are disproportionately employed in low-income jobs; this increases their likelihood of not having access to EBI. By expanding coverage, the ACA helps ameliorate long-standing disparities in access to care. The ACA also helps narrow the nation's widely discussed income gap by increasing the payroll tax rate on upper-income earners and subsidizing individuals and families earning below 400% of the poverty line (Gorin et al., 2010).

COSTS AND FINANCING ISSUES

Cost and financing have long been central issues in the nation's debate over health care reform. Starting in the early 1970s, health care spending increased more rapidly in the United States than in other "high-income" countries in the Organization for Economic Cooperation and Development (OECD, 2011), "increasing five-fold in real terms, even taking account [of] population growth" (p. 10). Between 1999 and 2009, the rapid growth of health care costs "wiped out real income gains for an average U.S. family" (Auerbach & Kellermann, 2011). The primary factors driving the high cost of health care in the United States have been "substantially higher prices" and a "fragmented" delivery system, which results in duplication of resources and extensive use of poorly coordinated specialists (Squires, 2011).

The ACA attempts to address both the expanding costs and the complex financing issues in the U.S. health care system. Funding for the ACA comes from several sources. These include increased taxes on individuals earning more than $200,000, "phasing out overpayments to ... private sector Medicare Advantage insurance companies, ... not delivering value for health care dollars," and "new fees" agreed to by the "health care industry," not including physicians; Mahar, 2011a, p. 4. According to Mahar (2011a), these and other funds amounted to $750 billion in reliable revenues and savings and an additional $196 billion in "less-certain savings." In addition, Peter Orszag (cited in Mahar, 2011a) and others argued that the ACA would bring about billions more in savings through structural changes that the Congressional Budget Office (CBO) could not calculate. According to Aaron (2011b), the ACA incorporated "virtually every method that analysts have advanced for slowing growth of spending in a rational fashion" (p. 2379).

Given the attention paid to fiscal concerns in recent years, it is reasonable to ask: How will the ACA affect the federal budget deficit? According to the CBO, between 2012 and 2021, the health-related provisions of the ACA (the bill also included education-related provisions) will reduce the federal deficit by $210 billion, with additional savings during the following decade (Elmendorf, 2011). A later CBO analysis of H.R. 2, the Repealing the Job-Killing Health Care Law Act—a bill to repeal the ACA, which the House of Representatives passed in 2011, but which did not become law—confirmed this estimate of deficit savings. [*See Chapter 7 in this volume for further discussion of the federal budget.*]

On June 28, 2012, the Supreme Court upheld most of the provisions in the ACA (*National Federation of Independent Business v. Sebelius*, 2012). In the days leading up to the decision, there was much speculation in particular about the constitutionality of the individual mandate. To the surprise of many, however, Chief Justice John Roberts, speaking for the majority, stated that the mandate was justified under the "power" of Congress to "tax and spend" (Jost, 2012). Although Congress cannot require individuals to purchase insurance, it "can tax people who fail to do so." Ironically, the Obama Administration had downplayed the impression that the individual mandate was a "tax," referring to it instead as a "penalty" for non-compliance with the law.

Perhaps even more surprising than the court's decision to uphold the mandate was its ruling on Medicaid. The ACA required states to extend Medicaid coverage to individuals earning below 138% of the FPL. States failing to do this would forfeit all federal funding for Medicaid. The Act attempted to incentivize states' compliance by substantially increasing the proportion of the cost paid by the federal government. The court, however, found this provision unconstitutional, noting that because many states need Medicaid funds to balance their budgets, they have "no real option to decline" (Dworkin, 2012). As a result, states could decline to expand coverage without losing all Medicaid funds. This was the first time the court "struck down conditions on federal grants to states that it determined 'cross the line from enticement to coercion'" (Swendiman & Baumrucker, 2012, p. 10).

It is difficult to understand why a state would refuse to undertake the Medicaid expansion. Between 2016 and 2025, the federal government will assume almost 95% of the cost of the expansion (CBO estimate, cited by the Center on Budget and Policy Priorities (CBPP), 2015), and the expansion will cost the states only 2.8% more than they "would have spent … on Medicaid in the absence of health reform" (Angeles, 2012). Despite this, as of 2015, 22 states had either rejected or were considering rejecting the expansion (CBPP, 2015) by 2016, this number had only dropped to 17 states (Advisory Board Company, 2016). This failure to expand Medicaid coverage is particularly troubling since Medicaid expansions reduce mortality, particularly among middle-age adults, "minorities, and residents of poor counties" (Sommers, Baicker, & Epstein, 2012, p. 1025) and protect many elderly, middle-class persons from destitution if they need nursing care. In this light, it is difficult to avoid concluding that opposition to the Medicaid expansion is at least in part motivated by ideology and political considerations (Cohn, 2012).

Subsequent Supreme Court decisions continued to affirm the constitutionality of the ACA. Despite this, the future of the ACA and its overall impact depend on the outcome of the 2016 presidential election. During the past 6 years, the Obama Administration has contended with fiscal battles between the White House and Congressional Republicans, particularly in the House of Representatives, numerous Congressional attempts to repeal or defund the ACA and challenges to the basis of its existence, and state governors questioning whether to establish insurance exchanges. All of the 2016 Republican presidential candidates, including the Republicans' eventual nominee, Donald Trump, vowed to eliminate "Obamacare," while the Democratic candidates pledged either to enhance it or work to replace it with a single payer system.

Even if the ACA continues to be implemented as intended under the next president, it may prove unsuccessful in "bending" the health care cost curve (Frakt, 2011). Since the 1970s, analysts have proposed numerous, apparently promising, cost-cutting reforms that have failed to produce lasting results. Failure to control costs could strengthen demands for the ACA's repeal or give rise to support for more extensive regulation, such as an all-payer system, in which health care prices are "set by government or negotiated on a regional basis between associations of health insurers and associations of providers of health care," or even a single-payer system such as that in Canada (Reinhardt, 2011, p. 2125).

QUALITY OF CARE

During the past two decades, informed observers have raised concern about the quality of health care in the United States (Moniz & Gorin, 2014). In 1998, President Clinton's Commission on Consumer Protection and Quality in the Health Care Industry noted that while most patients received high-quality

Figure 14.5 The enhancement of rehabilitative and end-of-life care is another critical component of the Affordable Care Act.

care, "too many" received "substandard care," including "avoidable errors, ... underuse" and "overuse of services, and ... variation in services" (President's Advisory Commission on Consumer Protection and Quality in the Health Care Industry, 1998). In a 2011 study, Classen et al. (2011) found that "adverse events" were at least 10 times more common than previously thought and occurred in one-third of hospital admissions. Donald Berwick, the outgoing director of the Centers for Medicare and Medicaid Services and a leading expert on health care quality, described our system as "fragmented, unsafe, not patient-centered, full of waste and unreliable" (cited in Galewitz, 2011, p. 1).

The ACA addresses health care quality in several ways (Fleming, 2011). It calls for development of a national plan for improving health care delivery, patient outcomes, and the general health of the population (U.S. Department of Health and Human Services, 2011b). The ACA also provides incentives for hospitals to reduce readmission rates for "chronically ill patients" and imposes penalties on those that fail to "exceed a particular target." It encourages the development of voluntary Accountable Care Organizations under Medicare, which will give providers "incentives" to collaborate in treating patients "across care settings" and encourage coordination and communication (Centers for Medicare and Medicaid Services, 2011c). The ultimate aim of the legislation is to replace traditional, fee-for-service medicine, which many believe promotes unnecessary and wasteful care, with a system that focuses on quality, while at the same time "softening the blow of reduced volume of care (and thus reduced revenue)" (Wennberg, 2010, p. 266). Recently, however, there have been some concerns expressed regarding the means employed by the Obama Administration to incentivize cost-savings and improve the quality of care.

For example, one of the more controversial aspects of the ACA was its creation of an Independent Payment Advisory Board (IPAB). The members of the IPAB were to be appointed by the President and approved by the Senate. The purpose of the board was to monitor Medicare spending and recommend ways to curb spending if it exceeded a "target growth rate" ("Health Policy Brief," 2011). The law also imposed limitations on the power of the IPAB. It cannot ration care or make "major ... changes that directly affect beneficiaries." Its recommendations are sent to Congress, which must either approve them or substitute provisions of its own. Aaron (2011b) called the IPAB "Congress's 'Good Deed,'" an effort to "mobilize the power of the country's largest health care buyer to effect health system change" (p. 2379). However, the IPAB remains controversial (opposed by the American Medical Association) and has not yet become operational. Members have not been appointed to the board. (Table 14.2 provides a summary of the ACA.)

THE FUTURE OF MEDICARE

For years, conservatives and others have argued that the United States cannot afford to sustain Medicare in its current form. This claim is somewhat misleading. Between 1970 and 2009, real Medicare costs per **beneficiary** did grow rapidly, but they still increased one-third more slowly than health insurance premiums

Table 14.2 Affordable Care Act (2010): Overview of Major Reforms.

Title I. Quality, Affordable Health Care for All Americans

Immediate insurance reforms (effective 2010):
—Eliminates lifetime and unreasonable annual limits on benefits
—Prohibits rescissions of health insurance policies
—Provides assistance for those who are uninsured because of a preexisting condition
—Bans preexisting condition exclusions for children
—Requires coverage of preventive services and immunizations
—Extends dependent coverage up to age 26
—Develops uniform coverage documents so consumers can compare policies
—Caps insurance company nonmedical, administrative expenditures
—Ensures consumers have access to an effective appeals process and provides a means for consumer assistance with appeals and accessing coverage
—Creates a temporary reinsurance program to support coverage for early retirees
—Establishes an internet portal to assist with identifying coverage options
—Facilitates administrative simplification to lower health system costs

By 2014:
—Establishes an "individual mandate," which requires nearly all individuals not already covered by an employer or public insurance to buy an approved private insurance policy or pay a penalty for noncompliance
—Requires employers with 50 or more full-time-equivalent employees to provide coverage or pay a penalty for noncompliance
—Provides subsidies to low-income individuals to help purchase the mandated coverage
—Bans preexisting condition exclusions for children
—Expands access to mental health services by increasing funding for community health centers

Title II. The Role of Public Programs
—Expands Medicaid and essentially assumes federal responsibility for cost (all children, parents, and childless adults up to 133% FPL covered by 2014)
—Increases federal support for the State Children's Health Insurance Program (S-CHIP)
—Simplifies Medicaid and S-CHIP enrollment
—Improves Medicaid services
—Provides new options for long-term services and supports
—Improves coordination for dual-eligibles
—Improves Medicaid quality for patients and providers

Title III. Improving the Quality and Efficiency of Health Care
—Payment for services linked to better quality outcomes
—Funding for research to inform consumers about treatment and patient outcomes
—New Center for Medicare and Medicaid Innovation to disseminate new patient care models
—Improvements for rural patient care
—Improvements in payment system
—Enhancements to Medicare Part D prescription drug benefit
—Reductions in Medicare coverage gap, or the "donut hole"
—Independent Medicare Advisory Board to address long-term fiscal stability

Title IV: Prevention of Chronic Disease and Improving Public Health
—Health promotion initiatives
—New interagency prevention council
—Increases access to clinical preventive services
—Support for prevention and public health innovation to develop health communities

(Continued)

Title V: Health Care Workforce
—Innovations in health workforce training, recruitment, and retention
—Establishes a new workforce commission
—New workforce training and education infrastructure to support increased supply of health care workers (including mental and behavioral health education and training grants to schools for the development, expansion, or enhancement of training programs in social work)
—Funds the expansion, construction, and operation of community health centers across the country

Title VI: Transparency and Program Integrity
—New requirements to provide information to the public about providers in the health system, including physician-owned hospitals, nursing homes, Medicare, Medicaid, and S-CHIP suppliers and providers, and to protect consumers from high-risk providers
—Enhanced requirements to combat fraud and abuse in public and private programs
—Establishes a private, nonprofit Patient-Centered Outcomes Research Institute governed by a public-private board to conduct comparative clinical outcomes research

Title VII: Improving Access to Innovative Medical Therapies
—Price competition and innovation in generic drugs
—More affordable medicines for children and underserved communities
—Extends drug discounts to hospitals and communities that serve low-income patients

Title VIII: Community Living Assistance Services and Supports (CLASS)
—Establishes new, voluntary, self-funded long-term care insurance program, the CLASS Independence Benefit Plan (*This program was soon discontinued for lack of participation*)

Title IX: Revenue Provisions
—New excise tax of 40% on insurance companies for charging annual premium that exceeds established thresholds
—New tax credits for families with incomes below $250,000 to help reduce premium costs and purchase insurance

Source: U.S. Department of Health and Human Services (2012a).

in the private sector (van de Water, 2011a). The real problem lies not with Medicare but with the structure of the U.S. health care system, which is more expensive than those in other industrialized nations due to its lack of a central mechanism for regulating and controlling costs. If the growth of health care costs in the United States were comparable to that in other nations, "our budget deficits" would "not rise uncontrollably in the future" (Center for Economic and Policy Research, n.d.).

Nor is Medicare's situation as dire as some have argued. In their 2011 report, the Medicare Trustees noted that the Hospital Insurance Trust Fund, or Medicare Part A, will be solvent through 2024, after which the program will still be able to meet between 88% and 90% of its obligations (Centers for Medicare and Medicaid Services, 2011b). (Medicare Parts B and D are funded by beneficiary contributions and general revenues.) Closing the gap between Part A's obligations and its projected revenues will take $3 trillion over the next 75 years.

While this is a considerable sum, it amounts to only 0.3% of the nation's projected **gross domestic product (GDP)** during this period. Moreover, in 2010 and 2011, Medicare inflation fell rapidly, due at least in part, some experts believe, to changes anticipated under the ACA (Mahar, 2011c). Inflation also fell among private insurers but not as dramatically. Some evidence suggests that the decline in Medicare inflation could well continue (Mahar, 2011b).

To address Medicare's "crisis," conservatives and other critics of Medicare have advocated the introduction of a premium support, or voucher, system. Under this approach, reflected most recently in the budget proposal passed by the Republican-controlled House of Representatives (Kogan & Shapiro, 2016), beneficiaries would receive a "flat payment" they could use to buy private coverage. However, as van de Water noted, any premium-support model would likely lead to a "two-tier health care system," in which affluent individuals would obtain the care they needed, while "those of modest means" would not (van de Water, 2011a, p. 1). Aaron (2011a), an originator of the idea of premium support, has subsequently repudiated the entire approach. He has argued that "Medicare's size confers power, so far largely untapped, that no private plan can match to promote the systemic change that can improve quality and reduce cost" (p. 1589).

In March 2012, the Republican majority in the House of Representatives passed a premium support bill developed by Representative Paul Ryan (R-WI) (Gorin, 2012). In addition to repealing the ACA, this bill "would [have ended] Medicare as we have known it, shift costs to beneficiaries, undermine traditional Medicare, and increase the program's retirement age. It would also [have] undermine[d] Medicaid and Social Security" (Gorin, 2012, p. 131). Although the reelection of President Obama in 2012 prevented Ryan and his allies from enacting this legislation, similar proposals, with similar consequences have resurfaced during the past four years (Park, 2014). Under different political circumstances, such proposals could become law and profoundly affect the nature of Medicare in the future.

CONCLUSION

Enactment of the ACA marked a turning point in the history of social welfare in the United States. By 2021, it was initially projected that 95% of the population would have health care coverage (compared with 82% without the law). The uninsured population will largely consist of "unauthorized immigrants," individuals who fail to enroll in Medicaid or who lived in states which refused to implement the expansion of Medicaid included in the ACA, people who either do not or choose not to receive subsidies, and others who fail to "comply with the mandate" (Elmendorf, 2011, pp. 1–2). While the ACA will not achieve universal coverage, this is clearly an important step toward that long-sought goal.

Despite these gains, the law faces serious fiscal, judicial, and political challenges in the years ahead. Health care costs may continue to grow more quickly than the rate of inflation, and opponents may succeed in repealing or changing the law through legislation, budget proposals, or court challenges. Social workers and other supporters of universal coverage, therefore, must continue to remain vigilant, oppose efforts to undermine the law, and continue their century-old advocacy of health care for all.

Discussion Questions

1. What connection did early health care reform campaigns have with efforts to expand public health measures? What obstacles did public health advocates face?
2. Why did Franklin D. Roosevelt decide not to include national health insurance as part of the Social Security Act?
3. What connection did individuals with links to social work have with the development of Medicare?
4. What factors helped contribute to the defeat of Bill Clinton's Health Security Act?
5. What problems did the Affordable Care Act seek to address?
6. What features of the Affordable Care Act are controversial, and why have they generated this controversy?
7. Do you think the United States is finally on the path to universal coverage?

Suggested Websites

Commonwealth Fund: http://www.commonwealthfund.org/

Families USA: http://www.familiesusa.org/

HealthCare.gov: http://www.healthcare.gov/law/full/index.html

Kaiser Family Foundation: www.kff.org

Medicaid.gov: http://www.medicaid.gov/

Medicare.gov: http://www.medicare.gov/default.aspx

U.S. Centers for Medicare and Medicaid Services: http://www.cms.gov/

U.S. Department of Health and Human Services: http://www.hhs.gov/

World Health Organization: http://www.who.int/en/

Suggestions for Further Reading

Johnson, H., & Broder, D. S. (1996). *The system: The American way of politics at the breaking point.* Boston: Little, Brown.
McDonough, J. E. (2011). *Inside national health reform.* Berkeley: University of California Press.
Moniz, C., & Gorin, S. (2014). *Health care policy and practice: A biopsychosocial perspective* (4th ed.) New York: Routledge.
Starr, P. (1982). *The social transformation of American medicine.* New York: Basic Books.
Starr, P. (2011). *Remedy and reaction: The peculiar American struggle over health care reform.* New Haven, CT: Yale University Press.

References

Aaron, H. J. (2011a, April 28). How not to reform Medicare. *New England Journal of Medicine, 364*(17), 1588–1589. Retrieved December 23, 2011 from http://www.nejm.org/doi/pdf/10.1056/NEJMp1103764
Aaron, H. (2011b, June 23). The Independent Payment Advisory Board—Congress's "Good Deed." *New England Journal of Medicine, 364*, 2377–2379. Retrieved from http://www.nejm.org/doi/pdf/10.1056/NEJMp1105144
Advisory Board Company (2016, January 13). *Where the states stand on medicaid expansion.* Retrieved from https://www.advisory.com/daily-briefing/resources/primers/medicaidmap
Altmeyer, A. J. (1965, December 9). *Social Security—Yesterday and tomorrow.* Presented at the 10th Anniversary Award Banquet, NASW. Retrieved December 10, 2011, from http://www.ssa.gov/history/aja1265.html

Anderson, O. Y. (1968). *The uneasy equilibrium: Private and public financing of health services in the United States, 1875–1965*. New Haven, CT: College and University Press.

Angeles, J. (2012, July 25). How health reform's Medicaid expansion will impact state budgets. *Center on Budget and Policy Priorities*. Retrieved from http://www.cbpp.org/cms/index.cfm?fa=view&id=3801

Auerbach, D., & Kellermann, A. (2011, September). A decade of health care cost growth has wiped out real income gains for an average U.S. family. *Health Affairs, 39*(9), 1630–1636.

Barr, D. A., Lee, P. R., Benjamin, A. E., & Estes, C. L. (2003). Health care and health care policy in a changing world. In P. R. Lee (Ed.), *The nation's health* (pp. 199–212). Boston: Jones & Bartlett.

Berenson, R. A. (2004). Medicare disadvantaged and the search for the elusive 'level playing field.' *Health Affairs*. doi: 10.1377/hlthaff.w4.572

Bernstein, I. (1991). *Promises kept: JFK's new frontier*. New York: Oxford University Press.

Birn, A.-E., Brown, T. M., Fee, E., & Lear, W. J. (2003). Struggles for national health reform in the United States. *American Journal of Public Health, 93*(1), 86–91. Retrieved from http://www.ncbi.nlm.nih.gov/pmc/articles/PMC1447697/

Bok, D. (1998). The great health care debate of 1993–94. *Public Talk*. Retrieved December 11, 2011, from http://www.upenn.edu/pnc/ptbok.html

Center for Economic and Policy Research (n.d.). *Health care budget deficit calculator*. Retrieved from http://www.cepr.net/calculators/hc/hc-calculator.html

Center on Budget and Policy Priorities (2015, June 15). *Policy basics: Introduction to Medicaid*. Washington, DC: Author. Retrieved from http://www.cbpp.org/research/health/policy-basics-introduction-to-medicaid

Centers for Medicare and Medicaid Services (2011a). *Annual report of the Boards of Trustees of the federal hospital insurance and federal supplementary medical insurance trust funds*. Retrieved December 22, 2011, from http://www.cms.gov/ReportsTrustFunds/downloads/tr2011.pdf

Centers for Medicare and Medicaid Services (2011b, March 31). *Medicare fact sheet: Improving quality of care for Medicare patients: Accountable care organizations*. Retrieved December 21, 2011 from http://www.kaiserhealthnews.org/Stories/2011/March/31/~/media/Files/2011/CMS%20ACO%20Fact%20Sheet%20Quality%20Scoring%2020110331.pdf

Centers for Medicare and Medicaid Services (2011c, November 14). *Prospective Payment Systems—general information: Overview*. Retrieved December 11, 2011, from https://www.cms.gov/ProspMedicareFeeSvcPmtGen/

Christensen, S. (1988, October). *The Medicare Catastrophic Coverage Act of 1988* (U.S., Congressional Budget Office). Retrieved December 11, 2011, from http://www.cbo.gov/ftpdocs/84xx/doc8430/88doc14.pdf

Classen, D., Resar, R., Friffin, E., Federico, F., Frankel, T., Kimmel, N., et al. (2011, April). 'Global trigger tool' shows that adverse events in hospitals may be ten times greater than previously measured. *Health Affairs, 30*(4), 581–589.

Clinton, H. R. (2003). *Living history*. New York: Simon & Schuster.

Cohn, J. (2012, June 29). Did the court undermine the Medicaid expansion? *New Republic*. Retrieved from http://www.tnr.com/blog/plank/104510/supreme-court-roberts-ruling-on-medicaid-expansion-obamacare-impact

Commonwealth Fund (2008–2009, December–January). The prospects for health reform in 2009. *States in Action Archive*. Retrieved December 18, 2011 from http://www.commonwealthfund.org/Newsletters/States-in-Action/2009/Jan/December-2008-January-2009/Feature/The-Prospects-for-Health-Reform-in-2009.aspx

Corning, P. (1969). The evolution of Medicare … from idea to law. *Social Security Online*. Retrieved December 10, 2011, from http://www.ssa.gov/history/corning.html

DeNavas-Walt, C., Proctor, B. D., & Smith, J. C. (2011, September). *Income, poverty, and health insurance coverage in the United States: 2010*. Washington, DC: U.S. Census Bureau. Retrieved from http://www.census.gov/prod/2011pubs/p60-239.pdf

Doherty, K. A., & Jenkins, J. A. (2009, January 7). *Examining a failed moment: National health care, the AMA, and the U.S. Congress, 1948–50*. Retrieved December 10, 2011, from http://faculty.virginia.edu/jajenkins/health_care.pdf

Domestic Policy Council (1993). *The President's health security plan: The complete draft and final reports of the White House Domestic Policy Council*. New York: Times Books.

Doty, M. M., Collins, S. R., Nicholson, J. L., & Rustgi, S. D. (2009, July 21). *Failure to protect: Why the individual insurance market is not a viable option for most U.S. families* (Issue brief). Retrieved from http://www.commonwealthfund.org/~/media/Files/Publications/Issue%20Brief/2009/Jul/Failure%20to%20Protect/1300_Doty_failure_to_protect_individual_ins_market_ib_v2.pdf

Downey, K. (2009). *The woman behind the New Deal: The life and legacy of Frances Perkins: Social Security, unemployment insurance, and the minimum wage*. New York: Anchor Books.

Dworkin, R. (2012, August 16). A bigger victory than we knew. *New York Review of Books*. Retrieved from http://www.nybooks.com/articles/archives/2012/aug/16/bigger-victory-we-knew/?pagination=false

Eichner, J., & Vladeck, B. C. (2005). Medicare as a catalyst for reducing health disparities. *Health Affairs, 24*(2), 365–375. doi: 10.1377/hlthaff.24.2.365

Elmendorf, D. (2011, March 30). *CBO's analysis of the major health care legislation enacted in March 2010. Testimony before the Subcommittee on Health Committee on Energy and Commerce U.S. House of Representatives*. Washington, DC: U.S. Congressional Budget Office. Retrieved December 18, 2011, from http://www.cbo.gov/ftpdocs/121xx/doc12119/03-30-healthcarelegislation.pdf

Enthoven, A. (1993). The history and principles of managed competition. *Health Affairs, 12*(Suppl. 1), 24–48.

Falk, I. S. (1973). Medical care in the USA 1932–1972: Problems, proposals and programs. From the Committee on the Costs of Medical Care to the Committee for National Health Insurance. *Milbank Quarterly, 51*, 1–32.

Feldman, R., Parente, S. T., Abraham, J., Christianson, J. B., & Taylor, R. (2005). Health savings accounts: Early estimates of national take-up. *Health Affairs, 24*(6), 1582–1591. doi: 10.1377/hlthaff.24.6.1582

Fleming, C. (2011a, December 16). Health policy brief: The Independent Payment Advisory Board. *Health Affairs Blog*. Retrieved from http://healthaffairs.org/blog/2011/12/16/health-policy-brief-the-independent-payment-advisory-board/

Frakt, A. (2011, November 11). Why the ACA is not enough. *Incidental Economist*. Retrieved December 21, 2011, from http://theincidentaleconomist.com/wordpress/why-the-aca-is-not-enough/

Fuchs, J. R. (1969, May 1). History interview with Oscar R. Ewing. *Harry S. Truman Library & Museum*. Retrieved December 10, 2011, from http://www.trumanlibrary.org/oralhist/ewing3.htm

Galewitz, P. (2011, December 12). Berwick: Don't blame Medicare, Medicaid. It's the delivery system. *Kaiser Health News*. Retrieved December 21, 2011, from http://www.kaiserhealthnews.org/Stories/2011/December/11/berwick-medicare-medicaid.aspx?p=1

Garrett, L. (2000). *Betrayal of trust: The collapse of global public health*. New York: Hyperion.

Gorin, S. H. (2001). The crisis of public health: Implications for social workers. *Health & Social Work, 25*(1), 49–53.

Gorin, S. H. (2009). Health care reform: The importance of a public option. *Health & Social Work, 34*(2), 83–85.

Gorin, S.H. (2012, August). The Ryan plan redux. *Health & Social Work, 37*(3), 131–132.

Gorin, S. H., Gehlert, S. J., & Washington, T. A. (2010, November). Health care reform and health disparities: Implications for social workers. *Health & Social Work, 35*(4), 243–247.

Haines, M. R. (1991). Birthrate and mortality. In E. Foner & J. A. Garraty (Eds.), *Readers' companion to American history* (pp. 103–105). Boston: Houghton Mifflin.

Health Policy Alternatives (2003, December 10). *Prescription drug coverage for Medicare beneficiaries: A summary of the Medicare Prescription Drug, Improvement, and Modernization Act of 2003*. Washington, DC: Kaiser Family Foundation. Retrieved December 16, 2011, from http://www.kff.org/medicare/upload/Prescription-Drug-Coverage-for-Medicare-Beneficiaries-A-Summary-of-the-Medicare-Prescription-Drug-Improvement-and-Modernization-Act-of-2003.pdf

Health policy brief: Improving quality and safety (2011, April 15). *Health Affairs, 39*(4). Retrieved December 21, 2011, from http://www.healthaffairs.org/healthpolicybriefs/brief.php?brief_id=45

Jost, T. (2012, June 28). The Supreme Court on the individual mandate's constitutionality: An overview. *Health Affairs Blog*. Retrieved from http://healthaffairs.org/blog/2012/06/28/the-supreme-court-on-the-individual-mandates-constitutionality-an-overview/

Kaiser Commission on Medicaid and the Uninsured (2010, August). *Community health centers: Opportunities and challenges of health reform*. Retrieved from http://www.kff.org/uninsured/8098.cfm

Kaiser Family Foundation (2011a, November). *The Medicare prescription drug benefit* (Fact sheet). Washington, DC: Author. Retrieved December 16, 2011, from http://www.kff.org/medicare/upload/7044-12.pdf

Kaiser Family Foundation (2016, March 4). Assessing ACA Marketplace Enrollment. Retrieved from http://kff.org/health-reform/issue-brief/assessing-aca-marketplace-enrollment/

Kaiser Family Foundation (2011b). The requirement to buy coverage under the Affordable Care Act. *Kaiser Family Foundation Health Reform Source*. Retrieved from http://healthreform.kff.org/The-Basics/Requirement-to-buy-coverage-flowchart.aspx

Kaiser Family Foundation (2009, February). *Children's Health Insurance Program Reauthorization Act of 2009 (CHIRPA). The Kaiser Commission on Medicaid and the Uninsured Medicaid Facts*. Washington, DC: The Kaiser Family Foundation.

Kenney, G., & Yee, J. (2007). SCHIP at a crossroads: Experiences to date and challenges ahead. *Health Affairs, 26*(2), 356–369. doi: 10.1377/hlthaff.26.2.356

Kogan, R., & Shapiro, I. (2016, March 28). *House GOP budget gets 62 percent of budget cuts from low- and moderate-income programs*. Washington, DC: Center on Budget and Policy Priorities. Retrieved from http://www.cbpp.org/research/federal-budget/house-gop-budget-gets-62-percent-of-budget-cuts-from-low-and-moderate-income

Madrick, J. (2012, July 30). The Republicans' Medicaid cruelty. *NYRBlog*. Retrieved from http://www.nybooks.com/blogs/nyrblog/2012/jul/30/medicaid-cruelty/

Mahar, M. (2011a). *Better care for less: How the Affordable Care Act pays for itself and cuts the deficit*. New York: Century Foundation. Retrieved December 21, 2011, from http://tcf.org/publications/pdfs/Mahar_BetterCareforLess.pdf/++atfield++file

Mahar, M. (2011b, September 6). Medicare spending slows: Proof that providers can trim fat—Part 3. *Health Beat*. Retrieved from http://www.healthbeatblog.com/2011/09/medicare-spending-slows-proof-that-providers-can-trim-fat-part-3-.html

Mahar, M. (2011c, November 11). You heard it here first: Medicare spending slows. *Health Beat*. Retrieved December 22, 2011, from http://www.healthbeatblog.com/2011/11/you-heard-it-here-first-medicare-spending-slows-.html

Marmor, T. R. (1973). *The politics of Medicare: With the assistance of Jan S. Marmor*. Chicago: Aldine.

McCuan, D. (2010). *There at the creation: The case of Whitaker Baxter as pioneer of political marketing.* Retrieved December 10, 2011, from http://www.psa.ac.uk/journals/pdf/5/2010/1174_1536.pdf

Moniz, C. D. (1990). *The National Council of Senior Citizens: The role of the elderly in the enactment of Medicare.* Unpublished doctoral dissertation, Brandeis University.

Moniz, C., & Gorin, S. H. (2014). *Health care policy and practice: A biopsychosocial perspective,* (4th ed.) New York and London: Routledge.

National Association of Social Workers (2011). NASW Social Work Pioneers. *NASW Foundation.* Retrieved December 23, 2011, from www.naswfoundation.org/pioneer.asp

National Federation of Independent Business et al. v. Sebelius, Secretary of Health and Human Services et al. (2012). Retrieved from http://www.law.cornell.edu/supremecourt/text/11-393

Oberlander, J.B. (2007, April). Through the looking glass; The problem of the Medicare Prescription Drug, Improvement, and Modernization Act. *Journal of Health Politics, Policy and Law, 32*(2), 187–219.

Oberlander, J. B., & Lyons, B. (2009). Beyond incrementalism? SCHIP and the politics of health reform. *Health Affairs, 28*(3), W399–W410. doi: 10.1377/hlthaff.28.3.w399

Organization for Economic Cooperation and Development (2011). *Health at a glance 2011: OECD indicators.* Retrieved December 18, 2011, from http://www.oecd.org/dataoecd/6/28/49105858.pdf

Park, E. (2006, June 12). Health savings accounts unlikely to significantly reduce health care spending. *Center on Budget and Policy Priorities.* Retrieved December 16, 2011 from http://www.cbpp.org/cms/?fa=view&id=381

Park, E. (2014, September 14). *New research shows limits of risk adjustment in protecting traditional Medicare under premium support.* Washington, DC: Center on Budget and Policy Priorities. Retrieved from http://www.cbpp.org/research/new-research-shows-limits-of-risk-adjustment-in-protecting-traditional-medicare-under

Patel, K., & Rushefsky, M. E. (1999). *Health care politics and policy in America.* Armonk, NY: M. E. Sharpe.

Pear, R. (2011, December 14). Lawmakers offer bipartisan plan to overhaul Medicare. *New York Times.* Retrieved December 23, 2011, from http://www.nytimes.com/2011/12/15/us/politics/lawmakers-offer-bipartisan-plan-to-overhaul-medicare.html

Pepper Commission (1990, September). *A call for action: U.S. Bipartisan Commission on Comprehensive Health Care, final report.* Washington, DC: U.S. Government Printing Office. Retrieved December 11, 2011 from http://www.allhealth.org/publications/Uninsured/Pepper_Commission_Final_Report_Executive_Summary_72.pdf

President's Advisory Commission on Consumer Protection and Quality in the Health Care Industry (1998). *Quality first: Better health care for all Americans.* Retrieved December 21, 2011, from http://www.hcqualitycommission.gov/final/chap01.html

President's New Freedom Commission on Mental Health (2003, July 22). *Achieving the promise: Transforming mental health care* [Cover letter]. Retrieved December 16, 2011, from http://govinfo.library.unt.edu/mentalhealthcommission/reports/FinalReport/CoverLetter.htm

President's New Freedom Commission on Mental Health (n.d.). *Achieving the promise: Transforming mental health care in America.* Retrieved December 16, 2011, from http://govinfo.library.unt.edu/mentalhealthcommission/reports/FinalReport/FullReport.htm

Quadagno, J. S. (2005). *One nation, uninsured: Why the U.S. has no national health insurance.* New York: Oxford University Press.

Reinhardt, U. (2011, November). The many different prices paid to providers and the flawed theory of cost shifting: Is it time for a more rational all-payer system? *Health Affairs, 30*(11), 2125–2133.

Rice, T., Desmond, K., & Gabel, J. (1990). The Medicare Catastrophic Coverage Act: A post-mortem. *Health Affairs, 9*(3), 75–87. doi: 10.1377/hlthaff.9.3.75

Schlabach, T. (1969). Rationality and welfare: Public discussion of poverty and social insurance in the United States, 1875–1935. *U.S. Social Security Administration.* Retrieved December 10, 2011, from http://www.ssa.gov/history/reports/schlabach.html

Schoen, C., Doty, M., Robertson, R., & Collins, S. (2011, September). Affordable Care Act reforms could reduce the number of underinsured U.S. adults by 70 percent. *Health Affairs, 30*(9), 1762–1771.

Sommers, B. D., Baicker, K., & Epstein, A. M. (2012, July 25). Mortality and access to care among adults after state Medicaid expansions. *New England Journal of Medicine, 367,* 1025–1034. Retrieved from http://www.nejm.org/doi/full/10.1056/NEJMsa1202099#t=articleTop

Squires, D. (2011, July). *The U.S. health system in perspective: A comparison of twelve industrialized nations.* Retrieved from http://www.commonwealthfund.org/~/media/Files/Publications/Issue%20Brief/2011/Jul/1532_Squires_US_hlt_sys_comparison_12_nations_intl_brief_v2.pdf

Starr, P. (1982). *The social transformation of American medicine.* New York: Basic Books.

Stockman, D. A. (1981). Premises for a medical marketplace: A neo-conservative's vision of how to transform the health system. *Health Affairs, 1*(1), 5–18.

Swendiman, K. S., & Baumrucker, E. P. (2012, July 16). *Selected issues related to the effect of NFIB v. Sebelius on the Medicaid expansion requirements in Section 2001 of the Affordable Care Act* [Congressional Research Service Memorandum]. Retrieved from http://www.healthreformgps.org/wp-content/uploads/crs-medicaid-update.pdf

Transcript, Wilbur Mills Oral History Interview II (March 25, 1987). By Michael L. Gillette. Internet Copy, LBJ Library, Austin, Texas.

Trattner, W. I. (1999). *From poor law to welfare state: A history of social welfare in America,* (6th ed.) New York: The Free Press.

Truman, H. S. (1945, November 19). Public papers of the presidents: Harry Truman 1945–1953: Special message to the Congress recommending a comprehensive health program. *Truman Library.* Retrieved December 10, 2011, from http://www.trumanlibrary.org/publicpapers/index.php

U.S. Census Bureau (2015, September). Health Insurance Coverage in the United States: 2014. *Current Population Reports.* Retrieved from http://www.census.gov/content/dam/Census/library/publications/2015/demo/p60-253.pdf

U.S. Centers for Medicare and Medicaid Services (2012). *Medicare and you.* Baltimore, MD: U.S. Department of Health and Human Services. Retrieved from http://www.medicare.gov/publications/pubs/pdf/10050.pdf

U.S. Congress (1938). *Report of the Technical Committee on Medical Care.* Retrieved December 10, 2011, from http://www.socialsecurity.gov/history/reports/Interdepartmental.html

U.S. Department of Health and Human Services (2007). *Condensed version of a primer on how to use Medicaid to assist persons who are homeless to access medical, behavioral health, and support services.* Retrieved from http://www.hhs.gov/homeless/research/condensedprimer.html

U.S. Department of Health and Human Services (2011a). Patient's Bill of Rights. *HealthCare.gov.* Retrieved December 18, 2011, from http://www.healthcare.gov/law/features/rights/bill-of-rights/index.html

U.S. Department of Health and Human Services (2011b, March 21). Report to Congress: National strategy for quality improvement in health care. *HealthCare.gov.* Retrieved December 21, 2011, from http://www.healthcare.gov/law/resources/reports/quality03212011a.html

U.S. Department of Health and Human Services (2012a). *The health care law and you.* Retrieved from http://www.healthcare.gov/law/full/index.html

U.S. Department of Health and Human Services (2012b). *Medicaid and Chip program information.* Retrieved from http://www.medicaid.gov/Medicaid-CHIP-Program-Information/By-Topics/By-Topic.html

U.S. Department of the Treasury (2011, August 15). *Health savings accounts (HSAs).* Retrieved December 16, 2011, from http://www.treasury.gov/resource-center/faqs/Taxes/Pages/Health-Savings-Accounts. aspx

U.S. Social Security Administration (1944, October 28). FDR's statements on Social Security: Campaign address on the "Economic Bill of Rights." *Social Security Online.* Retrieved December 10, 2011, from http://www.ssa.gov/history/fdrstmts.html#bill%20of%20rights

U.S. Social Security Administration (1948, November). *Report on the nation's health.* Retrieved December 10, 2011, from http://www.ssa.gov/policy/docs/ssb/v11n11/v11n11p9.pdf

U.S. Social Security Administration (2011a, July 27). Prohibition against any federal interference. In *Compilation of the Social Security Laws* (Sec. 1801). Retrieved December 18, 2011, from http://www.ssa. gov/OP_Home/ssact/title18/1801.htm

U.S. Social Security Administration (2011b, July 27). Purpose: State child health plans. *Social Security Online.* Retrieved December 16, 2011 from http://www.ssa.gov/OP_Home/ssact/title21/2101.htm

U.S. Social Security Administration (n.d.). *Medicare and Medicaid: Oscar Ewing, Administrator of the Federal Security Agency during the Truman Administration, makes the case for health care coverage for the elderly* [Video]. Retrieved December 21, 2011, from http://www.socialsecurity.gov/history/mpeg/ videosound.html

van de Water, P. N. (2010, May 14). Employer responsibility in health reform. *Center on Budget and Policy Priorities.* Retrieved December 18, 2011 from http://www.cbpp.org/cms/?fa=view&id=3163

van de Water, P. N. (2011a, September 26). *Converting Medicare to premium support would likely lead to two-tier health care system.* Retrieved from http://www.cbpp.org/cms/?fa=view&id=3589

van de Water, P. N. (2011b, December 21). Ryan-Wyden Premium Support Proposal not what it may seem: Likely would shift substantial costs to beneficiaries, threaten traditional Medicare, and produce few savings. *Center on Budget and Policy Priorities.* Retrieved December 23, 2011, from http://www.cbpp. org/cms/?fa=view&id=3645

Wennberg, J. E. (2010). *Tracking medicine: A researcher's quest to understand health care.* New York: Oxford University Press.

White, C. (2008). Why did Medicare spending growth slow down? *Health Affairs, 27*(3), 793–802. doi: 10.1377/hlthaff.27.3.793.

Zelman, W. A. (1994). The rationale behind the Clinton health care reform plan. *Health Affairs, 13*(1), 9.

Credits

HUMAN SERVICES IN THE U.S.

Safety Net Programs for Racial & Ethnic Minorities and Immigrant Families

Julian Chun-Chung Chow, PhD, Catherine M. Vu, PhD, and Isabel García

The United States has developed a complex and multifaceted human service delivery system to respond to the needs of low-income individuals, families, and communities. The demographic diversity of these groups has produced an equally diverse system that aims to provide culturally appropriate and responsive programs and services that help low-income racial and ethnic minority and immigrant families and children who are overrepresented among the population who lives in poverty. In 2014, African Americans constitute 13% of the U.S. population but represent over 26% of the population in poverty; Hispanics make up nearly 18% of the population but represent almost 24% of the poor; and Asian Americans and Pacific Islanders are just under 6%% of the population but comprise 12% of those living below the poverty line (U.S. Census Bureau, 2014).

This chapter will provide an overview of the human service delivery system with particular attention to its impact on low-income racial and ethnic minority and immigrant families and children. Although the effects of the recent Great Recession transcend socioeconomic status, the high unemployment rates and reduced household incomes that typically characterize economic downturns were particularly detrimental to ethnic minorities because a significant proportion of this population was already struggling prior to the recession. Despite this greater need, developing policies, programs, and services for ethnic and racial minorities is particularly difficult because of the administrative, structural, cultural, and linguistic barriers they face. As a result, it is important to explore strategies that can be used by human service organizations to engage minority families and children effectively.

The renowned social scientist Richard Titmuss (1963) defined **human services** (also called social services) as "a series of collective interventions that contribute to the general welfare" (p. 16). These interventions are delivered by a system of human service organizations whose goals are to maintain or improve the basic social, physical, psychological, and financial well-being of the populations they aim to serve. Human service organizations include federal, state, and local government-run programs, and private not-for-profit and for-profit agencies.

The United States has a distinct history of human service delivery that is different from other industrialized nations. Beyond the family, traditional assistance has historically been provided by local groups to address the needs of the community through **voluntary associations**, such as self-help groups and mutual aid societies, which provide material and social support for members to achieve specific common goals (Katz, 1981). The underlying principle of early voluntary associations was that communities should help themselves. This principle was derived from the Elizabethan Poor Laws, which stated that assistance to the poor should be provided and administered by local parishes and communities (Social Security Administration, 2011). The principles of the Elizabethan Poor Laws were brought across the Atlantic Ocean by early colonists and used as a framework to provide aid to those who deserved it through the collection of membership dues or local taxes to fund services and activities. [*See Chapter 2 for further discussion of the role of voluntary associations in the history of U.S. social welfare.*]

Voluntary associations were typically organized by lay people and based on the special interests, trades, and needs of their members. Racial, ethnic, immigrant, and religious minorities, in particular, relied on these organizations for financial, spiritual, and emotional support (Gamm & Putnam, 1999; Lee & De Vita, 2008). In the early 20th century, African Americans created a number of mutual aid societies and support groups to mitigate the negative effects of discrimination and prejudice. Immigrants from Mexico, China, Japan, Korea, the Philippines, Italy, Ireland, Germany, Poland, and other nations from Eastern and Southern Europe also provided various services that targeted their own ethnic groups through mutual aid and free-loan societies, social and recreational clubs, and newspapers. Religious institutions played a prominent role in human service delivery for many minority groups and immigrants, as they brought together communities that may have shared common faiths but felt isolated or disenfranchised due to their race, ethnicity, religion, or recent immigration status. As a result, churches, temples, and synagogues not only provided a gathering place for members to congregate but also venues for services to be offered and received.

Although human services in the United States have evolved into more complex systems of delivery, they still reflect the principles of the Poor Laws and the practices of early voluntary associations. Their diverse roots can be seen in the fragmented nature of the nation's human services, while the continuing influence of the Poor Laws can be seen in the decentralization of American service delivery and the preference for local service provision. While many **social welfare policies** are created at the federal level, these policies are often used primarily as guidelines by state and local governments; this frequently results in a wide range of program models and service delivery systems which have considerably different degrees of effectiveness.

Similar to early voluntary associations formed to meet the specific needs and interests of their members, human service organizations in the United States typically provide services that address a specific problem or issue, such as domestic violence or homelessness. Organizations can also target specific ethnic and immigrant groups (i.e., ethnic organizations) or develop ethnic-specific services to work with diverse client populations, a unique feature of American human services. While the flexibility of service delivery is an important component of the system's capacity to serve diverse populations with varying needs in a manner that is specific and individualized, the decentralized and fragmented system through which services are delivered can create administrative barriers that prevent racial and ethnic minorities and recent immigrants from participating in programs and services.

As discussed elsewhere in this volume, human services are part of a larger system of interventions that are the consequences of social welfare policies developed at the federal and state level. [*See Chapters 1, 2, 11–14 in this volume.*] These policies attempt to respond to social problems through legislation and regulations that provide guidelines regarding the type and level of benefits provided, set eligibility requirements, and stipulate how programs and services should be implemented to meet the needs of vulnerable populations. One set of interventions created through social welfare policies is **safety net programs**. These government-funded, means-tested programs are available to low-income vulnerable populations and can be categorized as cash assistance or in-kind supports. To qualify for cash assistance and/or in-kind benefits, individuals and families must meet income eligibility requirements as defined by federal poverty guidelines. [*See Chapter 12 in this volume.*]

Beneficiaries of **cash assistance** programs typically receive temporary cash aid in the form of checks that can be exchanged for cash or directly deposited into bank accounts. Examples of cash assistance programs include Temporary Assistance for Needy Families (TANF) for low-income individuals and families, Supplemental Security Income for elderly or disabled persons, and General Assistance for single childless adults who do not qualify for federal cash assistance (administered by individual states or counties). Cash assistance can also be provided in the form of tax transfers such as the Earned Income Tax Credit, which gives low-income working families with children a credit that reduces their tax liability or provides them with a tax refund. [*See Chapters 7, 11, 12, and 13 in this volume for a detailed discussion of these programs.*]

In-kind supports do not provide direct cash assistance but, rather, benefits that assist individuals and families with a specific need. For example, as discussed in Chapter 14, Medicaid is an in-kind support that pays the costs of medical and health-related services for low-income children and adults directly to health care providers. Similarly, housing assistance programs subsidize the rents of eligible residents by providing them with low-cost housing units (such as public housing or mixed-income developments) or by paying rent directly to landlords (for example, through the Housing Choice Voucher Program, formerly Section 8).

While social welfare policies create the framework for cash assistance and in-kind support programs through legislation and regulations, human service organizations actually deliver and administer these programs and services to eligible populations. In other words, social welfare policies establish the legal bases for programs and services while human service organizations facilitate the receipt of benefits. Because the programs and services delivered by human service organizations are closely related to social welfare policies, changes in policies can significantly affect the human service delivery system and the practice of social work within them.

This occurred when Congress passed the Personal Responsibility and Work Reconciliation Act (PRWORA) in 1996. [*See Chapter 13 in this volume for further discussion of welfare and welfare reform.*] PRWORA significantly changed the way social welfare programs and services are administered, because it transformed public assistance from an entitlement program (formerly known as Aid to Families with Dependent Children) that provided cash assistance into a service-based program (TANF) that adopts a "work-first" approach. This approach requires welfare participants to engage in work or work-related activities such as basic education, job training, and community service. These services are typically delivered by community-based organizations (CBOs), although they have also been delivered by private, for-profit companies. Participants who do not comply with welfare-to-work requirements risk penalties and/or sanctions. Once recipients reach the 60-month time limit, cash assistance for adults is significantly decreased or entirely cut off. In cases where parents have timed out of TANF, children may still receive cash aid, known as "child-only" cases (Anthony, Vu, & Austin, 2008). Because human services are now the primary means of assistance for low-income individuals and families, these organizations are essential to the provision of services that will help low-income families meet their basic needs (Edin & Shaefer, 2015). [*See Chapters 1, 4, 5, and 13 in this volume for further discussion of TANF.*]

Although the changes produced by welfare reform affect all beneficiaries, they have had particularly significant implications for racial and ethnic minority participants, especially immigrants. Prior to welfare reform, legal immigrants were generally able to receive welfare benefits as long as they met states' eligibility requirements, which were similar to the requirements required of citizens. Following the passage of welfare reform, however, some immigrants[1] who arrived after August 22, 1996 (the date when PRWORA was enacted) became ineligible for federal assistance and had to wait for at least 5 years before they could apply. PRWORA, however, gave states the option to use their own funding for means-tested programs to immigrants during the 5-year ban (Fortuny & Chaudry, 2011). This option has resulted in disparate safety net programs for low-income immigrants, as the availability of benefits and benefit levels vary by state.

The changes created by welfare reform have also altered the way racial and ethnic minorities perceive benefits and service utilization. TANF's complex rules and requirements have produced confusion, stress, and frustration for immigrant welfare participants, many of whom have language barriers (Geronimo, 2001; Truong, 2007). Children of undocumented parents are especially vulnerable to "chilling effects" because the confusion, fear, or stigma that accompanies receipt of government assistance or human services discourages their families from seeking help. Low-income undocumented parents who fear deportation or retribution from the government may be less inclined to apply for safety net benefits for their children even though they may be legally eligible.

In light of the changes produced by welfare reform, this chapter provides an overview of human service organizations and their capacity to address the gap in service delivery for racial and ethnic minority and immigrant families with children, specifically in programs that provide in-kind supports. While cash assistance programs still play a significant role in alleviating poverty for vulnerable populations, participation in in-kind support programs is important to understand because these programs provide critical benefits, such as food, housing, and education, that help individuals and families meet their basic needs. The role of human service organizations and in-kind supports is particularly critical for racial and ethnic minority groups because they have substantially higher rates of poverty (U.S. Census Bureau, 2014). Because of this disparity, the chapter examines engagement strategies that can be used by human service organizations to increase minority participation in their programs as a means to alleviate poverty.

This chapter is divided into three sections. The first section provides an overview of several in-kind benefits that support families with children and the participation rates of racial and ethnic minority groups in these programs. The second section explores the factors that contribute to utilization disparities and the role of CBOs as the administrator of programs and provider of services. The concluding section discusses the strategies CBOs can use to increase participation in safety net programs and to improve service delivery to low-income racial and ethnic minority populations and immigrants.

IN-KIND SUPPORTS FOR RACIAL AND ETHNIC MINORITIES

According to the most recent Census reports, nearly 50 million people in the United States, or almost 15% of the population, live in poverty (U.S. Census Bureau, 2014). Figure 15.1 shows that racial and ethnic minorities have consistently higher rates of poverty when compared with whites.[2]

Figure 15.1 Poverty Rates by Race and Ethnicity, 1987–2014.

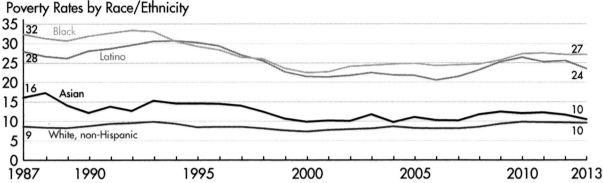

There Is a Persistent Racial/Ethnic Gap in U.S. Poverty Rates.

Poverty Rates by Race/Ethnicity

Note: Data for American Indians are not shown because of sampling error, but the poverty rate for American Indians/Alaska Natives was estimated to be 27 percent in 2013.

Source: U.S. Census Bureau, Current Population Survey. Starting in 2000, racial categories reflect those who selected only one race.

Of those living in poverty, over 21% are children under the age of 18. Child poverty rates by ethnic group mirror the poverty rates of the overall racial and ethnic populations living below poverty. African American children have the highest poverty rate (37%), followed by Hispanic children (nearly 32%), Asian American children (14%), and white non-Hispanic children (over12%).

In an effort to alleviate poverty and to respond to the many social problems associated with poverty, the United States has created a wide range of policies and programs to assist the poor (as described earlier in this chapter and in other chapters in this volume). The following discussion focuses on in-kind supports and their utilization by racial and ethnic minorities. These supports include child care subsidies, Head Start, the Supplemental Nutrition Assistance Program (SNAP, formerly food stamps), and the Special Supplemental Nutrition Program for Women, Infants, and Children (WIC). While many in-kind supports are available to low-income groups, these particular programs are chosen as examples of benefits that specifically assist families with children.

CHILD CARE

To support employment activities among working-poor parents and help them meet welfare-to-work requirements, PRWORA included funding for child care subsidies through the Child Care Development Fund (CCDF), which is the primary source of funding for child care assistance in the United States. States also have the ability to use a portion of their TANF block grant to provide child care subsidies for adult welfare participants with children. These subsidies usually come in the form of vouchers that can be used to purchase services from legally operating nonprofit or for-profit child care providers.

Although PRWORA significantly increased the funding available for child care subsidies (Adams & Rohacek, 2002), many eligible families do not utilize the subsidy due to a number of reasons, including lack of sufficient funding to meet demands. The overall use of child care subsidies between 2006 and 2008 decreased by 10% (Government Accountability Office, 2010), although this rate increased by 4.2% in 2010. According to the latest information available, the CCDF serves about 2.2 million children per month (U.S. Department of Health and Human Services, 2015).

The actual participation rate in child care subsidies for eligible children is somewhat difficult to determine because of the varying policies, samples, and methodologies used in studies to determine participation (Witte & Queralt, 2002) and the lack of systematic data on how CCDF funding is distributed among families with eligible children. The Government Accountability Office (2010) estimates that less than one-third of eligible children receive child care subsidies. More conservative estimates by the U.S. Department of Health and Human Services (2015), however, suggest that approximately 15% of federally eligible children receive assistance through the CCDF or related government funding in the average month. While estimates of the participation rates of child care subsidies vary, the consensus appears to be that these rates are generally lower than in other social welfare programs (Adams, Koralek, & Martinson, 2006; Witte & Queralt, 2002).

Application for and utilization of child care subsidies vary across ethnic groups. While some studies find that African American (Danziger, Ananat, & Browning, 2003; Schlay, Weinraub, & Harmon, 2010) and Latino (Blau & Tekin, 2003) families are more likely than whites to use child care subsidies, other research suggests that whites utilize child care subsidies at slightly higher rates than do Latinos—70% and 67%, respectively (Schlay et al., 2010). Studies on immigrant utilization have found that they are less likely to apply for child care assistance (Burnstein & Layzer, 2007) and utilize child care subsidies (Chapin Hall, 2011) than are native families.

HEAD START

Head Start is an important federally funded program that also provides child care services. Head Start focuses on low-income children from birth to age 5 and their families (U.S. Department of Health and Human Services, 2016). It promotes school readiness by improving children's social and cognitive development through education; medical, dental, and mental health care; and programs that help parents foster their children's growth. The program can also indirectly assist parents in working toward their own educational and employment goals by providing them with opportunities for leadership and professional development through active involvement in the program, linking them to community resources, and creating formal and informal connections to build social networks among community members (U.S. Department of Health and Human Services, 2016). In addition, Head Start programs can provide parents with additional services such as job training, adult education, and housing assistance (New York City Administration for Children's Services, 2012). Head Start programs are generally delivered through community-based schools or centers, family child care homes, in children's own homes, or through a combination of these approaches (U.S. Department of Health and Human Services, 2016).

The rate of racial and ethnic minority children entering Head Start programs has increased in recent years. A study that followed Head Start children from 2002 to 2006 found

Figure 15.2 President George H.W. Bush plays with children at the Emily Harris Head Start Center in Catonsville, Maryland

that newly entering 3-year-olds were 33% African American, 37% Latino, and 30% white/other children (U.S. Department of Health and Human Services, 2010). Of the entering 4-year-old cohort, 18% were African American and 52% were Latino, compared with 31% of children who were identified as white or other. In the 2009–2010 program year, white children had the highest participation rates in Head Start programs (40%), followed by African American children (29%), and children from other racial and ethnic groups, including Asian and Pacific Islanders (17%). Thirty-six percent of enrollees identified as Hispanic[3] (National Head Start Association, 2011). Although white children made up the highest proportion of students enrolled in Head Start programs, the majority of students came from racial and ethnic minority backgrounds.

National studies on immigrant children or children of foreign-born parents in Head Start programs have focused on the Migrant and Seasonal Head Start (MSHS) program which serves 3% of all children enrolled in Head Start (Schmit & Walker, 2016). Since 1969, MSHS programs have provided early childhood education, social services, and other types of support to migrant families (families who change residences to follow agricultural work) and, since 1999, to seasonal workers (families working in the agriculture industry who do not move) (Schmit, 2014; Schmit & Walker, 2016). Like Head Start, MSHS serves children from birth to 5 years old; these children account for 8% of all children enrolled in Head Start programs. According to Schmit and Walker (2016), Hispanic/Latino children comprise 97% of MSHS children (an estimated 30,276 children in fiscal year 2014 (U.S. Department of Health and Human Services, 2016), although national studies suggest that only about 28% of eligible children are served by MSHS (Office of Planning, Research and Evaluation, 2011).

SUPPLEMENTAL NUTRITION ASSISTANCE PROGRAM (SNAP)

SNAP, formerly known as food stamps, is a nutrition assistance program that gives low-income individuals and families the opportunity to purchase healthy food. It is an in-kind benefit that, in 2015, helped almost 46 million people obtain healthy food (U.S. Department of Agriculture, 2016). SNAP benefits now come in the form of a debit card that is issued to recipients which can be used to buy certain food items. (Prepared foods are not allowed to be purchased with SNAP benefits.) SNAP also provides free nutritional programs and services to help beneficiaries make healthy food choices for themselves and their families. For example, states have the option to provide educational programs through SNAP-Ed Guidance, a program that encourages SNAP beneficiaries to make healthy decisions regarding nutrition and physical activity (U.S. Department of Agriculture, 2011a). In addition, SNAP benefits local businesses in communities; every dollar spent on SNAP benefits generates about twice as much economic activity in the surrounding community (U.S. Department of Agriculture, 2011b).

A number of recent policy changes have significantly affected how SNAP is administered. PRWORA eliminated the eligibility of most legal immigrants for food benefits and limited the number of months that able-bodied adults without dependents could receive nutritional assistance (U.S. Department of Agriculture, 2012c). Subsequent legislation such as the Farm Bills of 2002 and 2008 later restored eligibility to some groups of legal immigrants (e.g., those who have been U.S. residents for at least 5 years and individuals with disabilities) and gave states the option to exempt some able-bodied adults without dependents from the time limits. Although funded by federal grants, SNAP is administered by state and local governments that determine eligibility requirements and distribute benefits. States choose their own definition of income and resources for applicant eligibility purposes and can provide additional services such as SNAP-Ed. The flexibility afforded to states to design and administer their food assistance programs is an example of the variation of social policies among the states and the patchwork nature of social services in the United States referred to at the beginning of this chapter.

Nationally, the number of SNAP participants parallels the number of people in poverty living in the United States. Between 2006 and 2015, the number of individuals receiving food assistance increased by 72.4%, (Food Research and Action Center (FRAC), 2016) due to a combination of factors, including an increase in the number of persons in poverty, a relaxation of eligibility requirements, the successful efforts of state outreach programs, and the infusion of additional funds through the 2009 American Reinvestment and Recovery Act. In 2009, about 72% of eligible individuals received SNAP benefits (Leftin, Eslami, & Strayer, 2011). While these rates are particularly high for a safety net program in the U.S., the data suggest that a significant proportion of people are still left without assistance for one of their most basic needs.

In 2013, the largest proportion of SNAP participants were white (38%), followed by African Americans (26%), Hispanic (16%), Native Americans (1%) and Asians (2%) (Briggs, Fisher, Lott, Miller, & Tessman, 2010).[4] Compared with other racial and ethnic minority groups, Hispanics have disproportionately low participation rates in SNAP; only about half of those who are eligible currently receive benefits (U.S. Department of Agriculture, 2011b). Low participation among Hispanic populations has been associated with the chilling effects associated with the receipt of benefits or services described above (Fix & Passel, 2003; Tumlin & Zimmerman, 2003).

SPECIAL SUPPLEMENTAL NUTRITION PROGRAM FOR WOMEN, INFANTS, AND CHILDREN (WIC)

WIC can be used as a supplement to SNAP by providing food to women who are pregnant, postpartum, or breastfeeding, as well as to their infants and young children. In addition, WIC programs provide nutrition education programs and other human services, such as counseling and peer support for breastfeeding mothers, and screening and referrals to other services provided through health departments, hospitals, schools, community centers, and other local institutions (U.S. Department of Agriculture, 2016). Similar to SNAP, WIC is funded by the Food and Nutrition Service at the federal level but is administered by state WIC agencies, which set specific eligibility requirements and benefit allocations for recipients. As a result, the WIC program differs from state to state, providing another example of the decentralized nature of human services in the United States.

In addition to meeting general income and residency requirements, women and children who receive other forms of government assistance such as SNAP and TANF are automatically eligible for WIC. In most states, WIC benefits come in the form of checks or vouchers that can be used to purchase infant foods and formula, fruits and vegetables, dairy products, juice and soy products, and/or other nutritious consumable items. By October 1, 2020, all states will issue electronic benefit transfer (EBT) cards to replace vouchers.

In 2013, WIC served about 8.6 million women, infants, and children per month (U.S. Department of Agriculture, 2015). Zedlewski and Martinez-Schiferl (2010) report that of families with children under the age of 5 who use emergency food assistance, WIC participation was highest among white families (61%), compared with rates of 60% for Hispanics and 40% for African Americans.[5]

The safety net programs briefly described above represent some of the largest antipoverty measures in the United States. As data on SNAP and WIC participation demonstrate, although these programs have been made available to low-income households, many eligible individuals and families are not receiving the benefits they need and to which they are legally entitled. The literature on the utilization rates of child care subsidies, Head Start, SNAP, and WIC suggests that participation varies among racial and ethnic populations across programs. Research also indicates that the participation rates of racial and ethnic minorities in these safety net programs remains relatively low, particularly in light of the high poverty rates they experience.

To improve participation rates in safety net programs, it is important to understand the unique challenges faced by low-income populations in general and ethnic minorities in particular. The next section describes barriers that may prevent low-income minority service users from participating in vital safety net programs.

BARRIERS TO PROGRAM AND SERVICE PARTICIPATION

Although social scientists have proposed a number of theories to explain the causes of poverty (Vu, 2010), these theories generally apply to the broader population and do not recognize the unique barriers faced by minorities of color and immigrants. For example, racial minorities tend to have lower levels of education and training relevant to the skills needed in current job markets (Ryu, 2009). This reduces their chances of obtaining jobs with wages adequate to support a family. For immigrants,

Figure 15.3 WIC provides food to women who are pregnant, postpartum, or breastfeeding, and to their infants and young children.

the lack of appropriate skills may be compounded by low levels of English proficiency. Language barriers can limit the types of jobs available to immigrants and force them to accept lower paying jobs that provide inadequate financial stability (Truong, 2007). In addition, discrimination has been widely cited as contributing to the poverty rates experienced by racial and ethnic minorities (Lang, 2007; Lin & Harris, 2008). Thus, the combination of administrative, structural, cultural, and language barriers may prevent ethnic and racial minority groups from receiving the human services they need and to which they are entitled.[6]

ADMINISTRATIVE BARRIERS

Administrative barriers include the nature of the multilayered human services system itself. The fragmented and decentralized structure of human services in the U.S. can be an overwhelming obstacle to uninformed racial and ethnic minorities or new immigrants. They are often unaware about the variety of services available, the range of eligibility requirements, and the different means of applying for benefits. The legal requirements and application procedures surrounding the receipt of services may be complicated and obscure, and may vary between cities or counties, making it difficult to navigate the human services system and frequently creating communication problems between social service organizations and the clients they seek to reach. The complexity of these policies may also deter ethnic and racial minorities, particularly non-English speakers, from receiving services. In a report surveying New York City parents with limited English capacity about their experiences attempting to access early childhood education services, respondents expressed frustration over the amount of confusing paperwork required to enroll their children in child care, Head Start, and universal pre-kindergarten programs (Kirmani & Leung, 2008). Even after the paperwork is completed, many respondents from the study cited long waiting lists that added an additional barrier to service access.

A lack of adequate outreach and easily accessible information about what programs exist and their eligibility requirements can also become an administrative barrier to the receipt of services. Clients' lack of awareness and difficulty understanding the safety net system may also be compounded by the receipt of inaccurate information. This can also create distrust of government agencies (Lincroft, Resner, Leung,

& Bussiere, 2006), particularly among undocumented or recent legal immigrants who may already be reluctant to apply for government-funded programs such as TANF or SNAP due to concerns about the legal consequences (Capps, Fix, Ost, Reardon-Anderson, & Passel, 2004). Miscommunication is also often cited as a barrier to nonparticipation among applicants for child care subsidies and food assistance. Schlay, Weinraub, Harmon, and Tran (2004) report that about 44% of study participants did not apply for child care assistance because they did not know they were eligible. A Government Accountability Office (2008) study found similar results among parents with limited English proficiency. In her extensive review of safety net program participation, Currie (2004) found that the lack of information about eligibility requirements consistently contributed to lower SNAP and WIC participation. In conducting recent ethnographic research on extreme poverty in the U.S., Edin and Shaefer (2015) discovered that in some communities residents even believed that cash assistance programs no longer existed.

STRUCTURAL BARRIERS

The location and spatial accessibility of social service programs also influence rates of participation. Studies demonstrate the importance of locating service providers in convenient areas that are easily accessible for low-income families. For example, Henly and Lyons (2000) observe that low-income mothers want child care centers located near their work or home. Other research suggests that greater proximity to service providers increases the likelihood of service utilization (Allard, 2009), particularly if services are accessible by public transportation (Kissane, 2003). Neidell and Waldfogel (2009) found that the enrollment of immigrant children in Head Start programs significantly increases when there is a center in the child's census tract. These findings are not surprising given that fewer low-income families own automobiles and more often live in areas with limited access to public transportation (Ong, 2002). Concerns about the safety of the neighborhood where a program is located may also affect participation rates. Kissane (2003, 2010) found that welfare participants are reluctant to obtain services from agencies in unsafe neighborhoods.

Barriers created by location and spatial accessibility can be further compounded by program regulations that often require in-person meetings to determine eligibility, regular check-ins with caseworkers, or attendance in class to receive benefits (Adams, Snyder, & Sandfort, 2002). These requirements create particular problems for adults with multiple jobs or irregular work schedules. Recertification for child care and food assistance subsidies may require multiple visits, which can be time-consuming and complicated for families lacking a reliable source of transportation or child care, and who might risk losing their jobs if they took off time from work for agency-mandated appointments.

CULTURAL AND LANGUAGE BARRIERS

Cultural barriers can prevent racial and ethnic minorities from utilizing services for a variety of reasons. Distrust of government programs, especially among new or undocumented immigrants, may prevent them from participating in early child care and education programs, food assistance programs, and other government sponsored social services. Cultural preferences for parental child care within the home may also decrease the participation rate for child care subsidy and Head Start participation (Karoly & Gonzalez, 2011). In addition, language barriers can be significant deterrents to participation because they can prevent non-English speakers from adequately expressing their needs or understanding the services available to them. Yeo (2004) suggests that the consequences of language barriers can range from miscommunication between staff and clients to inefficient use of services. In sum, as a result of cultural and language barriers, racial and ethnic minorities and immigrants may be discouraged from using services for which they are eligible, or the services they do utilize may be ineffective in addressing their unique needs.

The stigma associated with the receipt of publically funded social services also influences participation rates. Stuber and Schlesinger (2006) found that racial and ethnic minority welfare participants experience two forms of stigma: *identity stigma* (negative stereotypes and/or perceptions of welfare participants or individuals in poverty, in general) and *treatment stigma* (negative stereotypes and/or perceptions associated with the program itself). These types of stigmas occur *in addition to* the discrimination and racism that minorities of color experience irrespective of whether they receive public benefits. The combinations of these various forms of stigma can deter participants from utilizing benefits. Studies indicate that about 7% of eligible SNAP beneficiaries do not apply due to the stigma associated with receiving food assistance (Currie, 2003). Similarly, a study by Mabli, Cohen, Potter, and Zhao (2010) found that about 2.4% of food bank users did not apply for SNAP because of stigma.

Community-based human service organizations have developed a variety of strategies to reduce or eliminate these barriers and increase participation rates among racial and ethnic minority groups. The services provided by these organizations are usually contracted by local governments and are typically located in the communities they serve. As a result, CBOs have the capacity to understand the needs and barriers of local populations far better than more distant public or private agencies. CBOs also provide clients with a range of opportunities and activities that foster a sense of group identity and social support and reach out to those who cannot or will not seek help, making program and service participation more attractive to those who need them (Halpern, 1999; Holley, 2003; Lee & De Vita, 2008).

Figure 15.4 Cultural and language barriers can prevent some families from using available services.

Ethnic organizations, a subset of private not-for-profit CBOs, have played a particularly significant role in engaging racial and ethnic minority populations. Rooted in the traditions of early voluntary associations that provided human services to racial and ethnic minorities in the United States, ethnic organizations deliver human services to specific populations by providing programs and services that are compatible and responsive to the culture of ethnic and racial minority and immigrant groups (Iglehart & Becerra, 2011). Most ethnic and immigrant organizations refer to an ethnic group in the name of the agency and in their mission statements (Ramakrishnan & Viramontes, 2006). While ethnic and immigrant organizations can serve people from other ethnicities and non-immigrants in addition to their own, they hold a firm belief in the importance of culturally competent and ethnically sensitive approaches to service provision for their particular ethnic population. As a result, ethnic and immigrant organizations tend to be more approachable for racial and ethnic minority groups due to "the significance of the ethnic tie and the propensity to associate with others of like background" (Jenkins, 1988, p. 2).

Human service CBOs are particularly important for racial and ethnic minority and immigrant communities in light of welfare reform and the services it produced because the percentage of racial and ethnic minority participation in TANF (and, by proxy, in TANF-related required services) is higher than that of non-Hispanic whites (U.S. Department of Health and Human Services, 2009). The 60-month time limit is especially detrimental to racial and ethnic minorities and immigrants, as these populations, particularly non-English-speaking immigrants, reach the limit at a higher rate and more quickly than do English-speaking whites. For example, in a study of CalWORKs (California's welfare-to-work program), London and Mauldon (2006) found that 30% of the recipients close to reaching the 60-month time limit were African American, 29% were English-speaking Latinos, 20% were non-English-speaking immigrants (Latinos, Vietnamese, and other), and 21% were English-speaking whites. The increasing proportion of racial and ethnic minority and immigrant welfare participants and the replacement of cash aid with human services as the primary means of assistance (Allard, 2009) underscore the critical role CBOs can play in improving the lives of low-income racial and ethnic minority families.

In addition, participation in welfare-to-work activities can increase participation in other social services, such as child care (Layzer & Burnstein, 2007). As Currie (2004) argues, through participation in safety net programs, clients can learn about their eligibility for other programs such as food assistance and apply to multiple programs at the same time, thereby reducing the amount of time and effort required to participate in vital services. Because many welfare-to-work services are provided by CBOs, these organizations can play a critical role in connecting low-income minority groups to other critical services by informing them of their eligibility, clarifying questions about application procedures, and helping them apply for benefits. The final section of this chapter examines some strategies used by CBOs to increase racial and ethnic minority participation in safety net programs.

STRATEGIES TO INCREASE RACIAL AND ETHNIC MINORITY PARTICIPATION IN SAFETY NET PROGRAMS

CBOs are particularly well positioned to help vulnerable minority populations apply for and obtain safety net benefits. Research suggests that CBOs have used two major types of engagement strategies: (1) client-focused strategies and (2) organization-focused strategies. Client-focused strategies are used by staff to better assist clients who are already participating in programs. These strategies are designed to retain clients; they include ethnically matching staff and clients, utilizing community outreach workers, and including family members in service delivery. Organizational strategies are designed to attract and increase participation by new clients in existing programs and services. These include locating programs and services in areas with high concentrations of racial and ethnic minority and immigrant populations, recruiting racial and ethnically diverse board and staff members, and collaborating with other local organizations and institutions.

Table 15.1 summarizes the strategies used by CBOs attempting to expand services to racial and ethnic minority populations. Although these strategies have not been empirically evaluated systematically, they have been recommended by a number of programs and service providers as ways to encourage greater participation by racial and ethnic minorities in safety net programs.

Table 15.1 Strategies Used by CBOs to Increase Ethnic Minority Participation Rates.

Client-Focused Strategies	Organization-Focused Strategies
Ethnically match staff and clients	Provide programs in locations with high concentrations of minority populations
Utilize outreach workers	Recruit ethnically diverse board and staff members
Include family members in service delivery	Collaborate with local organizations and institutions

The cultural competence framework is used to guide approaches aimed at engaging racial and ethnic minorities and immigrant groups. The most widely accepted definition of cultural competence has been developed by Cross, Bazron, Dennis, and Isaacs (1989): "a set of congruent behaviors, attitudes, and policies that come together in a system, agency or amongst professionals and enables that system, agency or those professionals to work effectively in cross-cultural situations" (p. iv). Strategies to engage racial and ethnic minority and immigrant clients more effectively are based on different aspects of cultural competence models: Client-focused strategies use the individual-level cultural competence model, whereas organization-focused strategies use the organization-level model to guide their approaches to engage ethnic and racial minority and immigrant clients.

At the individual level, cultural competence focuses primarily on the interaction between staff and client. Such models are usually derived from research in the health and mental health fields. Culturally competent staff members are expected to be knowledgeable about clients' cultural beliefs, behaviors, and expectations to help overcome misunderstandings and facilitate better treatment outcomes (Kleinman, Eisenberg, & Good, 1978; Tervalon & Murray-Garcia, 1994).

In comparison, cultural competence at the organizational level expands the scope of the staff–client relationship to consider aspects of organizations and communities surrounding the areas where clients live. For example, Hernandez, Nesman, Mowery, Acevedo-Polakovich, and Callejas (2009) provide a conceptual model for organizational cultural competence that incorporates the community context, cultural characteristics of local residents, organizational infrastructure, and direct service support. This framework recognizes the role of social factors, particularly the community context and the cultural characteristics of residents, as potential barriers to and/or facilitators of utilization and tries to address them by institutionalizing practices across systems levels, especially in the organizational infrastructure and through direct service support. While the individual and organizational cultural competence models are usually presented from the perspectives of health and mental health care (Blank, Mahmood, Fox, & Guterbock, 2002; Chun & Akutsu, 2002; Sue, Fujino, Hu, Takeuchi, & Zane, 1991), the frameworks have applicability for staff and CBOs providing human services across all the sectors within which social workers are employed and their clients seek assistance.

CLIENT-FOCUSED STRATEGIES

Client-focused engagement strategies highlight the importance of the relationship between staff and clients in avoiding miscommunication and misunderstanding, increasing worker–client rapport, and fostering trusting relationships between them. To achieve these goals, CBOs have employed staff members who reflect the cultural diversity of the communities they serve. In a study of ethnic matching and client satisfaction, Chow and Wyatt (2003) found that Asian American and Pacific Islander service users preferred ethnic-specific services over services that were not ethnically specific. Focus group participants perceived higher levels of trust with staff that were from the same ethnic group and spoke the same language. Nevertheless, respect and courtesy within clients' cultural context were more important than ethnic matching *per se*. In fact, respondents complained about staff members who were too "Americanized" despite having the same ethnic and linguistic background.

Perceptions regarding trust, understanding, and comfort level were also found among immigrant domestic-violence service users who received assistance from ethnically matched staff (Senturia, Sullivan, Cixke, & Shiu-Thorton, 2000). It appears as though the presence of ethnically and linguistically diverse staff members increases not only the likelihood of engagement (Gordon, 1995; Solis, Marks, Garcia, & Shelton,

1990) but also the likelihood of achieving positive service outcomes. Chun and Akutsu (2002) found that employing ethnically diverse staff members who speak the same language as clients was related to shorter lengths of treatment for Asian and Mexican Americans, in particular for non-English-speaking immigrants from those groups.

A similar strategy involves the use of community members as outreach workers to engage and educate racial and ethnic minority and immigrant populations. Community outreach workers share common characteristics with local residents, such as racial/ethnic background, knowledge of verbal and nonverbal language skills, and an understanding of the community's social and cultural norms (Nemcek & Sabatier, 2003). For example, the *promotoras* model is used in many minority communities, particularly among Latinos, to connect those in need of services with service providers. *Promotoras* are members of the community who act as educators and advocates to inform their peers about social service and safety net programs for which they may be eligible by spreading the word through community centers, churches, and their own social networks. In addition to being credible outreach workers in the community, *promotoras* can also help human service organizations identify neighborhoods and families who need food assistance and can make referrals to relevant social service providers (U.S. Department of Agriculture, 2011b).

Family relationships can also be an influential means to engage racial and ethnic minorities and immigrants, who traditionally have strong connections to their extended families and often live in the same household and share similar resources (Chow, Bester, & Shinn, 2001; Jenkins, 1981; Kyriakakis, 2014). As a result, service plans aimed at enhancing participation should involve family members of recipients, especially if the plans involve issues of transportation, child care, and the sharing of benefits. Asian Americans, for example, are likely to frame issues in a family or community context, rather than an individual context (Chow et al., 2001).

ORGANIZATION-FOCUSED STRATEGIES

Organization-focused strategies involve administrative decision-making and the use of resources to incorporate cultural competence in the policies and administrative procedures of the CBO. To increase participation rates among low-income racial and ethnic minority groups, one organization-focused strategy could be to locate such programs in communities with high need and a high density of racial and ethnic minorities and immigrant families. Locating services in closer proximity to the populations with the greatest need can help reduce some of the structural barriers to service participation related to transportation and safety, making it easier for clients to be informed about and access services, or attend meetings with caseworkers to comply with program requirements.

The location of services closer to clients who need them can also help CBOs attract and racially and recruit ethnically similar board members, staff, and clients who live within the same communities, and use them as resources to better understand residents' needs and existing barriers to participation. Agencies with more racially and ethnically diverse boards and staff are also better able to engage clients by facilitating convenient access to services, creating clear channels of communication and understanding, and fostering trust and rapport in agency–community relationships (Holley, 2003). Clients who perceive a reciprocal sense of connectedness and familiarity may be more comfortable seeking help from organizations that understand and incorporate appropriate aspects from their culture into service delivery. One study found that parents were more likely to reenroll their children in Head Start programs if they felt the program reflected their cultural and linguistic needs (U.S. Department of Health and Human Services, 2010).

Beyond employing racially and ethnically representative board and staff members, CBOs can also collaborate with local institutions and leaders to work *with* the organization on advocacy and outreach efforts.

Partnering with community stakeholders such as churches, schools, mutual aid societies, community centers, and other human service organizations can make eligible recipients more comfortable applying for or receiving benefits knowing that the programs are recommended by trusted institutions and leaders in the community (De Graauw, 2016). Such collaborations can also familiarize staff members with additional resources to which they can connect and refer clients. Because minority clients, particularly immigrants, often need more than one service to address their social, economic, legal, and health care needs, collaboration with organizations providing different services broadens clients' exposure to the human service system and makes it easier for them to access services (Snowden, Masland, Ma, & Ciemens, 2006). In addition, collaboration enhances community building by cultivating positive relationships among individuals, groups, organizations, and their surrounding geographical areas (Weil, 1996). This is especially important for engaging ethnic minority groups who have been excluded or marginalized from mainstream society due to their immigration status, race, or ethnicity.

The application of information technology is another strategy that organizations can use to reach out to ethnic and racial minority and immigrant communities. As information technology has become more widely available, Benton (2014) suggests that access to smart phones and their applications can help to (1) reduce barriers for service usage, (2) provide easy access to new immigrants, and (3) encouraged civic engagement (p. 4). An example of an application is the California on-line and mobile application services, *MyBenefits CalWIN*, which provides Californians with information on medical, food, and cash assistance state programs. Responding to the needs of non-English speaking communities, the website provides user interface in over 10 different commonly used languages. In addition, the mobile application, *MyBenefits CalWIN*, available for iOS and Android devices, allows registered users to view their benefits, submit applications, and report and upload information (MyBenefits CalWIN, 2012). Yet, despite the promise of technology, there is little empirical evidence of actual [social] service usage or research that evaluates the quality of smart phones and phone applications.

In sum, client- and organization-focused strategies are aimed at increasing the participation and retention of ethnic and racial minority clients and immigrants in human service programs (Watson, 2005). While additional strategies have been identified to increase general participation rates in human services and safety net programs (Vu, Anthony, & Austin, 2009; Watson, 2005), the strategies highlighted in this chapter are meant to target the barriers that are more often experienced by low-income racial and ethnic minority populations, with the goal of increasing their participation in critical safety net programs.

CONCLUSION

Because of the current state of the U.S. economy, over the next several years an increasing number of individuals and families are likely to require assistance from safety net programs to help meet their basic needs. Although the impact of these economic conditions is widespread, they disproportionately affect racial and ethnic minority populations and immigrants, many of whom were already in or near poverty prior to the recent recession. Existing safety net programs can alleviate the economic hardships of these populations through cash assistance and job training, child care and early childhood education, and food aid. Although these programs continue to exist, a large proportion of eligible racial and ethnic minorities are not currently participating due to obstacles unique to these populations.

This chapter reviewed some of the strategies used by CBOs to help low-income racial and ethnic minorities overcome barriers to participation. Among the strategies discussed were client-focused strategies and organization-focused strategies, both of which operate under the cultural competence framework to address the obstacles racial and ethnic minorities confront. Although this chapter focuses specifically on strategies to increase minority participation in safety net programs, implications from this review warrant further consideration.

The safety net programs highlighted in this chapter represent only a few resources related to income support offered to low-income groups. However, a variety of other programs related to health and mental health, housing, and tax benefits that are available to low-income populations are underutilized by ethnic and racial minorities. [*See other chapters in this volume.*] Further research is needed to assess comparative participation rates in such programs and whether the strategies described here are relevant to the receipt of other social benefits.

In addition, as a group, racial and ethnic minorities generally have lower participation when compared with non-Hispanic whites. Disparities in participation exist, however, among different racial and ethnic groups and vary across programs. As a result, CBOs using the cultural competence framework to engage minorities should bear in mind the differences among racial and ethnic groups. For instance, African Americans and Latinos/Hispanics have different cultural characteristics and needs that influence their participation. Similarly, the participation of Latinos and Asian American populations that consist primarily of foreign-born immigrants are also influenced by different factors. Instead of making broad generalizations about ethnic and racial minority populations and immigrants it is important for CBOs to keep these differences in mind in their efforts to engage these populations and develop effective culturally competent approaches.

Finally, the effectiveness of each strategy should be empirically evaluated in terms of its impact on participation in vital social service programs. While a large body of literature exists on the issue of cultural competence, it is largely limited to the topic of health and mental health service utilization. Little is known about the impact of client-focused and organization-focused strategies on participation in other social service programs. Even less is known about the use of technology to enhance access to or the quality of services. Because engagement is the initial step for needy individuals and families to receive safety net benefits, it is essential that these strategies be empirically evaluated. Future research is needed to assess the impact of engagement strategies independently and in combination with one another to expand ethnic and racial minority group participation in the safety net programs they critically need.

Discussion Questions

1. Why is it important to provide equal access to safety net programs for all racial, ethnic, and immigrant groups?
2. Based on your own experiences or observations, how do the barriers faced by minority populations affect their ability to use programs and services?
3. What are some of the strengths and limitations of the current safety net programs discussed in this chapter?
4. In addition to those mentioned in this chapter, what other strategies could be effective in engaging vulnerable populations in safety net programs?
5. How can social workers be more prepared to provide services to ethnic and racial groups?

Class Exercises

1. Divide the class into subgroups. Each group is assigned to find out where (e.g., locations) and how (e.g., procedures, documentations needed) to apply for one specific, local safety net program mentioned in the chapter. Report back to the whole class to what extent the application process is "access-friendly" to racial and ethnic minority populations or not.

2. Ask permission from your field supervisor at your placement agency to conduct an informal interview of one service user who is a member of a racial and ethnic minority and one who is white. You should talk to each person individually. Ask them to identify up to three specific suggestions regarding how to make service access and utilization easier for them. As a class, compare the similarities and differences of the suggestions between racial and ethnic ethnic minority and white clients.

3. Divide the class into two teams, debate the question: Should non-citizen immigrants be eligible to receive the benefits of social safety net programs?

Suggested Websites

The Brookings Institute: www.brookings.edu

National Institute on Minority Health and Health Disparities: http://www.nimhd.nih.gov

The Urban Institute: www.urban.org

U.S. Department of Agriculture, Food and Nutrition Service: http://www.fns.usda.gov/fns/

U.S. Department of Health and Human Services, Office of the Assistant Secretary for Planning and Evaluation: http://aspe.hhs.gov/

Welfare Information: www.welfareinfo.org

Suggestions for Further Reading

Burnstein, N. R., Patrabansh, S., Hamilton, W. L, & Siegel, S. Y. (2009). *Understanding the determinants of Supplemental Nutrition Assistance Program participation.* Alexandria, VA: U.S. Department of Agriculture, Food and Nutrition Service, Office of Research and Analysis.

Burt, M. R., & Nightingale, D. S. (2010). *Repairing the U.S. social safety net.* Washington, DC: Urban Institute Press.

Chin, A. C., & Harris, D. R. (Eds.) (2008). *The colors of poverty: Why racial and ethnic disparities exist.* New York: Russell Sage Foundation.

Iglehart, A. P., & Becerra, R. M. (2011). *Social services and the ethnic community: History and analysis.* Long Grove, IL: Waveland Press.

Moffit, R. A. (Ed.). (2003). *Means-tested transfer programs in the United States.* Chicago: University of Chicago Press.

National Academies of Sciences, Engineering, and Medicine (2015). *The integration of immigrants into American society.* Panel on the Integration of Immigrants into American Society, M.C. Waters and M.G. Pineau, (Eds.). Committee on Population, Division of Behavioral and Social Sciences and Education. Washington, DC: The National Academies Press. doi: 10.17226/21746.

U.S. Department of Health and Human Services. (2001). *Mental health: Culture, race, and ethnicity—A supplement to mental health: A report of the Surgeon General.* Rockville: U.S. Department of Health and Human Services, Substance Abuse and Mental Health Services Administration, Center for Mental Health Services.

References

Adams, G., Koralek, R., & Martinson, K. (2006). *Child care subsidies and leaving welfare: Policy issues and strategies.* Washington, DC: Urban Institute. Retrieved September 20, 2011, from http://www.urban.org/UploadedPDF/311304_policy_issues.pdf

Adams, G., & Rohacek, M. (2002, February). *Child care and welfare reform* (Policy Brief No. 14). Retrieved September 29, 2011, from http://www.brookings.edu/es/wrb/publications/pb/pb14.pdf

Adams, G., Snyder, K., & Sandfort, J. (2002, March). *Navigating the child care subsidy system: Policies and practices that affect access and retention.* Washington, DC: Urban Institute. Retrieved September 20, 2011, from http://www.urban.org/UploadedPDF/310450.pdf

Allard, S. W. (2009). *Out of reach: Place, poverty, and the new American welfare state.* New Haven, CT: Yale University Press.

Anthony, E. K., Vu, C. M., & Austin, M. J. (2008). TANF child-only cases: Identifying the characteristics and needs of children living in low-income families. *Journal of Children and Poverty, 14*(1), 1–20.

Benton, M. (2014). *Smart inclusive cities: how new apps, big data, and collaborative technologies are transforming immigrant integration* (Transatlantic Council on Migration) (pp. 1–18). Washington, D.C.: Migration Policy Institute (MPI). Retrieved from http://www.migrationpolicy.org/research/smart-inclusive-cities-new-apps-big-data-and-collaborative-technologies

Blank, M. B., Mahmood, M., Fox, J. C., & Guterbock, T. (2002). Alternative mental health services: The role of the black church in the south. *American Journal of Public Health, 92*(10), 1668–1672.

Blau, T., & Tekin, E. (2003). *The determinants and consequences of child care subsidies for single mothers* (NBER Working Paper No. 9665). Cambridge, MA: National Bureau of Economic Research. Retrieved September 29, 2011, from http://www.nber.org/papers/w9665.pdf?new_window=1

Briggs, S., Fisher, A., Lott, M., Miller, S., & Tessman, N. (2010). *Real food, real choice*: Connecting SNAP recipients with farmers markets. Retrieved September 22, 2011, from http://www.foodsecurity.org/pub/RealFoodRealChoice_SNAP_FarmersMarkets.pdf

Burnstein, N., & Layzer, J. I. (2007, September 15). *National study of child care for low-income families: Patterns of child care use among low-income families.* Retrieved September 29, 2011, from http://www.acf.hhs.gov/programs/opre/cc/nsc_low_income/reports/patterns_cc/patterns_childcare.pdf

Capps, R., Fix, M., Ost, J., Reardon-Anderson, J., & Passel, J. S. (2004). *The health and well-being of young children of immigrants.* Washington, DC: Urban Institute. Retrieved September 23, 2011, from http://www.urban.org/UploadedPDF/311139_Childrenimmigrants.pdf

Chapin Hall, University of Chicago (2011). *Foreign-born and U.S. families: Who takes up supports?* Retrieved September 29, 2011, from http://www.chapinhall.org/research/inside/foreign-born-and-us-born- families-who-takes-supports

Chow, J. C., Bester, N., & Shinn, A. (2001). AsianWORKs: A TANF program for Southeast Asian Americans in Oakland, California. *Journal of Community Practice, 9*(3), 111–124.

Chow, J. C., & Wyatt, P. (2003). Ethnicity, language capacity, and perception of ethnic-specific services agencies in Asian American and Pacific Islander communities. *Journal of Immigrant and Refugee Services, 1*(3–4), 41–60.

Chun, K. M., & Akutsu, P. D. (2002). Acculturation processes among Asian American and Latino families. In G. Marin, P. Balls, K. Organista, & K. M. Chun (Eds.), *Acculturation: Advances in theory, measurement, and applied research* (pp. 95–119). Washington, DC: American Psychological Association.

Cross, T. L., Bazron, B. J., Dennis, K. W., & Isaacs, M. R. (1989). *Towards a culturally competent system of care: A monograph on effective services for minority children who are severely emotionally disturbed.* Washington, DC: CASSP Technical Assistance Center, Georgetown University Child Development Center.

Currie, J. (2003). U.S. food and nutrition programs. In R. Moffit (Ed.), *Means-tested transfer programs in the United States.* Chicago: University of Chicago Press.

Currie, J. (2004). *The take up of social benefits* (NBER Working Paper No. 10488). Cambridge, MA: National Bureau of Economic Research. Retrieved September 22, 2011, from http://www.nber.org/papers/w10488.pdf?new_window=1

Danziger, S. K., Ananat, E. O., & Browning, K. G. (2003). *Childcare subsidies and the transition from welfare to work.* National Poverty Center Working Paper Series No. 03–11. Retrieved September 29, 2011 from http://www.npc.umich.edu/publications/working_papers/paper11/03-11.pdf

De Graauw, E. (2016). *Making immigrant rights real: Nonprofits and the politics of integration in San Francisco.* Ithaca, NY: Cornell University Press.

Edin, K., & Shaefer, L. (2015). *$2 a day: Living on almost nothing in America.* Boston: Houghton Mifflin.

Fix, M. E., & Passel, J. (2003, January). *The scope and impact of welfare reform's immigrant provisions.* Retrieved September 23, 2011, from http://www.urban.org/UploadedPDF/410412_discussion02-03.pdf

Food Research and Action Center (2011). *SNAP/food stamp monthly participation data, 2011.* Retrieved February 12, 2012, from http://frac.org/reports-and-resources/snapfood-stamp-monthly-participation-data/

Food Research and Action Center (2016). *February 2016 participation tables—1-month change, 1-year change, 5-year change, and state-by-state analysis.* Washington, DC: Food Research and Action Center (FRAC). Retrieved from http://frac.org/wp-content/uploads/2011/01/snapdata2016_feb.pdf

Fortuny, K., & Chaudry, A. (2011). *A comprehensive review of immigrant access to health and human services.* Retrieved January 12, 2012, from http://www.urban.org/UploadedPDF/412425-Immigrant-Access-to-Health-and-Human-Services.pdf

Gamm, G., & Putnam, R. D. (1999). The growth of voluntary associations in America, 1840–1940. *Journal of Interdisciplinary History, 29,* 511–557.

Geronimo, V. (2001). *The impact of welfare reform on Asians and Pacific Islanders.* Retrieved February 12, 2007, from http://www.apalc.org/Welfare_Reform_Impact.pdf

Gordon, A. K. (1995). Deterrent to access and service for Blacks and Hispanics: The Medicare hospice benefit, healthcare utilization, and cultural barriers. In D. L. Infelt, A. K. Gordon, & B. C. Harpers (Eds.), *Hospice care and cultural diversity* (pp. 65–84). Binghamton, NY: Haworth Press.

Government Accountability Office (2008). *Child care and early childhood education: More information sharing and program review by HHS could enhance access for families with limited English proficiency.* Washington, DC: Author. Retrieved February 1, 2012, from http://www.gao.gov/new.items/d06807.pdf

Government Accountability Office (2010). *Multiple factors could have contributed to the recent decline in the number of children whose families receive subsidies.* Retrieved January 23, 2012, from http://www.gao.gov/new.items/d10344.pdf

Halpern, R. (1999). *Fragile families, fragile solutions: A history of supportive services for families in poverty.* New York: Columbia University Press.

Henly, J. R., & Lyons, S. (2000). The negotiation of child care and employment demands among low-income parents. *Journal of Social Issues, 56*(4), 683–706.

Hernandez, M., Nesman, T., Mowery, D., Acevedo-Polakovich, I. D., & Callejas, L. M. (2009). Cultural competence: A literature review and conceptual model for mental health services. *Psychiatric Services, 60*(8), 1046–1050.

Holley, L. (2003). Emerging ethnic agencies: Building capacity to build community. *Journal of Community Practice, 11*(4), 39–57.

Jenkins, S. (1981). *The ethnic dilemma in social services.* New York: Free Press.

Jenkins, S. (Ed.) (1988). *Ethnic associations and the welfare state: Services to immigrants in five countries.* New York: Columbia University Press.

Karoly, L. A., & Gonzalez, G. C. (2011). Early care and education for children in immigrant families. *Future of Children, 21*(1), 71–101.

Katz, A. H. (1981). Self-help and mutual aid: An emerging social movement? *Annual Review of Sociology, 7*, 129–155.

Kirmani, R., & Leung, V. (2008). *Breaking down barriers: Immigrant families and early childhood education in New York City.* Retrieved February 12, 2012, from http://www.cacf.org/resources_publications.html#breakingthebarriers

Kissane, R. J. (2003). What's need got to do with it? Barriers to use of nonprofit social services. *Journal of Sociology and Social Welfare, 30*(2), 127–148.

Kissane, R. J. (2010). "We call it the badlands": How social-spatial geographies influence social service use. *Social Service Review, 84*(1), 3–28.

Kleinman, A., Eisenberg, L., & Good, B. (1978). Culture, illness, and care: Clinical lessons from anthropologic and cross-cultural research. *Annals of Internal Medicine, 88*(2), 251–258.

Kyriakakis, S. (2014). Mexican immigrant women reaching out: The role of informal networks in the process of seeking help for intimate partner violence. *Violence against women, 20*(9), 1097–1116. http://doi.org/10.1177/1077801214549640

Lang, K. (2007). *Poverty and discrimination.* Princeton, NJ: Princeton University Press.

Layzer, J. I., & Burnstein, N. (2007, September 15). *National study of child care for low-income families: Patterns of child care use among low-income families.* Washington, DC: U.S. Department of Health and Human Services. Retrieved September 12, 2011, from http://www.acf.hhs.gov/programs/opre/cc/nsc_low_income/reports/patterns_cc_exsum/patterns_cc_execsum.pdf

Lee, A., & De Vita, C. J. (2008). *Community-based nonprofits serving ethnic populations in the Washington, D.C. metropolitan area.* Retrieved January 20, 2012, from http://www.urban.org/publications/411675.html

Leftin, J., Eslami, E., & Strayer, M. (2011). *Trends in Supplemental Nutrition Assistance Program participation rates: Fiscal year 2002 to fiscal year 2009.* Retrieved January 24, 2012, from http://www.mathematica-mpr.com/publications/PDFs/nutrition/trends2002-09.pdf

Levin-Epstein, J., & Lyons, W. (2006). *Targeting poverty: Aim at bull's eye.* Retrieved January 23, 2012, from http://www.clasp.org/publications/targetingpovertytakingaimatabullseye10_06.pdf

Lin, A. C., & Harris, D. R. (2008). *The colors of poverty: Why racial and ethnic disparities exist.* National Poverty Center Series on Poverty and Public Policy. New York: Russell Sage Foundation.

Lincroft, Y., Resner, J., Leung, M., & Bussiere, A. (2006). *Undercounted and underserved: Immigrant and refugee families in the child welfare system.* Baltimore, MD: Annie E. Casey Foundation.

London, R. A., & Mauldon, J. G. (2006). *Time running out: A portrait of California families reaching the CalWorks time limit in 2004.* Retrieved November 16, 2012, from http://ucdata.berkeley.edu/publication_record.php?recid=59

Mabli, J., Cohen, R., Potter, F., & Zhao, Z. (2010). *Hunger in America 2010: Report prepared for Food Bank of Central & Eastern North Carolina.* Princeton, NJ: Mathematica Policy Research. Retrieved February 16, 2012, from http://content.foodbankcenc.org/education/docs/HungerStudy2010.pdf

MyBenefits CalWIN (2012). *MyBenefits CalWIN.* Retrieved May 17, 2016, from http://www.calwin.org/CalWIN%20Mobile-Setting%20Up%20Your%20App.pdf

National Head Start Association (2011). *Basic Head Start facts.* Retrieved September 29, 2011, from http://www.nhsa.org/files/static_page_files/48BADE30-1D09-3519-ADED347C39FA16A4/Basic_Head_Start_Facts_rev02212011.pdf

Neidell, M., & Waldfogel, J. (2009). Program participation of immigrant children: Evidence from the local availability of Head Start. *Economics of Education Review, 28*(6), 704–715.

Nemcek, M., & Sabatier, R. (2003). State of evaluation: Community health workers. *Public Health Nursing, 20*(4), 260–270.

New York City Administration for Children's Services. (2012). *Child care and Head Start.* Retrieved February 13, 2012, from http://www.nyc.gov/html/acs/html/child_care/headstart.shtml

Office of Planning, Research and Evaluation. (2011, May 13). *Design for migrant and seasonal Head Start survey.* Retrieved September 13, 2011, from http://www.acf.hhs.gov/programs/opre/hs/migrant_mshs/reports/migrant_design.pdf

Ong, P. (2002). Car ownership and welfare-to-work. *Journal of Policy Analysis and Management, 21*(2), 239–252.

Ramakrishnan, S. K., & Viramontes, C. (2006, July). *Civic inequalities: Immigrant volunteerism and community organizations in California.* San Francisco: Public Policy Institute of California. Retrieved January 21, 2008, from http://www.ppic.org/main/publication.asp?i=531

Ryu, M. (2009). *Twenty-third status report: Minorities in higher education 2009 supplement.* Retrieved September 21, 2011, from http://www.acenet.edu/AM/Template.cfm?Section=Home&TEMPLATE=/CM/ContentDisplay.cfm&CONTENTID=34441

Schlay, A.B., Weinraub, M., & Harmon, M. (2010). Child care subsidies post TANF: Child care subsidy use by African American, White, and Hispanic TANF-leavers. *Children and Youth Services Review, 32*(12), 1711–1718.

Schlay, A., Weinraub, M., Harmon, M., & Tran, H. (2004). Barriers to subsidies: Why low-income families do not use child care subsidies. *Social Science Research, 33*(1), 134–157.

Schmit, S. (2014). *Migrant and seasonal Head Start participants, programs, families and staff in 2013.* Washington, DC: Center for Law and Social Policy, Inc. Retrieved from http://www.clasp.org/resources-and-publications/publication-1/MHSH-PIR-2013-Fact-Sheet.pdf

Schmit, S., & Walker, C. (2016). *Disparate access: Head Start and CCDBG data by race and ethnicity* (pp. 1–30). Washington, DC: Center for Law and Social Policy, Inc. Retrieved from http://www.clasp.org/resources-and-publications/publication-1/Disparate-Access.pdf

Senturia, K., Sullivan, M., Cixke, S., & Shiu-Thorton, S. (2000). *Cultural issues affecting domestic violence service utilization in ethnic and hard to reach populations: Executive summary.* Retrieved September 2, 2011, from www.ncjrs.gov/pdffiles1/nij/grants/185352.pdf

Snowden, L., Masland, M., Ma, Y., & Ciemens, E. (2006). Strategies to improve minority access to public mental health services in California: Description and preliminary evaluation. *Journal of Community Psychology, 34*(2), 225–235.

Social Security Administration (2011). *Historical background and development of Social Security.* Retrieved January 24, 2012 from http://www.ssa.gov/history/briefhistory3.html

Solis, J. M., Marks, G., Garcia, M., & Shelton, D. (1990, December). Acculturation, access to care, and use of preventative services by Hispanics: Findings from HHANES, 1982–1984. *American Journal of Public Health, 80,* 11–19.

Stuber, J., & Schlesinger, M. (2006). Sources of stigma for means-tested government programs. *Social Science & Medicine, 63*(4), 933–945.

Sue, S., Fujino, D. C., Hu, L. T., Takeuchi, D. T., & Zane, N. W. (1991). Community mental health services for ethnic minority groups: A test of the cultural responsiveness hypothesis. *Journal of Consulting and Clinical Psychology, 59*(4), 533–540.

Tervalon, M., & Murray-Garcia, J. (1994). Cultural humility versus cultural competence: A critical distinction in defining physician training outcomes in multicultural education. *Journal of Health Care for the Poor and Underserved, 9*(2), 117–125.

Titmuss, R. (1963). *Essays on the welfare state.* Boston: Beacon Press.

Truong, M. H. (2007). Welfare reform and liberal governance: Disciplining Cambodian-American bodies. *International Journal of Social Welfare, 16*(3), 258–268.

Tumlin, K. C., & Zimmerman, W. (2003). *Immigrants and TANF: A look at immigrant welfare recipients in three cities.* Washington, DC: Urban Institute. Retrieved September 12, 2007, from http://www.urban.org/url.cfm?ID=310874

U.S. Census Bureau (2014). *Poverty data—historical poverty tables: people.* Retrieved May 16, 2016, from http://www.census.gov/hhes/www/poverty/data/historical/people.html

U.S. Department of Agriculture (2016). *Supplemental Nutrition Assistance Program participation and costs.* Retrieved from http://www.fns.usda.gov/sites/default/files/pd/SNAPsummary.pdf

U.S. Department of Agriculture (2015). *National and state-level estimates of Special Supplemental Nutrition Program for Women, Infants, and Children (WIC) eligibles and program reach, 2013.* Washington, DC: U.S. Department of Agriculture: Food and Nutrition Service. Retrieved from http://www.fns.usda.gov/national-and-state-level-estimates-special-supplemental-nutrition-program-women-infants-and-childr-2

U.S. Department of Agriculture (2014). *Characteristics of Supplemental Nutrition Assistance Program households: Fiscal year 2013.* Retrieved from http://www.fns.usda.gov/sites/default/files/ops/Characteristics2013.pdf

United States Department of Agriculture (2011a). *Nutrition program facts: Supplemental Nutrition Assistance Program education*. Retrieved February 12, 2012 from http://www.nal.usda.gov/snap/SNAP-EdFactsheet2011.pdf.

United States Department of Agriculture (2011b). *Supplemental Nutrition Assistance Program (SNAP): Putting health foods within reach*. Retrieved September 17, 2011 from http://www.fns.usda.gov/snap/outreach/pdfs/toolkit/2011/Community/toolkit_complete.pdf.

U.S. Department of Health and Human Services (2016). *About us Head Start*. Retrieved May 17, 2016, from http://eclkc.ohs.acf.hhs.gov/hslc/hs/about

U.S. Department of Health and Human Services (2015, November 24). *Estimates of child care eligibility and receipt for fiscal year 2012*. Retrieved May 17, 2016, from https://aspe.hhs.gov/pdf-report/estimates-child-care-eligibility-and-receipt-fiscal-year-2012

U.S. Department of Health and Human Services (2011a*). FY 2010 Child Care and Development Fund data tables*. Retrieved February 4, 2012, from http://www.acf.hhs.gov/programs/ccb/data/ccdf_data/10acf800_preliminary/table1.htm

U.S. Department of Health and Human Services (2011b*). The Head Start parent, family, and community engagement framework: Promoting family engagement and school readiness, from prenatal to age 8*. Retrieved from http://www.hfrp.org/publications-resources/browse-our-publications/parent-family-and-community-engagement-framework-promoting-family-engagement-and-school-readiness-from-prenatal-to-age-8

U.S. Department of Health and Human Services (2010, January 15). *Head Start impact study final report: Executive summary*. Retrieved September 1, 2011, from http://www.acf.hhs.gov/programs/opre/hs/impact_study/reports/impact_study/executive_summary_final.pdf

U.S. Department of Health and Human Services (2009). *Temporary Assistance for Needy Families: Eighth annual report to Congress*. Retrieved September 29, 2011, from http://www.acf.hhs.gov/programs/ofa/resource/eighth-annual-report-to-congress

Vu, C. M. (2010). The influence of social science theories on the conceptualization of poverty in social welfare. *Journal of Human Behavior and the Social Environment, 20*(8), 989–1010.

Vu, C. M., Anthony, E. K., & Austin, M. J. (2009). Strategies to engage adults in welfare-to-work activities. *Families in Society, 90*(4), 359–366.

Watson, J. (2005). *Active engagement: Strategies to increase service participation by vulnerable families*. Retrieved September 2, 2011, from http://www.community.nsw.gov.au/docswr/_assets/main/documents/research_active_engagement.pdf

Weil, M. O. (1996). Community building: Building community practice. *Social Work, 41*(5), 481–499.

Witte, A. D., & Queralt, M. (2002). *Take-up rates and tradeoffs after the age of entitlement: Some thoughts and empirical evidence for child care subsidies* (NBER Working Paper No. 8886). Cambridge, MA: National Bureau of Economic Research. Retrieved September 29, 2011, from http://www.nber.org/papers/w8886.pdf

Yeo, S. (2004). Language barriers and access to care. In A. M. Villarruel & C. P. Porter (Eds.), *Annual review of nursing research: Eliminating health disparities among racial and ethnic minorities in the United States* (pp. 59–73). New York: Springer.

Zedlewski, S. R., & Martinez-Schiferl, M. (2010, October). *Low-income Hispanic children need both private and public food assistance*. Washington, DC: Urban Institute. Retrieved February 12, 2012, from http://feedingamerica.org/hunger-in-america/hunger-studies/~/media/Files/research/feeding-hispanic- children2.ashx?.pdf

Notes

[1]For further clarification on eligible immigrants, please refer to Fortuny and Chaudry (2011).

[2]Despite lower rates of poverty, whites have the highest *number* of people in poverty due to the higher proportion of whites in the United States (Levin-Epstein & Lyons, 2006).

[3]Hispanic or Latino origin was measured separately from other races, resulting in a number of 100%.

[4]The ethnicity of 25% of SNAP participants was unknown.

[5]Participation rates of families reporting other races were not given.

[6]While many of the barriers discussed below are associated with the participation rates of minorities of color, barriers to participation in means-tested programs can exist across low- and middle-income groups regardless of race or ethnicity.

Credits

GLOSSARY

access: An individual's ability to obtain health or mental health care or social services. Barriers to access are often financial (insufficient resources), geographic (distance to services), organizational (insufficient providers and services), and social (cultural, lingual, discriminatory).

administrative feasibility: Refers to the likelihood that a department or agency can implement the policy or deliver the program effectively and efficiently.

advocacy coalition framework: A means of analyzing the forces in support of or in opposition to a particular policy that assesses the learning that occurs by coalition members and its relationship to policy change within **policy subsystems** over time.

Affordable Care Act of 2010 (ACA): The comprehensive health care reform law enacted in March 2010 under the Obama Administration. (See Chapter 14)

American exceptionalism: The view that the United States has several distinctive political–economic and cultural features that made the development of its social policies different from that of the policies in other Western industrialized nations.

AmeriCorps: Begun in 1994, the AmeriCorps programs provide opportunities for Americans to make an intensive commitment to service. The AmeriCorps network of local, state, and national service programs engages more than 70,000 Americans in intensive service each year during the period covered by this chapter. Today, there are more than 75,000 AmeriCorps members annually at more than 21,000 locations. These include non-profits, schools, public agencies, faith-based, and other community organizations, helping meet critical needs in education, public safety, health, and the environment. The variety of service opportunities is almost unlimited. Members may tutor and mentor youth, build affordable housing, teach full-time in public schools, clean parks and streams, run after-school programs, and help communities respond to disasters. Upon completion of their service, AmeriCorps members earn an Education Award to help finance their education.

appropriations/appropriation process: Appropriation bills, enacted annually by Congress, determine the precise amount of money each federal agency or program receives.

authorization/authorizing process: Substantive legislation that creates or continues the legal operation of a federal program, either indefinitely or for a specific time. Each house of Congress is organized into authorizing committees with substantive jurisdiction and expertise. The authorizing process refers to the steps both houses of Congress take to create this legislation.

baby boomers: Refers collectively to a group of individuals born immediately after World War II (1946) and continuing until about 1964. The large number of babies born during these two decades generated a demographic group notable for the size of its cohort. The current and impending retirement of the baby boomer generation has created financial strain on the U.S. Social Security system and Medicare program.

bend points: The dollar amounts where the percentages applied to earnings in the **primary insurance amount** formula change; these are currently $9,204 and $55,448. They change annually with changes in the national average wage index.

beneficiary: An individual eligible for and enrolled in a health insurance plan, or the recipient of cash or in-kind benefits from a federal or state program.

block grants: A policy initiative that began in the late 1970s and early 1980s involving the consolidation of federal funding of various categorical programs into a single grant (often with fewer total dollars), which state governments could spend with greater discretionary authority.

case advocacy: Advocacy efforts meant to improve the situation of one or a limited number of individuals, families, or communities.

cash assistance: Financial help in the form of cash aid or tax transfers.

cause advocacy: Advocacy efforts meant to improve the situation of many individuals, families, or communities at one time, usually by changing laws or policies.

Charity Organization Societies (COS): Nonprofit organizations established in the last quarter of the 19th century that applied principles of "scientific charity" to the distribution of relief and later developed what became social casework.

Children's Aid Society (CAS): Established in 1853 by Charles Loring Brace to pioneer a form of foster and institutional care for low-income children, it is the oldest continuously operating nonprofit child welfare agency in the United States.

Children's Bureau: A federal agency established in 1912 and directed by social workers from the Settlement House Movement to conduct research on the needs of the nation's children.

color-blind racism: A type of new-style racism that suggests that acknowledging racial inequality and differences represents bigoted and biased thinking. By invalidating racial inequality and differences, the existence and continuation of systematic racism is denied. This denial often is justified by those who suggest that they are "color-blind" and, therefore, not racist.

Commerce Clause (of the U.S. Constitution): This clause gives the federal government the power "to regulate commerce with foreign nations, and among the several states, and with Indian Tribes." It has been used to determine the limits of federal power to legislate in certain areas and to establish the balance of power between federal and state governments.

common law: The body of cases and legal principles developed by judges. This body of law is distinct from legislative statutes or executive orders or regulations.

Community Action Programs: Neighborhood programs created by the Economic Opportunity Act of 1964 that required the "maximum feasible participation" of community residents in the development and implementation of the social services they provided.

community health centers: Outpatient or ambulatory health centers originally established by the federal government during the 1960s to serve low-income families in medically underserved areas; today, these centers primarily provide services to uninsured and Medicaid populations.

community mental health centers: An outpatient or ambulatory mental health center originally established by the federal government during the 1960s in response to a movement to deinstitutionalize public psychiatric hospitals; today, these centers continue to provide services primarily to the most vulnerable populations who are poor or low income.

concentration camps for Japanese Americans: Camps established by President Franklin Roosevelt's Executive Order 9066 to imprison Japanese Americans on the West Coast of the United States after the 1941 bombing of Pearl Harbor. The executive order was a result of the belief that Japanese Americans were a threat to American homeland security since Japan had bombed the U.S. base at Pearl Harbor, compelling the United States to enter into World War II.

Corporation for National and Community Service: A federal agency that engages more than 5 million Americans in service through Senior Corps and AmeriCorps. It was created in 1993 to engage Americans of all ages and backgrounds in service to meet community needs. Each year, more than 5 million individuals of all ages and backgrounds help meet local needs through a wide array of service opportunities. These include projects in education, the environment, public safety, homeland security, and other critical areas.

cost-of-living adjustment (COLA): Automatic annual increases in benefits (e.g., Social Security retirement benefits) to keep pace with inflation as determined by the consumer price index. If no inflation has occurred over the past year, no adjustment occurs in benefit levels.

coverage rate: Rate of receipt of a particular subsidy or social program, usually calculated as the proportion of how many persons use the subsidy or program compared with how much federal or state money is budgeted for the subsidy or program.

critical thinking: Refers to mental processes of conceptualizing, synthesizing, and evaluating information that is clear, rational, open-minded, and informed by evidence.

cultural oppression: A form of domination that regulates values, experiences, and behaviors that are endorsed and promulgated by institutions created and controlled by dominant group members. These values, experiences, and behaviors are usually promoted as being universally normative or pertinent to all cultural groups. Therefore, the unique culture and worldviews of subjugated groups are ignored, marginalized, or deemed nonexistent.

cultural pluralism: A remedy for cultural oppression that involves affirming and incorporating the unique history, experiences, and contributions of diverse cultural groups that share a common geophysical and political–economic space. Although cultural similarities are recognized, the focus is on how these groups can create social unity without social uniformity.

"culture of poverty" thesis: The belief, expressed in different ways since the 1960s, that poverty is the result of the intergenerational transfer of values and behaviors among the poor that deviate substantially from those of the dominant culture.

cyber-activism: The use of the Internet and social media technology to conduct advocacy and engage in community organization and mobilization.

debt (national): The *total amount* the federal government owes to all its creditors in principal and interest for past borrowing. Each year the federal government runs a deficit (see below), it must borrow more money and the national debt increases.

decentralization of policymaking: The shifting of decision-making authority from the national government to state, county, or local government.

decision-theoretic evaluations: The use of descriptive methods to produce reliable and valid information about policy outcomes that are explicitly valued by multiple stakeholders.

deficit: The *annual* difference between the revenues the federal government (or a state or local government) receives (primarily through taxes) and its total outlays or expenditures.

deficit spending: Refers to the practice of borrowing money to cover a fiscal shortfall (deficit). Only the federal government can engaged in deficit spending. Virtually all state governments are required by their constitutions to have a balanced budget.

defined benefit pension: A lifetime annuity paid by an employer to a former employee upon retirement.

defined contribution plans: Tax-favored individual retirement accounts—typically 401(k)s—sponsored by employers, to which a worker contributes with or without matching employer contributions.

delayed retirement credit: The percentage (8%) by which Social Security retirement benefits are increased for each year beyond the normal retirement age (currently 66). An individual can delay retirement up to the maximum retirement age of 70.

developmental view of social welfare: A form of social welfare system that supports the needs of individuals from birth to death regardless of their income, work status, or demographic category. The policies developed by Scandinavian nations, particularly Sweden, come closest to this view.

developmentalist: A method of constitutional interpretation based on the principle of a "living Constitution," which views the Constitution as a foundational but flexible document able to change and grow with society.

discouraged workers: The official term used by the Bureau of Labor Statistics to describe workers who have become so discouraged that they have stopped looking for employment and are, therefore, no longer deemed unemployed.

Dixiecrats: Members of the States' Rights Democratic Party, which was formed in opposition to the civil rights platform presented at the Democratic National Convention of 1948. The party was established by Southern Democrats who walked out of the convention in protest of the adoption of a civil rights plank in the party's platform that condemned racial segregation.

doctrinalist: A method of constitutional interpretation based on the accumulation of rules and principles decided by the U.S. Supreme Court over time. This approach relies heavily on the principles of precedent and *stare decisis.*

Due Process Clause (of the U.S. Constitution): This clause provides that no state shall deprive any person "of life, liberty, or property without due process of law." It has been used to define the parameters of core American values such as liberty and the right to privacy.

early retirement age: The earliest one can retire and claim Social Security benefits, currently age 62. For the first 3 years under the normal retirement age (currently age 66) that one retires, benefits are reduced by about 6.67% per year, and for the fourth year by an additional 5% (up to a maximum benefit reduction of 25%).

Earned Income Tax Credit (EITC): A form of fiscal welfare that provides financial assistance to low-income working families with children and enables them to escape poverty.

economic globalization: The transformation of the world economy that began in the 1970s, characterized by the dominance of market values, increased power of financial institutions, greater interdependence of national economies, and a widening of the gap between rich nations (the Global North) and poor nations (the Global South).

education award: After successfully completing a term of service, AmeriCorps members who were signed up for an education award are eligible to receive a Segal AmeriCorps Education Award. This education award can be used to pay education costs associated with higher education, to pay for educational training, and to repay qualified student loans. Recipients have up to 7 years after their term of service has ended to use the award. The amount of the education award is now tied to the maximum amount of the U.S. Department of Education's Pell Grant. Since the maximum amount of Pell Grants can change from year to year, so can the dollar amounts of education awards.

effect: Measuring the effect of a social policy requires analyzing the extent to which a service or benefit achieved the goals associated with instrumental values—that is, its overall impact on society and not merely its consequences for the target population.

effectiveness: The extent to which a service or benefit achieves the goals associated with terminal values, such as success. Measuring a policy's effectiveness determines if it is successful in addressing its target issue and achieving the policy's intended goals.

efficiency: The determination of a policy's short- and long-term costs and benefits. This involves identifying all costs and aspects of the service or benefit. A focus on efficiency is often associated with engaging in cost-benefit analysis and a utilitarian approach to social policy—that is, an approach that evaluates a policy in terms of its consequences rather than its underlying values. Efficiency can be interpreted as either the least cost for a given benefit or the largest benefit for a given cost.

Elizabethan Poor Laws: A generic name for the legislation passed in Great Britain between 1349 and 1664 that established a publically funded and administered system of relief, later adopted by the American colonies.

emergency appropriations: In 1990, Congress decided to allow spending outside of the normal budget-setting process if both the president and Congress designated that it was a "dire emergency." As a result, the federal government may make emergency appropriations that ordinarily do not need to be offset by cuts elsewhere in the budget. This budgetary device is most often used for military expenditures or to respond to natural disasters or epidemics.

employer-based insurance (EBI): Financial protection against medical expenses related to disease, illness, or disability provided by an employer as an employment benefit; it can cover all or some health services and all or some health service expenses.

employment–population ratio: The ratio of people who are employed, as a percentage of the employable adult population.

entitlement programs: A term applied to programs that are generally funded by the federal government that provide benefits based on a legal right to assistance. Examples include Social Security, Medicare, Medicaid, and the Supplemental Nutritional Assistance Program (formerly food stamps).

Equal Protection Clause (of the U.S. Constitution): This clause provides that "no State shall deny to any person within its jurisdiction the equal protection of the law." It is the basis for decisions on whether differential treatment based on gender or race is appropriate.

equity: Refers to fairness or justice in the distribution of a policy's costs, benefits, and risks across population subgroups.

evaluability assessment: A set of procedures designed to analyze decision-making systems that benefit from performance information by clarifying the goals, objectives, and assumptions against which performance is to be measured.

family maximum benefit: The maximum amount of Social Security benefits payable to an entire family on any one worker's record, typically ranging from about 150% to 180% of a worker's retirement benefit.

federal budget: An annual plan that forecasts the anticipated revenues and expenditures of the federal government. The budget may vary based on assumptions made about existing policies that influence revenue and expenditures, as well as the state of the economy and other external factors.

federal debt: The total amount of money (principal and interest) that the U.S. government owes to domestic and foreign creditors.

Federal Emergency Relief Administration (FERA): The federal agency that administered the first major policy initiative enacted by the Roosevelt Administration in 1933. Its goal was to distribute aid to "every needy person" to alleviate the effects of the Depression and stimulate the economy.

fee-for-service medicine: A traditional payment method that pays health care providers for each service provided. Beneficiaries with traditional fee-for-service indemnity insurance are reimbursed for all or part of the paid fee.

feminism: On the most basic level, feminism is a philosophy and a social movement that advocates women's rights and their political, social, and economic equality to men. It also has a broader meaning, which includes the larger movement to end oppression against women in all forms and that often incorporates the plight of other oppressed populations, including African Americans and the LGBTQ community.

finance capitalism: A stage of capitalist development in which the financial, real estate, and insurance sector displace manufacturing and play an increasingly important role.

fiscal welfare: Policies implemented through the tax system to support, reward, encourage, and discourage certain types of behavior. Examples of fiscal welfare in the United States include the home mortgage deduction, the oil depletion allowance, the child care tax credit, and the Earned Income Tax Credit (EITC). With the exception of the EITC, most fiscal welfare benefits middle- and upper-income households.

formal evaluations: The continuous monitoring of the accomplishment of the formal goals and objectives of policies and programs.

formative evaluations: Monitor continuously the accomplishment of formal goals and objectives of policies and programs.

Freedmen's Bureau: A federal agency established in the aftermath of the Civil War (April 1865) to provide a variety of assistance programs to newly freed African Americans in the South. Controversial from the start, its programs were terminated in 1871 after Congress refused to appropriate additional funding for the agency.

friendly visitors: Charity Organization Society volunteers, largely from the upper and middle classes, who attempted to use "moral suasion" to change the behaviors of relief recipients, particularly those from immigrant communities.

gladiators: A level of political activity characterized by extensive engagement in the political world. Gladiators typically volunteer time to participate in political campaigns, are active party members, solicit funds, and even run for or hold political office. (Compare with *spectators* below.)

governmental institutions: Legislative assemblies and governorships at the state level, county (or parish) governing bodies, and city councils and mayoral positions at the local level.

gross domestic product (GDP): The market value of all goods and services produced within a country in a given period.

Hayes-Tilden Compromise of 1877: An agreement reached between white Northern and Southern elites to end Northern military occupation of the South which had begun after the U.S. Civil War. To settle the 1876 presidential election dispute between Republican Rutherford Hayes and Democrat Samuel Tilden, Northern Republicans agreed to remove military troops from the South in return for Southern

Democratic support of Mr. Hayes as the new president. The primary implication of this compromise was that the Civil War Reconstruction Era, which helped protect and advance the rights of the newly freed African American slaves, was brought to a halt. Once the occupation of the South by the U.S. army ended, Southern Democrats were able to restore their racial discriminatory practices, which ultimately led to the passage of Jim Crow legislation throughout the South. In its 1896 *Plessy v. Ferguson* decision, the Supreme Court ruled that this legislation, based on the doctrine of "separate but equal," was constitutional.

health insurance: Financial protection against medical expenses related to disease, illness, or disability; it usually covers all or some of the costs and can be obtained on an individual or group basis, often through one's employment.

health maintenance organizations (HMOs): A health care plan that provides a comprehensive set of health care services to a group of beneficiaries, usually in a geographic area, for a predetermined, prepaid fixed fee per enrollee. The payment is fixed without regard to actual services provided (costs incurred). Beneficiaries are often restricted to care provided by the HMO's network of providers and hospitals. HMOs often provide integrated care and focus on prevention and wellness.

health savings accounts (HSAs): A change in the tax code created under President George W. Bush as part of the Medicare Prescription Drug, Improvement, and Modernization Act of 2003. The change allows individuals covered by high-deductible health plans to receive tax breaks for income set aside for medical expenses. Unlike a flexible spending account, funds roll over from year to year if not spent.

Health Security Act (1993): Health care reform legislation proposed by the Clinton Administration to achieve universal coverage. Due to a well-orchestrated campaign by its opponents, Congress failed to pass the legislation despite its initial popularity.

horizontal adequacy: A measure of whether a service or benefit is accessible to all persons who are eligible to receive it. Social Security and public education are examples of programs that have a high level of horizontal adequacy.

horizontal equity: A principle that states that all persons in the same circumstances should be treated equally regardless of other factors (e.g., income or past contributions).

House–Senate Conference Committee: When one house of Congress passes a different bill from the other, a conference committee, made up of representatives and senators from both parties, is usually convened to resolve the differences and produce a compromise bill. The members of the conference committee describe their efforts in a "statement of managers," which includes a section-by-section explanation of the agreement.

Housing Choice: The new name for the Section 8 housing program, which provides vouchers to help tenants obtain housing in the private market.

human services: Direct services that address the health, mental health, welfare, and other needs of individuals, families, and/or communities.

immigration policy: A type of social policy that regulates the flow of noncitizens who enter and may ultimately become citizens of a nation. In the United States, these policies often have been encouraged by the need for low-wage and low-skilled labor but have also been discouraged by nativist fear or xenophobia associated with demographic and cultural shifts. Historically, this fear has been especially targeted at people of color and, in recent years, prominently linked to Latino/Hispanic immigration.

inclusiveness of coverage: An evaluative concept that measures the extent to which a defined population-at-risk is protected against a specific hazard—for example, the number of jobless persons receiving unemployment benefits. This concept is linked to the determination of eligibility for a specific benefit.

income distribution: The measurement of how income is distributed among different segments of a society's population, usually divided into quintiles (fifths). The extent of inequality in a society's distribution of income is measured through the use of a Gini coefficient.

income inequality: The distribution of income among different groups of the population, which in recent years has shifted sharply upward so that the top 20% of the population now receive more than 51% of all income.

individual equity: A conception of equity that essentially states that "you get what you pay for."

indoor relief: Beginning in the 19th century, the provision of financial assistance to the poor in institutions (e.g., almshouses and workhouses) as an alternative to providing aid in their homes. Proponents of indoor relief argued that it was more efficient and better able to change the behavior of the poor.

in-kind supports: Non-cash benefits that assist individuals and families with a specific need, such as food, shelter, or medical attention.

institutional rational choice theory: A theory of policy analysis that focuses on the role of institutions, and the formal and informal rules that coordinate or constrain individual behavior in social interactions.

institutional view of social welfare: A view of social policy that regards a primary function of social welfare as the amelioration of the "diswelfare" effects of the market economy, such as unemployment, that emerged during the mid-20th century in response to the problems produced by industrialization. It is often associated with the development of universal social policies. (See below) This is the approach to social welfare that characterized U.S. social policy from the New Deal of the 1930s through the 1970s. Some of its features still exist today.

interest group politics: The means by which competing groups influence the policymaking process in the public arena, often associated with pluralist theories of policy development.

internalized oppression: The conscious and unconscious acceptance of beliefs, attitudes, and messages that distort and defame how members of oppressed groups view themselves. This form of domination is the internal manifestation of the external conditions of oppression. It is often associated with several self-negating behaviors that prevent members of oppressed groups from expressing their vast positive potential. Although this concept usually is limited to members of oppressed groups, it also can explain the dehumanizing effects of distortions of superiority among many members of privileged groups.

intersectionality: The understanding that power and oppression rest on many levels and are not confined solely to one's race, gender, and class, but are often the result of compounded layers of each acting in concert.

legitimation: A step in the policy development process by which a problem that has been recognized by the public (such as domestic violence or homelessness) becomes an issue worthy of action by policymakers.

less eligibility: The principle derived from the British Poor Law Reform Act of 1834 that no one receiving public assistance should have a higher standard of living than the lowest paid worker.

libertarian: A proponent of minimal government interference in the market economy (for example, through taxation, environmental regulations, or social welfare programs) based on a strong belief in individualism and individual freedom.

liberty: A condition that refers to the extent to which public policy extends or restricts people's privacy and individuals' rights and choices.

long-term care: Long-term personal care and social services provided to individuals who cannot function independently, regardless of age; services can be provided in an institution or at home but traditionally are provided in assisted-living and nursing care facilities.

managed care: A variety of clinical, financial, and organizational methods used to reduce health care costs and achieve greater cost efficiency.

maternalism/maternalist perspective: An ideology that values women's distinct role as caregivers and nurturers of the family and extends these values to society as a whole through the adoption of social policies, thus improving the quality of life for women and children as well as men.

means test: A process of determining individual or household eligibility for a particular government-funded social welfare benefit based solely on income. (See below) The use of a means test is generally associated with selective social policies such as Medicaid, SNAP, and TANF. (See below)

means-tested program: A program for which only those under a certain income and/or asset level are eligible.

Medicaid: A federal–state public health insurance system enacted in 1965 by the Johnson Administration that provides access to health care for certain low-income individuals who meet established eligibility criteria. States determine benefits, eligibility, provider payment rates, and program administration. The 2010 Affordable Care Act (ACA) significantly expanded Medicaid coverage to low-income individuals and families. However, nearly one half of the states refused to participate in this expansion. (See Chapter 14)

medicalization: Treating a social problem such as poverty as if it were an illness.

Medicare: A federal health insurance system enacted in 1965 by the Johnson Administration that provides access to health care for retired workers and their spouses over age 65, disabled workers eligible for Social Security disability benefits, and certain individuals who need kidney transplants or dialysis. The 2010 Affordable Care Act (ACA) expanded Medicare benefits to include preventive care and wellness programs for the elderly. (See Chapter 14.)

mental health parity: Federal legislation enacted in 1996 that requires that annual or lifetime spending limits on mental health benefits have parity with medical and surgical benefits offered through a health insurance plan. However, insurers were able to circumvent the law by imposing limits on the number of mental health provider visits and/or number of days for inpatient psychiatric hospitalizations covered. In 2008, new legislation prohibited all group health plans that offer mental health coverage from imposing greater limits on co-pays, co-insurance, number of visits, and/or number of days covered for hospital stays due to mental health conditions.

mothers' pensions: State-funded and state-administered financial assistance to widows, divorced, and abandoned women with children that were the antecedents to the welfare program established by the 1935 Social Security Act. By the early 1930s, nearly all states had some form of mothers' pensions program. They varied widely in their coverage and benefits, however, and discriminated against women of color.

multi-attribute utility analysis: A set of procedures designed to elicit from multiple stakeholders subjective judgments about the probability of occurrence and value of policy outcomes.

mutual aid organizations: Voluntary associations established by immigrant groups, trade unions, and racial, ethnic, or religious minority communities to aid their members and fill the gaps in services provided by government and mainstream nonprofit organizations. Many of their features have been incorporated into the social service programs developed by more traditional non-profit social service agencies.

National and Community Service Trust Act: The name given to the legislation that created the Corporation for National and Community Service and the AmeriCorps program. It was signed into law (Public Law 103-82) on September 21, 1993.

Native American boarding schools: Popular in the 19th through mid-20th centuries, these schools attempted to re-socialize Native American children so they could successfully assimilate and incorporate the values and behaviors of European American culture. Many writers believe that these schools represented a form of cultural hegemony aimed at devaluing and extinguishing Native American culture.

neoliberalism: A market-based policy regime that has emerged during the past four decades, concurrent with the advent of economic globalization. It emphasizes deregulation and lower taxes while equating the spread of democracy with the spread of markets. It produced a perspective on social policy based on the belief that government should play a smaller role in society and that market-oriented solutions are preferable means of addressing social problems. However, neoliberals recognize that specific social policies can advance the public good in a limited way and they are likely to support increased funding for human capital development—e.g., education and job training—to make the United States more competitive in the global economy. (See Chapter 13 for their impact on welfare and welfare reform.)

New Deal: The name given to the vast array of social and economic policies developed during the administration of Franklin D. Roosevelt (1933–1945) to combat the effects of the Great Depression.

new-style racism: Systematic racial subjugation and discrimination expressed in subtle, diffused, and covert forms. These forms have been increasingly dominant in the United States since the 1960s, when explicit legal racism was abolished through the enactment of civil rights legislation. A critical component of this form of racism is color-blind racism. Therefore, new-style racism can be thought of as "oppression by denial."

normal (or full-benefit) retirement age: The age at which a Social Security contributor can retire and receive a benefit equal to his or her **primary insurance amount.** At present, the age is 66.

objectivity: In its most common usage, refers to the attitude of the impartial or unbiased observer.

occupational welfare: Benefits that are provided to individuals through their employment, such as health insurance, pensions, transportation stipends, tuition assistance, and child care. Most of the beneficiaries of occupational welfare are in the middle or upper-middle class.

official unemployment rate: A calculation by the Bureau of Labor Statistics based on the number of persons seeking work who are unable to obtain employment. It does not take into account individuals who are not looking for work ("discouraged workers") or have never entered the labor force, and individuals who are employed part-time, or are under-employed, in the military, experiencing homelessness, or incarcerated.

off-year elections: Elections held in a year when there is not a presidential election. The year 2016, for example, is a presidential election year; 2014 was considered an off-year election because there was no vote for president that year. Members of the House of Representatives and one third of U.S. Senators are elected in off-year elections, as are countless state senators and state representatives, governors, mayors, city council members, and other elected officials.

old-style racism: Systematic racial subjugation and discrimination expressed in highly explicit and overt forms. These forms were dominant in the past, especially in legal prohibitions that prevented or restricted the civil and human rights of people of color. Because explicit and overt methods of fear are used to sustain this form of subjugation, it can be characterized as "oppression by terror."

organizational policies, procedures, and guidelines: Steps taken by social service agencies that shape how government policies are implemented—for example, through the application of eligibility regulations.

originalist: A method of constitutional interpretation that relies on both the text of the Constitution and the values and principles underlying it. This includes reference to what the framers intended, or what people at the time understood the words of the text to mean.

outcome equity: Often used interchangeably with *social justice*, this concept refers to the fair distribution of societal goods such as wealth, income, or political power.

outdoor relief: The provision of financial assistance to people in their homes, such as that provided by modern welfare programs.

paper entrepreneurialism: An economic activity where profits are made on paper from stock market and currency trades, rather than from any real contribution to the nation's economic well-being.

participation rates: The proportion of eligible persons accessing a particular social program or subsidy divided by the number of eligible persons.

paternalism: The treatment of individuals as if they are incapable of making their own decisions or in a manner that compels them to act in a particular way. Under welfare reform, this involved disciplining the poor (i.e., treating them like children) to make them more compliant with norms regarding work and family.

Personal Responsibility and Work Opportunity Reconciliation Act of 1996 (PRWORA): A public law, signed by President Bill Clinton, that eliminated the U.S. government's major income maintenance program, Aid to Families with Dependent Children (AFDC), and replaced it with a new and short-term program, known as Temporary Assistance for Needy Families (TANF), funded through block grants to the states. Unlike the lifetime entitlement to benefits that AFDC provided, the law limits aid to needy families with children to no more than five years. It also ended the federal jobs training program and rendered legal immigrants ineligible for many means-tested public benefits for their first 5 years of residence.

policy devolution: The transfer of responsibility for the funding and delivery of social policies from the federal government to the states that began in the 1970s. This process complemented the historic preference of U.S. policymakers for **decentralized** political decision making. (See above)

political feasibility: This concept refers to the likelihood that a policy would be adopted—that is, the extent to which elected officials accept and support a policy proposal.

poor or near poor: Households living on less than 125% of the poverty line. For a single person, this is less than $14,850 per year.

population-at-risk: The number and character of persons who are vulnerable to a particular social, economic, or environmental hazard. This could be determined by looking at such factors as gender, geography, age, occupation, and employment status.

post-racism era: The period after the 1960s but especially during the 1990s and first decade of the 21st century characterized by the increased visibility and advancement of people of color in high-profile positions of prestige and/or power, culminating in the election of President Barack Obama, the first African American president. Some conclude that the increased visibility of people of color as professionals, public officials, and entertainment figures provides evidence that the United States has finally achieved race neutrality.

poverty guidelines: A simplified version of the poverty thresholds used for administrative purposes, such as determining financial eligibility for certain federal or state programs; the federal poverty level.

poverty line: For 2016, the official poverty line for a family of four was $24,300 Each year, the federal government sets a new poverty threshold by adding the previous year's inflation rate to a formula developed in the 1960s.

poverty thresholds: The federal government's official statistical measure of poverty; it establishes the official poverty line.

precedents: Principles or rules established by a court that may apply when deciding subsequent cases with similar issues or facts.

primary insurance amount (PIA): The amount of a worker's Social Security retirement benefit prior to adjustments for early/delayed retirement, spouse and young children, etc. It is the sum of 90% of average earnings up to the first bend point, 32% of earnings between the first and second bend points, and 15% of earnings above the second bend point.

primary sector: A sector of the labor market that consists of jobs in large corporations and the financial industry. It is characterized by relatively high wages and, in some manufacturing industries, stronger unions.

privatization: The transfer of responsibility for social policy implementation or funding from government to either the for-profit or nonprofit sector.

process equity: A principle that refers to the justice of decision-making procedures or processes—that is, the extent to which they are voluntary, open, and fair to all participants.

Progressive Era: A period of future-oriented social reform (~1890–1918) in which the first major government and nonprofit social welfare programs emerged and the social work profession began.

pseudo-evaluations: The use of descriptive methods to produce reliable and valid information about policy outcomes.

public health: Organized health promotion activities, programs, and policies enacted by the federal government through the U.S. Public Health Service. Typical public health activities include immunizations, sanitation and health education programs, disease control such as HIV/AIDS, occupational health and safety programs, and programs that improve air, food, and water quality.

quintiles: Fifths of the population—the units by which income inequality is usually calculated.

racism-centered social policy analysis: A model of comprehending and evaluating social policies that views racism as a primary motive in their formulation and implementation. It allows for a more specific and thorough investigation of how white racial domination is manifested in the social policy racial regulation process.

redistributive effect: The use of social policies to reallocate societal resources, power, opportunities, or status, particularly to disadvantaged populations. The extent to which social policies should be used for this purpose is an ongoing subject of political debate.

residual: The conception of social policy typically associated with inadequacy and stigma, residual social policy involves means-tested social programs such as TANF and Medicaid for those recipients who have failed in the marketplace.

residual view of social welfare: Typically associated with individual inadequacy and the stigmatization of individuals who receive social welfare benefits, it is a view of social welfare that regards government intervention through social policies and services as a "last resort" and relies primarily on the market economy, the family, and private charity to address the needs of individuals. Proponents of a residual view oppose most social policies because they believe that government should not interfere with the operations of the market. For most of its history, the United States has adopted this view of social welfare. It is reflected in means-tested programs such as TANF, SNAP, and Medicaid for people who have "failed" in the marketplace.

revenues: The money collected through various forms of taxes to fund government services and programs.

safety net programs: Programs provided to populations that need assistance to prevent them from falling into or to help lift them out of poverty. Participants are often required to meet income eligibility requirements as defined by a government or organization providing the service or program.

sanctions: Financial penalties imposed on clients for failure to comply with welfare-to-work program rules.

Save AmeriCorps Coalition: Formed in response to devastating cuts in federal funding for national service programs in 2003, the coalition represented AmeriCorps programs throughout the country and led the campaign to reverse funding cuts and preserve the AmeriCorps program. The Save AmeriCorps Coalition evolved into Voices for National Service, a coalition of hundreds of service organizations.

scientific charity: The Charity Organization Societies' application of principles of scientific management to the administration of charity and relief programs.

secondary sector: A sector of the labor market that is highly competitive and consists of small and midsized businesses with few or no unions.

sectoral divisions in the labor market: A perspective on the labor market that divides it into three sectors: (a) the primary sector; (b) the secondary sector; and (c) the tertiary sector. The professional/technical labor market cuts across all three sectors and has been growing in recent years.

selective benefits: Government-funded programs or services available on the basis of individual need, usually determined by a means test.

selective social policies: Social policies whose benefits are determined either by a means test or by membership in a particular demographic category. Examples of selective policies in the United States include TANF (also known as welfare), the Supplemental Nutrition Assistance Program (also known as food stamps), and Medicaid.

separate-but-equal doctrine: Emerging from the 1896 *Plessy v. Ferguson* Supreme Court ruling, the legal doctrine or perspective that contended it was fair and constitutional for blacks and whites to have separate public accommodations as long as these accommodations were equal. This doctrine was challenged by the Civil Rights movement during the 1940s-1960s and rendered unconstitutional in large part by several important Supreme Court decisions (e.g., *Brown v. Board of Education*) and the 1964 Civil Rights Act.

settlement houses: Multipurpose social service agencies established during the Progressive Era by upper-class volunteers in low-income immigrant and racial minority communities. Because they were usually barred from settlement houses that provided services for European immigrants, African American and Latino communities created their own settlement houses.

single-payer health care system: A system of health care provision in which one entity, such as the federal government, acts as the financial administrator or payer to collect all health care fees and pay out all health care costs. In the current system in the United States, there are thousands of different payers, a situation that has raised concerns about wasteful spending associated with administrative costs.

SNAP: The Supplemental Nutritional Assistance Program, formerly called food stamps, an entitlement program that provides nutrition aid to low-income individuals and families.

social acceptability: The extent to which the public will accept and support a policy proposal.

social construction: A concept developed by postmodernists that postulates that reality is neither fixed nor objectively determined but is a subjective reflection of cultural values and beliefs, primarily of dominant groups. According to this perspective, views of conditions such as poverty, mental illness, crime, and sexual deviance and of institutions such as education, marriage, the market economy, and democracy are the products of social construction rather than some predetermined absolute. Analyzing issues through this lens provides a different interpretation of societal approaches to problems, assumptions about their causes, and preferences for particular solutions.

social construction framework: The notion that frameworks used to interpret our observations of the world can to some extent be altered by arguments, thereby providing an avenue for changing the political support for various policies.

Social Darwinism: The attempt to apply Charles Darwin's theory of evolution to human society to rationalize social inequality by explaining it as the natural outcome of societal competition.

social determinants of health: A perspective that postulates that health is determined by more than the availability of health care. It asserts that health is a state of complete physical, mental, and social well-being, and not merely the absence of disease or infirmity. According to this perspective, a person's health is affected by the social and economic conditions in which the person lives.

social division of welfare: A tripartite conception of welfare systems, developed by the British social policy expert Richard Titmuss, that asserts that individuals receive assistance through social, fiscal, and occupational welfare. This perspective is based on the assumption that in modern societies everyone receives welfare benefits in some form, not merely individuals who are poor.

social equity: A principle which states that individuals should get what they need regardless of their past, current, or potential future contribution to society. This principle more closely aligns with the idea of redistribution as a social justice goal.

social goals: Public statements or appeals to do something comprehensive about a social problem (e.g., poverty). Such appeals can be translated into specific social policies.

social insurance program: A pooled fund to which earners contribute during periods of employment and from which they and their families receive benefits when they are unable to work. Only families whose earners have contributed are eligible to receive benefits.

social media: Internet- or cell phone–based software that allows for asynchronous or synchronous interactive communication between two or more people.

social policies: Regulations and guidelines usually developed by ruling elites to manage, reduce, and sometimes solve social problems considered disruptive of societal relationships, norms, and institutions. These regulations and guidelines are usually developed through the legislative process at the national, state, or local governmental levels and frequently address basic human needs such as income, food, clothing, housing, and health care.

social policy racial regulation: The control and surveillance of people of color through the formulation and implementation of social policies. This control, which is motivated by white racial domination, seeks to minimize and preclude the possibility of people of color gaining sufficient power to resist and eliminate the political, economic, and cultural domination of non-Hispanic whites.

social programs: Acts of government designed to effect change around specific issues. They reflect efforts to implement social policies.

social reproduction: The process by which societal institutions pass down (reproduce) the values, customs, traditions, and behaviors of the dominant culture to maintain the status quo. Social policies in the United States engage in social reproduction by promoting work and individual responsibility and by placing greater reliance on the market economy than the state for the remediation of economic and social problems.

Social Security wage base: The income on which Social Security taxes are levied and on which benefits are based, up to the taxable maximum. In 2016, the taxable wage base is $118,500 of earned income.

social welfare policies: A smaller subset of social policies that regulate benefits to persons defined by society as "needy." They include not only policies that provide cash assistance, health care, and housing but also those that address issues in the areas of education, transportation, and environmental and criminal justice. Ideally, their goals are to optimize individual and family well-being and to redistribute societal resources more equitably.

societal policies: The sum of a society's actions, which affect individual and social development and both reflect and shape social norms of behavior. This is the broadest concept of policy.

socio-political: A term that signifies the combination or interaction of social and political factors.

spectators: A level of political activity characterized by minimal engagement in the political world. Spectators typically obey laws, vote, and may engage in political discussions. (Compare with *gladiators*.)

stare decisis: The legal principle that precedents are to be followed by the court in subsequent cases involving similar issues or facts. It derives from a Latin phrase meaning "to stand by decisions."

state budgets: Annual plans that forecast the anticipated revenues and expenditures of individual state governments.

state political culture: A state's political culture refers to its residents' orientations toward important aspects of their state's political system, including the role of the individual in how state politics operates. Elazar (1972) describes three ideal types of political culture: moralistic, traditionalistic, and individualistic.

stipend: Many AmeriCorps members receive a modest living allowance or stipend. These range from approximately $1,000-$2,000 a month plus, in some cases, an educational allowance.

street-level bureaucrats: Public sector positions that include police officers, teachers, social workers, nurses, doctors, lawyers, and other service providers such as lower court judges, corrections officers, and prison guards who occupy positions that have relatively high degrees of discretion and relative autonomy from organizational authority.

suffragettes: Advocates of women's right to vote in the 19th and early 20th centuries.

summative evaluations: A method of evaluation that monitors the accomplishment of formal goals and objectives after a policy or program has been in place for some period.

supplemental appropriations: Spending authority included in an appropriations bill in addition to funding that has already been provided. These appropriations are usually used to provide funding for unforeseen emergencies such as natural disasters, where Congress and the president conclude that the needs must be addressed before the next year's appropriations process.

Supplemental Security Income: A joint federal–state program of financial assistance to the elderly poor and individuals with physical or mental disabilities created by the Social Security amendments of 1972 through the consolidation of several programs established by the 1935 Social Security Act.

surplus: The excess amount that is created when government revenues are greater than expenditures in a particular fiscal year.

tax credits: Dollar-for-dollar reductions in the tax owed by an individual or household. Examples include the Child Care Tax Credit and the Earned Income Tax Credit (EITC).

tax expenditures: Exemptions in the tax code, such as deductibility of the interest on home mortgages, that allow taxpayers to retain income on which they would otherwise be taxed.

taxable maximum: The maximum amount of income from wages that is subject to the payroll (Social Security and Medicare) tax in a given year. In 2016, the maximum is $118,500 for Social Security. There is no ceiling on the earned income subject to the portion of the payroll tax dedicated to Medicare.

technical feasibility: Refers to the availability and reliability of technology needed for policy implementation.

tertiary sector: A sector of the labor market that includes government and nonprofit organizations.

textualist: A method of constitutional interpretation that relies only on the literal words of the Constitution, seeking their ordinary meaning without relying on other texts or outside sources.

think tanks: Institutions and organizations dedicated to problem solving and interdisciplinary research, usually in such areas as technology, social or political strategy, or the military.

Title XX: The 1975 Social Service amendment of the Social Security Act that funds a wide range of services not covered by income support or health care policies.

Treaty of Guadalupe Hidalgo of 1848: A treaty between Mexico and the United States that ended the U.S.-Mexican War. It required Mexico to relinquish more than half its territory and the United States to provide monetary compensation for damage to Mexican property. The treaty also provided civil and property rights protection for Mexicans who chose to remain in the new Texas territory, but many of these rights were violated and not enforced.

under-consumption: An economic condition in which the demand for goods is less than the supply. Under-consumption is often associated with a stagnating economy.

universal benefits: Government-funded benefits available to an entire population as a basic right and, for the most part, without means testing—that is, they are provided regardless of the income levels of recipients, their families, or households.

universal social policies: Policies whose benefits are made available to all citizens or all members of a particular demographic category (e.g., the aged) regardless of income. In the United States, examples of universal policies are public education, Social Security retirement benefits, and Medicare.

VA-HUD Appropriations Subcommittee: The appropriations subcommittee that had responsibility for funding AmeriCorps and the Corporation for National and Community Service when the events described in Chapter 8 occurred. Subsequently, jurisdiction has shifted to the Labor-Health and Human Services-Education appropriations subcommittee. The VA-HUD subcommittee is now known as the Subcommittee on Transportation, Housing and Urban Development, and Related Agencies.

value neutrality: A concept that refers to (1) the normative injunction that persons of science should be governed by the ethos of science in their role as scientists, but that this is not at all necessary in their role as citizens; and (2) the disjuncture between the world of facts and the world of values—the impossibility of deriving "ought statements" from "is statements."

value relevance: Refers to values that enter into the selection of problems investigators choose to examine.

vertical adequacy: A measure of whether a policy provides benefits that cover the needs of each recipient satisfactorily.

vertical equity: A principle used to justify the differential treatment of persons in different circumstances— for example, the allocation of greater resources to a person who has a more serious health condition or to a student who has special needs.

voluntary associations: Organizations made up of volunteers with similar interests, needs, and values who aim to work toward common objectives for the good of their members or targeted populations. These organizations are usually supported by a combination of government grants and contracts, philanthropic contributions from foundations, fees for services, or charitable donations from members and supporters.

War on Poverty: The initiative of the Johnson Administration during the mid- to late 1960s that included numerous policies and programs to address the needs of low-income Americans.

white racial domination: The ubiquitous control non-Hispanic whites exercise over the contour and character of the political, economic, educational, religious, military, and knowledge validation institutions in the United States. Having both overt and covert expressions, this influence primarily serves to protect and advance the political, economic, and cultural interests of non-Hispanic whites and to suppress the power and positive potential of people of color.

workforce development: Although there is no single definition, it can be aptly described as "a synthesis of the fields of employment and training, social services, economic development, and corporate human resources" (Meléndez, 2004, p. 2; see Chapter 12).

Works Progress Administration (WPA): An agency established during the New Deal that provided government-funded jobs to millions of unemployed Americans. WPA workers built the nation's physical infrastructure and engaged in many cultural projects.

"worthy" and "unworthy" poor: The distinction, established by the Elizabethan Poor Laws, between individuals who were poor through no fault of their own (e.g., the elderly, infirm, widows, and orphans) and those who were believed to be responsible for their own poverty (the able-bodied poor). This distinction persists today and is most visible in the U.S. in the differential treatment of individuals who receive entitlement programs, such as Social Security retirement benefits and Medicare, and those who receive means-tested programs like TANF and Medicaid.

yellow peril: A derogatory term used to characterize the fear many Americans, especially non-Hispanic white Americans, expressed over the growing immigration into the United States of persons of Asian or Pacific Islander origin during the late 19th and early 20th centuries. This fear was a chief reason for immigration laws that restricted the entry of these persons into the United States.

ABOUT THE AUTHORS

Joel Blau, DSW, is professor of social policy and director of the PhD program at the Stony Brook University School of Social Welfare. He has written three books, including *The Visible Poor: Homelessness in the United States* (Oxford, 1992) and (with Mimi Abramovitz) *The Dynamics of Social Welfare Policy*, 4th edition (Oxford, 2014), as well as numerous articles about income inequality, homelessness, and comparative social welfare.

Richard K. Caputo, PhD, is professor of social policy and research at Yeshiva University's Wurzweiler School of Social Work in New York City. He has authored six books, including most recently *Policy Analysis for Social Workers* and *U.S. Social Welfare Reform: Policy Transitions from 1981 to the Present*. He has also edited two books, including most recently *Basic Income Guarantee and Politics: International Experiences* and *Perspectives on the Viability of Income Guarantee*. He is on the editorial board of the *Journal of Family and Economic Issues*, *Families in Society*, the *Journal of Sociology & Social Welfare*, *Marriage & Family Review*, the *Journal of Poverty*, and *Race, Gender & Class*. In October 2015, the Commission on the Role and Status of Women in Social Work Education of the Council on Social Work Education named him a Mentor Recognition Honoree.

Julian Chun-Chung Chow, PhD, is a professor in the School of Social Welfare at the University of California, Berkeley. His specialty areas include community analysis, social service delivery, and community practice. His research focuses on understanding how social services could be more responsive to the needs of ethnic minorities, including recent immigrant populations. He has been active in Asian American communities and has served on many national, state, and local organizations, addressing issues such as welfare reform, poverty, immigration, health, and mental health. Currently, he is working on several projects concerning migrant workers in China and immigrant access to social services and social integration in Hong Kong, Taiwan, and the San Francisco Bay Area.

Richard C. Fording, PhD, is professor in the Department of Political Science at the University of Alabama. He earned his BA at the University of Florida (1986) and his PhD from Florida State University (1998). His primary teaching and research interests include social welfare policy, race and politics, state politics, and policy implementation. He is the author or coauthor of a number of articles related to social welfare policy that have appeared in a variety of journals, including the *American Sociological Review, American Journal of Sociology, Journal of Public Administration Research and Theory, Policy Studies Journal,* and *Social Service Review.* He is coauthor of *Disciplining the Poor: Neoliberal Paternalism and the Persistent Power of Race* (University of Chicago Press, 2011).

Isabel García is a doctoral student in the Department of Sociology at the University of California, Berkeley. Her research interests include immigration, family, the role of immigration law, and legal status. Her current research focuses on understanding how adult U.S. citizen children of undocumented parents/within undocumented-mixed status families experience their family's [il]legal status and the consequences for the family unit. In 2015, she received a National Science Foundation (NSF) Graduate Research Fellowship.

Stephen Gorin, PhD is professor emeritus of social work at Plymouth State University, University System of New Hampshire, and executive director of the New Hampshire Chapter of the National Association of Social Workers. He has a PhD in social welfare policy from the Heller School at Brandeis University. Gorin served on President Clinton's Health Care Task Force, as a member of the Advisory Council of the Center for Mental Health Services in the U.S. Department of Health & Human Services, and on the Coordinating Committee of the National Medicare Education Program. He is currently serving his second term as editor-in-chief of *Health & Social Work.* Gorin was a delegate to the 1995 and 2005 White House Conferences on Aging and to the 1998 White House Conference on Social Security. He is a member of the National Academy of Social Insurance, has been appointed to the Standing Editorial Board of Oxford Bibliographies Online: Social Work, and is serving a second term as a member of the New Hampshire State Committee on Aging. He is coauthor of *Health and Mental Health Care Policy: A Biopsychosocial Perspective* (2004, 2007, 2010, 2014).

Monica Healy is the president of Healy Strategies, a government affairs consulting firm that helps non-profits promote their agenda on Capitol Hill and within the executive branch, focusing on the education, national service, health care, and environmental fields. Prior to starting her consulting firm, Ms. Healy gained considerable experience in government and government relations, both in the public and private sector. She was a senior legislative assistant to Senator Charles (Mac) Mathias (R-MD) and later was staff director of the Senate Democratic Policy Committee, working for Senate Majority Leader George Mitchell (D-ME) and Senator Tom Daschle (D-SD). In between those two stints, she ran the State of Maryland's Washington, DC, office. Following her work for the U.S. Senate, Ms. Healy joined the Clinton Administration at the Department of Labor as liaison to the White House and Congress on health care issues. Ms. Healy also served as deputy executive director of the Pension Benefit Guaranty Corporation. Following her extensive career in government, Ms. Healy served as vice president of government relations for Teach for America where she helped lead the movement to save AmeriCorps. In addition to her advocacy work, Ms. Healy is currently board chair for the University of Maryland Center for American Politics and Citizenship and a frequent guest lecturer at the university, her Alma Mater.

Richard (Rick) Hoefer, PhD, is Roy E. Dulak Distinguished Professor for Community Practice Research at the School of Social Work, University of Texas at Arlington. Dr. Hoefer received his PhD from the University of Michigan (social work and political science). During his career, he has blended knowledge of policy processes with social work advocacy, such as in his recent books *Advocacy Practice for Social Justice* (3rd ed.) and *Social Welfare Policy: Responding to a Changing World* (with John McNutt). This theme also permeates his numerous articles delineating effective advocacy by human services interest groups. Dr. Hoefer's current research interests include U.S. social welfare policy, advocacy, and nonprofit management.

Roberta Rehner Iversen, PhD, MSS, is an associate professor in the School of Social Policy & Practice at the University of Pennsylvania and faculty director of the Master of Science in Social Policy program. Her ethnographic research concerns economic mobility among low-income urban families. Iversen's 2006 book, *Jobs Aren't Enough: Toward a New Economic Mobility for Low-Income Families* (coauthor, A. L. Armstrong; Temple University Press), illuminates how critical social institutions intersect to influence family mobility. In fall 2011, Iversen was invited to provide district-level TANF (Temporary Assistance for Needy Families) administrators with policy recommendations for TANF policy reauthorization. Iversen is currently working on a book about the meaning of work for low- and middle-earning workers over the past three decades of major labor market change. This book will conclude with ideas for creating a radically expanded view of "work" for all persons.

Vicki Lens is a professor at the City University of New York, Hunter College, Silberman School of Social Work. She has a JD and a PhD in social welfare. Prior to obtaining her PhD, Dr. Lens worked as a public interest lawyer. As a legal aid lawyer, she provided legal services to the poor in the areas of public assistance, Social Security disability benefits, SSI, and Medicaid. She brought several class action lawsuits establishing a right to shelter on behalf of homeless families and expanding entitlements to public assistance. As an Assistant Attorney General in New York State, she established the Suffolk County Public Advocacy Unit, which was responsible for prosecuting businesses for civil fraud and protecting the public from economic exploitation. Her primary research interest is in socio-legal studies, where she uses ethnographic and other methods to study legal settings, among them the welfare fair hearing system and family court. She is the author of *Poor Justice: How the Poor Fare in the Courts* (2016, Oxford University Press). She has also published several articles on the Supreme Court, including analyses of decisions involving gender discrimination, women's rights, and federalism.

Cynthia Moniz, PhD, is professor and director emeritus of the BSW program at Plymouth State University, University System of New Hampshire. She has a PhD in social welfare policy from the Heller School at Brandeis University. Moniz is coauthor of *Health and Mental Health Care Policy: A Biopsychosocial Perspective* (2004, 2007, 2010, 2014) and has published widely on health care and social policy. She is actively engaged as a national leader in social work education, both in the National Association of Social Workers (NASW) and the Council on Social Work Education (CSWE), where she has served in numerous capacities, including as a member of the NASW Board of Directors and the CSWE Commission on Professional Development. She was an invited participant to the Social Work Congress held in 2005 and 2010 by leading national social work organizations and associations. Her areas of interest and research are inequality and health, the social determinants of health, and health care policy.

Michael Reisch, PhD, is the Daniel Thursz Distinguished Professor of Social Justice at the University of Maryland. A former Woodrow Wilson Fellow and Fulbright Senior Scholar, he has held faculty and administrative positions at six major U.S. universities, and in Europe, Asia, and Australia, and leadership positions in national, state, and local advocacy, professional, and social change organizations and political campaigns. His 30 published books and monographs include *The Handbook of Community Practice* (Sage Publications); *The Road Not Taken: A History of Radical Social Work in the U.S.* (Brunner-Routledge); *From Charity to Enterprise: The Development of American Social Work in a Market Economy* (University of Illinois Press); *Social Work in the 21st Century* (Pine Forge Press); *For the Common Good* (Routledge); and *Social Work and Social Justice* (Oxford University Press). In 2013, he was named "Educator of the Year" by the Maryland Chapter of the National Association of Social Workers, and in 2014, he received both the Teacher of the Year Award from the University of Maryland, Baltimore, and the Significant Lifetime Achievement Award from the Council on Social Work Education. He is currently writing *Macro Practice in a Multicultural Society* (to be published by Cognella, Inc.) and a multicultural history of U.S. social welfare and social work.

Susan J. Roll, PhD, is an associate professor of social work at California State University, Chico. Her substantive area of research addresses housing, child care, and welfare policy, with an interest in how social scientists can influence and build better policies through empirical evidence. Susan teaches bachelor's and master's level courses on policy, community practice and social justice. Prior to pursuing her PhD, Susan was a social work administrator and community organizer in the fields of domestic violence and women's health for 10 years. She received her MSW from Arizona State University in 1998 and her PhD in social work from the University of Denver in 2010.

Jerome H. Schiele, PhD, is PROFESSOR and Dean of the College of Professional Studies at Bowie State University in Bowie, Maryland, a multi-disciplinary college that includes seven academic programs and over 1800 students. Dr. Schiele received his bachelor's degree in sociology from Hampton University in 1983, and both his master's and doctoral degrees in social work from Howard University. He has 26 years of higher education experience and has served in both faculty and administrative positions at the University of Georgia, Morgan State University, Norfolk State University, Clark Atlanta University, and the State University of New York at Stony Brook. Dr. Schiele's research focuses on social policy analysis, racial oppression, and cultural diversity. He has published numerous scholarly articles, essays, and book chapters, and is author of *Human Services and the Afrocentric Paradigm* (The Haworth Press, 2000—now Routledge Press), editor of *Social Welfare Policy: Regulation and Resistance among People of Color* (Sage Publications, 2011), and co-author with Phyllis Day of *A New History of Social Welfare, 7th edition* (Pearson Publishers, 2012).

Sanford F. Schram, PhD, teaches at Hunter College, CUNY, where he is a professor in the Political Science Department and a Faculty Associate at the Roosevelt House Public Policy Institute. He is the author of *The Return of Ordinary Capitalism: Neoliberalism, Precarity, Occupy* (2015) as well as *Words of Welfare: The Poverty of Social Science and the Social Science of Poverty* (1995) and *Disciplining the Poor: Neoliberal Paternalism and the Persistent Power of Race* (2011), coauthored with Joe Soss and Richard C. Fording.

Elliot Schreur is an Income Security Policy Analyst at the National Academy of Social Insurance (NASI), where he conducts research and policy analysis on Social Security, retirement policy, and unemployment insurance. Prior to joining NASI, he was a Policy Analyst with the Asset Building Program at the New American Foundation, where he researched policies to support retirement security for low-income families. He holds a Master's degree in Public Policy with a concentration in philosophy and social policy from the George Washington University and a Bachelor's degree from the University of Richmond.

Gene Sofer, PhD, is a founding partner of the Susquehanna Group, a Washington, DC–based consulting firm. Between 1980 and 1984, he served as majority associate staff on the House Budget Committee. From 1984 to 1993, he was counsel to the House Education and Labor Committee where he was responsible for passage of national service legislation in 1990, as well as for the introduction, consideration, and enactment of the National and Community Service Trust Act, which created the AmeriCorps program in 1993. Between 1994 and 1998, he served as the first director of Congressional and Intergovernmental Relations at the Corporation for National and Community Service. From 1998 to 2001, he was the deputy executive director of the Presidential Advisory Commission on Holocaust Assets in the United States. He is a graduate of New York University and received his PhD in history from UCLA. He is the author of *From Pale to Pampa: A Social History of the Jews of Buenos Aires*. He is a member of the Board of Directors of Avodah: The Jewish Service Corps and a member of the WAMU Community Council.

Joe Soss, PhD, is the inaugural Cowles Chair for the Study of Public Service at the University of Minnesota, where he holds faculty positions in the Hubert H. Humphrey Institute of Public Affairs, the Department of Political Science, and the Department of Sociology. His research and teaching explore the interplay of democratic politics, socioeconomic inequalities, and public policy. He is particularly interested in the political sources and consequences of policies that govern social marginality and shape life conditions for socially marginal groups. Soss is the author of *Unwanted Claims: The Politics of Participation in the U.S. Welfare System* (2000), coeditor of *Race and the Politics of Welfare Reform* (2003), coeditor of *Remaking America: Democracy and Public Policy in an Age of Inequality* (2007), and author or coauthor of numerous scholarly articles. His most recent book, *Disciplining the Poor: Neoliberal Paternalism and the Persistent Power of Race* (2011), coauthored with Richard C. Fording and Sanford F. Schram, was selected for the 2012 Michael Harrington Award (American Political Science Association, New Political Science) and the 2012 Oliver Cromwell Cox Book Award (American Sociological Association, Section on Racial and Ethnic Minorities).

Karen M. Staller, PhD, JD, is an associate professor at the University of Michigan School of Social Work. She teaches in the areas of social welfare policy, child and family policy, history and philosophy of social welfare programs and policies, and qualitative research methods. Her scholarship focuses on runaway and homeless youth, and the history of policies and programs for street youth. She is the author of *Runaways: How the Sixties Counterculture Shaped Today's Practices and Policies* (Columbia University Press) and serves on the Board of Directors of Ozone House, a local runaway and homeless youth shelter.

Benjamin Veghte, PhD, is Vice President for Policy at the National Academy of Social Insurance. In this role, Ben leads the Academy's research and policy initiatives. He has more than two decades of experience in the field of social insurance in diverse institutional environments in the United States and Germany. In Germany, he was an Assistant Professor of Political Science at the University of Bremen, and a consultant for the European Commission. His research, teaching, and policy work have been devoted to advancing our understanding of the role of social insurance in thriving economies and democratic societies. Ben earned his Master's in Public Administration from Harvard's Kennedy School and his PhD in Modern European History from the University of Chicago. He is a member of the Scholars' Strategy Network.

Catherine M. Vu, PhD, is the Director of Research in the Office of Research and Evaluation of the Santa Clara County, California Social Services Agency. She received her bachelor's degree in economics and management science from the University of California, San Diego. After working in the nonprofit sector, she received a master's in public administration from Cornell University and a master's in social work and a PhD from the University of California, Berkeley. Her research interests focus on strengthening the capacity of nonprofit community-based organizations to serve vulnerable low-income communities, social policy implementation, and poverty-related issues.

INDEX

A

Adarand Constructors, Inc. v. Pena, 300, 302

Advocacy
  state and local, 13, 33, 35, 54, 65, 74, 85–87, 96, 146, 193, 239, 265–269, 271–272, 275, 278, 280–282, 317, 348, 361, 371, 430, 435

Affirmative Action, 19, 23, 26, 149, 207, 209, 302, 388

African Americans
  poverty rates of, 433

"American dream", 80

American exceptionalism, 54, 60, 453

American Red Cross, 61

American Sociology Society, 198

Americans with Disabilities Act, 89

Annie E. Casey Foundation, 93, 182

Antipoverty programs
  Aid to Families with Dependent Children (AFDC), 63, 85, 144–145, 317, 383, 463
  child care assistance, 367, 369, 433–434, 438
  Earned Income Tax Credit (EITC), 32, 90, 207, 230, 354, 365, 394, 456, 458, 467
  housing assistance, 208, 368–369, 379, 431, 434
  SNAP (food stamps), 43, 327
  tax credit policies and, 370

  unemployment insurance program, 72, 363–364
  Work Opportunity Tax Credit (WOTC), 360, 365

Anti-tax movements, 86

Appropriation
  description of, 233
  FY 2003 emergency supplemental, 250

Aristotle, 21

Assessment
  evaluability, 216, 457
  multi-attribute utility analysis, 216, 461

B

Baby M case, 292

Black Lives Matter Movement, 129, 153, 179

Block grants, 86

Board of Trustees, 319, 334–335

Bowers v. Hardwick, 298

Brown v. Board of Education, 301, 306, 465

C

Cancian, M., 92

Capitalism

finance, 24, 42, 87, 114–116, 118, 121, 175, 191, 202, 208, 228, 233, 318–319, 326, 335, 341–342, 360, 411, 453, 458

Carnegie Corporation, 199

Carter administration, 86

Catholic Charities, 41

Cato Institute, 340, 386

Center for Economic and Policy Research, 336, 420

Center for Retirement Research, 332

Centers for Medicare and Medicaid Services, 410, 413, 418, 420

Chamber of Commerce, 78, 385

Child Care Aware of America, 369–370

Child Care Information Service, 370

Children's Bureau, 70–71, 407, 454

Children's Defense Fund, 88, 90, 389

Citizens for Tax Justice, 33

Citizens United v. Federal Election Commission, 387

Civilian Conservation Corps, 76–78, 358

Client advocate, 204

Client-focused strategies
    examples of, 14, 17, 33, 81, 139, 177, 180, 267, 311, 352, 433, 459, 468

Clinton administration
    social policy during, 173

Club for Growth, 387

Color-blind racism, 144

Colored Women Voters, 165

Commerce Clause, 76, 193, 289, 297, 304–306, 454

Community Action Programs, 81–82, 84, 454

Community Service Society, 58

Compania General De Tabacos De Filipinas v. Collector of Internal Revenue, 229

Comprehensive Employment and Training Act, 85, 358

Conference Report, 235, 247

Congressional Budget Office, 125, 204, 211, 238, 415–416

Conservative Keynesians, 38

"Contract with America", 391

Cornell Labor Program, 181

Council on Social Work Education, 199, 270, 471, 473–474

Court system
    the structure of the, 161, 193, 225, 289, 420

CQ-Roll Call, 265, 269

"Cult of Domesticity", 169

Cultural and language barriers, 439

Cultural competence
    definition of, 10, 19, 21, 24, 45, 92, 148, 435, 441

Cultural oppression
    description of, 233

Cyberacticism
    description of, 233

D

Dandridge v. Williams, 300

Decision-theoretic evaluations, 216

Developmentalists, 297

Disability benefits, 324–325

Divorce
    no-fault, 170, 182

Doctrinalists, 296

Due Process Clause, 170, 193, 289–291, 297–299, 303–304, 456

E

Eagle Forum, 386

Economic Policy Institute, 93, 117, 125, 130, 354

Economics
    "mixed economies", 37
    "Reaganomics", 87
    supply-side, 38
    trickle-down, 38, 236

Economic Security Index, 327, 330

Economy
    interaction of social policy and, 2

Elder Index, 327–328

Electronic advocacy
    description of, 233

Elementary and Secondary School Education Act, 82

EMILY's List, 175

Empire Zinc Corporation, 178

Employee Benefit Research Institute, 329

Empowerment Zone, 367

English Poor Laws, 56

Equal Opportunity Employment Commission, 294

Equal Protection Clause, 142, 291, 297–304, 308, 457

Evaluation
 decision-theoretic, 215–216, 456
 formal, 3, 10, 21, 34, 53, 55–56, 138, 142, 144, 162, 164–165, 167, 171–173, 175–176, 179, 183, 185, 200, 211, 213, 215–216, 304, 316, 362, 434, 458, 460, 467
 formative, 137, 215–216, 458
 pseudo-evaluation, 215, 464
 summative, 215, 467

Executive Order 139, 455, 9066

F

Families USA, 91

Family Research Council, 386

Federal budget
 an overview of the, 162, 429
 economic effects of the, 133

Federal deficit
 economic effects of the, 133

Federal Housing Administration, 78

Federal Insurance Contributions Act, 192, 229

Federal Register, 353

Federal Reserve Board, 77, 332–333

Feminism Ecological Model
 description of, 233
 illustration of the, 31

Flint, Michigan, 6, 269

Food Nutrition Service, 94, 120

Food Research and Action Center, 436

Formal evaluations, 215

Formative evaluations, 216

Fourteenth Amendment, 170, 193, 289, 295, 297–299

FY 2003 emergency supplemental appropriations bill, 250

G

Gallup Organization, 95

Gettysburg Address, 22

Gladiators, 458

Goldberg v. Kelly, 290, 306

Gonzales v. Raich, 291, 306

Gough, 127

Government Accountability Office, 364, 434, 438

Governmental institutions
 description of, 233

Government expenditures
 interest on the federal debt, 192
 purchase of goods and services, 192, 233, 240
 transfer payments, 192, 233–234, 239, 241

Government spending, 38

Gratz v. Bollinger, 302

Grutter v. Bollinger, 302–303

Gun Free School Zones Act, 305

Guttmacher Institute, 185

H

Habitat for Humanity, 250, 260

Harris v. Forklift, 294

Hayes-Tilden Compromise of 458, 1877

Health care system
 single-payer, 410–411, 417, 465

Health insurance
 employer-based insurance (EBI), 414, 457

Heart of Atlanta Motel Inc. v. United States, 304

HIV/AIDS programs, 91

Hobbs, D., 255

House Budget Committee, 238, 246, 475

House Ways and Means Committee, 125, 408

Housing market
 subsidized housing, 31

Hull House, 67–68, 142, 199
Human services
    definition of, 10, 19, 21, 24, 45, 92, 148, 435, 441

I

Indian Health Service, 414
In-kind supports
    description of, 233
    for racial and ethnic minorities, 338
    Head Start as, 82
In re Baby M, 290
Interest group politics, 211
Internal Revenue Service, 230, 365–366
International Tribunal on Crimes Against
        Women, 178
Issue advocate, 205

J

James, E., 91
"Jim Crow" laws, 62
Job Corps, 81, 124, 358, 361
Judiciaries
    developmentalists, 295, 297
    doctrinalists, 295
    originalists, 295–296
    textualists, 295–296

K

Kaiser Family Foundation, 92, 184, 412,
        414–415
Katzenbach v. McClung, 304
Keynesian economic theory, 37
Keynesian economic theory influencing the
    tax expenditures, 32, 127, 333–334, 365, 390,
        467
Korean War, 232
Ku Klux Klan, 65, 142

L

Labor unions
    decline of, 85, 149, 389, 394
Language barriers, 437
Lawrence v. Texas, 298
Legal Services, 81, 84
Legislation
    Americans with Disabilities Act, 89
    Civil Rights Act (1964), 182
    Elementary and Secondary School Education
        Act, 82
    Equal Pay Act (1963), 182
    Family and Medical Leave Act (FMLA), 171
    Family Medical Leave Act (1993), 171, 182
    Federal Emergency Relief Administration
        (FERA), 75, 458
    Gun Free School Zones Act, 305
    Hayes-Tilden Compromise of 458, 1877
    "Jim Crow" laws, 62
    National Labor Relations Act, 78
    National Recovery Administration (NRA), 75
    Taft-Hartley Act, 177
    Violence Against Women Act, 173, 179, 305
Legislative process
    appropriation, 236, 246–247, 249–256, 259, 453,
        457, 467–468
    authorization, 91, 246–247, 256–257, 259, 354,
        361, 412–413, 454, 473
"Leninist Strategy", 340
Liberal Keynesians, 38
Lochner v. New York, 290
Locke, J., 21
Lott, M., 436
Lowell Female Labor Reform Association, 177

M

MADRE, 180
Make Wealth History, 115
Marks, G., 441
Marriage

Defense of Marriage Act (DOMA), 171, 184, 298
Masland, M., 443
Medicare
future of, 96, 137, 332, 340, 417
Medicare Part D, 91, 412, 419
Medicare Prospective Payment System, 410
Miller, S., 216
Morrison, 149–150, 305–306
Muller v. Oregon, 167, 290, 306

N

NASW Code of Ethics, 282
NASW Social Work Pioneer, 407–408
National Academy of Social Insurance, 472, 474–475, 477
National Association for the Advancement of Colored People, 70
National Center for Health Statistics, 182
National Center for the Prevention and Control of Rape, 179
National Commission on Fiscal Responsibility and Reform, 349
National Conference of Social Work, 79
National Conference of State Legislatures, 122, 361
National Employment Law Project, 364
National Federation of Independent Business v. Sebelius, 241, 306, 416
National Head Start Association, 435
National Institute of Mental Health, 179
National Labor Relations Act, 78
National Organization for Women, 170, 179
National School Lunch Program, 94
National Skills Coalition, 361
National Study of Child Care of Low-Income Families, 184
National Welfare Rights Organization, 84
National Women's Law Center, 93
Native American boarding schools
Carlisle Indian Industrial School (1879–1918), 140

Natural law moralism, 198
Neighborhood Guild, 67
Neoliberalism paternalism
description of, 233
Nevada Department of Human Resources v. Hibbs, 306
New Deal
Fair Labor Standards or Wagner Act, 78
Federal Emergency Relief Administration (FERA), 75, 458
National Recovery Administration (NRA), 75
"New Federalism" philosophy, 358
New York Charity Organization Society, 58
New York City Administration for Children's Services, 434
Nicaragua's National Women's Association, 180
Nineteenth Amendment, 165, 173, 175

O

Objective technician, 204
O'Connor v. Donaldson, 299
Office of Economic Opportunity, 81, 85
Office of Management and Budget, 333, 352–353, 410
Office of Planning, Research and Evaluation, 435
Old Age Assistance, 76
One-Stop Career Center job connection services, 359
Oregon (State), 121
Organization-focused strategies
examples of, 14, 17, 33, 81, 139, 177, 180, 267, 311, 352, 433, 459, 468

P

Panic of 58, 1837
Personal income tax, 227, 240
Pew Research Center, 97
Planned Parenthood v. Casey, 298
Plato, 21
Plessy v. Ferguson, 142, 301, 459, 465

Points of Light Foundation, 248

Policy Advocacy Behavior Scale, 276

Policy analyst, 215

Political economy

of U.S. social policy, 1, 24, 55, 76, 82, 87, 96–97, 141, 167, 193, 267, 311–312

Politics

interest group, 28–29, 31, 210–211, 276–278, 307, 411, 460, 473

off-year elections, 275, 462

social policy development and, 1–2, 12, 20, 137–139, 191, 193, 267, 289, 308

Social Security, 2, 16–18, 20, 31–35, 43, 63, 70–72, 76–79, 81–82, 84–87, 90–92, 95–97, 113, 123–124, 144, 167, 172, 190, 192, 196, 207–208, 226–227, 231–233, 235, 268, 291, 311, 315–342, 348–349, 352, 363, 379, 381, 383, 389, 406–409, 411, 421, 430, 454–457, 459, 461–462, 464, 466–469, 472–474, 477

Population-at-risk, 43

Poverty

conservative myths about, 2

definition of, 10, 19, 21, 24, 45, 92, 148, 435, 441

Poverty measurement

definition of, 10, 19, 21, 24, 45, 92, 148, 435, 441

federal poverty level (FPL), 413

history of, 2, 10, 18, 39, 64, 138, 199, 294–295, 318, 364, 381, 392, 410, 421, 430, 474–475

official poverty line, 124, 327, 352–354, 463–464

poverty thresholds, 326–327, 337, 352–353, 463–464

Supplemental Poverty Measure (SPM), 327, 354

Private Industry Councils, 359

Privatization

description of, 233

social policy, 1–3, 9–12, 14–24, 26, 29, 31, 33–34, 40, 42–43, 45, 55, 61, 65, 71–72, 76, 79, 82, 84–85, 87–91, 95–98, 113–114, 120, 123, 125–126, 128–129, 135–139, 141–142, 144–146, 152–155, 161–165, 167, 170–171, 173, 175–176, 180, 182–185, 190–193, 227, 267–268, 274, 289–294, 299, 302, 306–308, 311–312, 333, 359, 365, 380, 395, 457, 459–460, 462, 464, 466, 471, 473–476

Process equity, 209

Pseudo-evaluations, 215

Q

Quincy, 57

R

"Race to the Top" program, 92

Racism

color-blind, 2, 144, 146, 302, 454, 462

of PRWORA, 91, 145, 171

Reagan administration

credited with "saving" Social Security, 233

Red Cross, 5, 61, 250

Republican Party

opposition to tax increases by, 33

Retirement benefits

eligibility for, 43, 182, 207, 327, 342, 353, 355, 360, 415, 440, 459, 461, 463

Retirement USA, 332

Revenues

description of, 233

tax, 2, 6, 19, 21, 23–24, 32–33, 35, 37–38, 42, 44, 56, 58, 76, 79, 85–90, 92–93, 95, 97, 113, 116–118, 123, 126–129, 142–143, 145–146, 149, 182, 184, 192, 201, 206–209, 212, 216, 226–241, 252, 266–269, 271–272, 281, 306, 317–319, 325–329, 332–334, 337–338, 340–342, 348, 352–353, 360, 363–367, 370–372, 385, 388, 390, 394, 409, 412, 416–417, 420, 430–431, 444, 454, 456, 458–460, 462, 464, 466–467

Rockefeller Foundation, 199, 406

Roe v. Wade, 170, 297

Roman Catholic Church, 272

Roosevelt administration

New Deal of the, 61, 71, 460

Rural Renewal County, 367

Russell Sage Foundation, 199

S

Safety net programs
    barriers to participation in, 452
    description of, 233
    Head Start as, 82
Sandfort, 438
Selective social policies
    description of, 233
September, 71, 90, 175, 237, 247–248, 252, 410, 461
Settlement House Movement, 66–67, 454
Sixth Amendment, 295, 297
Skinner, 93
Social Darwinism, 65, 466
Social equity, 44
Social justice
    different definitions of, 43, 54
Social policy
    advocacy of, 78, 421
    political feasibility of, 39
    privatization of, 381
    purpose of, 11, 17, 31, 55, 139, 203, 293, 296, 321, 359, 414, 418
Social policy analysis
    racism-centered, 2, 136–138, 145, 153, 155, 464
Social policy analysis studies
    emergence of, 41, 60, 62–63, 84, 96, 197, 201, 231, 303, 371
    value neutrality, value relevance, and critical thinking in, 195, 216
Social policy development
    models of, 1, 118, 277
    stages of, 1, 15–17, 23
Social policy performance
    decision-theoretic evaluation, 215–216, 456
    description of, 233
    pseudo-evaluation, 215, 464
Social policy processes
    description of, 233
    making policy, 214
    practical considerations for, 213
Social policy products

description of, 233
    financing, 43, 91, 98, 175, 193, 233, 267, 311, 317, 340, 342, 409, 416
Social problems
    homelessness, 13, 15, 40, 57, 63, 74, 82, 84, 86, 88, 90, 236, 430, 460, 462, 471
    social construction of, 3, 15–16, 162
Social programs
    safety net, 11, 20, 79, 95, 117, 171–172, 214, 226, 236, 238, 268, 306, 312, 351, 353, 431–432, 436–438, 440, 442–444, 465
Social Security
    eligibility for, 43, 182, 207, 327, 342, 353, 355, 360, 415, 440, 459, 461, 463
    historical roots of, 195, 351
Social Security benefits
    disability benefits, 291, 324, 331, 337, 349, 461, 473
    eligibility for, 43, 182, 207, 327, 342, 353, 355, 360, 415, 440, 459, 461, 463
    levels of, 18, 33, 35, 95–96, 119, 163–164, 182–183, 185, 193, 197, 206, 211, 265–266, 269–270, 275–276, 292, 300, 323, 348, 358, 361, 384, 437, 441, 468
    retirement, 32, 43, 76, 85, 90, 95, 125, 172, 185, 190, 225, 230–233, 242, 315, 317–325, 327–339, 341–342, 348–349, 379, 383, 408, 421, 454–457, 462, 464, 468–469, 474–475
    survivors benefits, 331
Social Security Poster, 320
Social Security reform options
    to cut benefits, 270
Social Security wage base, 319, 466
Social Security Works, 319
Social welfare
    developmental view of, 17, 23, 456
    institutional view of, 17, 22, 460
    residual view of, 17, 22, 464
    social division of, 31, 466
Social welfare policies
    description of, 233
    main political and economic functions of, 127
Southern Poverty Law Center, 146
Spectators, 467

Starbucks, 251
State and local advocacy
    best practices for, 275
State budgets
    in the midst of the Great Recession, 229
State political culture
    description of, 233
Street-level bureaucrats, 214
Summative evaluations, 215
Supplemental Security Income, 76, 85, 124, 208,
        318, 320, 367, 394, 431, 467
Survivors benefits, 324–325

T

Taft-Hartley Act, 177
"Take Back the Night" rallies, 178–179
Tarasoff v. Regents of the University of California,
    292
Targeted Jobs Tax Credit, 367
Tax credits
    Child Tax Credit (CTC), 365
    definition of, 10, 19, 21, 24, 45, 92, 148, 435, 441
    Earned Income Tax Credit (EITC), 32, 90, 207,
        230, 354, 365, 394, 456, 458, 467
    participation rates in, 435–437, 443–444
    Targeted Jobs Tax Credit, 367
    Work Opportunity Tax Credit (WOTC), 360,
        365
Tax policies
    sales tax, 33, 44, 86, 192, 208, 239, 266, 269, 271
    tax cuts since the 1980s, 33
Tax revenues
    business or corporate taxes, 192, 229
    miscellaneous other taxes, 229
    personal income tax, 192, 229, 239, 337
Teach for America, 249–250, 253, 258, 260, 472
Tea Party movement, 22–23, 275
terrorist attacks, 90, 148, 237, 248
Textualists, 295
The Washington Post, 251, 340
Thomas Aquinas, 21
Thurman v. the City of Torrington, 290

U

Under-consumption, 468
Undocumented workers
    exploitation of, 85, 143, 146, 383
Unemployment
    official unemployment rate, 92, 116, 120, 462
    social costs of, 86, 96
    statistics on, 311
United States v. Lopez, 305
United States v. Morrison, 305
United States v. Virginia, 300–301
United Way of America, 74
Universal social policies
    description of, 233
USA Freedom Corps, 248
U.S. Bureau of Refugees, Freedmen, and
        Abandoned Lands, 62
U.S. Constitution
    Commerce Clause of the, 76
    Due Process Clause of the, 170, 290–291,
        297–299
    Equal Protection Clause of the, 142, 291, 299,
        308
    First Amendment, 291, 296–297, 387
    Fourteenth Amendment, 170, 193, 289, 295,
        297–299
    Nineteenth Amendment, 165, 173, 175
    Sixth Amendment, 295, 297
U.S. Department of Agriculture, 94, 352–353,
        435–436, 442
U.S. Department of Commerce, 167
U.S. Department of Health and Human Services,
        95, 139, 353, 392, 396, 413, 415, 418, 420,
        434–435, 439, 442
U.S. Department of Housing and Urban
        Development, 164, 368
U.S. Department of Justice, 148, 394
U.S. Department of Labor, 172, 178, 355, 357,
        360–363, 367, 370
U.S. Department of the Treasury, 412
U.S. General Accounting Office, 249, 394
U.S. human service barriers

administrative, 9, 14, 18, 57, 73, 78, 85, 184, 206, 209, 212–213, 215, 313, 333, 349, 353, 359, 361, 419, 430–431, 437, 442, 453, 463, 465, 474

cultural and language, 438

structural, 16, 44, 66, 72, 76, 81, 96, 162, 192, 205, 209, 265, 269, 271, 282, 313, 317, 388, 416, 430, 437, 442

U.S. human service delivery

cash assistance programs, 230, 431–432, 438

community-based organizations (CBOs), 431

in-kind supports, 431–433, 460

of social welfare policies, 126, 138, 380, 431

safety net programs, 172, 226, 268, 431–432, 436–437, 440, 442–444, 465

U.S. Public Health Service, 464

U.S. Sanitary Commission, 61

U.S. social policy

health and mental health, 2, 18, 20, 72, 91, 291, 312, 405, 441, 444

political economy of the, 2, 114

U.S. Social Security Administration, 318, 322–326, 329, 335–340, 407–409, 411

U.S. social welfare

new disciplinary regime of, 397

residual view of, 17, 22, 464

U.S. social welfare history

New Deal, 22, 38, 61, 71–73, 75–80, 87, 127, 199, 267, 304, 312, 317, 358, 379, 383–384, 460, 462, 469

racial regulation of, 139

War on Poverty, 22, 38, 81–85, 87, 201, 267, 352, 358, 379, 384, 398, 468

U.S. Supreme Court cases

Adarand Constructors, Inc. v. Pena, 300, 302

Bowers v. Hardwick, 298

Brown v. Board of Education, 301, 306, 465

Citizens United v. Federal Election Commission, 387

Dandridge v. Williams, 300

Goldberg v. Kelly, 290, 306

Gonzales v. Raich, 291, 306

Gratz v. Bollinger, 302

Grutter v. Bollinger, 302–303

Harris v. Forklift, 294

Heart of Atlanta Motel Inc. v. United States, 304

Katzenbach v. McClung, 304

Lawrence v. Texas, 298

Lochner v. New York, 290

Muller v. Oregon, 167, 290, 306

National Federation of Independent Business v. Sebelius, 241, 306, 416

Nevada Department of Human Resources v. Hibbs, 306

O'Connor v. Donaldson, 299

Planned Parenthood v. Casey, 298

Plessy v. Ferguson, 142, 301, 459, 465

Roe v. Wade, 170, 297

Thurman v. the City of Torrington, 290

United States v. Lopez, 305

United States v. Morrison, 305

United States v. Virginia, 300–301

Wyatt v. Aderholt, 299

U.S. Women's Bureau, 199

V

VA-HUD Appropriations Subcommittee, 249, 251, 256, 468

Value neutrality, 202

Veterans Health Administration, 414

Violence Against Women Act, 173, 179, 305

Voluntary associations

description of, 233

W

Wage movements

living wage movement, 371

Wallace, G., 90

Wal-Mart, 114–115, 120

Wal-Mart [China], 115

War on Terror, 237

WCF Foundation's Voices, 175

White House Project, 175

Wider Opportunities for Women, 327–328, 330

Women's Campaign Forum, 175

Works Progress Administration, 74–75, 77–78, 358–359, 469

World Bank

creation of, 20–21, 57, 63, 67, 70, 75, 80, 86, 98, 129, 162, 179–180, 199, 209, 211, 250, 279, 300, 360, 385–386, 388, 390, 406, 409, 412, 418

World War I, 17, 63, 70–72, 78, 80, 88, 115, 117–118, 166–167, 169, 177, 197, 199–200, 232, 312, 358, 385, 405, 454–455

Wyatt v. Aderholt, 299

Y

YouthBuild, 249, 361

CPSIA information can be obtained at www.ICGtesting.com
Printed in the USA
LVOW09s0041230816

501392LV00018B/153/P